PENGUIN NATURE LIBRARY

General Editor: Edward Hoagland

THE JOURNALS OF LEWIS AND CLARK

Meriwether Lewis was born in Virginia in 1774. He was a captain in the First U.S. Infantry when he was appointed private secretary to President Thomas Jefferson. In 1803, he was appointed commander of the Corps of Discovery with instructions to explore the continent from the Missouri River to the Pacific Ocean. He subsequently served as the governor of Louisiana Territory until his death in 1809.

William Clark was born in Virginia in 1770. As a soldier for six years, he served in both the militia and the regular army during frontier Indian campaigns and rose to the rank of captain in the Fourth U.S. Infantry. From 1804 to 1806 he served as co-commander of the Corps of Discovery. He subsequently served as the governor of Missouri Territory and as Superintendent of Indian Affairs at St. Louis. He died in St. Louis in 1838.

Frank Bergon is the editor of *The Wilderness Reader* and *A Sharp Lookout: Selected Nature Essays of John Burroughs*, and the author of *Shoshone Mike*, a novel based on the Nevada Indian massacre of 1911. He has been awarded fellowships from the American Council of Learned Societies and the National Endowment for the Humanities for his studies of American naturalists. He teaches at Vassar College.

THE
JOURNALS OF
Lewis
AND
Clark

EDITED AND WITH AN INTRODUCTION BY
FRANK BERGON

PENGUIN BOOKS

PENGUIN BOOKS
Published by the Penguin Group
Viking Penguin Inc., 40 West 23rd Street,
New York, New York 10010, U.S.A.
Penguin Books Ltd, 27 Wrights Lane,
London W8 5TZ, England
Penguin Books Australia Ltd, Ringwood,
Victoria, Australia
Penguin Books Canada Ltd, 2801 John Street,
Markham, Ontario, Canada L3R 1B4
Penguin Books (N.Z.) Ltd, 182–190 Wairau Road,
Auckland 10, New Zealand

Penguin Books Ltd, Registered Offices:
Harmondsworth, Middlesex, England

This edition first published in simultaneous hardcover and
paperback editions by Viking Penguin Inc. 1989
Published simultaneously in Canada

1 3 5 7 9 10 8 6 4 2

Library of Congress Cataloging in Publication Data
Lewis, Meriwether, 1774–1809.
The journals of Lewis and Clark.
1. Lewis and Clark Expedition (1804–1806).
2. West (U.S.)—Description and travel—to 1848.
3. Missouri River—Description and travel.
4. Columbia River—Description and travel.
5. United States—Exploring expeditions.
6. Lewis, Meriwether, 1774–1809.
7. Clark, William, 1770–1838.   I. Clark, William, 1770–1838.
II. Bergon, Frank.   III. Title.
F592.4   1989   917.8'042   88-22513
ISBN 0 14 017006 5

Printed in the United States of America
Set in Caslon 540
Designed by Ann Gold

PENGUIN NATURE LIBRARY

Nature is our widest home. It includes the oceans that provide our rain, the trees that give us air to breathe, the ancestral habitats we shared with countless kinds of animals that now exist only by our sufferance or under our heel.

Until quite recently, indeed (as such things go), the whole world was a wilderness in which mankind lived as cannily as deer, over-mastering with spears or snares even their woodsmanship and that of other creatures, finding a path wherever wildlife could go. Nature was the central theater of life for everybody's ancestors, not a hide-away where people went to rest and recharge after a hard stint in an urban or suburban arena, and many of us still do swim, hike, fish, birdwatch, sleep on the ground, or paddle a boat on vacation, and will loll like a lizard in the sun any other chance we have. We can't help grinning for at least a moment at the sight of surf, or sunlight on a river meadow, as if remembering in our mind's eye paleolithic pleasures in a home before memories officially began.

It is a thoughtless grin because nature predates "thought." Aristotle was a naturalist, and nearer to our own time, Darwin and Thoreau made of the close observation of bits of nature a lever to examine life in many ways on a large scale. Yet nature writing, despite its basis in science, usually rings with rhapsody as well—a belief that nature is an expression of God.

In this series we are presenting some nature writers of the past century or so, though leaving out great novelists like Turgenev, Melville, Conrad, and Faulkner, who were masters of natural description, and poets such as Homer (who was perhaps the first nature writer, once his words had been transcribed). Nature writing now combines rhapsody with science and connects science with rhapsody. For that reason it is a very special and a nourishing genre.

—Edward Hoagland

CONTENTS

INTRODUCTION

"Epic" is a word frequently used to describe Lewis and Clark's remarkable journey across the continent in 1804–1806. In terms of scale or magnitude, that journey certainly exhibits something in common with epics like *The Odyssey*, or even Hollywood's latest film of epic proportions. It was the largest and longest of United States expeditions into *terra incognita*. It was also the first. Now seen as the most skillfully managed expedition in the history of North American exploration, the one against which all others are measured, the expedition lasted twenty-eight months and covered eight thousand miles, between the mouth of the Missouri River and the Pacific outlet of the Columbia River. It was called the Voyage of Discovery, and it was a journey into an unknown wilderness.

To a young nation—the United States was barely a dozen years old at the time—Lewis and Clark brought back maps of previously uncharted rivers and mountains, specimens of previously unknown plants and animals, amazing artifacts, and even representatives of previously unseen peoples of the West. But their most valuable contribution came in an elkskin-bound field book and red morocco-bound journals, stored in tin boxes. To a nation with no commonly sung mystique of the State or of the Race or of the Empire, no national literature—no *Iliad* or *Chanson de Roland* or *Kalevala*—these uneven, fragmented, and unpolished journals offered the equivalent

of a national poem, a magnificent epic for an unfinished nation.
Of course, it is only from the hindsight of 180 years that it might
be suggested that these journals, with their daily logs of temperature
and weather, astronomical observations, tabulations of longitude and
latitude, technical descriptions of flora and fauna, anthropological
data, misspellings, and neologisms, might serve as an appropriate
American epic. They tell a heroic story of a people's struggles
through a wilderness and the return home. Better than more artfully
constructed poems or novels or plays, they embody with the col-
loquial directness and power of an oral epic the mythic history of a
nation. Like ancient epics, they tell the story of the tribe, in this
case the story of a people moving west. It is not the story of an
individual frontiersman but of a pluralistic, fluctuating community
of thirty-five to forty-five people, including soldiers, woodsmen,
blacksmiths, carpenters, cooks, French *engagés*, a black slave, a
Lemhi Shoshone woman, and a newborn baby of mixed race, all
heading west. In retrospect, that story portrays the fall of one civilization and the rise of another. It dramatizes the relationship of a
people to the natural world and the design of a nation committed
to the belief that—as William Gilpin expressed it seventy years
later—"the *untransacted* destiny of the American people is to subdue
the continent."
The primary heroes of this epic adventure were two American
soldiers. Meriwether Lewis, appointed by the President to lead the
expedition, had served in the militia during the Whiskey Rebellion
before joining the regular army and rising to the rank of captain in
the First U.S. Infantry. As an ensign, Lewis had served briefly in
a rifle company under the command of Captain William Clark, who
became his immediate choice as co-commander of the expedition.
At the time of his appointment, Clark had resigned his army commission as a captain in the infantry, and despite Lewis's promise
and President Jefferson's approval of his reappointment as a captain,
the Department of War's bureaucratic machinations led to Clark's
reappointment as a second lieutenant in the artillery, a subordinate
to Lewis. Defying military red tape, Lewis made it clear that his
former commanding officer was to be his co-equal on the expedition
and that the men under their authority would never know them as
other than Captain Clark and Captain Lewis, co-commanders of the
Corps of Discovery.

The effectiveness of this strange alliance, a sharing of command that defies military hierarchy, is unique to military history. But Lewis and Clark seemed to command as one, effortlessly and without conflict, remaining friends to the end. At the start of the trip, Lewis was twenty-nine and Clark was thirty-three. Although Lewis enjoyed eating dog meat and Clark hated it, and Lewis craved salt and Clark dismissed it as a luxury, and Lewis liked eating black currants and Clark favored yellow ones, the two leaders otherwise formed a perfectly harmonious relationship.

Like heroes of ancient epics, they were first of all men of demonstrated military leadership and physical courage. Clark had more experience in actual battle, against the Creek and Cherokee Indians, but both men were archetypal American frontiersmen, whose characters had been forged in confrontation with the wilderness. Also like earlier epic heroes, they both showed cunning, intelligence, and dignity in their leadership of others. But they were always men, not gods. In them we see the flip side of heroism, the human dimension that gives rise to excesses and weakness, as well as doubts and concerns about day-to-day details we all share.

It is now a commonplace to present the personalities of the two men as polar opposites: Lewis as a brooding, romantic introvert, Clark an even-tempered, sociable extrovert. Clark's subsequently long and distinguished career as Superintendent of Indian Affairs at St. Louis, and Lewis's subsequently short and troubled political career as governor of Louisiana Territory—abruptly terminated by his murky death as a probable suicide—provide reinforcing evidence for these contrasting views of the two men. But the journals don't bear them out. Although the two men complement each other marvelously, they do so in subtle and changing ways. They sometimes reverse roles. At times it is Clark who seems the melancholy loner depressed by bad weather and bugs, while it is Lewis who retains his *joie de vivre* amid misfortune and who longs for the companionship of friends and civil society. It is as if this division of the classical hero into two men allows Lewis and Clark to embody the heroic virtues and antiheroic impulses of the classical hero in believable ways. They are heroes cut down to credible size, eighteenth-century men who merge into a composite hero acceptable to the cynicism of a rational, modern era.

It is the composite character of these two leaders—their pervasive outpouring of intellectual and moral energy—that sustained the expedition and guaranteed its success. That composite character manifested itself in the thousands of right decisions the leaders jointly made to avert disaster. It was only when Lewis and Clark were apart, on the return journey, that tragedy struck and two Blackfeet Indians were killed. While they were still apart, Lewis himself was almost killed when accidentally shot by one of his own hunters. Reunited, the men concluded their journey without further incident. The unfortunate skirmish with the Blackfeet was the only eruption of violence during the hundreds of meetings with native peoples across the continent. Equally remarkable is that only one member of the expedition died, despite numerous accidents and incessant illnesses during the long trip. Sergeant Floyd suffered what was most likely a ruptured appendix early in the trip. His death, it has been pointed out, would probably have been unavoidable even in the best hospital of the time, since the first appendectomy was not performed in the United States until over eighty years later.

In chronicling their trials and achievements, the heroes of this epic adventure sing of themselves, becoming—in a modern literary twist—their own bards. Just as the success of the expedition is unimaginable without the joint leadership of the two captains, so too is the contemporary appeal of the journals without their coauthorship. Where modesty commends one to silence about his own achievement, history compels the other to document the worthiness of the event. Of all the heroic moments recorded in the journals, however, none surpasses the recording of the journals themselves. Under the unbearably difficult circumstances of their composition, the writing of carefully detailed and fully documented accounts of the expedition was the most heroic of acts. It is a wonder they were done at all. Anyone who has tried to keep a diary at the end of a day of hiking along modern trails with the guidance of modern maps can only marvel at the fortitude of the captains as they continue to record their experiences despite exhaustion and illness while forging through an uncharted wilderness in all extremes of heat and cold. The journals offer an understated catalogue of trials by mosquitoes, hunger, storms, and grizzlies. A touching moment occurs when Meriwether Lewis notes in his journal, "The ink f[r]iezes in my pen," and he continues to write. The journals appropriately end with Clark's last brief entry on September 25, 1806, "a fine morning we commenced wrighting &c."

Like an oral epic, the journals are episodic, expansive, and digressive. They contain repetitive formulaic phrases, like "we proceeded on." They also contain gaps. Except for a few fragments, Lewis's entire journal is missing for the first ten months of the trip, and Lewis ceased writing while recovering from his gunshot wound during the last leg of the trip home. There are also long stretches where Clark merely copies Lewis. The explorers were careful to duplicate and preserve their writings, just as they protected their scientific collections, but accidents took their toll of specimens. Whether some gaps in the journals are due to accidents rather than choice is unknown.

Despite their inventive spelling and punctuation, both men are extremely effective writers. Whereas Lewis is often more polished, detailed, and reflective, Clark is sometimes more forceful and vivid. When they copy each other's field notes or journals, original authorship, as in oral narratives, sometimes becomes blurred or lost. The "I" of some entries becomes that composite hero and author whom Clark seemed to honor, after his co-captain's death, when he named his son Meriwether Lewis Clark.

The Muse to these journals was the President of the United States, Thomas Jefferson. His influence informs them like a third presence. The Voyage of Discovery was his dream, and the journals were his inspiration. For twenty years Jefferson had tried to have someone do what Lewis and Clark were finally accomplishing. As a congressman in 1783, Jefferson had unsuccessfully tried to enlist General George Rogers Clark, the Revolutionary War hero and William's older brother, to explore the lands west of the Mississippi. As Minister to France in 1786, Jefferson supported the Connecticut adventurer John Ledyard in his daring but frustrated attempt to cross the continent by traveling westward over Russia and Siberia before returning eastward from the Pacific, over the Rockies, to the Missouri River. In 1793, as Secretary of State and vice-president of the American Philosophical Society, Jefferson again backed another aborted exploration when he instructed André Michaux, France's most accomplished botanist, to "find the shortest & most convenient route of communication between the U.S. & the Pacific ocean." It was not until he was President, in 1803, that Jefferson sent a secret message to Congress in which he requested and finally received funds to launch his expedition across the continent.

In 1803, the vast stretch of lands that Jefferson wanted to explore was still a foreign territory. At the time of his inauguration, the Territory of Louisiana, between the Mississippi and the Rocky Mountains, was Spanish territory. In January 1803, when he sent his secret message to Congress, it had been ceded back to France. Beyond the Rockies, the territory bifurcated by the Columbia River—Oregon country—was a vague region controlled by Indians and subject to murky claims by Great Britain, Spain, France, the United States, and Russia. Jefferson couched his secret congressional request for exploratory funds in careful terms. He was interested primarily in looking for trade routes, he told Congress, for external commerce, and he tried to assure foreign powers that his encroachment into their territory was in the disinterested spirit of expanding scientific and geographical knowledge. Everyone knew otherwise, especially the European powers who were anxious to keep the original colonies of the United States tidily contained along the continental Eastern Seaboard. The real design of Jefferson's plan was imperial, to make way for American expansion from sea to shining sea.

"Westward the course of Empire makes its way" was the eighteenth-century sentiment that seemingly became reality when Napoleon, abandoning his own imperial designs in North America and trying to frustrate Britain's, surprisingly sold the vast Louisiana Territory to the United States for three cents an acre. The United States suddenly doubled its territory, and expansion to the Pacific became a virtual certainty. "The consequences of the cession of Louisiana," President Jefferson predicted, "will extend to the most distant posterity." Scarcely six months after congressional ratification of the sale in October 1803, Lewis and Clark were on their way across the continent, and the United States was on its way to becoming a world power. After hearing of the Louisiana Purchase, the Federalist Fisher Ames fearfully predicted, "We rush like a comet into infinite space!"

The political and commercial ramifications of the Lewis and Clark expedition are well known, but they should not overshadow what Jefferson told Congress were the "literary purposes" of the venture. In fact, it might be argued that the expedition succeeded more spectacularly as Jefferson's "literary pursuit" than in some of its political and commercial aims. The expedition failed in its primary commercial purpose of finding a practical water route across the continent to link the United States in trade with China. There was no Northwest Passage as it had been envisioned by explorers since Columbus. The expedition also failed to establish workable trade routes up the northern tributaries of the Missouri to capture the Canadian fur trade for the United States. And it failed to establish a lasting peace with the native peoples, especially those who controlled passage on the Missouri; in the killings of two Blackfeet warriors, it aggravated relations with tribes of the Northern Plains. It is also questionable how firmly the expedition reinforced the nation's claim to the Oregon territory. But as a "literary pursuit"— a report on the lands, animals, and native peoples of the American West—the expedition succeeded in ways that are still being appreciated.

The literary success of the journals as a work of natural history is much to Jefferson's credit. A fine naturalist himself, with a particular interest in phenology (dealing with the relationship between climate and periodic biological phenomena), Jefferson gave Lewis and Clark careful instructions for observing and recording the natural world. Although he is sometimes criticized for not sending a trained botanist or zoologist on the expedition, Jefferson saw in Lewis "a natural talent for observation which had led him to an accurate knowledge of plants and animals." Recent studies have shown Lewis to be better trained and more scientifically competent than is often assumed. His careful descriptions of plants included the use of no fewer than two hundred technical botanical terms. He merely avoided classifying and describing his discoveries of new plants and animals according to a Latinate, binomial taxonomy.

Jefferson had had his eye on young Lewis ever since the nineteen-year-old boy had requested Jefferson's permission to accompany the French botanist Michaux on his purported expedition. Lewis had virtually lived with Jefferson for four years before the expedition, on detached duty from the army, serving ostensibly as the President's private secretary while training for the Voyage of Discovery. In 1803, when Jefferson sent Lewis to scientists and physicians in Philadelphia for brief but intensive instruction in botany, zoology, celestial navigation, and medicine, he confided to the botanist Benjamin Smith Barton that he needed not just a trained specialist but someone with "firmness of constitution & character, prudence, habits adapted to the woods, & a familiarity with Indian manners & character, requisite for the undertaking. All the latter qualifications Capt. Lewis has." In both Lewis and Clark, Jefferson found men whose character combined with "a remarkable store of accurate observation" and a talent for seeing. In their ability to keep "a sharp lookout"—as the naturalist John Burroughs describes it—Lewis and Clark shared with other naturalists, like Audubon, Thoreau, Muir, and Burroughs, a trait that surpassed their formal scientific training. They were not scientific specialists; they were natural historians whose range of observation included minerals, plants, amphibians, fishes, mammals, birds, rivers, trees—in short, everything observable in nature, including native peoples and their works.

In the journals, Lewis and Clark offer descriptions of a natural world never before seen by white men. They were no sooner embarked on their journey than Clark noted that "Capt. Lewis went out to the woods & found many curious Plants & S[h]rubs." The strange landforms and new watercourses the explorers encountered were the primary concerns of Clark, who served as the expedition's main cartographer and geographer, while Lewis was the botanist and zoologist. Both compiled a valuable ethnographic record of Indian people, especially of the Lemhi Shoshone, whose meeting with Lewis and Clark marked their first encounter with whites. From the Mandan villages, north of present Bismarck, North Dakota, where the explorers spent their first winter, they sent back to Jefferson specimens of plants and animals never before seen in the United States, including roots, seeds, and cuttings of numerous plants, skins of pronghorns, bighorns, white-tailed jackrabbits, coyotes, live magpies, and live prairie dogs, as well as Mandan buffalo-robe paintings and Hidatsa clothing.

The journals record the first descriptions of hundreds of other new animals and plants, including the cutthroat trout, mountain quail, western meadowlark, pack rats, kit foxes, and *Ursus horribilis*, the grizzly bear. Among their descriptions of 178 plants, the explorers are honored in the scientific names of new genera and new species like *Clarkia pulchella* and *Lewisia rediviva*, commonly called ragged-robin Clarkia and bitterroot. Many other plants still bear such ordinary names as Lewis flax and Lewis and Clark's synthyris, in honor of their scientific discoverers, as do two of the many birds the explorers described for the first time, Lewis's woodpecker and Clark's nutcracker.

Despite their scientific, literary, and historical importance, Lewis and Clark's journals were available only in a rephrased, bowdlerized and truncated version until the twentieth century, when, in 1904–1905, Reuben Thwaites published the *Original Journals of the Lewis and Clark Expedition*, composed of seven volumes with an eighth volume of maps. What follows is an abridged edition of the original journals, based on Thwaites's compilation, which includes much of the natural-history material omitted in earlier edited versions of the journals. For instance, the purpose of Bernard DeVoto's fine abridgment, published in 1953, was to emphasize the geographical and political importance of the expedition in a running narrative that omitted much of the detailed description of animals, plants, and native peoples. In serving his purpose of providing a full narrative history of the expedition, DeVoto included excerpts from the journals of four other members of the expedition, transitions from Biddle's rephrased edition, as well as his own transitional summaries of events and interpretations of native peoples, all of which are excluded from this edition. Only the journals of Lewis and Clark, as emended by Thwaites, are included in this edition. For purposes of comparison and duplication of the original journals' format, examples are also provided of instances where Lewis and Clark sometimes copy each other's writings, or give overlapping reports of the same events. The result, however, is only a sampling. No abridgment can fully convey the dazzling epic quality of the complete journals or their splendid achievement in the literature of natural history, for their effect is monumental and cumulative.

Today the journals offer contemporary readers a sense of a bygone era as Lewis and Clark begin their journey up the snag-infested Missouri River, its banks dangerously caving into the muddy water. There is nothing else like it in our literature. No other exploratory

report of North America is so vivid; no other evokes such a sense
of immediacy. As the explorers leave the fringes of white civilization
and move into the West, they seem to move back in time. At the
Mandan villages they abandon their masted keelboat and paddle
toward the headwaters of the Missouri in two pirogues and six small
canoes. At the Great Falls of the Missouri, Lewis watches as his
collapsible iron boat, designed and built in the East, sinks uselessly
into a Western river. In the Rockies they abandon their canoes and
depend on Indian horses to cross the Bitterroots to where they can
chop and carve native cottonwoods into dugouts for the final run
down the Snake and Columbia rivers to the sea.

Conventional rhetoric and cultural assumptions also break down
as the facts of the actual country, animals, and native peoples of the
West give shape to new forms of perception. Language itself has to
be altered to describe a new country and its native inhabitants; words
coined and twisted and adapted to the occasion in the journals produced the addition of over fifteen hundred new words to the American language. In gradually abandoning attempts to present their
experience through conventional aesthetic forms and expressions,
the explorers seem to let the wonder of the country and its incredible
wildlife speak more and more through plain fact and events. The
explorers do seem like new men in a new Eden, walking peacefully
among hundreds of animals that will not scare: "the whole face of
the country," Lewis writes, "was covered with herds of Buffaloe,
Elk & Antelopes; deer are also abundant, but keep themselves more
concealed in the woodland. the buffaloe Elk and Antelope are so
gentel that we pass near them while feeding, without appearing to
excite any alarm among them and when we attract their attention,
they frequently approach us more nearly to discover what we are."

Horror shatters this Edenic world in the form of enraged grizzly
bears, charging buffalo, violent storms, smashed boats, horses rolling
down hillsides, feet torn and bleeding from cactus needles, incessant
rain, fleas, and mosquitoes. The journals often become a story of
confrontations with monsters and dark powers. But the real snake
in the garden hideously follows the explorers themselves. In the
wanton smashing of a wolf's skull with a spontoon, the slaughtering
of animals and the proprietary attitudes toward the land and native
peoples, we get sad glimpses of the coming dark side of American

imperialism. As an expedition of American expansionism, the Voyage of Discovery made way for others, seemingly bent on transforming the land of plenty into a land of waste.

Hard as it may be to read the journals without a sense of what we have lost, without nostalgia, they still offer a vision for the future. In their timeless struggle through a pristine wilderness, Lewis and Clark present a counterimage to the mythical frontiersman alone in the wilderness. They are not alone in the wilderness. They are not the self-sufficient, independent, gunslinging Western loners so popular in American fiction and film. They are dependent on each other, on the other members of the expedition, on the native peoples of the West, and especially on the natural world through which they pass. Without the continual instruction and abundant assistance of Indians across the continent, Lewis and Clark would not be remembered today. Their story is not one of American individualism but of communalism.

When the expedition finally reaches the Pacific at the mouth of the Columbia River, we see the whole community—including a black man and an Indian woman—vote on where they wish to encamp for the winter. Rather than striving to conquer the wilderness, they learn to make a home within it. It is a moment of cooperation among people of differing races in recognition of their ties to the natural world. It is an epic moment in the story of a westering people. What they have learned is not independence but interdependence. It is still an important moment as an epic vision for this nation's unfinished story.

A NOTE
ON THE TEXT

The text for this edition of the Lewis and Clark journals is based on the *Original Journals of Lewis and Clark*, edited by Reuben Gold Thwaites and published in eight volumes by Dodd, Mead, and Company in 1904–1905.

Thwaites indicated emendations or textual interlineations in the following manner: those in brackets and roman type are his own; those in brackets and italics are usually William Clark's or Elliott Coues's; those in parentheses and italics are presumably Nicholas Biddle's with the assistance of George Shannon, a member of the expedition.

Other than deletions, no changes have been made in the spelling or punctuation of the journals as presented in the Thwaites edition. For the purpose of readability, however, blocks of texts have been indented into paragraphs, spaces in the text have been emphasized, and deletions have been made without ellipses.

Unless otherwise ascribed in parentheses, all footnotes are those of the present editor. References in footnotes to current names of towns and states are intended to help the reader trace the route of the expedition and to locate events and geographical features described in the journals. To this end, abbreviations of counties and states in attributed footnotes have been written out and the spelling of proper names in these footnotes has been changed to conform to modern usage.

Scientific identification of Lewis and Clark's botanical and zoological observations and discoveries is based on the annotations of Elliott Coues and C. V. Piper in the Thwaites edition of the *Original Journals of Lewis and Clark*, the zoological catalogue in Raymond Darwin Burroughs's *Natural History of the Lewis and Clark Expedition*, published by Michigan State University Press in 1961, and the botanical and zoological catalogues of Paul Russell Cutright in *Lewis and Clark: Pioneering Naturalists*, published by the University of Illinois Press in 1969. Scientific and common names of plants and animals identified in footnotes have been based wherever possible on current usage.

JEFFERSON'S
INSTRUCTIONS TO LEWIS

To Meriwether Lewis, esquire, Captain of the 1st. regiment of infantry of the United States of America: Your situation as Secretary of the President of the United States has made you acquainted with the objects of my confidential message of Jan. 18, 1803, to the legislature. you have seen the act they passed, which, tho' expressed in general terms, was meant to sanction those objects, and you are appointed to carry them into execution.

Instruments for ascertaining by celestial observations the geography of the country thro' which you will pass, have already been provided. light articles for barter, & presents among the Indians, arms for your attendants, say for from 10 to 12 men, boats, tents, & other travelling apparatus, with ammunition, medicine, surgical instruments & provisions you will have prepared with such aids as the Secretary of War can yield in his department; & from him also you will receive authority to engage among our troops, by voluntary agreement, the number of attendants above mentioned, over whom you, as their commanding officer are invested with all the powers the laws give in such a case.

As your movements while within the limits of the U.S. will be better directed by occasional communications, adapted to circumstances as they arise, they will not be noticed here. what follows will respect your proceedings after your departure from the U.S.

Your mission has been communicated to the Ministers here from France, Spain & Great Britain, and through them to their governments: and such assurances given them as to it's objects as we trust will satisfy them. the country of Louisiana having been ceded by Spain to France, the passport you have from the Minister of France, the representative of the present sovereign of the country, will be a protection with all it's subjects: And that from the Minister of England will entitle you to the friendly aid of any traders of that allegiance with whom you may happen to meet.

The object of your mission is to explore the Missouri river, & such principal stream of it, as, by it's course & communication with the waters of the Pacific Ocean, may offer the most direct & practicable water communication across this continent, for the purposes of commerce.

Beginning at the mouth of the Missouri, you will take observations of latitude & longitude, at all remarkable points on the river, & especially at the mouths of rivers, at rapids, at islands & other places & objects distinguished by such natural marks & characters of a durable kind, as that they may with certainty by recognized hereafter. the courses of the river between these points of observation may be supplied by the compass, the log-line & by time, corrected by the observations themselves. the variations of the compass too, in different places, should be noticed.

The interesting points of the portage between the heads of the Missouri & the water offering the best communication with the Pacific Ocean should also be fixed by observation, & the course of that water to the ocean, in the same manner as that of the Missouri.

Your observations are to be taken with great pains & accuracy, to be entered distinctly, & intelligibly for others as well as yourself, to comprehend all the elements necessary, with the aid of the usual tables, to fix the latitude and longitude of the places at which they were taken, & are to be rendered to the war office, for the purpose of having the calculations made concurrently by proper persons within the U.S. several copies of these, as well as your other notes, should be made at leisure times & put into the care of the most trustworthy of your attendants, to guard by multiplying them, against the accidental losses to which they will be exposed. a further guard would be that one of these copies be written on the paper of the birch, as less liable to injury from damp than common paper.

The commerce which may be carried on with the people inhabiting the line you will pursue, renders a knolege of these people important. you will therefore endeavor to make yourself acquainted, as far as a diligent pursuit of your journey shall admit,

 with the names of the nations & their numbers;

  the extent & limits of their possessions;

  their relations with other tribes or nations;

  their language, traditions, monuments;

  their ordinary occupations in agriculture, fishing, hunting, war, arts, & the implements for these;

  their food, clothing, & domestic accomodations;

  the diseases prevalent among them, & the remedies they use;

  moral & physical circumstances which distinguish them from the tribes we know;

  peculiarities in their laws, customs & dispositions;

  and articles of commerce they may need or furnish, & to what extent.

And considering the interest which every nation has in extending & strengthening the authority of reason & justice among the people around them, it will be useful to acquire what knolege you can of the state of morality, religion & information among them, as it may better enable those who endeavor to civilize & instruct them, to adapt their measures to the existing notions & practises of those on whom they are to operate.

 Other object worthy of notice will be

  the soil & face of the country, it's growth & vegetable productions; especially those not of the U.S.

  the animals of the country generally, & especially those not known in the U.S.

  the remains and accounts of any which may deemed rare or extinct;

  the mineral productions of every kind; but more particularly metals, limestone, pit coal & saltpetre; salines & mineral waters, noting the temperature of the last, & such circumstances as may indicate their character.

Volcanic appearances.

climate as characterized by the thermometer, by the proportion of rainy, cloudy & clear days, by lightening, hail, snow, ice, by the access & recess of frost, by the winds prevailing at different seasons, the dates at which particular plants put forth or lose their flowers, or leaf, times of appearance of particular birds, reptiles or insects.

Altho' your route will be along the channel of the Missouri, yet you will endeavor to inform yourself, by inquiry, of the character & extent of the country watered by it's branches, & especially on it's Southern side. the North river or Rio Bravo which runs into the gulph of Mexico, and the North river, or Rio colorado, which runs into the gulph of California, are understood to be the principal streams heading opposite to the waters of the Missouri, and running Southwardly. whether the dividing grounds between the Missouri & them are mountains or flatlands, what are their distance from the Missouri, the character of the intermediate country, & the people inhabiting it, are worthy of particular enquiry. The Northern waters of the Missouri are less to be enquired after, because they have been ascertained to a considerable degree, and are still in a course of ascertainment by English traders & travellers. but if you can learn anything certain of the most Northern source of the Missisipi, & of it's position relative to the lake of the woods, it will be interesting to us. some account too of the path of the Canadian traders from the Missisipi, at the mouth of the Ouisconsin river, to where it strikes the Missouri and of the soil & rivers in it's course, is desireable.

In all your intercourse with the natives treat them in the most friendly & conciliatory manner which their own conduct will admit; allay all jealousies as to the object of your journey, satisfy them of it's innocence, make them acquainted with the position, extent, character, peaceable & commercial dispositions of the U.S. of our wish to be neighborly, friendly & useful to them, & of our dispositions to a commercial intercourse with them, confer with them on the points most convenient as mutual emporiums, & the articles of most desirable interchange for them & us. if a few of their influential chiefs, within practicable distance, wish to visit us, arrange such a visit with them, and furnish them with authority to call on

our officers, on their entering the U.S. to have them conveyed to
this place at public expence. if any of them should wish to have
some of their young people brought up with us, & taught such arts
as may be useful to them, we will receive, instruct & take care of
them. such a mission, whether of influential chiefs, or of young
people, would give some security to your own party. carry with
you some matter of the kine-pox, inform those of them with whom
you may be of it's efficacy as a preservative from the small-pox; and
instruct & incourage them in the use of it. this may be especially
done wherever you winter.

As it is impossible for us to foresee in what manner you will be
recieved by those people, whether with hospitality or hostility, so
is it impossible to prescribe the exact degree of perseverance with
which you are to pursue your journey. we value too much the lives
of citizens to offer them to probable destruction. your numbers will
be sufficient to secure you against the unauthorised opposition of
individuals, or of small parties: but if a superior force, authorised or
not authorised, by a nation, should be arrayed against your further
passage, & inflexibly determined to arrest it, you must decline it's
further pursuit, and return. in the loss of yourselves, we should
lose also the information you will have acquired. by returning safely
with that, you may enable us to renew the essay with better calculated means. to your own discretion therefore must be left the
degree of danger you may risk, & the point at which you should
decline, only saying we wish you to err on the side of your safety,
& bring basck your party safe, even if it be with less information.

As far up the Missouri as the white settlements extend, an intercourse will probably be found to exist between them and the
Spanish posts at St. Louis, opposite Cahokia, or Ste. Genevieve
opposite Kaskaskia. from still farther up the river, the traders may
furnish a conveyance for letters. beyond that you may perhaps be
able to engage Indians to bring letters for the government to Cahokia
or Kaskaskia, on promising that they shall there receive such special
compensation as you shall have stipulated with them. avail yourself
of these means to communicate to us, at seasonable intervals, a copy
of your journal, notes & observations of every kind, putting into
cypher whatever might do injury if betrayed.

Should you reach the Pacific ocean [One full line scratched out, indecipherable.] inform yourself of the circumstances which may decide whether the furs of those parts may not be collected as advantageously at the head of the Missouri (convenient as is supposed to the waters of the Colorado & Oregon or Columbia) as at Nootka sound or any other point of that coast; & that trade be consequently conducted through the Missouri & U.S. more beneficially than by the circumnavigation now practised.

On your arrival on that coast endeavor to learn if there be any port within your reach frequented by the sea-vessels of any nation, and to send two of your trusty people back by sea, in such way as shall appear practicable, with a copy of your notes. and should you be of opinion that the return of your party by the way they went will be eminently dangerous, then ship the whole, & return by sea by way of Cape Horn or the Cape of good Hope, as you shall be able. as you will be without money, clothes or provisions, you must endeavor to use the credit of the U.S. to obtain them; for which purpose open letters of credit shall be furnished you authorising you to draw on the Executive of the U.S. or any of its officers in any part of the world, on which drafts can be disposed of, and to apply with our recommendations to the Consuls, agents, merchants or citizens of any nation with which we have intercourse, assuring them in our name that any aids they may furnish you, shall [be] honorably repaid, and on demand. Our consuls Thomas Howes at Batavia in Java, William Buchanan of the isles of France and Bourbon, & John Elmslie at the Cape of good hope will be able to supply your necessities by draughts on us.

Should you find it safe to return by the way you go, after sending two of your party round by sea, or with your whole party, if no conveyance by sea can be found, do so; making such observations on your return as may serve to supply, correct or confirm those made on your outward journey.

In re-entering the U.S. and reaching a place of safety, discharge any of your attendants who may desire & deserve it, procuring for them immediate paiment of all arrears of pay & cloathing which may have incurred since their departure; & assure them that they shall be recommended to the liberality of the legislature for the grant of a soldier's portion of land each, as proposed in my message to Congress & repair yourself with your papers to the seat of government.

To provide, on the accident of your death, against anarchy, dispersion & the consequent danger to your party, and total failure of the enterprise, you are hereby authorised, by any instrument signed & written in your hand, to name the person among them who shall succeed to the command on your decease, & by like instruments to change the nomination from time to time, as further experience of the characters accompanying you shall point out superior fitness: and all the powers & authorities given to yourself are, in the event of your death, transferred to & vested in the successor so named, with further power to him, & his successors in like manner to name each his successor, who, on the death of his predecessor, shall be invested with all the powers & authorities given to yourself.

Given under my hand at the city of Washington, this 20th. day of June 1803

TH. JEFFERSON
Pr. U.S. of America

CLARK'S QUESTIONS
CONCERNING INDIANS
OF THE WEST

Inquiries relitive to the *Indians* of Louisiana.[1]

1st *Physical History and Medicine*

What is their State of Life as to longivity?
at what age do both Sexes usially marry?
How long do the Woman usually succle their Children?
What is the diet of their Children after they wean them?
Is polygamy admited among them?
What is the State of the pulse in both Sexes, Children, grown
    persons, and in old age, by feeling the Pulse Morning, Noon
    & Night &c.?
What is their most general diet, manner of cooking, time and
    manner of eating; and how doe they preserve their provisions?
What time to they generally consume in Sleep?
What are their *acute* diseases?
Is rheumatism, Pluricy, or *bilious fevers* known among them? &
does the latter ever terminate in a vomiting of *black matter?*
What are their chronic diseases—are palsy, apoplexy, Epilepsy,

[1] Transcribed by William Clark.

Madness, the goiture (or Swelled Neck) and the Venereal disease known among them?

What is their mode of treating the *Small pox* particularly?

Have they any other disease amongst them, and what are they?

What are their remidies for their different diseases?

Are artificial discharges of blood used among them?

In what manner do they generally induce evacuation?

Do they ever use Voluntary fasting?

What is the nature of their baths, and at what time of the day do they generally use them?

at what age do their women begin and cease to menstruate?

2nd *Relative to Morrals*

What are the Vices most common among the Indians?

Do they ever resort to Suicide under the influence of their passions, particularly love?

Is murder common among them, and do their Laws punish it by Death?

Are the lives of the Wife and Children subject to the Capprice of the husband, and father, and in case of the murder by him of either do their Laws punish the Culprit with Death?

Can the crime of murder be paliated by precuniary Considerations?

do they use any liquor or Substitute to premote intoxication, besides ardent Spirits?

Are they much attached to Spiritous liquors, and is intoxication deemed a Crime among them?

Have they any and what are the *punishments* of Which their usuages admit of—for either crimes.

3rd *Relative to Religion*

What affinity is there between their religious ceremonies and those of the ancient Jews?

do they use animal sacrifices in their Worship?

What are the principal objects of their Worship?

Do they Consider *Mannatoe* or the *good Spirit* & *Michimannatoe* or the *bad Spirit* as two distinct powers, neither haveing the power of Controling the other?

Do they ever petition the *Good Spirit* to interfere with his power to avert or relieve them from the evils which the *bad Spirit* meditates or is practicing against them

Do they sacrifice to, or petition the *bad Spirit* in order to avert the pernicious design which they may conceive he has formed against them.

How do they dispose of their dead?

and with what ceremonies do they inter them?

do they ever use human sacrifices in any case

do they Mourn for their disceased friends and what [is] their cerimony on Such occasions.

4th *Traditions or National History*

From what quarter of the earth did they emigrate as related to them by their ansisters.

What the cause of their removal and the circumstancies attending their peregrination.

With what savage nations have they formed stricte allyance, or those of *offensive* and *Defensive* war

Have they any *Monuments* to perpetuate national events or the memory of a distinguished Chief—and if so what are they?

5th *Agriculture and Domestic economy*

do they obtain by the Cultivation of the Soil their principal mantainence?

what species of grain or pulse do they cultivate?

what are their implements of husbandry, and in what manner do they use them?

have they any domestic animals & what are they?

do their men engage in agriculture or any other domestic employments.

How do they prepare their culinary and other domistic utensils, and what are they?

At what time do they usually relinquish their hunt and return to their Village?

* What are the esculent plants, and how do they prepare them

* What are those that are Commonly used by them?

In what form and of what materials are their Lodges or *Houses* usially built

Of what does the furniture of those lodges Consist, for the accommodation of the necessary avocations of human life *eating Drinking & Sleeping*

What materials compose, and in what form do they erect their temperary tents

do more that [than] one family inhabit the same lodge and in such case, is the furniture of the lodge considered as the common property of the inhabitants of it.

6th *Fishing & Hunting*

do those furnish their principal employment?

do their [tear in MS; probably the word is "women"] participate in the fatigues of either?

How do they persue, and how take their game?

What are the employments used for those purposes, how prepare[d] & in what manner do they use them?

How do they preserve, and how prepare the Skins & furs of their games when taken for raiment or for Market.

7th *War*

What is the cerimony of declareing war, and making peace; or forming alliancies?

What the cerimony of setting out and the return of the War Party?

do their women ever accompany them on those th[e]ir hostile experditions.

at what season of the year do they usially go to war?

In what manner are those War parties organized?

What is their Disipline and the regulations by which they are governed?

do they burn or torture their prisoners?

do they eat the flesh of their prisoners?

do they ever adopt their Prisoners as Members of their Nation?

What are their implements of war, how do they prepare and how use them?

8th *Amusements*.

Have they any and what are they?
do they with a view to amusement only make a feest
do they play at any games of risk, & what are they?
Have their women any games particularly to themselves, or do
they ever engage in those common to the Men
do they ever dance and what is the cerimony of their Dance
Have they any music, and what are their musical instruments

9th *Clothing Dress & Orniments*

What garments do their dress usially Consist, in both Sexes?
What are the Shapes & Materials of those garments?
In what manner are they Worn?
What orniments do they use to decorate their person?
do they use paints of Various Colours on the surface of their
Skins, and what are the most usial Colours thus used?
do they tattoe (or scarify) their bodys and on what parts?
do they imprint with the aids of a sharp pointed instrument
and some colouring matter any figures on their Skins, and
what are the part of the body on which they are usially
imprinted.
Which are the usial figures?

Customs & Manners Generally

In what particularly do they differ from those nations in our
neighbourhood.
Have they any & what are their festivals or feasts
What is the cerimony of reciving a Stranger at their Village?
When publickly recived at the Lodge of the Chief of the Village
is there any Cerimony afterwards necessary to your admission
in any other Lodge

Any information of the Indians of Louisiana so far as you may be
inabled, at your Leasure dureing this winter either from Materials
which may be in your possession, or Such as you may have it in
your power to acquire would be most sinceerly acknowledged by
me; the Interest you feel for the extention of General science would
I have no doubt more than any other consideration form your inducement to comply with this request

LEWIS'S ESTIMATE
OF EXPENSES, 1803

Mathematical Instruments	$ 217
Arms & Accoutrements extraordinary . . .	" 81
Camp Ecquipage	" 255
Medecine & packing	" 55
Means of transportation	" 430
Indian presents	" 696
Provisions extraordinary	" 224
Materials for making up the various articles into portable packs	" 55
For the pay of hunters guides & Interpreters . .	" 300
In silver coin to defray the expences of the party from Nashville to the last white settlement on the Missisourie . .	" 100
Contingencies	" 87
	$2,500

INDIAN PRESENTS

		Wt.				
12	Pipe Tomahawks . . .	8¾		.	. .	18 "
6½	lbs. Strips Sheet Iron . .	6½		.	. .	1 62
1	Ps. red flannel 47½ yds .	12¾	5	12	0	14 94
11	Ps. Hanckercheifs assd .	13 lb	22	8	9	59 83
1	doz. Ivory Combs . . .	3 oz	1	5	0	3 33
½	Catty Inda. S. Silk . . .	7 oz	1	8	1½	3 75
21	lbs. Tread assd	21 lbs	8	13	9	23 17
1	Ps. Scarlet Cloth 22 yds	28¾	21	18	9	58 50
5½	doz fan: i Floss . . .6¾ ⎫	.	7	1	6	18 87
6	Gro: Binding . . .9¼ ⎪	.	4	8	5	11 79
2	Cards Beads . . . .1¾ ⎬ 26½		1	8	6	3 80
4	doz. Butcher Knives 8¾ ⎭	.	2	0	0	5 33
12	doz. Pocket Looking					
	Glasses	12½ lb	.	.	.	5 19
15	doz Pewter do . do.	3⁶⁄₁₆	.	.	.	3 99
8	doz. Burning do.	11¼	.	.	12	12 ..
2	doz. Nonesopretty . . .	3¼	.	.	.	2 94
2	doz. Red strip'd tapes .	1½	.	.	.	2 80
72	ps. Strip'd silk ribbon . .	3¼	.	.	.	39 60
3	lbs. Beads	3 lb	.	.	.	2 01

6	Papers Small Bells . . .	1¼	.	.	.	4 02
1	box with 100 larger do.	1³⁄₁₆	.	.	.	2 25
73	Bunches Beads assd. . .	20	.	.	.	41
3½	doz: Tinsel Bands assd .	9 oz	.	.	.	3 75
1	doz: Needle Cases . . .	5½ oz	.	.	.	30
2¾	doz Lockets	3 oz	.	.	.	3 56
8½	lbs. Red Beads . . .	8½	.	.	.	25 50
2	doz: Earings		4	.	.	1 . .
8	Brass Kettles a 4/ Per lb	20 lbs.	.	.	.	10 67
12	lbs. Brass Strips . . .	.	.	.	.	6 80
500	Broaches . . . . .}	1½ b	.	.	.	62 07
72	Rings	. .	.	.	.	6 00
2	Corn Mills	52¾	.	.	.	20 00
15	doz: Scissors	17¼	.	.	.	18 97
12	lbs. Brass Wire	.	2	18	6	7 80
14	lbs Knitting Pins . . .	14	1	9	2	3 89
4600	Needles assd.	2¼	3	13	.	9 73
2800	Fish Hooks assd. . . .	6⅛	3	.	.	8 . .
1	Gro: Iron Combs . . .	8½	1	1	.	2 80
3	Gro: Curtain Rings . .	1¾	.	14	.	1 87
2	Gro: Thimbles assd. . .	2½	1	4	3	3 21
11	doz: Knives	37	9	8	9	25 17
10	lbs. Brads	16	7	6	.	1 00
8	lbs. Red lead . . .	8	.	.	.	89
2	lbs. Vermillion	2	.	.	3	3 34
130	Rolls of Tobacco (pigtail)	63	.	.	14	14 25
48	Calico Ruffled Shirts . .	.	.	.	.	71 04
15	Blankets (from P. Store)	.	.	.	.	
1	Trunk to pack sundry Ind: Prests.	.	.	.	.	3 50
8	Groce Seat or Mockasin Awls	.	.	.	.	15 67
						669 50

FROM PUBLIC STORE—vizt 15 Blankets

[Endorsed] No. I: Indian Presents Dolls. 669 50

CAMP EQUIPAGE

4	Tin Horns	1¾	.	.	2 . .
2	" Lanthorns	1	.	.	2 . .
2	" Lamps	½	.	.	50

32	" Cannisters of P. Soup	193		.	.	8 . .
1	" Box sqr. of Small astd.	1½		.	.	1 . .
3	doz: Pint Tumblers . .	6½		.	.	4 20
125	Large fishg Hooks . . . ⎫	.		.	.	4 45
	Fishg Lines assorted . . ⎬	10½		.	.	18 09
1	Stand of Fishg do. with ⎭	.		.	.	3 . .
	hooks Complete					
1	Sportsmans flaske . . .	.		.	.	1 50
8	ps. Cat gut for Mosquito	11	5	16	3	15 50
	Cart					
6	Brass Kettles & Porterage					
	25 ft.	28		.	.	15 18
1	block tin Sauce pan . .	¾		.	.	1 50
1	Corn Mill	20		.	.	9 . .
1	Set of Gold Scales & Wts.	¼		.	.	2 33
1	Rule	1 oz		.	.	60
1	Sett Iron Weights . . .	4		.	.	75
2	pr. Large Shears . . .	3½		.	.	1 86
4	doz: Packg. Needles &					
	large Awls	1		8	6	1 13
2	doz: Table Spoons . . .	3	.	14	.	1 87
4	drawing Knives	2½	.	9	.	1 20
3	doz: Gimblets	5¼ lbs	1	3	.	3 60
17	do. files & Rasps & 1 Shoe					
	float	5	.	17	4	2 31
1¼	doz. Small cord	8½	13	5	5	1 79
2	Small Vices	.		.	6	1 67
2	pr. Plyers	.		.	3	97
1	Saw Sett . . . . . ⎫	10	.	7	9	10
9	Chisels . . . . . ⎭		.	.	3	1 77
2	Adzes	4	.	9	1	1 20
2	hand Saws	4½	1	3	.	3 06
6	Augers 6	3½		12	3	1 64
2	Hatchets . . . . . ⎫	.		6	3	83
1	Wetstone . . . . . ⎬	4½	.	3	6	47
2	p. Pocket Steel yards . . ⎭	.		3	6	47
	Pkg 12 lbs Castile Soap	.		.	.	1 68
						117 67

FROM PUBLIC STORE
8   Receipt Books
48   ps. Tape

6   Brass Inkstands
6   Papers Ink Powder
1   Common Tent
1   lb. Sealing Wax
100   Quils
1   Packing Hogshead

Bought by the Purveyor of Richd. Wevill 8 Tents

45 Bags

10 yd Country Linnen ⎱ Oiled

20 ″ Brown do. ⎰

[Endorsed] No 2 Camp Equipage

MATHEMATICAL INSTRUMENTS

1 Spirit level	4 ..
1 Case platting Instruments	14 ..
1 Two pole chain	2 ..
1 Pocket Compas plated	5 ..
1 Brass Boat Compass	1 50
3 Brass Pocket Compasses	7 50
1 Magnet	1 ..
1 Hadleys Quadrant Wt Tangt Screw	22 ..
1 Metal Sextant	90 ..
Microscope to index of d	7 ..
Sett of Slates in a case	4 ..
4 oz of Talc	1 25
1 Surveying Compass wt extra needles (P by L)	23 50
1 Circular protractor & index . . . do.	8 ..
1 Six In: Pocket Telescope . . . do.	7 ..
1 Nautical Ephemeris . . . do.	1 50
1 Requisite Tables . . . do.	2 50
Kirwan's Mineralogy . . . do.	5 ..
1 Chronometer & Keys	250 75
1 Copy of Bartons Bottany (pd. by C. L.)	6 ..
Kelleys Spherics . . . do.	3 ..
2 Nautical Ephemeris . . . do.	4 ..
Log line reel & log ship	1 95
Parrallel Glass for a Horison	1 ..

[Endorsed] No 3 Mathematical Instrumts.

ARMS & ACCOUTREMENTS & AMMN

1	Pair Pocket pistols . . . . . .(P. by L.)	.	10 . .
176	lb. Gun powder 176	.	155 75
52	leaden Cannisters for Gunpowr . . . 420	.	26 33
15	Powder Horns & Pouches	.	26 25

FROM PUBLIC STORE

  15 Powder Horns
  18 Tomahaws
  15 Scalpking Knives & Belts
  15 Gun Slings
  30 Brushes & Wires
  15 Cartouch Boxes
  15 painted Knapsacks
 500 Rifle Flints
 125 Musket do.
  50 lb best rifle Powder
   1 pr. Horsemans Pistols
 420 lbs Sheet Lead

[Endorsed] No. 4 Arms, Ammn. & Accoutrets.

MEDICINES &C

1	Box	Wt.	
1	do.	Wt.	$90.69
2	lbs. Tea & Cannister W. 2 lbs.		3.80
			94.49

[Endorsed] No 5 Medicine &c

PROVISIONS &C

193	lbs. P. Soup 193	.	298 50
30	Galls Spr of Wine in 6 Kegs	.	77 20
			366 70

[Endorsed] No 6 Provisions &c

		Dolls. Cts.
45	Flannel Shirts	71 10
16	Coatees	246 63
		317 73

FROM PUBLIC STORES VIZT
15 Blankets
15 Match Coats
15 Ps. blue wool: overalls
36 pairs Stockgs
20 Frocks
30 Pr. Shirts
20 Pr Shoes

[Endorsed] No 7 Clothing

[No. 3]

Invoice of Articles received from the Arsenal for the use of Capt Lewis
May 18th. 1803

Invoice of Articles to be Dld. Cap. Lewis—

A & A	15	Powder Horns	a & a	15	Paintd Knapsacks
do.	18	Tomhawks	do.	500	Rifle flints
do.	15	Scalping Knives & Belts	do.	125	Musket do.
do.	15	Gun Slings	do.	50	lb. best Rifle Powder
do.	30	Brushes & Wires	do.	1	P. Horsemans Pistols
do.	15	Cartouch Box Belts		420	lbs. Sheet lead
Camp	8	Rect. Books	Ind P	15	Blankets
do.	48	Pieces Tape	Camp	100	Quils
do.	6	Brass Ink Stands	Clothg.	20	Pr Shoes
do.	6	Papers Ink Powder.	Camp	1	packg Hhd
do.	1	Common Tent			
Clothg.	15	Blankets 3 pt.			
do.	15	Match Coats.			
do.	15	Priv. Wool Overalls (Blue)			
do.	36	Pair Stockings			
do.	20	Frocks			
do.	30	Priv Lin Shirts			
Camp	1	lb Sealg Wax.			

To be left at Mr. Whelens Office May 18″ 1803

[Endorsed] Wm. A. Bass—for Geo. Ingels Esqr. K M S

PHILA. May 18. 1803
Mr. Israel Wheelen

Bt of Geo R. Lawton

70 Large hooks	@ 30/ pts	$2.80
55 ditto	@ 22/6 pts	1.65
1 donl. drum Lines		4.—
1 do. Rock ditto		2.50
1½ do. India Lines $5		7.50
1 India Line		.42
2 Lines—$1		2.—
Sportsman Flask		1.50
8 Stave reel		3.—
		$25.37

Rec payt
GEO. R. LAWTON
Received the within Articles
MERIWETHER LEWIS.
Capt. 1st. US. Regt. Infty.

[No. 4]

List of Charges taken out of Cap Lewis's account to be charged to other accots. as specified

176 lbs. Gunpowder		No. 16 ordnance	$155.75
B. & H.			
Leaden Canesters		No. 4	26.33
for securing			
gunpowder	Ludlam		
15 Shot-pouches	Marten	Qr Mr. 26	26.25
1 Par of pistols	Barnhill	Ord	10. . .
6 Brass kettles from	Harbeson & Sons	No. 13	15.18
one to five gallons			
4 Drawing-knives	H & Worth	"	1.20
3 Doz. Gimblets	Do.	"	3.6
assortd			
2 Small vices	Do.	"	1.67
1 Saw-set	Do.	"	. .10
9 Chissels assorted	Do.	"	1.77
2 Hand saws	Do.	Ord. No. 10	3.6
6 Augers assorted	Do.	"	1.64
17 Files assorted	Do.	"	2.31
1 Whetstone	Do.	"	.47
Medecine & Sergecal instruments Hospl.		"	94.49

No. 5 & 7—GOS & P. Logan

Oil-cloth tents   Wevill—Qr Mr.

& Baggs   No. 27   119.39

Transportation of public stores from Philadelphia to Indian D.
Pittsburgh

1 Boat and her caparison, including spiked poles, boat-hooks & toe line
to be furnished at Pittsburgh

18 Small falling axes to be furnished at Do. Indian D.

$462.67

176 lbs. Gunpowder B. & H. $155.75
Leaden Canesters for securing gunpowder No 16 ordnance
No. 4   26.33
15 Shot pouches   Marten Ludlam Qr Mr   26   26.25

[No. 5]

Bill of Gillaspy & Strong for Medicine

Israel Wheelen Purveyor   Bought of Gillaspy & Strong
the following articles for the use of M. Lewis Esquire on his tour up the
Missisipi River, & supplied by his Order:—Viz

15 lb. Pulv. Cort. Peru	$30.00	4 oz. Laudanum .50
½ " " Jalap	.67	2 lb. Ung. Basilic Flav. 50 1.00
½ " " Rhei [Rhubarb]	1.	1 " " e lap Calimin 50 .50
4 oz. " Ipecacuan.	1.25	1 " " Epispastric 1.
2 lb. " Crem. Tart.	.67	1 " " Mercuriale 1.25
2 oz. Gum Camphor	.40	1. Emplast. Diach. S. .50
1 lb. " Assafoetid.	1.	1. Set Pocket Insts. small 9.50
½ lb " Opii Turk, opt.	2.50	1. " Teeth " " 2.25
¼ " " Tragacanth	.37	1. Clyster Syringe 2.75
6 lb. Sal Glauber 10	.67	4. Penis do. 1.
2 " " Nitri 33½	.67	3. Best Lancets .80 2.40
2 " " Copperas	.10	1. Tourniquet 3.50
6 oz. Sacchar. Saturn. opt.	.37	2. oz Patent Lint .25
4 " Calomel	.75	50. doz. Bilious Pills to Order
		of B. Rush. 10 5.00
1 " Tartar Emetic	.10	6. Tin Canisters 25 1.50
4 " Vitriol Alb.	.12	3. 8 oz Gd. Stopd. bottles 40 1.20
½ lb. Columbo Rad.	1.	5 4 " Tinctures do 1.85
¼ " Elix. Vitriol	.25	6. 4 " Salt mo. 2.22
¼ " Ess. Menth. pip.	.50	1. Walnut Chest 4.50

¼ " Bals. Copaiboe	.37	1. Pine do.	1.20
¼ " " Traumat.	.50	Porterage	.30
2. oz Magnesia	.20		
			$90.69

¼ lb. Indian Ink	1.50
2 oz Gum Elastic	.37
2 " Nutmegs	.75
2 " Cloves	.31
4 " Cinnamon	.20
	$46.52

PHILA May 26. 1803
Recd May 27, 1803 of Israel Whelen Ninety Dollars & 69 cents in full—
for Gillaspy & Strong.
$90.69   THOMAS H. DAWSON

Duplicate   Received the within articles—
                                                  MERIWETHER LEWIS.
                                                  Capt 1st U.S. Regt. Infty.

[Endorsed] No. 14   Gillaspy & Strong   Expedn to W. O. $90.69   May 27. 1803
Say Hospital Dr.

[No. 6]
Bill of Rich. Wevill for making tents, etc.

Mr Israel Whelen   To Richd Wevill Dr.
10103

June 15	To 107 Yds of ⅞ brown Linen	a 1/6	21.40
	To 45½ Yds of ⅝ Flanders Sheeting . . .	a 2/5	14.49
	Shod be 14.66 but no more pd than 14:49		
	To 10 Yds of ⅝ Country Linen	3/	4 . .
	To making the brown Linen into 8/ Tents,		
	with Eyelet-holes, laps, &c., thread &c. .		16 . .
	To making the Russia Sheeting into 45 bags.		
	thread & cord	a 1/6	9 . .
	To 2 Gross of Hooks & Eyes	a 3/9	1 . .
	To Oiling all the Linen & Sheeting		
	156 Square Yards	a 2/6	52 . .
	To Numbering all the Bags & Tents . . .		1.50
			$119.39

Rec'd June 18th 1803 of Israel Whelen One hundred Nineteen dollars 39 Cents infull & Signed Two Receipts

$119.39/100   RICHARD WEVIL

United States Arsenal July 20" 1803   Received the above specified Tents & Bags

G. W. INGELS

[Endorsed] No. 11   Richd. Wevill $119:39   June 17: 1803

Capt Lewis

This Box of Mathematical Instruments to be Sent for to Mr. Paterson's & well Secured with canvas—mark'd "This side up," on the top—& particular charge given to the waggoner respectg it.

Some copies of Bills to be sent him.

weight of remaining articles to be sent him

A Strong Waggon   Wt. from here 2700—to be increased to 3500 or more If he has left any small bills unpaid requests Mr W. to pay them.

[Endorsed] Mem: Capt Lewis.

THE JOURNALS OF
LEWIS AND CLARK

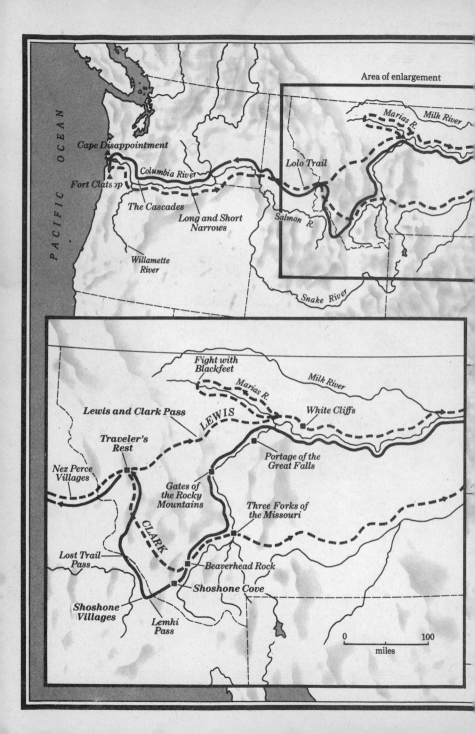

Area of enlargement

PACIFIC OCEAN

Cape Disappointment

Columbia River

Fort Clatsop

The Cascades

Long and Short
Narrows

Willamette
River

Lolo Trail

Marias R.

Milk River

Salmon R.

Snake River

Fight with
Blackfeet

Marias R.

Milk River

Lewis and Clark Pass

LEWIS

White Cliffs

Traveler's
Rest

Portage of the
Great Falls

Nez Perce
Villages

Gates of
the Rocky
Mountains

Three Forks of
the Missouri

CLARK

Lost Trail
Pass

Beaverhead Rock

Shoshone Cove

Shoshone
Villages

Lemhi
Pass

0   100

miles

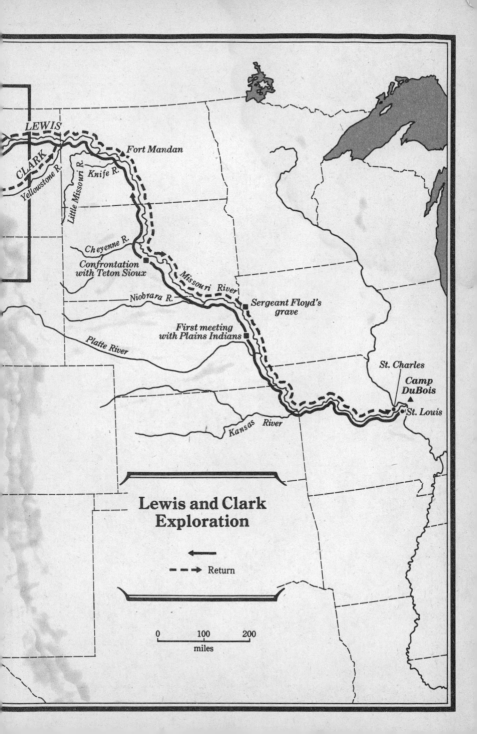

LEWIS

CLARK

Yellowstone R.

Little Missouri R.

Knife R.

Fort Mandan

Cheyenne R.

Confrontation
with Teton Sioux

Niobrara R.

Missouri River

Sergeant Floyd's
grave

First meeting
with Plains Indians

Platte River

St. Charles

Camp
DuBois

St. Louis

Kansas River

Lewis and Clark
Exploration

- - -> Return

0   100   200
miles

ONE

Up the Missouri

From Camp Dubois to Vermillion River
May 13–August 24, 1804

[Clark]   River a Dubois opposet the mouth of the Missourie River[1]
Sunday May the 13th. 1804.

I despatched an express this morning to Capt. Lewis at St. Louis, all our provisions Goods and equipage on Board of a Boat of 22 oars a large Perogue of 71 oares a Second Perogue of 6 oars, Complete with Sails &c. &c. Men compd. with Powder Cartragies and 100 Balls each, all in health and readiness to set out. Boats and everything Complete, with the necessary stores of provisions & such articles of merchandize as we thought ourselves authorised to procure—tho' not as much as I think nessy. for the multitude of Inds. thro which we must pass on our road across the Continent

Latd.   38°–55′–19″–6/10 North of equator
Longtd. 89 –57 –45 –West of Greenwich

Monday May 14th. 1804

Rained the fore part of the day I determined to go as far as St. Charles[2] a french Village 7 Leags. up the Missourie, and wait at

---

[1] River Dubois (Wood River, Illinois) was where the Corps of Discovery had prepared for the expedition during the winter of 1803–1804.

[2] St. Charles, Missouri, was then the oldest of the northern French settlements west of the Mississippi.

that place untill Capt. Lewis could finish the business in which he was obliged to attend to at St. Louis and join me by Land from that place 24 miles; by this movement I calculated that if any alterations in the loading of the Vestles or other Changes necessary, that they might be made at St. Charles

I set out at 4 oClock P.M, in the presence of many of the neighbouring inhabitents, and proceeded on under a jentle brease up the Missourie to the upper Point of the 1st Island 4 Miles and camped on the Island which is Situated Close on the right (or Starboard) Side, and opposit the mouth of a Small Creek called Cold water,[3] a heavy rain this after-noon

[Lewis]   Sunday May 20th 1804.

The morning was fair, and the weather pleasent;   at 10 OCk. A M. agreably to an appointment of the preceeding day, I was joined by Capt Stoddard, Lieuts. Milford & Worrell together with Messrs. A. Chouteau, C. Gratiot, and many other rispectable inhabitants of St. Louis, who had engaged to accompany me to the Vilage of St. Charles; accordingly at 12 OCk., after bidding an affectionate adieu to my Hostis, that excellent woman the spouse of Mr. Peter Chouteau, and some of my fair friends of St. Louis, we set forward to that vilage in order to join my friend companion and fellow labourer Capt. William Clark, who had previously arrived at that place with the party destined for the discovery of the interior of the continent of North America   the first 5 miles of our rout laid through a beatifull high leavel and fertile prarie which incircles the town of St. Louis from N. W. to S. E.   the lands through which we then passed are somewhat broken less fertile   the plains and woodlands are here indiscriminately interspersed untill you arrive within three miles of the vilage when the woodland commences and continues to the Missouri   the latter is extreemly fertile. At half after one P. M. our progress was interrupted by the near approach of a violent thunderstorm from the N. W. and concluded to take shelter in a little cabbin hard by untill the rain should be over; accordingly we alighted and remained about an hour and a half and regailed ourselves with a

[3] This creek was just above Bellefontaine, Missouri, where a U.S. military post was established in 1803 (Thwaites).

could collation which we had taken the precaution to bring with us from St. Louis.

The clouds continued to follow each other in rapaid succession, insomuch that there was but little prospect of it's ceasing to rain this evening; as I had determined to reach St. Charles this evening and knowing that there was now no time to be lost I set forward in the rain, most of the gentlemen continued with me, we arrived at half after six and joined Capt Clark, found the party in good health and sperits.

On consulting with my friend Capt C. I found it necessary that we should pospone our departure untill 2 P. M. the next day and accordingly gave orders to the party to hold themselves in readiness to depart at that hour.

Capt. Clark now informed me that having gotten all the stores on board the Barge and perogues on the evening of the 13th of May he determined to leave our winter cantonment at the mouth of River Dubois the next day, and to ascend the Missouri as far as the Vilage of St. Charles, where, as it had been previously concerted between us, he was to wait my arrival; this movement while it advanced us a small distance on our rout, would also enable him to determine whether the vessels had been judiciously loaded and if not timely to make the necessary alterations; accordingly at 4 P. M. on Monday the 14th. of May 1804, he embarked with the party in the presence of a number of the neighbouring Citizens who had assembled to witness his departure. during the fore part of this Day it rained excessively hard. In my last letter to the President dated at St. Louis I mentioned the departure of Capt. Clark from River Dubois on the 15th. Inst, which was the day that had been calculated on, but having completed the arrangements a day earlyer he departed on the 14th. as before mentioned. On the evening of the 14th. the party halted and encamped on the upper point of the first Island which lyes near the Larbord shore, on the same side and nearly opposite the center of this Island a small Creek disimbogues called *Couldwater*.

[Clark]   May 21st. 1804 Monday—
Set out at half passed three oClock under three Cheers from the gentlemen on the bank and proceeded on to the head of the Island (which is Situated on the Stbd. Side) 3 Miles Soon after we Set

out to day a hard Wind from the W. S W accompanied with a hard rain, which lasted with Short intervales all night, opposit our Camp a Small creek coms in on the Lbd Side.[4]

May 22nd Tuesday 1804—
This day we passed Several Islands, and Some high lands on the Starboard Side, verry hard water.

May 23rd. Wednesday 1804—
We Set out early ran on a Log and detained one hour, proceeded the Course of Last night 2 miles to the mouth of a Creek [R] on the Stbd. Side[5] called Osage Womans R, about 30 yds Wide, opposit a large Island and a [*American*] Settlement.[6]

Many people Came to See us, we passed a large *Cave* on the Lbd. Side (Called by the french the *Tavern*)—about 120 feet wide 40 feet Deep & 20 feet high many different immages are Painted on the Rock at this place the Inds. & French pay omage. Many names are wrote on the rock, Stoped about one mile above for Capt Lewis who had assended the Clifts which is at the Said Cave 300 fee[t] high, hanging over the waters, the water excessively Swift to day.

This evening we examined the arms and amunition found those mens arms in the perogue in bad order. a fair evening. Capt. Lewis near falling from the Pinecles of rocks 300 feet, he caught at 20 foot.

May 24th Thursday 1804—
Set out early. passed a verry bad part of the River Called the Deavels race ground, this is where the Current Sets against some projecting rocks for half a Mile on the Labd. Side

The Swiftness of the Current Wheeled the boat, Broke our *Toe* rope, and was nearly over Setting the boat, all hands jumped out on the upper Side and bore on that Side untill the Sand washed

---

[4] Larboard (or left) side.

[5] Starboard (or right) side.

[6] The American settlement just below this place was the Kentucky colony recently founded on Femme Osage River, about six miles above its mouth; among these settlers was Daniel Boone, who in 1798 had obtained a grant of land there from the Spanish authorities, whereon he resided until 1804 (Thwaites).

from under the boat and Wheeled on the next bank   by the time
She wheeled a 3rd Time   got a rope fast to her Stern and by the
means of swimmers was Carred to Shore and when her stern was
down whilst in the act of Swinging a third time into Deep Water
near the Shore,   we returned, to the Island where we Set out and
assended under the Bank which I have just mentioned, as falling
in,   here George Drewyer & Willard, two of our men who left us
at St. Charles to come on by land joined us,   we camped about 1
mile above where we were So nearly being lost, on the Labd. Side
at a Plantation.   all in Spirits.   This place I call the *retragrade* bend
as we were obliged to fall back 2 miles

Course & Distance of the 24th May
S. 63° W,   4 Ms. to a pt. on Stbd. Side
S. 68 W,   3 Ms. to a pt on Lbd. Side
S. 75° W,   3 Ms. to a pt. on Stbd. Side
          10

May 25th. Friday 1804—
Camped at the mouth of a Creek called River a Chouritte, [*La
Charrette*], above a Small french Village of 7 houses and as many
families,[7] settled at this place to be convt. to hunt, & trade with
the Indians

The people at this Village is pore, houses Small,   they sent us
milk & eggs to eat.

[Orderly Book; Lewis]   Detachment Orders.
                                         May 26th. 1804.

The Commanding Officers direct, that the three Squads under
the command of Sergts. Floyd Ordway and Pryor heretofore forming
two messes each, shall untill further orders constitute three messes
only, the same being altered and organized as follows (viz)

---

[7] Gass and Floyd, in their journals, call this place St. John's, and say that it was
"the last white settlement on the river" (Thwaites).

Sergt. Charles Floyd.

PRIVATES
Hugh Mc.Neal
Patric Gass
Reubin Fields
John B Thompson
John Newman
Richard Winsor
Francis Rivet & (*French*)
Joseph Fields

Sergt. John Ordway

PRIVATES
William Bratton
John Colter
Moses B. Reed (*Soldier*)

Alexander Willard
William Warner
Silas Goodrich
John Potts &
Hugh Hall

Sergt. Nathaniel Pryor

PRIVATES
George Gibson
George Shannon
John Shields
John Collins
Joseph Whitehouse
Peter Wiser
Peter Crusat &
Francis Labuche

The commanding officers further direct that the remainder of the detatchmen[t] shall form two messes; and that the same be constituted as follows.(viz)

Patroon, Baptist Dechamps

ENGAGES.
Etienne Mabbauf
Paul Primaut
Charles Hébert
Baptist La Jeunesse
Peter Pinaut
Peter Roi &
Joseph Collin

Corpl. Richard Warvington

Privates.
Robert Frasier
John Boleye
John Dame
Ebinezer Tuttle &
Isaac White.

Sergt. John Ordway will continue to issue the provisions and make the detales for guard or other duty.

The day after tomorrow lyed corn and grece will be issued to the party, the next day Poark and flour, and the day following indian meal and poark; and in conformity to that rotiene provisions will continue to be issued to the party untill further orders. should any of the messes prefer indian meal to flour they may recieve it accordingly—no poark is to be issued when we have fresh meat on hand.

Labuche and Crusat will man the larboard bow oar alternately, and the one not engaged at the oar will attend as the Bows-man, and when the attention of both these persons is necessary at the bow, their oar is to be manned by any idle hand on board.

MERIWETHER LEWIS Capt.

WM. CLARK Cpt

[Clark]   May 29th. Tuesday—
   Rained last night, Cloudy morning 4 hunters sent out with orders to return at 12 oClock

Took equal altitudes of Suns Lower limb found it 105°–31′–45″
                 A. M. 9h–25′–24″   P M 2h–35′–31″
                        9 –26 – 3   2 –37 –20
                        9 –27 –27   2 –38 –52
Error of Sextion 8′. 45″–
⊙8 Magnetic Azzamuth S. 83° W.
Time at place of obsvn. by bromtr. P. M. 4 h–4 m–44 s
Double altitude of ⊙ L Limb — 71°–24′–00″

Cap Lewis observed Meridean altitude of ⊙ U.L. back observation with the octant & artificeal horozen—gave for altitude on the Limb 38°.44′–00″. octant error—2–0–0 +

had the Perogues loaded and all prepared to Set out at 4 oClock after finishing the observations & all things necessary found that one of the hunters had not returned, we determined to proceed on & leave one perogue to wate for him, accordingly at half past four we set out and came on 4 miles & camped on the Lbd. Side above a small Creek called Deer Creek, Soon after we came too we heard several guns fire down the river, we answered them by a Discharge of a Swivell on the Bow.

May 31st. Thursday 1804—
   a *cajaux* of Bear Skins and pelteries came down from the Grand Osarge, one french man, one Indian, and a squaw, they had letters from the man Mr. Choteau Sent to that part of the Osarge nation settled on Arkansa River mentioning that his letter was commited

to the flaims,   the Inds. not believing that the Americans had possession of the Countrey they disregard'ed St. Louis & their Supplies
&c. Several *rats*[8] of Considerable Size was Caught in the woods to
day.   Capt. Lewis went out to the woods & found many curious
Plants & Srubs,   one Deer killed this evening.

June 2nd Satturday 1804
   George Drewyer & John Shields who we had sent with the horses
by Land on the N. Side joined us this evening much worsted, they
being absent Seven Days depending on their gun, the greater part
of the time rain,   they were obliged to raft or Swim many Creeks,
those men gave a flattering account of the Countrey[9] Commencing
below the first hill on the N Side and extend'g Parrelal with the
river for 30 or 40 Ms.   The Two Muddy rivers passing thro. & som
fine Springs & Streems   our hunters kill several Deer to day, Some
Small licks on the SE of the Osage River.

June 5th Tuesday 1804—
   after Jurking the meet killed yesterday and Crossing the hunting
party we Set out at 6 oClock
   at 11 oClock brought too a small Caissee [*raft made of two canoes
tied together*] in which was two french men, from 80 Leagues up the
Kansias [*Kanzas*] R. where they wintered, and Cought a great quantity of Beaver, the greater part of which they lost by fire from the
Praries,   those men inform [us] that the Kansas Nation are now out
in the plains hunting Buffalow,   they hunted last winter on this
river
   Passed a projecting rock on which was painted a figure
and a Creek at 2 ms. above Called Little Manitou Creek,
from the Painted rock   this Creek 20 yds. wide on the L.
Sd.   passed a Small Creek on L. S. opposit a verry bad Sand bar
of Several Ms. in extent, which we named *Sand C*,   here my Servent
York Swam to the Sand bar to geather Greens for our Dinner, and
returned with a Sufficient quantity wild *Creases* [*Cresses*] or Tung
grass,   we passed up for 2 ms. on the L. S. of this Sand and was

---

[8] Eastern wood rat (*Neotona floridana*).
[9] In the vicinity of Jefferson City, Missouri.

obliged to return, the watr. uncertain the quick Sand moveing we
had a fine wind, but could not make use of it, our Mast being broke
our Scout discovd. the fresh sign of about 10 Inds. I expect that
those Indians are on their way to war, against the Osages nation
probably they are the Saukees.

Course & Destance June 5th.

N. 51°, W. 5 Ms. to a pt. on S. S. psd. 3 C, 1 S. 2 L. S.
N 23° W 7½ Ms. a pt. L. S. psd. Mon. [Manitou.] Creek
<u>12½</u>

June 6th. Wednesday 1804
Mended our Mast this morning & Set out at 7 oClock under a
jentle breese from S. E. by S passed the large Island, and a Creek
Called Split rock Creek[10] the water excessivly Strong, so much so
that we Camped Sooner than the usual time to waite for the perogue, The banks are falling in verry much to day river rose last
night a foot.
I am Still verry unwell with a Sore throat & head ake

June 7th. Thursday 1804—
Set out early passed the head of the Island opposit which we
Camped last night, and braekfast at the Mouth of a large Creek on
the S. S. of 30 yds wide called big *Monetou*
a Short distance above the mouth of this Creek, is Several Cou-
rious paintings and carving on the projecting rock of Limestone
inlade with white red & blue' flint, of a verry good quallity, the
Indians have taken of this flint great quantities. We landed at this
Inscription and found it a Den of Rattle Snakes, we had not landed
3 Minites before three verry large Snakes was observed in the Crev-
ises of the rocks & killed. at the mouth of the last mentioned Creek
Capt. Lewis took four or five men & went to Some Licks or Springs
of Salt Water from two to four miles up the Creek, on Rt. Side
the water of those Springs are not Strong, say from 4 to 600 gs. of
water for a Bushel of Salt passed some Small willow Islands and
camped at the mouth of a small river Called *Good Womans* River[11]

---

[10] Perchee Creek, Missouri.
[11] Bonne Femme Creek, near Boonville, Missouri.

this river is about 35 yards Wide and said to be navagable for Perogues Several Leagues. Capt. Lewis with 2 men went up the Creek a short distance. our Hunters brought in three *Bear* this evening, and informs that the Countrey thro: which they passed from the last Creek is fine, rich land, & well watered.

10th of June 1804—
Cap. Lewis Killed a large Buck,   passed a large Isd. call'd Shecco[12] and camped in a Prarie on the L. S. I walked out three miles, found the prarie composed of good Land and plenty of water roleing & interspursed with points of timber land. Those Praries are not like those, or a number of those E. of the Mississippi void of every thing except grass,   they abound with Hasel Grapes & a wild plumb of a Superior quallity, Called the Osages Plumb Grows on a bush the hight of a Hasel (and is three times the sise of other Plumbs,) and hang in great quantities on the bushes I saw great numbers of Deer in the Praries,   the evening is Cloudy, our party in high Spirits.

12th of June. Tuesday 1804
at 1 oClock we brought too [to], two Chaussies one loaded with furs & Pelteries, the other with Greece [*buffalow grease & tallow*] we purchased 300 lbs of Greese, and finding that old Mr. Durioun was of the party we questioned him untill it was too late to Go further, and Concluded to Camp for the night,   those people inform nothing of much information.

Concluded to take old Durioun back as fur as the Soux nation with a view to get some of their Cheifs to visit the Presdt. of the United S. (This man being a verry confidential friend of those people, he haveing resided with the Nation 20 odd years) and to accompany them on[13]

June 17th. Sunday 1804 (S. 65° W. 1 Ml. S. Side.)
The party is much aflicted with *Boils*, and Several have the Deassentary, which I contribute to the water The Countrey about this

[12] Chicot (a French word, meaning "stump"), now Harrison Island (Coues). Clark enters the prairie country called Little Dixie in Missouri.

[13] Pierre Dorion, Sr., had married and settled down among the group of Lakota called the Yankton Sioux.

place is butifull on the river rich & well timbered the high lands
& Prarie coms. in the bank of the river and and continus back, well
watered and abounds in Deer Elk & Bear The Ticks & Musquiters
are verry troublesome.

June 20th. Wednesday

I saw *Pelicans* to day on a Sand bar, My Servent York nearly
loseing an Eye by a man throwing Sand into it, we came too at
the lower Point of a Small Island, the party on Shore we have not
Seen Since we passed Tiger R. The Land appear'd verry good on
each Side of the river to day and well timbered, We took Some
Loner observations, which detaind. us untill 1 oClock a butifull
night but the air exceedingly Damp, & the Mosquiters verry
troublesome

21st. June Thursday

at Sunset the atmespier presented every appearance of wind, Blue
& White Streeks centiring at the Sun as She disappeared and the
Clouds Situated to the S. W. Guilded in the most butifull manner.

The Countrey and Lands on each Side of the river is various as
useal, and may be classed as follows, viz: the low or overflown points
or bottom land, of the groth of Cotton & Willow, the 2nd. or high
bottom of rich furtile Soile of the groth of Cotton, Walnut, Som
ash, Hackberry, Mulberry, Lynn [Linden] & Sycamore. the third
or high Lands rises gradually from the 2nd. bottom (except whin it
Coms to the river then from the river) about 80 or 100 foot roleing
back Supplied with water (the small rivers of which loses themselves
in the bottom land) and are covered with a variety of timber Such
as Oake of different Kinds Blue ash, Walnut &c. &c. as far as the
Praries, which I am informed lie back from the river, at Some places
near & others a great Distance

24th June Sunday—

I joined the boat this morng at 8 oClock (I will only remark that
dureing the time I lay on the sand waiting for the boat, a large Snake
Swam to the bank imediately under the Deer which was hanging
over the water, and no great distance from it, I threw chunks and
drove this snake off Several times. I found that he was so determined on getting to the meet, I was compelld. to kill him, the

part of the Deer which attracted this Snake I think was the Milk from the bag of the Doe.) I observed great quts. of Bear Signs, where the had passed in all Directions thro the bottoms in Serch of Mulberries, which were in great numbers. in all the bottoms thro which our party passed)

Passed the mouth of a Creek 20 yds. wide name [named] *Hay Cabbin Creek*[14] from Camps of Straw built on it

28 June Thursday—[15]

To Describe the most probable of the various accounts of this great river of the Kansas, would be too lengthy & uncertain to insert here, it heads with the river Del Noird in the black Mountain or ridge which Divides the Waters of the Kansas *Del Nord,* & Callarado from those of the Missourie (and not well assertaind.) This river receves its name from a Nation which dwells at this time on its banks & [has] 2 villages one about 20 leagues & the other 40 Leagues up, those Indians are not verry noumerous at this time, reduced by war with their neighbours, &c, they formerly lived on the South Banks of the Missourie 24 Leagues above this river in a open & butifull plain, and were verry noumerous at the time the french first Settled the Illinois, I am told they are a fierce & warlike people, being badly Supplied with fire arms, become easily conquered by the Aiauway & Saukees who are better furnished with those materials of War, This Nation is now out in the Plains hunting the Buffalow our hunters killed Several Deer and Saw Buffalow, Men impd. [employed] Dressing Skins & makeing themselves comfortable, the high lands come to the river Kansas on the upper Side at about a mile, full in view, and a butifull place for a fort, good landing-place, the waters of the Kansas is verry disigreeably tasted to me.

[Orderly Book; Clark]   Camp Mouth of the Kansies June 29th. 1804
Ordered—A Court Martiall will Set this day at 11 oClock, to consist of five members, for the trial of *John Collins* and *Hugh Hall*, Confined on Charges exhibited against them by Sergeant Floyd, agreeable to the articles of War.

---

[14] Little Blue River, in Jackson County, Missouri (Coues).
[15] At the future site of Westport and Kansas City.

Detail for the Court
Sergt. Nat. Pryor presd.
2 John Colter ⎫
3 John Newmon ⎪
4 Pat.Gass   ⎬ Mbs.
1 J. B. Thompson ⎭

John Potts to act as Judge advocate.

The Court Convened agreeable to order and proceeded to the trial of the Prisoners Viz

John Collins Charged "with getting drunk on his post this Morning out of whiskey put under his charge as a Sentinal, and for Suffering *Hugh Hall* to draw whiskey out of the Said Barrel intended for the party."

To this Charge the prisoner plead *not Guilty*.

The Court after mature deliv[b]eration on the evidence adduced &c. are of oppinion that the prisoner is *Guilty* of the Charge exhibited against him, and do therefore sentence him to receive *one hundred Lashes on his bear Back*.

Hugh Hall was brought before the Court Charged with takeing whiskey out of a Keg this morning which whiskey was stored on the Bank (and under the Charge of the Guard) Contrary to all order, rule, or regulation."

To this Charge the prisoner "Pleaded Guilty."

The Court find the prisoner Guilty and Sentence him to receive *fifty* Lashes on his bear Back.

The Commanding Officers approve of the Sentence of the Court and orders that the Punishment take place at half past three this evening, at which time the party will Parrade for inspection.

[Clark]   July the 7th. Satturday 1804—

at 7 oClock a violent Ghust of Wind from the N. E with Some rain, which lasted half an hour (G D. informs me that he Saw in a Pond on the S. S. which we passed yesterday, a number of young Swans , one man verry sick, Struck with the Sun, Capt. Lewis bled him & gave Niter which has revived him much

July 12th. Thursday 1804—

Concluded to Delay here to day with a view of takeing equal altitudes & makeing observations as well as refreshing our men who

are much fatigued. after an early Brackfast I with five men in a
Perogue assended the River *Ne-Ma-haw*[16] about three Miles to the
Mouth of a Small creek on the Lower Side, here I got out of the
Perogue, after going to Several Small Mounds in a leavel plain, I
assended a hill on the Lower Side, on this hill Several artificial
Mounds were raised, from the top of the highest of those Mounds
I had an extensive view of the Serounding Plains, which afforded
one of the most pleasing prospect I ever beheld, under me a Butifull
River of Clear Water of about 80 yards wide Meandering thro: a
leavel and extensive meadow, as far as I could See, the prospect
much enlivened by the fiew Trees & Srubs which is bordering the
bank of the river, and the Creeks & runs falling into it, The bottom
land is covered with Grass of about 4½ feet high, and appears as
leavel as a smoth surfice, the 2d bottom is also covered with Grass
and rich weeds & flours, interspersed with copses of the Osage
Plumb, on the riseing lands, Small groves of trees are Seen, with
a numbers of Grapes and a Wild Cherry resembling the common
Wild Cherry, only larger and grows on a small bush on the tops of
those hills in every direction, I observed artifical Mounds (or as I
may more justly term graves) which to me is a strong evidence of
this Country being once thickly Settled. (The Indians of the Missouris Still keep up the Custom of Burrying their dead on high
ground) after a ramble of about two miles about I returned to the
perogue and decended down the river, gathd. Som *grapes* nearly
ripe, on a Sandstone Bluff about ¼ of a Mile from its mouth on
the Lower Side I observed some Indian Marks, went to the rock
which jucted over the water and marked my name & the day of the
month & year. This river heads near one of the villages of the
Pania [*Pawnee*] on the River Blue[17] a branch of the *Kansas* River.
above this river about half a mile the Prarie comes to the *Missouri*,
after my return to Camp on the Island completed Som observations.
Tri[e]d a man (W. C.) for Sleeping on his Post & inspected the
arms amunition &c. of the party found all complete, Took Some
Luner Observations. three Deer killed to day.

[16] In Richardson County, Nebraska.
[17] Big Blue River.

Latd. 39°–55′–56″ N.

[Orderly Book; Lewis]   Camp New Island July 12th. 1804.
A Court ma[r]tial consisting of the two commanding officers will
convene this day at 1 OCk. P.M. for the trial of such prisoners as
may be brought before them; one of the court will act as Judge
Advocate.

M. LEWIS
WM CLARK

[Clark]
The Commanding officers, Capts. M. Lewis & W. Clark consti-
tuted themselves a Court Martial for the trial of such prisoners as
are *Guilty* of *Capatal Crimes*, and under the rules and articles of *War*
punishable by DEATH.
Alexander Willard was brought foward Charged with *"Lying down
and Sleeping on his post" whilst a Sentinal, on the Night* of the 11th.
Instant" (by John Ordway Sergeant of the Guard)
To this Charge the prisoner pleads *Guilty of Lying Down, and Not
Guilty, of Going to Sleep.*
The Court after Duly Considering the evidence aduced, are of
oppinion that the *Prisoner* Alexdr. Willard is guilty of every part of
the Charge exhibited against him. it being a breach of the *rules*
and articles of *War* (as well as tending to the probable distruction
of the party) *do Sentience* him to receive *One hundred lashes, on his
bear back, at four different times in equal proportion.* and Order that
the punishment Commence this evening at Sunset, and Continue
to be inflicted (by the Guard) every evening until Completed

WM. CLARK
M. LEWIS

July 14th. Satturday 1804—
Some hard Showers of rain this morning prevented our Setting
out until 7 oClock,   at *half past Seven*, the atmispr. became Sudenly
darkened by a black and dismal looking Cloud,   at the time we
were in a Situation (not to be bettered,) near the upper point of the
Sand Island, on which we lay, and the opposit Shore, the *bank*
was falling in and lined with snags as far as we could See down,
in this Situation the Storm which passd. over an open Plain from

the N. E. Struck the our boat on the Starbd. quarter, and would have thrown her up on the Sand island dashed to pices in an Instant, had not the party leeped out on the Leward Side and kept her off with the assistance of the ancker & Cable, untill the *Storm* was over, the waves washed over her windward Side and she must have filled with water if the *Lockers* which is [had not been] covered with *Tarpoling* & threw of the Water prevented any quantity getting into Bilge of the Boat In this Situation we Continued about 40 Minits. when the Storm Sudenly Seased and the river become Instancetaniously as Smoth as Glass.

July 15th. Sunday—
after continueing at the mouth of this Creek[18] about an hour, I swam across and proceeded on about 3 miles and halted to waite for the boat, which was some distance below. In all this days march thro woods & Praries, I only Saw three Deer & 3 fawns. I had at one part of the Prarie a verry extensive view of all the Countrey around up and down the river a Considerable distance, on the Larbd. Sd. one continued Plain, on the S. S. Some timber on the bank of the river, for a Short distance back of this timber is a bottom Plain of four or five miles back to the hills and under the hills between them & the river this plain appeared to extend 20 or 30 miles, those hills have but little timber, and the Plain appears to Continue back of them, I saw Great quantities of Grapes, Plums of 2 kinds, Wild Cherries of 2 Kinds, Hazelnuts, and Goosberries.

July 21st. Satturday 1804—
at 7 oClock the wind luled and it Commns'd raining, arrived at the lower Mouth of the Great River *Platt* at 10 oClock

This Great river being much more rapid than the Missourie forces its Current against the opposit Shore. The Current of this river comes with great velosity roleing its Sands into the Missouri, filling up its Bead & Compelling it to incroach on the S [*North*] Shore. we found great dificuelty in passing around the Sand at the Mouth of this River. Capt. Lewis and Myself with 6 men in a perogue went up this Great river Platt about 2 Miles, found the Current verry rapid

---

[18] The Little Nemaha, at the edge of the Great Plains.

roleing over Sands, passing through different Channels none of them more than five or Six feet deep, about 900 [*600*] yards Wide at the Mouth,   I am told by one of our Party who wintered two winters on this river, that "it is much wider above, and does not rise more than five or six feet" Spreds verry wide and from its rapidity & roleing Sands Cannot be navagated with Boats or Perogues.   The Indians pass this river in Skin Boats which is flat and will not turn over.   The Otteaus[19] a Small nation reside on the South Side 10 Leagues up, the Panies on the Same Side 5 Leagues higher up. about 10 Leagues up this river on the S. Side a Small river Comes into the Platt Called Salt River, "the water So brackish that it Can't be Drank at Some Seasons, I went on Shore S. S. and proceeded up one mile thro: high Bottom land open   a great number of wolves about us this evening

July 22nd. Sunday 1804—
Set out verry early with a view of Getting Some Situation above in time to take equal altitudes and take observations, as well as one Calculated to make our party Comfortable in a Situation where they Could receve the benefit of a Shade.

This being a good Situation and much nearer the Otteaus town than the Mouth of the Platt, we Concluded to delay at this place a fiew days and Send for Some of the Chiefs of that nation, to let them know of the Change of Government the wishes of our government to Cultivate friendship with them, the Objects of our journy and to present them with a flag and Some Small presents.

Some of our Provisions in the French Perogue being wet it became necessary to Dry them a fiew days.   wind hard from N W.   five Deer Killed to day.   the river rise a little.

Camp White Catfish Nine [10] Miles above the Platt River,[20]
Monday the 23d. of July 1804—
A fair morning   Set a party to look for timber for Ores, two parties to hunt,   at 11 oClock Sent off George Drewyer & *Peter Crousett* with some tobacco to invite the Otteaus if at their town and Panies

[19] Otos.
[20] On the Iowa side of the Missouri, opposite Bellevue, Nebraska.

if they saw them, to come and talk with us at our Camp &c. &c.
(at this Season the Indians on this river are in the Praries hunting
the Buffalow, but from some signs of hunters, near this place & the
Plains being on fire near their towns induce a belief that they this
nation have returned to get some Green Corn or roasting Ears)
raised a flag Staff   Sund and Dryed our provisions &c.

I commence Coppying a Map of the river below to Send to the
P. [President] U. S.   five Deer Killed to day   one man with a tumer
on his breast,   Prepared our Camp the men put their arms in order

White Catfish Camp 10 Ms. above Platt
24th. of July 1804 Tuesday—
the wind blows hard from the South, the Breezes which are verry
frequent in this part of the Missouri is cool and refreshing.   Several
hunters out to day, but as the game of all kinds are Scerce   only
two Deer were brought in.   I am much engaged drawing off a map,
Capt. Lewis also much engaged in prepareing Papers to Send back
by a perogue—which we intended to Send back from the river Platt
observations at this place makes the Lattitude 41°. 3′ 19″ North.

This evening Guthrege Cought a *White Catfish*, its eyes Small &
tale much like that of a *Dolfin.*

White Catfish Camp 25th. of July Wednesday—
Several hunters out to day,   at 2 oClock *Drewyer & Peter* returned
from the *Otteau* village, and informs that no Indians were at their
towns,   they saw Some fresh Signs of a Small party But Could not
find them.   in their rout to the Towns (which is about 18 miles
West) they passed thro a open Prarie crossed papillion or Butterfly
Creek and a Small butifull river which run into the Plate a little
below the Town called *Corne de charf* [*corne de Cerf*] or *Elk Horn river*

Catfish which is White Camp—
26th. of July Thursday 1804—
the wind Blustering and hard from the South all day which blowed
the clouds of Sand in Such a manner that I could not complete my
pan [*plan*] in the tent,   the Boat roled in Such a manner that I could
do nothing in that,   was Compessed [compelled] to go to the woods
and combat with the Musquetors,   I opened the Tumer of a man
on the left breast, which discharged half a point [pint].

five Beaver Cough[t]   near the Camp the flesh of which we made use of.   This evening we found verry pleasant.

White Catfish Camp 10ms. above Platt 27th. of July Friday,—
Commence Loading the Boat & perogue, had all the ores completely fixed; Swam over the two remaining horses to the L. S. with the view of the Hunters going on that Side,   after getting everry thing complete, we Set Sale under a gentle breeze from the South and proceeded on

as we were Setting out to day one man Killed a Buck & another Cut his Knee verry bad.   Camped in a Bend to the L. Side in a coops [*copse*] of Trees,   a verry agreeable Breeze from the N. W. this evening.   I killed a Deer in the Prarie and found the Musquitors so thick & troublesom that it was disagreeable and painfull to Continue a moment still.

I took one man R. Fields and walked on Shore with a view of examoning Som Mounds on the L. S. of the river   those Mounds I found to be of Different hight Shape & Size, Some Composed of sand some earth & Sand,   the highest next to the river all of which covered about 200 acres of land, in a circular form,   on the Side from the river a low bottom & small Pond.   The Otteaus formerly lived here   I did not get to the boat untill after night.

July the 28th. Satturday 1804—
Drewyer brought in a *Missourie Indian* which he met with hunting in the Prarie   This Indian is one of the fiew remaining of that nation, & lives with the Otteauz, his Camp about 4 Miles from the river, he informs that the 'great gangue' of the Nation were hunting the Buffalow in the Plains.   his party was Small Consisting only of about 20 Lodges.   Miles further another Camp where there was a french man, who lived in the nation, this Indian appear'd Spritely, and appeared to make use of the Same pronouncation of the Osarge, Calling a Chief *Inea*

July 29th. Sunday 1804—
Sent a french man *la Liberty* with the Indian to Otteauze Camp to envite the Indians to meet us on the river above.   a Dark rainey morning wind from the W. N. W.   rained all the last night.
we stoped to Dine under Some high Trees near the high land on

the L. S. in a fiew minits Cought three verry large *Cat fish* one
nearly white,   those fish are in great plenty on the Sides of the river
and verry fat, a quart of Oile Came out of the surpolous fat of one
of those fish

above this high land & on the S. S. passed much falling timber
apparently the ravages of a Dreddfull harican which had passed
oblequely across the river from N. W. to S. E. about twelve months
Since,   many trees were broken off near the ground the trunks of
which were sound and four feet in Diameter

about ¾ of a Ml. above the Island on the S. S. a Creek coms in
Called Boyers R. this Creek is 25 yards wide,   one man in at-
tempting to cross this Creek on a log let his gun fall in,   R. Fields
Dived & brought it up   proceeded on to a Point on the S. S. and
Camped.

July 30th. Monday 1804—
posted out our guard and sent out 4 men, Captn. Lewis & [I]
went up the Bank and walked a Short Distance in the high Prarie
this Prarie is Covered with Grass of 10 or 12 inches in hight, Soil
of good quality & at the Distance of about a mile still further back
the Countrey rises about 80 or 90 feet higher, and is one Continued
Plain as fur as Can be seen, from the Bluff on the 2d. rise imediately
above our Camp, the most butifull prospect of the River up & Down
and the Countrey Opsd. prosented it Self which I ever beheld;
The River meandering the open and butifull Plains, interspursed
with Groves of timber, and each point Covered with Tall timber,
Such as Willow Cotton sum Mulberry, Elm, Sucamore Lynn & ash
(The Groves contain Hickory, Walnut, coffee nut & Oake in addition)   Two ranges of High Land parrelel to each other, and from
4 to 10 Miles Distant, between which the river & its bottoms are
Contained. (from 70 to 300 feet high)

Joseph Fields Killed and brought in an Anamale Called by the
French *Brarow*,[21] and by the Panies *Cho car tooch*   this Anamale
Burrows in the Ground and feeds on Flesh, (Prarie Dogs) Bugs &
Vigatables   "his Shape & Size is like that of a Beaver, his head
mouth &c. is like a Dogs with Short Ears, his Tail and Hair like

[21] Corruption of *blaireau,* French name of the badger (Thwaites).

that of a Ground Hog, and longer; and lighter. his Interals like the interals of a *Hog*, his Skin, thick and loose, his *Belly* is White and the Hair short, a white Streek from his nose to his Sholders. The toe nails of his fore feet is one Inch & ¾ long, & feet large; the nails of his hind feet ¾ of an Inch long, the hind feet Small and toes Crooked, his legs are short and when he moves Just sufficent to raise his body above the Ground He is of the Bear Species. We have his skin stuffed.

Jo. & R. Fields did not return this evening, Several men with verry bad *Boils*. Cat fish is cought in any part of the river Turkeys Geese & a Beaver Killed & Cought every thing in prime order men in high Spirits.

August the 1st. 1804—

a fair morning Despatched two men after the horses lost yesterday, one man back to the place from which the Messinger was Sent for the *Ottoes* to see if any Indians was or had been there sence our deptr. he return'd and informed that no person had been there Sence we left it. The Prarie which is situated below our Camp is above the high water leavel and rich covered with Grass from 5 to 8 feet high interspersed with copse of Hazel, Plumbs, Currents (like those of the U. S.) Rasberries & Grapes of Dift. Kinds. also producing a variety of Plants and flowers not common in the United States, two Kind of honeysuckle one which grows to a kind of a Srub Common about Harrodsburgh in Kentucky the other are not so large or tall and bears a flour in clusters short and of a light Pink colour, the leaves differ from any of the other Kinds in as much as the Lieves are destinct & does not surround the stalk as all the other kind do.

The Indians not yet arrived we fear Something amiss with our messenger or them.

August 2nd. Thursday 1804—

The Two men Drewyer & Colter returned with the horses loaded with Elk, those horses they found about 12 miles in a Southerly Derection from Camp.

The Countrey thro which they passed is Similar to what we see from Camp. one Beaver & a foot [*of Beaver caught in trap*] Cought this morning at Sunset Mr. Fairfong [*Ottoe interpreter resident with them*] and a pt. of Otteau & Missourie Nation Came to Camp, among those Indians 6 were Chiefs, (not the principal Chiefs) Capt. Lewis & myself met those Indians & informed them we were glad to see them, and would speak to them tomorrow, Sent them Some rosted meat, Pork flour & meal, in return they sent us Water *millions*. every man on his Guard & ready for any thing.

Three fat Bucks Killed this evening, the 4 qrs. of one weighed 147 lbs

August 3rd. Friday 1804—

Mad up a Small preasent for those people in perpotion to their Consiquence, also a package with a Meadle to accompany a Speech for the Grand Chief   after Brackfast we collected those Indians under an owning of our Main Sail, in presence of our Party paraded & Delivered a long Speech to them expressive of our journey the wishes of our Government, Some advice to them and Directions how they were to conduct themselves.   The principal Chief for the Nation being absent, we Sent him the Speech flag Meadel & Some Cloathes.   after hering what they had to say Delivered a Medal of Second Grade to one for the Ottos & one for the Missourie and present 4 medals of a third Grade to the inferior chiefs two for each tribe.   (Those two parts of nations Ottos & Missouries now residing together is about 250 men in the Ottoes composeing ⅓d. and Missouris ⅓ part)

The names of the Chiefs made this day are as follows viz:

	Indian name		English signfts.
1st.	*We ár ruge nor*	Ottoe *call'd*	*Little Thief*
2 {	Shōn gŏ tōn gŏ	" "	Big Horse
	We–the–à	Miss: "	Hospatality
	Shon Guss càn.	Ottoe	White horse
3 {	Wau pe ùh	M.	
	Āh hŏ ning gă.	M.	
	Baza cou jà.	Ottoe	
	Āh hŏ nē gă	M.	

Those Chiefs all Delivered a Speech, acknowledgeing their approbation to the Speech and promissing two prosue the advice & Derections given them that they wer happy to find that they had fathers which might be depended on &c.

We gave them a Cannister of Powder and a Bottle of Whiskey and delivered a few presents to the whole, after giveing a Br. Cth. [Breech Cloth] some Paint guartering & a Meadell to those we *made* Chiefs, after Capt. Lewis's Shooting the air gun a fiew Shots (which astonished those nativs) we Set out and proceeded on five miles on a Direct line passed a point on the S. S. & around a large Sand bar on the L. S. & Camped on the upper point, the Misquitors excessively troublesom this evening. Great appearance of wind and rain to the N. W. we prepare to rec've it, The man *Liberty* whome we Sent for the Ottoes has not Come up he left the Ottoes Town one Day before the Indians. This man has either tired his horse or, lost himself in the Plains Some Indians are to hunt for him.

The Situation of our last Camp *Councile Bluff*[22] or Handsom Prarie, (25 Days from this to *Santafee*) appears to be a verry proper place for a Tradeing establishment & fortification The Soil of the Bluff well adapted for Brick, Great deel of timber above in the two Points—many other advantages of a small nature. and I am told Senteral to Several nations viz. one Days march from the Ottoe Town, one Day & a half from the great Pania village, 2 days from the Mahar[23] Towns, two ¼ Days from the *Loups* village, & convenient to the Countrey thro: which Bands of the Soux [*rove &*] hunt, perhaps no other Situation is as well Calculated for a Tradeing establishment.

The air is pure and helthy so far as we can judge.

5th. of August Sunday 1804—
Set out early great appearance of wind and rain (I have observed that Thunder & lightning is not as common in this Countrey as it is in the atlantic States) Snakes are not plenty, one was killed to day large and resembling the rattle Snake, only something lighter.

---

[22] This is the origin of the name now applied to the city in Iowa opposite Omaha, Nebraska (Thwaites).
[23] Omahas.

I walked on Shore this evening S. S. in Pursueing Some turkeys I [s]truck the river twelve miles below within 370 yards, the high water passes thro' this Peninsula, and agreeable to the customary changes of the river, I concld [*should calculate*] that in two years the main current of the river will pass through. In every bend the banks are falling in from the current being thrown against those bends by the Sand points which inlarges and the Soil I believe from unquestionable appearns of the entire Bottom from one hill to the other being the Mud or Ooze of the river at Some former Period mixed with Sand and Clay easily melts and Slips into the River, and the mud mixes with the water & the Sand is washed down and lodges on the points. Great quantities of Grapes on the banks, I observe three different kinds at this time ripe, one of the no. is large & has the flaver of the Purple grape, camped on the S. S. the Musquitors verry troublesom. The man who went back after his knife has not yet come up, we have some reasons to believe he has Deserted.

Course Distance & Refrd. August 5th

S. 60° E	1½	Ms Crossg a large Sd bar to a pt. on ms. S. Sd bet: a willow Isd. in S. Bend
N. 20 W.	¾	Ms. to a pt. above a sad. bar opsd. the upper point of the Sd Island (Beaver
N. 34 W.	3¼	Ms. to a pt. on the L.S. passed one on the Starboard Side
North	¾	Ms. to a pt. on the right of Sand isd. makeing from the L. pt.
S. 45° W.	3¼	Ms. to 3 small trees in Prarie & bend to the L.S. pased a Sand pt. S. S.
N. 45°W.	4½	Ms. to a pt. on S. S.
North	1¼	Ms. on the S. S. to the pt. of a Sand bar river narrow
N. 70° E	¼	Ms. on the Sand bar S. S.
S. 30 E	2	Ms. to the pt. of a Sand bar making out from the L. pt. psd. a Sand.
S. 30 E	½	Ml. on the point
N. 45° E	2½	Mls. to the lower point of an Island Close to the S. S.
	20½	behind this Island on the S.S. the *Soldiers* river disimboques itself.

6th. August, Monday 1804—

At twelve oClock last nigh[t] a violent Storm of wind from the N. W. Some rain, one pt. of colours lost in the Storm from the bige Perogue. Set out early and proceeded on passed a large Island on the S. S. back of this Isd. Soldiers River Mouths, I am told by one of the men that this river is about the size of Nadawa river *40* yards wide at the mouth. Reed has not yet come up, neither has La Liberty the frenchman whome we Sent to the Indian Camps a fiew miles below the *Council Bluffs.*

7th. August Tuesday 1804—
dispatched George Drewyer, R. Fields, Wm. Bratten & Wm. Labieche back after the Deserter reed with order if he did not give up Peaceibly to put him to Death &c. to go to the Ottoes Village & enquire for La Liberty and bring him to the Mahar Village also with a Speech on the occasion to the Ottoes & Missouries, and derecting a few of their Chiefs to come to the Mahars, & we would make a peace between them & the Mahars and Souex, a String of Wompom & a Carrot of Tobacco. proceeded on and Camped on the S. S.

[Lewis]   August 8th. 1804.
we had seen but a few aquatic fouls of any kind on the river since we commenced our journey up the Missouri, a few geese accompanied by their young, the wood duck which is common to every part of this country & crains of several kinds which will be discribed in their respective places this day after we had passed the *river* Souix as called by Mr. Mackary (or as is more properly called the stone river, I saw a great number of feathers floating down the river those feathers had a very extraordinary appearance as they appeared in such quantities as to cover prettey generally sixty or seventy yards of the breadth of the river. for three miles after I saw those feathers continu[e] to run in that manner, we did not percieve from whence they came, at length we were surprised by the appearance of a flock of Pillican [*Pelecanus erythrorhynchus*] at rest on a large sand bar attatched to a small Island the number of which would if estimated appear almost in credible; they apeared to cover several acres of ground, and were no doubt engaged in procuring their ordinary food; *which is fish;* on our approach they flew and left behind them several small fish of about eight inches in length, none of which I had seen before. the Pellican rested again on a sand bar above the Island which we called after them from the number we saw on it. we now

approached them within about three hundred yards before they flew; I then fired at random among the flock with my rifle and brought one down; the discription of this bird is as follows.

HABITS.

They are a *bird* of *clime* remain on the coast of Floriday and the borders of the Gulph of mexico & even the lower portion of the Mississippi during the *winter,* and in the Spring (see for date my *thermometrical observations at the river Dubois*), visit this country and that fa[r]ther north for the purpose of raising their young. this duty seems now to have been accomplished from the appearance of a young Pilacon which was killed by one of our men this morning, and they are now in large flocks on their return to their winter quarters. they lay usually two eggs only and chuise for a nest a couple of logs of drift wood near the water's edge and with out any other preperation but the thraught formed by the proximity of those two logs which form a trought they set and hatch their young which after[wards they] nurture with fish their common food

MEASURE.

	F	I
F[r]om beak to toe	5.	8
Tip to tip of wing	9 .	4.
Beak Length	1 .	3.
Do. Width from	.	2. to 1½

	F	
Neck Length	1 .	11.
1st Joint of wing	1 .	1.
2ed Do.	1 .	4.½
3rd. Do.	— .	7.
4th Do.	— .	2¾
Length of leg including foot	.	10.
Do. of thy	.	11.

Discription of Colour &c. The beak is a whiteish yellow the under part connected to a bladder like pouch, this pouch is connected to both sides of the lower beak and extends down on the under side of the neck and terminates in the stomach this pouch is uncovered with feathers, and is formed [of] two skins the one on

the inner and the other on the outer side a small quantity of flesh
and strings of which the anamal has at pleasure the power of moving
or drawing in such manner as to contract it at pleasure. in the
present subject I measured this pouch and found it's contents 5.
gallons of water The feet are webbed large and of a yellow colour,
it has four toes the hinder toe is longer than in most aquatic fouls,
the nails are black, not sharp and ½ an inch in length. The plumage
generally is white, the feathers are thin compared with the swàn
goose or most aquatic fouls and has but little or no down on the
body. the upper part of the head is covered with black f[e]athe[r]s
short, as far as the back part of the head. the yellow skin unfeath-
ered extends back from the upper beak and opening of the mouth
and comes to a point just behind the eye The large f[e]athers of
the wings are of a deep black colour the 1st. & 2nd. joint of [the
wings] from the body above the same is covered with a second layer
of white feathers which extend quite half the length of those large
feathers of the wing the thye is covered with feathers within a
quarter of an inch of the knee.

1st Joint of wing has feather[s]	No. 21 Length.	9	Inch
			Black
2ed.	Do.	No. 17 Length	13	Inch
3rd.	Do.	No. 5 Length . . .	
		18	.Inch
4th.	Do	No. 3 Lenth . . .	
		19.	Ich

it has a curious frothy subs[t]ance which seems to divide its feathers from the flesh of the body and seems to be composes of
Glob[u]les of air and perfectly imbraces the part of the feather which
extends through the skin. the wind pipe terminates in the center
of the lower part of the upper and unf[e]athered part of the pouch
and is secured by an elastic valve commanded at pleasure.

The green insect known in the U'States by the name of the *sawyer*
or *chittediddle*, [*Katydid*] was first heard to cry on the 27th. of July,
we were then in latitude 41°. some minutes.

The *prarie hen* or *grouse*, was seen in the praries betwen the Missouri and the river *platte*

[Clark]   11th. August Satturday 1804.—

after the rain was over, Capt. Lewis myself & 10 men assended the Hill on the L. S. (under which there was some fine Springs) to the top of a high point where the *Mahars King Black* Bird was burried 4 years ago. [Died of small pox]   a mound of earth about 12 (*feet*) Diameter at the base, & 6 feet high is raised over him turfed, and a pole 8 feet high in the Center   on this pole we fixed a white flage bound with red Blue & white,   this hill about 300 feet above the water forming a Bluff between that & the water of various hight from 40 to 150 feet in hight, yellow soft Sand stone   from the top of this Nole the river may be Seen Meandering for 60 or 70 miles, we Decended & set out N. 24°. W. ½ Ml. passing over a Sand bar on the S. pt. along the willows to the river opposit a Small Beyeau on the L. S. which is the Conveyance of the high water from a bend which appears near in a northerly derection, haveing passed a Creek in a Deep bend to the L. S. Called by the *Mahars Wau can di Peeche* (Great Spirrit is bad)[24]   on the Creek & Hills near it about 400 of the *Mahars* Died with the Small Pox

                                        August 13th. Monday 1804
Detached Sergt. Ordeway Peter Crusatt, George Shannon. Werner & Carrn. [Carson] to the Mahar Village[25] with a flag & Some Tobacco to envite the Nation to See & talk with us on tomorrow. we took some Luner observation this evening. the air Pleasant.

                                        14th. August Tuesday 1804—
The men Sent to the Mahar Town last evining has not returned we Conclude to send a Spye to Know the Cause of their delay,   at about 12 oClock the Party returned and informd. us that they Could not find the Indians, nor any fresh Sign, those people have not returned from their Buffalow hunt.   Those people haveing no houses no Corn or anything more than the graves of their ansesters to attach them to the old Village, Continue in purseute of the Buffalow longer than others who has greater attachments to their native village.   The ravages of the Small Pox (which Swept off 400 men

[24] Blackbird Creek, near Macy, Nebraska.
[25] A little south of Dakota City, Nebraska, north of the Omaha Indian Reservation. (Coues).

& Womin & children in perpopotion) has reduced this nation not exceeding 300 men and left them to the insults of their weaker neighbours, which before was glad to be on friendly turms with them. I am told when this fatal malady was among them they Carried their franzey to verry extroadinary length, not only of burning their Village, but they put their *wives* & children to *Death* with a view of their all going together to some better Countrey. they burrey their Dead on the top of high hills and rais Mounds on the top of them. The cause or way those people took the Small Pox is uncertain, the most Probable, from Some other nation by means of a warparty.

August 15th, Wednesday, 1804.
Camp three Miles N. E. of the Mahar Village
I went with ten men to a Creek Damed by the Beavers about half way to the Village, with Some small Willows & Bark we made a Drag and hauled up the Creek, and Cought 318 fish of different kind i. e. Pike, Bass, Salmon, perch, red horse, small cat, and a kind of perch Called Silver fish, on the Ohio. I cought a Srimp prosisely of Shape Size & flavour of those about N. Orleans & the lower part of the Mississippi in this Creek which is only the pass or Streight from [one] Beaver Pond to another, is Crouded with large Musstlcs verry fat, Ducks, Plover of different kinds are on those Ponds as well as on the river. in my absence Capt. Lewis Sent Mr. Durione the Souix interpeter & three men to examine a fire which threw up an emence Smoke from the Praries on the NE. Side of the River and at no great distance from Camp. the Object of this party was to find Some Bands of Seouex which the intptr. thought was near the Smoke and get them to come in. in the evening this Party returned and informed, that the fire arose from Some trees which had been left burning by a small party of Seoux, who had passed [*by that place*] Several Days. the wind Setting from that point, blew the Smoke from that pt. over our Camp. our party all in health and Sperrits. The men Sent to the Ottoes & in pursute of the Deserter Reed has not yet returned or joined our party.

16th. August Thursday 1804.
Fishing Camp 3 Ms. N. E. of the Mahars.
Cap. Lewis took 12 men and went to the Pond & Creek between Camp and the old village and Cought upwards of 800 fine fish, 79

Pike, 8 salmon resembling Trout 1 Rock, 1 flat Back, 127 Buffalow
& red horse 4 Bass & 490 Cats, with many Small Silver fish. I had
a Mast made and fixed to the Boat to day, the Party Sent to the
ottoes not yet joined us. the wind shifted around to the S. E.
everry evening a Breeze rises which blows off the Musquitors &
cools the atmispeere.

17th. August Friday 1804.—
    I collected a grass much resembling Wheet in its grouth the grain
like Rye, also Some resembling Rye & Barly. a kind of Timothey,
the Seed of which branches from the main Stalk & is more like a
flax Seed than that of Timothey.
    at 6 oClock this evening *Labieche* one of the Party sent to the
Ottoes joined, and informed that the Party was behind with one of
the Deserters M. B. Reed and the 3 principal Chiefs of the Nations.
La Liberty they cought but he decived them and got away. the
object of those Chiefs comeing forward is to make a peace with the
Mahars thro: us. as the Mahars are not at home this great Object
cannot be accomplished at this time. Set the Praries on fire to bring
the Mahars & Soues if any were near, this being the useal Signal.
    a cool evening two Beaver cought to day.

18th. August, Sat'day 1804.—
    in the after part of the Day the Party with the Indians arrivd.
we meet them under a Shade near the Boat and after a Short talk
we gave them Provisions to eat & proceeded to the trial of Reed,
he confessed that he "Deserted & stold a public Rifle Shot-pouch
Powder & Ball" and requested we would be as favourable with him
as we Could consistantly with our Oathes—which we were and only
Sentenced him to run the Gantlet four times through the Party &
that each man with 9 Swichies Should punish him and for him not
to be considered in future as one of the Party. The three principal
Chiefs petitioned for Pardin for this man after we explained the
injurey such men could doe them by false representations, & ex-
plan'g the Customs of our Countrey they were all Satisfied with the
propriety of the Sentence & was Witness to the punishment. after
which we had Some talk with the Chiefs about the orrigan of the
war between them & the Mahars &c &c. it Commenced in this

way in two of the Misouries Tribes resideing with the Ottoes went
to the Mahars to steel horses, they Killed them both which was a
cause of revenge on the part of the Missouris & Ottoes, they also
brought war on themselves Nearly in the same way with the Pania
Loups, and they are greatly in fear of a just revenge from the Panies
for takeing their Corn from the Pania Towns in their absence hunting
this Summer. Cap L. Birth day the evening was closed with an
extra gill of whiskey and a Dance until 11 oClock.

19th. August Sunday 1804—
prepared a Small Present for the Chiefs and Warriors present.
the main chief Brackfast with us & beged for a Sun glass, those
People are all naked, Covered only with Breech Clouts Blankets or
Buffalow Roabes, the flesh Side Painted of Different colours and
figures. At 10 oClock we assembled the Chiefs and warriors 9 in
number under an owning, and Cap. Lewis explain the Speech Sent
to the Nation from the Council Bluffs by Mr. Faufon. The 3 Chiefs
and all the men or warriors made short Speeches approving the
advice & Council their great father had Sent them, and concluded
by giving themselves some Credit for their acts.

We then brought out the presents and exchanged the *Big horses*
Meadel and gave him one equal to the one Sent to the Little Thief
& gave all Some Small articles & 8 Carrots of Tobacco, we gave
one Small Meadel to one of the Chiefs and a Sertificate to the others
of their good intentions.

Names.		
The Little Thief	{	Grd. Chiefs I have
The Big Horse	{	mentioned before.
Crows Head (or)		*Kar Ka paha*—Missory
Black Cat (or)		*Ne na Sa wa*—do
Iron Eyes (or)		*Sar na no no*—Ottoe
Big Ax (or)		*Nee Swar Unja*—do
Big Blue Eyes—		*Star gea Hun ja* do
Brave Man (or)		*War sar Sha Co*

one of those Indians after receiving his Certificate delivd. it again
to me the *Big blue eyes* the Chief petitioned for the Ctft. again,
we would not give the Certft., but rebuked them verry roughly for

haveing in object goods and not peace with their neighbours. this language they did not like at first, but at length all petitioned for us to give back the Certificate to the Big blue eyes   he came forward and made a plausible excuse,   I then gave the Certificate [to] the Great Chief to bestow it to the most Worthy, they gave it to him, we then gave them a Dram and broke up the Council,   the Chiefs requested we would not leave them this evening   we determined to Set out early in the morning   we Showed them many Curiosities and the air gun which they were much astonished at.   those people beged much for Whiskey. Serjeant Floyd is taken verry bad all at once with a Biliose Chorlick   we attempt to relieve him without success as yet, he gets worst and we are much allarmed at his Situation, all [give] attention to him.

20th. August Monday 1804.—
Sergeant Floyd much weaker and no better.   Made Mr. Faufonn the interpter a fiew presents, and the Indians a Canister of Whiskey We Set out under a gentle breeze from the S. E. and proceeded on verry well.   Serjeant Floyd as bad as he can be no pulse & nothing will Stay a moment on his Stomach or bowels.   Passed two Islands on the S. S. and at the first Bluff on the S. S. Serj. Floyd Died with a great deal of Composure,   before his death he Said to me, "I am going away" I want you to write me a letter."   We buried him on the top of the bluff ½ Mile below a Small river to which we Gave his name,   he was buried with the Honors of War much lamented, a Seeder post with the Name Sergt. C. Floyd died here 20th. of august 1804 was fixed at the head of his grave.[26]   This Man at all times gave us proofs of his firmness and Determined resolution to doe Service to his Countrey and honor to himself   after paying all the honor to our Deceesed brother we camped in the Mouth of floyds River about 30 yards wide,   a butifull evening.

Course Dists. & reffr. 20th. Augt.
N. 56.° W. 3   Ms. to pt. of a Willow Isd. S. S.
North   ¾ ml. on the left of the Island

[26] He was buried at a spot which is now in the southern part of Sioux City, Iowa (Thwaites).

N. 72. E. 2¼ Ml. to the upr. pt. of the Isd.

N. 18. E. 2½ Ms. to the lower pt. of an Isd. on the S. S. passed Sand bars.

North 3½ Ms. to Sj. Floyds Bluff on S. S. the 1st above Aiaways Village a fiew miles above Platt R.

1 To the Mo. of Floyds River on S. S. and Camped.

13

22nd. August Friday 1804.—

we landed at a Bluff where the two men Sent with the horses were waiting with two Deer, by examonation this Bluff Contained Alum, Copperas, Cobalt, Pyrites; a Alum Rock Soft & Sand Stone. Capt. Lewis in proveing the quality of those minerals was Near poisoning himself by the fumes & tast of the *Cobalt* which had the appearance of Soft Isonglass. Copperas & alum is verry pisen

Capt. Lewis took a Dost of Salts to work off the effects of the arsenic, we camped on the S. S.[27] Sailed the greater part of this day with a hard wind from the S. E. Great deel of Elk Sign, and great appearance of wind from the N. W.

ordered a Vote for a Serjeant to chuse one of three which may be the highest number. the highest numbers are P. Gass had 19 votes, Bratten & Gibson.

23rd. August Thursday 1804—

J. Fields Sent out to hunt Came to the Boat and informed that he had Killed a Buffalow in the plain a head. Cap. Lewis took 12 Men and had the buffalow brought to the boat in the next bend to the S. S. 2 Elk Swam the river, and was fired at from the boat R. Fields came up with the Horses and brought two Deer one Deer killed from the Boat. Several Prarie Wolves Seen to day Saw Elk Standing on the Sand bar. The Wind blew hard and raised the Sands off the bar in Such Clouds that we Could Scercely [*see.*] this Sand being fine and verry light Stuck to everry thing it touched, and in the Plain for a half a mile the distance I was out, every Spire of Grass was covered with the Sand or Durt.

[27] Near Elk Point, Union County, South Dakota (Thwaites).

24th. August Friday 1804.—
I took my Servent and a french boy and Walked on Shore, Killed
Two Buck Elks and a fawn, and intersepted the Boat, and had all
the Meat butchered and in by Sun Set at which time it began to
rain and rained hard, Cap. Lewis & My self walk out & got verry
wet, a Cloudy rainey night In my absence the Boat Passed a Small
River Called by the Indians White Stone River[28] this river is about
30 yards wide and runs thro: a Plain or Prarie in its whole Course
In a northerley derection from the Mouth of this Creek in an emence
Plain a high Hill is Situated, and appears of a Conic form, and by
the different nations of Indians in this quarter is Suppose to be the
residence of Deavels.[29] that they are in human form with remarkable large heads, and about 18 Inches high, that they are very watchfull and are arm'd with Sharp arrows with which they Can Kill at a
great distance; they are Said to kill all persons who are So hardy as
to attempt to approach the hill; they State that tradition informs
them that many Indians have Suffered by those little people, and
among others three *Mahar* Men fell a sacrefise to their murceless
fury not many Years Sence. So Much do the Maha, Soues, Ottoes
and other neighbouring nations believe this fable, that no Consideration is Suffecient to induce them to approach the hill.

[28] Vermillion River.
[29] Spirit Mound, north of Vermillion, South Dakota.

TWO

Meeting the Lakota

From Vermillion River to the Mandan Villages
August 25–October 26, 1804

[Clark]   25th. August Satturday 1804.—

A cloudy morning Capt. Lewis & Myself concluded to go and See the Mound which was Viewed with Such turror by all the different Nations in this quarter, we Selected Shields; J. Fields, W. Bratten, Sergt. Ordway, J. Coller, Carr, and Corpl. Worbington & Frasure, also G. Drewyer and droped down to the Mouth of White Stone River, where we left the Perogue with two men and at 200 yards we assended a riseing ground of about Sixty feet, from the top of this High land the Countrey is leavel & open as far as can be Seen, except Some few rises at a great Distance, and the *Mound* which the Indians Call Mountain of *little people or Spirits,* this Mound appears of a conic form & is N. 20°. W. from the mouth of the Creek,[1] we left the river at 8 oClock, at 4 miles we Crossed the Creek 23 yards wide in an extensive Valley and Contin[u]ed on at two miles further— our Dog was so Heeted and fatigued we was obliged [to] Send him back to the Creek, at 12 oClock we arrived at the hill Capt. Lewis much fatigued from heat the day it being verry hot & he being in a debilitated State from the Precautions he was obliged to take to prevent the effects of the Cobalt, &

[1] Spirit Mound, South Dakota.

Minl Substance which had like to have poisened him two days ago,
his want of water, and Several of the men complaining of Great
thirst, determined us to make for the first water which was the Creek
in a bend N. E. from the Mound, about 3 miles.   after a Delay of
about 1 hour & a half to recrut our party we set out on our return
down the Creek thro: the bottom of about 1 mile in width,   crossed
the creek 3 times to the place we first struck it, where we gathered
some delisious froot such as Grapes, Plumbs, & Blue Currents   after
a Delay of an hour we set out on our back trail & arrived at the
Perogue at Sun set.   We proceeded on to the Place we Campd last
night and Stayed all night.

The reagular form of this hill would in Some measure justify a
belief that it owed its orrigin to the hand of man; but as the earth
and loos pebbles and other substances of which it was Composed,
bore an exact resemblance to the Steep Ground which border on
the Creek in its neighbourhood we concluded it was most probably
the production of nature.

The only remarkable Charactoristic of this hill admiting it to be
a natural production is that it is insulated or Seperated a considerable
distance from any other, which is verry unusial in the natural order
or disposition of the hills.

The Surrounding Plains is open Void of Timber and leavel to a
great extent, hence the wind from whatever quarter it may blow,
drives with unusial force over the naked Plains and against this hill;
the insects of various kinds are thus involuntaryly driven to the
Mound by the force of the wind, or fly to its Leeward Side for
Shelter;   the Small Birds whoes food they are, Consequently resort
in great numbers to this place in Surch of them; Perticularly the
Small brown Martin of which we saw a vast number hovering on
the Leward Side of the hill, when we approached it in the act of
catching those insects; they were so gentle that they did not quit
the place untill we had arrivd within a fiew feet of them.

One evidence which the Inds give for believeing this place to be
the residence of Some unusial Sperits is that they frequently discover
a large assemblage of Birds about this Mound [this] is in my opinion
a Sufficent proof to produce in the Savage Mind a Confident belief
of all the properties which they ascribe [to] it.

from the top of this Mound we beheld a most butifull landscape;

Numerous herds of buffalow were Seen feeding in various directions; the Plain to North N. W. & N. E. extends without interuption as far as Can be seen.

if all the timber which is on the Stone Creek was on 100 acres it would not be thickly timbered, the Soil of those Plains are delightfull.

Great numbers of Birds are seen in those Plains, Such as black bird, ren, [*wren*] or Prarie burd, a kind of larke about the sise of a Partridge with a Short tail

the Boat under the Comd of Serjt. Pryor proceeded on in our absence, (after jurking the Elk I Killed yesterday) Six Miles and Camped on the Larboard Side R. Fields brought in five Deer, George Shannon Killed an Elk Buck Som rain this evening.

We Set the Praries on fire as a signal for the Soues to Come to the River.

26th. August Sunday 1804.—
after jurking the meat Killed yesterday and prepareing the Elk Skins for a Toe Roape, we Set out Leaveing Drewyer & Shannon to hunt the horses which was lost with directions to follow us keeping on the high lands.

[Orderly Book; Lewis]   Orders August 26th. 1804.
The commanding officers have thought proper to appoint Patric Gass, a Sergeant in *the corps of volunteers for North Western Discovery;* he is therefore to be obeyed and respected accordingly.

Sergt. Gass is directed to take charge of the late Sergt. Floyd's mess, and immediately to enter on the discharge of such other duties, as have by their previous orders been prescribed for the government of the Sergeants of this corps.

[Clark]   27th. August Monday 1804.—
This morning the Star calld the morning Star much larger than Common, G. Drewyer came up and informed that he could neither find Shannon nor horses, we Sent Shields & J Fields, back to hunt Shannon & the horses, with derections to keep on the Hills to the Grand Calumet above on River *Kacure²*

² A corruption of *Rivière qui Court*, the French name of the Niobrara (or Rapid) River (Thwaites).

We Set Sail under a gentle Breeze from the S. E. at 7 miles passed a *White* Clay Marl or Chalk Bluff under this Bluff [which] is extensive I discovered large Stone much like lime incrusted with a clear substance which I believe to be *Cobalt*, also Ore is embeded in the Dark earth, resembling Slate [but] much Softer. above this Bluff we had the Prarie Set on fire to let the Soues See that we were on the river, and as a Signal for them to Come to it.

At 2 oClock passed the Mouth of *River Jacque* [*or Yeankton*,][3] one Indian at the mouth of this river Swam to the Perogue, we landed and two others Came to us, those Inds. informed that a large Camp of Soues, were on R. Jacque near the mouth. We sent Serjt. Pryor & a Frenchman with Mr. Durion, the Soues interpeter to the Camp with directions to invite the principal Chiefs to Council with us at a Bluff above Called the Calumet. two of those Indians accompanied them and the third continued in the Boat Showing an inclination to Continue, this boy is a Mahar, and inform that his nation, were gone to the Parnies [*Panies*][4] to make a peace with that nation.

We proceeded on about one and a half miles and inCamped on a bar makeing out from the S. S. the wind blew hard from the South. A cool and Pleasent evening, The river has fallen verry slowly and is now low.

28th. August Tuesday 1804.—

Capt. Lewis & my Self much indisposed owing to Some cause for which we cannot account one of the Perogues run a Snag thro her and was near Sinking in the opinions of the Crew. we came too below the *Calumet Bluff* and formed a Camp in a Butifull Plain near the foot of the high land which rises with a gradual assent near this Bluff[5] I observe more timber in the Valeys & on the Points than useal. The Perogue which was injured I had unloaded and the Loading put into the other Perogue which we intended to Send back & changed the Crew after examoning her & finding that She was unfit for service determined to Send her back by the party Some load which was in the Perogue much Injur'd.

[3] The James (or Dakota) River (Thwaites).
[4] Pawnee.
[5] In Cedar County, Nebraska.

The wind blew hard this afternoon from the South. J. Shields & J. Fields who was Sent back to look for Shannon and the Horses joined us and informed that Shannon had the horses ahead and that they Could not overtake him   This man not being a first rate Hunter, we deturmined to Send one man in pursute of him with some Provisions.

29th. August Wednesday 1804.—
Some rain last night & this morning,   Sent on Colter with Provisions in pursute of Shannon,   had a Toe roap made of Elk Skin, I am much engaged riteing. at 4 oClock P. M. Sergt. Pryor and Mr. Dorion with 5 Cheifs and about 70 men & boys arrived on the opposit Side   we Sent over a Perogue & Mr. Dorrion & his Son who was tradeing with the Indians[6] came over with Serjt. Pryor, and informed us that the Chiefs were there   we sent Serjt. Pryor & young Mr. Dorion[7] with Som Tobacco, Corn and a few Kittles for them to Cook in, with directions to inform the Chiefs that we would Speek to them tomorrow.

Those Indians brought with them for their own use 2 Elk & 6 Deer which the young men Killed on the way from their Camp 12 Miles distant.

Serjt. Pryor informs me that when [they] came near the Indian Camp they were met by men with a Buffalow roabe to carry them, Mr. Dorion informed they were not the owners of the Boats & did not wish to be carried   the Scioues Camps are handsom of a Conic form Covered with Buffalow Roabs Painted different colours and all compact & handsomly arranged,   Covered all round an open part in the Centre for the fire, with Buffalow roabs,   each Lodg has a place for Cooking detached,   the lodges contain from 10 to 15 persons. a Fat Dog   was presented as a mark of their Great respect for the party of which they partook hartily and thought it good and well flavored.

30th. of August Thursday 1804.
a verry thick fog this morning   after Prepareing Some presents for the Cheifs which we intended [to] make by giving Meadels, and

---

[6] Yankton Sioux.
[7] The son of Pierre Dorion, Sr., and his Yankton Sioux wife.

finishing a Speech which we intended to give them, we sent Mr.
Dorion in a Perogue for the Cheifs and Warriers to a Council under
an Oak Tree near where we had a flag flying on a high flagstaff at
12 oClock we met and Cap. L. Delivered the Speach & then made
one great Chiff by giving him a Meadel & Some Cloathes, one 2d.
Chief & three Third Chiefs in the same way, they recd. those
things with the goods and tobacco with pleasure To the Grand
Chief we gave a Flag and the parole [*certificate*] & Wampom with a
hat & Chiefs. Coat, We Smoked out of the pipe of peace, & the
Chiefs retired to a Bourey made of bushes by their young men to
Divide their presents and Smoke eate and Council Capt. Lewis &
My self retired to dinner and consult about other measures. Mr.
Daurion is much displeased that we did not invite him to dine with
us (which he was Sorry for afterwards). The Souex is a Stout bold
looking people, (the young men handsom) & well made, the greater
part of them make use of Bows & arrows, Some fiew fusees[8] I
observe among them, notwith standing they live by the Bow and
arrow, they do not Shoot So Well as the Nothern Indians the Warriers
are Verry much deckerated with Paint Porcupine quils & feathers,
large leagins and mockersons, all with buffalow roabs of Different
Colours. the Squars wore Peticoats & a White Buffalow roabe with
the black hare turned back over their necks and Sholders.

I will here remark a SOCIETY which I had never before this day
heard was in any nation of Indians, four of which is at this time
present and all who remain of this Band. Those who become Members of this Society must be brave active young men who take a
Vow never to give back let the danger be what it may, in War
Parties they always go forward without screening themselves behind
trees or anything else to this Vow they Strictly adhier dureing their
Lives. an instance which happened not long sence, on a party in
Crossing the R Missourie on the ice, a whole was in the ice imediately in their Course which might easily have been avoided by
going around, the foremost man went on and was lost the others
wer draged around by the party. in a battle with the Crow Indians
who inhabit the *Cout Noir*[9] or black Mountain out of 22 of this Society

---

[8] Fusils or muskets.

[9] That is, *Côte Noir.* "Our authors use the term 'Black mountains' for any of the
elevated country to the west of the Missouri in Northern Nebraska and both Dakotas"
(Coues).

18 was Killed, the remaining four was draged off by their Party Those men are likely fellows the[y] Set together Camp & Dance together. This Society is in imitation of the Societies of the de Curbo or Crow Indians, whom they imitate.

31st. of August, 1804—

After Dinner we gave Mr. Peter Dorion, a Commission to act with a flag and some Cloathes & Provisions & instructions to bring about a peace with the Seioux, Mahars, Panies, Poncaries, [Poncas.] Ottoes & Missouries, and to employ any trader to take Some of the Cheifs of each or as many of those nations as he Could Perticularly the Seuouex I took a Vocabulary of the Suoux Language, and the Answer to a fiew quaries such a[s] refured to their Situation, Trade, Number, War, &c. &c. This Nation is Divided into 20 Tribes, possessing Seperate interests. Collectively they are noumerous say from 2 to 3000 men, their interests are so unconnected that Some bands are at war with Nations [with] which other bands are on the most friendly terms. This Great Nation who the French has given the Nickname of Suouex, Call themselves *Dar co tar* [Dakota[10]]

THE NAMES OF THE DEFFERENT TRIBES OR BANDS OF THE SCEOUX, OR DAR CO TAR NATION.

1st   *Che cher ree Yankton* (or bois ruley) (*brulé*) now present inhabit the Suouex & Demoin Rivers and the Jacque. (*200 men.*)

2nd.   *Ho in de borto* (Poles) they live [rove] on the heads of Souex and Jacques Rivers.

3rd.   *Me Ma car jo* (Make fence on the river) rove on the Country near the big bend of the Missouries.

4th.   *Sou on, Te ton* (People of the Prarie) the[y] rove in the Plains N. of the Riv Missourie above this.

5th.   *Wau pa coo tar* (Leaf Beds) the[y] live near the Prarie de Chain Near the Missippi.

6th.   *Te Car ton* (or Village of Prarie) rove on the waters of the Mississippi above Prarie de Chain.

[10] The Dakota, or Lakota (meaning "allies"), as they called themselves, are the largest of the Siouian-speaking peoples, composed of "Seven Council Fires," two of which are the Yankton and Teton encountered by Lewis and Clark.

7th.   *Ne Was tar ton* (big Waters Town) rove on the Missippi above the
         St. Peters River.
8th.   *Wau pa tone* (Leaf Nation) live 10 Leagues up St. Peters River.
9th.   *Cas Carba* (White Man) live 35 Leagues up St. Peters river.
10th.   *Mi ca cu op si ba* (Cut bank) rove on the head of St. Peters.
11th.   *Sou on* (———) rove on St. Peters river in the Praries.
12th.   *Sou se toons* (———) live 40 Leages up the St. Peters river.

The names of the other bands neither of the Souex's interpters
could inform me. in the evening late we gave Mr. Dourion a bottle
of whiskey, & he with the Cheifs & his Son Crossed the river and
Camped on the Opposit bank. Soon after night a violent wind from
the N. W. with rain the rain Continud the greater part of the night.
The river is riseing a little.

                                           Sept. 7th. Friday—
a verry Cold morning wind S. E. Set out at day light we landed
after proceeding 5½ Miles, near the foot of a round Mounting, which
I saw yesterday, resembling a dome.[11] Cap. Lewis & Myself walked
up to the top which forms a Cone and is about 70 feet higher than
the high lands around it, the Base is about 300 foot in decending
this Cupola, discovered a Village of Small animals that burrow in
the grown (those animals are Called by the french Petite Chien)[12]
Killed one and Caught one a live by poreing a great quantity of
Water in his hole we attempted to dig to the beds of one of those
animals, after diging 6 feet, found by running a pole down that we
were not half way to his Lodge, we found 2 frogs in the hole, and
Killed a Dark rattle Snake near with a Ground rat (*or prairie dog*) in
him, (those rats are numerous) the Village of those animals Covd.
about 4 acres of Ground on a gradual decent of a hill and Contains
great numbers of holes on the top of which those little animals Set
erect make a Whistleing noise and whin allarmed Step into their
hole. we por'd into one of the holes 5 barrels of Water without
filling it. Those Animals are about the Size of a Small Squ[ir]rel
Shorter (*or longer*) & thicker, the head much resembling a Squirel

---

[11] A conspicuous landmark, now known as "the Tower" (Thwaites) in Boyd
County, Nebraska.
[12] Black-tailed prairie dog (*Cynomys ludovicianus*).

in every respect, except the ears which is Shorter, his tail like a ground squirel which they shake & whistle when allarmd. the toe nails long,   they have fine fur & the longer hairs is gray,   it is Said that a kind of Lizard also a Snake reside with those animals. (*did not find this correct.*)   Camped.

9th. September Sunday 1804—

Capt. Lewis went out to fill a buffalow.   I walked on Shore all this evening with a view to Kill a goat or Some Prarie Dogs   in the evening after the boat landed, I Derected My Servent York with me to kill a Buffalow near the boat from a Numbr. then Scattered in the Plains.   I saw at one view near the river at least 500 Buffalow, those animals have been in View all day feeding in the Plains on the L. S.   every Copse of timber appear to have Elk or Deer. D. Killed 3 Deer, I Kiled a Buffalow Y. 2, R. Fields one.

Sept. 11th. Tuesday 1804—

I saw a Village of Barking Squirel 970 yds. long, and 800 yds. Wide Situated on a jentle Slope of a hill,   those anamals are noumerous, I killed 4 with a View to have their Skins Stufed.

here the Man who left us with the horses 22 (*16*) days ago (*George Shannon   He started 26 Augt.*) and has been a head ever since joined us nearly Starved to Death,   he had been 12 days without any thing to eate but Grapes & one Rabit, which he Killed by shooting a piece of hard Stick in place of a ball. This Man Supposeing the boat to be a head pushed on as long as he could,   when he became weak and feable deturmined to lay by and waite for a tradeing boat, which is expected, Keeping one horse for the last resorse,   thus a man had like to have Starved to death in a land of Plenty for the want of Bullitts or Something to kill his meat.

14th. Sept. Friday 1804.—

I Killed a Buck Goat[13] of this Countrey, about the hight of the Grown Deer, its body Shorter   the Horns which is not very hard and forks ⅔ up one prong Short the other round & Sharp arched, and is imediately above its Eyes   the Colour is a light gray with

[13] Pronghorn (*Antilocapra americana*).

black behind its ears down its neck, and its face white round its neck, its Sides and its rump round its tail which is Short & white: Verry actively made, has only a pair of hoofs to each foot, his brains on the back of his head, his Norstrals large, his eyes like a Sheep he is more like the Antilope or Gazella of AFRICA than any other Species of Goat.

Shields killed a *Hare* like the mountain hare of Europe, waighing 6¼ pounds (altho pore) his head narrow, its ears large i, e. 6 Inches long & 3 Inches Wide one half of each White, the other & out part a lead Grey from the toe of the hind foot to toe of the for foot is 2 feet 11 Inches, the hith is 1 foot 1 Inch & ¾, his tail long thick & white.[14]

Passed 2 Small Creeks on the L. S. and Camped below the third, (the place that Shannon the man who went a head lived on grapes) Som heavy Showers of rain all wet,   had the Goat & rabit Stufed rained all night.

[Lewis]   September 14th. 1804.
this day Capt. Clark killed a male *wild goat* [antelope] so called it's weight 65 bs.

	F	I
length from point of nose to point of tail	4.	9.
hight to the top of the wethers	3.	
Do. behind	3.	
girth of the brest	3.	1.
girth of the neck *close to the* sholders	2.	2.
do. near the head	1.	7

Eye deep see green, large percing and reather prominent, & at or near the root of the horn within one ¼ inches.

Shields killed a *hare of the prarie* weight six pounds and ¼

	F.	I.
Length from point of hind to extremity fore feet	2	. 11
hight when standing erect	1	. 1¾

[14] White-tailed jack rabbit (*Lepus townsendi*).

		F	I
length from nose to tale		2 .	1.
girth of body		1 .	2¾
length of tale		.	6½
length of the year [ear]		.	5½
width of do. do.		.	3⅛
from the extremity of the hip to the toe of the hind foot		1 .	3½

the eye is large and prominent the sight is circular, deep sea green, and occupyes one third of the width of the eye the remaining two thirds is a ring of a bright yellowish silver colour. the years ar[e] placed at the upper part of the head and very near to each other, the years are very flexable, the anamall moves them with great ease and quickness and can contra[c]t and foald them on his back or delate them at pleasure. the front outer foald of the year is a redis[h] brown, the inner foalds or those which ly together when the years are thrown back and w[h]ich occupy two thirds of the width of the year is of a clear white colour except one inch at the tip of the year which is black, the hinder foald is of a light grey. the head back sholders and outer part of the thighs are of a ledcoloured grey the sides as they aproache the belly grow lighter becomeing greadually more white the belly and brest are white with a shad[e] of lead colour. the furr is long and fine. the tale is white round and blount[l]y pointed the furr on it is long and extreemly fine and soft when it runs it carry's it's tale strait behind in the direction of the body. the body is much smaller and more length than the rabbit in proportion to it's height. the teeth are like those of the hair or rabbit as is it's upper lip split. it's food is grass or herbs. it resorts the open plains, is extreemly fleet and never burrows or takes shelter in the ground when pursued, I measured the leaps of one which I surprised in the plains on the 17th. Inst. and found them 21 feet the ground was a little decending they apear to run with more ease and to bound with greater agility than any anamall I ever saw. this anamal is usually single seldom associating in any considerable numbers

Sept. 17th.

one of the hunters killed a bird of the *Corvus genus* and order of the pica[15] & about the size of a jack-daw. with a remarkable long tale. beautifully variagated. it[s] note is not disagreeable though loud—it is twait-twait-twait, twait; twait, twait twait twait.

	F		I
from tip to tip of wing	1	.	10
Do. beak to extremity of tale	1	.	8½
of which the tale occupys		.	11
from extremity of middle toe to hip	5	.	5½

it's head, beak, and neck are large for a bird of it's size; the beak is black and of a convex and cultrated figure, the chops nearly equal, and it's base large and beset with hairs. the eyes are black encircled with a narrow ring of yellowish black it's head, neck, brest & back within one inch of the tale are of a fine glossey black, as are also the short f[e]athers of the under part of the wing, the thies and those about the root of the tale. the belly is of a beatifull white which passes above and arround the but of the wing, where the feathers being long reach to a small white spot on the rump one inch in width. the wings have nineteen feathers, of which the ten first have the longer side of their plumage white in the midd[l]e of the feather and occupying unequal lengths of the same from one to three inches, and forming when the wing is sp[r]ead a kind [of] triangle, the upper and lower part of these party coloured feathers on the under side of the wing being of dark colour but not jut or shining black. the under side of the remaining feathers of the wing are darker. the upper side of the wing, as well as the short side of the plumage of the party-coloured feathers is of a dark blackis[h] or bluish green sonetimes presenting as light orange yellow or bluish tint as it happens to be presented to different exposures of lig[h]t.

the plumage of the tale consists of 12 feathers of equal lengths by pair[s], those in the center are the longest, and the others on each side deminishing about an inch each pair. the underside of the feathers is a pale black, the upper side is a dark blueish green

---

[15] Black-billed magpie (*Pica pica*).

and which like the outer part of the wings is changable as it reflects different portions of light. towards the extremity of these feathers they become of an orrange green, then shaded pass to a redish indigo blue, and again at the extremity assume the predominant colour of changable green. the tints of these feathers are very similar and equally beatiful and rich as the tints of blue and green of the peacock.

it is a most beatifull bird. the legs and toes are black and imbricated. it has four long toes, three in front and one in rear, each terminated with a black sharp tallon of from ⅜ths to ½ an inch in length. these birds are seldom found in parties of more than three or four and most usually at this season single as the halks and other birds of prey usually are. it's usual food is flesh. this bird dose not spread it's tail when it flys and the motion of it's wings when flying is much like that of a Jay-bird.

[Clark]   17th. of September Monday 1804—
Dried all our wet articles, this fine Day, Capt. Lewis went out with a View to See the Countrey and its productions, he was out all day he killed a Buffalow and a remarkable *Bird* (*Magpy*) of the *Corvus* Species long tail the upper part of the feathers & also the wings is of a purplish variated Green, the back & a part of the wing feathers are white edged with black, white belly, while from the root of the wings to Center of the back is White, the head nake [neck] breast & other parts are black the Beeke like a Crow, abt. the Size of a large Pigion, a butifull thing.

I took equal altitudes and a meridian altitude. Capt. Lewis returned at Dark, Colter Killed a Goat like the one I killed and a curious kind of Deer of a Dark gray Colr.[16] more so than common, hair long & fine, the ears large & long, a Small reseptical under the eyes; like an Elk, the Taile about the length of Common Deer, round (like a Cow) a tuft of black hair about the end, this Spec[i]es of Deer jumps like a goat or Sheep

8 fallow Deer[17] 5 Common & 3 Buffalow killed to day. Capt. Lewis saw a *hare* & killed a Rattle snake in a village of B.[arking] Squarels the wind from S. W. Dryed our provisions, Some of which was much Damaged.

[16] Mule deer (*Odocoileus hemionus*).
[17] Virginia white-tailed deer (*Odocoileus virginius*).

[Lewis]   Monday September 17th. 1804.

Having for many days past confined myself to the boat, I determined to devote this day to amuse myself on shore with my gun
and view the interior of the country lying between the river and the
Corvus Creek.[18] accordingly before sunrise I set out with six of my
best hunters, two of whom I dispatched to the lower side of Corvus
creek, two with orders to hunt the bottums and woodland on the
river, while I retained two others to acompany me in the intermediate country. one quarter of a mile in rear of our camp which was
situated in a fine open grove of cotton wood passed a grove of plumb
trees loaded with fruit and now ripe, observed but little difference
betwen this fruit and that of a similar kind common to the Atlantic
States. the trees are smaller and more thickly set. this forrest of
plumb trees garnish a plain about 20 feet more elivated than that
on which we were encamped; this plain extends back about a mile
to the foot of the hills one mile distant and to which it is gradually
ascending this plane extends with the same bredth from the creek
below to the distance of near three miles above parrallel with the
river, and it is intirely occupied by the burrows of the *barking squiril*
hertefore described; this anamal appears here in infinite numbers
and the shortness and virdu[r]e of grass gave the plain the appearance
throughout it's whole extent of beatifull bowling-green in fine order. it's aspect is S. E. a great number of wolves of the small
kind, halks [hawks] and some pole-cats were to be seen. I presume
that those anamals feed on this squirril.

found the country in every direction for about three miles intersected with deep revenes and steep irregular hills of 100 to 200 feet
high; at the tops of these hills the country breakes of[f] as usual
into a fine leavel plain extending as far as the eye can reach. from
this plane I had an extensive view of the river below, and the
irregular hills which border the opposite sides of the river and creek.
the surrounding country had been birnt about a month before and
young grass had now sprung up to hight of 4 Inches presenting the
live green of the spring to the West a high range of hills, strech
across the country from N. to S. and appeared distant about 20
miles; they are not very extensive as I could plainly observe their

---

[18] Crow Creek, near Oacoma, South Dakota.

rise and termination   no rock appeared on them and the sides were covered with virdu[r]e similar to that of the plains   this senery already rich pleasing and beatiful was still farther hightened by immence herds of Buffaloe, deer Elk and Antelopes which we saw in every direction feeding on the hills and plains.   I do not think I exagerate when I estimate the number of Buffaloe which could be compre[hend]ed at one view to amount to 3000.

my object was if possible to kill a female Antelope having already procured a male; I pursued my rout on this plain to the west flanked by my two hunters untill eight in the morning when I made the signal for them to come to me which they did shortly after. we rested our selves about half an hour, and regailed ourselves on half a bisquit each and some jirks of Elk which we had taken the precaution to put in our pouches in the morning before we set out, and drank of the water of a small pool which had collected on this plain from the rains which had fallen some days before.   we had now after various windings in pursuit of several herds of antelopes which we had seen on our way made the distance of about eight miles from our camp. we found the Antelope extreemly shye and watchfull   insomuch that we had been unable to get a shot at them; when at rest they generally seelect the most elivated point in the neighbourhood, and as they are watchfull and extreemly quick of sight and their sense of smelling very accute it is almost impossible to approach them within gunshot; in short they will frequently discover and flee from you at the distance of three miles.

I had this day an opportunity of witnessing the agility and the superior fleetness of this anamal which was to me really astonishing. I had pursued and twice surprised a small herd of seven,   in the first instance they did not discover me distinctly and therefore did not run at full speed, tho' they took care before they rested to gain an elivated point where it was impossible to approach them under cover, except in one direction and that happened to be in the direction from which the wind blew towards them;   bad as the chance to approch them was, I made the best of my way towards them, freqeuntly peeping over the ridge with which I took care to conceal myself from their view   the male, of which there was but one, frequently incircled the summit of the hill on which the females stood in a group, as if to look out for the approach of danger.   I got within about 200 paces of them when they smelt me and fled; I gained the top of the eminence on which they stood, as soon as possible from whence I had an extensive view of the country the antilopes which had disappeared in a steep reveene now appeared at the distance of about three miles on the side of a ridge which passed obliquely across me and extended about four miles. so soon had these antelopes gained the distance at which they had again appeared to my view I doubted at ferst that they were the same that I had just surprised, but my doubts soon vanished when I beheld the rapidity of their flight along the ridge before me it appeared reather the rappid flight of birds than the motion of quadrupeds. I think I can safely venture the asscertion that the speed of this anamal is equal if not superior to that of the finest blooded courser.

[Clark]   September 18th. Tuesday 1804—
   the hunters Killed 10 Deer to day and a Prarie wolf,[19] had it all jurked & Skins Stretchd. after Camping.
   I walked on Shore Saw Goats, Elk, Buffalow, Black tail Deer, & the Common Deer, I Killed a Prarie Wollf, about the Size of a gray fox bushey tail head & ears like a Wolf, Some fur Burrows in the ground and barks like a Small Dog.
   What has been taken heretofore for the Fox was those Wolves, and no Foxes has been Seen; The large Wolves[20] are verry numourous, they are of a light colr. large & has long hair with Coarse fur.

                                     21st. of September Friday 1804—
   at half past one o'clock this morning the Sand bar on which we Camped began to under mind and give way which allarmed the Serjeant on Guard, the motion of the boat awakened me; I got up & by the light of the moon observed that the Sand had given away both above and below our Camp & was falling in fast. I ordered all hands on as quick as possible & pushed off, we had pushed off but a few minits before the bank under which the Boat & perogus lay give way, which would Certainly have Sunk both Perogues, by

---

[19] Coyote (*Canis latrans*).
[20] Gray wolf (*Canis lupus*).

the time we made the opsd. Shore our Camp fell in, we made a
2d. Camp for the remainder of the night. & at Daylight proceeded
on to the Gouge of this Great bend and Brackfast

We Saw Some Camps and tracks of the Seaux which appears to
be old, three or four weeks ago, one frenchman I fear has got an
abscess on his they [thigh], he Complains verry much we are
makeing every exertion to reliev him

The Praries in this quarter Contains great qts. of Prickley Pear.

23rd of September Sunday 1804—
the river is nearly Streight for a great distance wide and Shoal
passed a Creek on the S. S. 16 yards wide we Call Reuben Creek,[21]
as R. Fields found it. Camped on the S. S. below the mouth of a
Creek on the L. S. three Souex boys Came to us Swam the river
and informd that the Band of Seauex called the *Tetongues* (*Tetons*) of
80 Lodges were Camped at the next Creek above, & 60 Lodges
more a Short distance above, we gave those boys two Carrots of
Tobacco to Carry to their Chiefs, with directions to tell them that
we would Speek to them tomorrow

24th. September Monday 1804—
we prepared Some Clothes and a fiew Meadels for the Chiefs of
the Teton's bands of Seoux which we expect to See to day at the
next river, observe a great Deel of Stone on the Sides of the hills
on the S. S. we Saw one Hare, to day, prepared all things for
Action in Case of necessity, our Perogus went to the Island for the
Meet, Soon after the man on Shore run up the bank and reported
that the Indians had Stolen the horse We Soon after Met 5 Inds.
and ankered out Som distance & Spoke to them informed them
we were friends, & Wished to Continue So but were not afraid of
any Indians, Some of their young men had taken the horse Sent
by their Great father for their Cheif and we would not Speek to
them untill the horse was returned to us again.

25th. Sept.—
A fair Morning the Wind from the S. E. all well, raised a Flag
Staff & made a orning or Shade on a Sand bar in the mouth of Tet

---

[21] East Medicine Knoll Creek (Coues) or Medicine Creek, in Hughes
South Dakota.

River, for the purpose of Speeking with the Indians under,　the
Boat Crew on board at 70 yards Distance from the bar　The 5 Indians
which we met last night Continued,　about 11 OClock the 1t. &
2d. Chief Came we gave them Some of our Provisions to eat, they
gave us great Quantitis of Meet Some of which was Spoiled　we
feel much at a loss for the want of an interpeter the one we have
can Speek but little.

Met in Council at 12 oClock and after Smokeing, agreeable to
the useal Custom, Cap. Lewis proceeded to Deliver a Speech which
we [were] oblige[d] to Curtail for want of a good interpeter　all our
party paraded.　gave a Medal to the Grand Chief Calld. in Indian
Un ton gar Sar bar in French *Beeffe nure* [Beuffle noir] Black Buffalow.　Said to be a good Man,　2nd Chief *Torto hon gar* or the *Parti
sin* or Partizan *bad*　the 3rd. is the Beffe De Medison [Beuffe de
Medecine] his name is *Tar ton gar Wa ker*　1st. Considerable Man,
War zing go.　2nd. Considerable Man　*Second Bear—Mato co que
par.*

Envited those Cheifs on board to Show them our boat and such
Curiossities as was Strange to them,　we gave them ¼ a glass of
whiskey which they appeared to be verry fond of, Sucked the bottle
after it was out & Soon began to be troublesom, one the 2d. Cheif
assumeing Drunkness, as a Cloake for his rascally intentions　I went
with those Cheifs (which left the boat with great reluctiance) to
Shore with a view of reconsileing those men to us,　as Soon as I
landed the Perogue three of their young Men Seased the Cable of
the Perogue, the Chiefs Soldr. Huged the mast, and the 2d. Chief
was verry insolent both in words & justures (*pretended Drunkenness
& staggered up against me*) declareing I should not go on, Stateing he
had not receved presents sufficent from us,　his justures were of
Such a personal nature I felt My self Compeled to Draw my Sword
(*and Made a Signal to the boat to prepare for action*)　at this Motion
Capt. Lewis ordered all under arms in the boat,　those with me also
Showed a Disposition to Defend themselves and me, the grand
Chief then took hold of the roap & ordered the young Warrers away,
I felt My Self warm & Spoke in verry positive terms.

Most of the Warriers appeared to have ther Bows strung and took
out their arrows from the quiver.　as I (*being surrounded*) was not
permited to return, I Sent all the men except 2 Inps. [Interpreters]

to the boat, the perogue Soon returned with about 12 of our determined men ready for any event. this movement caused a no: of the Indians to withdraw at a distance. Their treatment to me was verry rough & I think justified roughness on my part, they all lift my Perogue, and Councild. with themselves the result I could not lern and nearly all went off after remaining in this Situation Some time I offered my hand to the 1. & 2. Chiefs who refusd. to receve it. I turned off & went with my men on board the perogue, I had not prosd. more the [than] 10 paces before the 1st. Cheif 3rd. & 2 Brave Men Waded in after me. I took them in & went on board

We proceeded on about 1 Mile & anchored out off a Willow Island placed a guard on Shore to protect the Cooks & a guard in the boat, fastened the Perogues to the boat, I call this Island bad humered Island as we were in a bad humer.[22]

26th. of September Wednesday 1804—
Set out early proceeded on and Came to by the Wish of the Chiefs for to let their Squars [squaws] & boys see the Boat and Suffer them to treat us well great numbers of men womin & children on the banks viewing us, these people Shew great anxiety, they appear Spritely, Generally ill looking & not well made their legs Small generally, they Grese & Black themselves when they dress make use of a hawks feathers about their heads. the men [wear] a robe & each a polecats Skin, for to hold ther *Bawe roley* [*Bois roule*] for Smoking,[23] fond of Dress & Show badly armed with fusees, &c. The Squaws are Chearfull fine look'g womin not handsom, High Cheeks Dressed in Skins a Peticoat and roab which foldes back over ther Sholder, with long wool, do all their laborious work & I may Say perfect Slaves to the Men, as all Squars of Nations much at War, or where the Womin are more noumerous than the men.

Capt. Lewis & 5 men went on Shore with the Cheifs, who ap-

[22] Near Pierre, South Dakota.

[23] *Bois roulé*, literally "rolled wood,"—better known by its Algonkin name, Kinikinik (Kinnikinnic),—a mixture of tobacco with scrapings or shavings from various woods, especially that of sumac, red osier, and other dogwoods, and bearberry (Thwaites).

peared disposed to make up & be friendly,   after Captain Lewis
had been on Shore about 3 hours I became uneasy for fear of De-
ception & Sent a Serjeant to See him and know his treatment which
he reported was friendly, & they were prepareing for a Dance this
evening The[y] made frequent Selicitiations for us to remain one
night only and let them Show their good disposition towards us, we
deturmined to remain,   after the return of Capt. Lewis, I went on
Shore   on landing I was receved on a elegent painted B.[uffalo]
Robe & taken to the Village by 6 Men & was not permited to touch
the ground untill I was put down in the grand Concill house on a
White dressed Robe.   I saw Several Maha Prissners and Spoke to
the Chiefs [telling them that] it was necessary to give those prisoners
up & become good friends with the Mahas if they wished to follow
the advice of their great father

I was in Several Lodges neetly formed as before mentioned as to
the Baureily (*Bois brulé*—Yankton) Tribe. I was met by about 10
Well Dressd. young Men who took me up in a roabe Highly ade-
crated and Set me Down by the Side of their Chief on a Dressed
Robe in a large Council House,   this house formed a ¾ Circle of
Skins Well Dressed and Sown together   under this Shelter about
70 Men Set forming a Circle   in front of the Cheifs a plac of 6 feet
Diameter was Clear and the pipe of peace raised on Sticks under
which there was swans down scattered,   on each Side of this Circle
two Pipes, the (*two*) flags of Spain 2 & the Flag we gave them in
front of the Grand Chief   a large fire was near in which provisions
were Cooking, in the Center about 400 lbs. of excellent Buffalo
Beef as a present for us.

Soon after they Set me Down, the Men went for Capt. Lewis
brought him in the same way and placed him also by the Chief   in
a fiew minits an old man rose & Spoke aproveing what we had done
& informing us of their situation requesting us to take pity on them
& which was answered.   The great Chief then rose with great State
[speaking] to the Same purpote as far as we Could learn & then
with Great Solemnity took up the pipe of Peace & after pointing it
to the heavins the 4 quarters of the Globe & the earth, he made
Some disertation, lit it and presented the Stem to us to Smoke,
when the Principal Chief Spoke with the Pipe of Peace he took in

one hand some of the most Delicate parts of the Dog which was prepared for the fiest & made a Sacrefise to the flag. after A Smoke had taken place, & a Short Harange to his people, we were requested to take the Meal

We Smoked for an hour (*till*) Dark & all was Cleared away a large fire made in the Center, about 10 Musitions playing on tambereens (*made of hoops & Skin stretched*), long Sticks with Deer & Goats Hoofs tied so as to make a gingling noise, and many others of a Similer Kind, those Men began to Sing, & Beet on the Tamboren, the Women Came foward highly Deckerated in their Way, with the Scalps and Tropies of War of their fathers Husbands Brothers or near Connections & proceeded to Dance the War Dance which they done with great Chearfullness untill about 12 oClock when we informed the Cheifs that they were fatigued. they then retired & we Accompd. by 4 Cheifs returned to our boat, they Stayed with us all night.

Those people have Some brave men which they make use of as Soldiers those men attend to the police of the Village Correct all errors I saw one of them to day whip 2 Squars, who appeared to have fallen out, when he approachd. all about appeared to flee with great turrow [terror]. at night they keep two 3, 4 5 men at different Distances walking around Camp Singing the accurrunces of the night

All the Men on board 100 paces from Shore Wind from the S. E. moderate one man verry sick on board with a Dangerass Abscess on his Hip. All in Spirits this evening.

In this Tribe I saw 25 Squars and Boys taken 13 days ago in a battle with the Mahars in this battle they Destroyd 40 Lodges, Killed 75 Men, & som boys & Children, & took 48 Prisoners Womin & boys which they promis both Capt. Lewis and my self Shall be Delivered up to Mr. Durion at the Bous rulie (*Bois brulé*) Tribe, those are a retched and Dejected looking people the Squars appear low & Corse but this is an unfavourable time to judge of them

We gave our Mahar inteptr. some fiew articles to give those Squars in his name Such as Alls, needles &c. &c.

I saw & eat Pemitigon the Dog, Groud. potatoe made into a Kind of homney, which I thought but little inferior. I also Saw a Spoon

Made of a horn of an Animell of the Sheep Kind[24]   the Spoon will hold 2 quarts.

                                    27th. of Sept. Thursday 1804—

I rose early after a bad nights Sleep   found the Chief[s] all up, and the bank as useal lined with Spectators   we gave the 2 great Cheifs a Blanket a peace, or rether they took off agreeable to their Custom the one they lay on and each one Peck of corn.   after Brackfast Capt. Lewis & the Cheifs went on Shore, as a verry large part of their nation was comeing in, the Disposition of whome I did not know   one of us being sufficent on Shore, I wrote a letter to Mr. P.Durion & prepared a meadel & Some Comsns. (*Certificates*) & Sent to Cap Lewis   at 2 oClock Capt. Lewis Returned with 4 Chiefs & a Brave Man named *War cha pa* or on his Guard   when the friends of those people die they run arrows through their flesh above and below their elbows as a testimony of their Greaf.

after Staying about half an hour, I went with them on Shore, Those men left the boat with reluctience,   I went first to the 2d. Cheifs Lodge, where a croud came around   after Speeking on various Subjects I went to a princpal mans lodge from them to the grand Chiefs lodge,   after a fiew minits he invited me to a Lodge within the Circle in which I Stayed with all their principal Men untill the Dance began, which was Similer to the one of last night performed by their women with poles on which Scalps of their enemies were hung, Some with the Guns Spears & War empliments of their husbands in their hands.

Capt. Lewis Came on Shore and we Continued untill we were Sleepy & returned to our boat,   the 2nd. Chief & one principal Man accompanied us,   Those two Indians accompanied me on board in the Small Perogue; Capt. Lewis with a guard Still on Shore   the man who Steered not being much acustomed to Steer, passed the bow of the boat & the peroge Came broad Side against the Cable & broke it which obliged me to order in a loud voice all hands up & at their ores,   my preemptry order to the men and the bustle of their getting to their ores allarmd the Cheifs, together with the appearance of the Men on Shore, as the boat turnd.   The Cheif

---

[24] Bighorn sheep (*Ovis canadensis*).

hollowaed & allarmed the Camp or Town informing them that the Mahars was about attacking us. In about 10 minits the bank was lined with men armed the 1st. Cheif at their head, about 200 men appeared and after about ½ hour returned all but about 60 men who continued on the bank all night, the Cheifs Contd. all night with us. This allarm I as well as Capt. Lewis Considered as the Signal of their intentions (which was to Stop our proceeding on our journey and if Possible rob us) we were on our Guard all night, the misfortune of the loss of our Anchor obliged us to Lay under a falling bank much exposd. to the accomplishment of their hostile intentions. P. C. our Bowman who cd. Speek Mahar informed us in the night that the Maha Prisoners informed him we were to be Stoped. we Shew as little Sighns of a Knowledge of their intentions as possible all prepared on board for any thing which might hapen, we kept a Strong guard all night in the boat, no Sleep

                              28th. of September 1804 Friday—
Made many attemps in different ways to find our anchor, but Could not, the Sand had Covered it, from the Misfortune of last night our boat was laying at Shore in a verry unfavourable Situation, after finding that the anchor Could not be found we deturmined to proceed on, with great difficuelty got the Chiefs out of our boat, and when we was about Setting out the Class Called the Soldiers took possession of the Cable the 1st. Cheif which was Still on board, & intended to go a Short distance up with us. I told him the men of his nation Set on the Cable, he went out & told Capt. Lewis who was at the bow the men Who Set on the roap was Soldiers, and wanted Tobacco Capt. L. [*said*] would not agree to be forced into any thing, the 2d. Chief Demanded a flag & Tobacco which we refusd. to Give Stateing proper reasons to them for it after much Dificuelty—which had nearly reduced us to necessity to hostilites I threw a Carrot of Tobacco to 1st. Chief took the port fire from the gunner. Spoke so as to touch his pride The Chief gave the Tobacco to his Soldiers & he jurked the rope from them and handed it to the bowsman

we then Set out under a Breeze from the S. E. about 2 miles up we observed the 3rd. Chief on Shore beckining to us we took him on board he informed us the roap was held by the order of the 2d. Chief who was a Double Spoken man, Soon after we Saw a man Comeing full Speed, thro: the plains left his horse & proceeded across a Sand bar near the Shore we took him on board & observed that he was the Son of the Chief we had on board we Sent by him a talk to the nation Stateint [stating] the cause of our hoisting the red flag undr. the white, if they were for peace Stay at home & do as we had Directed them, if the[y] were for war or were Deturmined to stop us we were ready to defend our Selves, we halted one houre & ½ on the S. S. & made a Substitute of Stones for a ancher, refreshed our men and proceeded on about 2 Miles higher up & Came to a verry Small Sand bar in the middle of the river & Stayed all night, I am verry unwell for want of Sleep Deturmined to Sleep to night if possible, the Men Cooked & we rested well.

29th. of Septr. Satturday 1804.—
Set out early Some bad Sand bars, proceeded on at 9 oClock we observed the 2d. Chief & 2 principal Men one Man & a Squar on Shore, they wished to go up with us as far as the other part of their band, which they Said was on the river a head not far Distant we refused Stateing verry Sufficint reasons and was Plain with them on the Subject, they were not pleased observed that they would walk on Shore to the Place we intended to Camp to night, we observed it was not our wish that they Should for if they did we Could not take them or any other Tetons on board except the one we had now with us who might go on Shore whenever he pleased. they proceeded on, the Chief on board askd. for a twist of Tobacco for those men we gave him ½ of a twist, and Sent one by them for that part of their band which we did not See, & Continued on

30th. of Sept. Sunday 1804—
Set out this morning early had not proceeded on far before we discovered an Indn. running after us, he came up with us at 7 oClock & requested to come on bord and go up to the *Recorees*[25] we refused to take any of that band on board if he chose to proceed on Shore it was verry Well Soon after I descovered on the hills at a great distance great numbers of Indians which appeared to be

[25] Otherwise called Ricaree, Ree, or, more correctly, Arikara (Thwaites).

makeing to the river above us, we proceeded on under a Double reafed Sail, & some rain at 9 oClock observed a large band of Indians the Same which I had before seen on the hills incamping on the bank the L. S. we Came too on a Sand bar Brackfast & proceeded on & Cast the anchor opposit their Lodge at about 100 yards distant, and informed the Indians which we found to be a part of the Band we had before Seen, that (*we*) took them by the hand and Sent to each Chief a Carrot of tobacco, as we had been treated badly by some of the band below, after Staying 2 days for them, we Could not delay any time, & referred them to Mr. Durion for a full account of us and to here our Talk Sent by him to the Tetons, those were verry selicitious for us to land and eate with them, that they were friendly &c. &c. we appoligised & proceeded on,

This day is Cloudy & rainey. refresh the men with a glass of whisky after Brackfast.

we proceeded on under a verry Stiff Breeze from the S. E., the Stern of the boat got fast on a log and the boat turned & was verry near filling before we got her righted, the waves being verry high, The Chief on board was So fritened at the Motion of the boat which in its rocking Caused Several loose articles to fall on the Deck from the lockers, he ran off and hid himself, we landed, he got his gun and informed us he wished to return, that all things were cleare for us to go on, we would not see any more Tetons &c. we repeated to him what had been Said before, and advised him to keep his men away, gave him a blanket a Knife & some Tobacco, Smokd. a pipe & he Set out. We also Set Sale and Came to at a Sand bar, & Camped, a verry Cold evening, all on guard.

Sand bars are So noumerous, that it is impossible to describe them, & think it unnecessary to mention them.

1st. of October Monday 1804—

Continued on with the wind imediately a head, we Saw a man opposit to our Camp on the L. S. which we discovd. to be a Frenchman

This Mr. *Jon Vallie*[26] informs us that he wintered last winter 300

[26] Evidently meant for Jean Vallé (Thwaites)—near the mouth of the Cheyenne River in South Dakota.

Leagues up the Chien River under the Black mountains, he informs that this river is verry rapid and dificuelt even for Perogues to assend and when riseing the Swels is verry high,   one hundred Leagues up it forks   one fork Comes from the S. the other at 40 Leagues above the forks enters the black Mountain.[27]   The Countrey from the Missourie to the black mountains is much like the Countrey on the Missourie, less timber. & a great perpotion of Ceder.

The black mountains he Says is verry high, and Some parts of it has Snow on it in the Summer   great quantities of Pine Grow on the Mountains,   a great Noise is heard frequently on those Mountains.   No beever on Dog river,   on the Mountains great numbers of goat, and a kind of anamale with large circular horns, this animale is nearly the Size of an Elk. White bears is also plenty   The Chien (*Chayenne*) Inds. are about 300 Lodges   they inhabit this river principally, and Steel horses from the Spanish Settlements, to the S W.   this excurtion they make in one month   the bottoms & Sides of R Chien is corse gravel.   This frenchman gives an account of a white booted turkey an inhabitent of the Cout Noir (*Prairie Cock*)

1st. of October Monday 1804.
at the Mouth of River Chien or Dog R—
We proceeded now from the mouth of this river 11 miles and camped on a Sand bar in the river opposit to a Tradeing house verry windy & cold.   *11 miles above—Chien R—*

2nd. of October Tuesday 1804—
we proceeded on   passed a large Island, on the S. S. here we expected the Tetons would attempt to Stop us and under that idear we prepared our selves for action which we expected every moment.   opsd. this Island on the L. S. a Small Creek Coms in,   This Island we call Isd. of *Caution*[28]

4th. of October Thursday 1804—
Several Indians on the Shore viewing of us called to us to land one of them gave 3 yels & Sciped [*skipped*] a ball before us, we payed no attention to him,   proceeded on

[27] The Black Hills of South Dakota.
[28] Now Plum Island (Thwaites).

8th. of October Monday 1804.—
passed the mouth of a River called by the Ricares *We tar hoo*[29] on the L.S. this river is 120 yards wide, the water of which at this time is Confined within 20 yards, dischargeing but a Small quantity, throwing out mud with Small propotion of Sand, great quantities of the red Berries, ressembling Currents, are on the river in every bend.

2 of our men discovered the ricckerree village, about the Center of the Island on the L. Side on the main Shore. this Island is about 3 miles long, Seperated from the L.S. by a Channel of about 60 yards wide verry Deep, The Isld. is covered with fields, where those People raise their Corn Tobacco Beens Great numbers of those people came on the Island to See us pass, we passed above the head of the Island & Capt. Lewis with 2 interpeters & 2 men went to the Village I formed a Camp of the french & the guard on Shore, with one Sentinal on board of the boat at anchor, a pleasent evening all things arranged both for Peace or War, Several french men Came up with Capt. Lewis in a Perogue, one of which is a Mr. Gravellin[30] a man well versed in the language of this nation and gave us some information relitive to the Countrey nat[i]on &c.

River Maropa 9th. of October 1804. Tuesday—
a windey rainey night, and cold, So much So we Could not speek with the Indians to day the three great Chiefs and many others Came to see us to day, we gave them some tobacco and informed them we would Speek on tomorrow, the day continued Cold & windey some rain Sorry Canoos of Skins passed down from the 2 Villages a Short distance above, and many Came to view us all day, much astonished at my black Servent, who did not lose the opportunity of [displaying] his powers Strength &c. &c. this nation never Saw a black man before.

Several hunters Came in with loades of meat, I observed Several Canoos made of a Single Buffalow Skin with 3 thre squars Cross the river to day in waves as high as I ever Saw them on this river, quite uncomposed I have a Slite Plursie this evening verry cold

[29] Now Grand River (Thwaites).
[30] Joseph Gravelines, a trader residing among the Arikara tribe, in company with Antoine Tabeau (Thwaites).

10th. of October Wednesday 1804.
a fine morning wind from the S.E.   at about 11 oClock the wind Shifted, to the N. W.   we prepare all things ready to Speak to the Indians, Mr. Tabo & Mr. Gravolin came to brackfast with us   the Cheefs &c. came from the lower Town, but none from the 2 upper Towns, which is the largest,   we Continue to delay & waite for them   at 12 oClock Despatchd Gravelin to envite them to come down,   we have every reason to believe that a gellousy exists between the Villages for fear of our makeing the 1st. Cheif from the lower Village,   at one oClock the Cheifs all assembled & after Some little Cerremony the council Commenced,   we informd them what we had told the others before i. e. Ottoes & Seaux.   made 3 Cheif 1 for each Village;   gave them presents.   after the Council was over we Shot the air guns which astonished them much, the[y] then Departed and we rested Secure all night,   Those Indians wer much astonished at my Servent, they never Saw a black man before,   all flocked around him & examind him from top to toe,   he Carried on the joke and made himself more turribal than we wished him to doe.   Those Indians are not fond of Spirts Liquer. of any kind

11th. October Thursday 1804—
Those people gave us to eate bread made of Corn & Beens, also Corn & Beans boild. a large Been (*of*) which they rob the mice of the Prarie (*who collect & discover it*) which is rich & verry nurrishing also [*S*]quashes &c.   all Tranquillity.

12th. October Friday 1804—
I rose early   after brackfast we joined the Indians who were waiting on the bank for us to come out and go and councel, we accordingly joined them and went to the house of the 2nd. Cheif *Lassel* where there was many Cheif and Warriers & we Set Some time before the Councill Commenced   this man Spoke at Some length declareing his dispotion to believe and prosue our Councils, his intention of going to Visit his great father   acknowledged the Satisfaction in receiveing the presents &c. rais'g a Doubt as to the Safty in passing the Nations below particularly the Souex.   requested us to take a Chief of their nation and make a good peace with Mandins & nations above.   after answering those parts of the 2d Cheifs Speech which required it, which appeared to give general Satisfac-

tion we went to the Village of the 3rd. Chief and as usial Some
Serimony took place before he Could Speek to us on the Great
Subject. This Chief Spoke verry much in the [same] Stile on nearly
the Same Subjects of the other Chief who Set by his Side, more
Sincear & pleasently, he presented us with about 10 bushels of
Corn Some beens & [s]quashes all of which we acksepted with much
pleasure, after we had ansd. his Speech & give them Some account
of the Magnitude & power of our Countrey which pleased and
astonished them verry much we returned to our boat, the Chiefs
accompanied us on board, we gave them Some Sugar a little Salt
and a Sun Glass, & Set 2 on Shore & the third proceeded on with
us to the Mandens by name

The Nation of the Rickerries is about 600 men (Mr. Taboe says,
I think 500 men) able to bear arms a Great perpotion of them have
fusees they appear to be peacefull, their men tall and perpotiend,
womin Small and industerous, raise great quantities of Corn Beens
Simnins &c. also Tobacco for the men to Smoke they collect all
the wood and do the drugery as Common amongst Savages.

This nation is made up of 10 Different Tribes of the Pania (*Panies*),
who had formerly been Seperate, but by Commotion and war with
their neighbours have Come reduced and compelled to come together for protection, The curruption of the language of those
different Tribes has So reduced the language that the Different
Villages do not understan all the words of the others. Those people
are Durtey, Kind, pore, & extravigent. pursessing national pride,
not beggarley recive what is given with great pleasure, Live in warm
houses, large and built in an oxigon [octagon] form forming a cone
at top which is left open for the smoke to pass, those houses are
Generally 30 or 40 foot Diamiter, Covd. with earth on poles willows
& grass to prevent the earths passing thro'. Those people express
an inclination to be at peace with all nations. The Seaux who trade
the goods which they get of the Brituish Traders for their Corn, and
[have] great influence over the Rickeres, poison their minds and
keep them in perpetial dread.

a curious custom with the Souix as well as the rickeres is to give
handsom squars to those whome they wish to Show some acknowl-
edgements to. The Seauex we got clare of without taking their
squars, they followed us with Squars two days. The Rickores we

put off dureing the time we were at the Towns but 2 [*handsom young*] Squars were Sent by a man to follow us, they came up this evening, and pursisted in their civilities.

Dress of the men of this nation is Simply a pr. mockerson, Leagin, flap in front & a Buffalow roabe, with ther hair arms & ears Deckorated.

The womin, wore Mockersons leagins fringed and a Shirt of Goat Skins, Some with Sleaves this garment is longe & Genly. white & fringed, tied at the waste[,] with a roabe, in Summer without hair.

13th. of October Satturday 1804—

one man J. Newmon confined for mutinous expression Set out early proceeded on, passd. a camp of Seauex on the S.S. those people only viewed us & did not Speak one word.

at 21 Miles above the Village passed a Creek about 15 yards wide on the L.S. we call after 2d. Chief Pocasse (or Hay). nearly opposit this Creek a fiew miles from the river on the S.S.[31] 2 Stones resembling humane persons & one resembling a Dog is Situated in the open Prarie, to those Stones the Rickores pay Great reverance make offerings whenever they pass (Informtn. of the Chief & Intepeter) those People have a curious Tredition of those Stones, one was a man in Love, one a Girl whose parents would not let [them] marry the Dog went to morn with them all turned to Stone gradually, commenceing at the feet. Those people fed on grapes untill they turned, & the woman has a bunch of grapes yet in her hand, on the river near the place those are Said to be Situated, we obsd. a greater quantity of fine grapes than I ever Saw at one place.

we Tried the Prisoner Newmon last night by 9 of his Peers they did "Centence him 75 Lashes & Disbanded [from] the party."[32]

[Orderly Book; Clark]   Orders 13th. of October 1804

A Court Martial to Consist of nine members will set to day at 12 oClock for the trial of John Newmon now under Confinement. Capt. Clark will attend to the forms & rules of a president without giveing his opinion.

Detail for the Court Martial

[31] In Corson County, South Dakota.
[32] Near Fort Yates, North Dakota.

Sergt. John Ordaway Wm Werner
Sergeant Pat: Gass Wm Bratten
  Jo: Shields Geo: Shannon
  H.: Hall Silas Goodrich
  Jo. Collins

MERIWETHER LEWIS Capt.
1st. U'S. Regt. Infty
WM CLARK Capt
 or E. N W D [Engineer North Western Discovery.]

[Lewis]

In conformity to the above order the Court martial convened this day for the trial of John Newman, charged with "having uttered repeated expressions of a highly criminal and mutinous nature; the same having a tendency not only to distroy every principle of military discipline, but also to alienate the affections of the individuals composing this detatchment to their officers, and disaffect them to the service for which they have been so sacredly and solemnly engaged." The Prisonar plead *not guil*[*t*]*y* to the charge exhibited against him. The court after having duly considered the evidence aduced, as well as the defence of the said prisonor, are unanimously of opinion that the prisonor John Newman is guilty of every part of the charge exhibited against him, and do sentence him agreeably to the rules and articles of war, to receive seventy five lashes on his bear back, and to be henceforth discarded from the perminent party engaged for North Western discovery; two thirds of the Court concurring in the sum and nature of the punishment awarded. the commanding officers approve and confirm the sentence of the court, and direct the punishment take place tomorrow between the hours of one and two P.M. The commanding officers further direct that John Newman in future be attatched to the mess and crew of the red Perogue as a labouring hand on board the same, and that he be deprived of his arms and accoutrements, and not be permited the honor of mounting guard untill further orders; the commanding officers further direct that in lue of the guard duty from which Newman has been exempted by virtue of this order, that he shall be exposed to such drudgeries as they may think proper to direct from time to time with a view to the general relief of the detatchment.

[Clark]   14th. of October Sunday 1804.—

at 1 oClock we halted on a Sand bar & after Dinner executed the
Sentence of the Court Martial so far a[s] giveing the Corporal
punishment

The punishment of this day allarmd. the Indian Chief verry much,
he cried aloud (or effected to cry) I explained the Cause of the
punishment and the necessity (*of it*) which he (*also*) thought examples were also necessary, & he himself had made them by
Death, his nation never whiped even their Children, from their
burth.

                               15th. of October Monday 1804—
at Sunset we arrived at a Camp of Recares of 10 Lodges on the
S.S. we came too and camped near them Capt. Lewis and my
self went with the Chief who accompanis us, to the Huts of Several
of the men all of whome Smoked & gave us something to eate also
Some meat to take away, those people were kind and appeared to
be much plsd. at the attentioned paid them.

Those people are much pleased with my black Servent. Their
womin verry fond of carressing our men &c.

                  Course Distance & Reffurences—15th Oct

West   2½   Miles to a Creek on the L.S. passing over a Sand bar
                makeing from the S. pt.
North   4   Miles to a point of wood on the L. S. passing over a sand
                point on the S.S.
N. 34° W. 3½   Miles to a point of wood on the S. S. passing old Village
                of the *Shăr há* or Chien Indians on the L.S. below to
                Creek on the same Side.   passed a Camp of Ricares on
                S.S.

          ——
          10

                               16th. of October Tuesday 1804—
Some rain this morning,   2 young squars verry anxious to accompany us, we Set out with our Chief on board by name *Ar ke tar na
shar* or Chief of the Town

Saw great numbers of Goats on the Shore S.S.[33] proceeded on Capt. Lewis & the Indian Chief walked on Shore, soon after I discovered great numbers of Goats in the river, and Indians on the Shore on each Side, as I approached or got nearer I discovered boys in the water Killing the goats with Sticks and halling them to Shore, Those on the banks Shot them with arrows and as they approachd. the Shore would turn them back of this Gangue of Goats I counted 58 of which they had killed on the Shore, one of our hunters out with Cap Lewis killed three Goats, we passed the Camp on the S.S. and proceeded ½ mile and camped on the L.S. many Indians came to the boat to See, Some came across late at night, as they approach they hollowed and Sung, after Staying a short time 2 went for Some meat, and returned in a Short time with fresh & Dried Buffalow, also goat, those Indians Stayed all night, they Sung and was verry merry the greater part of the night.

17th. of October Wednesday 1804.—

I walked on Shore with the Indian Chief & Interpeters, Saw Buffalow, Elk and Great numbers of Goats in large gangues (I am told by Mr. G. that those animals winter in the Black Mountains) and this is about the Season they cross from the East of the Missouries to go to that Mountain, they return in the Spring and pass the Missouries in great numbers. This Chief tells me of a number of their Treditions about Turtles, Snakes, &c. and the power of a perticeler rock or Cove on the next river which informs of every thing none of those I think worth while mentioning.

18th. of October Thursday 1804—

We met 2 frenchmen in a perogue Decending from hunting, & complained of the Mandans robing them of 4 Traps their furs & Several other articles. Those men were in the imploy of our Ricaree interpeter Mr. Gravelin the[y] turned & followered us.

19th. October Friday 1804.—

I walked out on the Hills & observed Great numbers of Buffalow feeding on both Sides of the river I counted 52 Gangues of Buffalow

---

[33] Near Big Beaver Creek; at its mouth is the town of Emmonsburg, North Dakota (Thwaites). The goats are pronghorn.

& 3 of Elk at one View,   all the runs which come from the high
hills which is Generally about one or 2 miles from the water is
brackish and near the Hills (the Salts are) and the Sides of the Hills
& edges of the Streems, [*the mineral salts appear*] I saw Some remarkable round hills forming a cone at top one about 90 foot one
60 & several others Smaller,   the Indian Chief say that the Callemet
bird[34] live in the holes of those hills,   the holes form by the water
washing [away] this Some parts in its passage Down from the top
—near one of those noles [Knolls], on a point of a hill 90 feet above
the lower plane I observed the remains of an old village, which had
been fortified,   the Indian Chief with us tels me, a party of Mandins
lived there

                                20th. of October Satturday 1804—
I saw an old remains of a village[35] on the Side of a hill which the
Chief with Too né tels me that nation lived in 2 [*a number*] villages
1 on each Side of the river and the Troublesom Seaux caused them
to move about 40 miles higher up where they remained a fiew years
& moved to the place they now live.

Camped on the L.S. above a Bluff containing coal (5) of an inferior
quallity,   this bank is imediately above the old Village of the Mandans. The Countrey is fine, the high hills at a Distance wtih gradual
assents, *I kild. 3 Deer* The Timber confined to the bottoms as
useal which is much larger than below.

Great numbers of Buffalow Elk & Deer, Goats. our hunters killed
10 Deer & a Goat to day and wounded a white Bear,[36] I saw several
fresh tracks of those animals which is 3 times as large as a mans
track.

                                22nd. October Monday 1804—
last night at 1 oClock I was violently and Suddenly attacked with
the Rhumetism in the neck which was So violent I could not move
Capt. [Lewis] applied a hot Stone raped in flannel, which gave me

---

[34] The golden eagle (*Aquila chrysaetos*)—thus named because its tail-feathers are
used to decorate the calumet-pipes of the Indians, who attach great value to these
ornaments (Thwaites).
[35] Now Slant Indian Village in Fort Abraham Lincoln State Park, North Dakota.
[36] Their first encounter with a grizzly bear. See chapter 4, notes 9 and 12.

some temporey ease. We Set out early, the morning Cold at 7 oClock we came too at a camp of Teton Seaux on the L. S. those people 12 in number were nackd. and had the appearance of war, we have every reason to believe that they are going or have been to Steel Horses from the Mandins, they tell two Stories, we gave them nothing after takeing brackfast proceeded on. my Neck is yet verry painfull at times Spasms.

24th. October Wednesday 1804—
Set out early a cloudy day Some little Snow in the morning I am Something better of the Rhumitism in my neck. a butiful Countrey on both Sides of the river. the bottoms covd. with wood, we have Seen no game on the river to day—Indians hunting in the neighbourhood passed a Island on the S. S. made by the river Cutting through a point, by which the river is Shortened Several miles. on this Isld. we Saw one of the Grand Chiefs of the Mandins, with five Lodges hunting, this Chief met the Chief of the *Ricares* who accompanied us with great Cordiallity & serimony Smoked the pipe & Capt. Lewis with the Interpeter went with the Chiefs to his Lodges at 1 mile distant, after his return we admited the Grand Chief & his brother for a few minits on our boat. proceeded on a Short distance and camped on the S. S. below the old village of the Mandins & *ricares*.[37] Soon after our land'g 4 mandins came from a camp above, the Ricares Chief went with them to their Camp.

Several parties of Mandins rode to the river on the S. S. to view us indeed they are continuelly in Sight Satisfying their Curiossities as to our apperance &c. We are told that the Seaux has latterly fallen in with & Stole the horses of the *Big bellies*,[38] on their way home they fell in with the Ossiniboin who killed them and took the horses. a frenchman has latterly been killed by the Indians on the Track to the tradeing establishment on the Ossinebine R. in the North of this place (or British fort) This frenchman has lived

[37] Near Washburn, North Dakota (Thwaites).

[38] A common but somewhat erroneous translation of Gros Ventres, the French appellation of a tribe who form a division of the Arapaho people. The name Gros Ventres is also applied, as here, to the Siouan Minitaree (more correctly known as Hidatsa). The Assiniboin are a division of the Siouan family; most of them dwell in British territory (Thwaites).

many years with the Mandins. we were frequently called on to land & talk to parties of the Mandins on the Shore; wind Shifted to the S. W at about 11 oClock and blew hard until 3 oClk. clouded up   river full of Sand bars & we are at a great loss to find the channel of the river, frequently run on the Sand bars which Delais us much passed a verry bad riffle of rocks in the evening by takeing the L. S. of a sand bar and camped on a Sand point on the S. S. opposit a high hill on the L. S.   Several Indians came to see us this evening, amongst others the Sun of the late Great Chief of the Mandins (*mourning for his father*),   this man has his two little fingers off; on inquireing the cause, was told it was customary for this nation to Show their greaf by some testimony of pain, and that it was not uncommon for them to take off 2 Smaller fingers of the hand (*at the 2d joints*) and some times more with other marks of Savage effection

26th. of October Friday 1804—
proceeded on   saw numbers of the Mandins on Shore,   we set the Ricare Chief on Shore, and we proceeded on to the Camp of two of their Grand Chiefs where we delayed a fiew minits, with the Chiefs and proceeded on takeing two of their Chiefs on board & Some of the heavy articles of his house hold, Such as earthen pots & Corn,   proceeded on,   at this Camp Saw a (*Mr.*) McCracken Englishmon from the N. W. Company   this man Came nine Days ago to trade for *horses* & *Buffalow* robes,—one other man came with him.   the Indians continued on the banks all day.   but little wood on this part of the river, many Sand bars and bad places, water much devided between them

We came too and camped about ½ a mile below the 1st. Mandin Town on the L. S.[39]   soon after our arrival many men womin & children flocked down to See us, Capt. Lewis walked to the village with the principal Chiefs and our interpters,   my Rhumatic complaint increasing I could not go.   if I was well only one would have left the Boat & party until we niew the Disposition of the Inds.   I Smoked with the Chiefs who came after.   Those people apd. much pleased with the Corn Mill which we were obliged to use, & was fixed in the boat.

[39] Not far from Stanton, North Dakota (Thwaites).

THREE

Winter Among the Mandan

October 27, 1804–March 21, 1805

[Clark] 27th. of October Satturday 1804, Mandans.—
came too at the Village on the L.S. this village is situated on an
eminance of about 50 feet above the Water in a handsom plain it
containes [blank space in MS.] houses in a kind of Picket work,
the houses are round and verry large containing several families, as
also their horses which is tied on one Side of the enterance, a
Description of those houses will be given hereafter, I walked up
& Smoked a pipe with the Chiefs of the Village they were anxious
that I would stay and eat with them, my indisposition provented
my eating which displeased them, untill a full explenation took
place, I returned to the boat and Sent 2 Carrots of Tobacco for
them to smoke, and proceeded on, passed the 2d. Village and
camped opsd. the Village of the *Weter soon* [*or Ah wah har ways*]
which is Situated on an eminance in a plain on the L.S. this Village
is Small and Contains but fiew inhabitents. above this Village also
above the Knife river on the Same Side of the Missouri the Big
bellies Towns are Situated a further Description will be given
hereafter as also of the Town of Mandans on this side of the river
i.e. S. Side.

we met with a frenchman by the name of *Jessomme*[1] which we imploy as an interpeter. This man has a wife & Children in the village. Great numbers on both Sides flocked down to the bank to view us as we passed. Capt. Lewis with the Interpetr walked down to the village below our camp After delaying one hour he returned and informed me the Indians had returned to their village &c. &c., we Sent three twists [*carrots*] of Tobacco by three young men, to the three villages above enviting them to come Down & Council with us tomorrow. many Indians came to view us Some stayed all night in the Camp of our party. We procured some information of Mr. Jessomme of the Chiefs of the Different Nations

.   Sunday. 28th. of October 1804—
Many of the *Grosvantres* (or Big Bellies)[2] and Watersones Came to See us and hear the Council the wind being So violently hard from the S.W. provented our going into Council, (indeed the Chiefs of the Mandans from the lower village Could not Cross, we made up the presents and entertained Several of the Curious Chiefs whome, wished to see the Boat which was verry curious to them viewing it as great medison, as they also Viewed my black Servent The Black Cat Grand Chief of the Mandans, Capt Lewis & myself with an Interpeter walked up the river about 1½ miles our views were to examine the Situation & Timber for a fort, we found the Situation good but the Timber scerce
we had Several presents from the woman of Corn boil'd homney, Soft Corn I prosent a jar to the Chiefs wife who received it with much pleasure. our men verry chearfull this evening. We Sent the Chiefs of the Gross Vantres to Smoke a a pipe with the Grand Chef of the Mandans in his Village, & told them we would Speek tomorrow.

29th. October Monday 1804.—
after Brackfast we were visited by the old Cheaf of the *Big bellies* this man was old and had transfired his power to his Sun, who was

[1] René Jessaume was originally a "free trader" (one to whom certain quantities of goods would be advanced by a trading company), and had spent many years among the Mandan (Thwaites).

[2] "Big Bellies" or "Gros Ventres" or "Minitarees," are names applied to the Hidatsa.

then out at War against the Snake Indians who inhabit the Rockey Mountains.[3] at 10 oClock the S.W. wind rose verry high, we Collected the Chiefs and Commenced a Councel ounder a orning, and our Sales Stretched around to keep out as much wind as possible, we delivered a long Speech the Substance of which [was] Similer to what we had Delivered to the nations below. the old Chief of the Grosvanters was verry restless before the Speech was half ended observed that he Could not wait long that his Camp was exposed to the hostile Indians, &c. &c. he was rebuked by one of the Chiefs for his uneasiness at Such a time as the present, we at the end of the Speech mentioned the *Recare* who accompanied us to make a firm Peace, they all Smoked with him (I gave this Cheaf a Dollar of the American Coin as a Meadel with which he was much pleased) In Councel we presented him with a certificate of his sin[c]errity and good Conduct &c. We also Spoke about the fur which was taken from 2 frenchmen by a Mandan, and informd of our intentions of Sending back the french hands. after the Council we gave the presents with much serimoney, and put the Meadels on the Chiefs we intended to make viz. onc for each Town to whome we gave coats hats & flags, one Grand Chief to each nation to whome we gave meadels with the presidents likeness in Council we requested them to give us an answer tomorrow or as Soon as possible to Some Points which required their Deliberation. after the Council was over we Shot the air gun which appeared to astonish the nativs much, the greater part then retired Soon after.

The Prarie was Set on fire (or cought by accident) by a young man of the Mandins, the fire went with such velocity that it burnt to death a man & woman, who Could not get to any place of Safty, one man a woman & Child much burnt and Several narrowly escaped the flame. a boy half white was saved unhurt in the midst of the flaim, Those ignerent people say this boy was Saved by the Great Medison Speret because he was white. The couse of his being Saved was a Green buffalow Skin was thrown over him by his mother who perhaps had more fore Sight for the pertection of her Son, and [l]ess for herself than those who escaped the flame, the Fire did not burn under the Skin leaveing the grass round the boy. This

[3] The Shoshone commonly called Snake Indians (Thwaites).

fire passed our Camp last [night] about 8 oClock P.M.   it went with great rapitidity and looked Tremendious

The following Chiefs were made in Council to day

Ma-too-ton-ha or Lower Village of the Mandans
1st. Chief *Sha-ha-ka*—or *Big White*
2   do   *Ka-goh-ha-mi*.   or *Little Raven*

Roop-tar-hee or Second Village of the Mandans.
1st. and Grand Chief, Pose-cop-sa-he. or *black cat*
2nd. Chief Car-gar-no-mok-she raven man Cheaf

Mah-har-ha   3rd. Village
1st Cheaf Ta-tuck-co-pin-re-ha white Buffalow robe unfolded

Me-ne-tar-re   Me-te-har-tan
1st. Cheif—*Omp-se-ha-ra*.   Black Mockerson
2   do.   *Oh-harh*   or *Little fox*

We Sent the presents intended for the Grand Chief of the *Mi-ne-tar-re* or Big Belley, and the presents flag and Wompom by the old Chief and those intended for the Chief of the Lower Village by a young Chief.

The following Chiefs were recommended in addition to those viz.—

1st. Village
Oh-hee-nar Big Man a *Chien* (*a Chayenne prisoner adopted by them*)
Sho-ta-har-ro-ra (*or Coal*)

2d. Village
Taw-nuh-e-o Bel-lar-sara
Ar-rat-tana-mock-she—Wolf man Chief

3rd. Village
Min-nis-sur-ra-ree—Neighing horse
Lo-Cong-gar-ti-har—old woman at a distance

4th. Village
Mar-noh-tah. the big Steeler out at war (*who was then out at war & was killed afd.*)
Mar-se-rus-se—tale of Callumet bird
Ea pa no pa—Two taled Calumet bird young Chief
War ke ras sa The red Shield young Chief of Big belley—big town

5th. Village

Shà-hakó ho pin nee—Little Wolfs Medison

Ar-rat-toé-no-mook-ge—man wolf Chief (*at war*)

Cal-tar-co ta—cherry (grows (*growing*) on a bush) old Chief and father to the above mentd. chief

Mau-pah'-pir-re-cos-sa too—This chief is near this hunting and a verry considerable man

To the 1st. Chiefs we gave a Medal with the Impn. of the President of the U. S.

To the 2d. Chiefs a Medel of weaveing & Domestic animals.

To the 3rd. Chiefs a Medel with the impression of a man Sowing Wheat.

30th October Tuesday 1804—

Two chiefs came to have Some talk one the principal of the lower Village the other the one who thought himself the principal man, & requested to hear Some of the Speech that was Delivered yesterday   they were gratified, and we put the medal on the neck of the Big white to whome we had Sent Clothes yesterday & a flag, those men did not return from hunting in time to join the Councell, they were all pleased (2d. of those is a Chien) I took 8 men in a Small perogue and went up the river as fur as the 1st Island about 7 miles to see if a Situation could be got on it for our Winter quarters,   found the wood on the Isd. as also on the pt. above so Distant from the water that, I did not think that we could get a good wintering ground there, and as all the white men here informed us that wood was scerce, as well as game above, we Deturmined to drop down a fiew miles near wood and game

on my return found maney Inds. at our Camp,   gave the party a dram,   they Danced as is verry Comn. in the evening which pleased the Savages much.   Wind S. E.

31st of October Wednesday 1804—

the Chief of the Mandans Sent a 2d. Chief to invite us to his Lodge to receive Som corn & here what he had to say I walked down, and with great ceremoney was Seeted on a roabe by the Side of the Chief,   he threw a handsom Roabe over me and after smokeing the pipe with Several old men around, the Chief spoke

Said he believed what we had told them, and that peace would be general, which not only gave him Satisfaction but all his people,

they now could hunt without fear, & ther womin could work in the
fields without looking everry moment for the enemey, and put off
their mockersons at night,   as to the *Ri[c]ares* we will Show you that
we wish peace with all, and do not make War on any without cause,
that Chief—pointing to the 2d. and Some brave men will accompy.
the ricare Chief now with you to his village & nation, to Smoke
with that people,   when you came up the Indians in the neighbouring Villages, as well as those out hunting when they heard of
you had great expectations of receving presents .those hunting imediately on hearing returned to the Village and all was Disapointed,
and Some Dissatisfied,   as to himself he was not much So but his
village was. he would go and see his great father &c. &c.

he had put before me 2 of the Steel traps which was robed from
the french a Short time ago, [and] about 12 bushels of Corn which
was brought and put before me by the womin of the Village after
the Chief finishd & Smoked in great cerrimony, I answered the
Speech which Satisfied them verry much, and returned to the boat.
met the princapal Chief of the 3d. Village and the Little Crow both
of which I invited into the Cabin and Smoked & talked with for
about one hour. Soon after those Chiefs left us, the Grand Chief of
the Mandans came Dressed in the Clothes we had given with his
2 small Suns, and requested to See the men Dance which they verry
readily gratified him in,   the wind blew hard all the after part of
the day from the N. E. and continud all night to blow hard from
that point

1st. of November. Thursday 1804—
at about 10 oClock the Chiefs of the Lower Village came and
after a Short time informed us they wished us to call at their Village
& take Some corn,   [They said] that they would make peace with
the *Ricares* they never made war against them but after the *Rees*
killed their Chiefs they killed them like the birds, and were tired
and would Send a Chief and Some brave men to the Ricares to
Smoke with that people.

4th. November Sunday 1804—
a fine morning we continud to cut Down trees and raise our
houses, a Mr. Chaubonie (*Chaboneau*), interpeter for the Gross
Ventre nation Came to See us, and informed that the came Down

with Several Indians from a hunting expidition up the river, to here
what we had told the Indians in Council   this man wished to hire
as an interpiter

5 November Monday 1804—

I rose verry early and commenced raising the 2 range of Huts[4]
the timber large and heavy all to carry on on Hand Sticks, cotton
wood & Elm Som ash Small,   our Situation Sandy, great numbers
of Indians pass to and from hunting   a camp of Mandans, A fiew
miles below us Cought within two days 100 Goats, by Driveing
them in a Strong pen, derected by a Bush fence widening from the
pen &c. &c.   the Greater part of this day Cloudy, wind moderate
from the N. W.   I have the Rhumitism verry bad, Cap Lewis write-
ing all Day   we are told by our interpeter that 4 Ossiniboins Indians,
have arrived at the Camps of the Gross Venters, & 50 Lodges are
Comeing.

6th. November Tuesday 1804   Fort Mandan—

last night late we wer awoke by the Sergeant of the Guard to See
a Nothern light, which was light, (*but*) not red, and appeared to
Darken and Some times nearly obscured, and open,   many times
appeared in light Streeks, and at other times a great Space light &
containing floating collomns which appeared to approach each other
& retreat leaveing the lighter space   at no time of the Same
appearance

9th Nov. Friday 1804—

The Mandans Graze their horses in the Day on Grass, and at
night give them a Stick of Cotton wood to eate,   Horses Dogs &
people all pass the night in the Same Lodge or round House, Covd.
with earth with a fire in the middle[5]   great number of wild gees
pass to the South, flew verry high.

[4] Fort Mandan, the wintering-place of the expedition, was located on the left
bank of the Missouri, seven or eight miles below the mouth of Knife River; it was
nearly opposite the site of the later Fort Clark (Thwaites).

[5] These earth lodges of the Mandan differentiated them from the other Indians
of the plains, and are described by all early travellers (Thwaites).

12th. November Monday 1804—
a verry Cold night early this morning the Big White princapal
Chief of the lower Village of the Mandans came Down, he packd
about 100 lb. of fine meet on his squar for us, we made Some Small
presents to the Squar, & child gave a Small ax [with] which She
was much pleased Wind Changeable verry cold evening, freesing
all day some ice on the edges of the river.

Swans passing to the South, the Hunters we Sent down the river
to hunt has not returned

The interpeter says that the Mandan nation as they (old men)
Say came out of a Small lake where they had Gardins, maney years
ago they lived in Several Villages on the Missourie low down, the
Small pox destroyed the greater part of the nation and reduced them
to one large village and Some Small ones, all the nations before
this maladey was affrd. of them, after they were reduced the Seaux
and other Indians waged war, and killed a great maney, and they
moved up the Missourie, those Indians Still continued to wage
war, and they moved Still higher, until got in the Countrey of the
Panias, whith this Ntn. they lived in friendship maney years, inhabiting the Same neighbourhood untill that people waged war,
they moved up near the *Watersoons* & *Winataras* where they now
live in peace with those nations, the Mandans Speake a language
peculial to themselves verry much they can rase about 350 men
the Winataries about 80 (*the Wittassoons or Maharha 80*) and the Big
bellies (*or Minitarees*) about 600 or 650 men.

The Big bellies & Watersoons are at war with the Snake Indians
& Seauex and were at war with the *Ricares* untill we made peace a
fiew days passd. The Mandans are at war with all who make war
only, and wish to be at peace with all nations, Seldom the ogressors

14th. of November Wednesday 1804. Fort Mandan—
a cloudy morning, ice runing, verry thick, river rose ½ Inch last
night Some snow falling, only two Indians visit us to day owing
to a Dance at the Village last night in Concluding a serimoney of
adoption, and interchange of property, between the Ossinboins,
Christinoes[6] and the nations of this neighbourhood.

[6] Now known as Cree (Thwaites).

18th. Nov. Sunday 1804—

a cold morning Some wind the Black Cat, Chief of the Mandans came to see us, he made great inquiries respecting our fashions, he also Stated the Situation of their nation, he mentioned that a Council had been held the day before and it was thought advisable to put up with the resent insults of the Ossiniboins & Christinoes untill they were convinced that what had been told them by us [was true], Mr. Evins had deceived them & we might also, he promised to return & furnish them with guns & amunition, we advised them to remain at peace & that they might depend upon Getting Supplies through the Channel of the Missourie, but it required time to put the trade in opperation. The Ossiniboins &c. have the trade of those nations in their power and treat them badly, as the Soux does the *Ricarees*, and they cannot resent, for fear of loseing their trade.

20th. November Tuesday 1804—

Cap Lewis & my Self move into our hut, a verry hard wind from the W. all the after part of the day a temperate day Several Indians came Down to Eat fresh meat, three Chiefs from the 2d. Mandan Village Stay all Day, they are verry Curious in examining our works.

22nd. of November Thursday 1804—

I was allarmed about 10 oClock by the Sentinal, who informed that an Indian was about to kill his wife in the interpeters fire about 60 yards below the works, I went down and Spoke to the fellow about the rash act which he was like to commit and forbid any act of the kind near the fort. Some misunderstanding took place between this man & his fife [wife] about 8 days ago, and she came to this place, & continued with the Squars of the interpeters, 2 days ago She returned to the vill'ge. in the evening of the Same day She came to the interpeters fire appearently much beat, & Stabed in 3 places. We Derected that no man of this party have any intercourse with this woman under the penalty of Punishment. he the Husband observed that one of our Serjeants Slept with his wife & if he wanted her he would give her to him, We derected the Serjeant (Odway) to give the man Some articles, at which time I told the Indian that I believed not one man of the party had touched his wife except the one he had given the use of her for a nite, in his own bed, no man of the party Should touch his squar, or the wife of any Indian, nor did I believe they touch a woman if they knew her to be the wife of another man, and advised him to take his squar home and live hapily together in future

29th November Thursday 1804—

A verry cold windey day wind from the N.W. by W. Some snow last night the detph of the Snow is various in the wood about 13 inches, The river Closed at the Village above and fell last night two feet

Sergeant Pryor in takeing down the mast put his Sholder out of Place, we made four trials before we replaced it a cold afternoon wind as useal N W. river begin to rise a little.

30th. of November Friday 1804—

This morning at 8 oClock an Indian called from the other Side and informed that he had Something of Consequence to Communicate, we Sent a perogue for him & he informed us as follows. Viz: "five men of the Mandan nation out hunting in a S.W. derection about Eight Leagues, was Suprised by a large party of *Seeoux* & Panies, one man was Killed and two wounded with arrows & 9 Horses taken, 4 of the We ter soon nation was missing, and they expected to be attacked by the Souex &c. &c. we thought it well to Show a Disposition to ade and assist them against their enemies, perticulary those who Came in oppersition to our Councels; and I Deturmined to go to the town with Some men, and if the Seeoux were comeing to attact the Nation to Collect the worriers from each Village and meet them, those Ideas were also those of Capt Lewis, I crossed the river in about an hour after the arrival of the Indian express with 23 men including the interpeters and flankd the Town & came up on the back part. The Indians not expecting to receive Such Strong aide in So Short a time was much supprised, and a littled allarmed at the formadable appearence of my party. The principal Chiefs met me Some Distance from the town (say 200 yards) and invited me in to town. I ord[ered] my pty into dift. lodges &c. I explained to the nation the cause of my comeing in this formadable manner to their Town, was to assist and Chastise the enemies of our Dutifull Children, I requested the Grand Cheif to repeat the Circumstancies as they hapined, which he did as was mentioned by the *express* in the morning. I then informed them that if they would assemble their warrers and those of the Different Towns, I would [go] to meet the Army of *Souex* &c. chastise them for takeing the blood of our dutifull Children &c.

after a conversation of a fiew minits amongst themselves, one Chief. the Big Man (Cien). Said they now Saw that what we hade told them was the trooth, when we expected the enemies of their Nation was Comeing to attact them, or had Spilt their blood [we] were ready to protect them, and kill those who would not listen to our Good talk. his people had listened to what we had told them and fearlessly went out to hunt in Small parties believing themselves to be Safe from the other nations, and have fearlessly been killed by the *Panies* & Seauex, "I knew Said he that the Panies were liers, and told the old Chief who Came with you (to Confirm a piece with us) that his people were *liers* and bad men and that we killed them like the Buffalow, when we pleased, we had made peace several times and you Nation have always commenced the war, we do not want to kill you, and will not Suffer you to kill us or Steal our horses, we will make peace with you as our two fathers have derected, and they Shall See that we will not be the Ogressors, but we fear the Ricares will not be at peace long. My father those are the words I spoke to the Ricare in your presents. you See they have not opened their ears to your good Councels but have Spuilt our blood. two Ricaries whom we sent home this day for fear of our peoples killing them in their greaf, informed us when they came here Several days ago, that two Towns of the *Ricares* were makeing their Mockersons, and that we had best take care of our horses &c. a numbers of Seauex were in their Towns, and they believed not well disposed towards us. four of the *Wetersoons* are now absent they were to have been back in 16 days, they have been out 24 we fear they have fallen. My father the Snow is deep and it is cold our horses Cannot travel thro the plains, those people who have Spilt our blood have gone back? if you will go with us in the Spring after the Snow goes off we will raise the warriers of all the Towns & Nations around about us, and go out with you."

I told this nation that we should be always willing and ready to defend them from the insults of any nation who would dare to Come to doe them injury dureing the time we would remain in their neighbourhood after about two hours conversation on various Subjects all of which tended towards their Situation &c. I informed them I should return to the fort, the Chief said they all thanked me verry much for the fatherly protection which I shewed towards them, that the village had been crying all the night and day for the death of the brave young man, who fell but now they would wipe away their tears, and rejoice in their fathers protection, and cry no more.

I then Paraded & Crossed the river on the ice and Came down on the N. Side, the Snow So Deep, it was verry fatigueing arived at the fort after night, gave a little Taffee (*dram to my party*), a cold night the river rise to its former hite. The Chief frequently thanked me for comeing to protect them—and the whole village appeared thankfull for that measure

7th. of December Friday 1804—

the Big White Grand Chief of the 1st Village, came and informed us that a large Drove of Buffalow was near and his people was wating for us to join them in a chase Capt. Lewis took 15 men & went out joined the Indians, who were at the time he got up, Killing the Buffalow on Horseback with arrows which they done with great dexterity, his party killed 10 Buffalow, *five* of which we got to the fort by the assistance of a horse in addition to what the men Packed on their backs. one cow was killed on the ice after drawing her out of a vacancey in the ice in which She had fallen, and Butchered her at the fort. those we did not get in was taken by the indians under a Custom which is established amongst them i e. any person seeing a buffalow lying without an arrow Sticking in him, or some purticular mark takes possession, many times (as I am told) a hunter who kills maney Buffalow in a chase only Gets a part of one, all meat which is left out all night falls to the *Wolves* which are in great numbers, always in [the neighbourhood of] the Buffalows. the river Closed opposit the fort last night 1½ inches thick, The Thermometer Stood this Morning at 1 d. below 0. three men frost bit badly to day.

8th. December Satturday 1804—

in the evening on my return to the fort Saw great numbers of Buffalow Comeing into the Bottom on both Sides of the river this day being Cold Several men returned a little *frost bit*, one of [the]

men with his feet badly frost bit   my Servents feet also *frosted* &
his P——s a little,   I felt a little fatigued haveing run after the
Buffalow all day in Snow many Places 18 inches Deep, generally 6
or 8,   two men hurt their hips verry much in Slipping down.   The
Indians kill great numbers of Buffalow to day. 2 reflectings Suns
to day.

11th. December Tuesday 1804—
a verry Cold morning Wind from the north The Thermometer
at 4 oClock A M. at 21° below 0 which is 53°. below the freesing
point and getting colder,   the Sun Shows and reflects two imigies,
the ice floating in the atmospear being So thick that the appearance
is like a fog Despurceing.

21st. December Friday 1804—
a fine Day warm and wind from the NW by W,   the Indian whome
I stoped from Commiting Murder on his wife, 'thro jellosy of one
of our interpeters, Came & brought his two wives and Shewed great
anxiety to make up with the man with whome his joulussey Sprung.
a Womon brought a Child with an abcess on the lower part of the
back, and offered as much Corn as she Could Carry for some Medison,   Capt. Lewis administered &c.

22nd. December Satturday 1804—
worm. a number of Squars & men Dressed in Squars Clothes[7]
Came with Corn to Sell to the men for little things, We precured
two horns of the animale the french Call the rock Mountain Sheep
those horns are not of the largest kind The Mandans Indians Call
this Sheep *Ar-Sar-ta* it is about the Size of a large Deer, or Small
Elk,   its Horns Come out and wind around the head like the horn
of a Ram and the tecture (*texture*) not unlike it

25th. December Christmass Tuesday—
I was awakened before Day by a discharge of 3 platoons from the
Party and the french, the men merrily Disposed,   I give them all
a little Taffia and permitted 3 Cannon fired, at raising Our flag,

[7] Commonly called "berdashes" (a corruption of Fr. *bardache*) (Thwaites).

Some Men Went out to hunt & the others to Danceing and Continued untill 9 oClock P.M. when the frolick ended &c.

Fort Mandan on the NE bank of the Missouries 1600 Miles up   Tuesday
January the 1st. 1805.—
The Day was ushered in by the Descharge of two Cannon, we
Suffered 16 men with their Musick to visit the 1st. Village for the
purpose of Danceing, by as they Said the perticular request of the
Chiefs of that Village,   about 11 oClock I with an inturpeter & two
men walked up to the Village, (my views were to alay Some little
Miss understanding which had taken place thro jelloucy and mortification as to our treatment towards them   I found them much
pleased at the Danceing of our men,   I ordered my black Servent
to Dance which amused the Croud Verry much, and Somewhat
astonished them, that So large a man should be active

5th. of January Satturday 1805—
a cold day Some Snow,   Several Indians visit us with their axes
to get them mended,   I imploy my Self Drawing a Connection of
the Countrey[8] from what information I have rec[e]ved.   a Buffalow
Dance for 3 nights passed in the 1st. Village, a curious Custom   the
old men arrange themselves in a circle & after Smoke[ing] a pipe
which is handed them by a young man, Dress[ed] up for the purpose,   the young men who have their wives back of the Circle go
[each] to one of the old men with a whining tone and request the
old man to take his wife (who presents [herself] necked except a
robe) and—(or Sleep with her)   the Girl then takes the Old Man
(who verry often can scarcely walk) and leades him to a convenient
place for the business, after which they return to the lodge; if the
old man (or a white man) returns to the lodge without gratifying the
Man & his wife, he offers her again and again; it is often the Case
that after the 2d. time without Kissing the Husband throws a new
robe over the old man &c. and begs him not to dispise him & his
wife   (We Sent a man to this Medisan Dance last night, they gave
him 4 Girls)   all this is to cause the buffalow to Come near So that
they may kill them

[8] This map was sent to President Jefferson, April 7, 1805, and preserved in the
archives of the War Department (Coues).

7th. of January Monday 1805—
The Themtr. Stood at 22° below 0 Wind NW., the river fell 1
inch Several indians returned from hunting, one of them the Big
White Chief of the Lower Mandan Village, Dined with us, and gave
me a Scetch of the Countrey as far as the high Mountains, & on
the South Side of the River Rejone, he Says that the river rejone
recvees (*receives*) 6 Small rivers on the S. Side, & that the Countrey
is verry hilley and the greater part Covered with timber Great numbers of *beaver* &c. the 3 men returned from hunting, they killd.,
4 Deer & 2 Wolves, Saw Buffalow a long ways off. I continue to
Draw a connected plott from the information of Traders, Indians &
my own observation & ideas. from the best information, the Great
falls is about (*800*) miles nearly West

10th. of January Thursday 1805
last night was excessively Cold the Murkery this morning Stood
at 40°. below 0 which is 72°. below the freesing point, The Indians
of the lower Villege turned out to hunt for a man & a boy who had
not returned from the hunt of yesterday, and borrow'd a Slay to
bring them in expecting to find them frosed to death about 10
oClock the boy about 13 years of age Came to the fort with his feet
frosed and had layed out last night without fire with only a Buffalow
Robe to Cover him, the Dress which he wore was a pr. of Cabra
(*antelope)* Legins, which is verry thin and mockersons we had his
feet put in cold water and they are Comeing too. Soon after the
arrival of the Boy, a Man Came in who had also Stayed out without
fire, and verry thinly Clothed, this man was not the least injured.
Customs & the habits of those people has anured [them] to bare
more Cold than I thought it possible for man to endure.

14th. of January 1805 Monday
This morning early a number of indians men women children
Dogs &c. &c. passed down on the ice to joine those that passed
yesterday, we Sent Sergt Pryor and five men with those indians to
hunt (Several men with the Venereal cought from the Mandan
women) one of our hunters Sent out Several days [ago] arived &
informs that one Man (Whitehouse) is frost bit and Can't walk home.

15th. January Tuesday 1805 Fort Mandan

between 12 & 3 oClock this Morning we had a total eclips of the Moon, a part of the observations necessary for our purpose in this eclips we got which is

at 12 h–57 m–54 s	Total Darkness of the Moon
at–1 –44 –00	End of total Darkness of The moon
at *2 –39 –10*	End of the eclips.

27th. of January Sunday 1805

a fine day, attempt to Cut our Boat and Canoos out of the Ice, a deficuelt Task I fear as we find water between the Ice, I bleed the man with the Plurisy to day & Swet him, Capt. Lewis took off the Toes of one foot of the Boy who got frost bit Some time ago, Shabonoe our interpeter returned, & informed that the Assiniboins had returned to their Camps, & brought 3 horses of Mr. Larock's to Stay here for fear of their being Stolen by the Assiniboins who are great rogues. cut off the boy['s] toes.

[Lewis]   3rd. of February Sunday 1805.

the situation of our boat and perogues is now allarming, they are firmly inclosed in the Ice and almost covered with snow—the ice which incloses them lyes in several stratas of unequal thicknesses which are seperated by streams of water. this [is] peculiarly unfortunate because so soon as we cut through the first strata of ice the water rushes up and rises as high as the upper surface of the ice and thus creates such a debth of water as renders it impracticable to cut away the lower strata which appears firmly attatched to, and confining the bottom of the vessels. the instruments we have hitherto used has been the ax only, with which, we have made several attempts that proved unsuccessfull from the cause above mentioned.
we then determined to attempt freeing them from the ice by means of boiling water which we purposed heating in the vessels by means of hot stones, but this expedient proved also fruitless, as every species of stone which we could procure in the neighbourhood partook so much of the calcarious genus that they burst into small particles on being exposed to the heat of the fire. we now determined as the dernier resort to prepare a parsel of Iron spikes and attatch them to the end of small poles of convenient length and

endeavour by means of them to free the vessels from the ice. we have already prepared a large rope of Elk-skin and a windless by means of which we have no doubt of being able to draw the boat on the bank provided we can free [it] from the ice.

4th. February, Monday 1805.
Capt Clark set out with a hunting party consisting of sixteen of our command and two frenchmen who together with two others, have established a small hut and resided this winter within the vicinity of Fort Mandane under our protection. visited by many of the natives today. our stock of meat which we had procured in the Months of November & December is now nearly exhausted; a supply of this articles is at this moment peculiarly interesting as well for our immediate consumption, as that we may have time before the approach of the warm season to prepare the meat for our voyage in the spring of the year. Capt. Clark therefore determined to continue his rout down the river even as far as the River bullet[9] unless he should find a plenty of game nearer.

6th. February Wednesday 1805.
had a sley prepared against the return of the horses which Capt Clark had promised to send back as soon as he should be able to procure a load of meat. visited by many of the natives among others the Big white, the Coal, big-man, hairy horn and the black man, I smoked with them, after which they retired, a deportment not common, for they usually pester us with their good company the ballance of the day after once being introduced to our apartment. Shields killed three antelopes this evening. the blacksmiths take a considerable quantity of corn today in payment for their labour. the blacksmith's have proved a happy reso[r]ce to us in our present situation as I believe it would have been difficult to have devised any other method to have procured corn from the natives. the Indians are extravegantly fond of sheet iron of which they form arrow-points and manufacter into instruments for scraping and dressing their buffaloe robes.

[9] The Cannonball River, which empties into the Missouri near Fort Rice, North Dakota (Thwaites).

11th. February Monday 1805.

about five Oclock this evening one of the wives of Charbono was delivered of a fine boy.[10] it is worthy of remark that this was the first child which this woman had boarn, and as is common in such cases her labour was tedious and the pain violent; Mr. Jessome informed me that he had frequently administered a small portion of the rattle of the rattle-snake, which he assured me had never failed to produce the desired effect, that of hastening the birth of the child; having the rattle of a snake by me I gave it to him and he administered two rings of it to the woman broken in small pieces with the fingers and added to a small quantity of water. Whether this medicine was truly the cause or not I shall not undertake to determine, but I was informed that she had not taken it more than ten minutes before she brought forth perhaps this remedy may be worthy of future experiments, but I must confess that I want faith as to it's efficacy.

[Clark]   [undated]

I returned last Night from a hunting party much fatigued, haveing walked 30 miles on the ice and through Points of wood land in which the Snow was nearly Knee Deep

The 1st. day [Feb 4] I left the fort proceeded on the ice to *new Mandan* Island, 22 miles & camped, killed nothing, & nothing to eat

The 2d. day—the morning verry Cold & Windey. I broke thro the ice and got my feet and legs wet, Sent out 4 hunters thro' a point to kill a Deer & cook it by the time the party should get up, those hunters killed a Deer & 2 Buffalow Bulls the Buffalow too Meagur to eat, we eate the Deer & proceeded on to an old Indian Lodge, Sent out the hunters & they brought in three lean Deer, which we made use of for food, walking on uneaven *ice* has blistered the bottoms of my feat, and walking is painfull to me.

15th. of February Friday 1805

at 10 oClock P M. last night the men that [were] despatched yesterday for the Meat, returned and informed us that as they were

[10] This was Sacagawea, the Shoshone captive purchased by Charboneau, who had two other wives among the Mandan (Thwaites).

on their march down at the distance of about 24 miles below the Fort (G. Drewyer Frasure, S Gutterage, & Newmon[11] with a broken Gun). about 105 Indians which they took to be *Soues* rushed on them and cut their horses from the Slays, *two* of which they carried off in great hast, the 3rd. horse was given up to the party by the intersetion of an Indian who assumd. Some authority on the occasion, probably more thro fear of himself or Some of the Indians being killed by our men who were not disposed to be Robed of all they had tamely, they also forced 2 of the mens knives & a tamahauk, the man obliged them to return the tamahawk [,but] the knives they ran off with

We dispatched two men to inform the Mandans, and if any of them chose to pursue those robers, to come down in the morning, and join Capt Lewis who intended to Set out with a party of men Verry early, by 12 oClock the Chief of the 2nd. Village Big White came down, and Soon after one other Chief and Several men. The Chief observed that all the young men of the 2 Villages were out hunting, and but verry fiew guns were left, Capt. Lewis Set out at Sunrise with 24 men, to meet those *Soues* &c. Several Indians accompanied him Some with Bows & arrows Some with Spears & Battle axes, 2 with fuzees (*fusils*).[12] the morning fine The Thermometer Stood at 16° below 0, *Nought*, visited by 2 of the *Big Bellies* this evening, one Chief of the Mandans returned from Capt Lewises Party nearly blind, this Complaint is as I am informd. Common at this Season of the year and caused by the reflection of the Sun on the ice & Snow, it is cured by "jentilley swetting the part affected, by throwing Snow on a hot Stone."

a Verry Cold part of the night one man Killed a verry large Red Fox to day.

20th. February Wednesday 1805
a Butifull Day, visited by the Little raven verry early this morning I am informed of the Death of an old man whome I saw in the Mandan Village this man, informed me that he "was 120 winters

[11] These men were George Drouillard, Robert Frazier, Silas Goodrich, and John Newman (Thwaites).

[12] Flintlock muskets (Thwaites).

old, he requested his grand Children to Dress him after Death &
Set him on a Stone on a hill with his face towards his old Village or
Down the river, that he might go Streight to his brother at their
old village under ground" I observed Several Mandans verry old
chiefly men

21st. February Thursday 1805

a Delightfull Day put out our Clothes to Sun. Visited by the
big White & Big Man they informed me that Several men of their
nation was gone to Consult their Medison Stone about 3 day march
to the South West to know what was to be the result of the ensuing
year. They have great confidence in this stone, and say that it
informs them of every thing which is to happen, & visit it everry
Spring & Sometimes in the Summer. "They haveing arrived at the
Stone give it smoke and proceed to the Wood at Some distance to
Sleep the next morning return to the Stone, and find marks white
& raised on the stone representing the peece or War which they are
to meet with, and other changes, which they are to meet" This
Stone has a leavel Surface of about 20 feet in Surcumfrance, thick
and porus, and no doubt has Some mineral quallites effected by the
Sun.

The Big Bellies have a Stone to which they ascribe nearly the
Same Virtues

Capt Lewis returned with 2 Slays loaded with meat, after finding
that he could not overtake the Soues War party, (who had in their
way distroyed all the meat at one Deposit which I had made &
Burnt the Lodges) deturmined to proceed on to the lower Deposit
which he found had not been observed by the Soues he hunted
two day Killed 36 Deer & 14 Elk, Several of them so meager, that
they were unfit for use, the meet which he killed and that in the
lower Deposit amounting to about 3000 lb. was brought up on two
Slays one Drawn by 16 men had about 2400 lb. on it

23rd. of February 1805 Satturday

All hands employed in Cutting the Perogues Loose from the ice,
which was nearly even with their top; we found great dificuelty in
effecting this work owing to the Different devisions of Ice & water.
after Cutting as much as we Could with axes, we had all the Iron
we Could get, & some axes put on long poles and picked through

the ice, under the first water, which was not more the [than] 6 or 8 inches Deep,   we disengaged one Perogue, and nearly disengaged the 2nd. in Course of this day which has been worm & pleasent vis'ed by a No of Indians,   Jessomme & familey went to the *Shoe* Indians Villag to day

The father of the Boy whose feet were frosed near this place, and nearly Cured by us, took him home in a Slay.

26th. February Tuesday 1805
a fine Day   Commenced verry early in makeing preparations for drawing up the Boat on the bank,   at Sunset by Repeated exertions the whole day, we accomplished this troublesom task,   just as we were fixed for hauling the Boat, the ice gave way near us for about 100 yds in length.   a number of Indians here to day to See the Boat rise on the Bank.

March 1st. Friday 1805
a fine Day   I am ingaged in Copying a Map, men building per-ogus, makeing Ropes, Burning Coal, Hanging up meat & makeing battle axes for Corn

6th. of March Wednesday 1805
a cloudy morning & Smokey all Day from the burning of the plains, which was set on fire by the *Minetarries* for an early crop of Grass, as an enducement for the Buffalow to feed on,   the horses which was Stolen Some time ago by the Assinniboins from the *Menetarries* were returned yesterday.   Visited by *Oh-harh* or the Little fox 2d. Chief of the lower Village of the Me ne tar rees.   one man *Shannon* Cut his foot with the ads [adze] in working at the perogue, George & Gravelene go to the Village,   the river rise a little to day.

11th. of March Monday 1805
We have every reason to believe that our *Menetarre* interpeter (whome we intended to take with his wife, as an interpeter through his wife to the Snake Indians of which nation She is) has been Corrupted by the [blank in MS] Company &c.   Some explenation has taken place which Clearly proves to us the fact,   we give him to night to reflect and deturmin whether or not he intends to go with us under the regulations Stated.

12th.

a fine day Some Snow last night   our Interpeter Shabonah, de-
turmins on not proceeding with us as an interpeter under the terms
mentioned yesterday,   he will not agree to work let our Situation
be what it may nor Stand a guard, and if miffed with any man he
wishes to return when he pleases, also have the disposal of as much
provisions as he Chuses to Carry   in admissable and we Suffer him
to be off the engagement which was only virbal

[Lewis]   [March 16th]
   Mr. Garrow a Frenchman who has lived many years with the
Ricares & Mandans shewed us the process used by those Indians
to make beads.   the discovery of this art these nations are said to
have derived from the Snake Indians who have been taken prisoners
by the Ricaras.   the art is kept a secret by the Indians among
themselves and is yet known to but few of them.   the Prosess is as
follows.—Take glass of as many different colours as you think
proper, then pound it as fine as possible, puting each colour in a
seperate vessel.   wash the pounded Glass in several waters throwing
off the water at each washing,   continue this opperation as long as
the pounded glass stains or colours the water which is poured off
and the residuum is then prepared for uce.   you then provide an
earthen pot of convenient size say of three gallons which will stand
the fire; a platter also of the same material sufficiently small be
admitted in the mouth of the pot or jar.   the pot has a nitch in it's
edge through which to watch the beads when in blast. You then
provide some well seasoned clay with a proportion of sand sufficient
to prevent it's becoming very hard when exposed to the heat.   this
clay must be tempered with water untill it is about the consistency
of common doe. of this clay you then prepare, a sufficient number
of little sticks of the size you wish the hole through the bead, which
you do by roling the clay on the palm of the hand with your finger.
this done put those sticks of clay on the platter and expose them to
a red heat for a few minutes when you take them off and suffer
them to cool.   the pot is also heated to cles [cleanse] it perfectly of
any filth it may contain.   small balls of clay are also mad[e] of about
an ounce weight which serve each as a pedestal for a bead.   these
while soft ar destributed over the face of the platter at su[c]h distance
from each other as to prevent the beads from touching.   some little

wooden paddles are now provided from three to four inches in length sharpened or brought to a point at the extremity of the handle. with this paddle you place in the palm of the hand as much of the wet pounded glass as is necessary to make the bead of the size you wish it. it is then arranged with the paddle in an oblong from [form], laying one of those little stick of clay crosswise over it; the pounded glass by means of the paddle is then roped in cilindrical form arround the stick of clay and gently roled by motion of the hand backwards an forwards untill you get it as regular and smooth as you conveniently can. if you wish to introduce any other colour you now purforate the surface of the bead with the pointed end of your little paddle and fill up the cavity with other pounded glass of the colour you wish forming the whole as regular as you can. a hole is now made in the center of the little pedestals of clay with the handle of your shovel sufficiently large to admit the end of the stick of clay arround which the bead is formed. the beads are then arranged perpendicularly on their pedestals and little distance above them supported by the little sticks of clay to which they are attatched in the manner before mentioned. thus arranged the platter is deposited on burning coals or hot embers and the pot reversed with the apparture in its edge turned towards covers the whole. dry wood pretty much doated is then plased arron [around] the pot in sush manner as compleatly to cover it [It] is then set on fire and the opperator must shortly after begin to watch his beads through the apparture of the pot le[s]t they should be distroyed by being over heated. he suffers the beads to acquire a deepred heat from which when it passes in a small degree to a pailer or whitish red, or he discovers that the beads begin to become pointed at their upper extremities he removes the fire from about the pot and suffers the whole to cool gradually. the pot is then removed and the beads taken out. the clay which fills the hollow of the beads is picked out with an awl or nedle. the bead is then fit for uce. The Indians are extreemly fond of the large beads formed by this process. they use them as pendants to their years, or hair and sometimes wear them about their necks.

[Clark]   17th. of March Sunday—
   a windey Day attempted to air our goods &c. Mr. Chabonah Sent a frenchman of our party [to say] that he was Sorry for the

foolish part he had acted and if we pleased he would accompany us agreeably to the terms we had perposed and doe every thing we wished him to doe &c. &c. had requested me Some thro our French inturpeter two days ago to excuse his Simplicity and take him into the cirvice, after he had taken his things across the River we called him in and Spoke to him on the Subject, he agreed to our tirms and we agreed that he might go on with us.

18th. of March 1805—

Mr. Tousent Chabono [Toussaint Charboneau], Enlisted as Interpreter this evening, I am not well to day,

21st. March Thursday 1805—

a Cloudy Day Some Snow, the men Carried the remaining Canoes to the River, and all except 3 left to take care & complete the Canoes returned to the *fort* with their baggage, on my return to day to the Fort I came on the points of the high hills, Saw an emence quantity of Pumice Stone on the Sides & foot of the hills and emence beds of Pumice Stone near the Tops of the[m], with evident marks of the Hills haveing once been on fire, I Collected Some [of] the different [sorts] i.e. Stone Pumice Stone & a hard earth, and put them into a furnace, the hard earth melted and glazed the others two and the hard Clay became a pumice Stone Glazed. I collected Some plants &c.

FOUR

The Great Unknown

From Fort Mandan to Marias River
March 29–June 7, 1805

[Clark]   29th. (28) of March Satturday (Thursday) 1805—
The ice has stoped running owing to Som obstickle above, repare the Boat & Perogues, and prepareing to Set out but few Indians visit us to day they are now attending on the river bank to Catch the floating Buffalow

                      30th. (29) of March Sunday (Friday) 1805—
The obstickle broke away above & the ice came down in great quantities the river rose 13 inches the last 24 hours I observed extrodanary dexterity of the Indians in jumping from one cake of ice to another, for the purpose of Catching the buffalow as they float down many of the cakes of ice which they pass over are not two feet square. The Plains are on fire in View of the fort on both Sides of the River, it is Said to be common for the Indians to burn the Plains near their Villages every Spring for the benefit of their hors[e]s; and to induce the Buffalow to come near to them.

           31st. (30th) Saturday. of March Monday (Saturday) (Sunday) 1805—
Gees and Ducks pass up the river. all the party in high Sperits they pass but fiew nights without amuseing themselves danceing possessing perfect harmony and good understanding towards each

other, Generally helthy except Venerials Complaints which is verry Common amongst the natives and the men Catch it from them

April the 1st. Tuesday (Monday) 1805—
The fore part of to day haile rain with Thunder & lightning, the rain continued by intimitions all day, it is worthey of remark that this is the 1st. rain which has fallen Sence we have been here or Sence the 15 of October last, except a fiew drops at two or three defferent times. had the Boat Perogues & Canoes all put into the Water.

April the 3rd Thursday (Wednesday) 1805—
we are all day engaged packing up Sundery articles to be sent to the President of the U.S.

Box No. 1, contains the following articles i. e.
In package No. 3 & 4 Male & female antelope, with their Skelitons.
No. 7 & 9 the horns of two mule or Black tailed deer. a Mandan bow an[d] quiver of arrows—with some Recara's tobacco seed.
No. 11 a Martin Skin, Containing the tail of a Mule Deer, a weasel and three Squirels from the Rockey mountains.
No. 12, The bones & Skeleton of a Small burrowing wolf of the Praries the Skin being lost by accedent.
No. 99. The Skeliton of the white and Grey *hare*.

Box No. 2, Contains 4 Buffalow *Robes*, and a ear of Mandan Corn.
The large Trunk Contains a male & female *Braro* or burrowing dog of the Praire and the female's *Skeliton*.
a carrote of Ricaras *Tobacco*
a red fox Skin Containing a *Magpie*
No. 14 Minitarras Buffalow robe Containing Some articles of Indian dress.
No. 15 a mandan *robe* containing two burrowing Squirels, a white *weasel* and the Skin of a Loucirvia. also
13 red fox Skins.
1 white Hare Skin &c.
4 horns of the mountain ram
1 Robe representing a battle between the Sioux & Ricaras against the Minetares and Mandans.

In Box No. 3.
Nos. 1 & 2 the Skins of the Male & female Antelope with their Skeletons.
& the Skin of a Yellow *Bear* which I obtained from the *Sieoux*

No. 4. Box. Specimens of plants numbered from 1. to 67.

Specimens of Plants numbered from 1 to 60.

1 Earthen pot Such as the Mandans manufacture and use for culinary purposes.

1 Tin box containing insects mice &c.

a Specimine of the fur of the antilope.

a Specimon of a plant, and a parcel of its roots higly prized by the natives as an efficatious remidy in cases of the bite of the rattle Snake or Mad Dog.

In a large Trunk

Skins of a male and female Braro, or burrowing Dog of the Prarie, with the Skeleton of the female.

1 Skin of the red fox Containing a Magpie

2 Cased Skins of the white hare.

1 Minitarra Buffalow robe Containing Some articles of Indian Dress.

1 Mandan Buffalow robe Containing a dressed Lousirva Skin, and 2 cased Skins of the Burrowing Squirel of the Praries.

13 red fox Skins

4 Horns of the Mountain Ram, or *big horn*.

1 Buffalow robe painted by a mandan man representing a battle fought 8 years Since by the Sioux & Recaras against the mandans, me ni tarras & Ah wah har ways. (Mandans &c. on horseback

Cage No. 6.

Contains a liveing burrowing Squirel of the praries

Cage No. 7.

Contains 4 liveing Magpies

Cage No. 9.

Containing a liveing hen of the Prairie

a large par of Elks horns containing [*contained*, i. e., held together] by the frontal bone.

[Lewis]   Fort Mandan April 7th. 1805.

Having on this day at 4. P.M. completed every arrangement necessary for our departure, we dismissed the barge and crew with orders to return without loss of time to St. Louis, a small canoe with two French hunters accompanyed the barge; these men had assended the missouri with us the last year as engages. The barge crew consisted of six soldiers and two [blank space in MS.] Frenchmen; two Frenchmen and a Ricara Indian also take their passage in her as far as the Ricara Vilages, at which place we expect Mr. Tiebeau [Ta-

beau] to embark with his peltry who in that case will make an
addition of two, perhaps four men to the crew of the barge. We
gave Richard Warfington, a discharged Corpl., the charge of the
Barge and crew, and confided to his care likewise our dispatches to
the government, letters to our private friends, and a number of
articles to the President the United States. One of the Frenchmen
by the Name of Gravline an honest discrete man and an excellent
boat-man is imployed to conduct the barge as a pilot; we have
therefore every hope that the barge and with her our dispatches will
arrive safe at St. Louis. Mr. Gravlin who speaks the Ricara language
extreemly well, has been imployed to conduct a few of the Recara
Chiefs to the seat of government who have promised us to decend
in the barge to St. Liwis with that view.

At same moment that the Barge departed from Fort Mandan,
Capt. Clark emba[r]ked with our party and proceeded up the River.
as I had used no exercise for several weeks, I determined to walk
on shore as far as our encampment of this evening; accordingly I
continued my walk on the N. side of the River about six miles, to
the upper Village of the Mandans, and called on the Black Cat or
Pose-cop'-se-ha', the great chief of the Mandans; he was not at
home; I rested myself a [few] minutes, and finding that the party
had not arrived I returned about 2 miles and joined them at their
encampment on the N. side of the river opposite the lower Mandan
village. Our part[y] now consisted of the following Individuals.
Sergts. John Ordway, Nathaniel Prior, & Patric Gass; Privates, William Bratton, John Colter, Reubin, and Joseph Fields, John Shields,
George Gibson, George Shannon, John Potts, John Collins, Joseph
Whitehouse, Richard Windsor, Alexander Willard, Hugh Hall, Silas
Goodrich, Robert Frazier, Peter Crouzatt, John Baptiest la Page,
Francis Labiech, Hue Mc.Neal, William Warner, Thomas P. How-
ard, Peter Wiser, and John B. Thompson. *Interpreters*, George Drewyer and Tauasant Charbono also a Black man by the name of York,
servant to Capt. Clark, an Indian Woman wife to Charbono with a
young child, and a Mandan man who had promised us to accompany
us as far as the Snake Indians with a view to bring about a good
understanding and friendly intercourse between that nation and his
own, the Minetares and Ahwahharways.

Our vessels consisted of six small canoes, and two large perogues.

This little fleet altho' not quite so rispectable as those of Columbus or Capt. Cook, were still veiwed by us with as much pleasure as those deservedly famed adventurers ever beheld theirs; and I dare say with quite as much anxiety for their safety and preservation. we were now about to penetrate a country at least two thousand miles in width, on which the foot of civilized man had never trodden; the good or evil it had in store for us was for experiment yet to determine, and these little vessells contained every article by which we were to expect to subsist or defend ourselves. however, as the state of mind in which we are, generally gives the colouring to events, when the immagination is suffered to wander into futurity, the picture which now presented itself to me was a most pleasing one. enterta[in]ing as I do, the most confident hope of succeeding in a voyage which had formed a da[r]ling project of mine for the last ten years, I could but esteem this moment of my departure as among the most happy of my life. The party are in excellent health and sperits, zealously attached to the enterprise, and anxious to proceed; not a whisper or murmur of discontent to be heard among them, but all act in unison, and with the most perfict harmony. I took an early supper this evening and went to bed. Capt. Clark myself the two Interpretters and the woman and child sleep in a tent of dressed skins.

April 8th.

Set out early this morning, the wind blew hard against us, from the N.W. we therefore traveled very slowly. I walked on shore, and visited the *black Cat*, took leave of him after smoking a pipe as is their custom, and then proceeded on slowly by land about four miles where I wated the arrival of the party, at 12 Oclock they came up and informed me that one of the small canoes was behind in distress. Capt. Clark returned fou[n]d she had filled with water and all her loading wet. we lost half a bag of bisquit, and about thirty pounds of powder by this accedent; the powder we regard as a serious loss, but we spread it to dry immediately and hope we shall still be enabled to restore the greater part of it. this was the only powder we had which was not perfectly secure from getting wet. we took dinner at this place, and then proceed on to oure

encampment, which was on the N. side opposite to a high bluff.[1]
the Mandan man came up after we had encamped and brought with
him a woman who was extremely solicitous to accompany one of
the men of our party, this however we positively refused to permit.

Tuesday April 9th.

we saw a great number of brant[2] passing up the river, some of
them were white, except the large feathers in the first and second
joint of the wing which are black. there is no other difference
between them and the common gray brant but that of their colour—
their note and habits are the same, and they are freequently seen
to associate together. I have not yet positively determined whether
they are the same, or a different species. Capt Clark walked on
shore to-day[3] and informed me on his return, that passing through
the prarie he had seen an anamal that precisely resembled the burrowing squrril, accept in point of size, it being only about one third
as large as the squirrel, and that it also burrows. I have observed
in many parts of the plains and praries, the work of an anamal[4] of
which I could never obtain a view. their work resembles that of
the salamander common to the sand hills of the States of South
Carolina and Georgia, and like that anamal also it never appears
above the ground. the little hillocks which are thrown up by these
anamals have much the appearance of ten or twelve pounds of loose
earth poared out of a vessel on the surface of the plain. in the state
they leave them you can discover no whole through which they
throw out this earth; but by removing the loose earth gently you
may discover that the soil has been broken in a circle manner for
about an inch and a half in diameter; where it appears looser than
the adjacent surface, and is certainly the place through which the
earth has been thrown out, tho' the operation is performed without
leaving any visible aperture. the Bluffs of the river which we passed
today were upwards of a hundred feet high, formed of a mixture of

[1] Near the present Hancock, North Dakota (Thwaites).

[2] Lesser snow goose (*Chen caerulescens caerulescens*). and Canada goose (*Branta
canadensis*).

[3] Thwaites notes that while Clark was on shore, Lewis recorded in his weather
diary for this date, "The perogue is so unsteady that I can scarcely write."

[4] Northern pocket gopher (*Thomomys talpoides*).

yellow clay and sand—many horizontal stratas of carbonated wood, having every appearance of pitcoal at a distance; were seen in the face of these bluffs. these stratas are of unequal thickness from 1 to 5 feet, and appear at different elivations above the water some of them as much as eighty feet.[5] the hills of the river are very broken, and many of them have the apearance of having been on fire at some former period. considerable quantities of pumice stone and lava appear in many parts of these hills where they are broken and washed Down by the rain and melting snow. when we halted for dinner the squaw busied herself in serching for the wild artichokes which the mice[6] collect and deposit in large hoards. this operation she performed by penetrating the earth with a sharp stick about some small collections of drift wood. her labour soon proved successful, and she procured a good quantity of these roots. the flavor of this root resembles that of the Jerusalem Artichoke, and the stalk of the weed which produces it is also similar, tho' both the root and stalk are much smaller than the Jerusalem Artichoke. the root is white and of an ovate form, from one to three inches in length and usually about the size of a man's finger. one stalk produces from two to four, and somitimes six of these roots.

Wednesday April 10th 1805.
The country on both sides of the missouri from the tops of the river hills, is one continued level fertile plain as far as the eye can reach, in which there is not even a solitary tree or shrub to be seen, except such as from their moist situations or the steep declivities of hills are sheltered from the ravages of the fire. about 1½ miles down this bluff from this point, the bluff is now on fire and throws out considerable quantities of smoke which has a strong sulphurious smell. the appearance of the coal in the blufs continues as yesterday.[7]

at 1 P.M. we overtook three french hunters who had set out a few days before us with a view of traping beaver; they had taken 12 since they left Fort Mandan. these people avail themselves of

[5] The so-called "coal" near Fort Mandan was lignite, extensive beds of which exist in that region (Thwaites).

[6] Meadow mouse (*Microtus pennsylvanicus*).

[7] Near Sakakawea State Park, North Dakota.

the protection which our numbers will enable us to give them against the Assinniboins who sometimes hunt on the Missouri; and intend ascending with us as far as the mouth of the Yellow stone river and continue there hunt up that river.   this is the first essay of a beaver hunter of any discription on this river. the beaver these people have already taken is by far the best I have ever seen.

Thursday April 11th.

the country much the same as yesterday.   on the sides of the hills and even the banks of the rivers and sandbars, there is a white substance t[h]at appears in considerable quantities on the surface of the earth, which tastes like a mixture of common salt and glauber salts.   many of the springs which flow from the base of the river hills are so strongly impregnated with this substance that the water is extreemly unpleasant to the taste and has a purgative effect.[8] saw some large white cranes pass up the river—these are the largest bird of that genus common to the country through which the Missouri and Mississippi pass.   they are perfectly white except the large feathers of the two first joints of the wing which are black.

Saturday April 13th.

the wind was in our favour after 9 A.M. and continued favourable untill three 3. P.M.   we therefore hoisted both the sails in the White Perogue, consisting of a small squar sail, and spritsail, which carried her at a pretty good gate, untill about 2 in the afternoon when a suddon squall of wind struck us and turned the perogue so much on the side as to allarm Sharbono who was steering at the time,   in this state of alarm he threw the perogue with her side to the wind, when the spritsail gibing was as near overseting the perogue as it was possible to have missed.   the wind however abating for an instant I ordered Drewyer to the helm and the sails to be taken in, which was instant[ly] executed and the perogue being steered before the wind was agin plased in a state of security.

this accedent was very near costing us dearly.   beleiving this

[8] The famous "alkali" of the West, often rendering the water undrinkable, and covering great areas like snow (Thwaites), followed by a description of the whooping crane (*Grus americana*).

vessell to be the most steady and safe, we had embarked on board of it our instruments, Papers, medicine and the most valuable part of the merchandize which we had still in reserve as presents for the Indians. we had also embarked on board ourselves, with three men who could not swim and the squaw with the young child, all of whom, had the perogue overset, would most probably have perished, as the waves were high, and the perogue upwards of 200 yards from the nearest shore; however we fortunately escaped and pursued our journey under the square sail, which shortly after the accident I directed to be again hoisted.

our party caught three beaver last evening; and the French hunters 7. as there was much appearance of beaver just above the entrance of the little Missouri these hunters concluded to remain some days, we therefore left them without the expectation of seeing them again. just above the entrance of the little Missouri the great Missouri is upwards of a mile in width, tho' immediately at the entrance of the former it is not more than 200 yards wide and so shallow that the canoes passed it with seting poles. at the distance of nine miles passed the mouth of a creek on the Stard. side which we called onion creek from the quantity of wild onions which grow in the plains on it's borders.

we found a number of carcases of the Buffaloe lying along shore, which had been drowned by falling through the ice in winter and lodged on shore by the high water when the river broke up about the first of this month. we saw also many tracks of the white bear[9] of enormous size, along the river shore and about the carcases of the Buffaloe, on which I presume they feed. we have not as yet seen one of these anamals, tho' their tracks are so abundant and recent. the men as well as ourselves are anxious to meet with some of these bear. the Indians give a very formidable account of the streng[t]h and ferocity of this anamal, which they never dare to attack but in parties of six eight or ten persons; and are even then frequently defeated with the loss of one or more of their party. the savages attack this anamal with their bows and arrows and the indifferent guns with which the traders furnish them, with these they shoot with such uncertainty and at so short a distance, that (*unless*

[9] Grizzly bear (*Ursus horribilis*). See note 12.

shot thro' head or heart wound not mortal) they frequently mis their aim & fall a sacrefice to the bear. two Minetaries were killed during the last winter in an attack on a white bear. this anamall is said more frequently to attack a man on meeting with him, than to flee from him. When the Indians are about to go in quest of the white bear, previous to their departure, they paint themselves and perform all those supersticious rights commonly observed when they are about to make war uppon a neighbouring nation.

O[b]served more bald eagles on this part of the Missouri than we have previously seen. saw the small hawk, frequently called the sparrow hawk, which is common to most parts of the U. States. great quantities of gees are seen feeding in the praries. saw a large flock of white brant or gees with black wings pass up the river; there were a number of gray brant with them; from their flight I presume they proceed much further still to the N.W. we have never been enabled yet to shoot one of these birds, and cannot therefore determine whether the gray brant found with the white, are their brude of the last year or whether they are the same with the grey brant common to the Mississippi and lower part of the Missouri.

Monday April 15th. 1805.

in a little pond of water fromed by this rivulet where it entered the bottom, I heard the frogs crying for the first time this season; their note was the same with that of the small frogs which are common to the lagoons and swam[p]s of the U. States. I saw great quantities of gees feeding in the bottoms, of which I shot one. saw some deer and Elk, but they were remarkably shy. I also met with great numbers of Grouse[10] or *prarie hens* as they are called by the English traders of the N.W. these birds appeared to be mating; the note of the male, is kuck, kuck, kuck, coo, coo, coo. the first part of the note both male and female use when flying. the male also dubbs (*drums with his wings*) something like the pheasant, but by no means as loud.

[10] Sharp-tailed grouse (*Pedioecetes phasianellus*).

Wednesday April 17th. 1805.
we saw immence quantities of game in every direction around us
as we passed up the river; consisting of herds of Buffaloe, Elk, and
Antelopes with some deer and woolves. tho' we continue to see
many tracks of the bear we have seen but very few of them, and
those are at a great distance generally runing from us; I the[re]fore
presume that they are extreemly wary and shy; the Indian account
of them dose not corrispond with our experience so far. one black
bear passed near the perogues on the 16th. and was seen by myself
and the party but he so quickly disappeared that we did not shoot
at him. at the place we halted to dine on the Lard. side we met
with a herd of buffaloe of which I killed the fatest as I concieved
among them, however on examining it I found it so poar that I
thought it unfit for uce and only took the tongue; the party killed
another which was still more lean. just before we encamped this
evening we saw some tracks of Indians who had passed about 24
hours; they left four rafts of tim[ber] on the Stard. side, on which
they had passed. we supposed them to have been a party of the
Assinniboins who had been to war against the rocky Mountain Indians, and then on their return. Capt. Clark saw a Curlou to-day.
there were three beaver taken this morning by the party. the men
prefer the flesh of this anamal, to that of any other which we have,
or are able to procure at this moment. I eat very heartily of the
beaver myself, and think it excellent; particularly the tale, and liver

Saturday April 20th. 1805.
saw the remains of some Indian hunting camps, near which stood
a small scaffold of about 7 feet high on which were deposited two
doog slays with their harnis. underneath this scaffold a human body
was lying, well rolled in several dressed buffaloe skins and near it
a bag of the same materials conta[in]ing sundry articles belonging
to the diseased; consisting of a pare of mockersons, some red and
blue earth, beaver's nails, instruments for dressing the Buffalo skin,
some dryed roots, several platts of the sweet grass, and a small
quantity of Mandan tobacco. I presume that the body, as well as
the bag containing these articles, had formerly been placed on the
scaffold as is the custom of these people, but had fallen down by
accedent. near the scaffold I saw the carcase of a large dog not yet

decayed, which I supposed had been killed at the time the human body was left on the scaffold; this was no doubt the reward, which the poor doog had met with for performing the [blank space in MS.] friendly office to his mistres of transporting her corps to the place of deposit. it is customary with the Assinniboins, Mandans, Mine-tares &c who scaffold their dead, to sacrefice the favorite horses and doggs of their disceased relations, with a view of their being serv-icable to them in the land of sperits. I have never heard of any instances of human sacrefices on those occasions among them.

Sunday April 21st. 1805.
the country through which we passed is very simelar in every respect to that through which we have passed for several days. We saw immence herds of buffaloe Elk deer & Antelopes. Capt. Clark killed a buffaloe and 4 deer in the course of his walk today; and the party with me killed 3 deer, 2 beaver, and 4 buffaloe calves. the latter we found very delicious. I think it equal to any veal I ever tasted.

Monday April 22nd 1805.
proceeded pretty well untill breakfa[s]t, when the wind became so hard a head that we proceeded with difficulty even with the assistance of our toe lines.
I asscended to the top of the cutt bluff this morning,[11] from whence I had a most delightfull view of the country, the whole of which except the vally formed by the Missouri is void of timber or underbrush, exposing to the first glance of the spectator immence herds of Buffaloe, Elk, deer, & Antelopes feeding in one common and boundless pasture. we saw a number of bever feeding on the bark of the trees alonge the verge of the river, several of which we shot, found them large and fat. walking on shore this evening I met with a buffaloe calf which attatched itself to me and continued to follow close at my heels untill I embarked and left it. it appeared allarmed at my dog which was probably the cause of it's so readily attatching itself to me. Capt Clark informed me that he saw a large drove of buffaloe pursued by wolves today, that they at length caught

[11] Near New Town, North Dakota.

a calf which was unable to keep up with the herd. the cows only defend their young so long as they are able to keep up with the herd, and seldom return any distance in surch of them.

Wednesday April 24th.
The wind blew so hard during the whole of this day, that we were unable to move. notwithstanding that we were sheltered by high timber from the effects of the wind, such was it's violence that it caused the waves to rise in such manner as to wet many articles in the small canoes before they could be unloaded. we sent out some hunters who killed 4 deer & 2 Elk, and caught some young wolves of the small kind. Soar eyes is a common complaint among the party. I believe it origenates from the immence quantities of sand which is driven by the wind from the sandbars of the river in such clouds that you are unable to discover the opposite bank of the river in many instances. the particles of this sand are so fine and light that they are easily supported by the air, and are carried by the wind for many miles, and at a distance exhibiting every appearance of a collumn of thick smoke. so penitrating is this sand that we cannot keep any article free from it; in short we are compelled to eat, drink, and breath it very freely. my pocket watch, is out of order, she will run only a few minutes without stoping. I can discover no radical defect in her works, and must therefore attribute it to the sand, with which, she seems plentifully charged, notwithstanding her cases are double and tight.

Thursday April 25th. 1805.
the water friezed on the oars this morning as the men rowed. about 10 oclock A.M. the wind began to blow so violently that we were obliged to lye too. my dog had been absent during the last night, and I was fearfull we had lost him altogether, however, much to my satisfaction he joined us at 8 oclock this morning. The wind had been so unfavorable to our progress for several days past, and seeing but little prospect of a favourable chang; knowing that the river was crooked, from the report of the hunters who were out yesterday, and beleiving that we were at no very great distance from the Yellow stone River; I determined, in order as mush as possible to avoid detention, to proceed by land with a few men to the entrance of that river and make the necessary observations to determine it's

position, which I hoped to effect by the time that Capt. Clark could arrive with the party; accordingly I set out at 11 OCk. on the Lard. side, accompanyed by four men. we proceeded about four miles, when falling in with some buffaloe I killed a yearling calf, which was in good order; we soon cooked and made a hearty meal of a part of it, and renewed our march. our rout lay along the foot of the river hills. when we had proceeded about four miles, I ascended the hills from whence I had a most pleasing view of the country, particularly of the wide and fertile vallies formed by the missouri and the yellowstone rivers, which occasionally unmasked by the wood on their borders disclose their meanderings for many miles in their passage through these delightfull tracts of country. I could not discover the junction of the rivers immediately, they being concealed by the wood; however, sensible that it could not be distant I determined to encamp on the bank of the Yellow stone river which made it's appearance about 2 miles South of me.

the whol face of the country was covered with herds of Buffaloe, Elk & Antelopes; deer are also abundant, but keep themselves more concealed in the woodland. the buffaloe Elk and Antelope are so gentle that we pass near them while feeding, without apearing to excite any alarm among them; and when we attract their attention, they frequently approach us more nearly to discover what we are, and in some instances pursue us a considerable distance apparenly with that view.

in our way to the place I had determined to encamp, we met with two large herds of buffaloe, of which we killed three cows and a calf. two of the former, wer but lean, we therefore took their tongues and a part of their marrow-bones only. I then proceeded to the place of our encampment with two of the men, taking with us the Calf and marrowbones, while the other two remained, with orders to dress the cow that was in tolerable order, and hang the meat out of the reach of the wolves, a precaution indispensible to it's safe keeping, even for a night. we encamped on the bank of the yellow stone river, 2 miles South of it's confluence with the Missouri. On rejoining Capt. Clark, the 26th. in the evening, he informed me, that at 5. P.M. after I left him the wind abated in some measure and he proceeded a few miles further and encamped.

Friday April 26th. 1805.
there is more timber in the neighbourhood of the junction of these
rivers, and on the Missouri as far below as the White-earth river,
than there is on any part of the Missouri above the entrance of the
Chyenne river to this place. the timber consists principally of Cottonwood, with some small elm, ash and boxalder. the under growth
on the sandbars and verge of the river is the small leafed willow;
the low bottoms, rose bushes which rise to three or four fe[e]t high,
the redburry, servicebury, and the redwood; the high bottoms are
of two discriptions, either timbered or open; the first lies next to
the river and it's under brush is the same with that of the low
timbered bottoms with the addition of the broad leafed willow,
Goosbury, choke cherry, purple currant, and honeysuckle bushis;
the open bottoms border on the hills, and are covered in many parts
by the wild hyssop which rises to the hight of two feet. I observe
that the Antelope, Buffaloe Elk and deer feed on this herb; the
willow of the sandbars also furnish a favorite winter food to these
anamals as well as the growse, the porcupine, hare, and rabbit.

about 12 O[c]lock I heard the discharge of several guns at the
junction of the rivers, which announced to me the arrival of the
pa[r]ty with Capt Clark; I afterwards learnt that they had fired on
some buffaloe which they met with at that place, and of which they
killed a cow and several Calves; the latter are now fine veal. I
dispatched one of the men to Capt Clark requesting him to send
up a canoe to take down the meat we had killed and our baggage
to his encampnt, which was accordingly complyed with.

after I had completed my observations in the evening I walked
down and joined the party at their encampment on the point of land
formed by the junction of the rivers; found them all in good health,
and much pleased at having arrived at this long wished for spot, and
in order to add in some measure to the general pleasure which semed
to pervade our little community, we ordered a dram to be issued to
each person; this soon produced the fiddle, and they spent the
evening with much hilarity, singing & dancing, and seemed as perfectly to forget their past toils, as they appeared regardless of those
to come.

in the evening, the man I had sent up the river this morning
returned, and reported that he had ascended it about eight miles
on a streight line; the country bordering on this river as far as he

could percieve, like that of the Missouri, consisted of open plains.
he saw several of the bighorned anamals in the cou[r]se of his walk;
but they were so shy that he could not get a shoot at them; he found
a large horn of one of these anamals which he brought with him.
the bed of the yellowstone river is entirely composed of sand and
mud, not a stone of any kind to be seen in it near it's entrance.

Capt Clark measured these rivers just above their confluence;
found the bed of the Missouri 520 yards wide, the water occupying
330. it's channel deep.   the yellowstone river including it's sandbar,
858 yds. of which, the water occupyed 297 yards; the depest part
12 feet; it was falling at this time & appeard to be nearly at it's
summer tide.   the Indians inform that the yellowstone river is navigable for perogues and canoes nearly to it's source in the Rocky
Mountains, and that in it's course near these mountains it passes
within less than half a day's march of a navigable part of the Missouri.   it's extreem sources are adjacent to those of the Missouri,
river platte, and I think probably with some of the South branch of
the Columbia river.

Monday April 29th. 1805.

I walked on shore with one man.   about 8 A.M. we fell in with
two brown or yellow [*white*] bear; both of which we wounded; one
of them made his escape, the other after my firing on him pursued
me seventy or eighty yards, but fortunately had been so badly
wounded that he was unable to pursue so closely as to prevent my
charging my gun; we again repeated our fir[e] and killed him.   it
was a male not fully grown, we estimated his weight at 300 lbs. not
having the means of ascertaining it precisely.   The legs of this bear
are somewhat longer than those of the black, as are it's tallons and
tusks incomparably larger and longer.   the testicles, which in the
black bear are placed pretty well back between the thyes and contained in one pouch like those of the dog and most quadrupeds, are
in the yellow or brown bear placed much further forward, and are
suspended in separate pouches from two to four inches assunder;
it's colour is yellowish brown, the eyes small, black, and piercing;
the front of the fore legs near the feet is usually black; the fur is
finer thicker and deeper than that of the black bear.   these are all
the particulars in which this anamal appeared to me to differ from

the black bear;[12] it is a much more furious and formidable anamal, and will frequently pursue the hunter when wounded. it is asstonishing to see the wounds they will bear before they can be put to death. the Indians may well fear this anamal equiped as they generally are with their bows and arrows or indifferent fuzees, but in the hands of skillfull riflemen they are by no means as formidable or dangerous as they have been represented.

[Clark]   29th. of April Monday 1805
had not proceeded far eer we Saw a female & her faun of the Bighorn animal on the top of a Bluff lying, the noise we made allarmed them and they came down on the side of the bluff which had but little slope being nearly purpindicular, I directed two men to kill those anamals, one went on the top and the other man near the water they had two shots at the doe while in motion without effect, Those animals run & Skiped about with great ease on this declivity & appeared to prefur it to the leavel bottom or plain.

I saw only a single tree in this fertile vallie The water of the River is clear of a yellowish colour, we call this river Martheys river[13] in honor to the Selebrated M.F.

Here the high land widen from five to Eight miles and much lower than below. Saw several of the big horn animals this evening. The Wolves distroy great numbers of the antilopes by decoying those animals singularly out in the plains and prosueing them alternetly, those antelopes are curious and will approach any thing which appears in motion near them &c.

30th. of April Tuesday 1805
I walked on Shore to day our interpreter & his squar followed, in my walk the squar found & brought me a bush something like the currunt, which she said bore a delicious froot and that great quantitis grew on the Rocky Mountains. This shrub was in bloom has a yellow flower with a deep cup, the froot when ripe is yellow and hangs in bunches like cheries, Some of those berries yet remained

---

[12] By "white bear," here and elsewhere in Lewis and Clark's journals, must be understood the animal now known as "grizzly bear" (*Ursus horribilis*), first adequately described by our explorers. It was technically named in 1815 (Thwaites).

[13] Now the Big Muddy River.

on the bushes.[14] The bottoms above the mouth of the last river is extencive level & fertile and covered with indifferent timber in the points, the upland appear to rise gradually, I saw Great numbers of antelopes, also scattering Buffalow, Elk, Deer, wolves, Gees, ducks & Crows. I Killed 2 Gees which we dined on to day. Capt Lewis walked on Shore and killed an elk this evening, and we came too & camped on the S.S. the countrey on both sides have a butifull appearance.

[Lewis]   Wednesday May 1st. 1805.

John Shields sick today with the rheumatism. Shannon killed a bird of the plover kind.[15] weight one pound. it measured from the tip of the toe, to the extremity of the beak, 1. foot 10. Inches; from tip to tip of wings when extended 2 F. 5 I.; Beak 3 ⅝ inches; tale 3⅛ inches; leg and toe 10 Ins. the eye black, piercing, prominent and moderately large. the legs are flat thin, slightly imbricated and of a pale sky blue colour, being covered with feathers as far as the mustle extends down it, which is about half of it's length. it has four toes on each foot, three of which, are connected by a web, the fourth is small and placed at the heel about the ⅛ of an inch up the leg. the nails are black and short, that of the middle toe is extreemly singular, consisting of two nails the one laping on or overlaying the other, the upper one somewhat the longest and sharpest. the tale contains eleven feathers of equal length, & of a bluish white colour. the boddy and underside of the wings, except the large feathers of the 1st. & 2nd. joints of the same, are white, as are also the feathers of the upper part of the 4th. joint of the wing and part of those of the 3rd. adjacent thereto. the large feathers of the 1st. or pinion and the 2nd. joint are black; a part of the larger feathers of the 3rd. joint on the upper side and all the small feathers which cover the upper side of the wings are black, as are also the tuft of long feathers on each side of the body above the joining of the wing, leaving however a stripe of white between them on the back. the head and neck are shaped much like the grey plover, and are of a light brickdust brown; the beak is black and flat, largest where it joins

---

[14] Probably the golden currant (*Ribes aureum*).
[15] American avocet (*Recurvirostra americana*).

the head, and from thence becoming thiner and tapering to a very sharp point, the upper chap being ⅛ of an inch the longest turns down at the point and forms a little hook. the nostrils, which commence near the head are long, narrow, connected and parallel with the beak; the beak is much curved, the curvature being upwards in stead of downwards as is common with most birds; the substance of the beak precisely resembles whalebone at a little distance, and is quite as flexable as that substance. their note resembles that of the grey plover, tho' is reather louder and more varied, their habits appear also to be the same, with this difference; that it sometimes rests on the water and swims which I do not recollect having seen the plover do. this bird which I shall henceforth stile the *Missouri plover*, generally feeds about the shallow bars of the river, to collect it's food which consists of [blank space in MS.], it immerces it's beak in the water and throws it's head and beak from side to side at every step it takes.

Thursday May 2nd. 1805.

The wind continued violent all night nor did it abate much of it's violence this morning, when at daylight it was attended with snow which continued to fall untill about 10 A.M. being about one inch deep, it formed a singular contrast with the vegitation which was considerably advanced. some flowers had put forth in the plains, and the leaves of the cottonwood were as large as a dollar. sent out some hunters who killed 2 deer 3 Elk and several buffaloe; on our way this evening we also shot three beaver along the shore; these anamals in consequence of not being hunted are extreemly gentle, where they are hunted they never leave their lodges in the day, the flesh of the beaver is esteemed a delecacy among us; I think the tale a most delicious morsal, when boiled it resembles in flavor the fresh tongues and sounds of the codfish, and is usually sufficiently large to afford a plentifull meal for two men.

[Clark]   May 2nd. Thursday 1805

the Snow which fell to day was about 1 In deep. a verry extraordernarey climate, to behold the trees Green & flowers spred on the plain, & Snow an inch deep. the evening verry cold, Ice freesing to the Ores.

[Lewis]   Friday May 3rd. 1805.

we saw vast quantities of Buffaloe, Elk, deer principally of the
long tale kind, Antelope or goats, beaver, geese, ducks, brant and
some swan.   near the entrance of the river mentioned in the 10th.
course of this day, we saw an unusual number of Porcupines from
which we determined to call the river after that anamal, and accordingly denominated it *Porcupine river.* [16]

I walked out a little distance and met with 2 porcupines which
were feeding on the young willow which grow in great abundance
on all the sandbars; this anamal is exceedingly clumsy and not very
watchfull   I approached so near one of them before it percieved me
that I touched it with my espontoon. [17]   found the nest of a wild
goose among some driftwood in the river from which we took three
eggs.   this is the only nest we have met with on driftwood, the
usual position is the top of a broken tree, sometimes in the forks of
a large tree but almost invariably, from 15 to 20 feet or upwards
high.

Saturday May 4th. 1805.

We were detained this morning untill about 9 Ock, in order to
repare the rudder irons of the red perogue which were broken last
evening in landing; we then set out, the wind hard against us.   I
walked on shore this morning, the weather was more plesant, the
snow has disappeared; the frost seems to have effected the vegetation much less than could have been expected   the leaves of the
cottonwood the grass the box alder willow and the yellow flowering
pea seem to be scarcely touched; the rosebushes and honeysuckle
seem to have sustaned the most considerable injury.   The country
on both sides of the Missouri continues to be open level fertile and
beautifull as far as the eye can reach which from some of the em-
inences is not short of 30 Miles.   the river bottoms are very extensive
and contain a much greater proportion of timber than usual; the fore
part of this day the river was bordered with timber on both sides,
a circumstance which is extreemly rare and the first which has occurred of any thing like the same extent since we left the Mandans.

[16] Now Poplar River in Montana.
[17] A spontoon, a short pike or halberd.

in the after part of the day we passed an extensive beautifull plain on the Stard. side which gradually ascended from the river. I saw immense quantities of buffaloe in every direction, also some Elk deer and goats; having an abundance of meat on hand I passed them without firing on them; they are extreemly gentle the bull buffaloe particularly will scarcely give way to you. I passed several in the open plain within fifty paces, they viewed me for a moment as something novel and then very unconcernedly continued to feed.

Sunday May 5th 1805

Capt Clark found a den of young wolves in the course of his walk today and also saw a great number of those anamals; they are very abundant in this quarter, and are of two species   the small woolf or burrowing dog of the praries are the inhabitants almost invariably of the open plains; they usually ascociate in bands of ten or twelve sometimes more and burrow near some pass or place much frequented by game;   not being able alone to take a deer or goat they are rarely ever found alone but hunt in bands; they frequently watch and seize their prey near their burrows;   in these burrows they raise their young and to them they also resort when pursued; when a person approaches them they frequently bark, their note being precisely that of the small dog. they are of an intermediate size between that of the fox and dog, very active fleet and delicately formed; the ears large erect and pointed the head long and pointed more like that of the fox; tale long and bushey;   the hair and fur also resembles the fox tho' is much coarser and inferior. they are of a pale redish brown colour. the eye of a deep sea green colour small and piercing. their tallons are reather longer than those of the ordinary wolf or that common to the atlantic States, none of which are to be found in this quarter, nor I believe above the river Plat.[18] The large woolf found here is not as large as those of the atlantic states. they are lower and thicker made shorter leged. their colour which is not effected by the seasons, is a grey or blackish brown and every intermediate shade from that to a creen [cream] coloured white;   these wolves resort [to] the woodlands and are also found

---

[18] A description of the coyote (*Canis latrans*), followed by that of the gray wolf (*Canis lupus*).

in the plains, but never take refuge in the ground or burrow so far as I have been able to inform myself. we scarcely see a gang of buffaloe without observing a parsel of those faithfull shepherds on their skirts in readiness to take care of the mamed wounded. the large wolf never barks, but howls as those of the atlantic states do.

Capt. Clark and Drewyer killed the largest brown bear this evening which we have yet seen. it was a most tremendious looking anamal, and extreemly hard to kill notwithstanding he had five balls through his lungs and five others in various parts he swam more than half the distance acoss the river to a sandbar, & it was at least twenty minutes before he died; he did not attempt to attack, but fled and made the most tremendous roaring from the moment he was shot. We had no means of weighing this monster; Capt. Clark thought he would weigh 500 lbs. for my own part I think the estimate too small by 100 lbs. he measured 8. Feet 7½ Inches from the nose to the extremety of the hind feet, 5 F. 10½ Ins. around the breast, 1 F. 11. I. arround the middle of the arm, & 3.F. 11.I. arround the neck; his tallons which were five in number on each foot were 4⅜ Inches in length. he was in good order, we therefore divided him among the party and made them boil the oil and put it in a cask for future uce; the oil is as hard as hogs lard when cool, much more so than that of the black bear. this bear differs from the common black bear in several respects; it's tallons are much longer and more blont, it's tale shorter, it's hair which is of a redish or bey brown, is longer thicker and finer than that of the black bear; his liver lungs and heart are much larger even in proportion with his size; the heart particularly was as large as that of a large Ox. his maw was also ten times the size of black bear, and was filled with flesh and fish. his testicles were pendant from the belly and placed four inches assunder in separate bags or pouches. this animal also feeds on roots and almost every species of wild fruit.

Monday May 6th 1805

saw a brown bear swim the river above us, he disappeared before we can get in reach of him; I find that the curiossity of our party is pretty well satisfyed with rispect to this anamal, the formidable appearance of the male bear killed on the 5th. added to the difficulty with which they die when even shot through the vital parts, has staggered the resolution [of] several of them, others however seem keen for action with the bear; I expect these gentlemen will give us some amusement sho[r]rtly as they soon begin now to coppolate. saw a great quantity of game of every species common here. Capt Clark walked on shore and killed two Elk, they were not in very good order, we therefore took a part of the meat only; it is now only amusement for Capt. C. and myself to kill as much meat as the party can consum; I hope it may continue thus through our whole rout, but this I do not much expect. two beaver were taken in traps this mo[r]ning and one since shot by one of the party. saw numbers of these anamals peeping at us as we passed out of their wholes which they form of a cilindric shape, by burrowing in the face of the abbrupt banks of the river.

Tuesday May 7th. 1805.

at 11. A.M. the wind became so hard that we were compelled to ly by for several hours, one of the small canoes by the bad management of the steersman filled with water and had very nearly sunk; we unloaded her and dryed the baggage; at one we proceed on the wind having in some measure abated. the country we passed today on the North side of the river is one of the most beautifull plains we have yet seen

we continue to see a great number of bald Eagles, I presume they must feed on the carcases of dead anamals, for I see no fishing hawks to supp[l]y them with their favorite food. the water of the river is so terbid that no bird wich feeds exclusively on fish can subsist on it; from it's mouth to this place I have neither seen the blue crested fisher nor a fishing hawk.

Wednesday May 8th. 1805.

we nooned it just above the entrance of a large river which disimbogues on the Lard. [*Starbd*] side; I took the advantage of this leasure moment and examined the river about 3 miles; from the quantity of water furnished by this river it must water a large extent of country; perhaps this river also might furnish a practicable and advantageous communication with the Saskashiwan river; it is sufficiently large to justify a belief that it might reach to that river if it's direction be such. the water of this river possesses a peculiar whiteness, being about the colour of a cup of tea with the admixture of a tablespoonfull of milk. from the colour of it's water we called it

Milk river.[19] we think it possible that this may be the river called
by the Minitares *the river which scoalds at all others*

The white apple is found in great abundance in this neighbourhood; it is confined to the highlands principally. The *whiteapple,*[20]
so called by the French Engages, is a plant which rises to the hight
of 6 or 9 Inhs. rarely exceeding a foot; it puts forth from one to four
and sometimes more stalks from the same root, but is most generally
found with one only, which is branched but not defusely, is cylindric
and villose; the *leafstalks,* cylindric, villose and very long compared
with the hight of the plant, tho' gradually diminish in length as they
ascend, and are irregular in point of position; the leaf, digitate, from
three to five in number, oval 1 Inch long, absolutely entire and
cottony: the whole plant of a pale green, except the under disk of
the leaf which is of a white colour from the cottony substance with
which it is covered. the radix a tuberous bulb; generally ova formed
[oviform], sometimes longer and more rarely partially divided or
branc[h]ing; always attended with one or more radicles at it's lower
extremity which sink from 4 to 6 inches deep. the bulb covered
with a rough black, tough, thin rind which easily seperates from the
bulb which is a fine white substance, somewhat porus, spungy and
moist, and reather tough before it is dressed; the center of the bulb
is penitrated with a small tough string or liga-ment, which passing
from the bottom of the stem terminates in the extremity of the
radicle, which last is also covered by a prolongation of the rind which
invellopes the bulb: The bulb is usually found at the debth of 4
inches and frequently much deeper. This root forms a considerable
article of food with the Indians of the Missouri, who for this purpose
prepare them in several ways. they are esteemed good at all seasons
of the year, but are best from the middle of July to the latter end
of Autumn when they are sought and gathered by the provident
part of the natives for their winter store. when collected they are
striped of their rhind and strung on small throngs or chords and
exposed to the sun or plased in the smoke of their fires to dry; when

[19] Twenty-five miles west of Wolf Point, Montana, "this is by far the largest of
the Missouri's northern tributaries" (Thwaites). The "River That Scolds All Others"
was actually the Marias River, farther west.

[20] Fr. *pomme blanche*; the edible tubers of *Psoralea esculenta* (Thwaites); also called
Indian bread root.

well dryed they will keep for several years, provided they are not permitted to become moist or damp;   in this situation they usually pound them between two stones placed on a piece of parchment, untill they reduce it to a fine powder,   thus prepared they thicken their soope with it; sometimes they also boil these dryed roots with their meat without breaking them; when green they are generally boiled with their meat, sometimes mashing them or otherwise as they think proper.   they also prepare an agreeable dish with them by boiling and mashing them and adding the marrow grease of the buffaloe and some buries, untill the whole be of the consistency of a haisty pudding.   they also eat this root roasted and frequently make hearty meals of it raw without sustaining any inconvenience or injury therefrom.   The White or brown bear feed very much on this root, which their tallons assist them to procure very readily. the white apple appears to me to be a tastless insippid food of itself, tho' I have no doubt but it is a very healthy and moderately nutricious food.   I have no doubt but our epicures would admire this root very much, it would serve them in their ragouts and gravies in stead of the truffles morella.

we can send out at any time and obtain whatever species of meat the country affords in as large quantity as we wish.   we saw where an Indian had recently grained, or taken the hair off of a goatskin; we do not wish to see those gentlemen just now as we presume they would most probably be the Assinniboins and might be troublesome to us.   Capt C. could not be certain but thought he saw the smoke and some Indian lodges at a considrable distance up Milk river.

Thursday May 9th. 1805.

Capt C. killed 2 bucks and 2 buffaloe, I also killed one buffaloe which proved to be the best meat, it was in tolerable order;   we saved the best of the meat, and from the cow I killed we saved the necessary materials for making what our wrighthand cook Charbono calls the *boudin* (*poudingue*) *blanc,* and immediately set him about preparing them for supper; this white pudding we all esteem one of the greatest del[ic]acies of the forrest, it may not be amiss therefore to give it a place.   About 6 feet of the lower extremity of the large gut of the Buffaloe is the first mo[r]sel that the cook makes love to,   this he holds fast at one end with the right hand, while the forefinger and thumb of the left he gently compresses it, and discharges what he says *is not good to eat*, but of which in the s[e]quel we get a moderate portion;   the mustle lying underneath the shoulder blade next to the back, and fillets are next saught,   these are needed up very fine with a good portion of kidney suit[suet]; to this composition is then added a just proportion of pepper and salt and a small quantity of flour;   thus far advanced, our skilfull opporator C——o seizes his receptcle, which has never once touched the water, for that would intirely distroy the regular order of the whole procedure; you will not forget that the side you now see is that covered with a good coat of fat provided the anamal be in good order; the operator sceizes the recepticle I say, and tying it fast at one end turns it inward and begins now with repeated evolutions of the hand and arm, and a brisk motion of the finger and thumb to put in what he says is *bon pour manger;*   thus by stuffing and compressing he soon distends the recepticle to the utmost limmits of it's power of expansion, and in the course of it's longtudinal progress it drives from the other end of the recepticle a much larger portion of the [blank space in MS.] than was prev[i]ously discharged by the finger and thumb of the left hand in a former part of the operation; thus when the sides of the recepticle are skilfully exchanged the outer for the iner, and all is compleately filled with something good to eat, it is tyed at the other end, but not any cut off, for that would make the pattern too scant;   it is then baptised in the missouri with two dips and a flirt, and bobbed into the kettle; from whence, after it be well boiled it is taken and fryed with bears oil untill it becomes brown, when it is ready to esswage the pangs of a keen appetite or such as travelers in the wilderness are seldom at a loss for.

we saw a great quantity of game today particularly of Elk and Buffaloe,   the latter are now so gentle that the men frequently throw sticks and stones at them in order to drive them out of the way. we also saw this evening emence quantities of timber cut by the beaver which appeared to have been done the preceeding year,   in [one] place particularly they had cut all the timber down for three acres in front and on nearly one back from the river and had removed a considerable proportion of it,   the timber grew very thick and some of it was as large as a man's body.   the river for several days has been as wide as it is generally near it's mouth, tho' it is much shallower or I should begin to dispair of ever reaching it's source; it has been crouded today with many sandbars; the water also appears to become clearer, it has changed it's complexin very considerably. I begin to feel extreemly anxious to get in view of the rocky mountains.

I killed four plover this evening of a different species from any I have yet seen;[21] it resembles the grey or whistling plover more than any other of this family of birds; it is about the size of the yellow legged or large grey plover common to the lower part of this river as well as most parts of the Atlantic States where they are sometimes called the Jack curloo; the eye is moderately large, are black with a narrow ring of dark yellowish brown; the head, neck, upper part of the body and coverts of the wings are of a dove coloured brown, which when the bird is at rest is the predominant colour; the brest and belley are of a brownish white; the tail is composed of 12 feathers of 3 Ins. being of equal length, of these the two in the center are black, with traverse bars of yellowish brown; the others are a brownish white. the large feathers of the wings are white tiped with blacked. the beak is black, 2½ inches in length, slightly tapering, streight, of a cilindric form and blontly or roundly pointed; the chaps are of equal length, and nostrils narrow longitudional and connected; the feet and legs are smoth and of a greenish brown; has three long toes and a sho[r]t one on each foot, the long toes are unconnected with a web, and the short one is placed very high up the leg behind, insomuch that it dose not touch the ground when the bird stands erect. the notes of this bird are louder and more various than any other of this family that I have seen.

Friday May 10th. 1805
the wind continued violent all day, the clouds were thick and black, had a slight sprinkle of rain several times in the course of the day. we sent out several hunters to scower the country, to this we were induced not so much from the want of provision as to discover the Indians whome we had reasons to believe were in the neighbourhood, from the circumstance of one of their dogs comeing to

[21] Willet (*Catoptrophorus semipalmatus*), near the site of Fort Peck, Montana.

us this morning shortly after we landed;   we still beleive ourselves
in the country usually hunted by the Assinniboins, and as they are
a vicious illy disposed nation we think it best to be on our guard;
accordingly we inspected the arms and accoutrements of the party
and found them all in good order.   The hunters returned this evening having seen no tents or Indians nor any fresh sign of them;
they killed two Mule deer, one common fallow or longtailed deer,
2 Buffaloe and 5 beaver, and saw several deer of the Mule kind of
immence size, and also three of the Bighorned anamals.

from the appearance of the Mule deer and the bighorned anamals
we beleive ourselves fast approaching a hilly or mountainous country; we have rarely found the mule deer in any except a rough
country;   they prefer the open grounds and are seldom found in the
woodlands near the river; when they are met with in the woodlands
or river bottoms and are pursued, the[y] invariably run to the hills
or open country as the Elk do.   the contrary happens with the
common deer.

ther are several esscential differences between the Mule and common deer as well in form as in habits.   they are fully a third larger
in general, and the male is particularly large;   I think there is somewhat greater disparity of size between the male and female of this
species than there is between the male and female fallow deer; I
am convinced I have seen a buck of this species twice the volume
of a buck of any other species.   the ears are peculiarly large, I
measured those of a large buck which I found to be eleven inches
long and 3½ in width at the widest part;   they are not so delicately
formed, their hair in winter is thicker longer and of a much darker
grey, in summer the hair is still coarser longer and of a paleer red,
more like that of the Elk; in winter they also have a considerable
quantity of a very fine wool intermixed with the hair and lying next
to the skin as the Antelope has.   the long hair which grows on the
outer sides of the 1st. joint of the hinder legs, and which in the
common deer do not usually occupy more than 2 inches in them
occupys from 6 to eight;   their horns also differ, these in the common
deer consist of two main beams from which one or more points
project the beam gradualy deminishing as the points procede from
it,   with the mule deer the horns consist of two beams which at the
distance of 4 or 6 inches from the head divide themselves each into

two equal branches which again either divide into two other equal branches or terminate in a smaller, and two equal ones; having either 2. 4 or 6 points on a beam; the horn is not so rough about the base as the common deer and are invariably of a much darker colour. the most striking difference of all, is the white rump and tale. from the root of the tail as a center there is a circular spot perfectly white of abot 3 inches radius, which occupys a part of the rump and extremitys of the buttocks and joins the white of the belley underneath; the tail which is usually from 8 to 9 inches long, for the first 4 or 5 inches from it's upper extremity is covered with sho[r]t white hairs, much shorter indeed than the hairs of the body; from hence for about one inch further the hair is still white but gradually becomes longer, the tail then terminates in a tissue of black hair about 3 Inches long. from this black hair of the tail they have obtained among the French engages the appelation of the black taled deer, but this I conceive by no means characteristic of the anamal as much the larger portion of the tail is white. the year and the tail of this anamal when compared with those of the common deer, so well comported with those of the mule when compared with the horse, that we have by way of distinction adapted the appellation of the mule deer which I think much more appropriate. on the inner corner of each eye there is a drane or large recepicle which seems to answer as a drane to the eye which gives it the appearance of weeping, this in the common deer of the atlantic states is scarcely perceptable but becomes more conspicuous in the fallow deer, and still more so in the Elk; this recepticle in the Elk is larger than in any of the pecora order with which I am acquainted.

Boils and imposthumes [i.e., abscesses] have been very common with the party Bratton is now unable to work with one on his hand; soar eyes continue also to be common to all of us in a greater or less degree. for the imposthume I use emmolient poltices, and for soar eyes a solution of white vitriol and the sugar of lead in the proportion of 2 grs. of the former and one of the latter to each ounce of water.

Saturday May 11th. 1805.
the banks are falling in very fast; I sometimes wonder that some of our canoes or perogues are not swallowed up by means of these immence masses of earth which are eternally precipitating themselves into the river; we have had many hairbreadth escapes from

them but providence seems so to have ordered it that we have as yet sustained no loss in consequence of them.

About 5.P.M. my attention was struck by one of the Party runing at a distance towards us and making signs and hollowing as if in distress, I ordered the perogues to put too, and waited untill he arrived; I now found that it was Bratton the man with the soar hand whom I had permitted to walk on shore, he arrived so much out of breath that it was several minutes before he could tell what had happened; at length he informed me that in the woody bottom on the Lard. side about 1½ [miles] below us he had shot a brown bear which immediately turned on him and pursued him a considerable distance but he had wounded it so badly that it could not overtake him; I immediately turned out with seven of the party in quest of this monster, we at length found his trale and persued him about a mile by the blood through very thick brush of rosbushes and the large leafed willow; we finally found him concealed in some very thick brush and shot him through the skull with two balls; we proceeded [to] dress him as soon as possible, we found him in good order; it was a monstrous beast, not quite so large as that we killed a few days past but in all other rispects much the same the hair is remarkably long fine and rich tho' he appears parshally to have discharged his winter coat; we now found that Bratton had shot him through the center of the lungs, notwithstanding which he had pursued him near half a mile and had returned more than double that distance and with his tallons had prepared himself a bed in the earth of about 2 feet deep and five long and was perfectly alive when we found him which could not have been less than 2 hours after he received the wound; these bear being so hard to die reather intimedates us all; I must confess that I do not like the gentlemen and had reather fight two Indians than one bear; there is no other chance to conquer them by a single shot but by shooting them through the brains, and this becomes difficult in consequence of two large muscles which cover the sides of the forehead and the sharp projection of the center of the frontal bone, which is also of a pretty good thickness. the flece and skin were as much as two men could possibly carry. by the time we returned the sun had set and I determined to remain here all night, and directed the cooks to render the bear's oil and put it in the kegs which was done. there was about eight gallons of it.

there is another growth that begins now to make it's appearance in the bottom lands and is becoming extreemly troublesome;[22] it is a shrub which rises to the hight of from two to four feet, much branched, the bark of the trunk somewhat rough hard and of light grey colour; the wood is firm and stif, the branches beset with a great number of long, sha[r]p, strong, woody looking thorns; the leaf is about ¾ or an inch long, and one ⅛ of an inch wide, it is obtuse, absolutely entire, veinless fleshy and gibbose; has no perceptable taste or smell, and no anamal appears to eat it by way of designating when I mention it hereafter I shall call it the *fleshey leafed thorn.*

Sunday May 12th. 1805.

I walked on shore this morning for the benefit of exersize which I much wanted, and also to exmaine the country and it's productions, in these excurtions I most generally went alone armed with my rifle and espontoon; thus equiped I feel myself more than an equal match for a brown bear provided I get him in open woods or near the water, but feel myself a little diffident with respect to an attack in the open plains, I have therefore come to a resolution to act on the defencive only, should I meet these gentlemen in the open country. I ascended the hills and had a view of a rough and broken country on both sides of the river; on the North side the summits of the hills exhibit some scattering pine and cedar, on the South-side the pine has not yet commenced tho' there is some cedar on the face of the hills and in the little ravines. the choke cherry also grows here in the hollows and at the heads of the gullies; the choke Cherry has been in blume since the ninth inst. this growth has freequently made it's appearance on the Missouri from the neighbourhood of the *Bald pated Prarie,* to this place. in the form of it's leaf, colour and appearance of it's bark, and general figure of it's growth it resembles much the Marillar [Morello] cherry, tho' much smaller not generally rising to a greater hight than from 6 to 10 feet and ascoriating in thick clusters on clumps in their favorit situations which is usually the head of small ravines or along the sides of small brooks which flow from the hills. the flowers which are small and

---

[22] Greasewood (*Sarcobatus vermiculatus*).

white are supported by a common footstalk as those of the common wild cherry are, the corolla consists of five oval petals, five stamen and one pistillum, and of course of the Class and order Pentandria Monogynia. it bears a fruit which much resembles the wild cherry in form and colour tho' larger and better flavoured; it's fruit ripens about the begining of July and continues on the trees untill the latter end of September. The Indians of the Missouri make great uce of this cherry which they prepare for food in various ways, sometimes eating when first plucked from the trees or in that state pounding them mashing the seed boiling them with roots or meat, or with the prarie beans and white apple; again for their winter store they geather them and lay them on skins to dry in the sun, and frequently pound them and make them up in small roles or cakes and dry them in the sun; when thus dryed they fold them in skins or put them in bags of parchment and keep them through the winter either eating them in this state or boiling them as before mentioned. the bear and many birds also feed on these burries. the wild hysop sage, *fleshey leaf thorn*, and some other herbs also grow in the plains and hills, particularly the arromatic herb on which the Antelope and large hare feed.

[Clark]   13th. of May Monday 1805
I killed two deer this evening one a mule deer & the other a common Deer, the party killed several this morning all for the use of their Skins which are now good, one man Gibson wounded a verry large *brown bear*, too late this evening to prosue him. We passed two creeks in a bend to the Lard Side neither [of] them had any water,

Course & Distance 13th. of May 1805
                   miles
S. 35° W. 1½   along the Std. Shore to a point of high timber opposit a bluff, passing the enterence of two creeks on the L.S. neither of which discharge any water at this time. 1st. 18. 2d. 30 yds. wide
S. 50° W. 1   along the Std. point oppsd. a high bluff
N. 75° W. 2   to a point of wood land on the Lard. Side
S. 80° W 2½   along the Lard Shore to a point of wood land near which we incamped on the Lard Side
    miles 7

[Lewis]   Tuesday May 14th. 1805.

In the evening the men in two of the rear canoes discovered a large brown bear lying in the open grounds about 300 paces from the river, and six of them went out to attack him, all good hunters; they took the advantage of a small eminence which concealed them and got within 40 paces of him unperceived,   two of them reserved their fires as had been previously conscerted, the four others fired nearly at the same time and put each his bullet through him, two of the balls passed through the bulk of both lobes of his lungs,   in an instant this monster ran at them with open mouth, the two who had reserved their fir[e]s discharged their pieces at him as he came towards them, boath of them struck him, one only slightly and the other fortunately broke his shoulder, this however only retarded his motion for a moment only,   the men unable to reload their guns took to flight, the bear pursued and had very nearly overtaken them before they reached the river; two of the party betook themselves to a canoe and the others seperated an[d] concealed themselves among the willows, reloaded their pieces, each discharged his piece at him as they had an opportunity   they struck him several times again but the guns served only to direct the bear to them,   in this manner he pursued two of them seperately so close that they were obliged to throw aside their guns and pouches and throw themselves into the river altho' the bank was nearly twenty feet perpendicular; so enraged was this anamal that he plunged into the river only a few feet behind the second man he had compelled [to] take refuge in the water, when one of those who still remained on shore shot him through the head and finally killed him;   they then took him on shore and butch[er]ed him when they found eight balls had passed through him in different directions;   the bear being old the flesh was indifferent, they therefore only took the skin and fleece, the latter made us several gallons of oil

it was after the sun had set before these men come up with us, where we had been halted by an occurrence, which I have now to recappitulate, and which altho' happily passed without ruinous injury, I cannot recollect but with the utmost trepidation and horror; this is the upsetting and narrow escape of the white perogue.   It happened unfortunately for us this evening that Charbono was at the helm of this Perogue, in stead of Drewyer, who had previously steered her; Charbono cannot swim and is perhaps the most timid waterman in the world; perhaps it was equally unluckey that Capt. C. and myself were both on shore at that moment, a circumstance which rarely happened; and tho' we were on the shore opposite to the perogue, were too far distant to be heard or to do more than remain spectators of her fate; in this perogue were embarked, our papers, Instruments, books medicine, a great part of our merchandize and in short almost every article indispensibly necessary to further the views, or insure the success of the enterprize in which we are now launched to the distance of 2200 miles.

surfice it to say, that the Perogue was under sail when a sudon squawl of wind struck her obliquely, and turned her considerably, the steersman allarmed, in stead of puting, her before the wind, lufted her up into it,   the wind was so violent that it drew the brace of the squarsail out of the hand of the man who was attending it, and instantly upset the perogue and would have turned her completely topsaturva, had it not have been from the resistance mad[e] by the oarning [awning] against the water; in this situation Capt. C. and myself both fired our guns to attract the attention if possible of the crew and ordered the halyards to be cut and the sail hawled in, but they did not hear us;   such was their confusion and consternation at this moment, that they suffered the perogue to lye on her side for half a minute before they took the sail in, the perogue then wrighted but had filled within an inch of the gunwals;   Charbono still crying to his god for mercy, had not yet recollected the rudder, nor could the repeated orders of the Bowsman, Cruzat, bring him to his recollection untill he threatend to shoot him instantly if he did not take hold of the rudder and do his duty,   the waves by this time were runing very high, but the fortitude resolution and good conduct of Cruzat saved her; he ordered 2 of the men to throw out the water with some kettles that fortunately were convenient, while himself and two others rowed her as[h]ore, where she arrived scarcely above the water

we now took every article out of her and lay them to drane as well as we could for the evening, baled out the canoe and secured her. there were two other men beside Charbono on board who could not swim, and who of course must also have perished had the perogue gone to the bottom. while the perogue lay on her side, finding I could not be heard, I for a moment forgot my own situation, and involluntarily droped my gun, threw aside my shot pouch and was in the act of unbuttoning my coat, before I recollected the folly of the attempt I was about to make; which was to throw myself into the river and inde[a]vour to swim to the perogue; the perogue was three hundred yards distant the waves so high that a perogue could scarcely live in any situation, the water excessively could, and the stream rappid; had I undertaken this project therefore, there was a hundred to one but what I should have paid the forfit of my life for the madness of my project, but this had the perogue been lost, I should have valued but little. After having all matters arranged for the evening as well as the nature of circumstances would permit, we thought it a proper occasion to console ourselves and cheer the sperits of our men and accordingly took a drink of grog and gave each man a gill of sperits.

Thursday May 16th.

The morning was fair and the day proved favorable to our operations; by 4 oClock in the evening our Instruments, Medicine, merchandize provision &c, were perfectly dryed, repacked and put on board the perogue. the loss we sustained was not so great as we had at first apprehended; our medicine sustained the greatest injury, several articles of which were intirely spoiled, and many others considerably injured, the ballance of our losses consisted of some gardin seeds, a small quantity of gunpowder, and a few culinary articles which fell overboard and sunk. the Indian woman to whom I ascribe equal fortitude and resolution, with any person onboard at the time of the accedent, caught and preserved most of the light articles which were washed overboard.

Friday May 17th.

we employed the toe line the greater part of the day; the banks were firm and shore boald which favoured the uce of the cord. I find this method of asscending the river, when the shore is such as will permit it, the safest and most expeditious mode of traveling, except with sails in a steady and favourable breze.

a few scattering cottonwood trees are the only timber near the river; the sandbars, and with them the willow points have almost entirely disappeared. the great number of large beds of streams perfectly dry which we daily pass indicate a country but badly watered, which I fear is the case with the country through which we have been passing for the last fifteen or twenty days.

Capt. Clark narrowly escaped being bitten by a rattlesnake in the course of his walk, the party killed one this evening at our encampment, which he informed me was similar to that he had seen; this snake is smaller than those common to the middle Atlantic States, being about 2 feet 6 inches long;[23] it is of a yellowish brown colour on the back and sides, variagated with one row of oval spots of a dark brown colour lying transversely over the back from the neck to the tail, and two other rows of small circular spots of the same colour which garnis the sides along the edge of the scuta. it's bely contains 176 [s]cuta on the belly and 17 on the tale.

Capt Clark informed me that he saw some coal which had been brought down by the water of the last creek we passed; this creek also throws out considerable quantities of Drift-wood, though there is no timber on it which can be perceived from the Missouri; we called this stream rattlesnake creek.

Capt Clark saw an Indian fortifyed camp this evening, which appeared to have been recently occupyed, from which we concluded it was probable that it had been formed by a war party of the Menetares who left their vilage in March last with a view to attack the blackfoot Indians in consequence of their having killed some of their principal warriors the previous autumn.

we were roused late at night by the Sergt. of the guard, and warned of the danger we were in from a large tree that had taken fire and which leant immediately over our lodge. we had the loge removed, and a few minutes after a large proportion of the top of the tree fell on the place the lodge had stood; had we been a few minutes later we should have been crushed to attoms. the wind blew so hard, that notwithstanding the lodge was fifty paces distant from the fire it sustained considerable injury from the burning coals which were thrown on it; the party were much harrassed also by this fire which

[23] Prairie rattlesnake (*Crotalus viridis viridis*).

communicated to a collection of fallen timber, and could not be extinguished.

[Clark]   May 17th. Friday 1805
We set out at an early hour and proceeded on verry well by the assistance of the Toe rope principally, the countrey verry rugged & hills high and the river washing the bace on each side, great appearances of the Salt substance. a fiew cotton trees is the only timber which is scattered in the bottom & the hills contain a fiew Pine & cedar, which is scattered, river much narrower than below from 2 to 300 yards wide, the bottoms muddey & hills rich earth except near their tops. We passed 2 large creeks to day one on the Starbd Side and the other just below our camp on the Lard Side each of those creeks has a little running water near their mouthes which has a brackish taste, I was nearly treading on a small fierce rattle snake different from any I had ever seen &c. one man [of] the party killed another of the same kind. I walked on Shore after dinner & killed an Elk. the party in my absence killed a female Brown or Yellow Bear which was meagre the appearances of the Hills & countrey is as before mentioned except a greater appearance of the white appearances of salts or tarter and some coal which has been thrown out by the floods in the last creek. Buffalow & Deer is not plenty to day. *Elk* is yet to be seen in abundance we camped in the upper part of a small timbered bottom on the Lard. Side in which I saw a fortified Indian camp, which I suppose is one of the camps of a *Minetarre* war party of about 15 men, that set out from their village in March last to war against the Blackfoot Indians.
We were roused late at night and warned of the danger of fire from a tree which had cought and leaned over our Lodge, we had the lodge moved soon after the Dry limbs & top of the tree fell in the place the lodge stood, the wind blew hard and the dry wood cought & fire flew in every direction, burnt our Lodge verry much from the coals which fell on it altho at some distance in the plain, the whole party were much disturbed by this fire which could not be extinguished &c.

[Lewis]   Saturday May 18th. 1805.
Capt Clark walked on shore with two of the hunters and killed a brown bear; notwithstanding that it was shot through the heart it

ran at it's usual pace near a quarter of a mile before it fell. one of the party wounded a beaver, and my dog as usual swam in to catch it; the beaver bit him through the hind leg and cut the artery; it was with great difficulty that I could stop the blood; I fear it will yet prove fatal to him.

Monday May 20th. 1805.

passed the entrance of a large Creek, affording but little water; this stream we named *Blowing Fly Creek*, from the immence quantitites of those insects found in this neighbourhood, they infest our meat while roasting or boiling, and we are obliged to brush them off our provision as we eat. At 11. A.M. we arrived at the entrance of a handsome bold river which discharges itself into the Missouri on the Lard. side; this stream we take to be that called by the Minnetares the [blank space in MS.] or Muscleshell River

The hunters returned this evening and informed us that the country continued much the same in appearance as that we saw where we were or broken, and that about five miles abe (*above*) the mouth of shell river a handsome river of about fifty yards in width discharged itself into the shell river on the Stard. or upper side; this stream we called Sâh-câ-ger we-âh (*Sah ca gah we a*) or bird woman's River,[24] after our interpreter the Snake woman.

Thursday May 23rd. 1805.

passed the entrance of a creek 15 yds. wide on Stard. side, this we called Teapot Creek, it affords no water at it's mouth but has runing water at some small distance above, this I beleive to be the case with many of those creeks which we have passed since we entered this hilley country, the water is absorbed by the earth near the river and of course appear dry; they afford but little water at any rate, and that is so strongly impregnated with these salts that it is unfit for uce; all the wild anamals appear fond of this water; I have tryed it by way of experiment & find it moderately pergative, but painfull to the intestens in it's opperation.

just above the entrance of Teapot Creek on the stard. there is a large assemblage of the burrows of the Burrowing Squirrel they

---

[24] At present called Crooked Creek. (Thwaites).

generally seelect a south or a south Easterly exposure for their residence, and never visit the brooks or river for water, I am astonished how this anamal exists as it dose without water, particularly in a country like this where there is scarcely any rain during ¾ of the year and more rarely any due [dew]; yet we have sometimes found their villages at the distance of five or six miles from any water, and they are never found out of the limits of the ground which their burrows occupy; in the Autumn when the hard frosts commence they close their burrows and do not venture out again untill spring, indeed some of them appear to be yet in winter quarters. passed 3 Islands the two first covered with tall cottonwood timber and the last with willows only. river more rappid, & the country much the same as yesterday. some spruce pine of small size appears among the pitch pine, and reather more rock than usual on the face of the hills. The musquetoes troublesome this evening, a circumstance I did not expect from the temperature of the morning. The Gees begin to lose the feathers of their wings and are unable to fly.

The wild rose which is now in blume are very abundant, they appear to differ but little from those common to the Atlantic States, the leaves of the bushes and the bush itself appear to be of somewhat smaller size.

Friday May 24th. 1805.
the high country in which we are at present and have been passing for some days I take to be a continuation of what the Indians as well as the French Engages call the Black hills. This tract of country so called consists of a collection of high broken and irregular hills and short chain of mountains sometimes 120 miles in width and again becomeing much narrower, but always much higher than the country on either side

the air is so pure in this open country that mountains and other elivated objects appear much nearer than they really are; these mountains do not appear to be further than 15 M. we sent a man up this creek to explore the country he returned late in the evening and informed that he had proceeded ten miles directly towards these mountains and that he did not think himself by any mean[s] half way these mountains are rockey and covered with some scattering pine.

game is becoming more scarce, particularly beaver, of which we

have seen but few for several days   the beaver appears to keep pace
with the timber   as it declines in quantity they also become more
scarce.

Saturday May 25th 1805
as we ascended the river today I saw several gangs of the bighorned
Anamals[25] on the face of the steep bluffs and clifts on the Stard.
side and sent drewyer to kill one which he accomplished; Capt.
Clark and Bratton who were on shore each killed one of these anamals this evening.   The head and horns of the male which Drewyer
killed weighed 27 lbs.   it was somewhat larger than the male of the
common deer, the boddy reather thicker deeper and not so long in
proportion to it's hight as the common deer; the head and horns are
rema[r]kably large compared with the other part of the anamal;   the
whole form is much more delicate than that of the common goat,
and there is a greater disparity in the size of the male and female
than between those of either the deer or goat.   the eye is large and
prominant, the puple of a deep sea green and small, the iris of a
silvery colour much like the common sheep; the bone above the
eye is remarkably promenant;   the head nostrils and division of the
upper lip are precisely in form like the sheep.   there legs resemble
the sheep more than any other animal with which I am acquainted
tho' they are more delicately formed,   like the sheep they stand
forward in the knee and the lower joint of the foreleg is smallest
where it joins the knee,   the hoof is black & large in proportion, is
divided, very open and roundly pointed at the toe, like the sheep,
is much hollowed and sharp on the under edge like the Scotch goat,
has two small hoofs behind each foot below the ankle as the goat
sheep and deer have.   the belley, inerside of the legs, and the
extremity of the rump and butocks for about two inches arround the
but of the tale, are white, as is also the tale exce[p]t just at it's
extremety on the upper side which is of a dark brown.   the tail is
about three inches in length covered with short hair, or at least not
longer than that of the boddy; the outher parts of the anamal are of
a duskey brown or reather a leadcoloured light brown; the anamal
is now sheding it's winter coat which is thick not quite as long as

[25] Bighorns (*Ovis canadensis*), near the site of James Kipp State Park, Montana.

that of the deer and appears to be intermixed with a considerable quantity of a fine fur which lyes next to the skin & conceald by the coarcer hear; the shape of the hair itself is celindric as that of the antelope is but is smaller, shorter, and not compressed or flattened as that of the deer's winter coat is, I believe this anamal only sheds it's hair once a year. it has eight fore teeth in the under jaw and no canine teeth.

The horns are la[r]gest at their base, and occupy the crown of the head almost entirely. they are compressed, bent backwards and lunated; the surface swelling into wavy rings which incircleing the horn continue to succeed each other from the base to the extremity and becoming less elivated and more distant as they recede from the head. the horn for about two thirds of it's length is filled with a porus bone which is united with the frontal bone. I obtained the bones of the upper part of the head of this animal at the big bone lick.[26] the horns of the female are small, but are also compressed and bent backwards and incircled with a succession of wavy rings. the horn is of a light brown colour; when dressed it is almost white extreemly transparent and very elastic. this horn is used by the natives in constructing their bows; I have no doubt but it would [make] eligant and usefull hair combs, and might probably answer as many valuable purposes to civilized man, as it dose to the savages, who form their water-cups, spoons and platters of it.

the females have already brought forth their young, indeed from the size of the young I suppose that they produce them early in March. they have from one to two at a birth. they feed on grass but principally on the arromatic herbs which grow on the clifts and inaccessable hights which they usually frequent. the places they ge[ne]rally celect to lodg is the cranies or c[r]evices of the rocks in the faces of inacessable precepices, where the wolf nor bear can reach them and where indeed man himself would in many instancies find a smiliar deficiency; yet these anamals bound from rock to rock and stand apparently in the most careless manner on the sides of precipices of many hundred feet. they are very shye and are quick of both sent and sight.

[26] In Kentucky (Thwaites).

[Clark]   May 25th. Satturday 1805[27]

I walked on shore and killed a female *Ibi* or big horn animal   in my absence Drewyer & Bratten killed two ⟨image⟩ others,   this animal is a species peculiar to this upper ⟨image⟩ part of the Missouri, the head and horns of the male   which Drewyer killed to day weighed 27 lbs.   it was somewhat larger than the mail of the Common Deer; the body reather thicker deeper and not so long in proportion to it's hight as the common Deer; the head and horns of the male are remarkably large compared with the other parts of the animal; the whole form is much more delicate than that of the common goat, and there is a greater disparity in the size of the mail and female than between those of either the deer or goat. the eye is large and prominant, the puple of a deep sea green and small, the iris of a silvery colour much like the common Sheep; the bone above the Eye is remarkably prominant; the head nostrils and division of the upper lip are precisely in form like the sheep.   their legs resemble the sheep more than any other animal with which I am acquainted tho' they are more delicately formed,   like the sheep they stand foward in the knee and the lower joint of the fore leg is smallest where it joins the knee, the hoof is black and large in perpotion, is divided, very open and roundly pointed at the toe; like the sheep; is much hollowed and Sharp on the under edge like the Scotch goat,   has two small Hoofs behind each foot below the ankle as the goat Sheep and Deer have.   the belley, iner side of the legs, and the extremity of the rump and buttock's for about two inches ½ around the but of the tail, are white, as is also the tail except just at its extremity on the upper side which is of a dark brown.   the tail is about 3 inches in length covered with short hair, or at least not longer than that of the body; the outer part of the animal are of a duskey brown or reather a lead coloured light brown; the animal is now Sheding its winter coat which is thick not quite as long as that of the Deer and appears to be inter mixt with a considerable quantity of fine fur which lies next to the Skin and concealed by the coarcer hair; the shape of the hair itself is cylindric as that of the Antilope is, but is smaller, shorter and not compressed or flattened as that of the deers winter coat is.   I believe this animal

[27] Clark here copies from Lewis.

only sheds it's hair once a year. it has Eight fore teeth in the under jaw and no canine teeth. The *Horns* are large at their base, and occupy the crown of the head almost entirely, they are compressed, bent backwards and lunated; the surface swelling into wavey rings which incircleing the horn continue to succeed each other from the base to the extremity and becomeing less elivated and more distant as they receed from the head. The horn for about two thirds of its length is filled with a porus bone which is united with the frontal bone (Capt. Lewis obtained the bones of the upper part of the head of this animal at the *big Bone Lick* in the State of Kentucky which I saw and find to be the same in every respect with those of the Missouri and the Rockey Mountains) the horns of the *female* are small, but are also compressed and bent backwards and incircled with a succession of wavy rings. the horn is of a light brown colour; when Dressed it is almost white extreamly transparent and very elastic. this horn is used by the natives in constructing their bows; I have no doubt of it's elegance and usefullness in hair combs, and might probably answer as maney valuable purpoces to civilized man, as it does to the native indians, who form their water cups, spoons and platters of it. the females have already brought forth their young, indeed from the size of the young, I suppose that they produce them early in March. they have from one to two at a birth. they feed on grass, but principally on the arramatic herbs which grow on the clifts and inaxcessable hights which they frequent most commonly, and the places they generally collect to lodge is the cranies of c[r]evices of the rocks in the face of inaccessable prece- pices, where the wolf nor Bear can reach them, and where indeed man himself would in maney instances find a similar deficiency; yet those animals bound from rock to rock and stand apparently in the most careless manner on the Side of precipices of maney hundred feet. they are very shy and quick of both sent and sight. The flesh of this animal is dark and I think inferior to the flesh of the common Deer, and superior to the antilope of the Missouri and the Columbian Plains.

[Lewis]   Sunday May 26th. 1805.

In the after part of the day I also walked out and ascended the river hills which I found sufficiently fortiegueing. on arriving to the summit [of] one of the highest points in the neighbourhood I thought

myself well repaid for my labour; as from this point I beheld the
Rocky Mountains for the first time,[28] these points of the Rocky
Mountains were covered with snow and the sun shone on it in such
manner as to give me the most plain and satisfactory view. while
I viewed these mountains I felt a secret pleasure in finding myself
so near the head of the heretofore conceived boundless Missouri;
but when I reflected on the difficulties which this snowey barrier
would most probably throw in my way to the Pacific, and the suf-
ferings and hardships of myself and party in thim, it in some measure
counterballanced the joy I had felt in the first moments in which I
gazed on them; but as I have always held it a crime to anticipate
evils I will believe it a good comfortable road untill I am compelled
to believe differently.

on my return to the river I passed a creek about 20 yds. wide
near it's entrance it had a handsome little stream of runing water;
in this creek I saw several softshelled Turtles which were the first
that have been seen this season; this I believe proceeded reather
from the season than from their non existence in the portion of the
river from the Mandans hither. on the Stard. shore I killed a fat
buffaloe which was very acceptable to us at this moment;

it was after Dark before we finished butchering the buffaloe, and
on my return to camp I trod within [a] few inches of a rattle snake
but being in motion I passed before he could probably put himself
in a striking attitude and fortunately escaped his bite, I struck about
with my espontoon being directed in some measure by his nois untill
I killed him. Our hunters had killed two of the Bighorned Anamals
since I had left them. we also passed another creek a few miles
from Turtle Creek late this evening we passed a very bad rappid
which reached quite across the river, the party had considerable
difficulty in ascending it altho' they doubled their crews and used
both the rope and the pole. while they were passing this rappid a
female Elk and it's fawn swam down through the waves which ran
very high, hence the name of Elk rappids which they instantly gave
this place, these are the most considerable rappids which we have
yet seen on the missouri and in short the only place where there

---

[28] Lewis mistakes the Bear's Paw range for the actual Rocky Mountains a hundred
miles farther west.

has appeared to be a suddon decent.[29] opposite to these rappids there is a high bluff and a little above on Lard. a small cottonwood bottom in which we found sufficient timber for our fires and encampment. here I rejoined the party after dark. The appearances of coal in the face of the bluffs, also of birnt hills, pumice stone salts and quarts continue as yesterday. This is truly a desert barren country and I feel myself still more convinced of it's being a continuation of the black hills.

[Clark]   May 26th Sunday, 1805
This Countrey may with propriety I think be termed the Deserts of America, as I do not conceive any part can ever be settled, as it is deficent in water, Timber & too steep to be tilled. We pass old Indian lodges in the woody points everry day

                                          Tuesday May 28th 1805.
at 10 A. M. a few drops of rain again fell and were attended with distant thunder which is the first we have heared since we left the Mandans. This evening we encamped on Stard. opposite to the entrance of a small [*Bull*] Creek.[30] I believe the bighorn have their young at a very early season, say early in March, for they appear now to be half grown.

[Lewis]   Wednesday May 29th. 1805
Last night we were all allarmed by a large buffaloe Bull, which swam over from the opposite shore and coming along side of the white perogue, climbed over it to land, he then allarmed ran up the bank in full speed directly towards the fires, and was within 18 inches of the heads of some of the men who lay sleeping before the centinel could allarm him or make him change his course, still more alarmed, he now took his direction immediately towards our lodge, passing between 4 fires and within a few inches of the heads of one range of the men as they yet lay sleeping, when he came near the tent, my dog saved us by causing him to change his course a second time, which he did by turning a little to the right, and was quickly

---

[29] Identified by Coues as Lone Pine Rapids, above Sturgeon Island (Thwaites).
[30] The present Dog Creek, 2½ miles below Judith River (Thwaites). See note 31.

out of sight, leaving us by this time all in an uproar with our guns in o[u]r hands, enquiring of each other the ca[u]se of the alarm, which after a few moments was explained by the centinel: we were happy to find no one hirt.   The next morning we found that the buffaloe in passing the perogue had trodden on a rifle, which belonged to Capt. Clark's black man, who had negligently left her in the perogue,   the rifle was much bent, he had also broken the spindle; pivit, and shattered the stock of one of the blunderbushes on board,   with this damage I felt well content, happey indeed, that we had sustaned no further injury,   it appears that the white perogue, which contains our most valuable stores is attended by some evil genii.

This morning we set out at an early hour and proceded as usual by the Chord.   at the distance of 2½ Miles passed a handsome river which discharged itself on the Lard. side,   I walked on shore and acended this river about a mile and a half in order to examine it. I found this river about 100 yds. wide from bank to bank, the water occupying about 75 yards.   the bed was formed of gravel and mud with some sand; it appeared to contain much more water as (*than*) the Muscle-Shell river, was more rappid but equally navigable; there were no large stone or rocks in it's bed to obstruct the navigation; the banks were low yet appeared seldom to overflow; the water of this River is clearer much than any we have met with   great abundance of the Argalia or Bighorned animals in the high country through which this river passes.   Cap. C. who assended this R. much higher than I did has thought proper to call (*called*) it *Judieths* River.[31]   the bottoms of this stream as far as I could see were wider and contained more timber than the Missouri; here I saw some box alder intermixed with the Cottonwood willow; rose bushes and honeysuckle with some red willow constitute the undergrowth.   on the Missouri just above the entrance of the *Big Horn (Judith) River* I counted the remains of the fires of 126 Indian lodges which appeared to be of very recent date perhaps 12 or 15 days.   Capt. Clark also saw a large encamp[m]ent just above the entrance of this river on

[31] The Judith River, at first named "Bighorn" by Lewis, was afterwards renamed by Clark in honor of Miss Julia Hancock of Fincastle, Virginia, who later became his wife (Thwaites).

the Stard. side of reather older date, probably they were the same Indians. The Indian woman with us ex[a]mined the mockersons which we found at these encampments and informed us that they were not of her nation the Snake Indians, but she believed they were some of the Indians who inhabit the country on this side of [the] Rocky Mountains and North of the Missoury and I think it most probable that they were the Minetaries of Fort de Prarie.

today we passed on the Stard. side the remains of a vast many mangled carcases of Buffalow which had been driven over a precipice of 120 feet by the Indians and perished; the water appeared to have washed away a part of this immence pile of slaughter and still their remained the fragments of at least a hundred carcases they created a most horrid stench. in this manner the Indians of the Missouri distroy vast herds of buffaloe at a stroke; for this purpose one of the most active and fleet young men is scelected and disguised in a robe of buffaloe skin, having also the skin of the buffaloe's head with the years and horns fastened on his head in form of a cap, thus caparisoned he places himself at a convenient distance between a herd of buffaloe and a precipice proper for the purpose, which happens in many places on this river for miles together; the other indians now surround the herd on the back and flanks and at a signal agreed on all shew themselves at the same time moving forward towards the buffaloe; the disguised indian or decoy has taken care to place himself sufficiently nigh the buffaloe to be noticed by them when they take to flight and runing before them they follow him in full speede to the precipice, the cattle behind driving those in front over and seeing them go do not look or hesitate about following untill the whole are precipitated down the precepice forming one common mass of dead an[d] mangled carcases: the decoy in the mean time has taken care to secure himself in some cranney or crivice of the clift which he had previously prepared for that purpose. the part of the decoy I am informed is extreamly dangerous, if they are not very fleet runers the buffaloe tread them under foot and crush them to death, and sometimes drive them over the precipice also, where they perish in common with the buffaloe. we saw a great many wolves in the neighbourhood of these mangled carcases they were fat and extreemly gentle, Capt. C. who was on shore killed one of them with his espontoon. just above this place we came too for

dinner opposite the entrance of a bold runing river 40 Yds. wide
which falls in on Lard. side. this stream we called Slaughter river.³²
   soon after we landed it began to blow & rain, and as there was
no appearance of even wood enough to make our fires for some
distance above we determined to remain here untill the next morning, and accordingly fixed our camp and gave each man a small
dram. notwithstanding the allowance of sperits we issued did not
exceed ½ [*jill*] pr. man several of them were considerably effected
by it; such is the effects of abstaining for some time from the uce
of sperituous liquors; they were all very merry.

                                        Thursday May 30th. 1805.
   many circumstances indicate our near approach to a country whos
climate differs considerably from that in which we have been for
many months. the air of the open country is asstonishingly dry as
well as pure. I found by several experiments that a table spoon
full of water exposed to the air in a saucer would avaporate in 36
hours when the murcury did not stand higher than the temperate
point at the greatest heat of the day; my inkstand so frequently
becoming dry put me on this experiment. I also observed the well
seasoned case of my sextant shrunk considerably and the joints
opened. The water of the river still continues to become clearer
and notwithstanding the rain which has fallen it is still much clearer
than it was a few days past. this day we proceded with more labour
and difficulty than we have yet experienced; in addition to the
imbarrasments of the rappid courant, riffles, & rockey point[s] which
were as bad if not worse than yesterday, the banks and sides of the
bluff were more steep than usual and were now rendered so slippery
by the late rain that the men could scarcely walk. the chord is our
only dependance for the courant is too rappid to be resisted with
the oar and the river too deep in most places for the pole. the earth
and stone also falling from these immence high bluffs render it
dangerous to pass under them. the wind was also hard and against
us. our chords broke several times today but happily without injury
to the vessels. we had slight showers of rain through the course of
the day, the air was could and rendered more disagreeable by the
rain.

   ³² Now Arrow Creek, as named on the maps (Thwaites).

Friday May 31st. 1805.—

soon after we got under way it began to rain and continued untill meridian when it ceased but still remained cloudy through the ballance of the day. The obstructions of rocky points and riffles still continue as yesterday; at those places the men are compelled to be in the water even to their armpits, and the water is yet very could, and so frequent are those point[s] that they are one fourth of their time in the water, added to this the banks and bluffs along which they are obliged to pass are so slippery and the mud so tenacious that they are unable to wear their mockersons, and in that situation draging the heavy burthen of a canoe and walking acasionally for several hundred yards over the sharp fragments of rocks which tumble from the clifts and garnish the borders of the river; in short their labour is incredibly painfull and great, yet those faithfull fellows bear it without a murmur. The toe rope of the white perogue, the only one indeed of hemp, and that on which we most depended, gave way today at a bad point, the perogue swung and but slightly touched a rock; yet was very near overseting; I fear her evil gennii will play so many pranks with her that she will go to the bottomm some of those days.

Capt. C. walked on shore this morning but found it so excessively bad that he shortly returned. at 12 OC.M. we came too for refreshment and gave the men a dram which they received with much cheerfullness, and well deserved.

The hills and river Clifts which we passed today exhibit a most romantic appearance.[33] The bluffs of the river rise to the hight of from 2 to 300 feet and in most places nearly perpendicular; they are formed of remarkable white sandstone which is sufficiently soft to give way readily to the impression of water; two or thre thin horizontal stratas of white freestone, on which the rains or water make no impression, lie imbeded in these clifts of soft stone near the upper part of them; the earth on the top of these Clifts is a dark rich loam, which forming a gradluy ascending plain extends back from ½ a mile to a mile where the hills commence and rise abruptly to a hight of about 300 feet more. The water in the course of time in decending from those hills and plains on either side of the river

[33] White Cliffs in Chouteau County, Montana.

has trickled down the soft sand clifts and woarn it into a thousand grotesque figures, which with the help of a little immagination and an oblique view, at a distance are made to represent eligant ranges of lofty freestone buildings, having their parapets well stocked with statuary; collumns of various sculpture both grooved and plain, are also seen supporting long galleries in front of those buildings; in other places on a much nearer approach and with the help of less immagination we see the remains or ruins of eligant buildings; some collumns standing and almost entire with their pedestals and capitals; others retaining their pedestals but deprived by time or accident of their capitals, some lying prostrate an broken othe[r]s in the form of vast pyramids of conic structure bearing a serees of other pyramids on their tops becoming less as they ascend and finally terminating in a sharp point. nitches and alcoves of various forms and sizes are seen at different hights as we pass. a number of the small martin which build their nests with clay in a globular form attatched to the wall within those nitches, and which were seen hovering about the tops of the collumns did not the less remind us of some of those large stone buildings in the U. States. the thin stratas of hard freestone intermixed with the soft sandstone seems to have aided the water in forming this curious scenery. As we passed on it seemed as if those seens of visionary inchantment would never have and [an] end; for here it is too that nature presents to the view of the traveler vast ranges of walls of tolerable workmanship, so perfect indeed are those walls that I should have thought that nature had attempted here to rival the human art of masonry had I not recollected that she had first began her work.

Sunday June 2nd. 1805.

Game becomeing more abundant this morning and I thought it best now to loose no time or suffer an opportunity to escape in providing the necessary quantity of Elk's skins to cover my leather boat which I now expect I shall be obliged to use shortly. Accordingly I walked on shore most of the day with some of the hunters for that purpose and killed 6 Elk 2 buffal[o]e 2 Mule deer and a bear, these anamals were all in good order we therefore took as much of the meat as our canoes and perogues could conveniently carry. the bear was very near catching Drewyer; it also pursued Charbono who fired his gun in the air as he ran but fortunately

eluded the vigilence of the bear by secreting himself very securely in the bushes untill Drewyer finally killed it by a shot in the head; the (*only*) shot indeed that will conquer the farocity of those tremendious anamals.

in the course of the day we passed 9 Islands all of them small and most of them containing some timber. we came too on the Lard. side in a handsome bottom of small cottonwood timber opposite to the entrance of a very considerable river; but it being too late to ex[a]mine these rivers minutely to night we determined to remain here untill the morning, and as the evening was favourable to make some observations.

Courses and distances June 2nd. 1805.

N. 85.° W.	¾	to a few trees on a Lard. point.	
S. 60.° W.	¼.	Along the Lard. point opposite to a bluff.	
S. 40.° W.	½	to some trees in a Stard. Bend.	
S. 20.° E.	1.	to some willows on the Lard. side	
S. 30.° E.	1.	to a bush on a Stard. point opposite to a low bluff	
South	¼.	Along the Stard. point.	
S. 45.° W.	½.	to a tree in a Lard. bend	
West	2.	to a point on Lard. side opposite to a bluff	
S. 68.° W.	¼.	Along the Lard. shore oppst. an Island.	
S. 35.° W.	¼.	Along the Lard. shore	
S. 25.° W.	1.	to the point of a timbered bottom on Lard.	
South	2 ¾.	to a point on Stard. oppst. a dark bluff, passing three Islands; small.	
S. 60.° W.	1.	Along the Stard. side passing two small Islands on Lard.	
N. 80.° W.	1 ¾	to a Lard. point opposite to a bluff.	
S. 10.° W.	1 ½	to the Lower point of an Island near a Stard. point.	
S. 65.° W.	2.	to a point of timber on the Lard. side opposite a bluff the Island and also another small one near the Stard. side.	
S. 20.° W.	½	to the head of an island	
South	½	to a Point of timber on the Stard. side.	
S. 72.° W.	¼	to a point between two large rivers one of which is 362 Yd. and the 2nd. or right hand fork [*Maria's*] is 200 Yds. wide. encamped on the Lard. shore	
Miles—18.		opposite the junction of those rivers.	

Point of observation No. 25. June 2nd.

On the Lard. side, one mile from the commencement of the 12th. course of this day, observed Meridian Altd. of ☉s. L. L. with Octant by the back observation 57.° 52′. Latitude deduced from this observation [blank space in MS.]

Point of Observation No. 26.

At our encampment of this evening on the Lard. side of the Missouri. Observed time and distance of ☽'s. Western limb from Spica ♍., ✳ East, with Sextant.

	Time	Distance		Time	Distance
	h m s			h m s	
P.M.	10. 58. 53	53.° 56.′ 45 ″	P.M.	11. 30. 43.	53.° 42′ 45 ″
	11. 3. 33	″ 55. 30.		″ . 33. 46	″ 41. 15
	″ . 5. 52	″ . 54. 30.		″ . 36. 2	″ . 40. 15.
	″ . 8. 15.	″ . 52. 30.		″ . 38. 35.	″ . 38. 45.
	″ . 10. 52.	″ . 52. 30.		″ . 41. 28.	″ . 36. 30.
	″ . 13. 16.	″ . 50. 45.		″ . 43. 16.	″ . 36. 15.
	″ . 15. 6.	″ . 49. 15.		″ . 45. 12.	″ . 34. 45.
	″ . 18. 22.	″ . 48. —		″ . 47. —	33. —

Point of Observation No. 27. June 3rd.

On the point formed by the junction of Maria's River and the Missouri, Observed equal altds. of ☉ with Sextant.

	h m s		h m s	
A.M.	8. 57. 19	P.M. 5. 42. 39	⎫	Altd. at the time
	″ . 58. 55.	″ . 44. 14	⎬	of observation.
	Lost by Clouds.	″ 45. 48.	⎭	65.° 12′ —″.

Observed Meridian Altd. of ☉'s. L. L. with	⎫	56.° 6′
Octant by the back observation	⎬	
Latitude deduced from this observation		47.° 24′ 12″ .8

Observed time and distance of ☉.'s and ☽.'s nearest limbs with Sextant ☉. West.

Time.			Distance.				Time.			Distance.		
h	m	s					h	m	s			
P.M.	5.	54.	49.	85.°	47′	30 ″	P.M.	6.	14.	30	85.°	53′	45 ″
	″.	57.	7.	″.	48.	—		″.	16.	56	″.	55.	—
	″.	58.	19	″.	48.	15.		″.	17.	12	″.	55.	30.
	″.	59.	47	″.	48.	45.		″.	18.	12.	″.	55.	30
	6.	2.	8	″.	49.	45.		″.	20.	46.	″.	56.	45
	″.	3.	36	″.	49.	45.		″.	21.	49.	″.	57.	15
	″.	5.	7.	″.	50.	15.		″.	22.	33.	″.	55.	15.
	″.	6.	4.	″.	51.	—		″.	23.	11.	″.	58.	15.

Monday June 3rd. 1805.

This morning early we passed over and formed a camp on the point formed by the junction of the two large rivers. here in the course of the day I continued my observations as are above stated. An interesting question was now to be determined; which of these rivers was the Missouri, or that river which the Minnetares call *Amahte Arz⁻zha* or Missouri, and which they had discribed to us as approaching very near to the Columbia river.[34] to mistake the stream at this period of the season, two months of the traveling season having now elapsed, and to ascend such stream to the rocky Mountain or perhaps much further before we could inform ourselves whether it did approach the Columbia or not, and then be obliged to return and take the other stream would not only loose us the whole of this season but would probably so dishearten the party that it might defeat the expedition altogether. convinced we were that the utmost circumspection and caution was necessary in deciding on the stream to be taken. to this end an investigation of both streams was the first thing to be done; to learn their widths, debths, comparitive rappidity of their courants and thence the comparitive bodies of water furnished by each; accordingly we dispatched two light canoes with three men in each up those streams; we also sent out several small parties by land with instructions to penetrate the country as far as they conveniently can permitting themselves time to return this evening and indeavour if possible to discover the distant bearing of those rivers by ascending the rising grounds.

[34] On May 8, 1805, Lewis and Clark had mistaken the Milk River, which enters the Missouri from the north, as the "River That Scolds All Others." They had not expected the appearance of this second river from the north.

The no[r]th fork is deeper than the other but it's courant not so swift; it's waters run in the same boiling and roling manner which has uniformly characterized the Missouri throughout it's whole course so far; it's waters are of a whitish brown colour very thick and terbid, also characteristic of the Missouri; while the South fork is perfectly transparent runds very rappid but with a smoth unriffled surface it's bottom composed of round and flat smooth stones like most rivers issuing from a mountainous country.   the bed of the N. fork composed of some gravel but principally mud; in short the air & character of this river is so precisely that of the missouri below that the party with very few exceptions have already pronounced the N. fork to be the Missouri; myself and Capt. C. not quite so precipitate have not yet decided but if we were to give our opinions I believe we should be in the minority, certain it is that the North fork gives the colouring matter and character which is retained from hence to the gulph of Mexico.   I am confident that this river rises in and passes a great distance through an open plain country   I expect that it has some of it's sou[r]ces on the Eastern side of the rocky mountain South of the Saskashawan, but that it dose not penetrate the first range of these Mountains. and that much the greater part of it's sources are in a northwardly direction towards the lower and middle parts of the Saskashawan in the open plains. convinced I am that if it penetrated the Rocky Mountains to any great distance it's waters would be clearer unless it should run an immence distance indeed after leaving those mountains through these level plains in order to acquire it's turbid hue.   what astonishes us a little is that the Indians who appeared to be so well acquainted with the geography of this country should not have mentioned this river on wright hand if it be not the Missouri;   *the river that scolds at all others,* as they call it if there is in reallity such an one, ought agreeably to their account, to have fallen in a considerable distance below,   and on the other hand if this right hand or N. fork be the Missouri I am equally astonished at their not mentioning the S. fork which they must have passed in order to get to those large falls which they mention on the Missouri.   thus have our cogitating faculties been busily employed all day.

Those who have remained at camp today have been busily engaged in dressing skins for cloathing, notwithstanding that many of them have their feet so mangled and bruised with the stones and rough ground over which they passed barefoot, that they can scarcely walk or stand; at least it is with great pain they do either. for some days past they were unable to wear their mockersons; they have fallen off considerably, but notwithstanding the difficulties past, or those which seem now to mennace us, they still remain perfectly cheerfull.

In the evening the parties whom we had sent out returned agreeably to instructions. The parties who had been sent up the rivers in canoes informed that they ascended some distance and had then left their canoes and walked up the rivers a considerable distance further barely leaving themselves time to return; the North fork was not so rappid as the other and afforded the easiest navigation of course; Their accounts were by no means satisfactory nor did the information we acquired bring us nigher to the decision of our question or determine us which stream to take.

Capt. C. and myself concluded to set out early the next morning with a small party each, and ascend these rivers untill we could perfectly satisfy ourselves of the one, which it would be most expedient for us to take on our main journey to the Pacific. accordingly it was agreed that I should ascend the right hand fork and he the left.

Thursday June 6th. 1805.

I now became well convinced that this branch of the Missouri had it's direction too much to the North for our rout to the Pacific, and therefore determined to return the next day after taking an observation of the ☉'s. Meridian Altitude in order to fix the latitude of the place. I had sent Sergt. Pryor and Windsor early this morning with orders to procede up the river to some commanding eminence and take it's bearing as far as possible. in the mean time the four others and myself were busily engaged in making two rafts on which we purposed descending the river; we had just completed this work when Sergt. Pryor and Windsor returned, it being about noon

we now took dinner and embarcked with our plunder and five Elk's skins on the rafts but were soon convinced that this mode of navigation was hazardous particularly with those rafts they being too small and slender. we wet a part of our baggage and were near loosing one of our guns; I therefore determined to abandon the rafts

and return as we had come, by land. I regretted much being obliged
to leave my Elk's skins, which I wanted to assist in forming my
leather boat; those we had prepared at Fort Mandan being injured
in such manner that they would not answer.

Friday June 7th. 1805.—

It continued to rain almost without intermission last night and as
I expected we had a most disagreable and wrestless night. our camp
possessing no allurements, we left our watery beads at an early hour
and continued our rout down the river. it still continues to rain the
wind hard from N. E. and could. the grownd remarkably slipry,
insomuch that we were unable to walk on the sides of the bluffs
where we had passed as we ascended the river. notwithstanding
the rain that has now fallen the earth of these bluffs is not wet to a
greater depth than 2 inches; in it's present state it is precisely like
walking over frozan grownd which is thawed to small debth and
slips equally as bad. this clay not only appears to require more
water to saturate it as I before observed than any earth I ever observed but when saturated it appears on the other hand to yeald it's
moisture with equal difficulty.

In passing along the face of one of these bluffs today I sliped at
a narrow pass of about 30 yards in length and but for a quick and
fortunate recovery by means of my espontoon I should been precipitated into the river down a craggy pricipice of about ninety feet.
I had scarcely reached a place on which I could stand with tolerable
safety even with the assistance of my espontoon before I heard a
voice behind me cry out god god Capt. what shall I do on turning
about I found it was Windsor who had sliped and fallen ab[o]ut the
center of this narrow pass and was lying prostrate on his belley, with
his wright hand arm and leg over the precipice while he was holding
on with the left arm and foot as well as he could which appeared
to be with much difficulty. I discovered his danger and the tre-
pedation which he was in gave me still further concern for I expected
every instant to see him loose his strength and slip off; altho' much
allarmed at his situation I disguised my feelings and spoke very
calmly to him and assured him that he was in no kind of danger, to
take the knife out of his belt behind him with his wright hand and
dig a hole with it in the face of the bank to receive his wright foot
which he did and then raised himself to his knees; I then directed

him to take off his mockersons and to come forward on his hands and knees holding the knife in one hand and the gun in the other this he happily effected and escaped.

those who were some little distance b[e]hind returned by my orders and waded the river at the foot of the bluff where the water was breast deep. it was useless we knew to attempt the plains on this part of the river in consequence of the numerous steep ravines which intersected and which were quite as bad as the river bluffs. we therefore continued our rout down the river sometimes in the mud and water of the bottom lands, at others in the river to our breasts and when the water became so deep that we could not wade we cut footsteps in the face of the steep bluffs with our knives and proceded. we continued our disagreeable march th[r]ough the rain mud and water untill late in the evening having traveled only about 18 Miles, and encamped in an old Indian stick lodge which afforded us a dry and comfortable shelter. during the day we had killed six deer some of them in very good order altho' none of them had yet entirely discarded their winter coats. we had reserved and brought with us a good supply of the best peices; we roasted and eat a hearty supper of our venison not having taisted a mo[r]sel before during the day; I now laid myself down on some willow boughs to a comfortable nights rest, and felt indeed as if I was fully repaid for the toil and pain of the day, so much will a good shelter, a dry bed, and comfortable supper revive the sperits of the w[e]aryed, wet and hungry traveler.

FIVE

The Thundering Falls

From Marias River to Great Falls
June 8–July 13, 1805

[Lewis]   Saturday June 8th. 1805.—
   we breakfasted and set out about sunrise and continued our rout
down the river bottoms through the mud and water as yesterday,
tho' the road was somewhat better than yesterday and we were not
so often compelled to wade in the river.   we passed some dangerous
and difficult bluffs.   The river bottoms affording all the timber which
is to be seen in the country they are filled with innumerable little
birds that resort thither either for shelther or to build their nests.
when sun began to shine today these birds appeared to be very gay
and sung most inchantingly; I observed among them the brown
thrush, Robbin, turtle dove linnit goaldfinch, the large and small
blackbird, wren and several other birds of less note.   some of the
inhabitants of the praries also take reffuge in these woods at night
or from a storm.
   The whole of my party to a man except myself were fully
pe[r]suaided that this river was the Missouri, but being fully of
opinion that it was neither the main stream, nor that which it would
be advisable for us to take, I determined to give it a name and in

honour of Miss Maria W——d.[1] called it Maria's River. it is true
that the hue of the waters of this turbulent and troubled stream but
illy comport with the pure celestial virtues and amiable qualifications
of that lovely fair one; but on the other hand it is a noble river; one
destined to become in my opinion an object of contention between
the two great powers of America and Great Britin with rispect to
the adjustment of the Northwestwardly boundary of the former;
and that it will become one of the most interesting branc[h]es of
the Missouri in a commercial point of view, I have but little doubt,
as it abounds with anamals of the fur kind, and most probably
furnishes a safe and direct communication to that productive country
of valuable furs exclusively enjoyed at present by the subjects of
his Britanic Majesty; in adition to which it passes through a rich
fertile and one of the most beatifully picteresque countries that I
ever beheld, through the wide expance of which, innumerable herds
of living anamals are seen, it's borders garnished with one continued
garden of roses, while it's lofty and open forrests are the habitation
of miriads of the feathered tribes who salute the ear of the passing
traveler with their wild and simple, yet s[w]eet and cheerfull mel-
ody. I arrived at camp about 5 OClock in the evening much fatiegued, where I found Capt. Clark and the ballance of the party
waiting our return with some anxiety for our safety having been
absent near two days longer than we had engaged to return.

I now gave myself this evening to rest from my labours, took a
drink of grog and gave the men who had accompanyed me each a
dram. Capt. Clark ploted the courses of the two rivers as far as we
had ascended them.

Sunday June 9th. 1805.
We determined to deposite at this place the large red perogue all
the heavy baggage which we could possibly do without and some
provision, salt, tools powder and Lead &c with a view to lighten
our vessels and at the same time to strengthen their crews by means

---

[1] Maria Wood was Lewis's cousin. Lewis correctly determines Marias River to be
a tributary of the Missouri; however, if the explorers had mistaken it for the Missouri
itself, their route up the Marias and through Marias Pass would ironically have saved
them two months of travel.

of the seven hands who have been heretofore employd. in navigating the red perogue; accordingly we set some hands to diging a hole or cellar for the reception of our stores.   these holes in the ground or deposits are called by the engages *cashes* (*cachés*); on enquiry I found that Cruzatte was well acquainted [with] this business and therefore left the management of it intirely to him.   today we examined our maps, and compared the information derived as well from them as [from] the Indians and fully settled in our minds the propryety of addopting the South fork for the Missouri, as that which it would be most expedient for us to take.

The Indian information also argued strongly in favour of the South fork.   they informed us that the water of the Missouri was nearly transparent at the great falls, this is the case with the water of the South fork; that the falls lay a little to the South of sunset from them; this is also probable as we are only a few minutes North of Fort Mandan and the South fork bears considerably South from hence to the Mountains;   another impression on my mind is that if the Indians had passed any stream as large as the South fork on their way to the Missouri that they would not have omitted mentioning it; and the South fork from it's size and complexion of it's waters must enter the Ry. Mountains and in my opinion penetrates them to a great distance, or els whence such an immence body of water as it discharges;   it cannot procede from the dry plains to the N.W. of the Yellow Stone river on the East side of the Rocky Mountains for those numerous large dry channels which we witnessed on that side as we ascended the Missouri forbid such a conjecture

Those ideas as they occurred to me I indevoured to impress on the minds of the party all of whom except Capt. C. being still firm in the belief that the N. Fork was the Missouri and that which we ought to take;   they said very cheerfully that they were ready to follow us any wher we thought proper to direct but that they still thought that the other was the river and that they were affraid that the South fork would soon termineate in the mountains and leave us at a great distance from the Columbia.   Cruzatte who had been an old Missouri navigator and who from his integrity knowledge and skill as a waterman had acquired the confidence of every individual of the party declared it as his opinion that the N. fork was the true

genuine Missouri and could be no other. finding them so determined
in this beleif, and wishing that if we were in an error to be able to
detect it and rectify it as soon as possible it was agreed between
Capt. C. and myself that one of us should set out with a small party
by land up the South fork and continue our rout up it untill we
found the falls or reached the snowy Mountains by which means we
should be enabled to determine this question prety accurately. this
expedition I prefered undertaking as Capt. C. [is the] best waterman
&c. and determined to set out the day after tomorrow; I wished
to make some further observations at this place, and as we had
determined to leave our blacksmith's bellows and tools here it was
necessary to repare some of our arms, and particularly my Airgun
the main spring of which was broken, before we left this place.
these and some other preperations will necessarily detain us two
perhaps three days. I felt myself very unwell this morning and took
a portion of salts from which I feel much releif this evening.

The cash being completed I walked to it and examined it's construction. it is in a high plain about 40 yards distant from a steep
bluff of the South branch on it's no[r]thern side; the situation a dry
one which is always necessary. a place being fixed on for a cash,
a circle ab[o]ut 20 inches in diameter is first discribed, the terf or
sod of this circle is carefully removed, being taken out as entire as
possible in order that it may be replaced in the same situation when
the chash is filled and secured. this circular hole is then sunk
perpendicularly to the debth of one foot, if the ground be not firm
somewhat deeper. they then begin to work it out wider as they
proceed downwards untill they get it about six or seven feet deep
giving it nearly the shape of the kettle or lower part of a large still.
it's bottom is also somewhat sunk in the center. the dementions
of the cash is in proportion to the quantity of articles intended to
be deposited. as the earth is dug it is handed up in a vessel and
carefully laid on a skin or cloth and then carryed to some place where
it can be thrown in such manner as to conseal it usually into some
runing stream wher it is washed away and leaves no traces which
might lead to the discovery of the cash. before the goods are deposited they must be well dryed; a parsel of small dry sticks are
then collected and with then [them] a floor is maid of three or four
inches thick which is then covered with some dry hay or a raw hide

well dryed; on this the articles are deposited, taking care to keep
them from touching the walls by putting other dry sticks between
as you stoe away the merchandize,   when nearly full the goods are
covered with a skin and earth thrown in and well ramed untill with
the addition of the turf furst removed the whole is on a level with
the serface of the ground.   in this manner dryed skins or merchandize will keep perfectly sound for several years.   the traders of the
Missouri particularly those engaged in the trade with the Siouxs are
obliged to have frequent recourse to this method in order to avoyd
being robed.

most of the men are busily engaged dressing skins for cloathing.
In the evening Cruzatte gave us some music on the violin and the
men passed the evening in dancing singing &c and were extreemly
cheerfull.

Monday June 10th. 1805.

Shields renewed the main-spring of my air-gun we have been
much indebted to the ingenuity of this man on many occasions;
without having served any regular apprenticeship to any trade, he
makes his own tools principally and works extreemly well in either
wood or metal, and in this way has been extreemly servicable to us,
as well as being a good hunter and an excellent waterman.

At 3 P.M. we had a hard wind from the S. W. which continued
about an hour attended with thunder and rain.   as soon as the shower
had passed over we drew out our canoes, corked, repared and loaded
them.   I still feel myself somewhat unwell with the disentary, but
determined to set out in the morning up the South fork or Missouri
leaving Capt. Clark to compleat the deposit and follow me by water
with the party; accordingly gave orders to Drewyer, Joseph Fields,
Gibson and Goodrich to hold themselves in readiness to accompany
me in the morning.   *Sah-câh-gâh, we â,* our Indian woman is very
sick this evening; Capt. C. blead her.   the night was cloudy with
some rain.

I saw a small bird today which I do not recollect ever having seen
before, it is about the size of the blue thrush or catbird, and it's
contour not unlike that bird.   the beak is convex, moderately
curved, black, smoth, and large in proportion to its size.   the legs
were black, it had four toes of the same colour on ea[c]h foot, and
the nails appeared long and somewhat in form like the tallons of

the haulk [hawk], the eye black and proportionably large. a bluish brown colour occupyed the head, neck, and back, the belly was white; the tail was reather long in proportion and appeared to be composed of feathers of equal length of which a part of those in the center were white the others black. the wings were long and were also varigated with white and black. on each side of the head from the beak back to the neck a small black stripe extended imbrasing the eye. it appeared to be very busy in catching insects which I presume is it's usual food; I found the nest of this little bird, the female which differed but little in size or plumage from the male was seting on four eggs of a pale blue colour with small black freckles or dots.[2]

the bee martin or *Kingbird* is common to this country; tho' there are no bees in this country, nor have we met with a honey bee since we passed the entrance of the Osage River.

[Clark]   June 10th. Monday 1805
we drew up our large Perogue into the middle of a small Island in the North fork and covered her with bushes after makeing her fast to the trees, branded several trees to prevent the Indians injureing her, at 3 oClock we had hard wind from the S.W. thunder and rain for about an hour after which we repaired & corked the canoes & loadded them. Sahcahgagweâ our Indian woman verry sick I blead her, we deturmined to assend the South fork, and one of us, Capt. Lewis or my self to go by land as far as the Snow mountains S. 20° W. and examine the river & countrey course &c. to be certain of our assending the proper river, Capt. Lewis inclines to go by land on this expedition, according selects 4 men George Drewyer, Gibson, J. Fields & S. Gutrich to accompany him & deturmine to set out in the morning. The after noon or night cloudy some rain, river riseing a little.

[Lewis]   Tuesday June 11th. 1805.
This morning I felt much better, but somewhat w[e]akened by my disorder. at 8 A.M. I swung my pack, and set forward with my little party. proceeded to the point where Rose River a branch [of]

---

[2] Loggerhead shrike (*Lanius ludovicianus*).

Maria's River approaches the Missouri so nearly. from this hight we discovered a herd of Elk on the Missouri just above us to which we desended and soon killed four of them. we butchered them and hung up the meat and skins in view of the river in order that the party might get them. I determined to take dinner here, but before the meal was prepared I was taken with such violent pain in the intestens that I was unable to partake of the feast of marrow-bones. my pain still increased and towards evening was attended with a high fever; finding myself unable to march, I determined to prepare a camp of some willow boughs and remain all night. having brought no medecine with me I resolved to try an experiment with some simples; and the Choke cherry which grew abundantly in the bottom first struck my attention; I directed a parsel of the small twigs to be geathered striped of their leaves, cut into pieces of about 2 Inches in length and boiled in water untill a strong black decoction of an astringent bitter tast was produced; at sunset I took a point [pint] of this decoction and ab[o]ut an hour after repeated the d[o]ze by 10 in the evening I was entirely releived from pain and in fact every symptom of the disorder forsook me; my fever abated, a gentle perspiration was produced and I had a comfortable and refreshing nights rest Goodrich who is remarkably fond of fishing caught several douzen fish of two different species—one about 9 inches long of white colour round and in form and fins resembles the white chub common to the Potomac; this fish has a smaller head than the Chubb and the mouth is beset both above and below with a rim of fine sharp teeth; the eye moderately large, the puple dark and the iris which is narrow is of a yellowish brown colour, they bite at meat or grasshoppers. this is a soft fish, not very good, tho' the flesh is of a fine white colour.[3]

[Clark]   June 11th. Tuesday 1805
a fair morning wind from the S W. hard we burry 1 keg in the cach & 2 canisters of Powder in 2 seperate places all with Lead; & in the cach 2 axes, auger, Plains, 1 keg flour, 2 kegs Pork, 2 Kegs Parched meal 1 keg salt, files, chisel, 2 Musquits, some tin cups, Howel, 3 bear skins, Beaver Skins, Horns, & parts of the mens

---

[3] Mooneye (*Hiodon tergisus*).

robes & clothes.   Beaver Traps and blacksmith's tools.   Capt. Lewis set out at 8 oClock   we delayed to repair some guns out of order & complete our deposit, which took us the day   the evening fair and fine wind from the N.W.   after night it became cold & the wind blew hard,   the Indian woman verry sick,   I blead her which appeared to be of great service to her,   both rivers riseing fast

[Lewis]   Wednesday June 12th. 1805.
This morning I felt myself quite revived, took another portion of my decoction and set out at sunrise. I left a note on a stick near the river for Capt. Clark, informing him of my progress &c.

This evening I ate very heartily and after pening the transactions of the day amused myself catching those white fish mentioned yesterday; they are here in great abundance   I caught upwards of a douzen in a few minutes; they bit most freely at the melt [milt] of a deer which goodrich had brought with him for the purpose of fishing.

The narrow leafed cottonwood grows here in common with the other species of the same tree with a broad leaf or that which has constituted the major part of the timber of the Missouri from it's junction with the Mississippi to this place. The narrow-leafed cottonwood differs only from the other in the shape of it's leaf and greater thickness of it's bark.   the leaf is a long oval acutely pointed, about 2½ or 3 Inches long and from ¾ to an inch in width; it is thick, sometimes slightly grooved or channeled; margin slightly serrate; the upper disk of a common green while the under disk is of a whitish green; the leaf is smoth.   the beaver appear to be extremely fond of this tree and even seem to scelect it from among the other species of Cottonwood, probably from it's affording a deeper and softer bark than the other species.

[Clark]   June 12th. 1805 Wednesday
last night was clear and cold, this morning fair   we set out at 8 oClock & proceeded on verry well   wind from the S.W. The enterpreters wife verry *sick* so much so that I move her into the back part of our covered part of the Perogue which is cool, her own situation being a verry hot one in the bottom of the Perogue exposed to the Sun.   Saw a number of rattle snakes to day one of the men cought one by the head in catchig hold of a bush on which his head

lay reclined   three canoes were in great danger to day one diped
water, another very near turning over &c.   at 2 oClock P M a fiew
drops of rain   I walked thro' a point and killed a Buck Elk & Deer,
and we camped on the Stard Side,   the Interpreters woman verry
sick   one man have a fellon riseing on his hand   one other with the
Tooth ake has taken cold in the Jaw &c.

[Lewis]   Thursday June 13th. 1805.
   I had proceded about two miles with Goodrich at some distance
behind me whin my ears were saluted with the agreeable sound of
a fall of water and advancing a little further I saw the spray arrise
above the plain like a collumn of smoke which would frequently
dispear again in an instant caused I presume by the wind which
blew pretty hard from the S.W. I did not however loose my direction
to this point which soon began to make a roaring too tremendious
to be mistaken for any cause short of the great falls of the Missouri.
   I hurryed down the hill which was about 200 feet high and difficult
of access, to gaze on this sublimely grand specticle.
   immediately at the cascade the river is about 300 yrds. wide; about
ninty or a hundred yards of this next the Lard. bluff is a smoth even
sheet of water falling over a precipice of at least eighty feet,   the
remaining part of about 200 yards on my right formes the grandest
sight I ever beheld,   the hight of the fall is the same of the other
but the irregular and somewhat projecting rocks below receives the
water in it's passage down and brakes it into a perfect white foam
which assumes a thousand forms in a moment sometimes flying up
in jets of sparkling foam to the hight of fifteen or twenty feet and
are scarcely formed before large roling bodies of the same beaten
and foaming water is thrown over and conceals them.   in short the
rocks seem to be most happily fixed to present a sheet of the whitest
beaten froath for 200 yards in length and about 80 feet perpendicular.
the water after decending strikes against the butment before mentioned or that on which I stand and seems to reverberate and being
met by the more impetuous courant they roll and swell into half
formed billows of great hight which rise and again disappear in an
instant.
   the buffaloe have a large beaten road to the water, for it is but in
very few places that these anamals can obtain water near this place
owing to the steep and inaccessible banks.   I see several skelletons

of the buffaloe lying in the edge of the water near the Stard. bluff which I presume have been swept down by the current and precipitated over this tremendious fall.

from the reflection of the sun on the sprey or mist which arrises from these falls there is a beatifull rainbow produced which adds not a little to the beauty of this majestically grand senery. after wrighting this imperfect discription I again viewed the falls and was so much disgusted with the imperfect idea which it conveyed of the scene that I determined to draw my pen across it and begin agin, but then reflected that I could not perhaps succeed better than pening the first impressions of the mind; I wished for the pencil of Salvator Rosa or the pen of Thompson, that I might be enabled to give to the enlightened world some just idea of this truly magnificent and sublimely grand object, which has from the commencement of time been concealed from the view of civilized man; but this was fruitless and vain. I most sincerely regreted that I had not brought a crimee [camera] obscura with me by the assistance of which even I could have hoped to have done better but alas this was also out of my reach; I therefore with the assistance of my pen only indeavoured to trace some of the stronger features of this seen by the assistance of which and my recollection aided by some able pencil I hope still to give to the world some faint idea of an object which at this moment fills me with such pleasure and astonishment; and which of it's kind I will venture to ascert is second to but one in the known world. I retired to the shade of a tree where I determined to fix my camp for the present and dispatch a man in the morning to inform Capt. C. and the party of my success in finding the falls and settle in their minds all further doubts as to the Missouri.

Goodrich had caught half a douzen very fine trout and a number of both species of the white fish. these trout are from sixteen to twenty three inches in length, precisely resemble our mountain or speckled trout in form and the position of their fins, but the specks on these are of a deep black instead of the red or goald colour of those common to the U'. States. these are furnished long sharp teeth on the pallet and tongue and have generally a small dash of red on each side behind the front ventral fins; the flesh is of a pale yellowish red, or when in good order, of a rose red.[4]

[4] Cutthroat trout (*Salmo clarkii*).

I am induced to believe that the Brown, the white and the Grizly bear of this country are the same species only differing in colour from age or more probably from the same natural cause that many other anamals of the same family differ in colour. one of those which we killed yesterday was of a creem-coloured white while the other in company with it was of the common bey or r[e]dish brown, which seems to be the most usual color of them.

My fare is really sumptuous this evening; buffaloe's humps, tongues and marrowbones, fine trout parched meal pepper and salt, and a good appetite; the last is not considered the least of the luxuries.

[Clark]   June 13th. Thursday 1805
a fair morning, some dew this morning   the Indian woman verry sick   I gave her a doste of salts.   we set out early,   at a mile & ½ passed a small rapid stream on the Lard Side which heads in a mountain to the S.E 12 or 15 miles, which at this time is covered with Snow,   we call this stream Snow river,[5] as it is the conveyance of the melted snow from that mountain at present.   numbers of Gees & Goslings, the gees cannot fly at this season.   goose berries are ripe and in great abundance, the yellow current is also common, not yet ripe   killed a buffalow & camped on the Lard Side near an old Indian fortified camp one man sick & 3 with swellings,   the Indian woman verry sick.   Killed a goat & fraser 2 Buffalow
The river verry rapid maney sholes great nos of large stones, passed some bluffs or low cliffts of slate to day

[Lewis]   Friday June 14th. 1805.
This morning at sunrise I dispatched Joseph Fields with a letter to Capt. Clark and ordered him to keep sufficiently near the river to observe it's situation in order that he might be enabled to give Capt. Clark an idea of the point at which it would be best to halt to make our portage.   about ten O'Clock this morning while the men were engaged with the meat I took my Gun and espontoon and thought I would walk a few miles and see where the rappids

[5] Now Shonkin River, falling into the Missouri just below Fort Benton, Montana (Thwaites).

termineated above, and return to dinner. after passing one continued rappid and three small cascades of ab[o]ut for or five feet each
at the distance of about five miles I arrived at a fall of about 19 feet;
the river is here about 400 yrds. wide. this pitch which I called
the crooked falls occupys about threefourths of the width of the
river

I should have returned from hence but hearing a tremendious
roaring above me I continued my rout across the point of a hill a
few hundred yards further and was again presented by one of the
most beatifull objects in nature, a cascade of about fifty feet perpendicular streching at rightangles across the river from side to side
to the distance of at least a quarter of a mile. here the river pitches
over a shelving rock, with an edge as regular and as streight as if
formed by art, without a nich or brake in it; the water decends in
one even and uninterupted sheet to the bottom wher dashing against
the rocky bottom [it] rises into foaming billows of great hight and
rappidly glides away, hising flashing and sparkling as it departs   the
sprey rises from one extremity to the other to 50f. I now thought
that if a skillfull painter had been asked to make a beautifull cascade
that he would most probably have p[r]esented the precise immage
of this one; nor could I for some time determine on which of those
two great cataracts to bestoe the palm, on this or that which I had
discovered yesterday; at length I determined between these two
great rivals for glory that this was *pleasingly beautifull*, while the other
was *sublimely grand*.[6]

a beatifull little Island well timbered is situated about the middle
of the river. in this Island on a Cottonwood tree an Eagle has placed
her nest; a more inaccessable spot I beleive she could not have
found; for neither man nor beast dare pass those gulphs which seperate her little domain from the shores. the water is also broken
in such manner as it decends over this pitch that the mist or sprey
rises to a considerable hight. this fall[7] is certainly much the greatest
I ever behald except those two which I have mentioned below. it
is incomparably a g[r]eater cataract and a more noble interesting
object than the celibrated falls of Potomac or Soolkiln [Schuylkill]
&c.

[6] Colter Falls and Rainbow Falls.
[7] Black Eagle Falls.

just above this is another cascade of about 5 feet, above which the water as far as I could see began to abate of it's volosity, and I therefore determined to ascend the hill behind me which promised a fine prospect of the adjacent country, nor was I disappointed on my arrival at it's summit. from hence I overlooked a most beatifull and extensive plain reaching from the river to the base of the Snow-clad mountains to the S. and S. West; I also observed the missoury streching it's meandering course to the South through this plain to a great distance filled to it's even and grassey brim; in these plains and more particularly in the valley just below me immence herds of buffaloe are feeding. the missouri just above this hill makes a bend to the South where it lies a smoth even and unruffled sheet of water of nearly a mile in width bearing on it's watry bosome vast flocks of geese which feed at pleasure in the delightfull pasture on either border. the young geese are now completely feathered except the wings which both in the young and old are yet deficient. after feasting my eyes on this ravishing prospect and resting myself a few minutes I determined to procede as far as the river which I saw discharge itself on the West side of the Missouri convinced that it was the river which the Indians call *medecine river* and which they informed us fell into the Missouri just above the falls.

I decended the hill and directed my course to the bend of the Missouri near which there was a herd of at least a thousand buffaloe; here I thought it would be well to kill a buffaloe and leave him untill my return from the river and if I then found that I had not time to get back to camp this evening to remain all night here there being a few sticks of drift wood lying along shore which would answer for my fire, and a few s[c]attering cottonwood trees a few hundred yards below which would afford me at least the semblance of a shelter. under this impression I scelected a fat buffaloe and shot him very well, through the lungs; while I was gazeing attentively on the poor anamal discharging blood in streams from his mouth and nostrils, expecting him to fall every instant, and having entirely forgotten to reload my rifle, a large white, or reather brown bear, had perceived and crept on me within 20 steps before I discovered him; in the first moment I drew up my gun to shoot, but at the same instant recolected that she was not loaded and that he was too near for me to hope to perform this opperation before he reached me, as he was then briskly advancing on me; it was an open level plain, not a bush within miles nor a tree within less than three hundred yards of me; the river bank was sloping and not more than three feet above the level of the water; in short there was no place by means of which I could conceal myself from this monster untill I could charge my rifle;   in this situation I thought of retreating in a brisk walk as fast as he was advancing untill I could reach a tree about 300 yards below me, but I had no sooner terned myself about but he pitched at me, open mouthed and full speed,   I ran about 80 yards and found he gained on me fast, I then run into the water   the idea struk me to get into the water to such debth that I could stand and he would be obliged to swim, and that I could in that situation defend myself with my espontoon; accordingly I ran haistily into the water about waist deep, and faced about and presented the point of my espontoon,   at this instant he arrived at the edge of the water within about 20 feet of me; the moment I put myself in this attitude of defence he sudonly wheeled about as if frightened, declined the combat on such unequal grounds, and retreated with quite as great precipitation as he had just before pursued me.   as soon as I saw him run of[f] in that manner I returned to the shore and charged my gun, which I had still retained in my hand throughout this curious adventure. I saw him run through the level open plain about three miles, till he disappeared in the woods on medecine river; during the whole of this distance he ran at full speed, sometimes appearing to look behind him as if he expected pursuit.

I now began to reflect on this novil occurrence and indeavoured to account for this sudden retreat of the bear.   I at first thought that perhaps he had not smelt me bofore he arrived at the waters edge so near me, but I then reflected that he had pursued me for about 80 or 90 yards before I took [to] the water and on examination saw the grownd toarn with his tallons immediately on the imp[r]ession of my steps; and the cause of his allarm still remains with me misterious and unaccountable.   so it was and I felt myself not a little gratifyed that he had declined the combat.   my gun reloaded I felt confidence once more in my strength; and determined not to be thwarted in my design of visiting medecine river, but determined never again to suffer my peice to be longer empty than the time she necessarily required to charge her.

having examined Medecine river[8] I now determined to return, having by my estimate about 12 miles to walk. I looked at my watch and found it was half after six P.M. in returning through the level bottom of Medecine river and about 200 yards distant from the Missouri, my direction led me directly to an anamal that I at first supposed was a wolf; but on nearer approach or about sixty paces distant I discovered that it was not, it's colour was a brownish yellow; it was standing near it's burrow, and when I approached it thus nearly, it couched itself down like a cat looking immediately at me as if it designed to spring on me. I took aim at it and fired, it instantly disappeared in it's burrow; I loaded my gun and ex[a]mined the place which was dusty and saw the track from which I am still further convinced that it was of the tiger kind. whether I struck it or not I could not determine, but I am almost confident that I did; my gun is true and I had a steady rest by means of my espontoon, which I have found very serviceable to me in this way in the open plains.

It now seemed to me that all the beasts of the neighbourhood had made a league to distroy me, or that some fortune was disposed to amuse herself at my expence, for I had not proceded more than three hundred yards from the burrow of this tyger cat, before three bull buffaloe, which wer feeding with a large herd about half a mile from me on my left, seperated from the herd and ran full speed towards me, I thought at least to give them some amusement and altered my direction to meet them; when they arrived within a hundred yards they mad[e] a halt, took a good view of me and retreated with precipitation. I then continued my rout homewards passed the buffaloe which I had killed, but did not think it prudent to remain all night at this place which really from the succession of curious adventures wore the impression on my mind of inchantment; at sometimes for a moment I thought it might be a dream, but the prickley pears which pierced my feet very severely once in a while, particularly after it grew dark, convinced me that I was really awake, and that it was necessary to make the best of my way to camp.

it was sometime after dark before I returned to the party; I found them extremely uneasy for my safety; they had formed a thousand

[8] Now known as Sun River (Thwaites).

conjectures, all of which equally forboding my death, which they had so far settled among them, that they had already agreed on the rout which each should take in the morning to surch for me. I felt myself much fortiegued, but eat a hearty supper and took a good night's rest.

[Clark]   June 14th. Friday 1805
a fine morning   the Indian woman complaining all night & excessively bad this morning.   her case is somewhat dangerous.   two men with the Tooth ake 2 with Tumers, & one man with a Tumor & a slight fever   passed the camp Capt. Lewis made the 1st night at which place he had left part of two bear their skins &c.   three men with Tumers went on shore and stayed out all night   one of them killed 2 buffalow, a part of which we made use of for brackfast, the current excesevely rapid more so as we assend   we find great dificuelty in getting the Perogue & canoes up in safety, canoes take in water frequently,   at 4 oClock this evening Jo: Fields returned from Capt. Lewis with a letter for me,   Capt. Lewis dates his letter from the Great falls of the Missouri, which Fields informs me is about 20 miles in advance & about 10 miles above the place I left the river the time I was up last week   Capt L informs the [me] that those falls, in part answer the discription given of them by the Indians, much higher the Eagles nest which they describe is there, from those signs he is convinced of this being the river the Indians call the Missouri

[Lewis]   Saturday June 15th. 1805.
This morning the men again were sent to bring in some more meat which Drewyer had killed yesterday, and continued the opperation of drying it.   I amused myself in fishing, and sleeping away the fortiegues of yesterday.   I caught a number of very fine trout which I made goodrich dry; goodrich also caught about two douzen and several small cat of a yellow colour which would weigh about 4 lbs.   the tail was seperated with a deep angular nitch like that of the white cat of the missouri from which indeed they differed only in colour.   when I awoke from my sleep today I found a large rattlesnake coiled on the leaning trunk of a tree under the shade of which I had been lying at the distance of about ten feet from him. I killed the snake and found that he had 176 scuta on the abdomen

and 17 half formed scuta on the tale; it was of the same kinde which I had frequently seen before; they do not differ in their colours from the rattle-snake common to the middle attlantic states, but considerably in the form and figures of those colours. This evening after dark Joseph Fields returned and informed me that Capt Clark had arrived with the party at the foot of a rappid about 5 miles below which he did not think proper to ascend and would wait my arrival there. I had discovered from my journey yesterday that a portage on this side of the river will be attended by much difficulty in consequence of several deep ravenes which intersect the plains

[Clark]   June the 15th. Satturday 1805
    a fair morning and worm, we set out at the usial time and proceeded on with great dificuelty as the river is more rapid we can hear the falls this morning verry distinctly. our Indian woman sick & low spirited I gave her the bark & apply it exteranely to her region which revived her much. the current excessively rapid and dificuelt to assend great numbers of dangerous places, and the fatigue which we have to encounter is incretiatable the men in the water from morning untill night hauling the cord & boats walking on sharp rocks and round sliperery stones which alternately cut their feet & throw them down, notwith standing all this dificuelty they go with great chearfulness, aded to those dificuelties the rattle snakes [are] inumerable & require great caution to prevent being bitten. below this little [river], we pass a white clay which mixes with water like flour in every respect

                                        June 16th. of Sunday 1805
    the Indian woman verry bad, & will take no medisin what ever, untill her husband finding her out of her sences, easyly provailed on her to take medison, if she dies it will be the fault of her husband as I am now convinced.

[Lewis]   Sunday June 16th. 1805.
    J. Fields set out early on his return to the lower camp, at noon the men arrived and shortly after I set out with them to rejoin the party, we took with us the dryed meat consisting of about 600 lbs. and several douzen of dryed trout.
    about 2 P.M. I reached the camp found the Indian woman ex-

treemly ill and much reduced by her indisposition. this gave me some concern as well for the poor object herself, then with a young child in her arms, as from the consideration of her being our only dependence for a friendly negociation with the Snake Indians on whom we depend for horses to assist us in our portage from the Missouri to the columbia river.

one of the small canoes was left below this rappid in order to pass and repass the river for the purpose of hunting as well as to procure the water of the Sulpher spring, the virtues of which I now resolved to try on the Indian woman. the water is as transparent as possible strongly impreganted with sulpher, and I suspect Iron also, as the colour of the hills and bluffs in the neighbourhood indicate the existence of that metal. the water to all appearance is precisely similar to that of Bowyer's Sulpher spring in Virginia.

I found that two dozes of barks and opium which I had given her since my arrival had produced an alteration in her pulse for the better; they were now much fuller and more regular. I caused her to drink the mineral water altogether. w[h]en I first came down I found that her pulse were scarcely perceptible, very quick frequently irregular and attended with strong nervous symptoms, that of the twitching of the fingers and leaders of the arm; now the pulse had become regular much fuller and a gentle perspiration had taken place; the nervous symptoms have also in a great measure abated, and she feels herself much freer from pain. she complains principally of the lower region of the abdomen, I therefore continued the cataplasms of barks and laudnum which had been previously used by my friend Capt. Clark. I beleive her disorder originated principally from an obstruction of the mensis in consequence of taking could. I determined to remain at this camp in order to make some celestial observations, restore the sick woman, and have all matters in a state of readiness to commence the portage immediately on the return of Capt. Clark, who now furnished me with the dayly occurrences which had taken place with himself and party since our seperation

Monday June 17th. 1805.
Capt. Clark set out early this morning with five me[n] to examine the country and survey the river and portage as had been concerted last evening. I set six men at work to p[r]epare four sets of truck

wheels with couplings, toungs and bodies, that they might either be used without the bodies for transporting our canoes, or with them in transporting our baggage I found that the Elk skins I had prepared for my boat were insufficient to compleat her, some of them having become dammaged by the weather and being frequently wet; to make up this deficiency I sent out two hunters this morning to hunt Elk

we found much difficulty in geting the canoes up this creek to the distance we were compelled to take them, in consequence of the rappids and rocks which obstruct the channel of the creek. one of the canoes overset and was very near injuring 2 men essentially.

just above the canoes the creek has a perpendicular fall of 5 feet and the cliffs again become very steep and high. we were fortunate enough to find one cottonwood tree just below the entrance of portage creek that was large enough to make our carrage wheels about 22 Inchis in diameter; fortunate I say because I do not beleive that we could find another of the same size perfectly sound within 20 miles of us. the cottonwood which we are obliged to employ in the other parts of the work is extreemly illy calculated for it being soft and brittle. we have made two axeltrees of the mast of the white perogue, which I hope will answer tolerably well tho' it is reather small.

The Indian woman much better today; I have still continued the same course of medecine; she is free from pain clear of fever, her pulse regular, and eats as heartily as I am willing to permit her of broiled buffaloe well seasoned with pepper and salt and rich soope of the same meat; I think therefore that there is every rational hope of her recovery.

saw a vast number of buffaloe feeding in every direction arround us in the plains, others coming down in large herds to water at the river; the fragments of many carcases of these poor anamals daily pass down the river, thus mangled I p[r]esume in decending those immence cataracts above us. as the buffaloe generally go in large herds to water and the passages to the river about the falls are narrow and steep the hi[n]der part of the herd press those in front out of their debth and the water insta[n]tly takes them over the cataracts where they are instantly crushed to death without the possibility of escaping. in this manner I have seen ten or a douzen disappear

in a few minutes. their mangled carcases ly along the shores below
the falls in considerable quantities and afford fine amusement for
the bear wolves and birds of prey; this may be one reason and I
think not a bad one either that the bear are so tentatious of their
right of soil in this neighbourhood.

[Clark]   June 17th. Monday 1805.
we proceeded up the river passing a succession of rapids & cascades to the Falls, which we had herd for several miles makeing a
dedly sound   I beheld those cateracts with astonishment   the whole
of the water of this great river confined in a channel of 280 yards
and pitching over a rock of 97 feet ¾ of an [inch],   from the foot
of the falls arrises a continued mist which is extended for 150 yds
down & to near the top of the clifts on L. Sd.   the river below is
confined [in] a narrow Chan of 93 yards leaveing a small bottom of
timber on the Stard Side which is defended by a rock, rangeing
cross wise the river a little below the Shoot [chute],   a short distance
below this cateract a large rock divides the stream.   I in desending
the clifts to take the hite of the fall was near slipping into the water,
at which place I must have been sucked under in an instant, and
with dificuelty and great risque I assended again, and deceded the
clift lower down (but few places can be deceded to the river) and
took the hite with as much accurecy as possible with a Sperit Leavels
&c.   dined at a fine spring 200 yards below the pitch near which
place 4 cotton willow trees grew.   on one of them I marked my
name the date, and hight of the falls

[Lewis]   Tuesday June 18th 1805.
examined the frame of my Iron boat and found all the parts complete except one screw, which the ingenuity of Sheilds can readily
replace, a resource which we have very frequent occasion for.   about
12 O'Clk. the hunters returned; they had killed 10 deer but no Elk.
I begin to fear that we shall have some difficulty in procuring skins
for the boat.   I wo[u]ld prefer those of the Elk because I beleive
them more durable and strong than those of the Buffaloe, and that
they will not shrink so much in drying.
The waggons are completed this evening, and appear as if they
would answer the purpose very well if the ax[l]etrees prove sufficiently strong.   the wind blew violently this evening, as they fre-

quently do in this open country where there is not a tree to brake or oppose their force. The Indian woman is recovering fast she set up the greater part of the day and walked out for the fi[r]st time since she arrived here; she eats hartily and is free from fever or pain. I continue same course of medecine and regimen except that I added one doze of 15 drops of the oil of vitriol today about noon.

There is a species of goosberry which grows very common about here in open situations among the rocks on the sides of the clifts. they are now ripe of a pale red colour, about the size of a common goosberry, and like it is an ovate pericarp of soft pulp invelloping a number of smal whitish coloured seeds; the pulp is a yello[w]ish slimy muselaginous substance of a sweetish and pinelike tast, not agreeable to me. the surface of the berry is covered with a glutinous adhesive matter, and the frut altho' ripe retains it's withered corollar. this shrub seldom rises more than two feet high and is much branched; the leaves resemble those of the common goosberry only not so large; it has no thorns. the berry is supported by seperate peduncles or footstalks of half an inch in length.[9]

immence quantities of small grasshoppers of a brown colour in the plains, they no doubt contribute much to keep the grass as low as we find it which is not generally more than three inches, the grass is a narrow leaf, soft, and affords a fine pasture for the Buffaloe.

[Clark]   June 18th. Tuesday 1805
we set out early and arrived at the second great cateract a[t] about 200 yds above the last of 19 feet pitch. this is one of the grandest views in nature and by far exceeds any thing I ever saw,

I decended the clift below this cateract with ease measured the hight of the purpendicular fall of 47 feet 8 Inches at which place the river is 473 yards wide as also the hight of the cascade a continual mist quite across this fall after which we proceeded on up the river a little more than a mile to the largest fountain or spring I ever saw, and doubt if it is not the largest in America known, this water boils up from under the rocks near the edge of the river and falls imediately into the river 8 feet, and keeps its colour for ½ a mile which

[9] Squaw currant (*Ribes cereum*).

is emencely clear and of a bluish cast, proceeded on up the river passed a succession of rapids to the next great fall of 26 feet 5 Inches river 580 yards wide this fall is not intirely perpenducular a short bench gives a curve to the water as it falls a butifull small Island at the foot of this fall near the center of the channel covered with trees, a considerable mist rises at this fall occasionally

this evening, one man A. Willard going for a load of meat at 170 yards distance on an Island was attact by a white bear and verry near being caught, prosued within 40 yards of camp where I was with one man I collected 3 others of the party and prosued the bear (who had prosued my track from a buffalow I had killed on the Island at about 300 yards distance and chance[d] to meet Willard) for fear of his attacking one man Colter at the lower point of the Island, before we had got down the bear had allarmed the man and prosued him into the water, at our approach he retreated, and we relieved the man in the water, I saw the bear but the bushes was so thick that I could not shoot him and it was nearly dark, the wind from the S W & cool killed a beaver & an elk for their skins this evening.

[Lewis]   Wednesday June 19th 1805.

The wind blew violently the greater part of the day. the Indian woman was much better this morning she walked out and gathered a considerable quantity of the white apples of which she eat so heartily in their raw state, together with a considerable quantity of dryed fish without my knowledge that she complained very much and her fever again returned. I rebuked Sharbono severely for suffering her to indulge herself with such food he being privy to it and having been previously told what she must only eat. I now gave her broken dozes of diluted nitre untill it produced perspiration and at 10 P.M. 30 drops of laudnum which gave her a tolerable nights rest. I amused myself in fishing several hours today and caught a number of both species of the white fish, but no trout nor Cat. I employed the men in making up our baggage in proper packages for transportation; and waxed the stoppers of my powder canesters anew. had the frame of my Iron boat clensed of rust and well greased.

[Clark] June 19th. Wednesday 1805

We went on the Island to hunt the white bear this morning but could not find him, after plotting my courses &c. I deturmined to dry the meat we killed and leave here, and proceed up the river as far as it bent to the S.E. and examine a small creek above our camp, I returned to camp late and deturmined that the best nearest and most eassy rout would be from the lower part of the 3rd. or white bear Islands

the wind all this day blew violently hard from the S. W. off the snowey mountains, cool, in my last rout I lost a part of my notes which could not be found as the wind must have blown them to a great distance. summer duck setting great numbers of buffalow all about our camp.

[Lewis] Thursday June 20th. 1805.

This morning we had but little to do; waiting the return of Capt. Clark; I am apprehensive from his stay that the portage is longer than we had calculated on.

[Clark] June 20th. Thursday 1805

When I arrived at camp found all well with great quantites of meet, the canoes Capt Lewis had carried up the Creek 1¼ miles to a good place to assend the land & taken up. Not haveing seen the Snake Indians or knowing in fact whither to calculate on their friendship or hostillity, we have conceived our party sufficiently small, and therefore have concluded not to dispatch a canoe with a part of our men to St. Louis as we have entended early in the Spring. we fear also that such a measure might also discourage those who would in such case remain, and migh[t] possibly hazard the fate of the expedition. We have never hinted to any one of the party that we had such a scheem in contemplation, and all appear perfectly to have made up their minds to Succeed in the expedition or perish in the attempt. We all believe that we are about to enter on the most perilous and dificuelt part of our Voyage, yet I see no one repineing; all appear to meet those dificuelties which await us with resolution and becomeing fortitude.

[Lewis] Friday June 21st. 1805.

This morning I employed the greater part of the men in transporting a part of the bagage over portage creek to the top of the high plain about three miles in advance on the portage. I also had one canoe carryed on truck wheles to the same place and put the baggage in it, in order to make an early start in the morning, as the rout of our portage is not yet entirely settled, and it would be inconvenient to remain in the open plain all night at a distance from water, which would probably be the case if we did not set out early as the latter part of the rout is destitute of water for about 8 miles.

having determined to go to the upper part of the portage tomorrow, in order to prepare my boat and receive and take care of the stores as they were transported, I caused the Iron frame of the boat and the necessary tools my private baggage and Instruments to be taken as a part of this load, also the baggage of Joseph Fields, Sergt. Gass and John sheilds, whom I had scelected to assist me in constructing the leather boat. Th[r]ee men were employed today in shaving the Elk skins which had ben collected for the boat.

The growth of the neighbourhood what little there is consists of the broad and narrow leafed cottonwood, box alder, the large or sweet willow, the narrow and broad leafed willow. the sweet willow has not been common to the Missouri below this or the entrance of Maria's river; here [it] attains to the same size and in appearance much the same as in the Atlantic States. the undergrowth consists of rosebushes, goosberry and current bushes, honeysuckle small, and the red wood, the inner bark of which the engages are fond of smoking mixed with tobacco.

Saturday June 22nd. 1805.

This morning early Capt. Clark and myself with all the party except Sergt. Ordway Sharbono, Goodrich, York and the Indian woman, set out to pass the portage with the canoe and baggage to the Whitebear Island, where we intend that this portage shall end. Capt. Clarke piloted us through the plains. about noon we reached a little stream about 8 miles on the portage where we halted and dined; we were obliged here to renew both axeltrees and the tongues and howns of one set of wheels which took us no more than 2 hours. these parts of our carriage had been made of cottonwood and one axe[l]tree of an old mast, all of which proved deficient and had broken down several times before we reached this place we have now renewed them with the sweet willow and hope that they will answer better. after dark we had reached within half a mile of our intended camp when the tongues gave way and we were obliged to leave the canoe, each man took as much of the baggage as he could carry on his back and proceeded to the river where we formed our encampment much fortiegued. the prickly pears were extreemly troublesome to us sticking our feet through our mockersons.

there is a kind of larke[10] here that much resembles the bird called the oldfield lark with a yellow brest and a black spot on the croop; tho' this differs from ours in the form of the tail which is pointed being formed of feathers of unequal length;   the beak is somewhat longer and more curved and the note differs considerably; however in size, action, and colours there is no perceptable difference; or at least none that strikes my eye.

after reaching our camp we kindled our fires and examined the meat which Capt. Clark had left, but found only a small proportion of it, the wolves had taken the greater part.   we eat our suppers and soon retired to rest.

Sunday June 23rd. 1805.

this evening the men repaired their mockersons, and put on double souls to protect their feet from the prickley pears.   during the late rains the buffaloe have troden up the prarie very much which having now become dry the sharp points of earth as hard as frozen ground stand up in such abundance that there is no avoiding them. this is particular[l]y severe on the feet of the men who have not only their own weight to bear in treading on those hacklelike points but have also the addition of the burthen which they draw and which in fact is as much as they can possibly move with.   they are obliged to halt and rest frequently for a few minutes,   at every halt these poor fellows rumble down and are so much fortiegued that many of them are asleep in an instant; in short their fatiegues are incredible; some are limping from the soreness of their feet, others faint and unable to stand for a few minutes, with heat and fatigue, yet no one complains, all go with cheerfullness.   in evening Reubin Fields returned to the lower camp and informed Capt. Clark of the absence of Shannon, with rispect to whome they were extreemly uneasy. Fields and Drewyer had killed several buffaloe at the bend of the

[10] Western meadowlark (*Sturnella neglecta*).

missouri above the falls and had dryed a considerable quantity of meat; they had also killed several deer but no Elk.

[Clark]   June 23rd Sunday 1805
to state the fatigues of this party would take up more of the journal than other notes which I find scercely time to set down.

June 24th. Monday 1805
had the remaining canoe hauled out of the water to dry and devided the baggage into 3 parcels, one of which the party took on their backs & one waggon with truck wheels to the canoes 3 miles in advance (Those canoes or 5 of our canoes were carried up the creek 1¾ of a mile taken out on the bank and left to dry from which place they are taken up a point and [that] intersects this rout from the mouth of the creek at 3 miles from the foot of the rapids)   after getting up their loads they devided men & load & proceeded on with 2 canoes on truck wheels as before,   I accompaned them 4 miles and returned, my feet being verry sore from the walk over ruts stones & hills & thro the leavel plain for 6 days proceeding carrying my pack and gun.

[Lewis]   Tuesday June 25th. 1805.
about noon Fields returned and informed me that he had seen two white bear near the river a few miles above and in attempting to get a shoot [at] them had stumbled uppon a third which immediately made at him being only a few steps distant; that in runing in order to escape from the bear he had leaped down a steep bank of the river on a stony bar where he fell cut his hand bruised his knees and bent his gun, that fortunately for him the bank hid him from the bear when he fell and that by that means he had escaped. this man has been truly unfortunate with these bear, this is the second time that he has narrowly escaped from them.
in the evening Drewyer and Frazier arrived with about 800 lb. of excellent dryed meat and about 100 lbs. of tallow.
it is worthy of remark that the winds are sometimes so strong in these plains that the men informed me that they hoisted a sail in the canoe and it had driven her along on the truck wheels.   this is really sailing on dry land.

[Clark]   June 25th. Tuesday 1805
a fair worm morning,   clouded & a few drops of rain at 5 oClock
A.M. fair   I feel my self a little unwell with a looseness &c. &c.
put out the stores to dry & set Chabonah &c. to cook for the party
against their return he being the only man left on this side with
me.   I had a little coffee for brackfast which was to me a necessity
as I had not tasted any since last winter.

This countrey has a romantick appearance river inclosed between
high and steep hills cut to pices by revines   but little timber and
that confined to the Rivers & creek,   the Missouri has but a fiew
scattering trees on its borders, and only one solitary cotton tree in
sight of my camp

at 5 oClock the party returned, fatigued as usial, and proceeded
to mend their mockersons   a powerfull rain fell on the party on
their rout yestirday   Wet some fiew articles, and caused the rout to
be so bad, wet & Deep thay could with dificuelty proceed, Capt
Lewis & the men with him much employed with the Iron Boat in
fitting it for the Water

[Lewis]   Wednesday June 26th. 1805.
Shields and Gass had killed seven buffaloe in their absence, the
skins of which and a part of the best of the meat they brought with
them.   if I cannot procure a sufficient quantity of Elk's skins I shall
substitute those of the buffaloe.   late in the evening the party arrived
with two more canoes and another portion of the baggage. Whitehouse one of them much heated and fortiegued on his arrivall d[r]ank
a very hearty draught of water and was taken almost instantly extreemly ill.   his pulse were full and I therefore bled him plentifully
from which he felt great relief.   I had no other instrument with
which to perform this opperation but my penknife, however it answered very well.

Friday June 28th. 1805.
The White bear have become so troublesome to us that I do not
think it prudent to send one man alone on an errand of any kind,
particularly where he has to pass through the brush.   we have seen
two of them on the large Island opposite to us today but are so much
engaged that we could not spare the time to hunt them but will
make a frolick of it when the party return and drive them from these

islands   they come close arround our camp every night but have
never yet ventured to attack us and our dog gives us timely notice
of their visits, he keeps constantly padroling all night.   I have made
the men sleep with their arms by them as usual for fear of accedents.

Saturday June 29th. 1805.

I continued my rout to the fountain[11] which I found much as
Capt. C: had discribed & think it may well be retained on the list
of prodegies of this neighbourhood towards which, nature seems to
have dealt with a liberal hand, for I have scarcely experienced a day
since my first arrival in this quarter without experiencing some novel
occurrence among the party or witnessing the appearance of some
uncommon object.   I think this fountain the largest I ever beheld,
and the ha[n]dsome cascade which it affords over some steep and
irregular rocks in it's passage to the river adds not a little to it's
beauty.   the water of this fountain is extreemly tran[s]parent and
cold; nor is it impregnated with lime or any other extranious matter
which I can discover, but is very pure and pleasent.   it's waters
marke their passage as Capt. Clark observes for a considerable distance down the Missouri notwithstanding it's rapidity and force.
the water of the fountain boil up with such force near it's center
that it's surface in that part seems even higher than the surrounding
earth which is a firm handsom terf of fine green grass.   after amusing
myself about 20 minutes in examining the fountain I found myself
so chilled with my wet cloaths that I determined to return and
accordingly set out

[Clark]   June 29th. Satturday 1805.

a little rain verry early this morning after[wards] clear, finding that
the Prarie was so wet as to render it impossible to pass on to the
end of the portage, deturmined to send back to the top of the hill
at the creek for the remaining part of the baggage left at that place
yesterday, leaveing one man to take care of the baggage at this
place.   I deturmined my self to proceed on to the falls and take the

[11] This fountain, fan-shaped and between 300 and 400 feet wide, is known as the
Giant Spring. The volume of water thrown out is enormous, being 680 cubic feet
per second, with but little variation (Wheeler).

river,   according we all set out,   I took my servent & one man, Chabono our Interpreter & his Squar accompanied,   soon after I arrived at the falls, I perceived a cloud which appeared black and threaten imediate rain.

the first shower was moderate accompanied with a violent wind, the effects of which we did not feel,   soon after a torrent of rain and hail fell more violent than ever I saw before,   the rain fell like one voley of water falling from the heavens and gave us time only to get out of the way of a torrent of water which was Poreing down the hill in[to] the River with emence force tareing every thing before it takeing with it large rocks & mud,   I took my gun & shot pouch in my left hand, and with the right scrambled up the hill pushing the Interpreters wife (who had her child in her arms) before me, the Interpreter himself makeing attempts to pull up his wife by the hand much scared and nearly without motion,   we at length reached the top of the hill safe where I found my servent in serch of us greatly agitated, for our wellfar.   before I got out of the bottom of the reveen which was a flat dry rock when I entered it, the water was up to my waste & wet my watch,   I scercely got out before it raised 10 feet deep with a torrent which [was] turrouble to behold, and by the time I reached the top of the hill, at least 15 feet water, I derected the party to return to the camp at the run as fast as possible to get to our Lode where Clothes could be got to cover the child whose clothes were all lost, and the woman who was but just recovering from a severe indisposition, and was wet and cold, I was fearfull of a relaps   I caused her as also the others of the party to take a little spirits, which my servent had in a canteen, which revived [them] verry much.   on arrival at the camp on the willow run met the party who had returned in great confusion to the run leaveing their loads in the Plain, the hail & wind being so large and violent in the plains, and them naked, they were much brused, and some nearly killed   one knocked down three times, and others without hats or any thing on their heads bloody & complained verry much, I refreshed them with a little grog.   Soon after the run began to rise and rose 6 feet in a fiew minets.   I lost at the river in the torrent the large *compas*, an elegant fusee, Tomahawk *Humbrallo*, [Um-brella] shot pouch & horn with powder & Ball, Mockersons, & the woman lost her childs Bear & Clothes bedding &c.   The Compass, is a serious loss, as we have no other large one.

[Lewis]   Sunday June 30th. 1805.

I begin to be extremely impatient to be off as the season is now waisting a pace   nearly three months have now elapsed since we left Fort Mandan and not yet reached the Rocky Mountains   I am therefore fully preswaded that we shall not reach Fort Mandan again this season if we even return from the ocean to the Snake Indians.

There are a number of large bat or goatsucker[12] here I killed one of them and found that there was no difference between them and those common to the U'States; I have not seen the leather winged bat for some time nor is there any of the small goatsuckers in this quarter of the country.   we have not the whip-poor-will either.   this last is by many persons in the U'States confounded with the large goat-sucker or night-hawk as it is called in the Eastern States, and are taken for the same bird.   it is true that there is a great resemblance but they are distinct species of the goatsucker.   here the one exists without the other.   the large goat sucker lays it's eggs in these open plains without the preperation of a nest.   we have found their eggs in several instances   they lay only two before they set nor do I beleive that they raise more than one brood in a season; they have now just hatched their young.

This evening the bark was shaved and the leather covering for the sections were also completed and I had them put into the water, in order to toughen the bark, and prepare the leather for sewing on the sections in the morning.   it has taken 28 Elk skins and 4 Buffaloe skins to complete her.   the cross bars are also finished this evening; we have therefore only the way strips now to obtain in order to complete the wood work, and this I fear will be a difficult task. The party have not returned from the lower camp   I am therefore fearfull that some uncommon accedent has happened.

[Clark]   June 30th. Sunday 1805

I set 4 men to make new axeltrees & repare the carrages, others to take the load across the river which had fallen & is about 3 feet water,   Men complain of being Soore this day dull and lolling about,   The two men dispatched in serch of the articles lost yesterday returned and brought the compass which they found in the

[12] Common nighthawk (*Chordeiles minor*).

mud & stones near the mouth of the reveen, no other articles
found, the place I sheltered under filled up with hugh Rocks.

July 1st. Monday 1805.

We set out early this morning with the remaining load, and proceeded on verry well to Capt Lewis's camp where we arrived at 3
oClock, the Day worm and party much fatigued, found Capt. Lewis
and party all buisey employed in fitting up the Iron boat, the wind
hard from the S.W. one man verry unwell, his legs & thies broke
out and Swelled, the hail which fell at Capt. Lewis camp 17 Int.
was 7 Inches in circumference & waied 3 ounces fortunately for
us it was not so large in the plains, if it had [been] we should most
certainly fallen victims to its rage as the men were mostly naked,
and but few with hats or any covering on their heads, The hunters
killed 3 white bear one large, the fore feet of which measured 9
Inches across, the hind feet 11 Inches ¾ long & 7 Inches wide a
bear [came] naarly catching Joseph Fields chased him into the
water, bear about the camp every night & seen on an Isld in the
day

[Lewis]   Tuesday July 2nd. 1805.

After I had completed my observation of Equal altitudes today
Capt. Clark Myself and 12 men passed over to the large Island to
hunt bear. the brush in that part of it where the bear frequent is
an almost impenitrable thicket of the broad leafed willow; this brush
we entered in small parties of 3 or four together and surched in
every part. we found one only which made at Drewyer and he shot
him in the brest at the distance of about 20 feet, the ball fortunately
passed through his heart, the stroke knocked the bear down and
gave Drewyer time to get out of his sight; the bear changed his
course we pursued him about 100 yards by the blood and found him
dead; we surched the thicket in every part but found no other,
and therefore returned. this was a young male and would weigh
about 400 lbs. the water of the Missouri here is in most places
about 10 feet deep.

after our return, in moving some of the baggage we caught a large
rat.[13] it was somewhat larger than the common European rat, of

---

[13] Pack rat or bushy-tailed wood rat (*Neotoma cinerea*).

lighter colour; the body and outer part of the legs and head of a light lead colour, the belly and inner side of the legs white as were also the feet and years. the toes were longer and the ears much larger than the common rat; the ears uncovered with hair. the eyes were black and prominent the whiskers very long and full. the tail was reather longer than the body and covered with fine fur or poil of the same length and colour of the back. the fur was very silkey close and short. I have frequently seen the nests of these rats in clifts of rocks and hollow trees but never before saw one of them. they feed very much on the fruit and seed of the prickly pear; or at least I have seen large quantities of the hulls of that fruit lying about their holes and in their nests.

Wednesday July 3rd. 1805.
the Indians have informed us that we should shortly leave the buffaloe country after passing the falls; this I much regret for I know when we leave the buffaloe that we shal[l] sometimes be under the necessity of fasting occasionally. and at all events the white puddings will be irretrievably lost and Sharbono out of imployment. our tar-kiln which ought to have began to run this morning has yealded no tar as yet and I am much affraid will not yeald any, if so I fear the whole opperation of my boat will be useless. I fear I have committed another blunder also in sewing the skins with a nedle which has sharp edges these have cut the skin and as it drys I discover that the throng dose not fill the holes as I expected tho' I made them sew with a large throng for that purpose.

The current of the river looks so gentle and inviting that the men all seem anxious to be moving upwards as well as ourselves. we have got the boat prety well forward today and think we shall be able to complete her tomorrow except paying her, to do which will require some little time to make her first perfectly dry. she has assumed her shape and looks extreemly well. She will be very light, more so than any vessel of her size that I ever saw.

Thursday July 4th. 1805.
I employed a number of hands on the boat today and by 4 P.M. in the evening completed her except the most difficult part of the work that of making her seams secure. I had her turned up and some small fires kindled underneath to dry her.

we had a heavy dew this morning. the clouds near these mountains rise suddonly and discharge their contents partially on the
neighbouring plains; the same cloud will discharge hail alone in one
part hail and rain in another and rain only in a third within the space
of a few miles; and on the Mountains to the S.E. of us sometimes
snow. at present there is no snow on those mountains; that which
covered them when we first saw them and which has fallen on them
several times since has all disappeared. the Mountains to the N.W.
& W. of us are still entirely covered are white and glitter with the
reflection of the sun. I do not beleive that the clouds which prevail
at this season of the year reach the summits of those lofty mountains;
and if they do the probability is that they deposit snow only for
there has been no perceptible deminution of the snow which they
contain since we first saw them. I have thought it probable that
these mountains might have derived their appellation of *shining
Mountains*, from their glittering appearance when the sun shines in
certain directions on the snow which covers them.

since our arrival at the falls we have repeatedly witnessed a nois
which proceeds from a direction a little to the N. of West as loud
and resembling precisely the discharge of a piece of ordinance of 6
pounds at the distance of three miles. I was informed of it by the
men several times before I paid any attention to it, thinking it was
thunder most probably which they had mistaken   at length walking
in the plains the other day I heard this noise very disti[n]ctly, it was
perfectly calm clear and not a cloud to be seen, I halted and listened
attentively about an hour during which time I heard two other discharges and t[o]ok the direction of the sound with my pocket compass. I have no doubt but if I had leasure I could find from whence
it issued. I have thou[gh]t it probable that it might be caused by
runing water in some of the caverns of those immence mountains,
on the principal of the blowing caverns; but in such case the sounds
would be periodical & regular, which is not the case with this, being
sometimes heard once only and at other times, six or seven discharges in quick succession. it is heard also at different seasons of
the day and night. I am at a loss to account for this phenomenon.

our work being at an end this evening, we gave the men a drink
of Sperits, it being the last of our stock, and some of them appeared
a little sensible of it's effects   the fiddle was plyed and they danced

very merrily untill 9 in the evening when a heavy shower of rain put an end to that part of the amusement tho' they continued their mirth with songs and festive jokes and were extreemly merry until late at night. we had a very comfortable dinner, of bacon, beans, suit dumplings & buffaloe beaf &c. in short we had no just cause to covet the sumptuous feasts of our countrymen on this day. one Elk and a beaver were all that was killed by the hunters today; the buffaloe seem to have withdrawn themselves from this neighbour-hood; the men inform us that they are still abundant about the falls.

Friday July 5th. 1805.

This morning I had the boat removed to an open situation, scaf-fold[ed] her off the ground, turned her keel to the sun and kindled fires under her to dry her more expediciously. I then set a couple of men to pounding of charcoal to form a composition with some beeswax which we have and buffaloe tallow now my only hope and resource for paying my boat; I sincerely hope it may answer yet I fear it will not. the boat in every other rispect completely answers my most sanguine expectation; she is not yet dry and eight men can carry her with the greatest ease; she is strong and will carry at least 8,000 lbs. with her suit of hands; her form is as complete as I could wish it. the stitches begin to gape very much since she has began to dry; I am now convinced this would not have been the case had the skins been sewed with a sharp point only and the leather not cut by the edges of a sharp nedle.

Sunday July 7th. 1805.

we have no tents; the men are therefore obliged to have recourse to the sails for shelter from the weather and we have not more skins than are sufficient to cover our baggage when stoed away in bulk on land. many of the men are engaged in dressing leather to cloath themselves. their leather cloathes soon become rotton as they are much exposed to the water and frequently wet. Capt. Clarks black man York is very unwell today and he gave him a doze of tartar emettic which operated very well and he was much better in the evening. this is a discription of medecine that I never have recourse to in my practice except in cases of the intermittent fever.

the musquetoes are excessively troublesome to us. I have prepared my composition which I should have put on this evening but the rain prevented me.

Monday July 8th. 1805.
The party who were down with Capt. Clark also killed a small fox[14] which they brought with them. it was a female appeared to give suck, otherwise it is so much like the comm[on] small fox of this country commonly called the kit fox that I should have taken it for a young one of that species; however on closer examination it did apear to differ somewhat; it's colour was of a lighter brown, it's years proportionably larger, and the tale not so large or the hair not so long which formed it. they are very delicately formed, exceedingly fleet, and not as large as the common domestic cat. their tallons appear longer than any species of fox I ever saw and seem therfore prepared more amply by nature for the purpose of burrowing. ther is sufficient difference for discrimination between it and the kit fox, and to satisfy me perfectly that it is a distinct species.

the men also brought me a living ground squirrel[15] which is something larger than those of the U' States or those of that kind which are also common here. this is a much ha[n]dsomer anamal. like the other it's principal colour is a redish brown but is marked longitudinally with a much greater number of black or dark bro[w]n stripes; the spaces between which is marked by ranges of pure white circular spots, about the size of a brister blue shot. these colours imbrace the head neck back and sides; the tail is flat, or the long hair projecting horizontally from two sides of it only gives it that appearance. the belly and breast are of much lighter brown or nearly white. this is an inhabitant of the open plain altogether, wher it burrows and resides; nor is it like the other found among clifts of rocks or in the woodlands. their burrows sometimes like those of the mole run horizontally near the surface of the ground for a considerable distance, but those in which they reside or take refuge strike much deeper in the earth. slight rain this afternoon. musquetoes troublesome as usual.

[14] Swift fox (*Vulpes velox*).
[15] Thirteen-lined ground squirrel (*Citellus tridecemlineatus*).

Tuesday July 9th. 1805.

we corked the canoes and put them in the water and also launched the boat; she lay like a perfect cork on the water. five men would carry her with the greatest ease. I now directed seats to be fixed in her and oars to be fitted. the men loaded the canoes in readiness to depart.

just at this moment a violent wind commenced and blew so hard that we were obliged to unload the canoes again; a part of the baggage in several of them got wet before it could be taken out. the wind continued violent untill late in the evening, by which time we discovered that a greater part of the composition had seperated from the skins and left the seams of the boat exposed to the water and she leaked in such manner that she would not answer. I need not add that this circumstance mortifyed me not a little; and to prevent her leaking without pi[t]ch was impossible with us, and to obtain this article was equally impossible, therefore the evil was irraparable I therefore relinquished all further hope of my favorite boat and ordered her to be sunk in the water, that the skins might become soft in order the better to take her in peices tomorrow and deposited the iron fraim at this place as it could probably be of no further service to us. had I only singed my Elk skins in stead of shaving them I beleive the composition would have remained and the boat have answered; at least untill we could have reached the pine country which must be in advance of us from the pine which is brought down by the water and which is probably at no great distance where we might have supplyed ourselves with the necessary pi[t]ch or gum. but it was now too late to introduce a remidy and I bid adieu to my boat, and her expected services.

[Clark]   July 10th. Wednesday 1805
found two Trees which I thought would make Canoes, had them fallen, one of them proved to be hollow & Split at one End & verry much *wind Shaken* at the other, the other much win[d]-shaken, we serched the bottoms for better trees and made a trial of Several which proved to be more indifferent. I deturmined to make Canoes out of the two first trees we had fallen, to Contract their length so as to clear the hollow & winshakes, & ad to the width as much as the tree would allow. The Musquitors emencely noumerous & troublesom

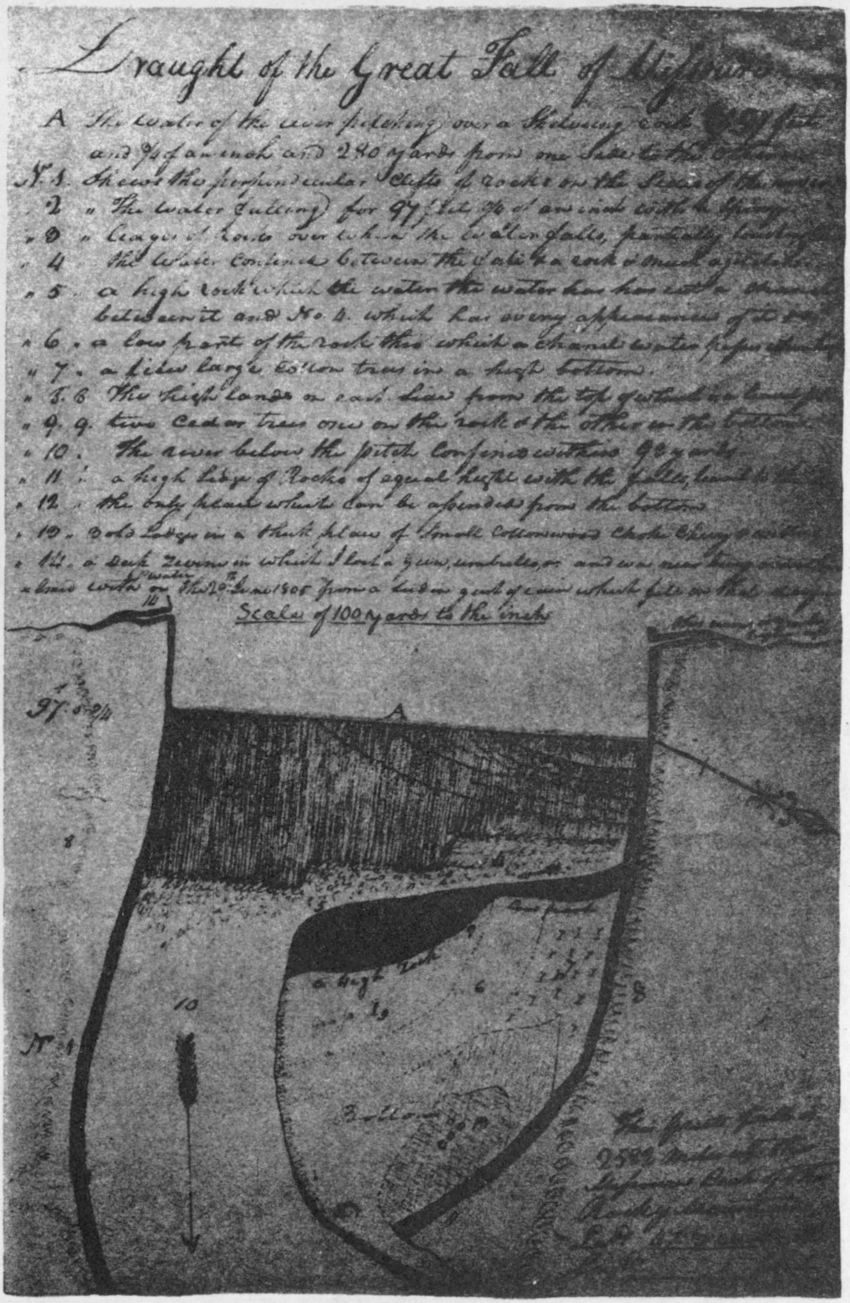

The Great Falls of the Missouri River.

[Lewis]   Thursday July 11th. 1805
We had now nothing to do but wait for the canoes; as they had not returned I sent out some of the small party with me to hunt; in the evening they returned with a good quantity of the flesh of a fat buffaloe which they had killed.   the canoes not arrived this evening.

this evening a little before the sun set I heared two other discharges of this unaccoun[t]able artillery of the Rocky Mountains proceeding from the same quarter that I had before heard it.   I now recollected the Minnetares making mention of the nois which they had frequently heard in the Rocky Mountains like thunder; and which they said the mountains made; but I paid no attention to the information supposing it either false or the fantom of a supersticious immagination.   I have also been informed by the engages that the Panis and Ricaras give the same account of the Black mountains which lye West. of them.   this phenomenon the philosophy of the engages readily accounts for; they state it to be the bursting of the rich mines of silver which these mountains contain.

                                            Friday July 12th. 1805.
Segt. Pryor got his sholder dislocated yesterday, it was replaced immediately and is likely to do him but little injury; it is painfull to him today.   Musquetoes extreemly troublesome to me today nor is a large black knat less troublesome which dose not sting, but attacks the eye in swarms and compells us to brush them off or have our eyes filled with them.[16]   I made the men dry the ballance of the freshe meet which we had abo[u]t the camp, amounting to about 200 lbs.

                                            Saturday July 13th. 1805.
This morning being calm and Clear I had the remainder of our baggage embarked in the six small canoes and man[n]ed them with two men each.   I now bid a cheerfull adue to my camp and passed over to the opposite shore.   Baptiest La Page one of the men whom I had reserved to man the canoes being sick I sent Charbono in his

[16] Coues identifies this as the buffalo gnat, a species of *Simulium* (Thwaites); (Family Simulüdae).

stead by water and the sick man and Indian woman accompanyed me by land.   from the head of the white bear Islands I passed in a S.W. direction and struck the Missouri at 3 Miles and continued up it to Capt. Clark's camp where I arrived about 9 A.M. and found them busily engaged with their canoes Meat &c.

SIX

In Search of the Shoshone

From Great Falls to the Beaverhead
July 15–August 10, 1805

[Lewis]   Monday July 15th. 1805

We arrose very early this morning, assigned the canoes their loads and had it put on board. we now found our vessels eight in number all heavily laden, notwithstanding our several deposits; tho' it is true we have now a considerable stock of dryed meat and grease. we find it extreemly difficult to keep the baggage of many of our men within reasonable bounds; they will be adding bulky articles of but little uce or value to them. At 10 A.M. we once more saw ourselves fairly under way much to my joy and I beleive that of every individual who compose the party.

the prickly pear is now in full blume and forms one of the beauties as well as the greatest pests of the plains. the sunflower is also in blume and is abundant. this plant is common to every part of the Missouri from it's entrance to this place. the lambsquarter, wild coucumber, sand rush and narrow dock are also common here.

early this morning we passed about 40 little booths formed of willow bushes to shelter them from the sun; they appeared to have been deserted about 10 days; we supposed that they were snake Indians. they appeared to have a number of horses with them. this appearance gives me much hope of meeting with these people shortly.

Drewyer killed a buffaloe this morning near the river and we halted and breakfasted on it. here for the first time I ate of the small guts of the buffaloe cooked over a blazing fire in the Indian stile without any preperation of washing or other clensing and found them very good. After breakfast I determined to leave Capt. C. and party, and go on to the point where the river enters the Rocky Mountains and make the necessary observations against their arrival; accordingly I set out with the two invalleds Potts and LaPage and Drewyer

we pursued our rout through a high roling plain to a rappid immediately at the foot of the mountain where the Missouri first enters them.[1]

the Musquetoes are extreemly troublesome this evening and I had left my bier, of course suffered considerably, and promised in my wrath that I never will be guil[t]y of a similar peice of negligence while on this voyage.[2]

Wednesday July 17th. 1805.

The sunflower is in bloom and abundant in the river bottoms. The Indians of the Missouri particularly those who do not cultivate maze make great uce of the seed of this plant for bread, or use it in thickening their soope. they most commonly first parch the seed and then pound them between two smooth stones untill they reduce it to a fine meal. to this they sometimes mearly add a portion of water and drink it in that state, or add a sufficient quantity of marrow grease to reduce it to the consistency of common dough and eate it in that manner. the last composition I think much best and have eat it in that state heartily and think it a pallatable dish. there is

[1] This was at the Half-breed Rapids; and Lewis encamped that night near Hardy, Montana (Thwaites).

[2] The word "bar" in the compound "mosquito-bar" is probably only a corruption of "baire." The Jesuit missionary Poisson in 1727 describes the torments endured by the voyagers on the lower Mississippi from mosquitoes, from which their only defense was the *baire*—"that is to say, a large canvas, the ends of which we carefully fold beneath the mattress; in those tombs, stifling with heat, we are compelled to sleep." By the time of Lewis and Clark the canvas was, at least sometimes, replaced by gauze or net (as affording fresh air), which would naturally retain the name *baire*, very easily corruptible to "bier" (Thwaites).

but little of the broad leafed cottonwood above the falls, much the greater portion being of the narrow leafed kind. there are a great abundance of red yellow perple & black currants, and service berries now ripe and in great perfection. I find these fruits very pleasant particularly the yellow currant which I think vastly preferable to those of our gardens.

the shrub which produces this fruit[3] rises to the hight of 6 or 8 feet; the stem simple branching and erect. they grow closly associated in cops either in the oppen or timbered lands near the watercou[r]ses. the leaf is petiolate of a pale green and resembles in it's form that of the red currant common to our gardens. the perianth of the fructification is one leaved, five cleft, abreviated and tubular, the corolla is monopetallous funnel-shaped, very long, superior, withering and of a fine orrange colour. five stamens and one pistillum; of the first, the fillaments are capillare, inserted into the corolla, equal, and converging; the anther ovate, biffid and incumbent. with rispect to the second the germ is roundish, smo[o]th, inferior pedicelled and small; the style, long, and thicker than the stamens, simple, cylindrical, smooth, and erect, withering and remains with the corolla untill the fruit is ripe. stigma simple obtuse and withering. the fruit is a berry about the size and much the shape of the red currant of our gardins, like them growing in clusters supported by a compound footstalk, but the peduncles which support the several berries are longer in this species and the berries are more scattered. it is quite as transparent as the red current of our gardens, not so ascid, & more agreeably flavored.

The survice berry differs somewhat from that of the U. States the bushes are small sometimes not more than 2 feet high and scarcely ever exceed 8 and are proportionably small in their stems, growing very thickly ascosiated in clumps. the fruit is the same form but for the most part larger more lucious and of so deep a perple that on first sight you would think them black. there are two species of goosbirris here allso but neither of them yet ripe. the choke cherries also abundant and not yet ripe.

[3] Golden currant (*Ribes aureum*) followed by a description of the serviceberry (*Amelanchier alnifolia*).

Thursday July 18th. 1805.

saw a large herd of the Bighorned anamals on the immencely high
and nearly perpendicular clift opposite to us; on the fase of this clift
they walked about and bounded from rock to rock with apparent
unconcern where it app[e]ared to me that no quadruped could have
stood, and from which had they made one false step the[y] must
have been precipitated at least a 500 feet.   this anamal appears to
frequent such precepices and clifts where in fact they are perfectly
secure from the pursuit of the wolf, bear, or even man himself.

we passed the entrance of a considerable river on the Stard. side;
about 80 yds. wide being nearly as wide as the Missouri at that
place.   this handsome bold and clear stream we named in honour
of the Secretary of war calling it Dearborn's river.

as we were anxious now to meet with the Sosonees or snake
Indians as soon as possible in order to obtain information relative to
the geography of the country and also if necessary, some horses we
thought it better for one of us either Capt. C. or myself to take a
small party & proceed on up the river some distance before the
canoes, in order to discover them, should they be on the river before
the daily discharge of our guns, which was necessary in procuring
subsistence for the party, should allarm and cause them to retreat
to the mountains and conceal themselves, supposing us to be their
enemies who visit them usually by the way of this river.   accordingly
Capt. Clark set out this morning after breakfast with Joseph Fields,
Pots and his servant York.   we proceeded on tolerably well; the
current st[r]onger than yesterday; we employ the cord and oars principally tho' sometimes the setting pole.   in the evening we passed
a large creek about 30 yds. wide which disembogues on the Stard.
side; it discharges a bold current of water it's banks low and bed
formed of stones altogether; this stream we called Ordway's creek[4]
after Sergt. John Ordway.

I have observed for several days a species of flax growing in the
river bottoms the leaf stem and pericarp of which resembles the
common flax cultivated in the U. States[5]   the stem rises to the hight
of about 2½ or 3 feet high; as many as 8 or ten of which proceede

[4] Now Little Prickly-pear Creek (Thwaites).
[5] Lewis flax or blueflax (*Linum lewisii*).

from the same root. the root appears to be perennial. the bark of the stem is thick strong and appears as if it would make excellent flax. the seed are not yet ripe but I hope to have an opportunity of collecting some of them after they are so. if it should on experiment prove to yeald good flax and at the same time admit of being cut without injury the perennial root it will be a most valuable plant, and I think there is the greatest probability that it will do so, for notwithstanding the seed have not yet arrived at maturity it is puting up suckers or young shoots from the same root and would seem therefore that those which are fully grown and which are in the proper stage of vegitation to produce the best f[l]ax are not longer essencial to the preservation or support of the root.

[Clark]   July 18th. Thursday 1805
    a fine morning   passed a Considerable river which falls in on the Stard Side and nearly as wide as the Missouri   we call [it] Dearbournes river after the Sety. of war. we thought it prudent for a partey to go a head for fear our fireing Should allarm the Indians and cause them to leave the river and take to the mountains for safety from their enem[ie]s who visit them thro this rout. I deturmined to go a head with a Small partey a few days and find the Snake Indians if possible   after brackfast I took J. Fields Potts & my Servent proceeded on. the Country So Hilley that we gained but little of the Canoes untill in the evening I passed over a mountain on an Indian rode by which rout I cut off Several Miles of the Meanderings of the river,   the roade which passes this mountain is wide and appears to have been dug in maney places,   we camped on a Small run of Clear cold water,   musquitors verry troublesom the forepart of the evening   I saw great maney Ibex.

[Lewis]   Friday July 19th. 1805.
    The Musquetoes are very troublesome to us as usual. this morning we set out early and proceeded on very well tho' the water appears to encrease in volocity as we advance. the current has been strong all day and obstructed with some rapids, tho' these are but little broken by rocks and are perfectly safe. the river deep from 100 to 150 yds. wide. I walked along shore today and killed an Antelope. wh[en] ever we get a view of the lofty summits of the mountains the snow presents itself, altho' we are almost suffocated

in this confined valley with heat. the pine cedar and balsum fir grow on the mountains in irregular assemb[l]ages or spots mostly high up on their sides and summits. this evening we entered much the most remarkable clifts that we have yet seen. these clifts rise from the waters edge on either side perpendicularly to the hight of 1200 feet. every object here wears a dark and gloomy aspect. the tow[er]ing and projecting rocks in many places seem ready to tumble on us.   the river appears to have forced it's way through this immence body of solid rock for the distance of 5¾ Miles and where it makes it's exit below has th[r]own on either side vast collumns of rocks mountains high. the river appears to have woarn a passage just the width of it's channel or 150 yds. it is deep from side to side nor is ther in the 1st. 3 Miles of this distance a spot except one of a few yards in extent on which a man could rest the soal of his foot. several fine springs burst out at the waters edge from the interstices of the rocks. it happens fortunately that altho' the current is strong it is not so but what it may be overcome with the oars for there is hear no possibility of using either the cord or Setting pole. it was late in the evening before I entered this place and was obliged to continue my rout untill sometime after dark before I found a place sufficiently large to encamp my small party; at length such an one occurred on the lard. side where we found plenty of lightwood and pi[t]ch pine. this rock is a black grannite below and appears to be of a much lighter colour above and from the fragments I take it to be flint of a yellowish brown and light creemcoloured yellow. from the singular appearance of this place I called it the *gates of the rocky mounatains.*[6]

[Clark]   July 19th. Fryday 1805
    I proceeded on in an Indian Parth   river verry Crooked   passed over two mountains   Saw Several Indians Camps which they have left this Spring. Saw trees Peeled and found poles &c.   at 11 oC. I saw a gange of Elk, as we had no provision Concluded to kill Some. Killd. two and dined being oblige[d] to substitute dry buffalow dung in place of wood,   this evening passed over a Cream Coloured flint which roled down from the Clifts into the bottoms,

---

[6] Gates of the Mountains, near Helena, Montana.

the Clifts Contain flint a dark grey Stone & a redish brown intermixed and no one Clift is solid rock, all the rocks of everry description is in Small pi[e]ces, appears to have been broken by Some
Convulsion passed a butifull Creek on the Std. Side this even[in]g
which meanders thro' a butifull Vallie of great extent, I call after
Sgt Pryor.[7] the countrey on the Lard Side a high mountain Saw
Several Small rapids to day the river keep[s] its width and appear[s]
to be deep, my feet is verry much brused & cut walking over the
flint, & constantly stuck full [of] Prickley pear thorns, I puled out
17 by the light of the fire to night

[Lewis] Saturday 20th. 1805
we saw the smoke arrise as if the country had been set on fire up
the valley of this creek about 7 Mi. distant we were at a loss to
determine whether it had been set on fire by the natives as a signall
among themselves on discovering us, as is their custom or whether
it had been set on fire by Capt. C. and party accedentally. the first
however proved to be the fact, they had unperceived by us discovered Capt. Clark's party or mine, and had set the plain on fire to
allarm the more distant natives and fled themselves further into the
interior of the mountains.

this evening we found the skin of an Elk and part of the flesh of
the anamal which Capt. C. had left near the river at the upper side
of the valley where he assended the mountain with a note informing
me of his transactions and that he should pass the mounts which
lay just above us and wate our arrival at some convenient place on
the river. the other elk which Capt. C. had killed we could not
find. about 2. in the evening we had passed through a range of low
mountains and the country bacame more open again, tho' still broken
and untimbered and the bottoms not very extensive.

we encamped on the Lard. side near a spring on a high bank[8]
the prickly pears are so abundant that we could scarcely find room

---

[7] Prickly Pear Creek is the "Pryor's Creek" of Lewis and Clark. Prickly Pear
Creek heads directly opposite the sources of Little Prickly Pear Creek, in the vicinity
of Marysville, Montana, and just north of Helena. In its relation to the river and to
the cañon just below its mouth, it is precisely a duplicate of Potts's Creek at Hilger's
and the Gates of the Mountains (Wheeler).

[8] Near El Dorado, about twelve miles northeast of Helena (Thwaites).

to lye. just above our camp the river is again closed in by the Mouts. on both sides. I saw a black woodpecker (or crow) today about the size of the lark woodpecker as black as a crow. I indevoured to get a shoot at it but could not. it is a distinct species of woodpecker; it has a long tail and flys a good deel like the jay bird.[9]

[Clark]　　　　　　　　　　　　　　　　July 20th. Satturday 1805
　The Misquetors verry troublesom　my man York nearly tired out, the bottoms of my feet blistered.　I observe a Smoke rise to our right up the Valley of the last Creek about 12 miles distant,　The Cause of this Smoke I can't account for certainly tho' think it probable that the Indians have heard the Shooting of the Partey below and Set the Praries or Valey on fire to allarm their Camps; Supposeing our party to be a war party comeing against them,　I left Signs to Shew the Indians if they should come on our trail that we were not their enemys. Camped on the river,　the feet of the men with me So Stuck with Prickley pear & cut with the Stones that they were Scerseley able to march at a Slow gate this after noon

[Lewis]　　　　　　　　　　　　　　　　Sunday July 21st. 1805.
　the Clifts high and covered with fragments of broken rocks.　the current strong; we employed the toe rope principally; and also the poles as the river is not now so deep but reather wider and much more rapid our progress was therefore slow and laborious.
　we saw three swans this morning, which like the geese have not yet recovered the feathers of the wing and could not fly　we killed two of them the third escaped by diving and passed down the current; they had no young ones with them therefore presume they do not breed in this country　these are the first we have seen on the river for a great distance.　we daily see great numbers of gees with their young which are perfectly feathered except the wings which are deficient in both young and old.　My dog caught several today, as he frequently dose.　the young ones are very fine, but the old gees are poor and unfit for uce.　saw several of the large brown or sandhill Crain today with their young. the young Crain is as large as a turkey and cannot fly they are of a bright red bey colour or that

---

[9] Lewis' woodpecker (*Melanerpes lewis*).

of the common deer at this season. this bird feeds on grass prin-
sipally and is found in the river bottoms. the grass near the river
is lofty and green that of the hill sides and high open grounds is
perfectly dry and appears to be scorched by the heat of the sun.
the country was rough mountainous & much as that of yesterday
untill towards evening when the river entered a beautifull and extensive plain country of about 10 or 12 miles wide which extended
upwards further that the eye could reach

[Clark]   July 21st. Sunday 1805
     a fine morning our feet So brused and cut that I deturmined
to delay for the Canoes, & if possible kill Some meet by the time
they arrived, all the Creeks which fall into the Missouri on the Std.
Side Since entering the Mountains have extencive valies of open
Plain, the river bottoms contain nothing larger than a Srub untill
above the last Creek, the Creeks & runs have timber on them
generally, the hills or mountains are in Some places thickly covered
with pine & Cedar &c. &c. I proceeded on about 3 miles this
morning finding no fresh Indian Sign returned down the river four
miles and Camped

[Lewis]   Monday July 22d. 1805.
     I passed through a large Island which I found a beautifull level
and fertile plain about 10 feet above the surface of the water and
never overflown. on this Island I met with great quantities of a smal
onion[10] about the size of a musquit ball and some even larger; they
were white crisp and well flavored I geathered about half a bushel
of them before the canoes arrived. I halted the party for breakfast
and the men also geathered considerable quantities of those onions.
it's seed had just arrived to maturity and I gathered a good quantity
of it. this appears to be a valuable plant inasmuch as it produces
a large quantity to the squar foot and bears with ease the rigor of
this climate, and withall I think it as pleasantly flavored as any
species of that root I ever tasted. I called this beatifull and fertile
island after this plant Onion Island.
     The Indian woman recognizes the country and assures us that this

---

[10] *Allium cernuum* (Coues), nodding onion.

is the river on which her relations live, and that the three forks are at no great distance. this peice of information has cheered the sperits of the party who now begin to console themselves with the anticipation of shortly seeing the head of the missouri yet unknown to the civilized world. the large creek which we passed on Stard. 15 yds. we call White Earth Creek[11] from the circumstances of the natives procuring a white paint on this crek.

late this evening we arrived at Capt. C[l]arks camp on the stard. side of the river; we took them on board with the meat they had collected and proceeded a short distance and encamped on an Island Capt. Clark's party had killed a deer and an Elk today and ourselves one deer and an Antelope only. altho' Capt C. was much fatiegued his feet yet blistered and soar he insisted on pursuing his rout in the morning nor weould he consent willingly to my releiving him at that time by taking a tour of the same kind. finding him anxious I readily consented to remain with the canoes, he ordered Frazier and Jo. & Reubin Fi[e]lds to hold themselves in readiness to accompany him in the morning. Sharbono was anxious to accompany him and was accordingly permitted. the musquetoes and knats more than usually troublesome to us this evening.

[Clark]   July 22nd. Monday 1805
    a fine morning wind from the S.E. the last night verry cold, my blanket being Small I lay on the grass & covered with it. I opened the bruses & blisters of my feet which caused them to be painfull dispatched all the men to hunt in the bottom for Deer, deturmined my Self to lay by & nurs my feet. haveing nothing to eat but Venison and Currents, I find my Self much weaker than when I left the Canoes and more inclined to rest & repose to day. I deturmined to proceed on in pursute of the Snake Indians on tomorrow and directed Jo [and] Ruben Fields [and] Frasure to get ready to accompany me. Shabono, our interpreter requested to go, which was granted

[Lewis]   Wednesday July 24th. 1805.
    I fear every day that we shall meet with some considerable falls or obstruction in the river notwithstanding the information of the

---

[11] Now Beaver Creek; at the forks is a town called Placer, on the road from Gallatin City to Helena. (Thwaites).

Indian woman to the contrary who assures us that the river continues much as we see it. I can scarcely form an idea of a river runing to great extent through such a rough mountainous country without having it's stream intersepted by some difficult and dangerous rappids or falls.

our trio of pests still invade and obstruct us on all occasions, these are the Musquetoes eye knats and prickley pear, equal to any three curses that ever poor Egypt laiboured under, except the *Mahometant yoke*. the men complain of being much fortiegued. their labour is excessively great. I occasionly encourage them by assisting in the labour of navigating the canoes, and have learned to *push a tolerable good pole* in their fraize [phrase]. This morning Capt. Clark set out early and pursued the Indian road which took him up a creek some miles abo[u]t 10.A.M. he discovered a horse about six miles distant on his left, he changed his rout towards the horse, on approaching him he found the horse in fine order but so wild he could not get within less than several hundred paces of him. he still saw much indian sign but none of recent date. from this horse he directed his course obliquely to the river where on his arrival he killed a deer and dined.

[Clark]   July 25th. Thursday 1805

we proceeded on a fiew miles to the three forks of the Missouri those three forks are nearly of a Size, the North fork appears to have the most water and must be Considered as the one best calculated for us to assend.[12]

after Brackfast (which we made on the ribs of a Buck killed yesterday), I wrote a note informing Capt. Lewis the rout I intended to take, and proceeded on up the main North fork thro' a Vallie, the day verry hot

Shabono our Intrepreter nearly tired [out] one of his ankles falling him. The bottoms are extencive and tolerable land covered with tall grass & prickley pears. The hills & mountains are high Steep & rockey.

[12] Jefferson River at Missouri Headwaters State Park near Three Forks, Montana.

[Lewis]   Friday July 26th. 1805.
   Capt. C. was so unwell that he had no inclination to eat.   after
a short respite he resumed his march   pass[ed] the North fork at a
large island; here Charbono was very near being swept away by the
current and cannot swim, Capt. C however risqued him[self] and
saved his life. Capt. C. continued his march to a small river which
falls into the North fork some miles above the junction of the 3
forks it being the distance of about four miles from his camp of last
evening   here finding himself still more unwell he determined to
encamp.

[Clark]   July 26th. Friday 1805
   I deturmined to leave Shabono & one man who had Sore feet to
rest & proceed on with the other two to the top of a mountain 12
miles distant west and from thence view the river & vallies a head,
we with great dificuelty & much fatigue reached the top at 11
oClock.   from the top of this mountain I could see the Course of
the North fork about 10 miles meandering through a Vallie but could
discover no Indians or sign which was fresh.   I could also See Some
distance up the Small River below, and also the Middle fork.   after
Satisfying my Self returned to the two me[n] by an old Indian parth,
on this parth & in the Mountain we came to a Spring of excessive
cold water, which we drank reather freely of as we were almost
famished; not with Standing the precautions of wetting my face,
hands, & feet, I soon felt the effects of the water. We Contind thro
a Deep Vallie without a Tree to Shade us scorching with heat to
the men who had killed a pore Deer, I was fatigued my feet with
Several blisters & Stuck with *prickley pears*.   I eate but verry little
deturmined to cross to the Middle fork and examine that.   we
crossed the Missouri which was divided by a verry large Island   the
first Part was knee deep the other waste deep & very rapid,   I felt
my Self verry unwell & took up Camp on the little river 3 miles
above its mouth & near the place it falls into the bottom   a fiew
Drops of rain this evening.
   We killed 2 bear which was imediately in our way.   both pore
emence number of Beaver and orter in this little river which forks
in the bottom

[Lewis]   Saturday July 27th 1805.—
   Capt Clark arrived very sick with a high fever on him and much
fatiegued and exhausted.   he informed me that he was very sick all
last night had a high fever and frequent chills & constant aking pains
in all his mustles.   this morning notwithstanding his indisposition
he pursued his intended rout to the middle fork about 8 miles and
finding no recent sign of Indians rested about an hour and came
down the middle fork to this place.   Capt. C. thought himself
somewhat bilious and had not had a passage for several days; I
prevailed on him to take a doze of Rushes pills, which I have always
found sovereign in such cases and to bath his feet in warm water
and rest himself.   Capt. C's indisposition was a further inducement
for my remaining here a couple of days; I therefore informed the
men of my intention, and they put their deer skins in the water in
order to prepare them for dressing tomorrow.   we begin to feel
considerable anxiety with rispect to the Snake Indians.   if we do
not find them or some other nation who have horses I fear the
successfull issue of our voyage will be very doubtfull or at all events
much more difficult in it's accomplishment.   we are now several
hundred miles within the bosom of this wild and mountanous country, where game may rationally be expected shortly to become scarce
and subsistence precarious without any information with rispect to
the country not knowing how far these mountains continue, or wher
to direct our course to pass them to advantage or intersept a navigable
branch of the Columbia,   or even were we on such an one the
probability is that we should not find any timber within these mountains large enough for canoes if we judge from the portion of them
through which we have passed.   however I still hope for the best,
and intend taking a tramp myself in a few days to find these yellow
gentlemen if possible.   my two principal consolations are that from
our present position it is impossible that the S.W. fork can head
with the waters of any other river but the Columbia, and that if any
Indians can subsist in the form of a nation in these mountains with
the means they have of acquiring food we can also subsist.

[Clark]   July 27th. Saturday 1805—
   I was verry unwell all last night with a high fever & akeing in all
my bones.   My fever &c. continus,   deturmind to prosue my intended rout to the Middle fork, accordingly Set out in great pain

across a Prarie 8 miles to the Middle [fork] this fork is nearly as
large as the North fork & appears to be more rapid, we examined
and found no fresh Sign of Indians, and after resting about an hour
proceeded down to the junction thro a wide bottom which appears
to be overflown every year, & maney parts Stoney. this river has
Several Islands and number of beaver & orter, but little timber,
we could See no fresh Sign of Indians just above the Point I found
Capt. Lewis encamped haveing arrived about 2 oClock. Several
Deer killed this evening. I continue to be verry unwell fever verry
high, take 5 of rushes pills & bathe my feet & legs in hot water.

[Lewis]   Sunday July 28th. 1805.
  My friend Capt. Clark was very sick all last night but feels himself
somewhat better this morning since his medicine has opperated.
  I dispatched two men early this morning up the S.E. Fork to
examine the river; and permitted sundry others to hunt in the neighbourhood of this place. Both Capt. C. and myself corrisponded in
opinon with rispect to the impropriety of calling either of these
streams the Missouri and accordingly agreed to name them after the
President of the United States and the Secretaries of the Treasury
and state having previously named one river in honour of the Secretaries of War and Navy. In pursuance of this resolution we called
the S.W. fork, that which we meant to ascend, Jefferson's River in
honor of that illustrious personage Thomas Jefferson. the Middle
fork we called Madison's River in honor of James Madison, and the
S.E. Fork we called Gallitin's River in honor of Albert Gallitin.[13]
  the beds of all these streams are formed of smooth pebble and
gravel, and their waters perfectly transparent; in short they are three
noble streams. there is timber enough here to support an establishment, provided it be erected with brick or stone either of which
would be much cheaper than wood as all the materials for such a
work are immediately at the spot. there are several small sand-bars
along the shores at no great distance of very pure sand and the earth
appears as if it would make good brick.
  Our present camp is precisely on the spot that the Snake Indians

[13] The three rivers form the beginning of the Missouri River, 2,475 miles from
the Mississippi.

were encamped at the time the Minnetares of the Knife R. first came in sight of them five years since. from hence they retreated about three miles up Jeffersons river and concealed themselves in the woods, the Minnetares pursued, attacked them, killed 4 men 4 women a number of boys, and mad[e] prisoners of all the females and four boys, *Sah-cah-gar-we-ah* o[u]r Indian woman was one of the female prisoners taken at that time; tho' I cannot discover that she shews any immotion of sorrow in recollecting this event, or of joy in being again restored to her native country; if she has enough to eat and a few trinkets to wear I beleive she would be perfectly content anywhere.

Monday July 29th. 1805.

This morning some of the hunters turned out and returned in a few hours with four fat bucks, the venison is now very fine we have killed no mule deer since we lay here, they are all of the longtailed red deer which appear qu[i]te as large as those of the United States.

the hunters brought in a living young sandhill crain; it has nearly obtained it's growth but cannot fly; they had pursued it and caught it in the meadows. it's colour is precisely that of the red deer. we see a number of the old or full grown crains of this species feeding in these meadows. this young animal is very f[i]erce and strikes a severe blow with his beak; after amusing myself with it I had it set at liberty and it moved off apparently much pleased with being releived from his captivity.

the men have been busily engaged all day in dising [dressing] skins and making them into various garments all are leather dressers and taylors. we see a great abundance of fish in the stream some of which we take to be trout but they will not bite at any bate we can offer them. the King fisher is common on the river since we have left the falls of the Missouri. we have not seen the summer duck since we left that place, nor do I beleive that it is an inhabitant of the Rocky mountains. the Duckanmallard were first seen with their young on the 20th. inst. and I forgot to note it; they are now abundant with their young but do not breed in the missouri below the mountains. the grasshopers and crickets are abundant in the plains as are also the small birds frequently mentioned. there is also in these plains a large ant with a redish brown body and legs, and a black head and abdomen; they construct little perimids of small gravel in a conic shape, about 10 or 12 inches high without a mixture of sticks and with but little earth. Capt. Clark is much better today, is perfectly clear of fever but still very languid and complains of a general soarness in all his limbs. I prevailed on him to take the barks which he has done and eate tolerably freely of our good venison.

Today I continued my observations. ⊙'s. magnetic Azimuth.

Time by Chronometer $\}$	$\{$ Azimuth by $\atop$ Circumferentor $\}$	$\{$ Altitude of ⊙ L. L. $\atop$ with Sextant.
h m s	°	° ′ ″
A.M. 8. 48. 9	N. 85. E.	73. –. –.
8. 53. 57	N. 86. E.	74. 58.15.

Observed Equal Altitudes of the Sun with Sextant.

A.M. 8. 57. 5.5	P.M. 4. 5. 50.	$\}$ Altitude by Sextant
″. 58. 41.	″. 7. 24.	at the time of Observts.
		° ′ ″
9. –. 14.	″. 8. 59	77. 4. 45.

Observed Meridian Altitude of the ⊙'s L.L. with $\atop$ Octant by the back observation $\}$	° ′ ″ $\atop$ 59. 7. –.

	° ′ ″
Latitude deduced from this observation N.	45. 23. 23.1.

	° ′ ″
Mean Latitude from 2 Merds. Altds. of ⊙'s. L.L. N.	45. 24. 8.5

Observed time and Distance of ⊙'s. and ☽'s. nearest Limbs with Sextant. ⊙ West.

Time	Distance.		Time.	Distance.
h m s	° ′ ″		h m s	° ′ ″
P.M. 4. 14. 42	49. 43. 30.	P.M.	4. 45. 25.	49. 54. –.
″. 17. 24	″. 44. –.		″. 46. 37.	″. 54. 45.
″. 19. 34	″. 44. 45.		″. 47. 40.	″. 55. 15
″. 21. 12	″. 45. –.		″. 48. 52.	″. 55. 45.
″. 22. 9	″. 45. 54.		″. 49. 47.	″. 56. 15.
″. 23. 12	″. 46. 30.		″. 50. 44.	″. 56. 45.
″. 24. 14	″. 46. 45.		″. 51. 36.	″. 57. 15
″. 25. 18	″. 47. –.		″. 52. 36.	″. 57. 45.
″. 26. 26	″. 47. 15.		″. 53. 37.	″. 58. –.
″. 27. 24	″. 47. 30.		″. 54. 36.	″. 58. 15.

Observed Magnetic Azimuth of the Sun.

| Time by Chronometer } | { Azimuth by } | { Altitude of ⊙'s. |
	Circumfert. }	L. L. by Sextant.
h m s	°	° ′ ″
P.M. 5. 7. 47.	S. 72. W.	55. 44. 30.
5. 13. 4.	S. 73. W.	53. 52. 45.

Observed time and Distance of ☽'s. Western limb from *a* Antares, with Sextant ✳ East.

Time	Distance		Time	Distance
h m s	° ′ ″		h m s	° ′ ″
P.M. 8. 42. 16	68. 56. –.	P.M.	9. 1. 12	68. 46. –.
″. 50. 55	″. 52. 30		″. 3. 1	″. 45. 30.
″. 54. 44	″. 49. 45		″. 4. 47	″. 45. –.
″. 55. 56	″. 49. –.		″. 6. 27	″. 44. –.
″. 58. 53	″. 47. 15.		″. 8. 31	″. 13. 45.

Observed the Azimuth of the Polar Star.

Time by Chronometer	Azimuth by Circumferenter
h m	
P.M. 9. 27.	N. 13° W.

[Clark]   July 29 Monday 1805

A fair morning wind from the North   I feel my Self something better to day,   made some Celestial observations took two Merdn.

altitudes which gave for Latd. *45° 22′ 34″ N* men all dressing skins &c.

[Lewis]   Tuesday July 30th. 1805.
    Capt. Clark being much better this morning and having completed my observations we reloaded our canoes and set out, ascending Jeffersons river. Sharbono, his woman two invalleds and myself walked through the bottom on the Lard. side of the river about 4½ miles when we again struck it at the place the woman informed us that she was taken prisoner.

    as the river now passed through the woods the invalleds got on board together with Sharbono and the Indian woman; I passed the river and continued my walk on the Stard. side. saw a vast number of beaver in many large dams which they had maid in various bayoes of the river which are distributed to the distance of three or four miles on this side of the river over an extensive bottom of timbered and meadow lands intermixed. in order to avoid these bayoes and beaver dams which I fou[n]d difficult to pass I directed my course to the high plain to the right which I gained after some time with much difficulty and waiding many beaver dams to my waist in mud and water. I would willingly have joined the canoes but the brush were so thick, the river crooked and bottoms intercepted in such manner by the beaver dams, that I found it uceless to attempt to find them, and therefore proceeded on up the river in order to intersept it where it came near the plain and woult be more collected into one channel.

    at length about sunset I arrived at the river only about six miles from my calculation on a direct line from the place I had left the canoes but I thought they were still below me. I found the river was divided where I reached it by an Island and was therefore fearfull that they might pass without my seeing them, and went down to the lower point of the large island; here I discovered a small Island, close under the shore on which I was; I passed the narrow channel to the small island and examined the gravly bar along the edge of the river for the tracks of the men, knowing from the appearance of the river at this place that if they had passed they would have used the cord on the side where I was. I saw no tracks and was then fully convinced that they were below me. I fired my gun and hallooed but counld hear nothing of them.

by this time it was getting nearly dark and a duck lit on the shore in about 40 steps of me and I killed it; having now secured my supper I looked our for a suitable place to amuse myself in combating the musquetoes for the ballance of the evening. I found a parsel of drift wood at the head of the little Island on which I was and immediately set it on fire and collected some willow brush to lye on. I cooked my duck which I found very good and after eating it layed down and should have had a comfortable nights lodge but for the musquetoes which infested me all night. late at night I was awakened by the nois of some animal runing over the stoney bar on which I lay but did not see it; from the weight with which it ran I supposed it to be either an Elk or a brown bear. the latter are very abundant in this neighbourhood. the night was cool but I felt very little inconvenience from it as I had a large fire all night.

[Clark]   July 30th. Monday 1805

We Set out 8 oClock and proceeded on 13½ miles up the N. fork the river verry rapid & Sholey the Channel entirely Corse gravel many Islands and a number of Chanels in different directions thro' the bottom &c. Passed the place the Squar interpretress was taken, one man with his Sholder Strained, 2 with Tumers, we Camped on the Std. Side the evening Cool. Capt Lewis who walkd on Shore did not join me this evening.

[Lewis]   Wednesday July 31st. 1805.

This morning I waited at my camp very impatiently for the arrival of Capt. Clark and party; I observed by my watch t[h]at it was 7.A.M. and they had not come in sight. I now became very uneasy and determined to wait until 8 and if they did not arrive by that time to proceed on up the river taking it as a fact that they had passed my camp some miles last evening. just as I set out to pursue my plan I discovered Charbono walking up shore some distance below me and waited untill [he] arrived I now learnt that the canoes were behind, they arrived shortly after. their detention had been caused by the rapidity of the water and the circuitous rout of the river. they halted and breakfasted after which we all set out again and I continued my walk on the Stard. shore

About one mile above Capt. Clark's encampment of the last eve-ning the principall entrance of a considerable river discharges itself into Jefferson's river. this stream is a little upwards of 30 yds. wide disc[h]arges a large quantity of very clear water it's bed like that of Jefferson's river is pebble and gravel. it takes it's rise in the snowclad mountains between Jefferson's and Madison's Rivers to the S.W. and discharges itself into the former by seven mouths it has some timber in it's bottoms and vas[t] numbers of beaver and Otter. this stream we call River Philosophy.[14] the rock of the clifts this evening is a hard black grannite like that of the clifts of most parts of the river below the limestone clifts at the 3 forks of the Missouri.

nothing killed today and our fresh meat is out. when we have a plenty of fresh meat I find it impossible to make the men take any care of it, or use it with the least frugallity. tho' I expect that necessity will shortly teach them this art. the mountiains on both sides of the river at no great distance are very lofty. we have a lame crew just now, two with tumers or bad boils on various parts of them, one with a bad stone bruise, one with his arm accedently dislocated but fortunately well replaced, and a fifth has streigned his back by sliping and falling backwards on the gunwall of the canoe. the latter is Sergt. Gass. it gives him great pain to work in the canoe in his present situation, but he thinks he can walk with convenience, I therefore scelected him as one of the party to accompany me to-morrow, being determined to go in quest of the Snake Indians. I also directed Drewyer and Charbono to hold themselves in readiness. Charbono thinks that his ankle is sufficiently recovered to stand the march but I entertain my doubts of the fact; he is very anxious to accompany me and I therefore indulge him

August 1st 1805—

At half after 8 A. M. we halted for breakfast and as had been previously agreed on between Capt. Clark and myself I set out with 3 men in quest of the Snake Indians. the men I took were the two Interpreters Drewyer and Sharbono and Sergt. Gass who by an accedental fall had so disabled himself that it was with much pain he could work in the canoes tho' he could march with convenience.

the mountains are extremely bare of timber and our rout lay

---

[14] Now known as Willow Creek; at its mouth is Willow City, Montana.

through the steep valleys exposed to the heat of the sun without shade and scarcely a breath of air; and to add to my fatiegue in this walk of about 11 miles I had taken a doze of glauber salts in the morning in consequence of a slight desentary with which I had been afflicted for several days; being weakened by the disorder and the opperation of the medecine I found myself almost exhausted before we reached the river. I felt my sperits much revived on our near approach to the river at the sight of a herd of Elk of which Drewyer and myself killed two. we then hurried to the river and allayed our thirst. I ordered two of the men to skin the Elk and bring the meat to the river while myself and the other prepared a fire and cooked some of the meat for our dinner. we made a comfortable meal of the Elk and left the ballance of the meat on the bank of the river [for] the party with Capt. Clark. this supply was no doubt very acceptable to them as they had had no fresh meat for near two days except one beaver Game being very scarce and shy.

as I passed these mountains I saw a flock of the black or dark brown phesants; the young phesant is almost grown we killed one of them.[15] this bird is fully a third larger than the common phesant of the Atlantic states. it's form is much the same. it is booted nearly to the toes and the male has not the tufts of long black feathers on the sides of the neck which are so conspicuous in those of the Atlantic. their colour is a uniform dark brown with a small mixture of yellow or yelloish brown specks on some of the feathers particularly those of the tail, tho' the extremities of these are perfectly black for about one inch. the eye is nearly black, the iris has a small dash of yellowish brown. the feathers of the tail are reather longer than that of our phesant or pattridge as they are Called in the Eastern States; are the same in number or eighteen and all nearly of the same length, those in the intermediate part being somewhat longest. the flesh of this bird is white and agreeably flavored.

I also saw near the top of the mountain among some scattering pine a blue bird about the size of the common robbin. it's action and form is somewhat that of the jay bird and never rests long in any one position but constantly flying or hoping from sprey to sprey.

[15] Blue grouse (*Dendragapus obscurus*), also called dusky or sooty grouse.

I shot at one of them but missed it. their note is loud and frequently repeated both flying and when at rest and is char âh', cha'r-âh, char-âh', as nearly as letters can express it.

[Clark]   August 1st. Wednesday 1805
    I entered a verrey high mountain which jutted its treme[n]dious Clifts on either Side for 9 Miles, the rocks ragide Some verry dark & other part verry light rock the light rocks is Sand Stone. The water Swift & very Sholey. I killed a *Ibix* on which the whole party Dined

[Lewis]   Friday August 2ed. 1805.
    this is the first time that I ever dared to wade the river, tho' there are many places between this and the forks where I presume it might be attempted with equal success. The valley[16] along which we passed today, and through which the river winds it's meandering course is from 6 to 8 miles wide and consists of a bea[u]tifull level plain with but little timber and that confined to the verge of the river; the land is tolerably fertile, and is either black or dark yellow loam, covered with grass from 9 inches to 2 feet high. the plain ascends gradually on either side of the river to the bases of two ranges of high mountains, which lye parallel to the river and pre-scribe the limits of the plains. the tops of these mountains are yet covered partially with snow, while we in the valley are nearly suf-focated with the intense heat of the mid-day sun; the nights are so cold that two blankets are not more than sufficient covering. soon after passing the river this morning Sergt. Gass lost my tommahawk in the thick brush and we were unable to find it, I regret the loss of this usefull implement, however accedents will happen in the best families, and I consoled myself with the recollection that it was not the only one we had with us.
    we saw some very large beaver dams today in the bottoms of the river several of which wer five feet high and overflowed several acres of land; these dams are formed of willow brush mud and gravel and are so closely interwoven that they resist the water perfectly. the base of this work is thick and rises nearly perpendicularly on the

[16] Beaverhead Valley, Montana.

lower side while the upper side or that within the dam is gently
sloped. the brush appear to be laid in no regular order yet acquires
a strength by the irregularity with which they are placed by the
beaver that it would puzzle the engenuity of man to give them.

[Clark]   August 2d. nd. Friday 1805
     a fine day set out early the river has much the Same kind of
banks Chanel Current &c. as it had in the last Vallie, I walked out
this morning on Shore & Saw Several rattle Snakes in the plain,
the wind from the NW we proceeded on with great dificuelty from
the rapidity of the current & rapids, abt. 15 miles and Encamped
on the Lard Side, saw a large Gangue of Elk at Sunset to the SW.
passed a Small Creek on the Stard Side called birth Creek[17] and
maney large and Small Islands. Saw a number of young Ducks as
we have also Seen everry Day, Some geese. I saw Black wood-
peckers. I have either got my foot bitten by Some poisonous insect
or a tumer is riseing on the inner bone of my ankle which is painfull

[Lewis]   Saturday August 3rd. 1805.
     the Mountains continue high on either side of the valley, and are
but scantily supplyed with timber; small pine apears to be the prevalent growth; it is of the pi[t]ch kind, with a short leaf. from the
appearance of the timber I supposed that the river forked above us
and resolved to examine this part of the river minutely tomorrow.
     Capt. Clark set out this morning as usual. he walked on shore
a small distance this morning and killed a deer. in the course of
his walk he saw a track which he supposed to be that of an Indian
from the circumstance of the large toes turning inward, he pursued
the track and found that the person had ascended a point of a hill
from which his camp of the last evening was visible; this circumstance also confirmed the beleif of it's being an Indian who had thus
discovered them and ran off.
     they found the river as usual much crouded with islands, the
currant more rapid & much more shallow than usual. in many places
they were obliged to double man the canoes and drag them over

[17] Named for Clark's birthday (August 1); it is now White Tail Deer Creek, near
Whitehall, Montana.

the stone and gravel. this morning they passed a small creek on
Stard. at the entrance of which Reubin Fields killed a large Panther.
we called the creek after that animal Panther Creek.[18]

[Clark]   August 3rd. Saturday 1805
I saw a fresh track which I took to be an Indian from the Shape
of the foot as the toes turned in, I think it probable that this Indian
Spied our fires and Came to a Situation to view us from the top of
a Small knob on the Lard Side. the river more rapid and Sholey
than yesterday one man R. F. killed a large *Panthor* on the Shore
We are oblige to haul over the Sholes [the] Canoes in maney places
where the Islands are numerous and bottom Sholey

[Lewis]   August 4th 1805
below our encampment of the last evening this river forms a
junction with a river 50 yards wide which comes from the N. W.
and falling into the S. valley runs parallel with the middle fork about
12 miles.[19] this is a bould rappid & clear stream it's bed so broken
and obstructed by gravel bars and Islands that it appeared to me
impossible to navigate it with safety. the middle fork is gentle and
possesses about ⅔ds. as much water as this rappid stream, it's cours
so far as I can observe it is about S. W. and it appears to be navigable:
its water is much warmer than that of the rappid fork and somewhat
turbid, from which I concluded that it had it's source at a greater
distance in the mountains and passed through an opener country
than the other. under this impression I wrote a note to Capt. Clark
recommending his taking the middle fork provided he should arrive
at this place before my return which I expect will be the day after
tomorrow. the note I left on a pole at the forks of the river

[Clark]   August 4th. Sunday. 1805
The river continued to be crouded with Islands Sholey rapid &
clear, I could not walk on Shore to day as my ankle was sore from
a tumer on that part. the method we are compelled to take to get

___

[18] Now Pipestone Creek. Just across the range from the headwaters of this creek
lies Butte, Montana (Wheeler).
[19] This is the stream which the explorers, two days later, named Wisdom River
(Thwaites).

on is fatiguing & laborious in the extreen, haul the Canoes over the rapids, which Suckceed each other every two or three hundred yards and between the water rapid oblige to tow & walke on stones the whole day except when we have poleing, men wet all day sore feet &c. &c. Murcury at Sun rise 49 a. 0

[Lewis]   Monday August 5th. 1805.

As Charbono complained of being unable to march far today I ordered him and Sergt. Gass to pass the rappid river near our camp and proceed at their leasure through the level bottom to a point of high timber about seven miles distant on the middle fork which was in view; I gave them my pack that of Drewyer and the meat which we had, directing them to remain at that place untill we joined them. I took Drewyer with me and continued my rout up the stard. side of the river about 4 miles and then waded it; found it so rapid and shallow that it was impossible to navigate it.

the middle fork as I suspected dose bear considerably to the West of South and the gap formed by it in the mountains after the valley terminates is in the same direction. under these circumstances I did not hesitate in beleiving the middle fork the most proper for us to ascend. about South from me, the middle fork approached within about 5 miles. I resolved to pass across the plains to it and return to Gass and Charbono, accordingly we set out and decended the mountain among some steep and difficult precipices of rocks. here Drewyer missed his step and had a very dangerous fall, he sprained one of his fingers and hirt his leg very much. in fifteen or 20 minutes he was able to proceed and we continued our rout to the river where we had desighned to interscept it. I quenched my thirst and rested a few minutes examined the river and found it still very navigable. an old indian road very large and plain leads up this fork, but I could see no tracks except those of horses which appeared to have passed early in the spring.

[Clark]   August 5th. Monday 1805

a cold clear morning the wind from the S. E. the river Streight & much more rapid than yesterday, proceeded on with great dificuelity from the rapidity of the Current, and [in]numerable rapids we had to encounter. at 4 oClock PM Murcery 49 ab. 0, passed the mouth of principal fork which falls in on the Lard. Side, this fork is about the size of the Stard. one less water reather not to rapid, its Course as far as can be seen is S.E. & appear to pass through between two mountains, the NW. fork being the one most in our course i.e. 25 W. as far as I can See, deturmind me to take this fork as the principal and the one most proper the S E fork is of a Greenish Colour & contains but little timber. The SW fork contains more timber than is below for some distance, we assended this fork about one mile and Encamped on an Island which had been laterly overflown & was wet we raised our bead on bushes, we passed a part of the river above the forks which was divided and Scattered thro' the willows in such a manner as to render it dificuelt to pass through for a ¼ of a mile, we were oblige to Cut our way thro' the willows. Men much fatigued from their excessive labours in hauling the Canoes over the rapids &c. verry weak being in the water all day. my foot verry painfull

[Lewis] Tuesday August 6th. 1805.

We set out this morning very early on our return to the forks. having nothing to eat I se[n]t Drewyer to the woodlands to my left in order to kill a deer, sent Sergt. Gass to the right with orders to keep sufficiently near to discover Capt C. and the party should they be on their way up that stream, and with Sharbono I directed my course to the main forks through the bottom directing the others to meet us there. about five miles above the forks I hea[r]d the hooping of the party to my left and changed my rout towards them; on my arrival found that they had taken the rapid fork and learnt from Capt. Clark that he had not found the note which I had left for him at that place and the reasons which had induced him to ascend this stream. it was easiest & more in our direction, and apd. to contain as much water. he had however previously to my comeing up with him, met Drewyer who informed him of the state of the two rivers and was on his return. one of their canoes had just overset and all the baggage wet, the medecine box among other articles and several articles lost a shot pouch and horn with all the implements for one rifle lost and never recovered. I walked down to the point where I waited their return. on their arrival found that two other canoes had filled with water and wet their cargoes completely. Whitehouse had been thrown out of one of the canoes as she swing in a rapid current and the canoe had rubed him and pressed him to the bottom as she passed over him and had the water been 2 inches shallower must inevitably have crushed him to death. our parched meal, corn, Indian preasents, and a great part of our most valuable stores were wet and much damaged on this ocasion.

we sent out some men to hunt this evening, they killed 3 deer and four Elk which gave us a plentifull supply om[f] meat once more. Shannon had been dispatched up the rapid fork this morning to hunt, by Capt Clark before he met with Drewyer or learnt his mistake in the rivers. when he returned he sent Drewyer in surch of him, but he rejoined us this evening and reported that he had been several miles up the river and could find nothing of him. we had the trumpet sounded and fired several guns but he did not join us this evening. I am fearful he is lost again. this is the same man who was seperated from us 15 days as we came up the Missouri and subsisted 8 days of that time on grapes only. Whitehouse is in much pain this evening with the injury one of his legs sustained from the canoe today at the time it upset and swing over him. Capt Clarks ankle is also very painfull to him. we should have given the party a days rest some where near this place had not this accedent happened, as I had determined to take some observations to fix the Latitude and longitude of these forks. our merchandize medecine &c are not sufficiently dry this evening we covered them securely for the evening. Capt Clark had ascended the river about 9 miles from this place on a course of S 30° W. before he met with Drewyer.

we therefore determined that the middle fork was that which ought of right to bear the name we had given to the lower portion or *River Jefferson*, and called the bold rapid an[d] clear stream *Wisdom*, and the more mild and placid one which flows in from the S.E. *Philanthropy*, in commemoration of two of those cardinal virtues, which have so eminently marked that deservedly selibrated character through life.[20]

[Clark]   August 6th. Tuesday 1805
dureing the time of Brackfast Drewyer Came to me from Capt. Lewis and informed me that they had explored both forks for 30 or

[20] Wisdom River is now the Big Hole, Philanthropy is the Ruby River, and at Twin Bridges, Montana, the Jefferson becomes the Beaverhead.

40 miles & that the one we were assending was impracti[c]able much further up & turned imediately to the North,   The middle fork he reported was gintle and after a Short distance turned to the S. W. and that all the Indian roades leades up the middle fork.   this report deturmind me to take the middle fork, accordingly Droped down to the forks where I met with Capt Lewis & party,   Capt Lewis had left a Letter on a pole in the forks informing me what he had discovered & th[e] course of the rivers &c.   this letter was Cut down by the [beaver] as it was on a green pole & Carried off.   Three Skins which was left on a tree was taken off by the Panthers or wolves.   In decending to the Point one Can[o]e Struck & turned on a rapid & Sunk, and wet every thing which was in her,   this misfortune obliged us to halt at the forks and dry those articles, one other Canoe nearly turning over, filled half full of water & wet our medison & Some goods Corn &c. Several hunters out to day & killed a young Elk, antilope, & 3 Deer,   one man Shannon did not return to night.   The evening Cool   my anckle much wors than it has been.   this evening a Violent wind from the N. W accompanied with rain which lasted half an hour   wind NW

[Lewis]   Thursday August 8th. 1805.

t[h]e tumor on Capt. Clarks ankle has discharged a considerable quantity of matter but is still much swolen and inflamed and gives him considerable pain. the Indian woman recognized the point of a high plain to our right which she informed us was not very distant from the summer retreat of her nation on a river beyond the mountains which runs to the west.   this hill she says her nation calls the beaver's head from a conceived re[se]mblance of it's figure to the head of that animal.[21]   she assures us that we shall either find her people on this river or on the river immediately west of it's source; which from it's present size cannot be very distant.   as it is now all important with us to meet with those people as soon as possible I determined to proceed tomorrow with a small party to the source of the principal stream of this river and pass the mountains to the Columbia; and down that river until I found the Indians; in short

---

[21] The Beaverhead lies about twelve miles south from Twin Bridges and eighteen miles north from Dillon, Montana (Wheeler).

it is my resolusion to find them or some others, who have horses if it should cause me a trip of one month. for without horses we shall be obliged to leave a great part of our stores, of which, it appears to me that we have a stock already sufficiently small for the length of the voyage before us.

Friday August 9th. 1805.

I walked on shore across the land to a point which I presumed they would reach by 8. A. M. our usual time of halting. by this means I acquired leasure to accomplish some wrightings which I conceived from the nature of my instructions necessary lest any accedent should befall me on the long and reather hazardous rout I was now about to take. the party did not arrive and I returned about a mile and met them, here they halted and we breakfasted; I had killed two fine gees on my return. while we halted here Shannon arrived, and informed us that having missed the party the day on which he set out he had returned the next morning to the place from whence he had set out or furst left them and not finding [them] that he had supposed that they wer above him; that he then set out and marched one day up wisdom river, by which time he was convinced that they were not above him as the river could not be navigated; he then returned to the forks and had pursued us up this river. he brought the skins of three deer which he had killed which he said were in good order. he had lived very plentifully this trip but looked a good deel worried with his march.

Saturday August 10th. 1805.

I sent Drewyer to the wright to kill a deer which we saw feeding and halted on the river under an immencely high perpendicular clift of rocks where it entered the mountain here we kindled a fire and waited for Drewyer. he arrived in about an hour and a half or at noon with three deer skins and the flesh of one of the best of them; we cooked and eat a haisty meal and departed, returning a sho[r]t distance to the Indian road which led us the best way over the mountains, which are not very high but ar[e] ruggid and approach the river closely on both sides just below these mountains I saw several bald Eagles and two large white headed fishinghawks boath these birds were the same common to our country. from the number of rattle snakes about the Clifts at which we halted we called them the rattle snake clifts.　this serpent is the same before discribed with oval spots of yellowish brown.

we continued our rout along the Indian road which led us sometimes over the hills and again in the narrow bottoms of the river till at the distance of fifteen Ms. from the rattle snake Clifts we arrived in a ha[n]dsome open and leavel vally where the river divided itself nearly into two equal branches; here I halted and examined those streams and readily discovered from their size that it would be vain to attempt the navigation of either any further. here also the road forked one leading up the vally of each of these streams.[22]

the mountains do not appear very high in any direction tho' the tops of some of them are partially covered with snow.　this convinces me that we have ascended to a great hight since we have entered the rocky Mountains, yet the ascent has been so gradual along the vallies that it was scarcely perceptible by land.　I do not beleive that the world can furnish an example of a river runing to the extent which the Missouri and Jefferson's rivers do through such a mountainous country and at the same time so navigable as they are.　if the Columbia furnishes us such another example, a communication across the continent by water will be practicable and safe.　but this I can scarcely hope from a knowledge of its having in it[s] comparitively short course to the ocean the same number of feet to decend which the Missouri and Mississippi have from this point to the Gulph of Mexico.

this stream enters a beatifull and extensive plain about ten miles long and from 5 to six in width. this plain is surrounded on all sides by a country of roling or high wavy plains through which several little rivulets extend their wide vallies quite to the Mountains which surround the whole in an apparent Circular manner; forming one of the handsomest coves [*Shoshone*] I ever saw, of about 16 or 18 miles in diameter.[23]　here we killed a deer and encamped on the Stard. side and made our fire of dry willow brush, the only fuel which the country produces.

---

[22] The junction of Horse Prairie Creek and Red Rock River now lies beneath Clark Canyon Reservoir, south of Dillon, Montana.

[23] Shoshone Cove, site of the expedition's home camp for the rest of the month (near Clark Canyon Dam, Montana), is where the explorers would make a cache and sink their canoes until their return the following year.

[Clark]   August 10th. Satturday 1805

Some rain this morning at Sun rise and Cloudy we proceeded on passed a remarkable Clift point on the Stard. Side about 150 feet high, this Clift the Indians Call the *Beavers* head, opposit at 300 yards is a low clift of 50 feet which is a Spur from the Mountain on the Lard. about 4 miles, the river verry Crooked, at 4 oClock a hard rain from the S W accompanied with hail Continued half an hour, all wet, the men Sheltered themselves from the hail with bushes. We Encamped on the Stard. Side near a Bluff, only one Deer killed to day, the one killed [by] Jo Fields 3 Days past & hung up we made use of river narrow, & Sholey but not rapid.

SEVEN

Across the Great Divide

From the Beaverhead to the Snake River
August 11–October 10, 1805

[Lewis]   Sunday August 11th. 1805.—

I discovered an Indian on horse back about two miles distant coming down the plain towards us. with my glass I discovered from his dress that he was of a different nation from any that we had yet seen, and was satisfyed of his being a Sosone; his arms were a bow and quiver of arrows, and was mounted on an eligant horse without a saddle, and a small string which was attatched to the under jaw of the horse which answered as a bridle. I was overjoyed at the sight of this stranger and had no doubt of obtaining a friendly introduction to his nation provided I could get near enough to him to convince him of our being whitemen. I therefore proceeded towards him at my usual pace. when I had arrived within about a mile he mad[e] a halt which I did also and unloosing my blanket from my pack, I mad[e] him the signal of friendship known to the Indians of the Rocky mountains and those of the Missouri, which is by holding the mantle or robe in your hands at two corners and then th[r]owing [it] up in the air higher than the head bringing it to the earth as if in the act of spreading it, thus repeating three times. this signal of the robe has arrisen from a custom among all those nations of spreading a robe or skin for ther gests to set on when they are visited. this signal had not the desired effect, he still kept his position and seemed to view Drewyer an[d] Shields who were now comiming in sight on either hand with an air of suspicion, I wo[u]ld willingly have made them halt but they were too far distant to hear me and I feared to make any signal to them least it should increase the suspicion in the mind of the Indian of our having some unfriendly design upon him. I therefore haistened to take out of my sack some b[e]ads a looking glas and a few trinkets which I had brought with me for this purpose and leaving my gun and pouch with Mc.Neal advanced unarmed towards him.

he remained in the same stedfast poisture untill I arrived in about 200 paces of him when he turn[ed] his ho[r]se about and began to move off slowly from me; I now called to him in as loud a voice as I could command repeating the word *tab-ba-bone*, which in their language signifyes *white-man*. but l[o]oking over his sholder he still kept his eye on Drewyer and Sheilds who wer still advancing neither of them haveing segacity enough to recollect the impropriety of advancing when they saw me thus in parley with the Indian. I now made a signal to these men to halt, Drewyer obeyed but Shields who afterwards told me that he did not obse[r]ve the signal still kept on the Indian halted again and turned his hor[s]e about as if to wait for me, and I beleive he would have remained untill I came up whith him had it not been for Shields who still pressed forward. whe[n] I arrived within about 150 paces I again repepeated the word tab-ba-bone and held up the trinkits in my hands and striped up my shirt sleve to give him an opportunity of seeing the colour of my skin and advanced leasure towards him. but he did not remain until I got nearer than about 100 paces when he suddonly turned his ho[r]se about, gave him the whip leaped the creek and disapeared in the willow brush in an instant and with him vanished all my hopes of obtaining horses for the preasent.

I now felt quite as much mortification and disappointment as I had pleasure and expectation at the first sight of this indian. I fe[l]t soarly chargrined at the conduct of the men particularly Sheilds to whom I principally attributed this failure in obtaining an introduction to the natives. I now called the men to me and could not forbare abraiding them a little for their want of attention and imprudence on this occasion. they had neglected to bring my spye-glass which in haist I had droped in the plain with the blanket where I made

the signal before mentioned. I sent Drewyer and Shields back to
surche it, they soon found it and rejoined me. we now set out on
the track of the horse hoping by that means to be lead to an indian
camp

Monday August 12th. 1805.
      This morning I sent Drewyer out as soon as it was light, to try
and discover what rout the Indians had taken. he followed the track
of the horse we had pursued yesterday to the mountain wher it had
ascended, and returned to me in about an hour and a half. I now
determined to pursue the base of the mountains which form this
cove to the S.W. in the expectation of finding some Indian road
which lead over the Mountains
      after eating we continued our rout through the low bottom of the
main stream along the foot of the mountains on our right the valley
for 5 Mls. further in a S.W. direction was from 2 to 3 miles wide
the main stream now after discarding two stream[s] on the left in
this valley turns abruptly to the West through a narrow bottom
betwe[e]n the mountains. the road was still plain, I therefore did
not dispair of shortly finding a passage over the mountains and of
taisting the waters of the great Columbia this evening.
      at the distance of 4 miles further the road took us to the most
distant fountain[1] of the waters of the Mighty Missouri in surch of
which we have spent so many toilsome days and wristless nights.
thus far I had accomplished one of those great objects on which my
mind has been unalterably fixed for many years, judge then of the
pleasure I felt in all[a]ying my thirst with this pure and ice-cold
water which issues from the base of a low mountain or hill of a gentle
ascent for ½ a mile. the mountains are high on either hand leave
this gap at the head of this rivulet through which the road passes.
here I halted a few minutes and rested myself. two miles below
Mc.Neal had exultingly stood with a foot on each side of this little
rivulet and thanked his god that he had lived to bestride the mighty
& heretofore deemed endless Missouri. after refreshing ourselves
we proceeded on to the top of the dividing ridge[2] from which I

---

[1] The most distant source of the Missouri River is actually Upper Red Rock Lake
and its feeder streams, west of Yellowstone National Park.
[2] The Continental Divide at Lemhi Pass on the Montana-Idaho border.

discovered immence ranges of high mountains still to the West of us with their tops partially covered with snow. I now decended the mountain about ¾ of a mile which I found much steeper than on the opposite side, to a handsome bold runing Creek of cold Clear water. here I first tasted the water of the great Columbia river.[3] after a short halt of a few minutes we continued our march along the Indian road which lead us over steep hills and deep hollows to a spring on the side of a mountain where we found a sufficient quantity of dry willow brush for fuel, here we encamped for the night having traveled about 20 Miles.

[Clark]   August 12th. Monday 1805
the river much more Sholey than below which obliges us to haul the Canoes over those Sholes which Suckceed each other at Short intervales emencely laborious men much fatigued and weakened by being continualy in the water drawing the Canoes over the Sholes, encamped on the Lard Side men complain verry much of the emence labour they are obliged to undergo & wish much to leave the river. I passify them. the weather Cool, and nothing to eate but venison, thc hunters killed three Deer to day.

[Lewis]   Tuesday August 13th. 1805.
We set out very early on the Indian road which still led us through an open broken country in a westerly direction.
we had proceeded about four miles through a wavy plain parallel to the valley or river bottom when at the distance of about a mile we saw two women, a man and some dogs on an eminence immediately before us. they appeared to v[i]ew us with attention and two of them after a few minutes set down as if to wait our arrival we continued our usual pace towards them. when we had arrived within half a mile of them I directed the party to halt and leaving my pack and rifle I took the flag which I unfurled and a[d]vanced singly towards them the women soon disappeared behind the hill, the man continued untill I arrived within a hundred yards of him and then likewise absconded. tho' I frequently repeated the word

---

[3] This was the Lemhi River, whose waters at last find their way into the Columbia (Thwaites); actually a feeder stream into the Lemhi River.

tab-ba-bone sufficiently loud for him to have heard it. I now haistened to the top of the hill where they had stood but could see nothing of them. the dogs were less shye than their masters they came about me pretty close I therefore thought of tying a handkerchief about one of their necks with some beads and other trinkets and then let them loose to surch their fugitive owners thinking by this means to convince them of our pacific disposition towards them but the dogs would not suffer me to take hold of them; they also soon disappeared. I now made a signal fror the men to come on, they joined me and we pursued the back track of these Indians which lead us along the same road which we had been traveling. the road was dusty and appeared to have been much traveled lately both by men and horses. these praries are very poor the soil is of a light yellow clay, intemixed with small smooth gravel, and produces little else but prickly pears, and bearded grass about 3 inches high.

we had not continued our rout more than a mile when we were so fortunate as to meet with three female savages. the short and steep ravines which we passed concealed us from each other untill we arrived within 30 paces. a young woman immediately took to flight, an Elderly woman and a girl of about 12 years old remained. I instantly laid by my gun and advanced towards them. they appeared much allarmed but saw that we were to near for them to escape by flight they therefore seated themselves on the ground, holding down their heads as if reconciled to die which the[y] expected no doubt would be their fate; I took the elderly woman by the hand and raised her up repeated the word *tab-ba-bone* and strip[ped] up my shirt sleve to s[h]ew her my skin; to prove to her the truth of the ascertion that I was a white man for my face and ha[n]ds which have been constantly exposed to the sun were quite as dark as their own. they appeared instantly reconciled, and the men coming up I gave these women some beads a few mockerson awls some pewter looking-glasses and a little paint. I directed Drewyer to request the old woman to recall the young woman who had run off to some distance by this time fearing she might allarm the camp before we approached and might so exasperate the natives that they would perhaps attack us without enquiring who we were. the old woman did as she was requested and the fugitive soon returned almost out of breath. I bestoed an equ[i]volent portion of trinket on her with the others. I now painted their tawny cheeks with some vermillion which with this nation is emblematic of peace. after they had become composed I enformed them by signs that I wished them to conduct us to their camp that we wer anxious to become acquainted with the chiefs and warriors of their nation. they readily obeyed and we set out, still pursuing the road down the river.

we had marched about 2 miles when we met a party of about 60 warriors mounted on excellent horses who came in nearly full speed, when they arrived I advanced towards them with the flag leaving my gun with the party about 50 paces behi[n]d me. the chief and two others who were a little in advance of the main body spoke to the women, and they informed them who we were and exultingly shewed the presents which had been given them these men then advanced and embraced me very affectionately in their way which is by puting their left arm over you[r] wright sholder clasping your back, while they apply their left cheek to yours and frequently vociforate the word *âh-hí-e, âh-hí-e* that is, I am much pleased, I am much rejoiced. bothe partics now advanced and we wer all carresed and besmeared with their grease and paint till I was heartily tired of the national hug. I now had the pipe lit and gave them smoke; they seated themselves in a circle around us and pulled of[f] their mockersons before they would receive or smoke the pipe. this is a custom among them as I afterwards learned indicative of a sacred obligation of sincerity in their profession of friendship given by the act of receiving and smoking the pipe of a stranger. or which is as much as to say that they wish they may always go bearfoot if they are not sincere; a pretty heavy penalty if they are to march through the plains of their country. after smoking a few pipes with them I distributed some trifles among them, with which they seemed much pleased particularly with the blue beads and vermillion.

I now informed the chief that the object of our visit was a friendly one, that after we should reach his camp I would undertake to explain to him fully those objects, who we wer, from whence we had come and w[h]ither we were going; that in the mean time I did not care how soon we were in motion, as the sun was very warm and no water at hand. they now put on their mockersons, and the principal chief Ca-me-âh-wait made a short speach to the warriors. I gave him the flag which I informed him was an emblem of peace among whitemen and now that it had been received by him it was to be respected as the bond of union between us. I desired him to march on, which [he] did and we followed him; the dragoons moved on in squadron in our rear. after we had marched about a mile in this order he halted them and gave a second harang; after which six or eight of the young men road forward to their encampment and no further regularity was observed in the order of march. I afterwards understood that the Indians we had first seen this morning had returned and allarmed the camp; these men had come out armed cap a pe for action expecting to meet with their enimies the Minnatares of Fort de Prarie whome they Call Pâh'-kees. they were armed with b[o]ws arrow and Shields except three whom I observed with small pieces such as the N.W. Company furnish the natives with which they had obtained from the Rocky Mountain Indians on the Yellow stone river with whom they are at peace.

on our arrival at their encampmen[t] on the river in a handsome level and fertile bottom at the distance of 4 Ms. from where we had first met them they introduced us to a londge made of willow brush and an old leather lodge which had been prepared for our reception by the young men which the chief had dispatched for that purpose. Here we were seated on green boughs and the skins of Antelopes. one of the warriors then pulled up the grass in the center of the lodge forming a smal[l] circle of about 2 feet in diameter the chief next produced his pipe and native tobacco and began a long cerimony of the pipe when we were requested to take of[f] our mockersons, the Chief having previously taken off his as well as all the warriors present. this we complyed with; the Chief then lit his pipe at the fire kindled in this little magic circle, and standing on the oposite side of the circle uttered a speach of several minutes in length at the conclusion of which he pointed the stem to the four cardinal points of the heavens first begining at the East and ending with the North. he now presented the pipe to me as if desirous that I should smoke, but when I reached my hand to receive it, he drew it back and repeated the same c[e]remony three times, after which he pointed the stem first to the heavens then to the center of the magic circle smoked himself with three whifs and held the pipe untill I took as many as I thought proper; he then held it to each of the white persons and then gave it to be consumed by his warriors.

this pipe was made of a dense simitransparent green stone very highly polished about 2½ inches long and of an oval figure, the bowl being in the same direction with the stem. a small piece of birned clay is placed in the bottom of the bowl to seperate the tobacco from the end of the stem and is of an irregularly rounded figure not fitting the tube purfectly close in order that the smoke may pass. this is the form of the pipe. their tobacco is of the same kind of that used by the Minnetares Mandans and Ricares of the Missouri. the Shoshonees do not cultivate this plant, but obtain it from the Rocky mountain Indians and some of the bands of their own nation who live further south.

I now explained to them the objects of our journey &c. all the women and children of the camp were shortly collected about the lodge to indulge themselves with looking at us, we being the first white persons they had ever seen. after the cerimony of the pipe was over I distributed the remainder of the small articles I had brought with me among the women and children. by this time it was late in the evening and we had not taisted any food since the evening before. the Chief informed us that they had nothing but berries to eat and gave us some cakes of serviceberries and Choke cherries which had been dryed in the sun; of these I made a hearty meal, and then walked to the river, which I found about 40 yards wide very rapid clear and about 3 feet deep.[4] the banks low and abrupt as those of the upper part of the Missouri, and the bed formed of loose stones and gravel. Cameahwait informed me that this stream discharged itself into another doubly as large at the distance of half a days march which came from the S.W. but he added on further enquiry that there was but little more timber below the

[4] Lemhi River.

junction of those rivers than I saw here, and that the river was confined between inacessable mountains, was very rapid and rocky insomuch that it was impossible for us to pass either by land or water down this river to the great lake where the white men lived as he had been informed. this was unwelcome information but I still hoped that this account had been exagerated with a view to detain us among them. as to timber I could discover not any that would answer the purpose of constructing canoes or in short more than was bearly necessary for fuel consisting of the narrow leafed Cottonwood and willow, also the red willow Choke Cherry service berry and a few currant bushes such as were common on the Missouri.

these people had been attacked by the Minetares of Fort de prarie this spring and about 20 of them killed and taken prisoners. on this occasion they lost a great part of their horses and all their lodges except that which they had erected for our accomodation; they were now living in lodges of a conic figure made of willow brush. I still observe a great number of horses feeding in every direction around their camp and therefore entertain but little doubt but we shall be enable[d] to furnish ourselves with an adiquate number to transport our stores even if we are compelled to travel by land over these mountains. on my return to my lodge an indian called me in to his bower and gave me a small morsel of the flesh of an antelope boiled, and a peice of a fresh salmon roasted; both which I eat with a very good relish. this was the first salmon I had seen and perfectly convinced me that we were on the waters of the Pacific Ocean.

This evening the Indians entertained us with their dancing nearly all night. at 12 O'ck. I grew sleepy and retired to rest leaving the men to amuse themselves with the Indians. I observe no essential difference between the music and manner of dancing among this nation and those of the Missouri. I was several times awoke in the course of the night by their yells but was too much fortiegued to be deprived of a tolerable sound night's repose.

[Clark]   August 13th. Tuesday 1805—
    a verry Cool morning   the Thermometer Stood at 52, a, 0 all the fore part of the day.   Cloudy   at 8 oClock a mist of rain
    proceeded on and Encamped on the Lard. side   no wood except dry willows and them Small,   one Deer killed to day. The river

obliges the men to undergo great fatigue and labour in hauling the Canoes over the Sholes in the Cold water naked.

[Lewis] Wednesday August 14th.

In order to give Capt. Clark time to reach the forks of Jefferson's river I concluded to spend this day at the Shoshone[5] Camp and obtain what information I could with rispect to the country. as we had nothing but a little flour and parched meal to eat except the berries with which the Indians furnished us I directed Drewyer and Shields to hunt a few hours and try to kill something, the Indians furnished them with horses and most of their young men also turned out to hunt. the game which they principally hunt is the Antelope which they pursue on horseback and shoot with their arrows. this animal is so extreemly fleet and dureable that a single horse has no possible chance to overtake them or run them down. the Indians are therefore obliged to have recorce to strategem when they discover a herd of the Antelope they seperate and scatter themselves to the distance of five or six miles in different directions arround them generally scelecting some commanding eminence for a stand; some one or two now pursue the herd at full speed over the hills vallies gullies and the sides of precipices that are tremendious to view. thus after runing them from five to six or seven miles the fresh horses that were in waiting head them and drive them back persuing them as far or perhaps further quite to the other extreem of the hunters who now in turn pursue on their fresh horses thus worrying the poor animal down and finally killing them with their arrows. forty or fifty hunters will be engaged for half a day in this manner and perhaps not kill more than two or three Antelopes. they have but few Elk or black tailed deer, and the common red deer they cannot take as they secrete themselves in the brush when pursued, and they have only the bow and arrow w[h]ich is a very slender dependence for killing any game except such as they can run down with their horses.

I was very much entertained with a view of this indian chase; it was after a herd of about 10 Antelope and about 20 hunters. it

[5] The Shoshone Lewis has met at Shoshone Cove are Lemhi Shoshone, a group of Northern Shoshone of the Lemhi River Valley and the upper Salmon River.

lasted about 2 hours and considerable part of the chase in view from my tent.   about 1.A.M. the hunters returned had not killed a single Antelope, and their horses foaming with sweat.   my hunters returned soon after and had been equally unsuccessfull.   I now directed Mc.Neal to make me a little paist with the flour and added some berries to it which I found very pallatable.

The means I had of communicating with these people was by way of Drewyer who understood perfectly the common language of jesticulation or signs which seems to be universally understood by all the Nations we have yet seen.   it is true that this language is imperfect and liable to error but is much less so than would be expected.   the strong parts of the ideas are seldom mistaken.

I now told Cameahwait that I wished him to speak to his people and engage them to go with me tomorrow to the forks of Jeffersons river where our baggage was by this time arrived with another Chief and a large party of whitemen who would wait my return at that place.   that I wish them to take with them about 30 spare horses to transport our baggage to this place where we would then remain sometime among them and trade with them for horses, and finally concert our future plans for geting on to the ocean and of the traid which would be extended to them after our return to our homes. he complyed with my request and made a lengthey harrangue to his village. he returned in about an hour and a half and informed me that they would be ready to accompany me in the morning.   I promised to reward them for their trouble.   Drewyer who had had a good view of their horses estimated them at 400.   most of them are fine horses.   indeed many of them would make a figure on the South side of James River or the land of fine horses.   I saw several with spanish brands on them, and some mules which they informed me that they had also obtained from the Spaniards.   I also saw a bridle bit of spanish manufactary, and sundry other articles which I have no doubt were obtained from the same source.   notwithstanding the extreem poverty of those poor people they are very merry they danced again this evening untill midnight.   each warrior keep[s] one or more horses tyed by a cord to a stake near his lodge both day and night and are always prepared for action at a moments warning.   they fight on horseback altogether.   I observe that the large flies are extreemly troublesome to the horses as well as ourselves.

[Clark]   August 14th. Wednesday 1805
    a Cold morning wind from the S.W. The Thermometer Stood
at 51° a 0, at Sunrise the morning being cold and men Stiff. I
deturmind to delay & take brackfast at the place we Encamped.
we Set out at 7 oClock and proceeded on river verry Crooked and
rapid as below Some fiew trees on the borders near the mountain,
passed a bold running Stream at 1 mile on the Stard. Side which
heads in a mountain to the North on which there is Snow passed
a bold running Stream on the Lard. Side which heads in a Spring
undr. a mountain, the river near the mountain is one continued
rapid, which requres great labour to push & haul the Canoes up.
We Encamped on the Lard Side near the place the river passes thro'
the mountain. I checked our interpreter for Striking his woman at
their Dinner.
    The hunters Jo. & R. Fields killed 4 Deer & a antilope, I killed
a fat Buck in the evening, Several men have hurt themselves pushing up the Canoes. I am oblige to [use] a pole occasionally.

[Lewis]   Thursday August 15th. 1805.
    This morning I arrose very early and as hungary as a wolf. I had
eat nothing yesterday except one scant meal of the flour and berries
except the dryed cakes of berries which did not appear to satisfy
my appetite as they appeared to do those of my Indian friends. I
found on enquiry of Mc.Neal that we had only about two pounds
of flour remaining. this I directed him to divide into two equal
parts and to cook the one half this morning in a kind of pudding
with the burries as he had done eysterday and reserve the ballance
for the evening. on this new fashoned pudding four of us breakfasted, giving a pretty good allowance also to the Chief who declared
it the best thing he had taisted for a long time.
    I hurried the departure of the Indians. the Chief addressed them
several times before they would move they seemed very reluctant
to accompany me. I at length asked the reason and he told me that
some foolish persons among them had suggested the idea that
we were in league with the Pahkees and had come on in order to
decoy them into an ambuscade where their enimies were waiting to
receive them. but that for his part he did not believe it. I readily
perceived that our situation was not enterely free from danger as
the transicion from suspicion to the confermation of the fact would

not be very difficult in the minds of these ignorant people who have been accustomed from their infancy to view every stranger as an enemy.

I told Cameahwait that I was sorry to find that they had put so little confidence in us, that I knew they were not acquainted with whitemen and therefore could forgive them.   that among whitemen it was considered disgracefull to lye or entrap an enemy by falsehood. I told him if they continued to think thus meanly of us that they might rely on it that no whitemen would ever come to trade with them or bring them arms and amunition and that if the bulk of his nation still entertained this opinion I still hoped that there were some among them that were not affraid to die, that were men and would go with me and convince themselves of the truth of what I had asscerted.   that there was a party of whitemen waiting my return either at the forks of Jefferson's river or a little below coming on to that place in canoes loaded with provisions and merchandize.   he told me for his own part he was determined to go, that he was not affraid to die.   I soon found that I had touched him on the right string; to doubt the bravery of a savage is at once to put him on his metal.   he now mounted his horse and haranged his village a third time; the perport of which as he afterwards told me was to inform them that he would go with us and convince himself of the truth or falsity of what we had told him if he was sertain he should be killed, that he hoped there were some of them who heard him were not affraid to die with him and if there was to let him see them mount their horses and prepare to set out.   shortly after this harange he was joined by six or eight only and with these I smoked a pipe and directed the men to put on their packs being determined to set out with them while I had them in the humour

at half after 12 we set out,   several of the old women were crying and imploring the great sperit to protect their warriors as if they were going to inevitable distruction.   we had not proceeded far before our party was augmented by ten or twelve more, and before we reached the Creek which we had passed in the morning of the 13th. it appeared to me that we had all the men in the village and a number of women with us.   this may serve in some measure to ilustrate the capricious disposition of those people, who never act but from the impulse of the moment.   they were now very cheerfull and gay, and two hours ago they looked as sirly as so many imps of satturn.

[Clark]   August 15th. Thursday 1805
the men Complain much of their fatigue and being repetiedly in the water which weakens them much perticularly as they are obliged to live on pore Deer meet which has a Singular bitter taste. I have no accounts of Capt Lewis Sence he Set out
In walking on Shore I Saw Several rattle Snakes and narrowly escaped at two different times, as also the Squar when walking with her husband on Shore. I killed a Buck nothing else killed to day. This mountn. I call rattle Snake mountain. not one tree on either Side to day

[Lewis]   Friday August 16th. 1805.
I sent Drewyer and Shields before this morning in order to kill some meat as neither the Indians nor ourselves had any thing to eat. I informed the C[h]eif of my view in this measure, and requested that he would keep his young men with us lest by their hooping and noise they should allarm the game and we should get nothing to eat, but so strongly were there suspicions exited by this measure that two parties of discovery immediately set out one on e[a]ch side of the valley to watch the hunters as I beleive to see whether they had not been sent to give information of their approach to an enemy that they still preswaided themselves were lying in wait for them. I saw that any further effort to prevent their going would only add strength to their suspicions and therefore said no more.
after the hunters had been gone about an hour we set out. we had just passed through the narrows when we saw one of the spies comeing up the level plain under whip, the chief pawsed a little and seemed somewhat concerned, I felt a good deel so myself and began to suspect that by some unfortunate accedent that perhaps some of there enimies had straggled hither at this unlucky moment; but we were all agreeably disappointed on the arrival of the young man to learn that he had come to inform us that one of the whitemen had killed a deer. in an instant they all gave their horses the whip and I was taken nearly a mile before I could learn what were the tidings; as I was without [s]tirrups and an Indian behind me the

jostling was disagreeable I therefore reigned up my horse and forbid
the indian to whip him who had given him the lash at every jum[p]
for a mile fearing he should loose a part of the feast. the fellow
was so uneasy that he left me the horse dismounted and ran on foot
at full speed I am confident a mile.

when they arrived where the deer was which was in view of me
they dismounted and ran in tumbling over each other like a parcel
of famished dogs each seizing and tearing away a part of the intestens
which had been previously thrown out by Drewyer who killed it;
the seen was such when I arrived that had I not have had a pretty
keen appetite myself I am confident I should not have taisted any
part of the venison shortly. each one had a piece of some discription
and all eating most ravenously. some were eating the kidnies the
melt and liver and the blood runing from the corners of their mouths,
others were in similar situation with the paunch and guts but the
exuding substance in this case from their lips was of a different
discription. one of the last who att[r]acted my attention particularly
had been fortunate in his allotment or reather active in the division,
he had provided himself with about nine feet of the small guts one
end of which he was chewing on while with his hands he was squezz-
ing the contents out at the other. I really did not untill now think
that human nature ever presented itself in a shape so nearly allyed
to the brute creation. I viewed these poor starved divils with pity
and compassion I directed Mc.Neal to skin the deer and reserved
a quarter, the ballance I gave the Chief to be divided among his
people; they devoured the whole of it nearly without cooking.

being now informed of the place at which I expected to meat
Capt C. and the party they insisted on making a halt, which was
complyed with. we now dismounted and the Chief with much
cerimony put tippets about our necks such as they t[h]emselves
woar I redily perceived that this was to disguise us and owed it's
origine to the same cause already mentioned. to give them further
confidence I put my cocked hat with feather on the chief and my
over shirt being of the Indian form my hair deshivled and skin well
browned with the sun I wanted no further addition to make me a
complete Indian in appearance the men followed my example and
we were so[o]n completely metamorphosed. I again repeated to
them the possibility of the party not having arrived at the place

which I expected they were, but assured them they could not be far below, lest by not finding them at the forks their suspicions might arrise to such hight as to induce them to return precipitately.

we now set out and rode briskly within sight of the forks making one of the Indians carry the flag that our own party should know who we were.

when we arrived in sight at the distance of about 2 miles I discovered to my mortification that the party had not arrived, and the Indians slackened their pace. I now scarcely new what to do and feared every moment when they would halt altogether, I now determined to restore their confidence cost what it might and therefore gave the Chief my gun and told him that if his enimies were in those bushes before him that he could defend himself with that gun, that for my own part I was not affraid to die and if I deceived him he might make what uce of the gun he thought proper or in other words that he might shoot me. the men also gave their guns to other indians which seemed to inspire them with more confidence; they sent their spies before them at some distance and when I drew near the place I thought of the notes which I had left and directed Drewyer to go with an Indian man and bring them to mc which he did. the indian seeing him take the notes from the stake on which they had been placed.

I now had recource to a stratagem in which I thought myself justifyed by the occasion, but which I must confess set a little awkward. it had it's desired effect. after reading the notes which were the same I had left I told the Chief that when I had left my brother Chief with the party below where the river entered the mountain that we both agreed not to bring the canoes higher up than the next forks of the river above us wherever this might happen, that there he was to wait my return, should he arrive first, and that in the event of his not being able to travel as fast as usual from the difficulty of the water, that he was to send up to the first forks above him and leave a note informing me where he was, that this note was left here today and that he informed me that he was just below the mountains and was coming on slowly up, and added that I should wait here for him, but if they did not beleive me that I should send a man at any rate to the Chief and they might also send one of their young men with him, that myself and two others would remain with them at this place. this plan was readily adopted and one of the young men offered his services; I promised him a knife and some beads as a reward for his confidence in us.

most of them seemed satisfyed but there were several that complained of the Chief's exposing them to danger unnecessarily and said that we told different stories, in short a few were much dissatisfyed. I wrote a note to Capt. Clark by the light of some willow brush and directed Drewyer to set out early being confident that there was not a moment to spare. the chief and five or six others slept about my fire and the others hid themselves in various parts of the willow brush to avoid the enimy whom they were fearfull would attack tham in the course of the night. I now entertained various conjectures myself with rispect to the cause of Capt. Clarks detention and was even fearfull that he had found the river so difficult that he had halted below the Rattlesnake bluffs. I knew that if these people left me that they would immediately disperse and secrete themselves in the mountains where it would be impossible to find them or at least in vain to pursue them and that they would spread the allarm to all other bands within our reach & of course we should be disappointed in obtaining horses, which would vastly retard and increase the labour of our voyage and I feared might so discourage the men as to defeat the expedition altogether.

my mind was in reallity quite as gloomy all this evening as the most affrighted indian but I affected cheerfullness to keep the Indians so who were about me. we finally laid down and the Chief placed himself by the side of my musquetoe bier. I slept but little as might be well expected, my mind dwelling on the state of the expedition which I have ever held in equal estimation with my own existence, and the fait of which appeared at this moment to depend in a great measure upon the caprice of a few savages who are ever as fickle as the wind. I had mentioned to the chief several times that we had with us a woman of his nation who had been taken prisoner by the Minnetares, and that by means of her I hoped to explain myself more fully than I could do signs. some of the party had also told the Indians that we had a man with us who was black and had short curling hair, this had excited their curiossity very much. and they seemed quite anxious to see this monster as they wer[e] the merchandize which we had to barter for their horses.

Saturday August 17th. 1805.—
an Indian who had straggled some little distance down the river returned and reported that the whitemen were coming, that he had seen them just below. they all appeared transported with joy, & the ch[i]ef repeated his fraturnal hug. I felt quite as much gratifyed at this information as the Indians appeared to be. Shortly after Capt. Clark arrived with the Interpreter Charbono, and the Indian woman, who proved to be a sister of the Chief Cameahwait. the meeting of those people was really affecting, particularly between Sah-cah-gar-we-ah and an Indian woman, who had been taken prisoner at the same time with her and who, had afterwards escaped from the Minnetares and rejoined her nation. At noon the Canoes arrived, and we had the satisfaction once more to find ourselves all together, with a flattering prospect of being able to obtain as many horses shortly as would enable us to prosicute our voyage by land should that by water be deemed unadvisable.

[Clark]   August 17th. Satturday 1805
I had not proceeded on one mile before I saw at a distance Several Indians on horsback comeing towards me, The Interpreter & Squar who were before me at Some distance danced for the joyful sight, and She made signs to me that they were her nation,   as I aproached nearer them descovered one of Capt Lewis party With them dressed in their Dress; the[y] met me with great Signs of joy,   as the Canoes were proceeding on nearly opposit me, I turned those people & Joined Capt Lewis who had Camped with 16 of those Snake Indians at the forks 2 miles in advance.   those Indians Sung all the way to their Camp where the others had provd a cind [kind] of Shade of Willows Stuck up in a Circle   the Three Chiefs with Capt. Lewis met me with great cordiallity embraced and took a Seat on a white robe,   the Main Chief imediately tied to my hair Six Small pieces of Shells resembling *perl* which is highly Valued by those people and is pr[o]cured from the nations resideing near the *Sea* Coast. we then Smoked in their fassion without Shoes and without much ceremoney and form.
Capt. Lewis informed me he found those people on the *Columbia* River about 40 miles from the forks   at that place there was a large camp of them,   he had purswaded those with him to Come and see that what he said was the truth, they had been under great appre-

hension all the way, for fear of their being deceived. The Great Chief of this nation proved to be the brother of the *woman* with us and is a man of Influence Sence & easey & reserved manners, appears to possess a great deel of Cincerity. The Canoes arrived & unloaded. every thing appeared to astonish those people. the appearance of the men, their arms, the Canoes, the Clothing my black Servent & the Segassity of Capt Lewis's Dog.

we spoke a fiew words to them in the evening respecting our rout intentions our want of horses &c. & gave them a fiew presents & medals. we made a number of enquires of those people about the Columbia River[6] the Countrey game &c. The account they gave us was verry unfavourable, that the River abounded in emence falls, one perticularly much higher than the falls of the Missouri & at the place the mountains Closed so Close that it was impracticable to pass, & that the ridge Continued on each Side of perpendicular Clifts inpenetratable, and that no Deer Elk or any game was to be found in that Countrey, aded to that they informed us that there was no timber on the river Sufficiently large to make Small Canoes

This information (if true is alarming) I deturmined to go in advance and examine the Countrey, See if those dificueltes presented themselves in the gloomey picture in which they painted them, and if the river was practi[c]able and I could find timber to build Canoes, those Ideas & plan appear[e]d to be agreeable to Capt Lewis's Ideas on this point, and I selected 11 men, directed them to pack up their baggage Complete themselves with amunition, take each an ax and Such tools as will be Soutable to build Canoes, and be ready to Set out at 10 oClock tomorrow morning.

Those people greatly pleased. our hunters killed three Deer & an antilope which was eaten in a Short time the Indians being so harrassed & compelled to move about in those rugid mountains that they are half Starved liveing at this time on berries & roots which they geather in the plains. Those people are not begerley but generous, only one has asked me for anything and he for powder.

---

[6] Referring to the stream on which was the Shoshone village—the Lemhi River, which falls into the Salmon River (Thwaites).

[Lewis] Sunday August 18th. 1805.

This morning while Capt Clark was busily engaged in preparing for his rout, I exposed some articles to barter with the Indians for horses

This day I completed my thirty first year, and conceived that I had in all human probability now existed about half the period which I am to remain in this Sublunary world. I reflected that I had as yet done but little, very little, indeed, to further the hapiness of the human race, or to advance the information of the succeeding generation. I viewed with regret the many hours I have spent in indolence, and now soarly feel the want of that information which those hours would have given me had they been judiciously expended. but since they are past and cannot be recalled, I dash from me the gloomy thought, and resolved in future, to redouble my exertions and at least indeavour to promote those two primary objects of human existence, by giving them the aid of that portion of talents which nature and fortune have bestoed on me; or in future, to live *for mankind*, as I have heretofore lived *for myself*.

[Clark] August 18th. Sunday 1805

Purchased of the Indians three horses for which we gave a chiefs Coat Some Handkerchiefs a Shirt Legins & a fiew arrow points &c. I gave two of my coats to two of the under Chiefs who appeared not well satisfied that the first Chief was dressed so much finer than themselves, at 10 oClock I set out accompanied by the Indians except 3 the interpreter and wife, the fore part of the day worm, at 12 oClock it became hasey with a mist of rain wind hard from the S.W. and cold which increased untill night

[Lewis] Monday August 19th. 1805

from what has been said of the Shoshones it will be readily perceived that they live in a wretched stait of poverty. yet notwithstanding their extreem poverty they are not only cheerfull but even gay, fond of gaudy dress and amusements; like most other Indians they are great egotists and frequently boast of heroic acts which they never performed. they are also fond of games of wrisk. they are frank, communicative, fair in dealing, generous with the little they possess, extreemly honest, and by no means beggarly. each individual is his own sovereign master, and acts from the dictates of his own mind; the authority of the Cheif being nothing more than mere admonition supported by the influence which the prop[r]iety of his own examplary conduct may have acquired him in the minds of the individuals who compose the band. the title of cheif is not hereditary, nor can I learn that there is any cerimony of instalment, or other epo[c]h in the life of a Cheif from which his title as such can be dated. in fact every man is a chief, but all have not an equal influence on the minds of the other members of the community, and he who happens to enjoy the greatest share of confidence is the principal Chief.

The Shoshonees may be estimated at about 100 warriors, and about three times that number of woomen and children. they have more children among them than I expected to have seen among a people who procure subsistence with such difficulty. there are but few very old persons, nor did they appear to treat those with much tenderness or rispect. The man is the sole propryetor of his wives and daughters, and can barter or dispose of either as he thinks proper. a plurality of wives is common among them, but these are not generally sisters as with the Minnitares & Mandans but are purchased of different fathers. The father frequently disposes of his infant daughters in marriage to men who are grown or to men who have sons for whom they think proper to provide wives. the compensation given in such cases usually consists of horses or mules which the father receives at the time of contract and converts to his own uce. the girl remains with her parents untill she is conceived to have obtained the age of puberty which with them is considered to be about the age of 13 or 14 years. the female at this age is surrendered to her sovereign lord and husband agreeably to contract, and with her is frequently restored by the father quite as much as he received in the first instance in payment for his daughter; but this is discretionary with the father. Sah-car-gar-we-ah had been thus disposed of before she was taken by the Minnetares, or had arrived to the years of puberty. the husband was yet living with this band. he was more than double her age and had two other wives. he claimed her as his wife but said that as she had had a child by another man, who was Charbono, that he did not want her.

They seldom correct their children particularly the boys who soon become masters of their own acts. they give as a reason that it cows and breaks the sperit of the boy to whip him, and that he never recovers his independence of mind after he is grown. They treat their women but with little rispect, and compel them to perform every species of drudgery. they collect the wild fruits and roots, attend to the horses or assist in that duty, cook, dress the skins and make all their apparel, collect wood and make their fires, arrange and form their lodges, and when they travel pack the horses and take charge of all the baggage; in short the man dose little else except attend his horses hunt and fish. the man considers himself degraded if he is compelled to walk any distance; and if he is so unfortunately poor as only to possess two horses he rides the best himself and leavs the woman or women if he has more than one, to transport their baggage and children on the other, and to walk if the horse is unable to carry the additional weight of their persons. the chastity of their women is not held in high estimation, and the husband will for a trifle barter the companion of his bead for a night or longer if he conceives the reward adiquate; tho' they are not so importunate that we should caress their women as the siouxs were. and some of their women appear to be held more sacred than in any nation we have seen. I have requested the men to give them no cause of jealousy by having connection with their women without their knowledge, which with them, strange as it may seem is considered as disgracefull to the husband, as clandestine connections of a similar kind are among civilized nations. to prevent this mutual exchange of good officers altogether I know it impossible to effect, particularly on the part of our young men whom some months abstanence have made very polite to those tawney damsels. no evil has yet resulted and I hope will not from these connections.

notwithstanding the late loss of horses which this people sustained by the Minnetares the stock of the band may be very safely estimated at seven hundred of which they are perhaps about 40 coalts and half that number of mules. these people are deminutive in stature, thick ankles, crooked legs, thick flat feet and in short but illy formed, at least much more so in general than any nation of Indians I ever saw. their complexion is much that of the Siouxs or darker than the Minnetares Mandands or Shawnees. generally both men and women wear their hair in a loos lank flow over the sholders and face;

tho' I observed some few men who confined their hair in two equal
cues hanging over each ear and drawnn in front of the body. the
cue is formed with throngs of dressed leather or Otterskin
a[l]ternately crossing each other. at present most of them have their
hair cut short in the neck in consequence of the loss of their relations
by the Minnetares. Cameahwait has his cut close all over his head.
this constitutes their cerimony of morning for their deceased
relations.

the dress of the men consists of a robe long legings, shirt, tippet
and Mockersons, that of the women is also a robe, chemise, and
Mockersons; sometimes they make use of short legings. the ornements of both men and women are very similar, and consist of several
species of sea shells, blue and white beads, bras, and Iron arm bands,
plaited cords of the sweet grass, and collars of leather ornamented
with the quills of the porcupine dyed of various colours among which
I observed the red, yellow, blue, and black. the ear is purforated
in the lower part to receive various ornaments but the nose is not,
nor is the ear lasserated or disvigored for this purpose as among many
nations. the men never mark their skins by birning, cuting, nor
puncturing and introducing a colouring matter as many nations do.
there women sometimes puncture a small circle on their forehead
nose or cheeks and thus introduce a black matter usually soot and
grease which leaves an indelible stane. tho' this even is by no means
common. their arms offensive and defensive consist in the bow and
arrows shield, some, lances, and a weapon called by the Cippeways
who formerly used it, the pog-gar'-mag-gon'. in fishing they employ
wairs, gigs, and fishing hooks. the salmon is the principal object
of their pursuit, they snair wolves and foxes.

I was anxious to learn whether these people had the venerial, and
made the enquiry through the intrepreter and his wife; the information was that they sometimes had it but I could not learn their
remedy; they most usually die with it's effects. this seems a strong
proof that these disorders bothe ganaræhah and Louis Veneræ are
native disorders of America. tho' these people have suffered much
by the small pox which is known to be imported and perhaps those
other disorders might have been contracted from other indian tribes
who by a round of communications might have obtained from the
Europeans since it was introduced into that quarter of the globe.

but so much detatched on the other ha[n]d from all communication with the whites that I think it most probable that those disorders are original with them.

from the middle of May to the first of September these people reside on the waters of the Columbia where they consider themselves in perfect security from their enimies as they have not as yet ever found their way to this retreat; during this season the salmon furnish the principal part of their subsistence and as this fish either perishes or returns about the 1st. of September they are compelled at this season in surch of subsistence to resort to the Missouri, in the vallies of which, there is more game even within the mountains. here they move slowly down the river in order to collect and join other bands either of their own nation or the Flatheads, and having become sufficiently strong as they conceive venture on the Eastern side of the Rockey mountains into the plains, where the buffaloe abound. but they never leave the interior of the mountains while they can obtain a scanty subsistence, and always return as soon as they have acquired a good stock of dryed meat in the plains; thus alternately obtaining their food at the risk of their lives and retiring to the mountains, while they consume it. These people are now on the eve of their departure for the Missouri, and inform us that they expect to be joined at or about the three forks by several bands of their own nation, and a band of the Flatheads. as I am now two busily engaged to enter at once into a minute discription of the several articles which compose their dress, impliments of war hunting fishing &c I shall pursue them at my leasure in the order they have here occurred to my mind, and have been mentioned.

[Clark]   August 19th Monday 1805.

A verry Cold morning Frost to be seen   we Set out at 7 oClock and proceeded on thro a wide leavel Vallie[7]   the Chief shew[ed] me the place that a number of his nation was killed about 1 years past   this Vallie (wheel Vallie) Continues 5 miles & then becomes narrow,   the beaver has Damed up the River in maney places   we proceeded on up the main branch with a gradial assent to the head and passed over a low mountain and Decended a Steep Decent to

[7] Near Tendoy, Idaho.

a butifull Stream, passed over a Second hill of a verry Steep assent & thro' a hilley Countrey for 8 miles an[d] Encamped on a Small Stream, the Indians with us we wer oblige[d] to feed. one man met me with a mule & Spanish Saddle to ride, I gave him a westcoat a mule is considered a of great value among those people we proceeded on over a verry mountainous Countrey across the head of hollows & Springs

[Lewis]　　　　　　　　　　　　　　　　　Tuesday August 20th. 1805.

This morning I sent out the two hunters and employed the ballance of the party pretty much as yesterday. I walked down the river about ¾ of a mile and scelected a place near the river bank unperceived by the Indians for a cash, which I set three men to make, and directed the centinel to discharge his gun if he pereceived any of the Indians going down in that direction which was to be the signal for the men at work on the cash to desist and seperate, least these people should discover our deposit and rob us of the baggage we intend leaving here. by evening the cash was completed unperceived by the Indians, and all our packages made up. the Packsaddles and harnes is not yet complete. in this operation we find ourselves at a loss for nails and boards; for the first we substitute throngs of raw hide which answer verry well, and for the last [had] to cut off the blades of our oars and use the plank of some boxes which have heretofore held other articles and put those articles into sacks of raw hide which I have had made for the purpose. by this means I have obtained as many boards as will make 20 saddles which I suppose will be sufficient for our present exegencies.

The Indians with us behave themselves extreemly well; the women have been busily engaged all day making and mending the mockersons of our party. In the evening the hunters returned unsuccessfull. Drewyer went in search of his trap which a beaver had taken off last night; he found the beaver dead with the trap to his foot about 2 miles below the place he had set it. this beaver constituted the whole of the game taken today. the fur of this animal is as good as I ever saw any, and beleive that they are never out of season on the upper part of the Missouri and it's branches within the mountains. Goodrich caught several douzen fine trout today. I made up a small assortment of medicines, together with the specemines of plants, minerals, seeds &c, which, I have collected betwen this place and the falls of the Missouri which I shall deposit here.

the robe woarn by the Sho-sho-nees is the same in both sexes and is loosly thrown about their sholders, and the sides at pleasure either hanging loose or drawn together with the hands; sometimes if the weather is cold they confine it with a girdel arround the waist; they are generally about the size of a 2½ point blanket for grown persons and reach as low as the middle of the leg. this robe forms a garment in the day and constitutes their only covering at night. with these people the robe is formed most commonly of the skins of Antelope, Bighorn, or deer, dressed with the hair on, tho' they prefer the buffaloe when they can procure them. I have also observed some robes among them of beaver, moonox,[8] and small wolves.

their legings are most usually formed of the skins of the Antelope dressed without the hair. in the men they are very long and full each leging being formed of a skin nearly entire. the legs, tail and neck are also left on these, and the tail woarn upwards, and the neck deeply fringed and ornimented with porcupine qu[i]lls drags or trails on the ground behind the heel. the skin is sewn in such manner as to fit the leg and thye closely; the upper part being left open a sufficient distance to permit the legs of the skin to be dra[w]n underneath a girdle both before and behind, and the wide part of the skin to cover the buttock and lap before in such manner that the breechcloth is unnecessary. they are much more decent in concealing those parts than any nation on the Missouri the sides of the legings are also deeply fringed and ornimented. sometimes this part is ornimented with little fassicles of the hair of an enimy whom they have slain in battle. The tippet of the Snake Indians is the most eligant peice of Indian dress I ever saw. the neck or collar of this is formed of a strip of dressed Otter skin with the fur. it is about four or five inches wide and is cut out of the back of the skin the nose and eyes forming one extremity and the tail the other.

I now prevailed on the Chief to instruct me with rispect to the

[8] The monax or woodchuck. This was probably the Rocky Mountain species, *Arctomys flavienter* (Thwaites). Thwaites here refers to the yellow-bellied marmot (*Marmota flaviventris*).

geography of his country. this he undertook very cheerfully, by delienating the rivers on the ground. but I soon found that his information fell far short of my expectation or wishes. he drew the river on which we now are [*i.e.*, Lemhi] to which he placed two branches just above us, which he shewed me from the openings of the mountains were in view; he next made it discharge itself into a large river which flowed from the S.W. about ten miles below us, then continued this joint stream in the same direction of this valley or N.W. for one days march and then enclined it to the West for 2 more days march. here he placed a number of heaps of sand on each side which he informed me represented the vast mountains of rock eternally covered with snow through which the river passed. that the perpendicular and even juting rocks so closely hemned in the river that there was no possibil[it]y of passing along the shore; that the bed of the river was obstructed by sharp pointed rocks and the rapidity of the stream such that the whole surface of the river was beat into perfect foam as far as the eye could reach. that the mountains were also inaccessible to man or horse. he said that this being the state of the country in that direction that himself nor none of his nation had ever been further down the river than these mountains. I then enquired the state of the country on either side of the river but he could not inform me. he said there was an old man of his nation a days march below who could probably give me some information of the country to the N.W. and refered me to an old man then present for that to the S.W. the Chief further informed me that he had understood from the persed nosed[9] Indians who inhabit this river below the rocky mountains that it ran a great way toward the seting sun and finally lost itself in a great lake of water which was illy taisted, and where the white men lived.

I next commenced my enquiries of the old man to whom I had been refered for information relative the country SW. of us. this he depicted with horrors and obstructions scarcely inferior to that just mentioned. he informed me that the band of this nation to which he belonged resided at the distance of 20 days march from hence not far from the white people with whom they traded for horses mules cloth metal beads and the shells which they woar as

[9] Commonly known as Nez Perce, also named Chopunnish (Thwaites).

orniment being those of a species of perl oister. that the course to his relations was a little to the West of South. that in order to get to his relations the first seven days we should be obliged to climb over steep and rocky mountains where we could find no game to kill nor anything but roots such as a ferce and warlike nation lived on whom he called the broken mockersons or mockersons with holes, and said inhabited those mountains and lived like the bear of other countries among the rocks and fed on roots or the flesh of such horses as they could take or steel from those who passed through their country. that in passing this country the feet of our horses would be so much wounded with the stones many of them would give out.

the next part of the rout was about 10 days through a dry and parched sandy desert in which [there is] no food at this season for either man or horse, and in which we must suffer if not perish for the want of water. that the sun had now dryed up the little pools of water which exist through this desert plain in the spring season and had also scorched all the grass. that no animal inhabited this plain on which we culd hope to subsist. that about the center of this plain a large river passed from S.E. to N.W. which was navigable but afforded neither Salmon nor timber. that beyond this plain th[r]ee or four days march his relations lived in a country tolerable fertile and partially covered with timber on another large river which ran in the same direction of the former. that this last discharged itself into a large river on which many numerous nations lived with whom his relations were at war but whether this last discharged itself into the great lake or not he did not know. that from his relations it was yet a great distance to the great or stinking lake as they call the Ocean. that the way which such of his nation as had been to the Stinking lake traveled was up the river on which they lived and over to that on which the white people lived which last they knew discharged itself into the Ocean, and that this was the way which he would advise me to travel if I was determined to proceed to the Ocean but would advise me to put off the journey untill the next spring when he would conduct me. I thanked him for his information and advise and gave him a knife with which he appeared to be much gratifyed.

I now asked Cameahwait by what rout the Pierced nosed indians,

who he informed me inhabited this river below the mountains, came
over to the Missouri; this he informed me was to the north, but
added that the road was a very bad one as he had been informed
by them and that they had suffered excessively with hunger on the
rout being obliged to subsist for many days on berries alone as there
was no game in that part of the mountains which were broken rockey
and so thickly covered with timber that they could scarcely pass.
however knowing that Indians had passed, and did pass, at this
season on that side of this river to the same below the mountains,
my rout was instantly settled in my own mind, p[r]ovided the account of this river should prove true on an investigation of it, which
I was determined should be made before we would undertake the
rout by land in any direction. I felt perfectly satisfyed, that if the
Indians could pass these mountains with their women and Children,
that we could also pass them; and that if the nations on this river
below the mountains were as numerous as they were stated to be
that they must have some means of subsistence which it would be
equally in our power to procure in the same country.   they informed
me that there was no buffaloe on the West side of these mountains;
that the game consisted of a few Elk deer and Antelopes, and that
the natives subsisted on fish and roots principally.

in this manner I spent the day smoking with them and acquiring
what information I could with respect to their country.   they informed me that they could pass to the Spaniards by the way of the
yellowstone river in 10 days. I can discover that these people are
by no means friendly to the Spaniards.   their complaint is, that the
Spaniards will not let them have fire arms and amunition, that they
put them off by telling them that if they suffer them to have guns
they will kill each other, thus leaving them defenceless and an easy
prey to their bloodthirsty neighbours to the East of them, who being
in possession of fire arms hunt them up and murder them without
rispect to sex or age and plunder them of their horses on all occasions.   they told me that to avoid their enemies who were eternally
harrassing them that they were obliged to remain in the interior of
these mountains at least two thirds of the year where the[y] suffered
as we then saw great heardships for the want of food sometimes
living for weeks without meat and only a little fish roots and berries.
but this added Câmeahwait, with his ferce eyes and lank jaws grown

meager for the want of food, would not be the case if we had guns, we could then live in the country of buffaloe and eat as our enimies do and not be compelled to hide ourselves in these mountains and live on roots and berries as the bear do. we do not fear our enimies when placed on an equal footing with them.

I told them that the Minnetares Mandans & recares of the Missouri had promised us to desist from making war on them & that we would indevour to find the means of making the Minnetares of fort d Prarie or as they call them Pahkees desist from waging war against them also. that after our finally returning to our homes towards the rising sun whitemen would come to them with an abundance of guns and every other article necessary to their defence and comfort, and that they would be enabled to supply themselves with these articles on reasonable terms in exchange for the skins of the beaver Otter and Ermin so abundant in their country. they expressed great pleasure at this information and said they had been long anxious to see the whitemen that traded guns; and that we might rest assured of their friendship and that they would do whatever we wished them.

[Clark]   August 20th. Tuesday 1805 "So-So-ne" the Snake Indians
this evening passed a number of old lodges, and met a number of men women children & horses, met a man who appeared of Some Consideration who turned back with us, he halted a woman & gave us 3 Small Sammon, this man continued with me all night and partook of what I had which was a little Pork verry Salt. Those Indians are verry attentive to Strangers &c. I left our interpreter & his woman to accompany the Indians to Capt Lewis tomorrow the Day they informed me they would Set out I killed a Pheasent at the Indian Camp larger than a dungal [dunghill] fowl with f[l]eshey protubrances about the head like a turkey. Frost last night.

[Lewis]   Wednesday August 21st. 1805.
This morning was very cold. the ice ¼ of an inch thick on the water which stood in the vessels exposed to the air. some wet deerskins that had been spread on the grass last evening are stiffly frozen. the ink f[r]eizes in my pen. the bottoms are perfectly covered with frost, insomuch that they appear to be covered with snow.

The party pursued their several occupations as yesterday. by evening I had all the baggage, saddles, and harness completely ready for a march. after dark, I made the men take the baggage to the cash and deposit it. I beleve we have been unperceived by the Indians in this movement.

The mockersons of both sexes are usually the same and are made of deer Elk or buffaloe skin dressed without the hair. sometimes in the winter they make them of buffaloe skin dressed with the hair on and turn the hair inwards as the Mandans Minetares and most of the nations do who inhabit the buffaloe country. the mockerson is formed with one seem on the outer edge of the foot is cut open at the instep to admit *the foot and sewed up behind. in this rispect they are the same with the Mandans.* they sometimes ornament their mockersons with various figures wrought with the quills of the Porcupine. some of the dressey young men orniment the tops of their mockersons with the skins of polecats and trale the tail of that animal on the ground at their heels as they walk.

the robe of the woman is generally smaller than that of the man but is woarn in the same manner over the sholders. the Chemise is roomy and comes down below the middle of the leg the upper part of this garment is formed much like the shirt of the men except the sholder strap which is never used with the Chemise. in women who give suck, they are left open at the sides nearly as low as the waist, in others, close as high as the sleeve. the sleeve underneath as low as the elbow is open, that part being left very full. the sides tail and upper part of the sleeves are deeply fringed and sometimes orniment in a similar manner with the shirts of the men with the addition of little patches of red cloth about the tail edged around with beads. the breast is usually ornament[e]d with various figures of party colours rought with the quills of the Porcupine. it is on this part of the garment that they appear to exert their greatest engenuity. a girdle of dressed leather confines the Chemise around the waist. when either the man or the woman wish to disengage their arm from the sleeve they draw it out by means of the opening underneath the arm and throw the sleeve behind the body.

the legings of the women reach as high as the knee and are confined with a garter below. the mockerson covers and confins it's lower extremity. they are neither fringed nor ornamented. these legings are made of the skins of the antelope and the Chemise

usually of those of the large deer Bighorn and the smallest elk.
They seldom wear the beads they possess about their necks; at least
I have never seen a grown person of either sex wear them on this
part; some [of] their children are seen with them in this way. the
men and women were [wear] them suspen[ded] from the ear in little
bunches or intermixed with triangular peices of the shells of the perl
oister. the men also were them attached in a similar manner to the
hare of the fore part of the crown of the head; to which they sometimes make the addition of the wings and tails of birds.

the nose in neither sex is pierced nor do they wear any ornament
in it. they have a variety of small sea shells of which they form
collars woarn indiscriminately by both sexes. these as well as
the shell of the perl oister they value very highly and inform us
that they obtain them from their friends and relations who live
beyond the barren plain towards the Ocean in a S. Westerly direction. these friends of theirs they say inhabit a good country abound-
ing with Elk, deer, bear, and Antelope, and possess a much greater
number of horses and mules than they do themselves; or using their
own figure that their horses and mules are as numerous as the grass
of the plains. the warriors or such as esteem themselves brave men
wear collars made of the claws of the brown bear which are also
esteemed of great value and are preserved with great care. these
claws are ornamented with beads about the thick end near which
they are peirced through their sides and strung on a throng of dressed
leather and tyed about the neck commonly with the upper edge of
the tallon next the breast or neck but sometimes are reversed. it
is esteemed by them an act of equal celebrity the killing one of
these bear or an enimy, and with the means they have of killing
this animal it must really be a serious undertaking.

the sweet sented grass which grows very abundant on this river is
either twisted or plaited and woarn around the neck in ether sex,
but most commonly by the men. they have a collar also woarn by
either sex. it [is] generally round and about the size of a man's
finger; formed of leather or silk-grass twisted or firmly rolled and
covered with the quills of the porcupine of different colours. the
tusks of the Elk are pierced strung on a throng and woarn as an
orniment for the neck, and is most generally woarn by the women
and children. the men frequently wear the skin of a fox or a broad

strip of that of the otter around the forehead and head in form of a
bando. they are also fond of the feathers of the tail of the beautifull
eagle or callumet bird with which they ornament their own hair and
the tails and mains of their horses. also a collar of round bones which
look like the joints of a fishes back The dress of these people is
quite as desent and convenient as that of any nation of Indians I
ever saw.

   This morning early Capt. C. resumed his march; at the distance
of five miles he arrived at some brush lodges of the Shoshones
inhabited by about seven families. here he halted and was very
friendly received by these people, who gave himself and party as
much boiled salmon as they could eat; they also gave him several
dryed salmon and a considerable quantity of dryed chokecherries.
after smoking with them he visited their fish wear [weir] which was
abut 200 yds. distant. he found the wear extended across four
channels of the river which was here divided by three small islands.
three of these channels were narrow, and were stoped by means of
trees fallen across, supported by which stakes of willow were driven
down sufficiently near each other to prevent the salmon from
passing. about the center of each a cilindric basket of eighteen or
20 feet in length terminating in a conic shape at it's lower extremity,
formed of willows, was opposed to a small apperture in the wear
with it's mouth up stream to receive the fish. the main channel of
the water was conducted to this basket, which was so narrow at it's
lower extremity that the fish when once in could not turn itself
about, and were taken out by untying the small ends of the longitudinal willows, which form the hull of the basket. the wear in the
main channel was somewhat differently contrived. there were two
distinct wears formed of poles and willow sticks, quite across the
river, at no great distance from each other. each of these, were
furnished with two baskets; the one wear to take them ascending
and the other in decending. in constructing these wears, poles were
first tyed together in parcels of three near the smaller extremity;
these were set on end, and spread in a triangular form at the base,
in such manner, that two of the three poles ranged in the direction
of the intended work, and the third down the stream. two ranges
of horizontal poles were next lashed with willow bark and wythes

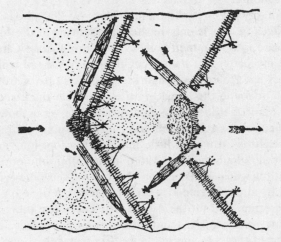

to the ranging poles, and on these willow sticks were placed perpendicularly, reaching from the bottom of the river to about 3 or
four feet above it's surface; and placed so near each other, as not
to permit the passage of the fish, and even so thick in some parts,
as with the help of gravel and stone to give a direction to the water
which they wished. the baskets were the same in form of the others.
this is the form of the work, and disposition of the baskets.

while Capt. Clark was at these lodges an Indian brought him a
tomehawk which he said he found in the grass near the lodge where
I had staid at the upper camp when I was first with his nation. the
tommahawk was Drewyer's he missed it in the morning before we
had set out and surched for it but it was not to be found I beleive
the young fellow stole it, but if he did it is the only article they
have pilfered and this was now returned.

[Clark]   August 21st. Wednesday 1805
Frost last night   proceeded on with the Indians I met about 5
miles to there Camp,   I entered a lodge and after smokeing with
all who Came about me I went to see the place those people take

the fish, a wear across the Creek in which there is Stuk baskets Set in different derections So as to take the fish either decending or assending

on my return to the Camp which was 200 yards only the different lodges (which is only bushes) brought in to the lodge I was introduced into, Sammon boiled, and dried Choke Chers. Sufficent for all my party. one man brought me a *tomahawk* which we expected they had Stolen from a man of Cap Lewis's party, this man informed me he found the tomak. in the grass near the place the man Slept.

Their method of takeing fish with a *gig* or bone is with a long pole, about a foot from one End is a Strong String attached to the pole, this String is a little more than a foot long and is tied to the middle of a bone from 4 to 6 inches long, one end Sharp the other with a whole to fasten on the end of the pole with a beard [*i.e.*, barb] to the large end, the[y] fasten this bone on one end & with the other, feel for the fish & turn and Strike them So hard that the bone passes through and Catches on the opposit Side, Slips off the End of the pole and holds the Center of the bone

Those Indians are mild in their disposition, appear Sincere in their friendship, punctial, and decided. kind with what they have, to spare. They are excessive pore, nothing but horses there Enemies which are noumerous on account of there horses & Defenceless Situation, have deprived them of tents and all the Small Conveniances of life.

The women are held more sacred among them than any nation we have seen and appear to have an equal Shere in all conversation, which is not the Case in any other nation I have seen. their boys & girls are also admited to speak except in Councels, the women doe all the drugery except fishing and takeing care of the horses, which the men apr. to take upon themselves. The men ware the hair loose flowing over ther Sholders & face, the women Cut Short, ornements of the back bones of fish Strung, plated grass grains of Corn Strung Feathers and orniments of Birds Claws of the Bear encurcling their necks the most sacred of all the orniments of this nation is the Sea Shells of various Sizes and Shapes and colours, of the bassterd perl kind, which they inform us they get from the Indians to the South on the other Side of a large fork of this river in passing to which they have to pass thro: Sandy & barron open

plains without water to which place they can travel in 15 or 20 days.
The men who passed by the forks informed me that the S W. fork
was double the Size of the one I came down, and I observed that
it was a handsom river at my camp I shall in justice to Capt. Lewis
who was the first white man ever on this fork of the Columbia Call
this Louis's [Lewis's] river.[10]

[Lewis] Thursday August 22ed. 1805.

This morning early I sent a couple of men to complete the covering
of the cash which could not be done well last night in the dark,
they soon accomplished their work and returned.

late last night Drewyer returned with a fawn he had killed and a
considerable quantity of Indian plunder. the anecdote with rispect
to the latter is perhaps worthy of relation. he informed me that
while hunting in the Cove yesterday about 12 OCk. he came suddonly upon an Indian Camp, at which there were a young man an
Old man and a boy and three women, that they seemed but little
supprised at seeing him and he rode up to them and dismounted
turning [his] horse out to graize. these people had just finished their
repast on some roots, he entered into conversation with them by
signs, and after about 20 minutes one of the women spoke to the
others of the party and they all went immediately and collected their
horses brought them to camp and saddled them. at this moment
he thought he would also set out and continue his hunt, and ac-
corgingly walked to catch his horse at some little distance and neglected to take up his gun which he left at camp. the Indians
perceiving him at the distance of fifty paces immediately mounted
their horses, the young man took the gun, and the whole of them
left their baggage and laid whip to their horses directing their course
to the pass of the mountains.

finding himself deprived of his gun he immediately mounted his
horse and pursued; after runing them about 10 miles the horses of
two of the women nearly gave out and the young fellow with the
gun from their frequent crys slackened his pace and being on a very
fleet horse road around the women at a little distance at length
Drewer overtook the women and by signs convinced them that he

[10] The Salmon River at Salmon, Idaho.

did not wish to hirt them　they then halted and the young fellow approached still nearer, he asked him for his gun but the only part of the answer which he could understand was pahkee which he knew to be the name by which they called their enimies.　watching his opportunity when the fellow was off his guard he suddonly rode along side of him seized his gun and wrest[ed] her out of his hands. the fellow finding Drewyer too strong for him and discovering that he must yeald the gun had p[r]esents of mind to open the pan and cast the priming before he let the gun escape from his hands; now finding himself devested of the gun he turned his horse about and laid whip leaving the women to follow him as well as they could.

Drewyer now returned to the place where they had left their baggage and brought it with him to my camp.　it consisted of several dressed and undressed skins; a couple of bags wove with the fingers of the bark of the silk-grass containing each about a bushel of dryed service burries some ch[ok]cherry cakes and about a bushel of roots of three different kinds dryed and prepared for uce which were foalded in as many parchment hides of buffaloe.　some flint and the instrument of bone for manufactureing the flint into arrow points. some of this flint was as transparent as the common black glass and much of the same colour, easily broken, and flaked of[f] much like glass leaving a very sharp edge.

one speceis of the roots were fusiform abo[u]t six inches long and about the size of a man's finger at the larger end tapering to a small point.　the radicles larger than in most fusiform roots.　the rind was white and thin. the body or consistence of the root was white mealy and easily reduced by pounding to a substance resembleing flour which thickens with boiling water something like flour and is agreeably flavored.　this rout is frequently eaten by the Indians either green or in it's dryed state without the preparation of boiling. another speceis was much mutilated but appeared to be fibrous; the parts were brittle, hard, of the size of a small quill, cilindric and as white as snow throughout, except some small parts of the hard black rind which they had not seperated in the preperation.　this the Indians with me informed were always boiled for use.　I made the exp[e]riment, found that they became perfectly soft by boiling, but had a very bitter taste, which was naucious to my pallate, and I transfered them to the Indians who had eat them heartily.　a third speceis were about the size of a nutmeg, and of an irregularly rounded form, something like the smallest of the Jarusalem artichoke, which they also resemble in every other appearance. they had become very hard by being dryed, these I also boiled agreeably to the instruction of the Indians and found them very agreeable. they resemble the Jerusalem Artichoke very much in their flavor and I thought them preferable, however there is some allowance to be made for the length of time I have now been without vegitable food to which I was always much attatched. these are certainly the best root[s] I have yet seen in uce among the Indians. I asked the Indians to shew me the plant of which these roots formed a part but they informed me that neither of them grew near this place.[11] I had set most of the men at work today to dress the deerskin belonging to those who had gone on command with Capt. Clark.

at 11.A.M. Charbono, the Indian Woman, Cameahwait and about 50 men with a number of women and children arrived. they encamped near us. after they had turned out their horses and arranged their camp I called the Cheifs and warriors together and addressed them a second time; gave them some further presents, particularly the second and third Cheifs who it appeared had agreeably to their promise exerted themselves in my favour, having no fresh meat and these poor devils half starved I had previously prepared a good meal for them all of boiled corn and beans which I gave them as soon as the council was over and I had distributed the presents. this was thankfully received by them. the Cheif wished that his nation could live in a country where they could provide such food. I told him that it would not be many years before the whitemen would put it in the power of his nation to live in the country below the mountains where they might cultivate corn beans and squashes. he appeared much pleased with the information. I gave him a few

[11] It is not easy to identify these roots fully, as Lewis could describe only the dried tuber, without seeing the plant. The first named was probably that of dill (*Carum*, or *Anethum*), called by the Shoshone Indians *yampah*. The third was probably the wild artichoke (*Helianthus tuberosus*). Coues thinks that the other is *Lewisia rediviva* (Fr. *racine amère*, "bitter root"—giving name to the Bitterroot Mountains) (Thwaites). Yampa (*Perideridia gairdneri*) is also called squawroot; *Helianthus tuberosus*, a species of sunflower, is called Jerusalem artichoke; and bitterroot (*Lewisia rediviva*), the Montana state flower, is also called rock rose.

dryed squashes which we had brought from the Mandans   he had them boiled and declared them to be the best thing he had ever tasted except sugar, a small lump of which it seems his sister Sah-cah-gar Wea had given him.

late in the evening I made the men form a bush drag, and with it in about 2 hours they caught 528 very good fish, most of them large trout,   among them I now for the first time saw ten or a douzen of a white speceis of trout. they are of a silvery colour except on the back and head, where they are of a bluish cast.   the scales are much larger than the speckled trout, but in their form position of their fins teeth mouth &c they are precisely like them.   they are not generally quite as large but equally well flavored.   I distributed much the greater portion of the fish among the Indians.   I purchased five good horses of them very reasonably, or at least for about the value of six dollars a peice in merchandize. the Indians are very orderly and do not croud about our camp nor attempt to disterb any article they see lying about.   they borrow knives kettles &c from the men and always carefully return them.

[Clark]   August 22d. Thursday 1805.
   passed a Small Creek on the right at 1 mile and the points of four mountains verry Steup high & rockey,   the assent of three was So Steup that it is incredeable to describe   the rocks in maney places loose & Sliped from those mountains and is a Solid bed of rugid loose white and dark brown loose rock for miles.   the Indian horses pass over those Clifts hills beds & rocks as fast as a man, the three horses with me do not detain me any on account of those dificulties, passed two bold rung. Streams on the right and a Small river[12] at the mouth of which Several families of Indians were encamped and had Several Scaffolds of fish & buries drying   we allarmed them verry much as they knew nothing of a white man being in their Countrey, and at the time we approached their lodges which was in a thick place of bushes   my guides were behind.   They offered every thing they possessed (which was verry little) to us, Some run off and hid in the bushes   The first offer of theirs were Elks tushes from around their childrens necks, Sammon &c.

[12] The north fork of Salmon River, near North Fork, Idaho.

my guide attempted [to] passify those people and they Set before me berri[e]s, & fish to eate, I gave a fiew Small articles to those fritened people which added verry much to their pasification but not entirely as some of the women & Childn. Cried dureing my Stay of an hour at this place, I proceeded on the Side of a verry Steep & rockey mountain for 3 miles and Encamped on the lower pt. of an Island we attempted to gig fish without Suckcess caught but one Small one. in this day passed Several womin and Children gathering and drying buries of which they were very kind and gave us a part. the river rapid and Sholey maney Stones Scattered through it in different directions. I saw to day [a] Bird of the woodpecker kind which fed on Pine burs its Bill and tale white the wings black every other part of a light brown, and about the Size of a robin.[13]

[Lewis]   Friday August 23rd. 1805.

I also laid up the canoes this morning in a pond near the forks; sunk them in the water and weighted them down with stone, after taking out the plugs of the gage holes in their bottoms; hoping by this means to guard against both the effects of high water, and that of the fire which is frequently kindled in these plains by the natives. the Indians have promised to do them no intentional injury and [I] beleive they are too laizy at any rate to give themselves the trouble to raise them from their present situation in order to cut or birn them. I reminded the chief of the low state of our stores of provision and advised him to send his young men to hunt, which he immediately recommended to them and most of them turned out. I wished to have purchased some more horses of them but they objected against disposing of any more of them untill we reach their camp beyond the mountains.

The metal which we found in possession of these people consi[s]ted of a few indifferent knives, a few brass kettles some arm bands of iron and brass, a few buttons, woarn as ornaments in their hair, a spear or two of a foot in length and some iron and brass arrow points which they informed me they obtained in exchange for horses from the Crow or Rocky Mountain Indians on the yellowstone

[13] Clark's nutcracker (*Nucifraga columbiana*).

River. the bridlebits and stirreps they obtained from the Spaniards, tho these were but few. many of them made use of flint for knives, and with this instrument, skined the animals they killed, dressed their fish and made their arrows; in short they used it for every purpose to which the knife is applyed. this flint is of no regular form, and if they can only obtain a part of it, an inch or two in length that will cut they are satisfyed. they renew the edge by flecking off the flint by means of the point of an Elk's or deer's horn. with the point of a deer or Elk's horn they also form their arrow points of the flint, with a quickness and neatness that is really astonishing. we found no axes nor hatchets among them; what wood they cut was done either with stone or Elk's horn. the latter they use always to rive or split their wood.

their culinary eutensils exclusive of the brass kettle before mentioned consist of pots in the form of a jar made either of earth, or of a white soft stone which becomes black and very hard by birning, and is found in the hills near the three forks of the Missouri betwen Madison's and Gallitin's rivers. they have also spoons made of the Buffaloe's horn and those of the Bighorn. Their bows are made of ceader or pine and have nothing remarkable about them. the back of the bow is covered with sinues and glue and is about 2½ feet long. much the shape of those used by the Siouxs Mandans Minnetares &c. their arrows are more slender generally than those used by the nations just mentioned but much the same in construction. Their sheild is formed of buffaloe hide, perfectly arrow proof, and is a circle of 2 feet 4 I. or 2 F. 6 I. in diameter. this is frequently painted with varios figures and ornamented around the edges with feather[s] and a fringe of dressed leather. they sometimes make bows of the Elk's horn and those also of the bighorn. those of the Elk's horn are made of a single peice and covered on the back with glue and sinues like those made of wood, and are frequently ornamented with a stran[d] wrought [of] porcupine quills and sinues raped around them for some distance at both extremities. the bows of the bighorns are formed of small peices laid flat and cemented with gleue, and rolled with siniws, after which, they are also covered on the back with sinews and glew, and highly ornamented as they are much prized.

forming the sheild is a cerimony of great importance among them, this implement would in their minds be devested of much of its protecting power were it not inspired with those virtues by their old men and jugglers. their method of preparing it is thus, an entire skin of a bull buffaloe two years old is first provided; a feast is next prepared and all the warriors old men and jugglers invited to partake. a hole is sunk in the ground about the same in diameter with the intended sheild and about 18 inches deep. a parcel of stones are now made red hot and thrown into the hole water is next thrown in and the hot stones cause it to emit a very strong hot steem, over this they spread the green skin which must not have been suffered to dry after taken off the beast. the flesh side is laid next to the groround and as many of the workmen as can reach it take hold on it's edges and extend it in every direction. as the skin becomes heated, the hair seperates and is taken of[f] with the fingers, and the skin continues to contract untill the who[l]e is drawn within the compas designed for the shield, it is then taken off and laid on a parchment hide where they pound it with their heels when barefoot. this operation of pounding continues for several days or as long as the feast lasts when it is delivered to the propryeter and declared by the jugglers and old men to be a sufficient defence against the arrows of their enimies or even bullets if [the] feast has been a satisfactory one. many of them beleive implisitly that a ball cannot penitrate their sheilds, in consequence of certain superna[t]ural powers with which they have been inspired by their jugglers.

[Clark]   August 23rd. Friday 1805
    proceed on with great dificuelty as the rocks were So sharp large and unsettled and the hill sides Steep that the horses could with the greatest risque and dificulty get on, no provisions as the 5 Sammon given us yesterday by the Indians were eaten last night, one goose killed this morning; at 4 miles we came to a place the horses Could not pass without going into the river, we passed one mile to a verry bad riffle the water confined in a narrow Channel & beeting against the left Shore, as we have no parth further and the Mounts. jut So close as to prevent the possibility of horses proceeding down, I Deturmined to delay the party here and with my

guide[14] and three men proceed on down to examine if the river continued bad or was practi[c]able

The River from the place I left my party to this Creek is almost one continued rapid, five verry considerable rapids the passage of either with Canoes is entirely impossible, as the water is Confined between huge Rocks & the Current beeting from one against another for Some distance below &c. &c. at one of those rapids the mountains close so Clost as to prevent a possibility of a portage with [out] great labour in cutting down the Side of the hill removeing large rocks this river is about 100 yards wide and can be forded but in a few places. below my guide and maney other Indians tell me that the Mountains Close and is a perpendicular Clift on each Side, and Continues for a great distance and that the water runs with great violence from one rock to the other on each Side foaming & roreing thro rocks in every direction, So as to render the passage of any thing impossible.[15]

[Lewis]   Saturday August 24th. 1805.

at twelve Oclock we set out and passed the river below the forks, directing our rout towards the cove. most of the horses were heavily laden, and it appears to me that it will require at least 25 horses to convey our baggage along such roads as I expect we shall be obliged to pass in the mountains. I had now the inexpressible satisfaction to find myself once more under way with all my baggage and party. an Indian had the politeness to offer me one of his horses to ride which I accepted with cheerfullness as it enabled me to attend better to the march of the party. I had reached the lower part of the cove when an Indian rode up and informed me that one of my men was very sick and unable to come on. I directed the party to halt at a small run which falls into the creek on Lard. at the lower part of the Cove and rode back about 2 Miles where I found Wiser very ill with a fit of the cholic. I sent Sergt. Ordway who had remained with him for some water and gave him a doze of the essence of Peppermint and laudinum which in the course of half an hour so far recovered him that he was enabled to ride my horse and I proceeded on foot and rejoined the party.

---

[14] The old Shoshone man called Toby.
[15] The Salmon River, west of North Fork, Idaho, called the River of No Return.

Goodrich who is our principal fisherman caught several fine trout. Drewyer came to us late in the evening and had not killed anything. I gave the Indians who were absolutely engaged in transporting the baggage, a little corn as they had nothing to eat. I told Cameahwait that my stock of provision was too small to indulge all his people with provision and recommended it to him to advise such as were not assisting us with our baggage to go on to their camp to morrow and wait our arrival; which he did accordingly. *Cameahwait* literally translated is *one who never walks.* he told me that his nation had also given him another name by which he was signalized as a warrior which was Too-et'-te-can'-e or *black gun.* these people have many names in the course of their lives, particularly if they become distinguished characters. for it seems that every important event by which they happen to distinguish themselves intitles them to claim another name which is generally scelected by themselves and confirmed by the nation. those distinguishing acts are the killing and scalping an enemy, the killing a white bear, leading a party to war who happen to be successfull either in destroying their enemies or robing them of their horses, or individually stealing the horses of an enemy. these are considered acts of equal heroism among them, and that of killing an enemy without scalping him is considered of no importance; in fact the whole honour seems to be founded in the act of scalping, for if a man happens to slay a dozen of his enemies in action and others get the scalps or first lay their hand on the dead person the honor is lost to him who killed them and devolves on those who scalp or first touch them. Among the Shoshones, as well as all the Indians of America, bravery is esteemed the primary virtue; nor can any one become eminent among them who has not at some period of his life given proofs of his possessing this virtue. with them there can be no preferment without some warlike achievement, and so completely interwoven is this principle with the earliest Elements of thought that it will in my opinion prove a serious obstruction to the restoration of a general peace among the nations of the Missouri.

I have seen a few skins among these people which have almost every appearance of the common sheep.[16] they inform me that they

[16] Mountain goat (*Oreamnos americanus*).

finde this animal on the high mountains to the West and S. W. of them. it is about the size of the common sheep, the wool is reather shorter and more intermixed with long hairs particularly on the upper part of the neck. these skins have been so much woarn that I could not form a just Idea of the animal or it's colour. the Indians however inform me that it is white and that it's horns are lunated comprest twisted and bent backward as those of the common sheep. the texture of the skin appears to be that of the sheep. I am now perfectly convinced that the sheep as well as the Bighorn exist in these mountains.

[Clark]   August 24th. Satturday 1805
I wrote a letter to Capt Lewis informing him of the prospects before us and information rec[ei]ved of my guide which I thought favourable &c. & Stating two plans one of which for us to pursue &c. and despatched one man & horse and directed the party to get ready to march back, every man appeared disheartened from the prospects of the river, and nothing to eate, I Set out late and Camped 2 miles above, nothing to eate but Choke Cherries & red haws, which act in different ways So as to make us Sick, dew verry heavy, my beding wet in passing around a rock the horses were obliged to go deep into the water.

The plan I stated to Capt Lewis if he agrees with me we shall adopt is. to procure as many horses (one for each man) if possible and to hire my present guide who I sent on to him to interigate thro' the Intptr. and proceed on by land to Some navagable part of the *Columbia* River, or to the *Ocean*, depending on what provisions we can procure by the gun aded to the Small Stock we have on hand depending on our horses as the last resort.

a second plan to divide the party one part to attempt this deficuelte river with what provisions we had, and the remainde[r] to pass by Land on ho[r]se back Depending on our gun &c. for Provisions &c. and come together occasionally on the river. the 1st. of which I would be most pleased with &c. I saw Several trees which would make Small Canoes and by putting 2 together would make a Siseable one, all below the last Indian Camp Several miles

[Lewis]   Sunday August 25th. 1805.

sometime after we had halted, Charbono mentioned to me with apparent unconcern that he expected to meet all the Indians from the camp on the Columbia tomorrow on their way to the Missouri. allarmed at this information I asked why he expected to meet them. he then informed me that the 1st. Cheif had dispatched some of his young men this morning to this camp requesting the Indians to meet them tomorrow and that himself and those with him would go on with them down the Missouri, and consequently leave me and my baggage on the mountain or thereabouts. I was out of patience with the folly of Charbono who had not sufficient sagacity to see the consequencies which would inevitably flow from such a movement of the indians, and altho' he had been in possession of this information since early in the morning when it had been communicated to him by his Indian woman yet he never mentioned it untill the after noon. I could not forbear speaking to him with some degree of asperity on this occasion. I saw that there was no time to be lost in having those orders countermanded, or that we should not in all probability obtain any more horses or even get my baggage to the waters of the Columbia.

I therefore Called the three Cheifs together and having smoked a pipe with them, I asked them if they were men of their words, and whether I could depent on the promises they had made me; they readily answered in the affermative; I then asked them if they had not promised to assist me with my baggage to their camp on the other side of the mountains, or to the place at which Capt. Clark might build the canoes, should I wish it. they acknowledged that they had. I then asked them why they had requested their people on the other side of the mountain to meet them tomorrow on the mountain where there would be no possibility of our remaining together for the purpose of trading for their horses as they had also promised. that if they had not promised to have given me their assistance in transporting my baggage to the waters on the other side of the mountain that I should not have attempted to pass the mountains but would have returned down the river and that in that case they would never have seen anymore white men in their country. that if they wished the white men to be their friends and to assist them against their enemies by furnishing them with arms and keeping their enemies from attacking them that they must never promis us anything which they did not mean to perform. that when I had first seen them they had doubted what I told them about the arrival of the party of whitemen in canoes, that they had been convinced that what I told them on that occasion was true, why then would they doubt what I said on any other point. I told them that they had witnessed my liberality in dividing the meat which my hunters killed with them; and that I should continue to give such of them as assisted me a part of whatever we had ourselves to eat. and finally concluded by telling them if they intended to keep the promises they had made me to dispatch one of their young men immediately with orders to their people to remain where they were untill our arrival.

the two inferior cheifs said that they wished to assist me and be as good as their word, and that they had not sent for their people, that it was the first Chief who had done so, and they did not approve of the measure. Cameahwait remained silent for some time, at length he told me that he knew he had done wrong but that he had been induced to that measure from seeing all his people hungry, but as he had promised to give me his assistance he would not in future be worse than his word. I then desired him to send immediately and countermand his orders; accordingly a young man was sent for this purpose and I gave him a handkerchief to engage him in my interest.

this matter being arranged to my satisfaction I called all the women and men together who had been assisting me in the transportation of the baggage and gave them a billet for each horse which they had imployed in that service and informed them when we arrived at the plaice where we should finally halt on the river I would take the billet back and give them merchandize for it. every one appeared now satisfyed and when I ordered the horses loaded for our departure the Indians were more than usually allert. we continued our march until late in the evening and encamped at the upper part of the cove where the creek enters the mountains; here our hunters joined us with another deer which they had killed, this I gave to the women and Children, and for my own part remained supperless.

[Clark]   August 25th. Sunday 1805
  Set out verry early and halted one hour at the Indian Camp, they were kind gave us all a little boiled Sammon & dried buries to eate, abt. half as much as I could eate, those people are kind with what they have but excessive pore & Durtey. we proceeded on over the mountains we had before passed to the Bluff we Encamped at on the 21st.

Course & Distance Down
Columbia [Lemhi and Salmon] river by Land, as I Decended &c.

N.W.	18	miles from the Indian Camp to the forks [of Salmon R] crossed the [Lemhi] river twice, passed Several old camps
[*Aug 20*]		on the East Side and a Camp of Several lodges at a were [weir] on the west Side, passed a roade on the left leading
[*Aug 21*]		up the main West fork [i.e. Salmon above the Lemhi] below the last Camp, Several Small branches falls in on each Side [of the Lemhi], a high mountain on eash Side, [of Salmon and Lemhi together]
N. 15.° W.	14	miles to a Island passed [a] high red Clift on the right Side passed a large [*Tower*] Creek [*on the right*] at 9 miles up which
[*Aug 21*]		a roade passes large bottom below. Several Spring runs
[*Aug 22*]		falling from the mountains on the left. passed a Creek on the right.
N. 30.° W.	2	to the top of a mountain the river one mile to the left
NW	10	miles with the general Course of the river, passed over the Spurs of four mountains almost inexcessable and two Small
Aug. 22]		runs on the right to Some Indian Camps at the mouth of a Small river [*Fish cr.*] on the right up which a road passes passed Several Islands, and Small bottoms between the mountains.
West	3	miles on the right Side to the assent of a mountain, passed over one Spur of the Same Mountain passed 2 Islands, & a bottom in which berris were plenty.
S.W.	5	miles to a verry bad rapid & *Camped*, a Small run on the left. passed perpendicular Clift where we were obliged to
[*Aug. 22*]		go into the water passed Several places on Stones & sides of Mountains, one Island & several rapids, all the way rapids at intervals
N.W.	3	miles high Clifts on each Side no road [*left men here*]

West	2	Miles do do. passed bad rapids Scercely possible to pass down or up
[*Aug. 23*]		
N.W.	6	miles to a large Creek on the Right Side, passed verry bad rapids & a number of riffles, Mountains high and Steep verry Stoney no bottoms except the Creek & a little above
South	1	Mile to the Mouth of a Small run on the right a Small Island and rapid
N.W.	6	Miles up the Run [*Berry Creek Aug. 23*] thro a piney countrey large & lofty hills high
S.W.	1	m. to the river at a Small bottom passed over a gap in the Mountns. from the top of which I could See the hollers of the river for 20 miles to a verry high Mountain on the Left,
[*End of recon-noissance*]		at which place my guide made Signs that the bad part of the river Comsd. and much worst than any I saw &c. &c.

miles   70

returned. 6 bad rapids.   many others

[Lewis]   Monday August 26th. 1805.
   we proceeded to a fine spring on the side of the mountain where
I had lain the evening before I first arrived at the Shoshone Camp.
here I halted to dine and graize our horses, there being fine green
grass on that part of the hillside which was moistened by the water
of the spring while the grass on the other parts was perfectly dry
and parched with the sun.
   I directed a pint of corn to be given each Indian who was engaged
in transporting our baggage and about the same quantity to each of
the men which they parched pounded and made into supe. one of
the women who had been assisting in the transportation of the
baggage halted at a little run about a mile behind us, and sent on
the two pack horses which she had been conducting by one of her
female friends. I enquired of Cameahwait the cause of her detention, and was informed by him in an unconcerned manner that she
had halted to bring fourth a child and would soon overtake us; in
about an hour the woman arrived with her newborn babe and passed
us on her way to the camp apparently as well as she ever was.
   It appears to me that the facility and ease with which the women
of the aborigines of North America bring fourth their children is
reather a gift of nature than depending as some have supposed on
the habitude of carrying heavy burthens on their backs while in the

state of pregnacy. if a pure and dry air, an elivated and cold country is unfavourable to childbirth, we might expect every difficult incident to that operation of nature in this part of the continent; again as the snake Indians possess an abundance of horses, their women are seldom compelled like those in other parts of the continent to carry burthens on their backs, yet they have their children with equal convenience, and it is a rare occurrence for any of them to experience difficulty in childbirth. I have been several times informed by those who were conversant with the fact, that the indian women who are pregnant by whitemen experience more difficulty in childbirth than when pregnant by an Indian. if this be true it would go far in suport of the opinion I have advanced.

on our near approach we were met by a number of young men on horseback. Cameahwait requested that we would discharge our guns when we arrived in sight of the Village, accordingly when I arrived on an eminence above the village in the plain I drew up the party at open order in a single rank and gave them a runing fire discharging two rounds. they appeared much gratifyed with this exhibition. we then proceeded to the village or encampment of brush lodges 32 in number. we were conducted to a large lodge which had been prepared for me in the center of their encampment which was situated in a beautifull level smooth and extensive bottom near the river about 3 miles above the place I had first found them encamped. here we arrived at 6 in the evening arranged our baggage near my tent and placed those of the men on either side of the baggage facing outwards. I found Colter here who had just arrived with a letter from Capt. Clark in which Capt. C. had given me an account of his perigrination and the description of the river and country

from this view of the subject I found it a folly to think of attemp[t]ing to decend this river in canoes and therefore determined to commence the purchase of horses in the morning from the indians in order to carry into execution the design we had formed of passing the rocky Mountains. I now informed Cameahwait of my intended expedition overland to the great river which lay in the plains beyond the mountains and told him that I wished to purchase 20 horses of himself and his people to convey our baggage. he observed that the Minnetares had stolen a great number of their horses this spring but hoped his people would spear me the number I wished. I also asked a guide, he observed that he had no doubt but the old man who was with Capt. C. would accompany us if we wished him and that he was better informed of the country than any of them. matters being thus far arranged I directed the fiddle to be played and the party danced very merily much to the amusement and gratification of the natives, though I must confess that the state of my own mind at this moment did not well accord with the prevailing mirth as I somewhat feared that the caprice of the indians might suddenly induce them to withhold their horses from us without which my hopes of prosicuting my voyage to advantage was lost; however I determined to keep the indians in a good humour if possible, and to loose no time in obtaining the necessary number of horses. I directed the hunters to turn out early in the morning and indeavor to obtain some meat. I had nothing but a little parched corn to eat this evening.

[Clark]   August 29th. Thursday 1805—
     I left our baggage in possession of 2 men and proceeded on up to join Capt. Lewis at the upper Village of Snake Indians where I arrived at 1 oClock found him much engaged in Councelling and attempting to purchase a fiew more horses. I Spoke to the Indians on various Subjects endeavoring to impress on theire minds the advantage it would be to them for to sell us horses and expedite the [*our*] journey the nearest and best way possibly that we might return as soon as possible and winter with them at Some place where there was plenty of buffalow, our wish is to get a horse for each man to carry our baggage and for Some of the men to ride occasionally, The horses are handsom and much acustomed to be changed as to their Parsture, we cannot calculate on their carrying large loads & feed on the Grass which we may calculate on finding in the Mountain thro' which we may expect to pass on our rout

                                          August 30th. Friday 1805
     finding that we Could purchase no more horse[s] than we had for our goods &c. (and those not a Sufficint number for each of our Party to have one which is our wish) I Gave my Fuzee to one of the men & Sold his musket for a horse which Completed us to 29 total horses, we Purchased pack cords Made Saddles & Set out on

our rout down the [*Lemhi*] river by land guided by my old guide [and] one other who joined him, the old gu[i]de's 3 Sons followed him, before we Set out our hunters killed three Deer proceeded on 12 Miles and encamped on the river South Side.[17]

at the time we Set out from the Indian Camps the greater Part of the Band Set out over to the waters of the Missouri. we had great attention paid to the horses, as they were nearly all Sore Backs, and Several pore, & young Those horses are indifferent, maney Sore backs and others not acustomed to pack, and as we cannot put large loads on them are Compelled to purchase as maney as we can to take our Small propotion of baggage of the Parties, (& Eate if necessary) Proceeded on *12* Miles to day.

September 2nd. Monday 1805
proceded on up the Creek,[18] proceded on thro' thickets in which we were obliged to Cut a road, over rockey hill Sides where our horses were in [per]peteal danger of Slipping to their certain distruction & up & Down Steep hills, where Several horses fell, Some turned over, and others Sliped down Steep hill Sides, one horse Crippeled & 2 gave out.

September 3rd. Tuesday 1805—
hills high & rockey on each Side, in the after part of the day the high mountains closed the Creek on each Side and obliged us to take on the Steep Sides of those Mountains, So Steep that the horses Could Scur[ce]lly keep from Slipping down, Several sliped & Injured themselves verry much, with great dificuelty we made [blank space in MS.] miles & Encamped on a branch of the Creek we assended after crossing Several Steep points & one mountain, but little to eate

The mouintains to the East Covered with Snow. we met with a great misfortune, in haveing our last Th[er]mometer broken, by accident This day we passed over emence hils and Some of the worst roads that ever horses passed, our horses frequently fell

[17] This camping-place was on the Lemhi River, about eight miles above the forks of Salmon River (Thwaites).

[18] North fork of the Salmon River, toward the Continental Divide.

Snow about 2 inches deep when it began to rain which termonated in a Sleet [storm]

Septr. 3rd. Tuesday 1805

N. 25.° W. 2½   Miles to a Small fork on the left Hilley and thick assending
N. 15.° W. 2   miles to a fork on the right assending
N. 22.° W. 2½   miles to a fork on the left passing one on the left Several
               Spring runs on the right   Stoney hills & much falling
               timber
N. 18.° E. 2   miles passing over Steep points & winding ridges to a high
               Point   passed a run on the right
N. 32.° W. 2   miles to the top of a high hill   passed 2 runs from the left,
               passing on the Side of a Steep ridge.   no road
N. 40.° W 3   miles leaveing the waters of the Creek to the right &
14   passing over a high pine Mountn.   o the head of a Drean
               running to the left

September 4th. Wednesday 1805—
a verry cold morning every thing wet and frosed,   Groun[d] covered with Snow,   we assended a mountain & took a Divideing
ridge[19] which we kept for Several Miles & fell on the head of a
Creek which appeared to run the Course we wished to go
prosued our Course down the Creek to the forks about 5 miles
where we met a part[y] of the Tushepau[20] nation, of 33 Lodges
about 80 men 400 Total and at least 500 horses,   those people
rec[e]ved us friendly, threw white robes over our Sholders & Smoked
in the pipes of peace,   we Encamped with them & found them
friendly but nothing but berries to eate a part of which they gave
us, those Indians are well dressed with Skin shirts & robes,   they
[are] Stout & light complected more So than Common for Indians,
The Chief harangued untill late at night, Smoked in our pipe and
appeared Satisfied.   I was the first white man who ever wer on the
waters of this river.[21]

[19] Lost Trail Pass into Montana on the west slope of the Continental Divide.
[20] Flathead.
[21] Headwaters of the Bitterroot River near Sula, Montana.

September 5th. Thursday 1805

we assembled the Chiefs & warriers and Spoke to them (with much dificuel[t]y as what we Said had to pass through Several languages before it got into theirs, which is a gugling kind of language Spoken much thro the throught [throat]) we informed them who we were, where we came from, where bound and for what purpose &c. &c. and requested to purchase & exchange a fiew horses with them, in the Course of the day I purchased 11 horses & exchanged 7 for which we gave a fiew articles of merchendize, those people possess ellegant horses.

September 6th. Friday 1805—

took a Vocabelary of the language litened our loads & packed up, rained contd. untill 12 oClock

all our horses purchased of the flat heads (*oote-lash-shutes*) we Secured well for fear of their leaveing of us, and Watched them all night for fear of their leaving us or the Indians prosuing & Steeling them.

[Lewis]   Monday September 9th. 1805.

two of our hunters have arrived, one of them brought with him a redheaded woodpecker of the large kind common to the U States. this is the first of the kind I have seen since I left the Illinois.[22] just as we were seting out Drewyer arrived with two deer. we continued our rout down the valley about 4 miles and crossed the river; it is hear a handsome stream about 100 yards wide and affords a considerable quantity of very clear water, the banks are low and it's bed entirely gravel. the stream appears navigable, but from the circumstance of their being no sammon in it I believe that there must be a considerable fall in it below. our guide could not inform us where this river[23] discharged itself into the columbia river, he informed us that it continues it's course along the mountains to the N. as far as he knew it and that not very distant from where we then were it formed a junction with a stream nearly as large as itself which took it's rise in the mountains near the Missouri to the East

---

[22] Red-headed woodpecker (*Melanerpes erythrocephalus*).
[23] Bitterroot River, originally named Clark's River by the explorers.

of us and passed through an extensive valley generally open prarie which forms an excellent pass to the Missouri. the point of the Missouri where this Indian pass intersects it, is about 30 miles above the *gates of the rocky Mountain*, or the place where the valley of the Missouri first widens into an extensive plain after entering the rockey Mountains. the guide informed us that a man might pass to the missouri from hence by that rout in four days.[24]

we continued our rout down the W. side of the river about 5 miles further and encamped on a large creek which falls in on the West. as our guide inform[ed] me that we should leave the river at this place and the weather appearing settled and fair I determined to halt the next day rest our horses and take some scelestial Observations. we called this Creek *Travellers rest.*[25]

[Clark]   September 11th Wednesday 1805—
    proceeded on up the *Travelers rest Creek*[26] accompanied by the Flat head Indian about 7 miles our guide tels us a fine large roade passes up this river to the Missouri. The loss of 2 of our horses detained us unl. 3 oClock P.M. our *Flat head* Indian being restless thought proper to leave us and proceed on alone, Sent out the hunters to hunt in advance as usial. (we have Selected 4 of the best hunters to go in advance to hunt for the party. This arrangement has been made long since)
    Encamped at Some old Indian Lodges, nothing killed this evening hills on the right high & ruged, the mountains on the left high & Covered with Snow. The day Verry worm

                                            September 12th Thursday 1805.
    The road through this hilley Countrey is verry bad passing over hills & thro' Steep hollows, over falling timber &c. &c. continued on & passed Some most intolerable road on the Sides of the Steep Stoney mountains, which might be avoided by keeping up the Creek which is thickly covered with under groth & falling timber, Crossed

---

[24] The route of Lewis's return in 1806. The current route has taken fifty-two days.
[25] At Lolo, Montana.
[26] The route of Highway 12, west of Lolo, Montana.

a Mountain 8 miles with out water & encamped on a hill Side on the Creek after Decending a long Steep mountain,   Some of our Party did not get up untill 10 oClock P M.

September 14th Thursday (*Saturday*) 1805
a verry high Steep mountain for 9 miles to a large fork from the left which appears to head in the Snow toped mountains we Encamped opposit a Small Island at the mouth of a branch on the right side of the river which is at this place 80 yards wide, Swift and Stoney,   here we were compelled to kill a Colt for our men & Selves to eat for the want of meat & we named the South fork Colt killed Creek, and this river we Call *Flat head* River   the flat head name is Koos koos ke[27]   The Mountains which we passed to day much worst than yesterday the last excessively bad & thickly Strowed with falling timber & Pine Spruce fur Hackmatak & Tamerack, Steep & Stoney   our men and horses much fatigued

Wednesday (*Sunday*) Septr. 15th. 1805
Several horses Sliped and roled down Steep hills which hurt them verry much   the one which Carried my desk & Small trunk Turned over & roled down a mountain for 40 yards & lodged against a tree, broke the Desk the horse escaped and appeared but little hurt Some others verry much hurt,   from this point I observed a range of high mountains Covered with Snow from S E. to S W with their tops bald or void of timber,
after two hours delay we proceeded on up the mountain Steep & ruged as usial, more timber near the top,   when we arrived at the top As we Conceved, we could find no water and Concluded to Camp and make use of the Snow we found on the top to cook the remns. of our Colt & make our Supe,   evening verry cold and cloudy. Two of our horses gave out, pore and too much hurt to proceed on and left in the rear.   nothing killed to day except 2 Phests.
From this mountain I could observe high ruged mountains in every direction as far as I could see.   with the greatest exertion we could only make 12 miles up this mountain

[27] Clearwater River, west of Lolo Pass on the Idaho-Montana border.

Saturday (*Monday*) Septr. 16th. 1805

began to Snow about 3 hours before Day and continued all day
the Snow in the morning 4 inches deep on the old Snow, and by
night we found it from 6 to 8 inches deep, I walked in front to
keep the road and found great dificuelty in keeping it as in maney
places the Snow had entirely filled up the track, and obliged me to
hunt Several minits for the track, at 12 oClock we halted on the
top of the mountain to worm & dry our Selves a little as well as to
let our horses rest and graze a little on Some long grass which I
observed, (*on*) The (*South*) Knobs Steep hill Sides & falling timber
Continue to day, and a thickly timbered Countrey of 8 different
kinds of pine, which are so covered with Snow, that in passing thro'
them we are continually covered with Snow,

I have been wet and as cold in every part as I ever was in my
life, indeed I was at one time fearfull my feet would freeze in the
thin Mockirsons which I wore, after a Short Delay in the middle
of the Day,[28] I took one man and proceeded on as fast as I could
about 6 miles to a Small branch passing to the right, halted and built
fires for the party agains[t] their arrival which was at Dusk, verry
cold and much fatigued, we Encamped at this Branch in a thickly
timbered bottom which was scurcely large enough for us to lie
leavil, men all wet cold and hungary. Killed a Second Colt which
we all Suped hartily on and thought it fine meat.

[Lewis]   Wednesday September 18th. 1805

Cap Clark set out this morning to go a head with six hunters.
there being no game in these mountains we concluded it would be
better for one of us to take the hunters and hurry on to the leavel
country a head and there hunt and provide some provisions while
the other remained with and brought on the party. the latter of these
was my part; accordingly I directed the horses to be gotten up early
being determined to force my march as much as the abilities of our
horses would permit.

this morning we finished the remainder of our last coult. we
dined & suped on a skant proportion of portable soupe, a few
canesters of which, a little bears oil and about 20 lbs. of candles

---

[28] Indian Post Office, Idaho.

form our stock of provision, the only resources being our guns &
packhorses. the first is but a poor dependance in our present situation where there is nothing upon earth ex[c]ept ourselves and a
few small pheasants, small grey Squirrels, and a blue bird of the
vulter kind about the size of a turtle dove or jay bird.

[Clark]   Monday (*Wednesday*) 18th Septr. 1805—
  I proceeded on in advance with Six hunters to try and find deer
or Something to kill

[Lewis]   Thursday September 19th 1805.
  Fraziers horse fell from this road in the evening, and roled with
his load near a hundred yards into the Creek. we all expected that
the horse was killed but to our astonishment when the load was
taken off him he arose to his feet & appeared to be but little injured,
in 20 minutes he proceeded with his load. this was the most won-
derfull escape I ever witnessed, the hill down which he roled was
almost perpendicular and broken by large irregular and broken rocks.
  we took a small quantity of portable soup, and retired to rest much
fatiegued. several of the men are unwell of the disentary. brakings
out, or irruptions of the Skin, have also been common with us for
some time.

[Clark]   Tuesday (*Thursday*) 19th Septr. 1805
  Set our early proceeded on up the [*Hungry*] Creek passing through
a Small glade at 6 miles at which place we found a horse. I derected
him killed and hung up for the party after takeing a brackfast off
for our Selves which we thought fine

[Lewis]   Friday September 20th. 1805.
  This morning my attention was called to a species of bird which
I had never seen before.[29] It was reather larger than a robbin, tho'
much it's form and action. the colours were a blueish brown on the
back the wings and tale black, as wass a stripe above the croop ¾
of an inch wide in front of the neck, and two others of the same
colour passed from it's eyes back along the sides of the head. the

[29] Steller's jay (*Cyanocritta stelleri*).

top of the head, neck brest and belley and butts of the wing were of a fine yellowish brick reed [red]. it was feeding on the buries of a species of shoemake or ash which grows common in [this] country & which I first observed on 2d. of this month. I have also observed two birds of a blue colour both of which I believe to be of the haulk or vulter kind. the one of a blue shining colour with a very high tuft of feathers on the head a long tale, it feeds on flesh the beak and feet black. it's note is chă-ăh, chă-ăh. it is about the size of a pigeon, and in shape and action resembles the jay bird.

Three species of Phesants,[30] a large black species, with some white feathers irregularly scattered on the brest neck and belley— a smaller kind of a dark uniform colour with a red stripe above the eye, and a brown and yellow species that a gooddeel resembles the phesant common to the Atlantic States.

we were detained this morning untill ten oclock in consequence of not being enabled to collect our horses. we had proceeded about 2 Miles when we found the greater part of a horse which Capt. Clark had met with and killed for us. he informed me by note that he should proceed as fast as possible to the leavel country which lay to the S. W. of us, which we discovered from the hights of the mountains on the 19th. there he intended to hunt untill our arrival. at one oclock we halted on a small branch runing to the left and made a hearty meal on our horse beef much to the comfort of our hungry stomachs. here I larnt that one of the Packhorses with his load was missing and immediately dispatched Baptiest Lapage who had charge of him, to surch for him. he returned at 3 OC. without the horse. The load of the horse was of considerable value consisting of merchandize and all my stock of winter cloathing. I therefore dispatched two of my best woodsmen in surch of him, and proceeded with the party.

our road was much obstructed by fallen timber particularly in the evening. we encamped on a ridge where ther was but little grass for our horses, and at a distance from water. however we obtained as much as served our culinary purposes and suped on our beef. the soil as you leave the hights of the mountains becomes gradually more fertile. the land through which we passed this evening is of

[30] Blue grouse, spruce grouse, and ruffed grouse.

an excellent quality tho' very broken, it is a dark grey soil. a grey
free stone appearing in large masses above the earth in many places.
saw the hucklebury, honeysuckle, and alder common to the Atlantic
states, also a kind of honeysuckle which bears a white bury and rises
about 4 feet high not common but to the western side of the rockey
mountains.[31] a growth which resembles the choke cherry bears a
black bury with a single stone of a sweetish taste, it rises to the
hight of 8 or 10 feet and grows in thick clumps. the Arborvita is
also common and grows to an immence size, being from 2 to 6 feet
in diameter.

[Clark]   Wednesday (*Friday*) 20th September 1805
    I set out early and proceeded on through a Countrey as ruged as
usial   at 12 miles decended the mountain to a leavel pine Countrey
proceeded on through a butifull Countrey for three miles to a Small
Plain in which I found maney Indian lodges,[32]   a man Came out to
meet me, & Conducted me to a large Spacious Lodge which he
told me (by Signs) was the Lodge of his great Chief who had Set
out 3 days previous with all the Warriers of the nation to war on a
South West derection & would return in 15 or 18 days. the fiew
men that were left in the Village and great numbers of women
geathered around me with much apparent signs of fear, and apr.
pleased   they those people gave us a Small piece of Buffalow meat,
Some dried Salmon beries & roots in different States, Some round
and much like an onion which they call Pas she co [*quamash*.[33] *the
Bread or Cake is called Pas-shi-co*] Sweet, of this they make bread &
Supe   they also gave us, the bread made of this root all of which
we eate hartily,   I gave them a fiew Small articles as preasents, and
proceeded on with a Chief to his Village 2 miles in the Same Plain,
where we were treated kindly in their way and continued with them
all night   Those two Villages consist of about 30 double lodges, but

[31] Snowberry (*Symphoricarpos albus*).

[32] At Weippe, Idaho.

[33] The quamash, or camas (with many other variants of the name), is an important
article of food among the Northwestern Indian tribes. It is the bulbous root of a
liliaceous plant (*Camassia*—of two species, *esculenta* and *leuchlini*; also named *Quamasia
quamash*, Coville) which grows in moist places from California to Montana and British
Columbia; it is dug in June and July, and may be eaten raw or cooked (Thwaites).

fiew men a number of women & children,   they call themselves
Cho pun-nish or *Pierced noses*[34] Their diolect appears verry different
from the flat heads, [*Tushapaws*], altho origineally the Same people

Emence quantity of the [*quawmash or*] *Pas-shi-co* root gathered &
in piles about the plain, those roots grow much like an onion in
marshey places the seed are in triangular Shells, on the Stalk. they
sweat them in the following manner i.e. dig a large hole 3 feet deep,
cover the bottom with Split wood on the top of which they lay Small
Stones of about 3 or 4 Inches thick, a Second layer of Splited wood
& Set the whole on fire which heats the Stones,   after the fire is
extinguished they lay grass & mud mixed on the Stones, on that
dry grass which Supports the Pâsh-shi-co root a thin Coat of the
Same grass is laid on the top, a Small fire is kept when necessary
in the Center of the kill &c.

I find myself verry unwell all the evening from eateing the fish
& roots too freely Sent out hunters they killed nothing

[Lewis]   Saturday September 21st. 1805.

we killed a few Pheasants, and I killed a prarie woolf which
together with the ballance of our horse beef and some crawfish which
we obtained in the creek enabled us to make one more hearty meal,
not knowing where the next was to be found.

the Arborvita increases in quantity and size. I saw several sticks
today large enough to form eligant perogues of at least 45 feet in
length. I find myself growing weak for the want of food and most
of the men complain of a similar deficiency, and have fallen off very
much.

[Clark]   Thursday (*Saturday*) 21st. Septr. 1805

A fine Morning Sent out all the hunters in different directions
to hunt deer, I my self delayed with the Chief to prevent Suspission
and to Collect by Signs as much information as possible about the
river and Countrey in advance. The Chief drew me a kind of chart
of the river, and informed me that a greater Chief than himself was

---

[34] The Chopunnish, or Nez Perces, were located on the Salmon and Snake rivers;
they were the principal tribe of the Sahaptin family, which formerly extended along
a considerable part of the lower Columbia and its tributaries, as far east as the
Bitterroot Mountains (Thwaites).

fishing at the river half a days march from his Village called the twisted hare [hair], and that the river forked a little below his Camp and at a long distance below & below 2 large forks one from the left & the other from the right the river passed thro' the mountains at which place was a great fall of the Water passing through the rocks, at those falls white people lived from whome they precured the white Beeds & Brass &c. which the womin wore

I am verry sick to day and puke which relive me

[Lewis]   Sunday September 22nd. 1805.

Notwithstanding my positive directions to hubble the horses last evening one of the men neglected to comply. he plead[ed] ignorance of the order. this neglect however detained us untill ½ after eleven OCk. at which time we renewed our march, our course being about west. we had proceeded about two and a half miles when we met Reubin Fields one of our hunters, whom Capt. Clark had dispatched to meet us with some dryed fish and roots that he had procured from a band of Indians, whose lodges were about eight miles in advance. I ordered the party to halt for the purpose of taking some refreshment. I divided the fish roots and buries, and was happy to find a sufficiency to satisfy compleatly all our appetites.

the pleasure I now felt in having tryumphed over the rockey Mountains and decending once more to a level and fertile country where there was every rational hope of finding a comfortable subsistence for myself and party can be more readily conceived than expressed, nor was the flattering prospect of the final success of the expedition less pleasing. on our approach to the village which consisted of eighteen lodges most of the women fled to the neighbouring woods on horseback with their children, a circumstance I did not expect as Capt. Clark had previously been with them and informed them of our pacific intentions towards them and also the time at which we should most probably arrive. the men seemed but little concerned, and several of them came to meet us at a short distance from their lodges unarmed.

[Clark]   Friday (*Sunday*) 22nd. Septr. 1805

Set out with the Chief & his Son on a young horse for the Village at which place I expected to meet Capt Lewis this young horse in fright threw himself & me 3 times on the Side of a Steep hill &

hurt my hip much,   Cought a Coalt which we found on the roade
& I rode it for Several miles untill we saw the Chiefs horses,   he
Cought one & we arrived at his Village at Sunset, & himself and
mys[el]f walked upto the 2d Village where I found Capt Lewis &
the party Encamped, much fatigued, & hungery, much rejoiced to
find something to eate of which they appeared to partake plentifully
I cautioned them of the Consequences of eateing too much &c.

The planes appeared covered with Spectators viewing the white
men and the articles which we had,   our party weakened and much
reduced in flesh as well as Strength

I got the Twisted hare to draw the river from his Camp down
which he did with great Cherfullness on a white Elk skin,   from
the 1st. fork which is few miles below, to the large fork on which
the *So So ne* or Snake Indians fish, is South 2 Sleeps;   to a large
river which falls in on the N W. Side and into which The *Clarks
river* empties itself is 5 Sleeps   from the mouth of that river to the
falls is 5 Sleeps   at the falls he places Establishments of white people
&c. and informs that the great numbers of Indians reside on all those
fo[r]ks as well as the main river;   one other Indian gave me a like
account of the Countrey.   Some few drops of rain this evening.   I
precured maps of the Countrey & river with the Situation of Indians,
Towns from Several men of note Seperately which varied verry little.

                          Saturday (*Monday*) 23rd. Septr. 1805
gave a Shirt to the *Twisted hare* & a knife & Handkerchief with
a Small pece of Tobacco to each.   Finding that those people gave
no provisions to day we deturmined to purchase with our Small
articles of Merchindize, accord[ingly] we purchased all we could,
Such as roots dried, in bread, & in their raw State, Berries of red
Haws & *Fish*

Capt. Lewis & 2 men Verry Sick this evening,   my hip Verry
Painfull,   the men trade a few old tin Canisters for dressed Elk Skin
to make themselves Shirts.   at dark a hard wind from the S W
accompanied with rain which lasted half an hour.   The *twisted hare*
envited Capt. Lewis & myself to his lodge which was nothin[g]
more than Pine bushes & bark, and gave us Some broiled dried
Salmon to eate,   great numbers about us all night.   at this village
the women were busily employed in gathering and drying the *Pas-
she-co* root of which they had great quantities dug in piles

Sunday (*Tuesday*) 24th. Septr. 1805
despatched J. Colter back to hunt the horses lost in the mountains
& bring up Some Shot left behind, and at 10 oClock we all Set out
for the river and proceeded on by the Same rout I had previously
traveled, and at Sunset we arrived at the Island on which I found
the *Twisted hare*, and formed a Camp on a large Island a little below,[35]
Capt. Lewis scercely able to ride on a jentle horse which was furnished by the Chief, Several men So unwell that they were Compelled to lie on the Side of the road for Some time others obliged
to be put on horses. I gave rushes Pills to the Sick this evening.
Several Indians follow us.

Monday (*Wednesy.*) 25th. of September 1805—
I Set out early with the Chief and 2 young men to hunt Some
trees Calculated to build Canoes, as we had previously deturmined
to proceed on by water, I was furnished with a horse and we
proceeded on down the river Passed down on the N side of the
river to a fork from the North we halted about an hour,[36] one of
the young men took his guig and killed 6 fine Salmon two of them
were roasted and we eate, I Saw fine timber for Canoes

Tuesday (*Thursday*) 26th. Septr. 1805
I had the axes distributed and handled and men apotned. [ap-
portioned] ready to commence building canoes on tomorrow, our
axes are Small & badly calculated to build Canoes of the large Pine,
Capt Lewis Still very unwell, Several men taken Sick on the way
down, I administered *Salts* Pils Galip, [jalap] Tarter emetic &c. I
feel unwell this evening, two Chiefs & their families follow us and
encamp near us, they have great numbers of horses. This day
proved verry hot, we purchase fresh Salmon of the Indians

Thursday (*Saturday*) 28th. Septr. 1805
Our men nearly all Complaining of their bowels, a heaviness at
the Stomach & Lax, Some of those taken first getting better, a

[35] Near Orofino, Idaho.
[36] This is the junction of the Middle and North forks of the Kooskooskee (Clearwater). The explorers called the North Fork the Chopunnish (Thwaites).

number of Indians about us gazeing   This day proved verry worm and Sultery,   nothing killed   men complaining of their diat of fish & roots.   all that is able working at the Canoes

October 5th Friday Saty. 1805

had all our horses 38 in number Collected and branded   Cut off their fore top and delivered them to the 2 brothers and one son of one of the Chiefs who intends to accompany us down the river   to each of those men I gave a Knife & Some Small articles &c.   they promised to be attentive to our horses untill we Should return.

Nothing to eate except dried fish & roots.   Capt Lewis & myself eate a Supper of roots boiled, which Swelled us in Such a manner that we were Scercely able to breath for Several hours.   finished and lanced (*launched*) 2 of our canoes this evening which proved to be verry good   our hunters with every diligence Could kill nothing. The hills high and ruged and woods too dry to hunt the deer which is the only game in our neighbourhood.   Several Squars Came with fish and roots which we purchased of them for Beeds, which they were fond of.   *Capt Lewis not So well to day as yesterday*

October 7th. Monday 1805—

I continue verry unwell but obliged to attend every thing all the Canoes put into the water and loaded, fixed our Canoes as well as possible and Set out   as we were about to Set out we missd. both of the Chiefs who promised to accompany us, I also missed my Pipe Tomahawk which could not be found.

The after part of the day cloudy   proceded on passed 10 rapids which wer dangerous   the Canoe in which I was Struck a rock and Sprung a leak in the 3rd. rapid,   we proceeded on

October 8th. Tuesday 1805—

passed 15 rapids four Islands and a Creek on the Stard Side at 16 miles just below which one canoe in which Sergt. Gass was Stearing and was nearle turning over,   she Sprung a leak or Split open on one side and Bottom filled with water & Sunk on the rapid,   the men, Several of which Could not Swim hung on to the Canoe, I

had one of the other Canoes unloaded & with the assistance of our
Small Canoe and one Indian Canoe took out every thing & toed the
empty Canoe on Shore

October 9th Wednesday 1805—
at Dark we were informed that our old guide & his son had left
us and had been Seen running up the river Several miles above,
we could not account for the cause of his leaveing us at this time,
without receiving his pay for the services he had rendered us, or
letting us know anything of his intention.

we requested the Chief to Send a horseman after our old guide
to come back and receive his pay &c. which he advised us not to
do as his nation would take his things from him before he passed
their camps. The Indians and our party were verry mery this after
noon a woman faind madness &c. &c. Singular acts of this woman
in giveing in small po[r]tions all she had & if they were not received
She would Scarrify her self in a horid manner &c. Capt Lewis
recovering fast.

October 10th Wednesday (*Thursday*)
passed 2 Islands and two bad rapids at 3 miles lower passed a
Creek[37] on the Lard. with wide cotton willow bottoms we arrived
at the heade of a verry bad riffle at which place we landed near 8
Lodges of Indians after viewg. this riffle two Canoes were taken
over verry well; the third stuck on a rock which took us an hour to
get her off which was effected without her receiving a greater injurey
than a Small Split in her Side which was repaired in a Short time,
we purchased fish & dogs of those people, dined and proceeded on.
here we met with an Indian from the falls at which place he Sais
he saw white people, and expressd an inclination to accompany us,
we passd. a few miles above this riffle 2 Lodges and an Indian
batheing in a hot bath made by hot stones thrown into a pon[d] of
water. at five miles lower and Sixty miles below the forks arived
at a large southerly fork which is the one we were on with the *Snake*
or *So-So-nee* nation (haveing passed 5 rapids) This South fork or

[37] This is Lapwai Creek. Up this stream is the site of Fort Lapwai, Idaho
(Thwaites).

Lewis's River[38] which has two forks which fall into it   on this fork a little above its mouth resides a Chief who as the Indian say has more horses than he can count and further sayeth that Louises River is navagable about 60 miles up with maney rapids at which places the Indians have fishing

I think Lewis's [Snake] River is about 250 yards wide, the *Koos koos ke* River about 150 yards wide and the river below the forks about 300 yards wide   a miss understanding took place between Shabono one of our interpreters and Jo & R Fields which appears to have originated in just [jest].   our diet extremely bad haveing nothing but roots and dried fish to eate,   all the Party have greatly the advantage of me, in as much as they all relish the flesh of the dogs, Several of which we purchased of the nativs for to add to our store of fish and roots &c. &c.—

The *Cho-pun-nish* or Pierced nose Indians are Stout likely men, handsom women, and verry dressey in their way,   the dress of the men are a White Buffalow robe or Elk Skin dressed with Beeds which are generally white, Sea Shells & the Mother of Pirl hung to the[i]r hair & on a piece of otter skin about their necks   hair Ceewed in two parsels hanging forward over their Sholders, feathers, and different Coloured Paints which they find in their Countrey Generally white, Green & light Blue.   Some fiew were a Shirt of Dressed Skins and long legins & Mockersons Painted, which appears to be their winters dress, with a plat of twisted grass about their Necks.

The women dress in a Shirt of Ibex or Goat [*Argalia*] Skins which reach quite down to their anckles with a girdle,   their heads are not ornemented, their Shirts are ornemented with quilled Brass, Small peces of Brass Cut into different forms, Beeds, Shells & curious bones &c.   The men expose those parts which are generally kept from few [view] by other nations but the women are more perticular than any other nation which I have passed [*in s[e]creting the parts*]

---

[38] At this point the expedition reaches the junction of the Clearwater (or Kooskooskee) River with the Snake River.   The stream which Clark first reached on the Pacific slope was the Lemhi, a tributary of the Salmon, and this latter of the Snake. It was the Salmon to which he gave the name Lewis's River, but intended it to apply to the entire stream as far as its junction with the Columbia (Thwaites). The camping place of the explorers for this night was near the site of the twin cities named in their honor, Lewiston, Idaho, and Clarkston, Washington.

EIGHT

Down the Rapids

Descending the Snake and the Columbia
October 11–November 21, 1805

[Clark]   October 11th. Friday 1805

We set out early and proceeded on   passed a rapid at *two* miles, at 6 miles we came too at Some Indian lodges and took brackfast, we purchased all the fish we could and Seven dogs of those people for Stores of Provisions down the river   at this place I saw a curious Swet house underground, with a Small whole at top to pass in or throw in the hot Stones, which those in[side] threw on as much water as to create the temperature of heat they wished   at 9 mile passed a rapid   at 15 miles halted at an Indian Lodge, to purchase provisions of which we prec[u]red some of the *Pash-he-quar* roots[1] and a few fish dried,   after takeing Some dinner of dog &c. we proceeded on.   Came to and encamped at 2 Indian Lodges at a great place of fishing[2]   here we met an Indian of a nation near the mouth of this river.   we purchased three dogs and a fiew fish of those Indians,   we Passed today nine rapids all of them great fishing places

---

[1] Camas root (*Camassia quamash*).
[2] Almota Creek, in Whitman County, Washington (Thwaites).

October 13th. Sunday 1805

Rained a little before day, and all the morning a hard wind from the S West untill 9 oClock, the rained seased & wind luled, and Capt Lewis with two canoes set out & passed down the rapid The thers soon followed and we passed over this bad rapid safe. We should make more portages if the season was no so far advanced and time precious with us.

October 14th. Monday 1805

passed rapids at 6 and 9 miles. at 12 miles we came too at the head of a rapid which the Indians told me was verry bad, we viewed the rapid found it bad in decending three Stern Canoes stuck fast for some time on the head of the rapid and one struck a rock in the worst part, fortunately all landed Safe below the rapid which was nearly 3 miles in length. here we dined, and for the first time for three weeks past I had a good dinner of Blue wing Teel,

after dinner we Set out and had not proceded on two miles before our Stern Canoe in passing thro a Short rapid opposit the head of an Island,[3] run on a Smothe rock and turned broad Side, the men got out on the [rock] all except one of our Indian Chiefs who swam on Shore, The canoe filed and sunk a number of articles floated out, Such as the mens bedding clothes & skins. the greater part of which were cought by 2 of the Canoes, whilst a 3rd. was unloading & Steming the Swift current to the relief of the men on the rock, who could with much dificuelty hold the Canoe however in about an hour we got the men an[d] canoe to shore with the Loss of Some bedding Tomahaw[k]s shot pouches skins Clothes &c &c. all wet we had every article exposed to the Sun to dry on the Island, our loss in provisions is verry considerable all our roots was in the canoe that Sunk, and Cannot be dried Sufficient to save, our loose powder was also in the Canoe and is all wete. This I think may be saved

In this Island we found some Spilt [Split] timber the parts of a house which the Indians had verry securely covered with Stone, we also observed a place where the Indians had buried their fish, we

---

[3] These were the Pine-tree Rapids, some 30 miles below Palouse River (Thwaites).

have made it a point at all times not to take any thing belonging to the Indians even their wood. but at this time we are Compelled to violate that rule and take a part of the split timber we find here bur[i]ed for fire wood, as no other is to be found in any direction.

October 16th. Wednesday 1805
A cool morning, deturmined to run the rapids, put our Indian guide in front our Small Canoe next and the other four followinig each other, the canoes all passed over Safe except the rear Canoe which run fast on a rock at the lower part of the Rapids, with the early assistance of the other Canoes & the Indians, who was extreamly ellert every thing was taken out and the Canoe got off without any enjorie further than the articles [with] which it was loaded [getting] all wet.

In every direction from the junction of those rivers[4] the countrey is one continued plain low and rises from the water gradually, except a range of high Countrey which runs from S.W. & N. E. and is on the opposit Side about 2 miles distant from the Collumbia and keeping its derection S. W. untill it joins a S. W. range of mountains.

We halted above the point on the river Kimooenim[5] to smoke with the Indians who had collected there in great numbers to view us, after we had our camp fixed and fires made, a Chief came from this camp which was about ¼ of a mile up the Columbia river at the head of about 200 men singing and beeting on their drums Stick and keeping time to the musik, they formed a half circle around us and Sung for Some time, we gave them all Smoke, and Spoke to their Chief as well as we could by signs informing them of our friendly disposition to all nations, and our joy in Seeing those of our Children around us

October 17th. Thursday 1805
Several men and woman offered Dogs and fish to Sell, we purchased all the dogs we could, the fish being out of season and dieing in great numbers in the river, we did not think proper to use them, send out Hunters to shute the Prarie Cock[6] a large fowl which I

---

[4] The confluence of the Snake and Columbia rivers.
[5] Snake River.
[6] Sage grouse (*Centrocercus urophasianus*).

Junction of Columbia and Lewis's [Snake] rivers.

have only Seen on this river, several of which I have killed, they are the size of a Small turkey, of the pheasant kind, one I killed on the water[s] edge to day measured from the Beak to the end of the toe 2 feet 6 & ¾ Inches; from the extremities of its wings 3 feet 6 inches; the tale feathers is 13 inches long: they feed on grasshoppers and the Seed of the wild plant which is also peculiar to this river and the upper parts of the Missoury somewhat resembling the whins.

Capt. Lewis took a Vocabelary of the Language of those people who call themselves *Sokulk*, and also one of the language of a nation resideing on a Westerly fork of the Columbia which mouthes a fiew miles above this place who Call themselves *Chim-ña-pum* Some fiew of this nation reside with the *Sokulks* nation. Their language differ but little from either the Sokulks or the *Chô-pun-nish* (or pierced nose) nation which inhabit the Koskoskea river and Lewis's R below.[7]

I took *two* men in a Small canoe and assended the Columbia river 10 miles to an Island near the Stard. Shore on which two large Mat Lodges of Indians were drying Salmon, (as they informed me by Signs for the purpose of food and fuel, & I do not think [it] at all improbable that those people make use of Dried fish as fuel, The number of dead Salmon on the Shores & floating in the river is incrediable to say—and at this Season they have only to collect the fish Split them open and dry them on their Scaffolds on which they have great numbers, how far they have to raft their timber they make their scaffolds of I could not lern; but there is no timber of any sort except Small willow bushes in sight in any direction. Saw great numbers of Dead Salmon on the Shores and floating in the water, great numbers of Indians on the banks viewing me and 18 canoes accompanied me from the point. The waters of this river is clear, and a Salmon may be seen at the deabth of 15 or 20 feet. West 4 miles to the lower point of a large Island near the Stard. Side at 2 Lodges, passed three large lodges on the Stard. Side near which great number of Salmon was drying on scaffolds

one of those Mat lodges I entered found it crouded with men women and children and near the enterance of those houses I saw

[7] Wanapams and Yakimas.

maney squars engaged [in] splitting and drying Salmon. I was furnished with a mat to set on, and one man set about prepareing me something to eate, first he brought in a piece of a Drift log of pine and with a wedge of the elks horn, and a malet of Stone curioesly carved he Split the log into Small pieces and lay'd it open on the fire on which he put round Stones, a woman handed him a basket of water and a large Salmon about half Dried, when the Stones were hot he put them into the basket of water with the fish which was soon sufficently boiled for use it was then taken out put on a platter of rushes neetly made, and set before me they boiled a Salmon for each of the men with me, dureing those preparations, I smoked, with those about me who chose to smoke which was but fiew, this being a custom those people are but little accustomed to and only Smok thro: form.

on my return I was followd. by 3 canoes in which there was 20 Indians I shot a large Prairie Cock Several grouse, Ducks and fish. on my return found Great numbs. of the nativs with Capt. Lewis, men all employ[e]d in dressing ther skins mending their clothes and putting their arms in the best order the latter being always a matter of attention with us. The Dress of those natives differ but little from those on the Koskoskia and Lewis's rivers, except the women who dress verry different, in as much as those above ware long leather Shirts which [are] highly orniminted with beeds shells &c. &c. and those on the main Columbia river only ware a truss or pece of leather tied around them at their hips and drawn tite between ther legs and fastened before So as bar[e]lly to hide those parts which are so sacredly hid & s[e]cured by our women. Those women are more inclined to Co[r]pulency than any we have yet Seen, with low Stature broad faces, heads flatened and the foward [forehead] compressed so as to form a Streight line from the nose to the Crown of the head, their eyes are of a Duskey black, their hair of a corse black without orniments of any kind braded as above.

The orniments of each Sects are Similar, Such as large blue & white beeds, either pendant from their ears or incircling their necks, wrists & arms. they also ware bracelets of Brass, Copper & horn, and trinkets of Shells, fish bones and curious feathers. Their garments consists of a short shirt of leather and a roabe of the Skins of Deer or the antilope, but fiew of them ware Shirts all have Short robes. Those peole appears to live in a State of comparitive happiness: they take a great[er] share [in the] labor of the woman, than is common among Savage tribes, and as I am informed [are] content with one wife (as also those on the Ki moo e nim river) Those people respect the aged with Veneration. I observed an old woman in one of the Lodges which I entered, She was entirely blind as I was informed by signs, had lived more than 100 winters, She occupied the best position in the house, and when She Spoke great attention was paid to what she Said.

Those people as also those of the *flat heads* which we had passed on the Koskoske and Lewis's rivers are subject to sore eyes, and many are blind of one and Some of both eyes. this misfortune must be owing to the reflections of the sun &c. on the waters in which they are continually fishing during the Spring Summer & fall, & the snows dureing the, winter Seasons, in this open countrey where the eye has no rest. I have observed amongst those, as well in all other tribes which I have passed on these waters who live on fish maney of different sectes who have lost their teeth about middle age, Some have their teeth worn to the gums, perticelar[ly] those of the upper jaw, and the tribes generally have bad teeth the cause of it I cannot account [for], sand attachd. to the roots & the method they have of useing the dried Salmon, which is mearly worming it and eating the rine & scales with the flesh of the fish, no doubt contributes to it.

The Houses or Lodges of the tribes of the main Columbia river is of large Mats made of rushes, those houses are from 15 to 60 feet in length generally of an Oblong squar form, Suported by poles on forks in the in[n]er Side, Six feet high, the top is covered also with mats leaveing a Seperation in the whole length of about 12 or 15 inches wide, left for the purpose of admitting light and for the Smok of the fire to pass which is made in the middle of the house. The roughfs are nearly flat, which proves to me that rains are not common in this open Countrey.

Those people appeare of a mild disposition and friendly disposed. They have in their huts independant of their nets gigs & fishing tackling each bows & large quivers of arrows on which they use flint Spikes. Their ammusements are similar to those of the Missouri. they are not beggerley, and receive what is given them with much joy.

I saw but fiew horses they appeared [to] make but little use of those animals principally useing Canoes for their uses of procuring food &c.

October 18th. Friday 1805

Several canoes of Indians came down and joined those with us, we had a council with those in which we informed of our friendly intentions towards them and all other of our red children, of our wish to make a piece between all of our red Children in this quarter &c &c. this was conveyed by signs thro: our 2 Chiefs who accompanied us, and was understood, we made a 2d. Chief and gave Strings of wompom to them all in remembrance of what we Said. four men in a Canoe came up from a large encampment on an Island in the River about 8 miles below, they delayed but a fiew minits and returned, without Speaking a word to us.

The Great Chief and one of the *Chim-nâ-pum*[8] nation drew me a sketch of the Columbia above and the tribes of his nation, living on the bank[s], and its waters, and the *Tâpe-tett* river which falls in 18 miles above on the westerly side

we thought it necessary to lay in a Store of Provisions for our voyage, and the fish being out of Season, we purchased forty dogs for which we gave articles of little value, such as bells, thimbles, knitting pins, brass wire and a few beeds [with] all of which they appeared well Satisfied and pleased.

every thing being arranged we took in our Two Chiefs, and set out on the great Columbia river, haveing left our guide and the two young men two of them enclined not to proceed on any further, and the 3d. could be of no service to us as he did not know the river below

Took our leave of the Chiefs and all those about us and proceeded on down the great Columbia river

October 19th. Saturday 1805

The great chief *Yel-lep-pit*[9] two other chiefs, and a chief of [a] Band below presented themselves to us verry early this morning.

[8] Yakima.
[9] Of the Wallawallas.

we Smoked with them, enformed them as we had all others above
as well as we could by signs of our friendly intentions towards our
red children perticelar those who opened their ears to our Councils.
we gave a Medal, a Handkercheif & a String of Wompom to *Yelleppit*
and a String of wompom to each of the others. *Yelleppit* is a bold
handsom Indian, with a dignified countenance about 35 years of
age, about 5 feet 8 inches high and well perpotiond. he requested
us to delay untill the Middle of the day, that his people might come
down and see us, we excused our Selves and promised to stay with
him one or 2 days on our return which appeared to Satisfy him

great numbers of Indians came down in Canoes to view us before
we Set out passed two Islands, one near the middle of the river
on which is Seven lodges of Indians drying fish, at our approach
they hid themselves in their Lodges and not one was to be seen
untill we passed, they then came out, in greater numbers than is
common in Lodges of their Size, it is probable that the inhabitants
of the 5 Lodges above had in a fright left their lodges and decended
to this place to defend themselves if attackted there being a bad
rapid opposit the Island thro which we had to pass prevented our
landing on this Island and passifying those people, about four miles
below this fritened Island we arrived at the head of a verry bad
rapid,[10] we came too on the Lardd. Side to view the rapid before
we would venter to run it,

I assended a high clift about 200 feet above the water from the
top of which is a leavel plain extending up the river and off for a
great extent, at this place the countrey becoms low on each Side
of the river, and affords a pros[pect] of the river and countrey below
for great extent both to the right and left; from this place I descovered a high mountain of emence hight covered with Snow, this
must be one of the mountains laid down by Vancouver, as seen from
the mouth of the Columbia River, from the course which it bears
which is *West* I take it to be Mt. St. Helens, destant about 120 miles
a range of mountains in the Derection crossing a conical mountain
S. W. toped with snow[11]

I landed in front of five Lodges which was at no great distance

[10] The Umatilla Rapid, near the mouth of the river of that name (Thwaites).
[11] The mountain was not Mt. St. Helens, but Mt. Adams (Wheeler).

from each other, Saw no person the enterance or Dores of the Lodges wer Shut with the Same materials of which they were built a Mat, I approached one with a pipe in my hand entered a lodge which was the nearest to me found 32 persons men, women and a few children Setting permiscuisly in the Lodge, in the greatest agutation, Some crying and ringing there hands, others banging their heads. I gave my hand to them all and made Signs of my friendly dispo[si]tion and offered the men my pipe to Smok and distributed a fiew Small articles which I had in my pockets, this measure passified those distressed people verry much, I then sent one man into each lodge and entered a Second myself the inhabitants of which I found more fritened than those of the first lodge I destributed Sundrey Small articles amongst them, and Smoked with the men, I then entered the third 4th. & fifth Lodge which I found Somewhat passified, the three men, Drewer Jo. & R. Fields, haveing useed everey means in their power to convince them of our friendly disposition to them, I then Set my self on a rock and made signs to the men to come and Smoke with me not one come out untill the canoes arrived with the 2 chiefs, one of whom spoke aloud, and as was their custom to all we had passed. the Indians came out & Set by me and smoked They said we came from the clouds &c &c. and were not men &c. &c. this time Capt. Lewis came down with the canoes in which the Indian[s were], as Soon as they Saw the Squar wife of the interperter they pointed to her and informed those who continued yet in the Same position I first found them, they imediately all came out and appeared to assume new life, the sight of This Indian woman, wife to one of our interprs. confirmed those people of our friendly intentions, as no woman ever accompanies a war party of Indians in this quarter.

October 21st. Monday 1805

last night we could not collect more dry willows the only fuel, than was barely Suffi[ci]ent to cook Supper, and not a sufficency to cook brackfast this morning, passd. a Small Island at 5½ miles a large one 8 miles in the middle of the river, some rapid water at the head and Eight Lodges of nativs opposit its Lower point on the Stard. Side, we came too at those lodges, bought some wood and brackfast, Those people recived us with great kindness, and examined us with much attention, their employments customs, Dress

Map from Clark field book, showing course and camping place, October 21, 1805.

and appearance Similar to those above, Speak the Same language, here we Saw two scarlet and a blue cloth blankets, also a Salors Jacket

we got from those people a fiew pounded roos [*roots*] fish and *Acorns* of white oake[12], those Acorns they make use of as food raw & roasted and inform us they precure them of the natives who live near the falls below which place they all discribe by the term *Timm* at 2 miles lower passed a rapid large rocks stringing into the river of large Size, opposit to this rapid on the Stard. Shore is Situated *two* Lodges of the Nativs drying fish here we halted a fiew minits to examine the rapid before we entered it which was our Constant Custom, and at all that was verry dangerous put out all who Could not Swim to walk around, after passing this rapid we proceeded a little below is a bad rapid which is bad crouded with hugh [huge] rocks scattered in every Direction which renders the pasage verry Difficult a little above this rapid on the Lard. Side emence piles of rocks appears as if Sliped from the clifts under which they lay, passed great number of rocks in every direction scattered in the river.

landed and encamped near *five* Lodges of nativs, drying fish those are the relations of those at the *great falls*, they are pore and have but little wood which they bring up the river from the falls as they Say, we purchased a little wood to cook our Dog meat and fish; those people did not receive us at first with the same cordiality of those above, they appear to be the Same nation Speak the Same language with a little curruption of maney words Dress and fish in the same way, all of whome have *pierced noses* and the men when Dressed ware a long taper'd piece of Shell or beed put through the nose.[13]

this part of the river is furnished with fine Springs which either rise high up the Sides of the hills or on the bottom near the river and run into the river. the hills are high and rugid a fiew scattering trees to be Seen on them either Small pine or Scrubey white oke.

---

[12] Oregon white oak (*Quercus garryana*).
[13] Inserting two small, tapering white shells, about two inches long, through the lower part of the cartilaginous division of the nose. These shells are of the genus *dentalium*, they inhabit the Pacific shore, and are an article of traffic among the natives. (Samuel Parker).

Collins made some excellent beer of the *Pasheco quarmash* bread of roots which was verry good. obliged to purchase wood at a high rate.

October 22d. Tuesday 1805

I beheld an emence body of water compressd in a narrow chanel of about 200 yds in width, fomeing over rocks maney of which presented their tops above the water, when at this place Capt. Lewis joined me haveing delayed on the way to examine a root of which the nativs had been digging great quantities in the bottoms of this River. this River haveing no Indian name that we could find out, except "the River on which the Snake Indians live", we think it best to leave the nameing of it untill our return.

we proceeded on pass[ed] the mouth of this river[14] at which place it appears to discharge ¼ as much water as runs down the Columbia. we landed and walked down accompanied by an old man to view the falls,[15] and the best rout for to make a portage at the lower part of those rapids we arrived at 5 Large Lod[g]es of nativs drying and prepareing fish for market, they gave us Philburts, and berries to eate.

Indians assisted us over the portage with our heavy articles on their horses, the waters is divided into Several narrow chanels which pass through a hard black rock forming Islands of rocks at this Stage of the water, on those Islands of rocks as well as at and about their Lodges I observe great numbers of Stacks of pounded Salmon neetly preserved in the following manner, i.e. after [being] suffi[c]ently Dried it is pounded between two Stones fine, and put into a speces of basket neetly made of grass and rushes better than two feet long and one foot Diamiter, which basket is lined with the Skin of Salmon Stretched and dried for the purpose, in this it is pressed down as hard as is possible, when full they Secure the open part with the fish Skins across which they fasten th[r]o. the loops of the basket that part very securely, and then on a Dry Situation they Set those baskets the corded part up, their common custom is to Set 7 as close as they can Stand and 5 on the top of them, and secure them

[14] Deschutes River.
[15] Celilo Falls at Celilo, Oregon.

with mats which is raped around them and made fast with cords and covered also with mats, those 12 baskets of from 90 to 100 lbs. each form a Stack. thus preserved those fish may be kept Sound and sweet Several years, as those people inform me, Great quantities as they inform us are sold to the whites people who visit the mouth of this river as well as to the nativs below.

October 23d. Wednesday 1805

I with the greater part of the men crossed in the canoes to opposit side above the falls and hauled them across the portage of 457 yards which is on the Lard. Side and certainly the best side to pass the canoes, I then decended through a narrow chanel of about 150 yards wide forming a kind of half circle in it[s] course of a mile to a pitch of 8 feet in which the chanel is divided by 2 large rocks, at this place we were obliged to let the Canoes down by strong ropes of Elk Skin which we had for the purpose, one Canoe in passing this place got loose by the cords breaking, and was cought by the Indians below.

I accomplished this necessary business and landed Safe with all the canoes at our Camp below the falls by 3 oClock P. M. nearly covered with flees which were so thick amongst the Straw and fish Skins at the upper part of the portage at which place the nativs had been Camped not long since; that every man of the party was obliged to Strip naked dureing the time of takeing over the canoes, that they might have an oppertunity of brushing the flees off[f] their legs and bodies. Great numbers of *Sea Otters*[16] in the river below the falls, I shot one in the narrow chanel to day which I could not get. Great numbers of Indians visit us both from above and below. one of the old Chiefs who had accompanied us from the head of the river, informed us that he herd the Indians Say that the nation below intended to kill us. we examined all the arms &c. complete the amunition to 100 rounds. The nativs leave us earlyer this evening than usial, which gives a Shadow of confermation to the information of our old Chief, as we are at all times & places on our guard, are under no greater apprehention than is common.

we purchased 8 Small fat dogs for the party to eate; the nativs

[16] Harbor seal (*Phoca vitulina*).

not being fond of Selling their good fish, compells us to make use of Dog meat for food, the flesh of which the most of the party have become fond of from the habits of useing it for Some time past.

I observed on the beach near the Indian Lodges two butifull canoes of different Shape & Size to what we had Seen above wide in the midd[l]e and tapering to each end, on the bow curious figures were cut in the wood &c. Capt. Lewis went up to the Lodges to See those Canoes and exchanged our Smallest canoe for one of them by giveing a Hatchet & few trinkets to the owner who informed that he purchased it of a white man below for a horse, these canoes are neeter made than any I have ever Seen and calculated to ride the waves, and carry emence burthens, they are dug thin and are suported by cross pieces of about 1 inch diamieter tied with Strong bark thro' holes in the Sides. our two old chiefs appeared verry uneasy this evening.

October 24th. Thursday 1805
The morning fare after a beautifull night, the nativs approached us this morning with great caution. our two old chiefs expressed a desire to return to their band from this place, Saying "that they could be of no further Service to us, as their nation extended no further down the river than those falls, (*they could no longer understand the language of those below the falls, till then not much difference in the vocabl.*) and as the nation below had expressed hostile intentions against us, would certainly kill them; perticularly as they had been at war with each other;" we requested them to Stay with us *two* nights longer, and we would See the nation below and make a peace between them, they replied they "were anxious to return and See our horses" we insisted on their staying with us two nights longer to which they agreed; our views were to detain those Chiefs with us, untill we should pass the next falls, which we were told were very bad, and at no great distance below, that they might inform us of any designs of the nativs, and if possible to bring about a peace between them and the tribes below.

At 9 oClock a. m. I Set out with the party and proceeded on down a rapid Stream of about 400 yards wide at 2-½ miles the river widened into a large bason to the Stard. Side on which there is five Lodges of Indians. here a tremendious black rock Presented itself high and Steep appearing to choke up the river; nor could I See where the water passed further than the current was drawn with great velocity to the Lard. Side of this rock at which place I heard a great roreing. I landed at the Lodges and the natives went with me to the top of this rock which makes from the Stard. Side, from the top of which I could See the dificuelties we had to pass for Several miles below; at this place the water of this great river is compressed into a chanel between two rocks not exceeding *forty five* yards wide and continues for a ¼ of a mile when it again widens to 200 yards and continues this width for about 2 miles when it is again intersepted by rocks. This obstruction in the river accounts for the water in high floods riseing to Such a hite at the last falls. The whole of the Current of this great river must at all Stages pass thro' this narrow chanel of 45 yards wide.[17] as the portage of our canoes over this high rock would be impossible with our Strength, and the only danger in passing thro those narrows was the whorls and swills [swells] arriseing from the Compression of the water, and which I thought (as also our principal watermen Peter Crusat) by good Stearing we could pass down Safe, accordingly I deturmined to pass through this place notwithstanding the horrid appearance of this agitated gut swelling, boiling & whorling in every direction, (which from the top of the rock did not appear as bad as when I was in it; however we passed Safe to the astonishment of all the Inds. of the last Lodges who viewed us from the top of the rock.

passed one Lodge below this rock, and halted on the Stard. Side to view a very bad place, the current divided by 2 Islands of rocks the lower of them large and in the midal of the river, this place being verry bad I sent by land all the men who could not Swim and such articles as was most valuable to us such as papers Guns & amunition, and proceeded down with the canoes two at a time to a village of 20 wood houses in a Deep bend to the Stard. Side below which [was] a rugid black rock about 20 feet hiter [higher] than the Common high fluds of the river with Several dry chanels which appeared to Choke the river up quite across; The nativs of this village re[ce]ived me verry kindly, one of whome envited me into his house, which I found to be large and comodious, and the first

[17] The so-called Short Narrows of the Columbia (Thwaites) at The Dalles, Oregon.

wooden houses in which Indians have lived Since we left those in the vicinty of the Illinois

I returned through a rockey open countrey infested with pole-cats to the village where I met with Capt. Lewis the two old Chiefs who accompanied us & the party & canoes who had all arrived Safe; the Canoes haveing taken in some water at the last rapids. here we formed a camp near the village, The principal chief from the nation below with Several of his men visited us, and afforded a favourable oppertunity of bringing about a Piece and good under-standing between this chief and his people and the two chiefs who accompanied us which we have the Satisfaction to say we have accomplished, as we have every reason to believe, and that those two bands or nations are and will be on the most friendly terms with each other, gave this great chief a Medal and some other articles, of which he was much pleased. Peter Crusat played on the *violin* and the men danced which delighted the nativs, who Shew every civility towards us. we Smoked with those people untill late at night, when every one retired to rest.

October 25th. Friday 1805

A cool morning Capt. Lewis and my Self walked down to See the place the Indians pointed out as the worst place in passing through the gut, which we found difficuelt of passing without great danger, but as the portage was impracti[c]able withour large canoes, we concluded to Make a portage of our most valuable articles and run the canoes thro.[18] accordingly on our return divided the party Some to take over the Canoes, and others to take our Stores across a portage of a mile to a place on the chanel below this bad whorl & Suck, with Some others I had fixed on the Chanel with roapes to throw out to any who Should unfortunately meet with difficuelty in passing through; great number of Indians viewing us from the high rocks under which we had to pass, the 3 fir[s]t canoes passed thro very well, the 4th. nearly filled with water, the last passed through by takeing in a little water, thus Safely below what I conceved to be the worst part of this chanel felt my self extreamly gratified and pleased.

[18] The Long Narrows (Thwaites).

October 28th. Monday 1805

as we were about to set out 3 canoes from above and 2 from below came to view us. in one of those canoes I observed an Indian with round hat Jacket & wore his hair cued [*he said he got them from Indians below the great rapid who bought them from the whites*] we proceeded on river inclosed on each Side in high clifts of about 90 feet of loose dark Coloured rocks at four miles we landed at a Village of 8 houses on the Stard. Side under some rugid rocks, Those people call themselves *Chil-luckit-te-quaw*, [19] live in houses similar to those described, Speake somewhat different language with maney words the Sam & understand those in their neighbourhood Capt. Lewis took a vocabilary of this Language I entered one of the houses in which I saw a British musket, a cutlash and Several brass Tea kittles of which they appeared verry fond Saw them boiling fish in baskets with Stones, I also Saw [*badly executed*] figures of animals & men cut & painted on boards in one Side of the house which they appeared to prize, but for what purpose I will not ventur to say, here we purchased five Small Dogs, Some dried buries, & white bread made of roots

October 29th. Tuesday 1805

at 4 miles further we landed to smoke a pipe with the people of a village of 11 houses we found those people also friendly They also inform that 10 nations live on this river by hunting and on buries &c. The Countrey begins to be thinly timbered with Pine & low white Oake verry rocky and hilley. [20] at the end of this Course is 3 rocks, the middle rock is large and has a number of graves on it we call it the Sepulchar Island. [21] The last River we call Caterack River from the number of falls which the Indians inform is on it The Indians are afraid to hunt or be on the Lard. Side of this Columbia river for fear of the Snake Inds. who reside on a fork of this river which falls in above the falls. a good situation for winter quarters if game can be had is just below Sepulchar rock

[19] Members of the Chinookan linguistic family.
[20] The beginning of the Cascade Range.
[21] At Memaloose, Oregon.

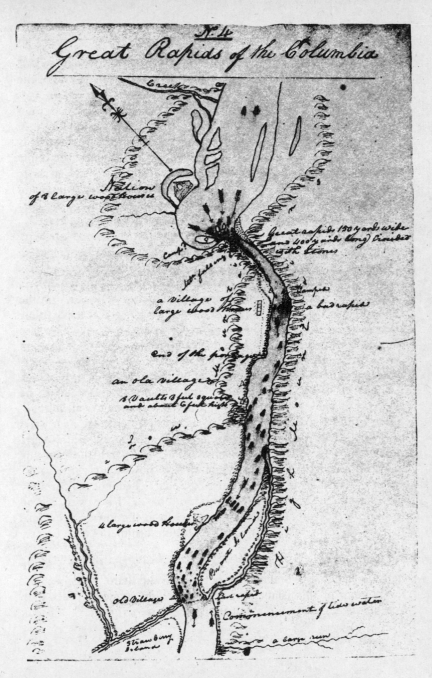

Great Rapids of the Columbia River, sketch-map by Clark.

October 31st Thursday 1805

I with Jo Fields proceeded on, at ½ a mile below the end of the portage passed a house where there had been an old town for ages past   as this house was old Decayed and a place of flees I did not enter it,   about ½ a mile below this house in a verry thick part of the woods is 8 Vaults, which appeared closely covered and highly deckerated with orniments.   Those vaults are all nearly the Same size and form 8 feet square, 6 feet high, sloped a little so as to convey off the rain, made of Pine or cedar boards Closely Connected & s[e]curely Covered with wide boards, with a Dore left in the East side which is partially stoped with wide boards curiously engraved.

In Several of those vaults the dead bodies w[e]re raped up verry securely in Skins tied around with cords of grass and bark, laid on a mat, all east & west and some of those vaults had as maney as 4 Bodies laying on the Side of each other.   the other Vaults containing bones only, Some contained bones for the debth of 4 feet.   on the tops and on poles attached to those vaults hung Brass kittles & frying pans pearced through their bottoms, baskets, bowls of wood, sea Shels, skins, bits of Cloth, hair, bags of Trinkets & Small pieces of bone &c. and independant of the [*Hieroglyphics, figures of men & animals*] curious engraveing and paintings on the boards which formed the Vaults I observed Several wooden Images, cut in the figure[s] of men and Set up on the Sides of the vaults all round, Some of those so old and worn by time, that they were nearly out of Shape,   I also observed the remains of Vaults rotted entirely into the ground and covered with moss. This must bee the burrying place for maney ages for the inhabitants of those rapids,   the vaults are of the most lasting timber Pine & Cedar.   I cannot say certainly that those nativs worship those wooden idols as I have every reason to believe they do not; as they are Set up in the most conspicious parts of their houses, and treated more like orniments than objects of adoration.

I deturmind to return to camp 10 miles distant,   a remarkable high detached rock Stands in a bottom on the Stard. Side near the lower point of this Island on the Stard. Side about 800 feet high and 400 paces around, we call the *Beaten* [*Beacon*] rock.[22]   a Brook

---

[22] Near North Bonneville, Washington.

falls into the narrow chanel which forms the [*what we call*] Strawberry Island, which at this time has no running water, but has every appearance of dischargeing emence torrents   I returned by the Same rout on our Indian parth passing up on the N. W. Side of the river to our Camp at the Great Shute   found Several Indians from the village, I Smoked with them;   Soon after my return two canoes loaded with fish & Bear grass for the trade below, came down from the village at the mouth of the Catterack River,   they unloaded and turned their canoes up Side down on the beech, & camped under a Shelving rock below our Camp.

One of the men shot a goose above this Great Shute,[23] which was floating into the Shute, when an Indian observed it, plunged! into the water & swam to the Goose and brought in on shore, at the head of the Suck, [*great danger, rapids bad, a descent close by him (150 feet off,) of all Columbia River, current dashed among rocks, if he had got in the Suck—lost*] as this Indian richly earned the goose I suffered him to keep it which he about half picked and Spited it up with the guts in it to roste.

This Great Shute or falls is about ½ a mile, with the water of this great river compressed within the space of 150 paces in which there is great numbers of both large and Small rocks, water passing with great velocity forming [foaming] & boiling in a most horriable manner, with a fall of about 20 feet,   below it widens to about 200 paces and current gentle for a Short distance.   a Short distance above is three Small rockey Islands and at the head of those falls, three Small rockey Islands are Situated crosswise the river,   Several rocks above in the river & 4 large rocks in the head of the Shute; those obstructions together with the high Stones which are continually braking loose from the mountain on the Stard. Side and roleing down into the Shute aded to those which brake loose from these Islands above and lodge in the Shute, must be the cause of the rivers daming up to such a distance above, where it shows such evidant marks of the common current of the river being much lower than at the present day.

[23] Formerly the Cascades at Cascade Locks, Oregon.

November 1st. Friday 1805

A verry cool morning wind hard from the N. E. The Indians who arrived last evening took their Canoes on ther Sholders and carried them below the Great Shute, we Set about takeing our Small canoe and all the baggage by land 940 yards of bad slippery and rockey way. The Indians we discovered took ther loading the whole length of the portage 2-½ miles, to avoid a second Shute which appears verry bad to pass, and thro' which they passed with their empty canoes. Great numbers of Sea Otters, they are so cautious that I with dificuelty got a Shot at one today, which I must have killed, but could not get him as he Sunk.

We got all our baggage over the Portage of 940 yards, after which we got the 4 large canoes over by slipping them over the rocks on poles placed across from one rock to another, and at some places along partial Streams of the river. in passing those canoes over the rocks &c. three of them rec[ei]ved injuries which obliged us to delay to have them repared. Several Indian Canoes arrived at the head of the portage, Some of the men acompanied by those from the village come down to Smoke with us, they appear to Speak the same language with a little different axcent

I cannot lern certainly as to the traffick those Inds. carry on below, if white people or the indians who trade with the whites who are either settled or visit the mouth of this river. I believe mostly with the latter as their knowledge of the white people appears to be verry imperfect, and the articles which they appear to trade mostly i.e. Pounded fish, Beargrass, and roots; cannot be an object of comerce wtih furin merchants. however they git in return for those articles Blue and white *beeds* copper [Tea] Kettles, brass arm bands, some scarlet and blue robes and a fiew articles of old clothes, they prefer beeds to any thing, and will part with the last mouthfull or articles of clothing they have for a fiew of those beeds, those beeds the[y] trafick with Indians Still higher up this river for roabs, Skins, cha-pel-el bread, beargrass &c. who in their turn trafick with those under the rockey mountains for Beargrass, *quarmash* [*Pashico*] roots & robes &c.

The nativs of the waters of the Columbia appear helthy, Some have tumers on different parts of their bodies, and Sore and weak Eyes are common, maney have lost their Sight entirely, great numbers with one eye out and frequently the other verry weak, This misfortune I must again asscribe to the water &c. They have bad teeth, which is not common with indians, maney have worn their teeth down and Some quite into their gums, this I cannot satisfactorily account for it, do ascribe it in some measure to their method of eateing, their food, roots pert[i]cularly, which they make use of as they are taken out of the earth frequently nearly covered with sand, I have not Seen any of their long roots offered for Sale clear of sand. They are rether below the Common Size high cheeks womin Small and homely, and have Swelled legs and thighs, and their knees remarkably large which I ascribe to the method in which they sit on their hams go nearly necked wareing only a piece of leather tied about their breast which falls down nearly as low as the waste, a small roabe about 3 feet square, and a piece of leather tied about their breach, They [*womin*] have all flat heads in this quarter both men and women. They are dirty in the extream, both in their person and cookery. ware their hare loose hanging in every direction. They ask high prices for what they Sell and Say that the white people below give great prices for every thing &c.

The noses are all pierced and when they are dressed they have a long tapered piece of white shell or wampum put through the nose, those Shells are about 2 inches in length. I observed in maney of the villeages which I have passed, the heads of the female children in the press for the purpose of compressing their heads in their infancy into a certain form, between two boards

> November 3d. Sunday 1805

The Fog so thick this morning that we could not see a man 50 Steps off, this fog detained us untill 10 oClock at which time we Set out, accompanied by our Indian friends who are from a village near the great falls

The Quick Sand river[24] appears to pass through the low countrey at the foot of those high range of mountains in a Southerly direction. A Mountain which we Suppose to be Mt. Hood, is S. 85° E about 47 miles distant from the mouth of quick sand river. This Mtn. is covered with Snow and in the range of mountains which we have passed through and is of a conical form but rugid.

[24] The Sandy River.

proceeded on to the center of a large Island in the middle of the river which we call Dimond Island from its appearance,[25] Capt. L walked out with his gun on the Island, sent out hunters & fowlers. the Countrey is low rich and thickly timbered on each Side of the river, the Islands open & some ponds river wide and emence numbers of fowls flying in every direction, Such as Swan, geese, Brants, Cranes, Stalks [*Storks*], white guls, comerants & plevers &c. also great numbers of Sea Otter in the river. a canoe arrived from the village below the last rapid with a man his wife and 3 children, and a woman whome had been taken prisoner from the Snake Inds. on Clarks River I sent the Interpreters wife who is a *So so ne* or Snake Indian of the Missouri, to Speake to this squar, they could not understand each other Sufficiently to converse. This family and the Inds. we met from below continued with us. Capt. Lewis borrowed a Small canoe of those Indians & 4 men took her across to a Small lake in the Isld. Capt. L. and 3 men set out after night in this canoe in serch of the Swans, Brants Ducks &c. &c.

Saw white geese with black wings. Saw a small crab-apple with all the taste & flavor of the common.

Mount Hellen bears N. 25°. E about 80 miles, this is the mountain we saw near the forks of this river. it is emensely high and covered with snow, riseing in a kind of cone perhaps the highest pinecal from the common leavel in America

November 4th. Monday 1805

we landed at a village[26] of *25 houses*: 24 of those houses we[re] thached with Straw, and covered with bark, the other House is built of boards in the form of those above, except that it is above ground and about 50 feet in length [*and covered with broad split boards*] This village contains about 200 Men of the *Skilloot* nation I counted 52 canoes on the bank in front of this village maney of them verry large and raised in bow.

we recognized the man who over took us last night, (*our pilot who came in his canoe*) he invited us to a lodge in which he had Some

---

[25] Now Government Island; nearly opposite whose lower end is East Portland, Oregon (Thwaites).

[26] A Chinookan village near Vancouver, Washington.

part and gave us a roundish roots about the Size of a Small Irish potato which they roasted in the embers until they became Soft, This root they call *Wap-pa-to* the *Bulb* of which the Chinese cultivate in great quantities called the *Sa-git ti folia* or common arrow head,[27] it has an agreeable taste and answers verry well in place of bread. we purchased about 4 bushels of this root and divided it to our party.

Several canoes of Indians from the village above came down, dressed for the purpose as I supposed of Paying us a friendly visit, they had scarlet & blue blankets Salor Jackets, overalls, Shirts and hats independant of their usial dress; the most of them had either Muskets or pistols and tin flasks to hold their powder, Those fellows we found assumeing and disagreeable, however we Smoked with them and treated them with every attention & friendship.

dureing the time we were at dinner those fellows Stold my pipe Tomahawk which they were Smoking with, I imediately serched every man and the canoes, but could find nothing of my Tomahawk, while Serching for the Tomahawk one of those Scoundals Stole a cappoe [*Capotte (gr: coat)*] of one of our interperters, which was found Stufed under the root of a tree, near the place they Sat, we became much displeased with those fellows, which they discovered and moved off on their return home to their village, except 2 canoes which had passed on down.

we proceeded on met a large & a Small canoe from below with 12 men the large canoe was orniminted with *Images* carved in wood the figures of a Bear in front & a man in Stern, Painted & fixed verry netely on the canoe, rising to near the hight of a man two Indians verry finely Dressed & with hats on was in this canoe passed the lower point of the Island[28] which is *nine* miles in length

November 5th. Tuesday 1805

Rained all the after part of last night, rain continues this morning, I [s]lept but verry little last night for the noise Kept [up] dureing the whole of the night by the Swans, Geese, white & Grey Brant Ducks &c. on a Small Sand Island close under the Lard. Side; they were emensely noumerous, and their noise horid.

---

[27] The roots of arrowhead (*Sagittaria cuneata*), also called swamp potato.

[28] Sauvie Island; originally called Image Canoe Island by the explorers, but changed to Wappato on the return trip.

We met 4 Canoes of Indians from below, in which there is 26 Indians, one of those canoes is large, and ornimented with *Images* on the bow & Stern. That in the Bow [is] the likeness of a Bear, and in Stern the picture of a man. we landed on the Lard. Side & camped a little below the mouth of a creek[29] on the Stard. Side a little below the mouth of which is an Old village which is now abandaned; This is certainly a fertill and a handsom valley, at this time crouded with Indians. The day proved cloudy with rain the greater part of it, we are all wet cold and disagreeable— I saw but little appearance of frost in this valley which we call Columbia [or] Wap-pa-too Valley (*Columbian valley*) from that root or plants growing Spontaniously in this valley only In my walk of to Day I saw 17 Striped Snakes I killed a grouse which was verry fat, and larger than common. This is the first night which we have been entirely clear of Indians since our arrival on the waters of the Columbia River. we made 32 miles to day by estimation.

November 6th. Wednesday 1805

we over took two Canoes of Indians going down to trade, one of the Indians Spoke a few words of english and Said that the principal man who traded with them was Mr. Haley, and that he had a woman in his Canoe who Mr. Haley was fond of &c. he Showed us a Bow of Iron and Several other things which he Said Mr. Haley gave him. we came too to Dine on the long narrow Island found the woods so thick with under groth that the hunters could not get any distance into the Isld. the red wood, and Green bryers interwoven, and mixed with pine, alder, a Speci[e]s of Beech, ash &c. we killed nothing to day.

November 7th. Thursday 1805

A cloudy foggey morning Some rain. we Set out early proceeded under the Stard. Side under a high rugid hills with Steep assent the Shore boalt and rockey, the fog so thick we could not See across the river, two cano[e]s of Indians met and returned with us to their village which is Situated on the Stard. Side behind a cluster of Marshey Islands, on a narrow chanl. of the river through which we

[29] The Creek was the present Kalama River, Washington (Thwaites).

passed to the *village* of 4 Houses, they gave us to eate Some fish, and Sold us, fish, *Wap pa to* roots three *dogs* and 2 otter skins for which we gave fish hooks principally of which they were verry fond.

Those people call themselves *War-ci-â-cum*[30] and Speake a language different from the nativs above with whome they trade for the *Wapato* roots of which they make great use of as food. their houses differently built, raised entirely above the ground eaves about 5 feet from the ground Supported and covered in the same way of those above, dores about the Same size but in the Side of the house in one corner, one fire place and that near the opposit end, around which they have their beads raised about 4 feet from the flore which is of earth, under their beads they Store away baskets of dried fish Berries & *Wappato*, over the fire they hang the fiesh as they take them and [of] which they do not make immediate use. Their Canoes are of the Same form of those above. The Dress of the men differ verry little from those above, The womin altogether different, their robes are Smaller only covering their Sholders & falling down to near the hip. and Sometims when it is cold a piec of fur curiously plated and connected so as to meet around the body from the arms to the hips. "The garment which occupies the Waist and thence as low as the knee before and mid leg behind, cannot properly be called a petticoat, in the common accep[ta]tion of the word; it is a *Tissue* formed of white cedar bark bruised or broken into Small Strans, which are interwoven in their center by means of Several cords of the same Materials which Serves as well for a girdle as to hold in place the Strans of bark which forms the tissue, and which Strans, confined in the middle, hang with their ends pendulous from the waist, the whole being of Suff[i]cent thickness when the female Stands erect to conceal those parts useally covered from familiar view, but when she stoops or places herself in any other attitude this battery of Venus is not altogether impervious to the penetrating eye of the amorite. This tissue is Sometims formed of little Strings of the Silk grass twisted and knoted at their ends" &c.[31]

Encamped under a high hill on the Stard. Side opposit to a rock[32]

---

[30] Wahkiakums are also Chinookan speakers.
[31] Clark is here quoting Lewis's journal.
[32] Pillar Rock, Washington.

Situated half a mile from the shore, about 50 feet high and 20 feet in Deamieter; we with dificuelty found a place clear of the tide and Sufficiently large to lie on and the only place we could get was on round stones on which we lay our mats rain continud. moderately all day our Small Canoe which got Seperated in the fog this morning joined us this evening

Great joy in camp we are in *view* of the *Ocian*[33] this great Pacific Octean which we been so long anxious to See. and the roreing or noise made by the waves brakeing on the rockey Shores (as I suppose) may be heard disti[n]ctly

We made 34 miles to day as computed.

November 8th. Friday 1805

Some rain all day at intervales, we are all wet and disagreeable, as we have been for Several days past, and our present Situation a verry disagreeable one in as much, as we have not leavel land Sufficient for an encampment and for our baggage to lie cleare of the tide, the High hills jutting in so close and steep that we cannot retreat back, and the water of the river too Salt to be used, added to this the waves are increasing to Such a hight that we cannot move from this place,[34] in this Situation we are compelled to form our camp between the hite of the Ebb and flood tides, and rase our baggage on logs. We are not certain as yet if the white people who trade with those people or from whome they precure their goods are Stationary at the mouth, or visit this quarter at stated times for the purpose of trafick &c. I believe the latter to be the most probable conjecture. The Seas roled and tossed the Canoes in such a manner this evening that Several of our party were Sea sick.

November 9th. Saturday 1805

at 2 oClock P M the flood tide came in accompanied with emence waves and heavy winds, floated the trees and Drift which was on the point on which we Camped and tosed them about in such a manner as to endanger the canoes verry much, with every exertion

[33] The explorers probably mistook the great bay of the river, which just below this point widens to fifteen miles, for the expanse of the ocean (Thwaites).

[34] This was Gray's Point, the western boundary of the bay of that name (Thwaites), near Megler, Washington.

and the Strictest attention by every individual of the party was scercely sufficient to Save our Canoes from being crushed by those monsterous trees maney of them nearly 200 feet long and from 4 to 7 feet through. our camp entirely under water dureing the hight of the *tide*, every man as wet as water could make them all the last night and to day all day as the rain continued all day, at 4 oClock P M the wind Shifted about to the S. W. and blew with great violence imediately from the Ocean for about two hours, notwithstanding the disagreeable Situation of our party all wet and cold (and one which they have experienced for Several days past) they are chearfull and anxious to See further into the Ocian, The water of the river being too Salt to use we are obliged to make use of rain water. Some of the party not accustomed to Salt water has made too free a use of it on them it acts as a pergitive.

At this dismal point we must Spend another night as the wind & waves are too high to proceed.

November 12th. Tuesday 1805

A Tremendious wind from the S. W. about 3 oClock this morning with Lightineng and hard claps of Thunder, and Hail which Continued untill 6 oClock a. m. when it became light for a Short time, then the heavens became sudenly darkened by a black cloud from the S. W. and rained with great violence untill 12 oClock, the waves tremendious brakeing with great fury against the rocks and trees on which we were encamped. our Situation is dangerous. we took the advantage of a low *tide* and moved our camp around a point to a Small wet bottom, at the Mouth of a Brook, which we had not observed when we came to this cove;[35] from its being verry thick and obscured by drift trees and thick bushes. It would be distressing to See our Situation, all wet and colde our bedding also wet, (and the robes of the party which compose half the bedding is rotten and we are not in a Situation to supply their places) in a wet bottom scercely large enough to contain us our baggage half a mile from us, and Canoes at the mercy of the waves, altho Secured as well as possible, Sunk with emence parcels of Stone to wate them down to prevent their dashing to pecies against the rocks

[35] Near Point Ellice, Washington.

November 14th. Thursday 1805

rained all the last night without intermission, and this morning.
wind blows verry hard, but our situation is Such that we cannot
tell from what point it comes. one of our canoes is much broken
by the waves dashing it against the rocks. 5 Indians came up in a
canoe, thro' the waves, which is verry high and role with great fury.
They made Signs to us that they saw the 3 men we Sent down
yesterday. only 3 of those Indians landed, the other 2 which was
women played off in the waves, which induced me to Suspect that
they had taken Something from our men below, at this time one
of the men Colter returnd. by land and informed us that those
Indians had taken his Gigg & basket, I called to the Squars to land
and give back the gigg, which they would not doe untill a man run
with a gun, as if he intended to Shute them when they landed, and
Colter got his gig & basket I then ordered those fellows off, and
they verry readily cleared out they are of the *War-ci-a-cum* N.

Colter informed us that "it was but a Short distance from where
we lay around the point to a butifull Sand beech, which continued
for a long ways, that he had found a good harber in the mouth of a
creek near 2 Indian Lodges—that he had proceeded in the canoe
as far as he could for the waves, the other two men Willard &
Shannon had proceeded on down["]

Capt. Lewis concluded to proceed on by land & find if possible
the white people the Indians say is below and examine if a Bay is
Situated near the mouth of this river as laid down by Vancouver in
which we expect, if there is white traders to find them &c. at 3
oClock he Set out with 4 men Drewyer Jos. & Ru. Fields & R.
Frasure, in one of our large canoes and 5 men to set them around
the point on the Sand beech. this canoe returned nearly filled with
water at Dark which it receved by the waves dashing into it on its
return, haveing landed Capt. Lewis & his party Safe on the Sand
beech.

The rain &c. which has continued without a longer intermition
than 2 hours at a time for ten days past has distroyd. the robes and
rotted nearly one half of the fiew clothes the party has, perticularley
the leather clothes fortunately for us we have no very cold weather
as yet. and if we have cold weather before we can kill & Dress
Skins for clothing the bulk of the party will Suffer verry much.

November 15th. Friday 1805
about 3 oClock the wind luled, and the river became calm, I had
the canoes loaded in great haste and Set Out, from this dismal nitch
where we have been confined for 6 days passed, without the possibility of proceeding on, returning to a better Situation, or get out
to hunt; Scerce of Provisions, and torents of rain poreing on us all
the time. proceeded on passed the blustering point below which
I found a butifull Sand beech thro which runs a Small river from
the hills, below the mouth of this Stream is a *village* of 36 houses
uninhabited by anything except flees, here I met G. Shannon and
5 Indians. Shannon informed me that he met Capt. Lewis at an
Indian Hut about 10 miles below who had sent him back to meet
me, he also told me the Indians were thievish, as the night before
they had Stolen both his and Willards rifles from under their heads
that they Set out on their return and had not proceeded far up the
beech before they met Capt. Lewis, whose arival was at a timely
moment and alarmed the Indians So that they instantly produced
the Guns. I told those Indians who accompanied Shannon that they
should not come near us, and if any one of their nation Stold anything
from us, I would have him Shot, which they understoot verry well.
as the tide was comeing in and the Seas became verry high imediately from the *ocian* (imediately faceing us) I landed and formed
a camp on the highest Spot I could find between the hight of the
tides, and the Slashers in a small bottom this I could plainly See
would be the extent of our journey by water, as the waves were too
high at any stage for our Canoes to proceed any further down. in
full view of the *Ocian* from *Point Adams or Rond* to Cape Disapointment, I could not see any Island in the mouth of this river as laid
down by Vancouver. the Bay which he laies down in the mouth is
imediately below me. This Bay we call Haley's bay[36] from a favourite
trader with the Indians which they Say comes into this Bay and
trades with them our men all comfortable in their Camps[37] which
they have made of boards from the old village above. we made 3
miles to day.

[36] Baker's Bay.

[37] Fort Columbia, opposite Astoria, is probably upon or near the site of the old
camp of Lewis and Clark (November 15–25, 1805), as well as that of the Chinook
village of their friend Concomly (Wheeler).

November 17th. Sunday 1805

Capt. Lewis returned haveing travesed Haley Bay to Cape Disapointment and the *Sea* coast to the North for Some distance.
Several *Chinnook* Indians followed Capt. L——, and a Canoe came
up with roots mats &c. to Sell. those Chinnooks made us a present
of a rute boiled much resembling the common liquorice in taste and
Size: in return for this root we gave more than double the value
to Satisfy their craveing disposttn. It is a bad practice to receive a
present from those Indians as they are never satisfied for what they
recive in return if ten time the value of the articles they gave. This
Chinnook Nation is about 400 Souls inhabid the countrey on the
Small rivers which run into the bay below us and on the Ponds to
the N. W. of us, live principally on fish and roots, they are well
armed with fusees

I directed all the men who wished to see more of the main *Ocian*
to prepare themselves to Set out with me early on tomorrow morning.

November 18th. Monday 1805

A little cloudy this morning I set out with 10 men and my man
York to the Ocian by land. i. e. Serjt. Ordway & Pryor, Jos. & Ru
Fields, Go. Shannon, W. Brattin, J. Colter, P. Wiser, W. Labieche
& P. Shabono one of our interpreters & York. I set out at Day
light and proceeded on a Sandy beech

made a fire and dined on 4 brant and 48 Plever which was killed
by Labiech on the coast as we came on. Rubin Fields Killed a
Buzzard [*Vulture*] of the large Kind[38] near the whale we Saw measured from the tips of the wings across 9½ feet, from the point of
the Bill to the end of the tail 3 feet 10-¼ inches, middle toe 5-½
inches, toe nale 1 inch & 3-½ lines, wing feather 2-½ feet long &
1 inch 5 lines diamiter, tale feathers 14-½ inches, and the *head* is
6-½ inches including the beak. after dineing we crossed the river
in an old canoe which I found on the sand near Some old houses
and proceeded on

to the iner extremity of *Cape Disapointment* passing a nitch in which
there is a Small rock island, a Small Stream falls into this nitch
from a pond which is imediately on the Sea coast passing through

---

[38] California condor (*Gymnogyps californianus*).

are 4½ inches
a whitish
with feathers,
entirely
not imbricated;
in number three
forward and that
in length, and of
colour uncovered
they are not
smooth but
the toe are four
of which one
is the center
much the longest; the fourth is short and is inserted
near the inner of the three other toes and rather projecting forward. the thigh is covered with feathers
as low as the knee the top or upper part of the toes
are imbricated with broad scales lying transversely
the nails are black and in proportion to the size of
the bird comparatively with those of the Hawk or
Eagle, short and bluntly pointed the under
side of the wing is covered with white down and
feathers. a white stripe of about 2 inches in
width, also marks the outer part of the wing, in-
bracing the lower points of the feathers, which
over the joints of the wing through their whole
length or width of that part of the wing. all

Head of a California condor by Clark.

a low isthmus. this Cape is an ellivated circlier [circular] point covered with thick timber on the iner Side and open grassey exposur next to the Sea and rises with a Steep assent to the hight of about 150 or 160 feet above the leavel of the water this cape as also the Shore both on the Bay & Sea coast is a dark brown rock.[39]

I crossed the neck of Land low and ½ of a mile wide to the main Ocian, at the foot of a high open hill projecting into the ocian, and about one mile in Si[r]cumfrance. I assended this hill which is covered with high corse grass. decended to the N. of it and camped. [walked] 19 Miles [to-day]. I picked up a flounder on the beech this evening

from Cape Disapointment to a high point of a Mountn. which we shall call [*Clarke's Point of View*] beares S. 20° W. about 40 [*25*] miles, point adams is verry low and is Situated within the derection between those two high points of land, the water appears verry Shole from off the mouth of the river for a great distance, and I cannot assertain the direction of the deepest chanel, the Indians point nearest the opposit Side. the waves appear to brake with tremendious force in every direction quite across a large Sand bar lies within the mouth nearest to point Adams which is nearly covered at high tide. I suped on brant this evening with a little pounded fish. Some rain in the after part of the night. men appear much Satisfied with their trip beholding with estonishment the high waves dashing against the rocks & this emence Ocian

                                November 19th Tuesday 1805
after takeing a Sumptious brackfast of Venison which was rosted on Stiks exposed to the fire, I proceeded on through ruged Country of high hills and Steep hollers on a course from the Cape N 20° W. 5 miles on a Direct line to the commencement of a Sandy coast which extended N. 10° W. from the top of the hill above the Sand Shore to a Point of high land distant near 20 miles. this point I have taken the Liberty of Calling after my particular friend Lewis.[40] at the commencement of this Sand beech the high lands leave the Sea Coast in a Direction to Chinnook river, and does not touch the

[39] Fort Canby State Park, Washington.
[40] The site of North Head Lighthouse.

Sea Coast again below point Lewis leaveing a low pondey Countrey, maney places open with small ponds in which there is great numbr. of fowl I am informed that the *Chinnook* Nation inhabit this low countrey and live in large wood houses on a river which passes through this bottom Parrilal to the Sea coast and falls into the Bay

I proceeded on the sandy coast[41] 4 miles, and marked my name on a Small pine, the Day of the month & year, &c. and returned to the foot of the hill, from which place I intended to Strike across to the Bay, I saw a Sturgeon which had been thrown on Shore and left by the tide 10 feet in length, and Several joints of the back bone of a Whale, which must have foundered on this part of the Coast. after Dineing on the remains of our Small Deer I proceeded through over a land S E with Some Ponds to the bay

The Deer[42] of this Coast differ materially from our Common deer in as muech as they are much darker, deeper bodied, Shorter ledged [legged] horns equally branched from the beem the top of the tail black from the rute [*root*] to the end. Eyes larger and do not lope but jump.

Wednesday November the 20th. 1805

I proceeded on up the Beech and was overtaken by three Indians one of them gave me Some dried Sturgeon and a fiew Wappato roots, I employ[e]d those Indians to take up one of our Canoes which had been left by the first party that Came down, for which Service I gave them each a fishing hook of a large Size. on my way up I met Several parties of Chinnooks which I had not before Seen, they were on their return from our Camp. all those people appeared to know my deturmonation of keeping every individual of their nation at a proper distance, as they were guarded and resurved in my presence &c. found maney of the *Chin nooks* with Capt. Lewis of whome there was 2 Cheifs *Com com mo ly* & *Chil-lar-la-wil* to whome we gave Medals and to one a flag. one of the Indians had on a roab made of 2 Sea Otter Skins the fur of them were more butifull than any fur I had ever Seen both Capt. Lewis & my self

---

[41] Long Beach, Washington.
[42] Mule deer (*Odocoileus hemionus*) of the northwest Pacific coast, sometimes called black-tailed deer.

endeavored to purchase the *roab* with differant articles   at length
we precured it for a belt of blue beeds which the Squar-wife of our
interpreter Shabono wore around her waste.

                                        Thursday November 21st. 1805.
     An old woman & Wife to a Cheif of the *Chunnooks* came and made
a Camp near ours.   She brought with her 6 young Squars I believe
for the purpose of Gratifying the passions of the men of our party
and receving for those indulgiences Such Small [presents] as She
(the old woman) thought proper to accept of.
     Those people appear to View Sensuality as a Necessary evel, and
do not appear to abhor it as a Crime in the unmarried State.   The
young females are fond of the attention of our men and appear to
meet the sincere approbation of their friends and connections, for
thus obtaining their favours,   the Womin of the Chinnook Nation
have handsom faces low and badly made with large legs & thighs
which are generally Swelled from a Stopage of the circulation in the
feet (which are Small) by maney Strands of Beeds or curious Strings
which are drawn tight around the leg above the ankle,   their legs
are also picked [i.e., tattooed] with defferent figures,   I saw on the
left arm of a Squar the following letters *J. Bowman*,   all those are
considered by the natives of this quarter as handsom deckerations,
and a woman without those deckorations is Considered as among
the lower Class   they ware their hair lose hanging over their back
and Sholders   maney have blue beeds threaded & hung from different parts of their *ears* and about ther neck and around their wrists,
their dress otherwise is prosisely like that of the Nation of *War ci a
cum* as already discribed.   a Short roab, and *tissue* or kind of peticoat
of the bark of Cedar which fall down in strings as low as the knee
behind and not so low before.   Maney of the men have blankets of
red blue or Spotted Cloth or the common three & 2½ point blankets,
and Salors old Clothes which they appear to prise highly, they also
have robes of *SeaOtter*, Beaver, Elk, Deer, fox and cat common to
this Countrey, which I have never Seen in the U States.   they also
precure a roabe from the nativs above, which is made of the Skins
of a Small animal about the Size of a cat, which is light and dureable
and highly prized by those people.   the greater numbers of the men
of the Chinnooks have Guns and powder and Ball.   The Men are
low homely and badly made, Small crooked legs large feet, and all

of both Sects have flattened heads. The food of this nation is principally fish & roots   the fish they precure from the river by the means of nets and gigs, and the Salmon which run up the Small branches together with what they collect drifted up on the Shores of the Sea coast near to where they live. The roots which they use are Several different kinds, the *Wap pa to* which they precure from the nativs above, a black root which they call *Shaw-na-tâh-que* & the Wild licquorish is the most Common,   they also kill a fiew Elk Deer & fowl.   maney of the Chinnooks appear to have Venerious and pustelus disorders.   one woman whome I saw at the Creek appeared all over in Scabs and ulsers &c.

We gave to the men each a pece of ribin. We purchased cramberies Mats verry netely made of flags and rushes, Some roots, Salmon and I purchased a hat made of Splits & Strong grass, which is made in the fashion which was common in the U States two years ago also small baskets to hold Water made of Split and Straw,   for those articles we gave high prices.

NINE

Winter at Fort Clatsop

November 22, 1805–March 22, 1806

[Clark]   Friday November 22nd. 1805.

O! how horriable is the day   waves brakeing with great violence against the Shore throwing the Water into our Camp &c.   all wet and confind to our Shelters,   Several Indian men and women crouding about the mens shelters to day, we purchased a fiew Wappato roots for which we gave Armban[d]s, & rings to the old Squar, those roots are equal to the Irish potato, and is a tolerable substitute for bread

                                    Saturday November 22 [3]rd. 1805.

in the evening Seven indians of the *Clot sop* Nation came over in a Canoe, they brought with them 2 Sea otter Skins for which they asked blue beads &c. and Such high pricies that we were unable to purchase them without reducing our Small Stock of Merchendize, on which we depended for Subcistance on our return up this river. mearly to try the Indian who had one of those Skins, I offered him my Watch, handkerchief a bunch of red beads and a dollar of the American coin, all of which he refused and demanded *"ti-â-co-mo-shack"* which is *Chief beads* and the most common blue beads, but fiew of which we have at this time

This nation is the remains of a large nation destroyed by the Small pox or Some other [disease] which those people were not acquainted with, they Speak the Same language of the Chinnooks and resemble them in every respect except that of Stealing, which we have not cought them at as yet.

November 24th. Sunday 1805

[A vote of the men, as to location of winter quarters.]

Sergt J. Ordway	cross & examine		S
Serjt. N. Pryor	do	do	S
Sgt. P. Gass	do	do	S
Jo. Shields	proceed to Sandy R		
G. Shannon	examn.	cross	falls
T. P. Howard	do	do	falls
P. Wiser	do	do	S.R.
J. Collins	do	do	S. R.
Jo. Fields	do	do	up
Al. Willard	do	do	up
R. Willard	do	do	up
J. Potts	do	do	falls
R. Frasure	do	do	up
Wm. Bratten	do	do	up
R. Fields	do	do	falls
J: B: Thompson	do	do	up
J. Colter	do	do	up
H. Hall	do	do	S. R.
Labeech	do	do	S. R.
Peter Crusatte	do	do	S R
J. P. Depage	do	do	up
Shabono	—	—	—
S. Guterich	do	do	falls
W. Werner	do	do	up
Go: Gibson	do	do	up
Jos. Whitehouse	do	do	up
Geo Drewyer	Exam other side		falls
Mc. Neal	do	do	up
York	"	"	lookout

| falls | Sandy River | lookout up |
| 5 | 10 | 12 |

Janey [Sacajawea] in favour of a place where there is plenty of Potas.

Sunday November 24th. 1805.

being now determined to go into Winter quarters as soon as possible, as a convenient Situation to precure the Wild animals of the
forest which must be our dependance for Subsisting this Winter,
we have every reason to believe that the Nativs have not provisions
Suffi[ci]ent for our consumption, and if they had, their prices are
So high that it would take ten times as much to purchase their *roots*
& Dried fish as we have in our possesion, encluding our Small remains
of Merchindize and Clothes &c. This certinly enduces every individual of the party to make diligient enquiries of the nativs [for] the
part of the Countrey in which the Wild animals are most plenty.
They generaly agree that the Most *Elk* is on the Opposit Shore, and
that the greatest Numbers of *Deer* is up the river at Some distance
above. The Elk being an animal much larger than Deer, easier to
Kill, & better meat (in the Winter when pore) and Skins better for
the Clothes of our party: added to [this] a convenient Situation to
the Sea coast where We Could make Salt, and a probibility of Vessels
comeing into the Mouth of Columbia ("which the Indians inform
us would return to trade with them in 3 months") from whome we
might precure a fresh Supply of Indian trinkets to purchase provisions on our return home: together with the Solicitations of every
individual, except one of our party induced us [to] Conclude to
Cross the river and examine the opposit Side, and if a Sufficent
quantity of Elk could probebly be precured to fix on a Situation as
convenient to the Elk & Sea Coast as we could find. added to the
above advantagies in being near the Sea Coast one most Strikeing
one occurs to me i.e, the Climate which must be from every appearance much milder than that above the 1st. range of Mountains,
The Indians are Slightly Clothed and give an account of but little
Snow, and the weather which we have experienced since we arrived
in the neighbourhood of the Sea coast has been verry warm, and
maney of the fiew days past disagreeably so. if this Should be the
case it will most Certainly be the best Situation of our Naked party
dressed as they are altogether in leather.

November 28th. Thursday 1805
we could find no deer, several hunters attempted to penetrate
the thick woods, to the main South Side without suckcess   the swan
& gees wild and cannot be approached,   and wind to high to go

either back or forward, and we have nothing to eate but a little Pounded fish which we purchasd. at the Great falls, This is our present situation! truly disagreeable. aded to this the robes of our selves and men are all rotten from being continually wet, and we cannot precure others, or blankets in these places. about 12 oClock the wind shifted about to the N.W. and blew with great violence for the remainder of the day at maney times it blew for 15 or 20 minits with such violence that I expected every moment to see trees taken up by the roots, some were blown down. Those squals were suckceeded by rain O! how Tremendious is the day. This dredfull wind and rain continued with intervales of fair weather, the greater part of the evening and night

[Lewis]   November 29th. 1805
    the wind being so high the party were unable to proceed with the perogues. I determined therefore to proceed down the river on it's E. side in surch of an eligible place for our winters residence and accordingly set out early this morning in the small canoe accompanyed by 5 men. Drewyer R. Fields, Shannon, Colter & labiesh, proceeded along the coast.[1]
    send out the hunters they killed 4. deer 2 brant a goat and seven ducks
    it rained up on us by showers all day. left three of these deer and took with us one encamped at an old Indian hunting lodge which afforded us a tolerable shelter from the rain. which continued by intervales throughout the night.

[Clark]   Friday 29th. of November 1805
    The winds are from Such points that we cannot form our Camp So as to prevent the Smoke which is emencely disagreeable, and painfull to the eyes. The Shore below the point at our camp[2] is formed of butifull pebble of various colours. I observe but fiew birds of the Small kind, great numbers of wild fowls of Various kinds, the large Buzzard with white wings, grey and bald eagle's, large red tailed Hawks, ravens & crows in abundance, the blue

---

[1] Site of Astoria, Oregon.
[2] At Tongue Point, Oregon.

Magpie, a Small brown bird which frequents logs & about the roots of trees, Snakes, Lizards, Small bugs, worms, Spiders, flyes & insects of different kinds are to be Seen in abundance at this time.

Saturday 30th. of November 1805

Several men Complain of a looseness and griping which I contribute to the diet, pounded fish mixed with Salt water, I derect that in future that the party mix the pounded fish with fresh water. The squar gave me a piece of bread made of flour which She had reserved for her child and carefully Kept untill this time, which has unfortunately got wet, and a little Sour. this bread I eate with great satisfaction, it being the only mouthfull I had tasted for Several months past. my hunters killed *three* Hawks, which we found fat and delicious, they saw 3 Elk but could not get a Shot at them. The fowlers killed 3 black Ducks with Sharp White beeks Keep in large flocks & feed on Grass, they have no Craw and their toes are seperate, Common in the U. States[3]

Sunday December 1st. 1805.

The emence Seas and waves which breake on the rocks & Coasts to the S.W. & N W roars like an emence fall at a distance, and this roaring has continued ever Since our arrival in the neighbourhood of the Sea Coast which has been 24 days Since we arrived in Sight of the Great Western; (for I cannot Say Pacific) Ocian as I have not Seen one pacific day Since my arrival in its vicinity, and its waters are forming and petially [perpetually] breake with emenc waves on the Sands and rockey coasts, tempestous and horiable. I have no account of Capt. Lewis Since he left me.

Monday 2nd. December 1805

I feel verry unwell, and have entirely lost my appetite for the Dried pounded fish which is in fact the cause of my disorder at present. The men are generally complaining of a lax and gripeing. In the evening Joseph Field came in with the Marrow bones of a elk which he killed at 6 miles distant, this welcome news to us. I dispatched Six men in a empty Canoe with Jo: imediately for the

[3] American coot (*Fulica americana*).

elk which he Said was about 3 miles from the Water this is the first Elk which has been killd on this Side of the rockey mountains

December 3rd. Tuesday 1805
I am still unwell and can't eate even the flesh of the Elk. an Indian Canoe of 8 Indians Came too, those Inds. are on their way down to the *Clât-sops* with *Wap pa to* to barter with that Nation, I purchasd. a fiew of those roots for which I gave Small fish hooks, those roots I eate with a little Elks Soupe which I found gave me great relief I found the roots both nurishing and as a check to my disorder. The Indians proceeded on down through emence high waves maney times their Canoe was entirely out of Sight before they were ½ a mile distant. Serjt. Pryor & Gibson who went hunting yesterday has not returned untill after night, they informed me that they had killed 6 Elk at a great distance which they left lying, haveing taken out their interals, that they had been lost and in their ramble saw a great deel of Elk Sign. after eateing the marrow out of two shank bones of an Elk, the Squar choped the bones fine boiled them and extracted a pint of Grease, which is Superior to the tallow of the animal. Some rain this evening I marked my name on a large pine tree imediately on the isthmus William Clark December 3rd. 1805. By Land from the U.States in 1804 & 1805.

Wednesday 4th. December 1805
Some rain all the last night, this morning it increased with the wind from the S.E. I Se[n]t out Sergiant Pryor and 6 men to the Elk he had killed with directions to carry the meat to a bay which he informed me was below and as he believed at no great distance from the Elk, and I Should proceed on to that bay as soon as the wind would lay a little and the tide went out in the evening. the Smoke is exceedingly disagreeable and painfull to my eyes, my appetite has returned and I feel much better of my late complaint. a Spring tide to day rose 2 feet higher than common flood tides and high water at 11 oClock. Hard wind from the South this evening, rained moderately all day and the waves too high for me to proceed in Safty to the bay as I intended, in Some part of which I expected would be convenient for us to make winter quarters, the reports of seven hunte[r]s agreeing that elke were in great abundance about

the Bay below. no account of Capt Lewis. I fear Some accident has taken place in his craft or party.

December 5th. Thursday 1805

Som hard showers of rain last night, this morn cloudy and drisley rain, in the bay above the showers appear harder. High water to day at 12 oClock this tide is 2 Ins. higher than that of yesterday all our stores again wet by the hard showers of last night Capt. Lewis's long delay below has been the cause of no little uneasiness on my part for him, a 1000 conjectures has crouded into my mind respecting his probable situation & safty. the repeeted rains and hard winds which blows from the S.W. renders it impossible for me to move with loaded Canoes along an unknown coast we are all wet and disagreeable, the party much better of indispositions

Capt. Lewis returned with 3 men in the Canoe and informs me that he thinks that a Sufficient number of Elk may be pr[o]cured convenient to a Situation on a Small river which falls into a Small bay a Short distance below, that his party had Killed 6 Elk & 5 Deer in his rout, two men of his party left behind to secure the Elk.

this was verry Satisfactory information to all the party. we accordingly deturmined to proceed on to the Situation which Capt. Lewis had Viewed as Soon as the wind and weather should permit and Comence building huts &c.

December 7th. Saturday 1805

have every thing put on board the Canoes and Set out to the place Capt. Lewis had viewed and thought well Situated for winter quarters. we proceeded on against the tide to a point about [blank space in MS.] miles here we met Sergt. Pryor and his party returning to the Camp we had left without any meat, the waves verry verry high, as much as our Canoes could bear rendered it impossible to land for the party, we proceeded on around the point into the bay and landed to take brackfast on 2 Deer which had been killed & hung up, one of which we found the other had been taken off by [s]ome wild animal probably Panthors or the Wild[cat?] of this Countrey here all the party of Sergt. Pryors joined us except my man York, who had stoped to rite his load and missed his way, Sergt. Pryor informed us that he had found the Elk, which was much further from the bay than he expected, that they missed the way for one day and a half, & when he found the Elk they were mostly spoiled, and they only brought the Skins of 4 of the Elk.

after brackfast I delayed about half an hour before York Came up, and then proceeded around this Bay which I call Meriwethers Bay the Cristian name of Capt. Lewis who no doubt was the 1st. white man who ever Surveyed this Bay, we assended a river which falls in on the South Side of this Bay 3 miles to the first point of high land on the West Side, the place Capt. Lewis had viewed and formed in a thick groth of pine about 200 yards from the river,[4] this situation is on a rise about 30 feet higher than the high tides leavel and thickly Covered with lofty pine. this is certainly the most eligable Situation for our purposes of any in its neighbourhood.

Wednesday 11th. December 1805
rained all the last night moderately   we are all employed putting up huts or Cabins for our winters quarters,   Sergeant Pryor unwell from a dislocation of his sholder, Gibson with the disentary, Jo. Fields with biles on his legs, & Werner with a Strained Knee.   The rain Continued moderately all day.

Monday 23rd. December 1805
Rained without intermition all the last night and to day with Thunder and Hail the fore and after part of this day.   Capt. Lewis and my self move into our hut to day unfinished.

Tuesday 24th. December 1805
hard rain at Different times last night and all this day without intermition.   men all employd. in finishing their huts and moveing into them.

Cuscalah the Indian who had treated me so politely when I was at the Clâtsops Village, come up in a canoe with his young brother & 2 Squars   he laid before Capt. Lewis and my self each a mat and a parcel of roots   Some time in the evening two files was demanded for the presents of mats and roots,   as we had no files to part with, we each returned the present which we had received, which dis-

---

[4] Lewis and Clark River and Young's Bay. The site is four miles from the ocean and ten miles southwest of Astoria, Oregon.

pleased Cuscalah a little. He then offered a woman to each of us which we also declined axcepting of, which displeased the whole party verry much—the female part appeared to be highly disgusted at our refuseing to axcept of their favours &c.

our Store of Meat entirely Spoiled, we are obliged to make use of it as we have nothing else except a little pounded fish, the remains of what we purchased near the Great falls of the Columbia, and which we have ever found to be a convenient resort, and a portable method of curing fish.

Christmas Wednesday 25th. December 1805

at day light this morning we we[re] awoke by the discharge of the fire arm[s] of all our party & a Selute, Shouts and a Song which the whole party joined in under our windows, after which they retired to their rooms was chearfull all the morning. after brackfast we divided our Tobacco which amounted to 12 carrots one half of which we gave to the men of the party who used tobacco, and to those who doe not use it we make a present of a handkerchief, The Indians leave us in the evening all the party Snugly fixed in their huts. I recved a pres[e]nt of Capt. L. of a fleece hosrie [hosiery] Shirt Draws and Socks, a pr. Mockersons of Whitehouse a Small Indian basket of Gutherich, two Dozen white weazils tails of the Indian woman, & some black root of the Indians before their departure. Drewyer informs me that he saw a Snake pass across the parth to day. The day proved Showerey wet and disagreeable.

we would have Spent this day the nativity of Christ in feasting, had we any thing either to raise our Sperits or even gratify our appetites, our Diner concisted of pore Elk, so much Spoiled that we eate it thro' mear necessity, Some Spoiled pounded fish and a fiew roots.

December 26th. Thursday 1805

rained and blew hard last night, some hard Thunder, The rain continued as usial all day and wind blew hard from the S.E. Joseph Fields finish a Table & 2 seats for us. we dry our wet articles and have the blankets fleed, The flees are so troublesom that I have slept but little for 2 night past and we have regularly to kill them out of our blankets every day for several past. maney of the men

Christmas

Wednesday 25th December 1805

at day light this morning we we awoke by
the discharge of the fire arm of all our party &
a Selute, Shout and a Song which the whole
party joined in under our windows, after which
they retired to their rooms were chearfull
all the morning—. after breakfast we divid-
-ed our tobacco which amounted to 12 carrots
one half of which we gave to the men of the
party who used tobacco, and to those who
doe not use it we make a present of a handkerchief. The Indians leave us in the evening
all the party Snugly fixed in their huts. I
recved a present of Capt. L. of a fleece hosrie shirt
Draws and Socks—, a pr. Mockersons of Whitehouse
a Small Indian basket of Guthrie's, two dozen
white weazils tails of the Indian woman, &
Some black root of the Indians before their
departure. Drewyer informs me that he Saw
a Snake pass across the parth to day—. The
day proved Showerey wet and disagreeable.

we would have Spent this day the nativity of Christ in feasting, had we any thing
either to raise our Spirits or even gratify
our appetites, our Diner conssisted of pore
Elk, so much Spoiled that we eate it thro'
mear necessity, Some Spoiled pounded fish &
a fiew roots.

Manuscript page by Clark, December 25, 1805.

have ther Powder wet by the horns being repeatedly wet,   hut smoke[s] verry bad.

Sunday 29th. December 1805

we were informed day before yesterday that a whale had foundered on the coast to the S.W. near the *Kil a mox* N. and that the greater part of the *Clatsops* were gorn for the oile & blubber,   the wind proves too high for us to proceed by water to See this Monster, Capt. Lewis has been in readiness Since we first heard of the whale to go and see it and collect Some of its Oil,   the wind has proved too high as yet for him to proceed.

The flees are So noumerous and hard to get rid of; that the Indians have different houses which they resort to occasionally, not withstanding all their precautions, they never Step into our house without leaveing Sworms of those tormenting insects; and they torment us in such a manner as to deprive us of half the nights Sleep frequently.

December 30th. Monday 1805

The fort was completed this evening and at sun set we let The Indians know that, our custom will be to shut the gates at sun set, at which time they must all go out of the fort.[5]   those people who are verry foward and disegreeable, left the huts with reluctiance. This day proved the best we have had since at this place, only 3 Showers of rain to day, cloudy nearly all day, in the evening the wind luled and the fore part of the night fair and clear.   I saw flies & different kinds of insects in motion to day   Snakes are yet to be seen, and Snales without cover is common and large,   fowls of every kind common to this quarter abound in the Creek & Bay near us

[5] The sketch-plan here given of the fort on the Pacific Coast, wherein the Lewis and Clark expedition spent the winter of 1805–06 was traced by Clark upon the rough elk-skin cover of his field-book.   In the original it is much faded, and the lines have been pulled out of shape by a fold in the skin; no doubt, when drawn, the walls of the fort were straight.   Apparently the stockade was 50 feet square, with a long cabin of three rooms ranged along the upper wall, each with what seems to be a central fireplace; and along the lower wall four cabins, two of them with fireplaces and one with an outside chimney; the gates are to the left and the parade ground is 20 × 48 feet. It would appear that the gates opened to the south (Thwaites).

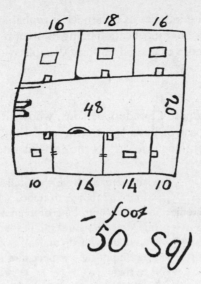

[Lewis]   Fort Clatsop. 1806.
                                  January 1st. Tuesday [*Wednesday*]

This morning I was awoke at an early hour by the discharge of a
volley of small arms, which were fired by our party in front of our
quarters to usher in the new year; this was the only mark of rispect
which we had it in our power to pay this celebrated day. our repast
of this day tho' better than that of Christmass, consisted principally
in the anticipation of the 1st. day of January 1807, when in the
bosom of our friends we hope to participate in the mirth and hilarity
of the day, and when with the zest given by the recollection of the
present, we shall completely, both mentally and corporally, enjoy
the repast which the hand of civilization has prepared for us. at
present we were content with eating our boiled Elk and wappetoe,
and solacing our thirst with our only beverage *pure water*. two of our
hunters who set out this morning reterned in the evening having
killed two bucks elk; they presented Capt. Clark and myself each
a marrow-bone and tonge, on which we suped. visited today by a
few of the Clatsops who brought some roots and burries for the
purpose of trading with us. we were uneasy with rispect to two of
our men, Willard and Wiser, who were dispatched on the 28th. ulto.
with the saltmakers, and were directed to return immediately; their

not having returned induces us to believe it probable that they have missed their way. our fourtification being now completed we issued an order for the more exact and uniform discipline and government of the garrison.

[Clark]   January 1st. 1806

A List of the names of Sundery persons, who visit this part of the Coast for the purpose of trade &c. &c. in large Vestles; all of which speake the English language &c. as the Indians inform us

Moore	Visit them in a large 4 masted ship, they expect him in 2 moons to trade.
1 Eyd [one-eyed] Skellie	in a large ship, long time gorn.
Youin	In a large Ship, and they expect him in 1 moon to trade with them.
Swepeton	In a Ship, they expect him in 3 month back to trade
Mackey	In a Ship, they expect him back in 1 or 2 Moons to trade with them.
Meship	In a Ship, the[y] expect him 2 moons to trade.
Jackson	Visit them in a Ship and they expect him back in 3 months to trade.
Balch	In a Ship and they expect him in 3 months to trade.
Mr. Haley	Visits them in a Ship & they expect him back to trade with them in 3 Moons to trade. he is the favourite of the Indians (from the number of Presents he gives) and has the trade principally with all the tribes.
Washilton	In a Skooner, they expect him in 3 months to return and trade with them—a favourite.
Lemon	In a Slupe, and they expect him in 3 moons to trade with them.
Davidson	Visits this part of the coast and river in a Brig for the purpose of Hunting the Elk returns when he pleases he does not trade any, kills a great many Elk &c. &c.
Fallawan	In a Ship with guns he fired on & killed several Indians, he does not trade now and they doe not know when he will return, well done

[Lewis]   Friday January 3d. 1806

At 11. A.M. we were visited by our near neighbours, Cheif or Tiá. Co-mo-wool, alias Conia and six Clatsops. the[y] brought for sale some roots buries and three dogs also a small quantity of fresh blubber. this blubber they informed us they had obtained from their neighbours the Callamucks[6] who inhabit the coast to the S.E. near whose vilage a whale had recently perished. this blubber the Indians eat and esteeme it excellent food. our party from necessaty having been obliged to subsist some lenth of time on dogs have now become extreemly fond of their flesh; it is worthy of remark that while we lived principally on the flesh of this anamal we were much more healthy strong and more flesshey than we had been since we left the Buffaloe country. for my own part I have become so perfectly reconciled to the dog that I think it an agreeable food and would prefer it vastly to lean Venison or Elk. a small Crow, the blue crested Corvus and the smaller corvus with a white brest, the little brown ren, a large brown sparrow, the bald Eagle and the beatifull Buzzard of the columbia still continue with us.

[Clark]   Friday the 3rd. January 1806

At 11 A. M. we were visisted by our near neighbour Chief or *tiá Co mo wool* alias *Conia* (*Coō̃ nê*) and six Clatsops. they brought for Sale Some roots berries and 3 Dogs also a Small quantity of fresh blubber. this blubber they informed us they had obtained from their neighbours the *Cal lá mox* who inhabit the coast to the S.E. near one of their Villages a Whale had recently perished. this blubber the Indians eat and esteem it excellent food. our party from necescity have been obliged to Subsist some length of time on dogs have now become extreamly fond of their flesh; it is worthey of remark that while we lived principally on the flesh of this animal we wer much more helthy strong and more flesshey then we have been Sence we left the Buffalow Country. as for my own part I have not become reconsiled to the taste of this animal as yet.

Capt. Lewis gave the Cheif Cania a par of Sattin breechies with which he appeared much pleased.

---

[6] A variant of Tillamook—once a large Salishan tribe on the Oregon coast (Thwaites).

[Lewis] Saturday January 4th. 1806.

Comowooll and the Clatsops who visited us yesterday left us in the evening. These people the Chinnooks and others residing in this neighbourhood and speaking the same language have been very friendly to us; they appear to be a mild inoffensive people but will pilfer if they have an opportunity to do so where they conceive themselves not liable to detection. they are great higlers in trade and if they conceive you anxious to purchase will be a whole day bargaining for a handfull of roots; this I should have thought proceeded from their want of knowledge of the comparitive value of articles of merchandize and the fear of being cheated, did I not find that they invariably refuse the price first offered them and afterwards very frequently accept a smaller quantity of the same article; in order to satisfy myself on this subject I once offered a Chinnook my watch two knives and a considerable quantity of beads for a small inferior sea Otter's skin which I did not much want, he immediately conceived it of great value, and refused to barter except I would double the quantity of beads; the next day with a great deal of importunity on his part I received the skin in exchange for a few strans of the same beads he had refused the day before. I therefore believe this trait in their character proceeds from an avaricious all grasping disposition. in this rispect they differ from all Indians I ever became acquainted with, for their dispositions invariably lead them to give whatever they are possessed off no matter how usefull or valuable, for a bauble which pleases their fancy, without consulting it's usefullness or value. nothing interesting occurred today, or more so, than our wappetoe being all exhausted.

Sunday January 5th. 1806.

At 5.P.M. Willard and Wiser returned, they had not been lost as we apprehended. they informed us that it was not untill the fifth day after leaving the Fort that they could find a convenient place for making salt; that they had at length established themselves on the coast about 15 Miles S.W. from this,[7] near the lodge of some Killamuck families; that the Indians were very friendly and had given them a considerable quantity of the blubber of a whale which

---

[7] At the site of Seaside, Oregon.

perished on the coast some distance S.E. of them; part of this blubber they brought with them, it was white & not unlike the fat of Poork, tho' the texture was more spongey and somewhat coarser. I had a part of it cooked and found it very pallitable and tender, it resembled the beaver or the dog in flavour. it may appear somewhat extraordinary tho' it is a fact that the flesh of the beaver and dog possess a very great affinity in point of flavour. These lads also informed us that J. Fields, Bratton and Gibson (the Salt Makers) had with their assistance erected a comfortable camp killed an Elk and several deer and secured a good stock of meat; they commenced the making of salt and found that they could obtain from 3 quarts to a gallon a day; they brought with them a specemine of the salt of about a gallon, we found it excellent, fine, strong, & white; this was a great treat to myself and most of the party, having not had any since the 20th. Ultmo.; I say most of the party, for my friend Capt. Clark. declares it to be a mear matter of indifference with him whether he uses it or not; for myself I must confess I felt a considerable inconvenience from the want of it; the want of bread I consider as trivial provided, I get fat meat, for as to the species of meat I am not very particular, the flesh of the dog the horse and the wolf, having from habit become equally formiliar with any other, and I have learned to think that if the chord be sufficiently strong, which binds the soul and boddy together, it dose not so much matter about the materials which compose it.

Colter also returned this evening unsuccessfull from the chase, having been absent since the 1st. Inst. Capt. Clark determined this evening to set out early tomorrow with two canoes and 12 men in quest of the whale, or at all events to purchase from the Indians a parcel of the blubber, for this purpose he prepared a small assortment of merchandize to take with him.

Monday January 6th. 1806.

Capt Clark set out after an early breakfast with the party in two canoes as had been concerted the last evening; Charbono and his Indian woman were also of the party; the Indian woman was very impo[r]tunate to be permited to go, and was therefore indulged; she observed that she had traveled a long way with us to see the great waters, and that now that monstrous fish was also to be seen, she thought it very hard she could not be permitted to see either (she had never yet been to the Ocean).

The Clatsops, Chinnooks, Killamucks &c. are very loquacious and inquisitive; they possess good memories and have repeated to us the names capasities of the vessels &c of many traders and others who have visited the mouth of this river; they are generally low in stature, proportionably small, reather lighter complected and much more illy formed than the Indians of the Missouri and those of our frontier;   they are generally cheerfull but never gay.   with us their conversation generally turns upon the subjects of trade, smoking, eating or their women; about the latter they speak without reserve in their presents, of their every part, and of the most formiliar connection.   they do not hold the virtue of their women in high estimation, and will even prostitute their wives and daughters for a fishinghook or a stran of beads.   in common with other savage nations they make their women perform every species of domestic drudgery.   but in almost every species of this drudgery the men also participate,   their women are also compelled to geather roots, and assist them in taking fish, which articles form much the greatest part of their subsistance; notwithstanding the survile manner in which they treat their women they pay much more rispect to their judgment and oppinions in many rispects than most indian nations; their women are permitted to speak freely before them, and some- times appear to command with a tone of authority; they generally consult them in their traffic and act in conformity to their opinions.

I think it may be established as a general maxim that those nations treat their old people and women with most differrence [deference] and rispect where they subsist principally on such articles that these can participate with the men in obtaining them; and that, that part of the community are treated with least attention, when the act of procuring subsistence devolves entirely on the men in the vigor of life.   It appears to me that nature has been much more deficient in her filial tie than in any other of the strong affections of the human heart, and therefore think, our old men equally with our women indebted to civilization for their ease and comfort.   Among the Siouxs, Assinniboins and others on the Missouri who subsist by hunting it is a custom when a person of either sex becomes so old and infurm that they are unable to travel on foot from camp to camp as they rome in surch of subsistance, for the children or near relations of such person to leave them without compunction or remo[r]se; on those occasions they usually place within their reach a small peace of meat and a platter of water, telling the poor old superannuated wretch for his consolation, that he or she had lived long enough, that it was time they should dye and go to their relations who can afford to take care of them much better than they could. I am informed that this custom prevails even among the Minetares Arwaharmays and Recares when attended by their old people on their hunting excurtions; but in justice to these people I must observe that it appeared to me at their vilages, that they provided tolerably well for their aged persons, and several of their feasts appear to have principally for their object a contribution for their aged and infirm persons.

This day I overhalled our merchandize and dryed it by the fire, found it all damp; we have not been able to keep anything dry for many days together since we arrived in this neighbourhood, the humidity of the air has been so excessively great. our merchandize is reduced to a mear handfull, and our comfort during our return the next year much depends on it, it is therefore almost unnecessary to add that we much regret the reduced state of this fund.

Monday (*Tuesday*) January 7th. 1806.

Last evening Drewyer visited his traps and caught a beaver and an otter; the beaver was large and fat we have therefore fared sumptuously today; this we consider a great prize for another reason, it being a full grown beaver was well supplyed with the materials for making bate with which to catch others. this bate when properly prepared will intice the beaver to visit it as far as he can smell it, and this I think may be safely stated at a mile, their sense of smelling being very accute.

To prepare beaver bate, the castor or bark stone is taken as the base, this is gently pressed out of the bladderlike bag which contains it, into a phiol of 4 ounces with a wide mouth; if you have them you will put from four to six stone in a phiol of that capacity, to this you will add half a nutmeg, a douzen or 15 grains of cloves and thirty grains of cinimon finely pulverized, stir them well together and then add as much ardent sperits to the composition as will reduce it the consistency [of] mustard prepared for the table; when thus prepared it resembles mustard precisely to all appearance. when you cannot procure a phiol a bottle made of horn or a tight earthen vessel will answer, in all cases it must be excluded from the air or it will soon loose it's virtue; it is fit for uce immediately it is prepared but becomes much stronger and better in about four or five days and will keep for months provided it be perfectly secluded from the air. when cloves are not to be had use double the quantity of Allspice, and when no spice can be obtained use the bark of the root of sausafras; when sperits can not be had use oil stone of the beaver adding mearly a sufficient quantity to moisten the other materials, or reduce it to a stif past[e.] it appears to me that the principal uce of the spices is only to give a variety to the scent of the bark stone and if so the mace vineller [vanilla] and other sweet-smelling spices might be employed with equal advantage.

The male beaver has six stones, two [of] which contain a substance much like finely pulvarized bark of a pale yellow colour and not unlike tanner's ooz in smell, these are called the *bark stones* or castors; two others, which like the bark stone resemble small bladders, contain a pure oil of a strong rank disagreeable smell, and not unlike train oil, these are called the *oil stones;* and 2 others of generation. the Bark-stones are about two inc[h]es in length, the others somewhat smaller all are of a long oval form, and lye in a bunch together between the skin and the root of the tail, beneath or behind the fundament with which they are closely connected and seem to communicate. the pride of the female lyes on the inner side much like those of the hog. they have no further parts of generation that I can perceive and therefore beleive that like the birds they copulate with the extremity of the gut. The female have from two to four young ones at a birth and bring fourth once a year only, which usually happens about the latter end of may and begining of June. at this stage she is said to drive the male from the lodge, who would otherwise destroy the young.

dryed our lodge and had it put away under shelter; this is the first day during which we have had no rain since we arrived at this place. nothing extraordinary happened today.

[Clark]   Wednesday 8th. January 1806
    proceeded to the place the whale had perished, found only the Skelleton of this Monster on the Sand between the Villages of the

Kil a mox nation; the Whale was already pillaged of every Valuable part by the Kilamox Inds. in the Vecinity of whose village's it lay on the Strand where the waves and tide had driven up & left it.

I returned to the Village of 5 Cabins on the creek which I shall call *E co-la* or Whale Creek,[8] found the nativs busily engaged boiling the blubber, which they performed in a large Squar wooden trought by means of hot stones; the oil when extracted was secured in bladders and the Guts of the whale; the blubber from which the oil was only partially extracted by this process, was laid by in their cabins in large flickes [flitches] for use; those flickes they usially expose to the fire on a wooden Spit untill it is prutty well wormed through and then eate it either alone or with roots of the rush, *Shaw na ták-we* or Diped in the oil. The *Kil a mox* although they possessed large quantities of this blubber and oil were so prenurious that they disposed of it with great reluctiance and in small quantities only; insomuch that my utmost exertion aided by the party with the Small Stock of merchindize I had taken with me were not able to precure more blubber than about 300lb. and a fiew gallons of oil; Small as this stock is I prise it highly; and thank providence for directing the whale to us; and think him much more kind to us than he was to jonah, having Sent this Monster to be *swallowed by us* in Stcd of *Swallowing of us* as jonah's did.

[Lewis]   Friday (*Thursday*) January 9th. 1806.

The persons who usually visit the entrance of this river[9] for the purpose of traffic or hunting I believe are either English or Americans; the Indians inform us that they speak the same language with ourselves, and give us proofs of their varacity by repeating many words of English, as musquit, powder, shot, [k]nife, file, damned rascal, sun of a bitch &c. whether these traders are from Nootka sound, from some other late establishement on this coast, or immediately from the U'States or Great Brittain, I am at a loss to determine, nor can the Indians inform us.

This traffic on the part of the whites consists in vending, guns, (principally old british or American musquits) powder, balls and shot,

[8] Between Tillamook Head and Cannon Beach, Oregon.
[9] Columbia River.

Copper and brass kettles, brass teakettles and coffee pots, blankets from two to three point, scarlet and blue Cloth (coarse), plates and strips of sheet copper and brass, large brass wire, knives, beads and tobacco with fishinghooks buttons and some other small articles; also a considerable quantity of Sailor's cloaths, as hats coats, trowsers and shirts. for these they receive in return from the natives, dressed and undressed Elk-skins, skins of the sea Otter, common Otter, beaver, common fox, spuck, and tiger cat; also dryed and pounded sammon in baskets, and a kind of buisquit, which the natives make of roots called by them shappelell. The natives are extravegantly fond of the most common cheap blue and white beads, of moderate size, or such that from 50. to 70. will weigh one penneyweight. the blue is usually p[r]efered to the white; these beads constitute the principal circulating medium with all the indian tribes on this river; for these beads they will dispose [of] any article they possess. the beads are strung on strans of a fathom in length and in that manner sold by the bredth or yard.

[Clark]   Thursday 9th. of January 1806
   last night about 10 oClock while Smokeing with the nativ's I was alarmed by a loud Srill voice from the cabins on the opposite side, the Indians all run immediately across to the village, my guide who continued with me made Signs that Some one's throat was Cut, by enquiry I found that one man Mc.Neal was absent, I imediately Sent off Sergt. N. Pryor & 4 men in quest of McNeal who' they met comeing across the Creak in great hast, and informed me that the people were alarmed on the opposit side at Something but what he could not tell, a Man had verry friendly envited him to go and eate in his lodge, that the Indian had locked armes with him and went to a lodge in which a woman gave him Some blubber, that the man envited him to another lodge to get Something better, and the woman [*Knowing his design*] held him [McNeal] by the blanket which he had around him [*This woman a Chinnook an old friend of McNeals*] and another ran out and hollow'd and his pretended friend disapeared. I emediately ordered every man to hold themselves in a State of rediness and Sent Sergt. Pryor & 4 men to know the cause of the alarm which was found to be a premeditated plan of the pretended friend of McNeal to ass[ass]anate [him] for his Blanket and what fiew articles he had about him, which was found out by

a Chinnook woman who allarmed the men of the village who were
with me in time to prevent the horred act. this man was of another
band at Some distance and ran off as soon as he was discovered.

we have now to look back and Shudder at the dreadfull road on
which we have to return of 45 miles S E of Point adams & 35 miles
from Fort *Clatsop*. I had the blubber & oil divided among' the party
and set out about Sunrise and returned by the Same rout we had
went out, met Several parties of men & women of the Chinnook
and Clatsops nations, on their way to trade with the *Kil a mox* for
blubber and oil; on the Steep decent of the Mountain I overtook
five men and Six women with emence loads of the Oil and blubber
of the Whale, those Indians had passed by Some rout by which
we missed them as we went out yesterday; one of the women in
the act of getting down a Steep part of the Mountain her load by
Some means had Sliped off her back, and She was holding the load
by a Strap which was fastened to the mat bag in which it was in, in
one hand and holding a bush by the other, as I was in front of my
party, I endeavoured to relieve this woman by takeing her load untill
She could get to a better place a little below, & to my estonishment
found the load as much as I could lift and must exceed 100 lbs the
husband of this woman who was below Soon came to her releif

[Lewis]   Monday (*Sunday*) January 12th. 1806.
   At 2.P.M. the ballance of the party who had been left by Capt.
C. arrived; about the same time the two hunters [*also arrived*] who
had been dispatched by Capt C. for the purpose of hunting, they
had killed nothing. We have heretofore usually divided the meat
when first killed among the four messes into which we have divided
our party leaving to each the care of preserving and the discretion
of using it, but we find that they make such prodigal use of it when
they hapen to have a tolerable stock on hand that we have determined to adapt a different system with our present stock of seven
Elk; this is to jirk it & issue to them in small quantities

[Clark]   Sunday the 12th. January 1806
   This morning Sent out Drewyer and one man to hunt, they returned in the evening Drewyer haveing killed 7 Elk; I scercely know
how we Should Subsist, I beleive but badly if it was not for the
exertions of this excellent hunter; maney others also exert them-

selves, but not being acquainted with the best method of finding and killing the elk and no other wild animals is to be found in this quarter, they are unsucksessfull in their exertions.

[Lewis]   Tuesday (*Monday*) January 13th. 1806.

 this evening we exhausted the last of our candles, but fortunately had taken the precaution to bring with us moulds and wick, by means of which and some Elk's tallow in our possession we do not yet consider oursleves destitute of this necessary article; the Elk we have killed have a very small portion of tallow.

                                                    Friday (*Thursday*) January 16th. 1806.

 we have plenty of Elk beef for the present and a little salt, our houses dry and comfortable, and having made up our minds to remain until the 1st. of April, every one appears content with his situation and his fare. it is true that we could even travel now on our return as far as the timbered country reaches, or to the falls of the river; but further it would be madness for us to attempt to proceede untill April, as the indians inform us that the snows lye knee deep in the plains of Columbia during the winter, and in these plains we could scarcely get as much fuel of any kind as would cook our provision as we descended the river; and even were we happyly over these plains and again in the woody country at the foot of the Rocky Mountains we could not possibly pass that immence barrier of mountains on which the snows ly in winter to the debth in many places of 20 feet; in short the Indians inform us that they are impracticable untill about the 1st. of June, at which time even there is an abundance of snow but a scanty subsistence may be obtained for the horses. we should not therefore forward ourselves on our homeward journey by reaching the rocky mountains. early than the 1st. of June, which we can easily effect by seting out from hence on the 1st. of April.

[Clark]   Wednesday February 12th. 1806.

 This morning we were visited by a Clatsop man who brought with him three dogs as a remuneration for the Elk which himself and Nation had stolen from us some little time sence, however the dogs took the alarm and ran off; we suffered him to remain in the fort all night.

There are two species of evergreen shrubs.[10] This is the leaf of one. which I first met with at the grand rapids of the Columbia River, and which I have sence found in this neighbourhood also; they usually grow in rich dry ground not far from some watercourse. the roots of both species are creeping and celindric. the stem of the first (as above) is from a foot to 18 inches high and as large as a goose quil; it is simple and erect. its leaves are cauline, and spredding. the leaf[l]its are jointed & oppositly poinnate 3 par and termonateing in one, cessile widest at the base and tapering to an accuminated point, an inch and ¼ the greatest width, & 3¼ inches in length. each point of their crenate margins armed with a thorn or spine, and are from 13 to 17 in number. they are also veined, glossy, crinated and wrinkled; their points obliquely pointing towards the extremity of the common footstalk.

The stem of the 2nd. is procumbent about the size of the former, jointed and umbracated. its leaves are cauline, compound and oppositly pointed; the rib from 14 to 16 inches long celendric and smooth the leaf[l]its 2½ inches long and 1 inch wide. the greatest width ½ inch from their base which they are regularly rounded, and from the same point tapering to an accute apex, which is mostly but not entirely termonated with a small subulate thorn. they are jointed and oppositly pointed, consisting of 6 par and termonateing in one (in this form.) sessile, serrate, or like the teeth of a whip-saw, each point terminating in a small subulate spine, being from

[10] Tall Oregon Grape (*Berberis aquifolium*) and Cascade Oregon Grape (*Berberis nervosa*); Clark's sketches accompany copies of Lewis's descriptions.

25 to 27 in numbr; veined, smoth, plane and of a deep green, their points tending obliquely towards the extremity of the rib or common footstalk. I do not know the frute or flower of either. the 1st resembles a plant common to maney parts of the United States called the Mountain Holly.

Friday February 14th. 1806

I compleated a *map* of the Countrey through which we have been passing from the Mississippi at the Mouth of Missouri to this place. In the Map the Missouri Jefferson's river the S.E. branch of the Columbia or Lewis's river, Koos-koos-ke and Columbia from the enterance of the S.E. fork to the pacific Ocian, as well as a part of Clark's river and our track across the Rocky Mountains are laid down by celestial observations and survey. the rivers are also conected at their sources with other rivers agreeably to the information of the nativs and the most probable conjecture arrising from their capacities and the relative positions of their respective enterances which last have with but fiew exceptions been established by celestial observations. We now discover that we have found the most practicable and navigable passage across the Continent of North America; it is that which we have traveled with the exception of that part of our rout from the foot of the Falls of the Missouri, or in neighbourhood of the enterance of the Rocky Mountains untill we arive on Clarks river at the enterence of *Travelers-rest* Creek; the distance between those two points would be traveled more advantagiously by land as the navigation of the Missouri above the *Falls* is crooked laborious and 521 miles distant by which no advantage is gained as the rout which we are compelled to travel by land from the source of Jeffersons River to the enterance of *Travellers rest* Creek is 220 miles being further by abt 600 miles than that from the Falls of the Missourie to the last mentioned point (Travellers rest Creek) and a much worse rout if indian information is to be relied on which is from the *Sosonee* or Snake Indians, and the Flatheads of the Columbia West of the rocky mountains.

considering therefore the dangers and deficuelties attending the navigation of the Columbia in this part, as well as the circuitous and distant rout formed by itself and that of Clark's River we conceive that even admitting that Clarks river contrary to information to be as navagable as the Columbia below its enterance, that the tract by land over the Rocky Mountains usually traveled by the nativs from the enterance of Travellers-rest Creek to the Forks of the Kooskooske is preferable; the same being a distance of 184 miles. The inferrence therefore deduced from these premises are, that the best and most practicable rout across the Continent is by way of the Missouri to the *Falls;* thence to *Clarks* river at the enterance of Travellers rest Creek, from thence up travillers rest Creek to the forks, from whence you prosue a range of mountains which divides the waters of the two forks of this Creek, and which still Continues it's westwardly course on the Mountains which divides the waters of the two forks of the Kooskooske river to their junction; from thence to decend this river to the S. E. branch of the Columbia, thence down that river to the Columbia, and down the Latter to the *Pacific Ocian.*

[Lewis]   Sunday February 23rd. 1806.
   not anything transpired during this day worthy of particular notice.   our sick are all on the recovery, except Sergt. Ordway who is but little wo[r]se and not very ill tho' more so than any of the others. the men have provided themselves very amply with mockersons and leather cloathing, much more so indeed than they ever have since they have been on this voige.
   The Sea Otter is found on the sea coast and in the salt water. this anamal when fully grown is as large as a common mastive dog. the ears and eyes are remarkab[l]y small, particularly the former which is not an inch in length thick fleshey and pointed covered with short hair.   the tail is about 10 inches in length thick where it joins the body and tapering to a very sharp point; in common with the body it is covered with a deep fur particularly on the upper side, on the under part the fur is not so long.   the legs are remarkably short and the feet which have five toes each are broad large and webbed. the legs are covered with fur and the feet with short hair. the body of this animal is long and nearly of the same thickness throughout.   from the extremity of the tail to that of the nose they will measure 5 feet or upwards.   the colour is a uniform dark brown and when in good order and season perfectly black and glossey.   it is the riches[t] and I think the most delicious fur in the world at least I cannot form an idea of any more so.   it is deep thick silkey in the extreem and strong.   the inner part of the fur when opened

is lighter than the surface in it's natural position.   there are some
fine black and shining hairs intermixed with the fur which are reather
longer and add much to it's beauty.   the nose, about the eyes ears
and forehead in some of these otter is of a lighter colour, sometimes
a light brown.   those parts in the young sucking Otter of this species
is sometimes of a cream coloured white, but always much lighter
than the other parts.   the fur of the infant Otter is much inferior in
point of colour and texture to that of the full grown otter, or even
after it has been weaned. there is so great a difference that I have
for some time supposed it a different animal; the Indians called the
infant Otter *Spuck,* and the full grow[n] or such as had obtained a
coat of good fur, *E-luck'-ke.* this still further confirmed the opinion
of their being distinct species; but I have since learned that the
Spuck is the young Otter.   the colour of the neck, body, legs and
tail is a dark lead brown.   The mink is found in the woody country
on this coast, and dose not differ in any particu[lar] from those of
the Atlantic coast.   the seal are found here in great numbers, and
as far up the Columbia river as the great falls, above which there
are none.

I have reason to beleive from the information of the men that
there are several species of the seal on this coast and in the river
but what the difference is I am unable to state not having seen them
myself sufficiently near for minute inspection nor obtained the different kinds to make a comparison.   the skins of such as I have
seen are covered with a short coarse stiff and glossey hair of a redish
bey brown colour.   tho' the anamal while in the water or as we saw
them frequently in the river appear to be black and spoted with
white sometimes.   when we first saw those animals at the great falls
and untill our arrival at this place we conseived they were the Sea
Otter. but the indians here have undeceived us.[11] I am not much
acquainted with the Seal but suppose they are the same common
also to the Atlantic Ocean in the same parallel of latitude.   the
skins I have seen are precisely such as our trunks are frequently
covered with.

[11] "The sea otter (*Enhydra lutris*) never leaves salt water. The seal which had
'every appearance of the sea otter' was the harbor or hair seal (*Phoca vitulina*)"
(Cutright).

Monday February 24th. 1806.

Our sick are still on the recovery. Shannon & Labuishe returned in the forenoon; they had killed no Elk and reported that they beleived the Elk have retired from their former haunts and gone further back in the country to a considerable distance from this place. this is very unwelcome information for poor and inferior as the flesh of this animal is it is our principal dependance for subsistence.

This evening we were visited by Comowooll the Clatsop Chief and 12 men women and children of his nation. Drewyer came a passenger in their canoe, and brought with him two dogs. The chief and his party had brought for sail a Sea Otter skin some hats, stergeon and a species of small fish[12] which now begin to run, and are taken in great quantities in the Columbia R. about 40 miles above us by means of skiming or scooping nets.

the rays of the fins are boney but not sharp tho' somewhat pointed. the small fin on the back next to the tail has no rays of bone being a thin membranous pellicle. the fins next to the gills have eleven rays each. those of the abdomen have eight each, those of the pinna-ani are 20 and 2 half formed in front. that of the back has eleven rays. all the fins are of a white colour. the back is of a bluish duskey colour and that of the lower part of the sides and belley is of a silvery white. no spots on any part. the first bone of the gills next behi[n]d the eye is of a bluis[h] cast, and the second of a light goald colour nearly white. the puple of the eye is black and the iris of a silver white. the under jaw exceeds the uper; and the mouth opens to great extent, folding like that of the herring. it has no teeth. the abdomen is obtuse and smooth; in this differing from the herring, shad, anchovey &c. of the Malacopterygious Order & Class Clupea, to which however I think it more nearly allyed than to any other altho' it has not their accute and serrate abdomen and the under jaw exceeding the upper. the scales of this little fish are so small and thin that without minute inspection you would suppose they had none. they are filled with roes of a pure white colour and have scarcely any perceptable alimentary duct. I find them best

[12] Eulachon or candlefish (*Thaleichthys pacificus*).

when cooked in Indian stile, which is by roasting a number of them together on a wooden spit without any previous preperation whatever. they are so fat they require no additional sauce, and I think them superior to any fish I ever tasted, even more delicate and lussious than the white fish of the lakes which have heretofore formed my standart of excellence among the fishes. I have heard the fresh anchovey much extolled but I hope I shall be pardoned for beleiving this quite as good. the bones are so soft and fine that they form no obstruction in eating this fish.

we purchased all the articles which these people brought us; we suffered these people to remain all night as it rained, the wind blew most violently and they had their women and children with them; the latter being a sure pledge of their pacific dispositions. the Sturgeon which they brought us was also good of it's kind. we determine to send a party up the river to procure some of those fish, and another in some direction to hunt Elk as soon as the weather will permit.

Sunday March 2nd.

The diet of the sick is so inferior that they recover their strength but slowly. none of them are now sick but all in a state of convalessence with keen appetites and nothing to eat except lean Elk meat. late this evening Drewyer arrived with a most acceptable supply of fat Sturgeon, fresh Anchovies and a bag containing about a bushel of Wappetoe. we feasted on Anchovies and Wappetoe.

The *Cock of the Plains*[13] is found in the plains of Columbia and are in Great abundance from the entrance of the S.E. fork of the Columbia to that of Clark's river. this bird is about ⅔rds. the size of a turkey. the beak is large short curved and convex. the upper exceeding the lower chap. the nostils are large and the b[e]ak black. the colour is an uniform mixture of dark brown reather borde[r]ing on a dove colour, redish and yellowish brown with some small black specks. in this mixture the dark brown prevails and has a slight cast of the dove colour at a little distance. the wider side of the large feathers of the wings are of a dark brown only. the tail is composed of 19 feathers of which that in the center is the

---

[13] Sage grouse (*Centrocercus urophasianus*).

longest, and the remaining 9 on each side deminish by pairs as they recede from the center; that is only one feather is equal in length to one equadistant from the center of the tail on the opposite side. the tail when foalded comes to a very sharp point and appears long in proportion to the body. in the act of flying the tail resembles that of a wild pigeon, tho' the motion of the wings is much that of the pheasant and Grouse. they have four toes on each foot of which the hinder one is short. the leg is covered with feathers about half the distance between the knee and foot. when the wing is expanded there are wide opening[s] between it's feathers the plumeage being so narrow that it dose not extend from one quill to the other. the wings are also proportionably short, reather more so than those of the pheasant or grouse. the habits of this bird are much the same as those of the grouse. only that the food of this fowl is almost entirely that of the leaf and buds of the pulpy leafed thorn; nor do I ever recollect seeing this bird but in the neighbourhood of that shrub. they sometimes feed on the prickley pear. the gizzard of it is large and much less compressed and muscular than in most fowls; in short it resembles a maw quite as much as a gizzard. when they fly they make a cackling noise something like the dunghill fowl. the flesh of the cock of the Plains is dark, and only tolerable in point of flavor. I do not think it as good as either the Pheasant or Grouse. it is invariably found in the plains. The feathers about it's head are pointed and stif. some hairs about the base of the beak. feathers short fine and stif about the ears.

Thursday March 13th. 1806.

This morning Drewyer Jos. Fields and Frazier returned; they had killed two Elk and two deer. visited by two Cathlahmahs who left us in the evening. we sent Drewyer down to the Clatsop village to purchase a couple of their canoes if possible. we sent Sergt. Ordway and a party for the flesh of one of the Elk beyond the bay with which they returned in the evening. the other Elk and two deer were at some distance. R. Fields and Thompson who set out yesterday morning on a hunting excurtion towards point Adams have not yet returned. The horns of some of the Elk have not yet fallen off, and those of others have shotten out to the length of six inches. the latter are in the best order; from which it would seem that the poor Elk retain their horns longest.

Observed Equal Altitudes of the ☉ with Sextant.

A.M.	8. 6. 16.	P.M.	2. 45. 10		Altitude given by Sext.
".	8. 6.	".	47. 3	}	at the time of Obsert.
".	10. –.	".	48. 54		48.° 26.' 45."

Chronometer too slow on Mean Time [blank space in MS.]

The Porpus is common on this coast and as far up the river as the water is brackish. the Indians sometimes gig them and always eat the flesh of this fish when they can procure it; to me the flavor is disagreeable. the Skaite is also common to the salt water, we have seen several of them that had perished and were thrown out on the beach by the tide. The flounder is also an inhabitant of the salt water, we have seen them also on the beach where they had been left by the tide. the Indians eat the latter and esteem it very fine. these several speceis are the same with those of the Atlantic coast.

the common Salmon and red Charr are the inhabitants of both the sea and rivers. the former is usually largest and weighs from 5 to 15 lbs. it is this speceis that extends itself into all the rivers and little creeks on this side of the Continent, and to which the natives are so much indebted for their subsistence. the body of this fish is from 2½ to 3 feet long and proportionably broad. it is covered with imbricated scales of a moderate size and is variagated with irregular black spots on it's sides and gills. the eye is large and the iris of a silvery colour the pupil black. the nostrum [rostrum] or nose extends beyond the under jaw, and both the upper and lower jaws are armed with a single series of long teeth which are subulate and infle[c]ted near the extremities of the jaws where they are also more closely arranged. they have some sharp teeth of smaller size and same shape placed on the tongue which is thick and fleshey. the fins of the back are two; the first is plaised nearer the head than the ventral fins and has rays, the second is placed far back near the tail is small and has no rays. the flesh of this fish is when in order of a deep flesh coloured red and every shade from that to an orrange yellow, and when very meager almost white. the roes of this fish are much esteemed by the natives who dry them in the sun and preserve them for a great length of time. they are about the size of a small pea nearly transparent and of a redish yellow colour. they resemble very much at a little distance the common currants of our gardens but are more yellow. this fish is sometimes red along the sides and belley near the gills; particularly the male. The red Charr are reather broader in proportion to their length than the common salmon, the skales are also imbricated but reather large.[14] the nostrum [rostrum] exceeds the lower jaw more and the teeth are neither as large nor so numerous as those of the salmon. some of them are almost entirely red on the belley and sides; others are much more white than the salmon and none of them are variagated with the dark spots which make the body of the other. their flesh roes and every other particular with rispect to their form is that of the Salmon. this fish we did not see untill we decended below the gr[e]at falls of the Columbia, but whether they are exclusively confined to this portion of the river or not at all seasons I am unable to determine.

[Clark]   Saturday March 15th 1806
This morning at 11 oClock the hunters arrived, haveing killed four Elk only. Labiesh it seams was the only Hunter who fell in with the Elk and haveing by some accident lost the foresight of his gun shot a great number of times and only killed four. as the Elk were scattered we sent two parties for them, they return in the evening with four skins, and the flesh of three Elk, that of one of them haveing become putred from the liver and pluck haveing been carelessly left in the animal all night.

We were visited this Afternoon in a canoe 4 feet 2 I. wide by *Delash-hel-wilt* a Chinnook Chief his wife and six women of his Nation, which the Old Boud his wife had brought for Market. this was the same party which had communicated the venereal to several of our party in November last, and of which they have finally recovered. I therefore gave the men a particular charge with respect to them which they promised me to observe. late this evening we were also visited by *Ca-tel* a Clatsop man and his family. he brought a Canoe and a sea otter skin for sale neither of which we could purchase of him. the Clatsops which had brought a Canoe for sale last evening

[14] "Common salmon" is Chinook or king salmon (*Oncorhynchus tshawytscha*); "red charr" is sockeye or blueback salmon (*Oncorhynchus nerka*).

left us this morning. Bratten is still very weak and unwell.

There is a third species of Brant in the neighbourhood of this place which is about the size and much the form of the b[p]ided brant. they weigh about 8½ lbs. the wings are not as long nor so pointed as the common pided brant. the following is a likeness of its head and beak.[15] a little distance around the base of the beak is white and is suddenly succeeded by a narrow line of dark brown. the ballance of the neck, head, back, wings and tail all except the tips of the feathers are of the blueish brown of the common wild goose, the breast and belly are white with an irregular mixture of black feathers which give that part a pided appearance. from the legs back underneath the tail, and around the junction of the same with the body above, the feathers are white. the tail is composed of 18 feathers; the longest of which are in the center and measure 6 inches with the barrel of the quill; those on the side of the tail are something shorter and bend with their extremities inwards towards the center of the tail. the extremities of these feathers are white. the beak is of a light flesh colour. the legs and feet which do not differ in structure from those of the Goose or brant of the other species, are of an orrange yellow colour. the eye is small; the iris of a dark yellowish brown, and puple black. the note of this brant is much that of the common pided brant from which in fact they are not to be distinguished at a distance, but they certainly are a distinct species of brant. the flesh of this fowl is as good as that of the common pided brant. they do not remain here dureing the winter in such numbers as the white brant do, tho' they have now returned in considerable quantities. we first met with this brant on tide water.

[Lewis]   Sunday March 16th 1806.

The *white Salmon Trout*[16] which we had previously seen only at the great falls of the Columbia has now made it's appearance in the creeks near this place. one of them was brought us today by an Indian who had just taken it with his gig. this is a likeness of it; it was 2 feet 8 Inches long, and weighed 10 lbs. the eye is mod-

---

[15] White-fronted goose (*Anser albifrons*).
[16] Coho or silver salmon (*Oncorhynchus kisutch*).

There is a third species of Brant in the neighbourhood of this place which is about the size and much the form of the pided brant. they weigh about 8 1/2 lb. the wings are not as long nor so pointed as the common pided brant. the following is a likeness of its head and beak. a little distance arround the base of the beak is white and is suddenly succeeded by a narow line of dark brown. the balance of the neck, head, back, wings and tail are except the tips of the feathers are of the bluish brown of the common wild goose. the breast and belly are white with an irregular mixture of black feathers which give that part a pided appearance. from the legs back underneath the tail, and around the junction of the same with the body above, the feathers are white. the tail is composed of 18 feathers; the longest of which are in the center and measure 6 inches with the barrel of the quill; those on the sides of the tail are something shorter and bend with their extremities inwards towards the center of the tail. the extremities of these feathers are white. the beak is of a light flesh colour. the legs and feet which do not differ in structure from those of the goose or brant of the other species, are of an orange yellow colour. the eye is small; the iris is of a dark yellowish brown, and pupil black. the note of this brant is much that of the common pided brant from which in fact they are not to be distinguished at a distance, but they certainly are a distinct species of brant. the flesh of this fowl is as good as that of the common pided brant. they do not remain

Head of a white-fronted goose by Clark.

erately large, the puple black and iris of a silvery white with a small
addmixture of yellow, and is a little terbid near it's border with a
yellowish brown. the position of the fins may be seen from the
drawing, they are small in proportion to the fish, the fins are boney
but not pointed except the tail and back fins which are a little so,
the prime back fin and ventral ones, contain each ten rays; those of
the gills thirteen, that of the tail twelve, and the small fins placed
near the tail above has no bony rays, but is a tough flexable substance
covered with smooth skin. it is thicker in proportion to it's width
than the salmon. the tongue is thick and firm beset on each border
with small subulate teeth in a single series. the teeth of the mouth
are as before discribed. neither this fish nor the salmon are caught
with the hook, nor do I know on what they feed.

Monday March 17th. 1806.

we have had our perogues prepared for our departure, and shal
set out as soon as the weather will permit. the weather is so precarious that we fear by waiting untill the first of April that we might
be detained several days longer before we could get from this to the
Cathlahmahs as it must be calm or we cannot accomplish that part
of our rout. Drewyer returned late this evening from the Cathlahmahs with our canoe which Sergt. Pryor had left some days since,
and also a canoe which he had purchased from those people. for
this canoe he gave my uniform laced coat and nearly half a carrot
of tobacco. it seems that nothing excep[t] this coat would induce
them to dispose of a canoe which in their mode of traffic is an article
of the greatest val[u]e except a wife, with whom it is equal, and is
generally given in exchange to the father for his daughter. I think
the U'States are indebted to me another Uniform coat for that of
which I have disposed on this occasion was but little woarn.

Tuesday March 18th. 1806.

Drewyer was taken last night with a violent pain in his side.
Capt. Clark blead him. several of the men are complaining of being
unwell. it is truly unfortunate that they should be sick at the moment of our departure. we directed Sergt. Pryor to prepare the two
Canoes which Drewyer brought last evening for his mess. they
wanted some knees to strengthen them and several cracks corked
and payed. he completed them except the latter operation which

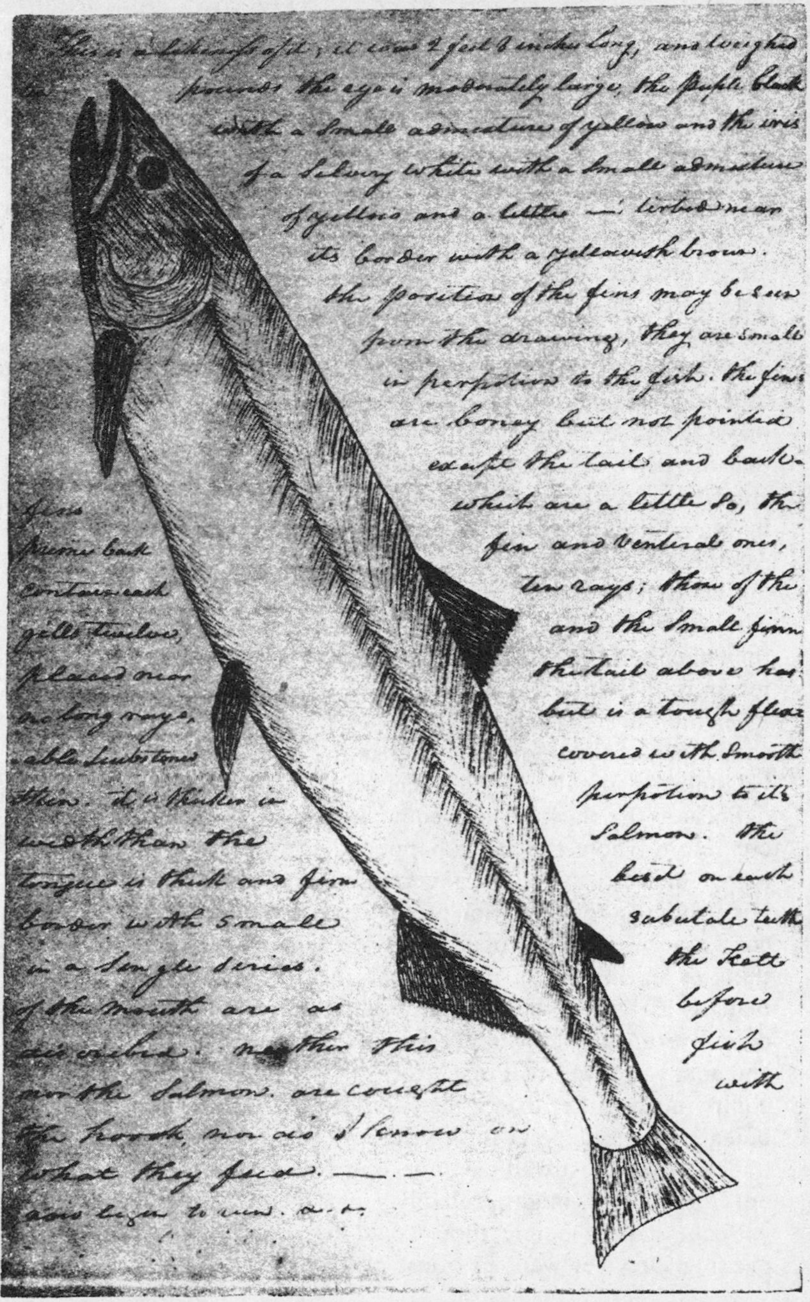

Clark's drawing of a silver salmon.

the frequent showers in the course of the day prevented as the canoes could not be made sufficiently dry even with the assistance of fire.

Comowooll and two Cathlahmahs visited us to-day; we suffered them to remain all night.   this morning we gave Delashelwilt a certificate of his good deportment &c. and also a list of our names, after which we dispatched him to his village with his female band. These lists of our names we have given to several of the natives and also paisted up a copy in our room.   the object of these lists we stated in the preamble of the same as follows (viz)   "The object of this list is, that through the medium of some civilized person who may see the same, it may be made known to the informed world, that the party consisting of the persons whose names are hereunto annexed, and who were sent out by the government of the U'States in May 1804. to explore the interior of the Continent of North America, did penetrate the same by way of the Missouri and Columbia Rivers, to the discharge of the latter into the Pacific Ocean, where they arrived on the 14th. of November 1805, and from whence they departed the [blank space in MS.] day of March 1806 on their return to the United States by the same rout they had come out."

on the back of some of these lists we added a sketch of the connection of the upper branches of the Missouri with those of the Columbia, particularly of it's main S.E. branch, on which we also delineated the track we had come and that we meant to pursue on our return where the same happened to vary.   There seemed so many chances against our government ever obtaining a regular report, through the medium of the savages and the traders of this coast that we declined making any.   our party are also too small to think of leaving any of them to return to the U'States by sea, particularly as we shall be necessarily divided into three or four parties on our return in order to accomplish the objects we have in view; and at any rate we shall reach the United States in all human probability much earlier than a man could who must in the event of his being left here depend for his passage to the United States on the traders of the coast who may not return immediately to the U'States or if they should, might probably spend the next summer in trading with the natives before they would set out on their return.   this evening Drewyer went in quest of his traps, and took an Otter.

Joseph Fields killed an Elk. The Indians repeated to us the names of eighteen distinct tribes residing on the S.E. coast who spoke the Killamucks language, and beyond those six others who spoke a different language which they did not comprehend.

Wednesday March 19th. 1806.

It continued to rain and hail today in such manner that nothing further could be done to the canoes. a party were sent out early after the Elk which was killed yesterday with which they returned in the course of a few hours. we gave Comowooll alias Connia, a cirtificate of his good conduct and the friendly intercourse which he has maintained with us during our residence at this place; we also gave him a list of our names.

The Killamucks, Clatsops, Chinnooks, Cathlahmahs and Wâc-ki-a-cums resemble each other as well in their persons and dress as in their habits and manners. their complexion is not remarkable, being the usual copper brown of most of the tribes of North America. they are low in statu[r]e reather diminutive, and illy shapen; poss[ess]ing thick broad flat feet, thick ankles, crooked legs wide mouths thick lips, nose moderately large, fleshey, wide at the extremity with large nostrils, black eyes and black coarse hair. their eyes are sometimes of a dark yellowish brown the puple black. I have observed some high acqualine noses among them but they are extreemly rare. the nose is generally low between the eyes.

the most remarkable trait in their physiognomy is the peculiar flatness and width of forehead which they artificially obtain by compressing the head between two boards while in a state of infancy and from which it never afterwards perfectly recovers. this is a custom among all the nations we have met with West of the Rocky mountains. I have observed the heads of many infants, after this singular bandage had been dismissed, or about the age of 10 or eleven months, that were not more than two inches thick about the upper edge of the forehead and reather thinner still higher. from the top of the head to the extremity of the nose is one streight line. this is done in order to give a greater width to the forehead, which they much admire. this process seems to be continued longer with their female than their mail children, and neither appear to suffer any pain from the operation. it is from this peculiar form of the head that the nations East of the Rocky mountains, call all the nations on this side, except the Aliohtans or snake Indians, by the generic name of Flatheads. I think myself that the prevalence of this custom is a strong proof that [of] those nations having originally proceeded from the same stock.

The nations of this neighbourhood or those recapitulated above, wear their hair loosly flowing on the back and sholders; both men and women divide it on the center of the crown in front and throw it back behind the ear on each side. they are fond of combs and use them when they can obtain them; and even without the aid of the comb keep their hair in better order than many nations who are in other rispects much more civilized than themselves. the large or apparently swolen legs particularly observable in the women are obtained in a great measure by tying a cord tight around the ankle. their method of squating or resting themselves on their hams which they seem from habit to prefer to siting, no doubt contributes much to this deformity of the legs by preventing free circulation of the blood.

the dress of the man consists of a smal robe, which reaches about as low as the middle of the thye and is attatched with a string across the breast and is at pleasure turned from side to side as they may have occasion to disencumber the right or left arm from the robe entirely, or when they have occasion for both hands, the fixture of the robe is in front with it's corners loosly hanging over their arms. they sometimes wear a hat which has already been discribed. this robe is made most commonly of the skins of a small animal which I have supposed was the brown Mungo, tho' they have also a number, of the skins of the tiger cat, some of those of the Elk which are used principally on their war excursions, others of the skins of the deer panther and bear and a blanket wove with the fingers of the wool of the native sheep. a mat is sometimes temperarily thrown over the sholders to protect them from rain. they have no other article of cloathing whatever neither winter nor summer. and every part except the sholders and back is exposed to view. they are very fond of the dress of the whites, which they wear in a similar manner when they can obtain them, except the shoe which I have never seen woarn by any of them. they call us pâh-shish'-e-ooks, or *cloth men*.

The dress of the women consists of a robe, tissue, and sometimes when the weather is uncommonly cold, a vest. their robe is much smaller than that of the men, never reaching lower than the waist nor extending in front sufficiently for to cover the body. it is like that of the men confined across the breast with a string and hangs loosly over the sholders and back. the most esteemed and valuable of these robes are made of strips of the skins of the Sea Otter net together with the bark of the white cedar or silk-grass. these strips are first twisted and laid parallel with each other a little distance assunder, and then net or wove together in such manner that the fur appears equally on both sides, and unites between the strands. it make[s] a warm and soft covering. other robes are formed in a similar manner of the skin of the Rackoon, beaver &c. at other times the skin is dressed in the hair and woarn without any further preperation. in this way one beaver skin, or two of those of the Raccoon or tiger catt forms the pattern of the robe. the vest is always formed in the manner first discribed of their robes and covers the body from the armpits to the waist, and is confined behind, and destitute of straps over the sholder to keep it up. when this vest is woarn the breast of the woman is concealed, but without it which is almost always the case, they are exposed, and from the habit of remaining loose and unsuspended grow to great length, particularly in aged women in many of whom I have seen the bubby reach as low as the waist. The garment which occupys the waist, and from thence as low as nearly to the knee before and the ham, behind, cannot properly be denominated a petticoat, in the common acceptation of that term; it is a tissue of white cedar bark, bruised or broken into small shreds, which are interwoven in the middle by means of several cords of the same materials, which serve as well for a girdle as to hold in place the shreds of bark which form the tissue, and which shreds confined in the middle hang with their ends pendulous from the waist, the whole being of sufficient thickness when the female stands erect to conceal those parts usually covered from formiliar view, but when she stoops or places herself in many other attitudes, this battery of Venus is not altogether impervious to the inquisitive and penetrating eye of the amorite.

the women as well as the men sometimes cover themselves from the rain by a mat woarn over the sholders. they also cover their heads from the rain sometimes with a common water cup or basket made of the cedar bark and beargrass. these people seldom mark their skins by puncturing and introducing a colouring matter. such of them as do mark themselves in this manner prefer their legs and arms on which they imprint parallel lines of dots either longitudinally or circularly. the women more frequently than the men mark themselves in this manner.

The favorite ornament of both sexes are the common coarse blue and white beads which the men wear tightly wound aro[u]nd their wrists and ankles many times untill they obtain the width of three or more inches. they also wear them in large rolls loosly arond the neck, or pendulous from the cartelage of the nose or rims of the ears which are purforated for the purpose. the women wear them in a similar manner except in the nose which they never purforate. they are also fond of a species of wampum which is furnished them by a trader whom they call Swipton. it seems to be the native form of the shell without any preperation. this shell is of a conic form somewhat curved, about the size of a raven's quill at the base, and tapering to a point which is sufficiently large to permit to hollow through which a small thred passes; it is from one to 1½ Inches in length, white, smooth, hard and thin. these are woarn in the same manner in which the beads are; and furnish the men with their favorite ornament for the nose. one of these shells is passed horizontally through the cartilage of the nose and serves frequently as a kind of ring to prevent the string which suspends other ornaments at the same part from chafing and freting the flesh.

the men sometimes wear collars of bears claws, and the women and children the tusks of the Elk variously arranged on their necks arms &c. both males and females wear braslets on their wrists of copper brass or Iron in various forms. I think the most disgusting sight I have ever beheld is these dirty naked wenches. The men of these nations partake of much more of the domestic drudgery than I had at first supposed. they collect and prepare all the fuel, make the fires, assist in cleansing and preparing the fish, and always cook for the strangers who visit them. they also build their houses, construct their canoes, and make all their wooden utensils. the peculiar provence of the woman seems to be to collect roots and manufacture various articles which are prepared of rushes, flags, cedar bark, bear grass or waytape. the management of the canoe for various purposes seems to be a duty common to both sexes, as also many other occupations which with most Indian nations devolves exclusively on the woman. their feasts of which they are very fond are always prepared and served by the men.

Comowool and the two Cathlahmahs left us this evening. it continued to rain so constantly today that Sergt. Pryor could not pitch his canoes.

Thursday March 20th. 1806.

Altho' we have not fared sumptuously this winter and spring at Fort Clatsop, we have lived quite as comfortably as we had any reason to expect we should; and have accomplished every object which induced our remaining at this place except that of meeting with the traders who visit the entrance of this river. our salt will be very sufficient to last us to the Missouri where we have a stock in store. it would have been very fortunate for us had some of those traders arrived previous to our departure from hence, as we should then have had it in our power to obtain an addition to our stock of merchandize which would have made our homeward bound journey much more comfortable.[17]

many of our men are still complaining of being unwell; Willard and Bratton remain weak, principally I beleive for the want of proper food. I expect when we get under way we shall be much more healthy. it has always had that effect on us heretofore. The guns of Drewyer and Sergt. Pryor were both out of order. the first was repared with a new lock, the old one having become unfit for uce; the second had the cock screw broken which was replaced by a duplicate which had been prepared for the lock at Harpers ferry where she was manufactured. but for the precaution taken in bringing on those extra locks, and parts of locks, in addition to the ingenuity of John Shields, most of our guns would at this moment [have] been untirely unfit for use; but fortunately for us I have it in my power here to record that they are all in good order.

[17] The brig "Lydia," from Boston, Captain Hill commanding, was in Columbia River in November, 1805, a fortnight after Lewis and Clark had passed down the river, possibly while they lay camped in Gray's Bay, or upon Point Ellice (Thwaites).

Saturday March 22ed 1806.

Drewyer and the Feildses departed this morning agreably to the order of the last evening.   we sent out seven hunters this morning in different directions on this side the Netul.   about 10 A.M.   we were visited by 4 Clatsops and a killamucks; they brought some dried Anchoveis[18] and a dog for sale which we purchased.   the air is perfectly temperate, but it continues to rain in such a manner that there is no possibility of geting our canoes completed.   at 12 OCk. we were visited by Comowooll and 3 of the Clatsops.   to this Chief we left our houses and fu[r]niture.   he has been much more kind an[d] hospitable to us than any other indian in this neighbourhood.   the Indians departed in the evening.   the hunters all returned except Colter, unsuccessfull.   we determined to set out tomorrow at all events, and to stop the canoes temperarily with Mud and halt the first fair day and pay them.

the leafing of the hucklebury riminds us of spring.

[18] Candlefish.

The Start
for Home

From Fort Clatsop to Three Forks
March 23–July 13, 1806

[Clark]   Sunday 23rd. March 1806
the rained seased and it became fair about Meridian, at which
time we loaded our canoes & at 1 P. M. left Fort Clatsop on our
homeward bound journey.

at this place we had wintered and remained from the 7th. of Decr.
1805 to this day and have lived as well as we had any right to expect,
and we can say that we were never one day without 3 meals of some
kind a day either pore Elk meat or roots, notwithstanding the repeated fall of rain which has fallen almost constantly since we passed
the long narrows on the [blank space in MS.] of Novr. last indeed
w[e] have had only [blank space in MS.] days fair weather since
that time.[1] Soon after we had set out from Fort Clatsop we were
met by Delashelwilt & 8 men of the Chinnook and Delashelwilts
wife the old boud and his six Girls,   they had, a canoe, a sea otter
skin, dried fish and hats for sale, we purchased a sea otter skin, and
proceeded on, thro' Meriwethers Bay,   there was a stiff breese from
the S.W. which raised considerable swells around Meriwethers point
which was as much as our canoes could ride.

[1] The journals note only about a dozen days without rain.

[Lewis]   Monday March 24th. 1806.
  we arrived at the Cathlahmah village[2] where we halted and purchased some wappetoe, a dog for the sick, and a hat for one of the
men. on one of the Seal Islands opposite to the village of these
people they have scaffolded their dead in canoes elivating them
above tidewater mark. these people are very fond of sculpture in
wood of which they exhibit a variety of specemines about their
houses. the broad peices supporting the center of the roof and
those through which the doors are cut, seem to be the peices on
which they most display their taist. I saw some of these which
represented human figures

[Clark]   Monday 24th. of March 1806
  The village of these people is the dirtiest and stinkingest place
I ever saw in any shape whatever, and the inhabitants partake of
the carrestick [characteristic] of the village. we proceeded on
through some difficult and narrow channels between the Seal Islands, and the South side to an old village on the South Side opposit
to the lower Warkiacom village, and Encamped. to this old villg a
very considerable deposit of the dead at a short distance below in
the usial and customary way of the nativs of this coast in canoes
raised from the ground as before described. Soon after we made
our camp 2 Indians visited us from the opposit side, one of them
spoke several words of English and repeated the names of the traders, and many of the salors. made 16 miles.

[Lewis]   Wednesday March 26th. 1806.
  we halted for dinner the two Wackiacums who have been pursuing
us since yesterday morning with two dogs for sale, arrived. they
wish tobacco in exchange for their dogs which we are not disposed
to give as our stock is now reduced to a very few carrots. our men
who have been accustomed to the use of this article (*Tobaco*) and to
whom we are now obliged to deny the uce of this article appear to
suffer much for the want of it. they substitute the bark of the wild
crab which they chew; it is very bitter, and they assure me they
find it a good substitute for tobacco. the smokers substitute the

---

[2] Apparently across the river from Cathlamet, Washington.

inner bark of the red willow and the sacacommis. here our hunters joined us having killed three Eagles and a large goose. I had now an oportunity of comparing the bald with the grey Eagle; I found that the greay Eagle was about ¼ larger, it's legs and feet were dark while those of the bald Eagle wer[e] of a fine orrange yellow; the iris of the eye is also of a dark yellowish brown while that of the other is of a bright silvery colour with a slight admixture of yellow.

Thursday March 27th. 1806.

We set out early this morning and were shortly after joined by some of the Skillutes who came along side in a small canoe for the purpose of trading roots and fish. at 10 A.M. we arrived at two houses of this nation on the Stard side where we halted for breakfast. here we overtook our hunters, they had killed nothing. the natives appeared extreemly hospitable, gave us dryed Anchovies, Sturgeon, wappetoe, quamash, and a speceis of small white tuberous roots about 2 inches in length and as thick as a man's finger; these are eaten raw, are crisp, milkey, and agreeably flavored. most of the party were served by the natives with as much as they could eat; they insisted on our remaining all day with them and hunting the Elk and deer which they informed us were very abundant in their neighbourhood. but as the weather would not permit us to dry our canoes in order to pitch them we declined their friendly invitation, and resumed our voyage

the principal village of these Skillutes reside on the lower side of the Cowe-lis'-kee river a few miles from it's entrance into the columbia. these people are said to be numerous. in their dress, habits, manners and language they differ but little from the Clatsops Chinnooks &c. they have latterly been at war with Chinnooks but peace is said now to be restored between them, but their intercourse is not yet resumed. no Chinnooks come above the marshey islands nor do the Skillutes visit the mouth of the Columbia. The Clatsops, Cathlahmahs and Wackkiacums are the carriers between these nations being in alliance with both.

late in the evening we passed our camp of the 5th. of November and encamped about 4½ [miles] above at the commencement of the bottom land on stard. below Deer Island. we had scarcely landed before we were visited by a large canoe with eight men; from them we obtained a dryed fruit which resembled the raspburry

and which I be[l]eive to be the fruit of the large leafed thorn frequently mentioned.[3] it is reather ascid tho' pleasently flavored.   I
preserved a specemine of this fruit   I fear that it has been baked
in the process of drying and if so the seed will not vegitate.   saw
the Cottonwood, sweet willow, oak, ash and the broad leafed ash,
the growth which resembles the beach &c. these form the growth
of the bottom lands while the hills are covered almost exclusively
with the various speceis of fir heretofore discribed.   the black Alder
appears as well on some parts of the hills as the bottoms.

Friday March 28th. 1806

  This morning we set out very early and at 9 A.M. arrived at the
old Indian village of Lard. side of Deer Island[4] where we found our
hunters   by 10 A.M. they all returned to camp having killed seven
deer.   these were all of the common fallow deer with the long tail.
I measured the tail of one of these bucks which was upwards of 17
Inches long; they are very poor, tho' they are better than the black
tailed fallow deer of the coast.   these are two very distinct speceis
of deer.[5] the Indians call this large Island E-lal-lar or deer island
which is a very appropriate name.   the hunters informed us that
they had seen upwards of a hundred deer this morning on this
island.   the interior part of the island is praries and ponds, with a
heavy growth of Cottonwood ash and willow near the river.
  we have seen more waterfowl on this island than we have previously seen since we left Fort Clatsop, consisting of geese, ducks,
large swan, and Sandhill crains.   I saw a few of the Canvis-back
duck.   the duckinmallard are the most abundant.   one of the hunters killed a duck which appeared to be the male, it was a size less
than the duckinmallard.[6] the head neck as low as the croop, the
back tail and covert of the wings were of a fine black with a small
addmixture of perple about the head and neck, the belley & breast
were white; some long feathers which lie underneath the wings and
cover the thye were of a pale dove colour with fine black specks;
the large feathers of the wings are of a dove colour.   the legs are

---

[3] Salmonberry (*Rubus spectabilis*).
[4] Near the town of Deer Island, Oregon.
[5] White-tailed deer (*Odocoileus virginianus*) as opposed to mule deer.
[6] Ring-necked duck (*Aythya collaris*).

dark, the feet are composed of 4 toes each of which there are three in front connected by a web, the 4th is short flat and placed high on the heel behind the leg. the tail is composed of 14 short pointed feathers. the beak of this duck is remarkably wide, and is 2 inches in length, the upper chap exceeds the under one in both length and width, insomuch that when the beak is closed the under is entirely concealed by the upper chap. the tongue, indenture of the margin of the chaps &c. are like those of the mallard. the nostrils are large longitudinal and connected. a narrow strip of white garnishes the upper part or base of the upper chap—this is succeeded by a pale skye blue colour which occupys about one inch of the chap, is again succeeded by a transverse stripe of white and the extremity is of a pure black. the eye is moderately large the puple black and iris of a fine orrange yellow. the feathers on the crown of the head are longer than those on the upper part of neck and other parts of the head; these feathers give it the appearance of being crested.

Tuesday April 1st. 1806.

We were visited by several canoes of natives in the course of the day; most of whom were decending the river with their women and children. they informed us that they resided at the great rapids and that their relations at that place were much streightened at that place for want of food; that they had consumed their winter store of dryed fish and that those of the present season had not yet arrived. I could not learn wheather they took the sturgeon but presume if they do it is in but small quantitites as they complained much of the scarcity of food among them. they informed us that the nations above them were in the same situation & that they did not expect the Salmon to arrive untill the full of the next moon which happens on the 2d. of May. we did not doubt the varacity of these people who seemed to be on their way with their families and effects in surch of subsistence which they find it easy to procure in this fertile valley. This information gave us much uneasiness with rispect to our future means of subsistence. above [the] falls or through the plains from thence to the Chopunnish there are no deer Antelope nor Elk on which we can depend for subsistence; their horses are very poor most probably at this season, and if they have no fish their dogs must be in the same situation. under these circumstances there seems to be but a gloomy prospect for subsistence on any terms; we therefore took it into serious consideration what measures we were to pursue on this occasion; it was at once deemed inexpedient to wait the arrival of the salmon as that would detain us so large a portion of the season that it is probable we should not reach the United States before the ice would close the Missouri; or at all events would hazard our horses which we left in charge of the Chopunnish who informed us they intended passing the rocky mountains to the Missouri as early as the season would permit them w[h]ich is as we believe about the begining of May. should these people leave their situation near kooskooske before our arrival we may probably find much difficulty in recovering our horses; without which there will be but little possibility of repassing the mountains; we are therefore determined to loose as little time as possible in getting to the Chopunnish Village.

Wednesday April 2ed. 1806.

This morning we came to a resolution to remain at our present encampment or some where in this neighbourhood untill we had obtained as much dryed meat as would be necessary for our voyage as far as the Chopunnish. to exchange our perogues for canoes with the natives on our way to the great falls of the columbia or purchase such canoes from them for Elkskins and Merchandize as would answer our purposes. these canoes we intend exchanging with the natives of the plains for horses as we proceed untill we obtain as many as will enable us to travel altogether by land. at some convenient point, perhaps at the entrence of the S.E. branch of the Columbia, we purpose sending a party of four or five men a head to collect our horses that they may be in readiness for us by our arrival at the Chopunnish; calculating by thus acquiring a large stock of horses we shall not only secure the means of transporting our baggage over the mountains but that we will also have provided the means of subsisting; for we now view the horses as our only certain resource for food, nor do we look forward to it with any detestation or horrow [horror], so soon is the mind which is occupied with any interesting object, reconciled to it's situation.

about this time several canoes of the natives arrived at our camp and among others one from below which had on board eight men of the Shah-ha-la nation   these men informed us that 2 young men whom they pointed out were Cash-hooks and resided at the falls of a large river which discharges itself into the Columbia on it's South side some miles below us. we readily prevailed on them to give us a sketch of this river which they drew on a mat with a coal. it appeared that this river which they called Mult-no-mâh[7] discharged itself behind the Island which we called the image canoe Island and as we had left this island to the S. both in ascending and decending the river we had never seen it. they informed us that it was a large river and run a considerable distance to the South between the mountains. Capt. Clark determined to return and examine this river

[Clark]   Wednesday April 2nd. 1806
I deturmined to take a small party and return to this river and examine its size and collect as much information of the nativs on it or near it's enterance into the Columbia of its extent, the country which it waters and the nativs who inhabit its banks
I landed at a large double house of the *Ne-er-che-ki-oo* tribe of the *Shah-ha-la* Nation.[8] at this place we had seen 24 aditional straw Huts as we passed down last fall and whome as I have before mentioned reside at the Great rapids of the Columbia.
I entered one of the rooms of this house and offered several articles to the nativs in exchange for wappato. they were sulkey and they positively refused to sell any. I had a small pece of port fire match in my pocket, off of which I cut a pece one inch in length & put it into the fire and took out my pocket compas and set myself down on a mat on one side of the fire, and [also showed] a magnet which was in the top of my ink stand the port fire cought and burned vehemently, which changed the colour of the fire; with the magnit I turned the needle of the compas about very briskly; which astonished and alarmed these nativs and they laid several parsles of wappato at my feet, & begged of me to take out the bad fire; to this I consented; at this moment the match being exhausted was of course extinguished and I put up the magnet &c. this measure alarmed them so much that the womin and children took shelter in their beads and behind the men, all this time a very old blind man was

[7] Williamette River.
[8] All members of the Chinookan language family.

speaking with great vehemunce, appearently imploring his god. I lit my pipe and gave them smoke, & gave the womin the full amount [value] of the roots which they had put at my feet. they appeared somewhat passified and I left them and proceeded on.

below the last village and at the place I had supposed was the lower point of the image canoe island, I entered this river which the nativs had informed us of, called *Multnomah* River so called by the nativs from a nation who reside on Wappato Island a little below the enterance of this river.

three small Islands are situated in it's mouth which hides the river from view from the Columbia. from the enterance of this river, I can plainly see Mt. Jefferson which is high and covered with snow S.E. Mt. Hood East, Mt. St. Helians [and] a high humped mountain [Mount Adams] to the East of Mt. St. Helians.

Thursday April 3rd. 1806

being perfectly satisfyed of the size and magnitude of this great river which must water that vast tract of Country between the western range of mountains and those on the sea coast and as far S. as the Waters of Callifornia about Latd. 37. North. I deturmined to return.[9]

we arived at the residence of our Pilot which consists of one long house with seven appartments or rooms in square form about 30 feet

back of this house I observe the wreck of 5 houses remaining of a very large village, the houses of which had been built in the form of those we first saw at the long narrows of the *E-lute* Nation with whome those people are connected. I indeavored to obtain from those people of the situation of their nation, if scattered or what had become of the nativs who must have peopled this great town. an old man who appeared of some note among them and father to my guide brought foward a woman who was badly marked with the Small Pox and made signs that they all died with the disorder which marked her face, and which she was verry near dieing with when a girl, from the age of this woman this Distructive disorder I judge must have been about 28 or 30 years past, and about the time the

---

[9] Clark ascended to a point at or near the present site of Portland, Oregon (Thwaites).

Clatsops inform us that this disorder raged in their towns and distroyed their nation.

Saturday April 5th. 1806.
Saw the Log cock, the humming bird, gees ducks &c. to-day. the tick has made it's appearance it is the same with those of the Atlantic States. the Musquetoes have also appeared but are not yet troublesome. The dogwood grows abundantly on the uplands in this neighbourhood. it differs from that of the United States in the appearance of it's bark which is much smoother, it also arrives here to much greater size than I ever observed it elsewhere sometimes the stem is nearly 2 feet in diameter.[10] we measured a fallen tree of fir N°. 1. which was 318 feet including the stump which was about 6 feet high. this tree was only about 3½ feet in diameter. we saw the martin, small gees, the small speckled woodpecker with a white back, the Blue crested Corvus, ravens, crows, eagles Vultures and hawks. the mellow [melon] bug and long leged spider have appeared, as have also the butterfly blowing fly and many other insects. I observe not any among them which appear to differ from those of our country or which deserve particular notice.

[Lewis] Monday April 7th. 1806.
last evening Reubin Field killed a bird of the quail kind it is reather larger than the quail, or partridge as they are called in Virginia. it's form is precisely that of our partridge tho' it's plumage differs in every part. the upper part of the head, sides and back of the neck, including the croop and about ⅓ of the under part of the body is of a bright dovecoloured blue, underneath the under beak, as high as the lower edge of the eyes, and back as far as the hinder part of the eyes and thence coming down to a point in front of the neck about two thirds of it's length downwards, is of a fine dark brick red. between this brick red and the dove colour there runs a narrow stripe of pure white. the ears are covered with some coarse stiff dark brown feathers. just at the base of the under chap there is [a] narrow transverse stripe of white. from the crown of the head two long round feathers extend backwards nearly in the direction

[10] Pacific dogwood (*Cornus nuttalli*).

of the beak and are of a black colour.　the longest of these feathers is two inches and an half, it overlays and conceals the other which is somewhat shorter and seems to be raped in the plumage of that in front which folding backwards colapses behind and has a round appearance.　the tail is composed of twelve dark brown feathers of nearly equal length.　the large feathers of the wings are of a dark brown and are reather short in proportion to the body of the bird in that rispect very similar to our common partridge.　the covert of the wings and back are of a dove colour with a slight admixture of redish brown.　a wide stripe which extends from side to side of the body and occupyes the lower region of the breast is beautifully variagated with the brick red white and black which p[r]edominate in the order they are mentioned and the colours mark the feathers transversely.

the legs are covered with feathers as low as the knee; these feathers are of a dark brown tiped with dark brick red as are also those between and about the joining of the legs with the body.　they have four toes on each foot of which three are in front and that in the center the longest, those one [on] each side nearly of a length; that behing[d] is also of good length and are all armed with long and strong nails. the legs and feet are white and imbrecated with proportionably large broad scales.　the upper beak is short, wide at it's base, black, convex, curved downwards and reather obtusely pointed. it exceeds the under chap considerably which is of a white colour, also convex underneath and obtusely pointed.　the nostrils are remarkably small, placed far back and low down on the sides of the beak.　they are covered by a thin protuberant elastic, black leatherlike substance.　the eyes are of a uniform piercing black colour.　this is a most beautifull bird.[11] I preserved the skin of this bird retaining the wings feet and head which I hope will give a just idea of the bird.　it's loud note is single and consists of a loud squall, intirely different from the whistling of our quales or partridge.　it has a cherping note when allarmed something like ours.　today there was a second of these birds killed [*by Capt C.*] which precisely resembled that just discribed.　I believe these to be the male bird the female, if so, I have not yet seen.

I provaled on an old indian to mark the Multnomah R down on

[11] Mountain quail (*Oreortyx pictus*).

the sand which hid [he did] and perfectly corisponded with the sketch given me by sundary others, with the addition of a circular mountain which passes this river at the falls and connects with the mountains of the Seacoast. he also lais down the Clarkamos [Clackamas] passing a high conical mountain near it's mouth on the lower Side and heads in Mount Jefferson which he lais down by raiseing the Sand as a very high mountain and covered with eternal snow.

the high mountain which this Indian lais down near the enterance of Clarkamos river, we have not seen as the hills in it's direction from this vally is high and obscures the sight of it from us. Mt Jefferson we can plainly see from the enterance of Multnomah from which place it bears S.E. this is a noble mountain and I think equally as high or something higher than Mt. St. Heleans but its distance being much greater than that of the latter, so great a portion of it does not appear above the range of mountains which lie between both those stupendious mountains and the mouth of Multnomah. like Mt. St. Heleans its figure is a regular cone and is covered with eturnial snow.

[Lewis]   Tuesday April 8th. 1806.

I took a walk today of three miles down the river; in the course of which I had an opportunity to correct an errow [error] which I have heretofore made with rispect to the shrub I have hithertoo called the large leafed thorn. the leaf of this thorn is small being only ab[o]ut 2½ inches long, is petiolate,, conjugate; the leafets are petiolate accutely pointed, having their margins cut with unequal angular insissures. the shrub which I have heretofore confounded with this grows in similar situations, has a stem precisely like it except the thorn and bears a large three loabed leaf.[12] this bryer is of the class Polyandria and order Polygynia. the flowers are single, the peduncle long and celindric. the calix is a perianth, of one leaf, five cleft & accutely pointed. the perianth is proper, erect, inferior with rispect to both petals and germen, and equal. the corolla consists of five accute pale scarlet petals, insirted in the recepticle with a short and narrow claw, the Corolla is smooth, moderately

---

[12] This briar is *Rubus macropetalus*, while the broad-leaved thorn is doubtless *R. spectabilis* (Piper), or the greenbriar and salmonberry (Cutright).

long, situated at the base of the germen, permament, and cup shaped. of the stamens the filaments are subulate, inserted into the recepticle, unequal and bent inwards concealing the pistillum; anther two loabed and inflected situated on the top of the fillaments of the pistillum the germ is conical, imbricated, superior, sessile and short. the styles are short with rispect to the stamen, capillary smooth, obtuse, distributed over the serface of the germ and deciduous. no perseptable stigma.

Wednesday April 9th. 1806.

John Colter one of our party observed the tomehawk in one of the lodges which had been stolen from us on the 4th of November last as we decended this river; the natives attempted to wrest the tomahawk from him but he retained it. they indeavoured afterwards to exculpate themselves from the odium of having stolen it, they alledged that they had bought it from the natives below; but their neighbours had several days previously, informed us that these people had stolen the Tommehawk and then had it at their village.

we passed several beautifull cascades[13] which fell from a great hight over the stupendious rocks which closes the river on both sides nearly, except a small bottom on the South side in which our hunters were encamped. the most remarkable of these casscades falls about 300 feet perpendicularly over a solid rock into a narrow bottom of the river on the south side. it is a large creek, situated about 5 miles above our encampment of the last evening. several small streams fall from a much greater hight, and in their decent become a perfect mist which collecting on the rocks below again become visible and decend a second time in the same manner before they reach the base of the rocks. the hills have now become mountains high on each side are rocky steep and covered generally with fir and white cedar. we saw some turkey buzzards this morning of the speceis common to the United states which are the first we have seen on this side the rocky mountains.

[Clark] Wednesday April 9th. 1806

last night at a late hour the old amsiated [emaciated?] Indian who was detected in stealing a Spoon yesterday, crept upon his belley

---

[13] Seven waterfalls, including Multnomah Falls, on the Oregon side of Columbia Gorge.

with his hands and feet, with a view as I suppose to take some of
our baggage which was in several defferent parcels on the bank.
the Sentinal observed the motions of this old amcinated retch untill
he got with[in] a fiew feet of the baggage at [that] he hailed him
and approached with his gun in a possion [position] as if going to
shoote which allarmed the old retch in such a manner that he ran
with all his powers tumbleing over brush and every thing in his way.

[Lewis]   Friday April 11th. 1806.

As the tents and skins which covered both our men and baggage
were wet with the rain which fell last evening, and as it continued
still raining this morning we concluded to take our canoes first to
the head of the rapids, hoping that by evening the rain would cease
and afford us a fair afternoon to take our baggage over the portage.
this portage is two thousand eight hundred yards along a narrow
rough and slipery road.[14] the duty of getting the canoes above the
rapid was by mutual consent confided to my friend Capt. C. who
took with him for that purpose all the party except Bratton who is
yet so weak he is unable to work, three others who were lamed by
various accedents and one other to cook for the party. a few men
were absolutely necessary at any rate to guard our baggage from the
War-clel-lars who crouded about our camp in considerable numbers. these are the greates[t] theives and scoundrels we have met
with.

by the evening Capt. C. took 4 of our canoes above the rapids
tho' with much difficulty and labour. the canoes were much damaged by being driven against the rocks in dispite of every precaution
which could be taken to prevent t. the men complained of being
so much fatiegued in the evening that we postponed taking up our
5th canoe untill tomorrow. these rapids are much worse than they
were [in the] fall when we passed them, at that time there were
only three difficult points within seven miles, at present the whole
distance is extreemly difficult of ascent, and it would be impracticable to decend except by leting down the empty vessels by a cord
and then even the wrisk would be greater than in taking them up
by the same means. the water appears to be (considerably) upwards

---

[14] Along the Cascades, or the explorers' "Grand Shute."

of 20 feet higher than when we decended the river. the distance by way of the river between the points of the portage is 3 Ms.

many of the natives crouded about the bank of the river where the men were engaged in taking up the canoes; one of them had the insolence to cast stones down the bank at two of the men who happened to be a little detached from the party at the time. on the return of the party in the evening from the head of the rapids they met with many of the natives on the road, who seemed but illy disposed; two of these fellows met with John Sheilds who had delayed some time in purchasing a dog and was a considerable distance behind the party on their return with Capt. C. they attempted to take the dog from him and pushed him out of the road. he had nothing to defend himself with except a large knife which he drew with an intention of puting one or both of them to death before they could get themselves in readiness to use their arrows, but discovering his design they declined the combat and instantly fled through the woods. three of this same tribe of villains the Wahclel-lars, stole my dog this evening, and took him towards their village; I was shortly afterwards informed of this transaction by an indian who spoke the Clatsop language, (*some of which we had learnt from them during the winter*) and sent three men in pursuit of the theives with orders if they made the least resistence or difficulty in surrendering the dog to fire on them; they overtook these fellows or reather came within sight of them at the distance of about 2 miles; the indians discovering the party in pursuit of them left the dog and fled. they also stole an ax from us, but scarcely had it in their possession before Thompson detected them and wrest[ed] it from them.

we ordered the centinel to keep them out of camp, and informed them by signs that if they made any further attempts to steal our property or insulted our men we should put them to instant death. a cheif of the Clah-clel-lah tribe informed us that there were two very bad men among the Wah-clel-lahs who had been the principal actors in these scenes of outradge of which we complained, and that it was not the wish of the nation by any means to displease us. we told him that we hoped it might be the case, but we should certainly be as good as our words if they persisted in their insolence. I am convinced that no other consideration but our number at this mo-

ment protects us. The Cheif appeared mortified at the conduct of
his people, and seemed friendly disposed towards us.

Wednesday April 16th. 1806.

I was visited today be several of the natives, and amused myself
in making a collection of the esculent plants in the neighbourhood
such as the Indians use, a specemine of which I preserved. I also
met with sundry other plants which were strangers to me which I
also preserved, among others there is a currant which is now in
blume and has [a] yellow blossom something like the yellow currant
of the Missouri but is a different speceis.[15] Reubin Feilds returned
in the evening and brought with him a large grey squ[i]rrel and two
others of a kind I had never before seen. they are a size less than
the grey squirrel common to the middle atlantic states and of a pided
grey and yellowish brown colour, in form it resembles our grey
squ[i]rrel precisely.[16] I had them skined leaving the head feet and
tail to them and placed in the sun to dry.

Joseph Feilds brought me a black pheasant which he had killed;
this I found on examination to be the large black or dark brown
pheasant I had met with on the upper part of the Missouri. it is as
large as a well grown fowl the iris of the eye is of a dark yellowish
brown, the puple black, the legs are booted to the toes, the tail is
composed of 18 black feathers tiped with bluish white, of which the
two in the center are reather shorter than the others which are all
of the same length. over the eye there is a stripe of a ¼ of an inch
in width uncovered with feathers of a fine orrange yellow. the wide
spaces void of feathers on the side of the neck are also of the same
colour. I had some parts of this bird preserved.[17]

our present station is the last point at which there is a single stick
of timber on the river for a great distance and is the commencement
of the open plains which extend nearly to the base of the rocky Mts

this evening Capt. C. informed me by some of the men whom
he sent over that that he had obtained no horses as yet of the natives.
that they promised to trade with him provided he would remove to

[15] *Ribes aureum* (Piper), or golden currant.
[16] Western gray squirrel (*Sciurus griseus*).
[17] Blue grouse (*Dendragapus obscurus*).

their village. to this he had consented and should proceede to the Skillute village above the long narrows as soon as the men returned whom he had sent to me for some other articles.

[Clark]   Wednesday April 16th. 1806
About 8 oClock this morning I passed the river with the two interpreters, and nine men in order to trade with the nativs for their horses, for which purpose I took with me a good part of our stock of merchindize.

Great numbers of Indians came from both villages and delayed the greater part of the day without tradeing a single horse. Drewyer returned with the principal Chief of the Skillutes who was lame and could not walk. after his arival some horses were offered for sale, but they asked nearly half the merchindize I had with me for one horse. this price I could not think of giveing. the Chief informed me if I would go to his town with him, his people would sell me horses. I therefore concluded to accompany him to his village 7 miles distant. we set out and arrived at the village at Sunset. after some serimony I entered the house of the Chief. I then informed them that I would trade with them for their horses in the morning for which I would give for each horse the articles which I had offered yesterd[ay]. The Chief set before me a large platter of onions which had been sweeted [sweated]. I gave a part of those onions to all my party and we all ate of them, in this state the root is very sweet and the tops tender. the nativs requested the party to dance which they very readily consented and Peter Cruzat played on the violin and the men danced several dances & retired to rest in the houses of the 1st. and second Chief.

This is the great mart of all this country.[18] ten different tribes who reside on Taptate and Catteract River visit those people for the purpose of purchaseing their fish, and the Indians on the Columbia and Lewis's river quite to the Chopunnish Nation visit them for the purpose of tradeing horses buffalow robes for beeds, and such articles as they have not. The Skillutes precure the most of their cloth knivs axes & beeds from the Indians from the North of them who trade with white people who come into the inlets to the

[18] Near The Dalles, Oregon.

North at no great distance from the Tapteet. their horses of which I saw great numbers, they precure from the Indians who reside on the banks of the Columbia above, and what fiew they take from the Towarnihooks or Snake Indians. I smoked with all the principal men of this nation in the house of their great Chief and lay my self down on a mat to sleep but was prevented by the mice and vermin with which this house abounded and which was very troublesom to me.

[Lewis]   Thursday April 17th. 1806.

Joseph Fields brought me today three eggs of the party coloured corvus,[19] they are about the size and shape of those of the pigeon. they are bluish white much freckled with dark redish brown irregular spots, in short it is reather a mixture of those colours in which the redish brown predominates, particularly towards the larger end. This evening Willard and Cruzatte returned from Capt. Clark and brought me a note in which Capt. C. informed me that he had s[t]ill been unsuccessfull having not obtained a single horse as yet from the natives and the state of our stores are so low that I begin to fear we shall not be enabled to obtain as many horses at this place as will convey our baggage and unless we do obtain a sufficient number for that purpose we shall not hasten our progress as a part of our baggage must still be conveyed by water.

there is a species of hiasinth in these plains the bulb of which the natives eat either boiled baked or dryed in the sun. this bulb is white, not entirely solid, and of a flat form; the bulb of the present year overlays, or crowns that of the last, and seems to be pressed close to it, the old bulb is withered much thiner equally wide with that of the present year and sends fourth from it's sides a number of small radicles. this hiasinth is of a pale blue colour and is a very pretty flower. I preserved a specemine of it.[20]

[Clark]   Thursday 17th. of April 1806

I rose early after [a] bad nights rest, and took my merchindize to a rock which afforded an eligable situation for my purpose, and at

---

[19] Black-billed magpie (*Pica pica*).
[20] This is *Brodiae douglasii*, Wats. The specimen preserved is dated April 20, 1806 (Piper); wild hyacinth.

a short distance from the houses, and divided the articles of merchindize into parsels of such articles as I thought best calculated to pleas the Indians. Maney of the nativs from different villages on the Columbia above offered to trade, but asked such things as we had not and double as much of the articles which I had as we could afford to give. I dispatched Crusat, Willard & McNeal and Peter Wiser to Capt Lewis at the Rock fort Camp with a note informing him of my ill suckcess in precureing horses, and advised him to proceed on to this place as soon as possible. that I would in the mean time proceed on to the Enesher Nation above the Great falls[21] and try to purchase some horses of that people.

Friday 18th. April 1806

Early this morning I was awoke by an indian man of the Chopunnish Nation who informed me that he lived in the neighbourhood of our horses. this man delivered me a bag of powder and ball which he had picked up this morning at the place the goods were exposed yesterday. I had a fire made of some poles purchased of the nativs at a short distance from the houses and the articles exposed yesterday. Collected the 4 horses purchased yesterday and sent Frazier and Shabono with them to the bason where I expected they would meet Cap L——s and commence the portage of the baggage on those horses. about 10 A. M. the Indians came down from the Eneesher Villages and I expected would take the articles which they had laid by yesterday. but to my estonishment not one would make the exchange to day. two other parcels of goods were laid by, and the horses promised at 2 P.M. I payed but little attention to this bargain, however suffered the bundles to lye.

I dressed the sores of the principal Chief gave some small things to his children and promised the chief some Medicine for to cure his sores. his wife who I found to be a sulky Bitch and was somewhat efflicted with pains in her back. this I thought a good opportunity to get her on my side giveing her something for her back. I rubed a little camphere on her temples and back, and applyed worm flannel to her back which she thought had nearly restored her to her former feelings. this I thought a favourable time to trade with the chief

[21] Celilo Falls.

who had more horses than all the nation besides. I accordingly made him an offer which he excepted and sold me two horses.   Great numbers of Indians from defferent derections visited me at this place to day.   none of them appeared willing to part with their horses, but told me that several were comeing from the plains this evening.

among other nations who visit this place for the purpose of trade is the *Skad-datt*'s.[22]   those people bartered the Skillutes to play at a singular kind of game.   in the course of the day the Skillutes won all their beeds skins arrows &c.   This game was composed of 9 men on a side.   they set down opposit to each other at the distance of about 10 feet.   in front of each party a long pole was placed on which they struck with a small stick to the time of their songs. after the bets were made up which was nearly half an hour after they set down, two round bones was produced about the size of a mans little finger or something smaller and 2¼ inches in length. which they held in their hands changeing it from one hand to the other with great dexterity.   2 men on the same side performed this part, and when they had the bone in the hand they wished, they looked at their advorsarys swinging arms around their sholders for their advorsary [to] Guess which they performed by the motion the hand either to the right or left.   if the opposit party guessed the hand of both of the men who had the bone, the bones were given to them.   if neither the bones was retained and nothing counted. if they guessed one and not the other, one bone was delivered up and the party possessing the other bone counted one. and one for every time the advorsary missguessed untill they guessed the hand in which the bone was in. in this game each party has 5 sticks. and one side wins all the sticks, once twice or thrice as the game may be set.

at 5 P. M. Capt. Lewis came up.   he informed me that he had [passed] the river to the bason with much dificuelty and danger, haveing made one portage.   as I had not slept but very little for the two nights past on account of mice & Virmen with which those indian houses abounded, and haveing no blanket with me, and the means of keeping a fire sufficent to keep me worm out [of doors]

---

[22] Sahaptin speakers, like the Chopunnish (Nez Perce), as opposed to the Chinookan-speaking Skilloots.

was too expensive I deturmined to proceed with Capt L. down to camp at the bason.

[Lewis]   Saturday April 19th. 1806.

there was great joy with the natives last night in consequence of the arrival of the Salmon; one of those fish was caught; this was the harbinger of good news to them.   They informed us that these fish would arrive in great quantities in the course of about 5 days.   this fish was dressed and being divided into small peices was given to each child in the village. this custom is founded in a supersticious opinion that it will hasten the arrival of the Salmon.

with much difficulty we obtained four other horses from the Indians today, we wer[e] obliged to dispence with two of our kettles, in order to acquire those.   we have now only one small kettle to a mess of 8 men. in the evening Capt. Clark set out with four men to the Enesher village at the grand falls in order to make a further attempt to procure horses.   these people are very faithless in their contracts; they frequently receive the merchandize in exchange for their horses and after some hours. insist on some additional article being given them or revoke the exchange. they have pilfered several small articles from us this evening. I directed the horses to be hubbled & suffered to graize at a little distance from our camp under the immediate eye of the men who had them in charge.

[Clark]   Saturday 19th. April 1806.

We deturmined to make the portage to the head of the long narrows with our baggage and 5 small canoes,   the 2 large canoes we could take no further and therefore cut them up for fuel.

The long narrows are much more formidable than they were when we decended them last fall, there would be no possibility of passing either up or down them in any vessle at this time.

I entered the largest house of the Eneeshers Village in which I found all the enhabitants in bead.   they rose and made a light of straw, they haveing no wood to burn.   Many men collected we smoked and I informed them that I had come to purchase a fiew horses of them.   they promused to sell me some in the morning.

[Lewis]   Sunday April 20th. 1806.

The Enesher an[d] Skillutes are much better clad than they were last fall, there men have generally legings mockersons and large robes; many of them wear shirts of the same form with those of the Shoshone Chopunnish &c. highly ornamented with porcupine quills. the dress of their women differs very little from those of the great rapids and above. their children frequently wear robes of the large grey squirrel skins, those of the men and women are principally deer skins, some wolf, elk, big horn and buffaloe; the latter they procure from the nations who sometimes visit the Missouri. indeed a considerable p[r]oportion of their wearing apparel is purchased from their neighbours to the N.W. in exchange for pounded fish copper and beads. at present the principal village of the Eneshur is below the falls

                                              Monday April 21st. 1806.

Notwithstanding all the precautions I had taken with rispect to the horses one of them had broken his cord of 5 strands of Elkskin and had gone off spanseled. I sent several men in surch of the horse with orders to return at 10 A.M. with or without the horse being determined to remain no longer with these villains. they stole another tomahawk from us this morning I surched many of them but could not find it. I ordered all the spare poles, paddles and the ballance of our canoe put on the fire as the morning was cold and also that not a particle should be left for the benefit of the indians. I detected a fellow in stealing an iron socket of a canoe pole and gave him several severe blows and mad[e] the men kick him out of camp. I now informed the indians that I would shoot the first of them that attempted to steal an article from us. that we were not affraid to fight them, that I had it in my power at that moment to kill them all and set fire to their houses, but it was not my wish to treat them with severity provided they would let my property alone. that I would take their horses if I could find out the persons who had stolen the tommahawks, but that I had reather loose the property altogether than take the ho[r]se of an inosent person. the chiefs [who] were present hung their heads and said nothing. at 9 A.M. Windsor returned with the lost horse, the others who were in surch of the horse soon after returned also. the Indian

who promised to accompany me as far as the Chopunnish country
produced me two horses one of which he politely gave me the liberty
of packing. we took breakfast and departed a few minutes after 10
OClock. having nine horses loaded and one which Bratton rode not
being able as yet to march; the two canoes I had dispatched early
this morning.

at 1 P.M. I arrived at the Enesher Village where I found Capt.
Clark and party; he had not purchased a single horse. he informed
me that these people were quite as unfriendly as their neighbours
the Skillutes, and that he had subsisted since he left me on a couple
of platters of pounded roots and fish which an old man had the
politeness to offer him. his party fared much better on dogs which
he purchased from those people.

we obtained two dogs and a small quantity of fuel of these people
for which we were obliged to give them a higher price than usual.
our guide continued with us, he appears to be an honest sincere
fellow. he tells us that the indians a little above will treat us with
much more hospitality than those we are now with. we purchased
another horse this evening but his back is in such a horid state that
we can put but little on him; we obtained him for a trifle, at least
for articles which might be procured in the U' States for 10 shillings
Virga Cory. we took the precautions of piqu[i]ting and spanseling
our horses this evening near our camp.

[Clark]   Wednesday 23rd. 1806
At day light this morning we were informed that the two horses
of our interpreter Shabono were missing on enquirey we were
informed that he had neglected to tie up his horses as derected last
evening. we imediately dispatch him, R. Fields & Labiech in serch
of the horses, one of them were found at no great distance. the
other was not found. R. Fields retd. without finding the horse set
out with Sergt. Gass in the Small Canoe at about 8 A M. at 10
Shabono and Labiech returned also unsucksessfull they had went
on the back tract nearly to the last Village and took a circle around
on the hills. as our situation was such that we could not detain for
a horse, which would prevent our makeing a timely stage which is
a great object with us in those open plains, we concluded to give
up the horse and proceed on to the next village which we were

informed was at some distance and would take us the greater part
of the day.

at 11 A.M. we packed up and set out and proceeded up on the
N. Side of the Columbia on a high narrow bottom and rockey for
12 miles to the *Wah-how-pum* village near the rock rapid of 12 tem-
porary mat Lodges, those people appeared pleased to see us. they
sold us 4 dogs some shapollell and wood for our small articles such
as awls pieces of Tin and brass. we passed several Lodges on the
bank of the river where they were fixed waiting for the salmon. I
over took a Choponish man whome I had seen at the long [narrows],
and who had found a bag of our powder and brought it to me at
that place. this man had his family on the [blank space in MS.]
and about 13 head of horses which appeared young and unbroke.
his spous as also that of the other gave me a cake of Chapellell and
proceeded on with me to the Wahhowpum village and formed his
camp near us. we caused all the old & brave men to set around and
smoke with us. we caused the fiddle to be played and some of the
men danced. after them the nativs danced. they dance different
from any Indians I have seen. they dance with their sholders together and pass from side to side, defferent parties passing each
other, from 2 to 7 and 4 parties danceing at the same time and
concluding the dance by pasing promiscuisly throu[gh] & between
each other. after which we sent of [f] the Indians and retired to
bed. Those people speak a language very similar to the Chopunish
and with a very inconsiderable difference. their dress and appearance is more like those of the Great falls of the Columbia.

we had all our horses side hobbled and let out to feed. at this
village a large creek falls in on the N. side which I had not observed
as I decended the river. the river is by no means as rapid as it was
at the time we decended. The nativs promised to give us a horse
for one of our canoes, and offer to sell us another for a scarlet robe
which we have not at present. Shabono made a bargin with one of
the Indian men going with us, for a horse for which he gave his
shirt, and two of the leather sutes of his wife. The sand through
which we walked to day is so light that [it] renders the march very
fatigueing. made 12 miles by land.

[Lewis]   Thursday April 24th. 1806.

we now sold our canoes for a few strands of beads, loaded up and departed at 2 P.M. the natives had tantalized us with an exchange of horses for our canoes in the first instance, but when they found that we had made our arrangements to travel by land they would give us nothing for them I determined to cut them in peices sooner than leave them on those terms, Drewyer struck one of the canoes and split of[f] a small peice with his tommahawk, they discovered us determined on this subject and offered us several strands of beads for each which were accepted.

we purchased three dogs and some shappellel of these people which we cooked with dry grass and willow boughs. many of the natives pased and repassed us today on the road and behaved themselves with distant rispect towards us. most of the party complain of the soarness of their feet and legs this evening; it is no doubt caused by walking over the rough stones and deep sands after b[e]ing for some months passed been accustomed to a soft soil. my left ankle gives me much pain. I baithed my feet in cold water from which I experienced considerable relief. The curloos are abundant in these plains and are now laying their eggs. saw the kildee[r], the brown lizzard, and a Moonax[23] which the natives had petted. the winds which set from Mount Hood or in a westerly direction are much more cold than those from the opposite quarter.

[Clark]   Thursday 24th: April 1806

rose early this morning and sent out after the horses all of which were found except Mc.Neals which I hired an Indian to find and gave him a Tomahawk   had 4 pack saddles made ready to pack the horses which we may purchase. we purchased 3 horses, and hired 3 others of the Chopunnish man who accompanies us with his family, and at 1 P.M. set out and proceeded on through a open countrey rugid & sandy between some high lands and the river to a village of 5 Lodges of the Met-cow-we band haveing passed 4 Lodges at 4 miles and 2 Lodges at 6 miles. Great numbers of the nativs pass us on hors back   maney meet us and continued with us to the Lodges. we purchased 3 dogs which were pore, but the fattest we

---

[23] Yellow-bellied marmot (*Marmota flaviventris*).

could precure, and cooked them with straw and dry willow. we sold
our canoes for a fiew strands of beeds. the nativs had tantelized us
with an exchange of horses for our canoes in the first instance, but
when they found that we had made our arrangements to travel by
land they would give us nothing for them. we sent Drewyer to cut
them up, he struck one and split her they discovered that we were
deturmined to destroy the canoes and offered us several strands of
beeds which were accepted most of the party complain of their
feet and legs this evening being very sore, it is no doubt caused
by walking over the rough stone and deep sand after being accustomed to a soft soil. my legs and feet give me much pain. I bathed
them in cold water from which I experienced considerable relief.
we directed that the 3 horses purchased yesterday should be hobbled
and confined to pickquets and that the others should be hobbled &
spanceled, and strictly attended to by the guard made 12 miles to
day.

[Lewis]   Sunday April 27th. 1806.

I now thought it best to halt as the horses and men were much
fatiegued altho we had not reached the Wallahwollah village as we
had been led to beleive by our guide who informed us that the
village was at the place we should next return to the river, and the
consideration of our having but little provision had been our inducement to make the march we had made this morning. we collected some of the dry stalks of weeds and the stems of a shrub
which resembles the southernwood; made a small fire and boiled a
small quantity of our jerked meat on which we dined; while here
the principal Cheif of the Wallahwallahs joined us with six men of
his nation. this Cheif by name *Yel-lept!* had visited us on the morning of the 19 of October at our encampment a little below this place;[24]
we gave him at that time a small medal, and promised him a larger
one on our return. he appeared much gratifyed at seeing us return,
invited us to remain at his village three or four days and assured us
that we should be furnished with a plenty of such food as they had
themselves, and some horses to assist us on our journey.

[24] His village was in Yakima County, Washington, opposite the mouth of the Walla
Walla River, where is the town of Wallula (Coues).

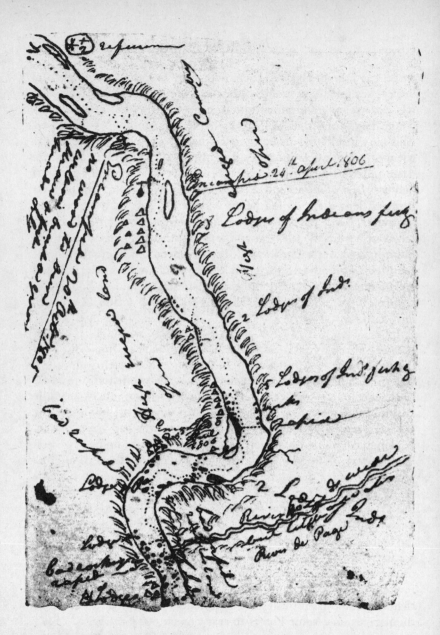

Map from Clark field book, showing position of Indian lodges, and places of encampment for October 20, 1805, and the return journey, April 24, 1806.

after our scanty repast we continued our march accompanyed by Yellept and his party to the village which we found at the distance of six miles situated on the N. side of the river at the lower side of the low country about 12 ms. below the entrance of Lewis's river. This Cheif is a man of much influence not only in his own nation but also among the neighbouring tribes and nations. Yellept haranged his village in our favour intreated them to furnish us with fuel and provision and set the example himself by bringing us an armfull of wood and a platter of 3 roasted mullets. the others soon followed his example with rispect to fuel and we soon found ourselves in possession of an ample stock. they birn the stems of the shrubs in the plains there being no timber in their neighbourhood of any discription. we purchased four dogs of these people on which the party suped heartily having been on short allowance for near two days. the indians retired when we requested them this evening and behaved themselves in every rispect extreemly well.

the indians informed us that there was a good road which passed from the columbia opposite to this village to the entrance of the Kooskooske on the S. side of Lewis's river;[25] they also informed us, that there were a plenty of deer and antelopes on the road, with good water and grass. we knew that a road in that direction if the country would permit it would shorten our rout at least 80 miles. the indians also informed us that the country was level and the road good, under these circumstances we did not hesitate in pursuing the rout recommended by our guide whos information was corroberated by Yellopt & others. we concluded to pass our horses over early in the morning.

[Clark]   Monday April 28th. 1806
This morning early the Great Chief Yelleppet brought a very eligant white horse to our camp and presented him to me, signifying his wish to get a kittle but being informed that we had already disposed of every kittle we could possibly spare he said he was content with whatever I thought proper to give him. I gave him my *Swoard*, 100 balls & powder and some small articles of which he appeared perfectly satisfied. it was necessary before we entered

[25] From the Columbia to the Clearwater, just south of the Snake River.

on our rout through the plains where we were to meet with no lodges
or resident Indians that we should lay in a stock of provisions and
not depend altogether on the gun.   we derected R. Frazer to whome
we have intrusted the duty of makeing the purchases, to lay in as
maney fat dogs as he could procure; he soon obtained 10, being
anxious to depart we requested the Chief to furnish us with canoes
to pass the river, but he insisted on our remaining with him this day
at least, that he would be much pleased if we would consent to
remain two or 3 days, but he would not let us have canoes to leave
him this day.   that he had sent for the *Chim-na-pums*[26] his neighbours
to come down and join his people this evening and dance for us.
We urged the necessity of our proceeding on imediately in order
that we might the sooner return to them, with the articles which
they wished brought to them but this had no effect, he said that
the time he asked could not make any considerable difference.   I
at length urged that there was no wind blowing and that the river
was consequently in good order to pass our horses and if he would
furnish us with canoes for that purpose we would remain all night
at our present encampment,   to this proposition he assented and
soon produced a canoe.   I saw a man who had his knee contracted
who had previously applyed to me for some medisene, that if he
would fournish another canoe I would give him some medisene.
he readily consented and went himself with his canoe by means of
which we passed our horses over the river safely and hobbled them
as usial.
    We found a *Sho-sho-ne* woman, prisoner among those people by
means of whome and *Sah-cah-gah-weah*, Shabono's wife we found
means of converceing with the *Wallahwallârs*.   we conversed with
them for several hours and fully satisfy all their enquiries with respect
to our Selves and the Objects of our pursute.   they were much
pleased.   they brought several disordered persons to us for whome
they requested some medical aid.   one had his knee contracted by
the Rhumitism (whome is just mentioned above) another with a
broken arm &c.   to all of whome we administered much to the
gratification of those pore wretches,   we gave them some eye water
which I believe will render them more essential sirvice than any

[26] Yakimas.

other article in the medical way which we had it in our power to
bestow on them   sore eyes seam to be a universal complaint among
those people; I have no doubt but the fine sands of those plains and
the river contribute much to the disorder. The man who had his
arm broken had it loosely bound in a piece of leather without any
thing to surport it.   I dressed the arm which was broken short above
the wrist & supported it with broad sticks to keep it in place, put
[it] in a sling and furnished him with some lint bandages &c. to
Dress it in future.

a little before sun set the Chimnahpoms arrived; they were about
100 men and a fiew women; they joined the Wallahwallahs who
were about 150 men and formed a half circle arround our camp
where they waited verry patiently to see our party dance.   the fiddle
was played and the men amused themselves with danceing about
an hour.   we then requested the Indians to dance which they very
chearfully complyed with; they continued their dance untill 10 at
night. the whole assemblage of Indians about 350 men women and
children sung and danced at the same time.   Most of them danced
in the same place they stood and mearly jumped up to the time of
their musick.   Some of the men who were esteemed most brave
entered the space around which the main body were formed in solid
column and danced in a circular manner side wise.   at 10 P M. the
dance ended and the nativs retired; they were much gratified in
seeing some of our party join them in their dance.

[Lewis]   Tuesday April 29th. 1806.

This morning Yellept furnished us with two canoes and we began
to transport our baggage over the river; we also sent a party of the
men over to collect the horses.   we purchased some dogs and shap-
pellell this morning.   we had now a store of 12 dogs for our voyage
through the plains.

[Clark]   Tuesday April 29th. 1806.

Several applyed to me to day for medical aide, one a broken arm
another inward fevers and several with pains across their loins, and
sore eyes.   I administered as well as I could to all.   in the evening
a man brought his wife and a horse both up to me.   the horse he
gave me as a present and his wife who was verry unwell the effects
of violent coalds was placed before me. I did not think her case a

bad one and gave such medesene as would keep her body open and
raped her in flannel.   left some simple medesin to be taken.

[Lewis]   Wednesday April 30th. 1806.
   we purchased two other horses this morning and several dogs.
we exchanged one of our most indifferent horses for a very good
one with the Chopunnish man who has his family with him.   this
man has a daugher new arrived at the age of puberty, who being in
a certain situation [mences] is not permitted to ascociate with the
family but sleeps at a distance from her father's camp and when
traveling follows at some distance behind.   in this state I am informed that the female is not permitted to eat, nor to touch any
article of a culinary nature or manly occupation.
   collected all our horses except the white horse which Yellept had
given Capt. C.   the whole of the men soon after returned without
being able to find this horse.   I lent my horse to Yellept to surch
Capt. C's   about half an hour after he set out our Chopunnish man
brought up Capt. C's horse   we now determined to leave one man
to bring on my horse when Yellept returned and to proceed on with
the party   accordingly took leave of these friendly honest people
the Wollahwollahs and departed at 11 A.M. accompanyed by our
guide and the Chopunnish man and family.   we continued our rout
N.30.E. 14 ms. through an open level sandy plain   there are many
large banks of pure sand which appear to have been drifted up by
the wind to the hight of 15 to 20 feet, lying in many parts of the
plain through which we passed today.   this plain as usual is covered
with arromatic shrubs hurbatious plants and a short grass.   many of
those plants produce those esculent roots which form a principal
part of the subsistence of the natives.   among others there is one
which produces a root somewhat like the sweet pittaitoe.   we encamped at the place we intersepted the creek[27] where we had the
pleasure once more to find an abundance of good wood for the
purpose of making ourselves comfortable fires, which has not been
the case since we left rockfort camp.

[27] On the Touchet River, east of Wallula and west of Walla Walla, Washington.

Thursday May 1st. 1806.

some time after he had encamped, three young men arrived from the Wallahwollah village bringing with them a steel trap belonging to one of our party which had been neglegently left behind; this is an act of integrity rarely witnessed among indians. during our stay with them they several times found the knives of the men which had been carelessly lossed by them and returned them. I think we can justly affirm to the honor of these people that they are the most hospitable, honest, and sincere people that we have met with in our voyage.

Friday May 2ed. 1806.

I observed considerable quantities of the quâmash in the bottoms through which we passed this evening now in blume. there is much appearance of beaver and otter among these creeks. saw two deer at a distance; also observed many sandhill crains Curloos and other fowls common to the plains. the soil appears to improve as we advance on this road. our hunters killed a duck only. the three young men of the Wallahwollah nation continued with us. in the course of the day I observed them eat the inner part of the young and succulent stem of a large coarse plant with a ternate leaf, the leafets of which are three loabed and covered with a woolly pubersence. the flower and fructification resembles that of the parsnip this plant is very common in the rich lands on the Ohio and it's branches the Mississippi &c. I tasted of this plant found it agreeable and eat heartily of it without feeling any inconvenience.[28]

[Clark]   Sunday, May 4th. 1806.

a Great portion of the Chopunnish we are informed are now distributed in small Villages through this plain Collecting the *Cowse*[29] a white meley root which is very fine in soup after being dried and pounded; the Salmon not yet haveing arived to call them to the river. The hills of the Creek which we decended this morning are high and in most parts rocky and abrupt. one of our pack horses

[28] *Heracleum lanatum* (Piper), or cow parsnip.
[29] Cous (*Lomatium cous*), a species of biscuitroot.

sliped from one of those hights and fell into the Creek with it's load consisting principally of amunition, but fortunately neither the horse nor load suffered any material injury. the amunition being secured in canisters the water did not effect it. after dinner we continued our rout up the West Side of the river 3 ms opposit 2 Lodges the one containing 3 and the other 2 families of the Chopunnish Nation; here we met with *Te-toh-ar-sky* the oldest of the two Chiefs who accompanied us last fall to the Great falls of the Columbia. here we also met with our old pilot who decended the river with us as low as the Columbia these indians recommended our passing the river [30] at this place and going up on the N E Side of the Kooskoske. they sayed it was nearer and a better rout to the forks of that river where the twisted hair resided in whose charge we had left our horses; thither they promised to conduct us.

we determined to take the advise of the indians and imediately prepared to pass the river which with the assistance of three indian canoes we effected in the course of the evening, purchased a little wood, some *Cows* bread and encamped, haveing traveled *15* miles to day only. We-ark-koomt whose people reside on the West Side of Lewis's river above left us when we deturmined to pass the river. before he left us he expressed his concern that his people would be deprived of the pleasure of seeing us at the forks at which place they had assembled to shew us sivilities &c. I gave him a small piece of tobacco and he went off satisfied. the evening was cold and disagreeable, and the nativs crouded about our fire in great numbers in so much that we could scercely cook or keep ourselves worm. at all those Lodges of the Chopunnish I observe an appen-dage of a small lodge with one fire, which seames to be the retreat of their women in a certain situation. the men are not permited to approach this Lodge within a certain distance, and if they have any thing to convey to the occupents of this little hospital they stand at the distance of 50 or 60 paces and throw it towards them as far as they can and retire.

[Lewis]   Monday May 5th. 1806.
     we passed an indian man [who] gave Capt. C. a very eligant grey mare for which he requested a phial of eyewater which was accord-

---

[30] Snake River, south of Clarkston, Washington.

ingly given him. while we were encamped last fall at the entrance
of the Chopunnish river Capt. C. gave an indian man some volitile
linniment to rub his k[n]ee and thye for a pain of which he complained, the fellow soon after recovered and has never ceased to
extol the virtues of our medicines and the skill of my friend Capt.
C. as a phisician. this occurrence added to the benefit which many
of them experienced from the eyewater we gave them about the
same time has given them an exalted opinion of our medicine. my
friend Capt. C. is their favorite phisician and has already received
many applications. in our present situation I think it pardonable
to continue this deseption for they will not give us any provision
without compensation in merchandize and our stock is now reduced
to a mere handfull. We take care to give them no article which can
possibly injure them.

while at dinner an indian fellow verry impertinently threw a poor
half starved puppy nearly into my plait by way of derision for our
eating dogs and laughed very heartily at his own impertinence; I
was so provoked at his insolence that I caught the puppy and th[r]ew
it with great violence at him and stru[c]k him in the breast and face,
siezed my tomahawk and shewed him by signs if he repeated his
insolence I would tommahawk him, the fellow withdrew apparently
much mortifyed and I continued my repast *on dog* without further
molestation.

after dinner we continued our rout 4 miles to the entrance of
Colter's Creek[31] about ½ a mile above the rapid where we sunk the
1st. canoe as we decended the river last fall. we encamped on
the lower side of this creek at a little distance from two lodges of
the Chopunnish nation having traveled *20½ Ms.* today. one of these
lodges contained eight families the other was much the largest we
have yet seen. it is 156 feet long and about 15 wide built of mats
and straw. in the form of the roof of a house having a number of
small doors on each side, is closed at the ends and without divisions
in the intermediate space this lodge contained at least 30 families.
their fires are kindled in a row in the center of the house and about
10 feet assunder. all the lodges of these people are formed in this
manner.

[31] The junction of the Potlatch and Clearwater, east of Lewiston, Idaho.

we arrived here extreemly hungry and much fatiegued, but no articles of merchandize in our possession would induce them to let us have any article of provision except a small quantity of bread of *cows* and some of those roots dryed.   we had several applications to assist their sick which we refused unless they would let us have some dogs or horses to eat.   a man [*Chief*] whose wife had an absess formed on the small of her back promised a horse in the morning provided we would administer to her accordingly Capt. C. opened the absess introduced a tent and dressed it with basilicon; [*Capt. C soon had more than 50 applications*]   I prepared some dozes of the flour of sulpher and creem of tarter which were given with directions to be taken on each morning.   a little girl and sundry other patients were offered for cure but we postponed our operations untill morning; they produced us several dogs but they were so poor that they were unfit for use.

We-ark-koomt rejoined us this evening.   this man has been of infinite service to us on several former occasions and through him we now offered our address to the natives.

Wednesday May 7th. 1806.
The Spurs of the Rocky Mountains which were in view from the high plain today were perfectly covered with snow.   the Indians inform us that the snow is yet so deep on the mountains that we shall not be able to pass them untill the next full moon or about the first of June; others set the time at still a more distant period. this [is] unwelcom inteligence to men confined to a diet of horsebeef and roots, and who are as anxious as we are to return to the fat plains of the Missouri and thence to our native homes.

Friday May 9th. 1806.
our rout lay through a level rich country similar to that of yesterday[32]; at the distance of 6 miles we arrived at the lodge of the twisted hair; this habitation was built in the usual form with sticks mats and dryed hay, and contained 2 fir[e]s and about 12 persons. even at this small habitation there was an appendage of the soletary lodge, the retreat of the tawney damsels when nature causes them

[32] Camas Prairie, Idaho.

to be driven into coventry; here we halted as had been previously concerted, and one man with 2 horses accompa[n]yed the twisted hair to the canoe camp,[33] about 4 ms. in quest of the saddles. the Twisted hair sent two young men in surch of our horses agreeably to his promis.

The country along the rocky mountains for several hundred miles in length and about 50 in width is level extreemly fertile and in many parts covered with a tall and open growth of the longleafed pine,[34] near the watercourses the hills are steep and lofty tho' [they] are covered with a good soil not remarkably stony and possess more timber than the level country, the bottom lands on the water-cou[r]ses are reather narrow and confined tho' fertile & seldom in-undated. this country would form an extensive settlement; the climate appears quite as mild as that of similar latitude on the Atlantic coast if not more so and it cannot be otherwise than healthy; it possesses a fine dry pure air. the grass and many plants are now upwards of knee high.

I have no doubt but this tract of country if cultivated would produce in great abundance every article essentially necessary to the comfort and subsistence of civillized man. to it's present inhabitants nature seems to have dealt with a liberal hand, for she has distributed a great variety of esculent plants over the face of the country which furnish them a plentifull store of provision; these are acquired with but little toil, when prepared after the method of the natives afford not only a nutricious but an agreeable food. among other roots those called by them the quawmash and Cows are esteemed the most agreeable and valuable as they are also the most abundant. the *cows* is a knobbed root of an irregularly rounded form not unlike the gensang in form and consistence. this root they collect, rub of[f] a thin black rhind which covers it and pounding it expose it in cakes to the sun. these cakes are about an inch and ¼ thick and 6 by 18 in width, when dryed they either eat this bread alone without any further preperation, or boil it and make a thick musilage; the latter is most common and much the most agreeable. the flavor of

---

[33] Referring to the camp made by the explorers at the forks of the Clearwater, September 26, 1805 (Thwaites).

[34] Ponderosa pine (*Pinus ponderosa*).

this root is not very unlike the gensang. this root they collect as early as the snows disappear in the spring and continue to collect it untill the quawmash supplys it's place which happens about the latter end of June. the quawmash is also collected for a few weaks after it first makes it's appearance in the spring, but when the scape appears it is no longer fit for use untill the seed are ripe which happens about the time just mentioned, and then the cows declines. the latter is also frequently dryed in the sun and pounded afterwards and then used in making soope. I observed a few trees of the larch and a few small bushes of the balsam fir near the lodge of the Twisted hair.

Saturday May 10th. 1806.

in the afternoon we decended the hills to Commearp Creek[35] and arrived at the Village of Tunnachemootoolt,[36] the cheif at whos lodge we had left the flag last fall. this flag was now displayed on a staff placed at no great distance from the lodge. underneath the flag the Cheif met my friend Capt. C. who was in front and conducted him about 80 yds. to a place on the bank of the creek where he requested we should encamp; I came up in a few minutes and we collected the Cheifs and men of consideration smoked with them and stated our situation with rispect to provision. the Cheif spoke to his people and they produced us about 2 bushels of the quawmas roots dryed, four cakes of the bread of *cows* and a dryed salmon trout.

we thanked them for this store of provision but informed them that our men not being accustomed to live on roots alone we feared it would make them sick, to obviate which we proposed exchangeing a horse in reather low order for a young horse in tolerable order with a view to kill. the hospitality of the cheif revolted at the eydea of an exchange, he told us that his young men had a great abundance of young horses and if we wished to eat them we should by [be] furnished with as many as we wanted. accordingly they soon produced us two fat young horses one of which we killed, the other we informed them we would pospone killing untill we had consumed the one already killed.

[35] This creek is sometimes called Kamai or Kamiah, but is generally known as Lawyer's Canyon Creek (Thwaites).

[36] Of the Nez Perce.

This is a much greater act of hospitality than we have witnessed from any nation or tribe since we have passed the Rocky mountains. in short be it spoken to their immortal honor it is the only act which deserves the appellation of hospitallity which we have witnessed in this quarter. we in formed these people that we were hungry and fatiegued at this moment, that when we had eaten and refreshed ourselves we would inform them who we were, from whence we had come and the objects of our resurches.

a principal Cheif by name Ho-hâst-ill-pilp arrived with a party of fifty men mounted on eligant horses. he had come on a visit to us from his village which is situated about six miles distant near the river. we invited this man into our circle and smoked with him, his retinue continued on horseback at a little distance. after we had eaten a few roots we spoke to them as we had promised, and gave Tinnachemootoolt and Hohâstillpilp each a medal; the former one of the small size with the likeness of Mr. Jefferson and the latter one of the sewing medals[37] struck in the presidency of Washington. we explained to them the desighn and the importance of medals in the estimation of the whites as well as the red men who had been taught their value. The Cheif had a large conic lodge of leather erected for our reception and a parsel of wood collected and laïd at the door after which he invited Capt. C. and myself to make that lodge our home while we remained with him. we had a fire lighted in this lodge and retired to it accompanyed by the Cheifs and as many of the considerate [considerable] men as could croud in a circcle within it. here after we had taken a repast on some horsebeef we resumed our council with the indians which together with smoking the pipe occupyed the ballance of the evening.

as these people had been liberal with us with rispect to provision I directed the men not to croud their lodge [in] surch of food in the manner hunger has compelled them to do at most lodges we have passed, and which the Twisted hair had informed me was disgreeable to the natives. but their previous want of hospitality had induced us to consult their enclinations but little and suffer our men to obtain provision from them on the best terms they could. the

[37] I. e., "sowing"—referring to the design on the "third-class" medal of a farmer sowing grain (Thwaites).

noise of their women pounding roots reminds me of a nail factory. The indians seem well pleased, and I am confident that they are not more so than our men who have their s[t]omachs once more well filled with horsebeef and mush of the bread of cows. the house of coventry is also seen here.

Monday May 12th 1806.

The indians formed themselves this evening into two large parties and began to gamble for their beads and other ornaments. the game at which they played was that of hiding a stick in their hands which they frequently changed accompanying their operations with a song. this game seems common to all the nations in this country, and dose not differ from that before discribed of the Shoshonees on the S.E. branch of Lewis's river.

we are anxious to procure some guides to accompany us on the different routs we mean to take from Travellers rest; for this purpose we have turned our attention to the Twisted hair who has several sons grown who are well acquainted as well as himself with the various roads in those mountains. we invited the old fellow to remove his family and live near us while we remained; he appeared gratifyed with this expression of our confidence and promised to do so. shot at a mark with the indians, struck the mark with 2 balls distce. 200 yds.

[Clark]   Monday 12th: May 1806

a fine morning   great numbers of Indians flock about us as usial. after brackfast I began to administer eye water and in a fiew minits had near 40 applicants with sore eyes, and maney others with other complaints most common Rhumatic disorders & weaknesses in the back and loins perticularly the womin. the Indians had a grand Council this morning after which we were presented each with a horse by two young men at the instance of the nation. we caused the chiefs to be seated and gave them each a flag a pint of Powder and 50 balls to the two young men who had presented the horses we also gave powder and ball. The broken arm or Tunnachemootoolt pulled off his leather shirt and gave me. In return gave him a shirt. We retired into the Lodge and the natives spoke to the following purpote, i.e. they had listened to our advice and that the whole nation were deturmined to follow it, that they had only one

heart and one tongue on this subject.   explained the cause of the
War with the *Shoshones.*   they wished to be at peace with all nations
&c.   Some of their men would accompany us to the Missouri &c.
&c.   as a great number of men women & children wre wateing and
requesting medical assistance maney of them with the most simple
coomplaints which could be easily releieved, independent of maney
with disorders intirely out of the power of Medison all requesting
something, we agreed that I should administer and Capt L to here
and answer the Indians.   I was closely employed untill 2 P.M.
administering eye water to about 40 grown persons. some simple
cooling medicenes to the disabled Chief, to several women with
rhumatic effections & a man who had a swelled hip, &c. &c.

[Lewis]   Wednesday May 14th. 1806.
   we arrose early and dispatched a few of our hunters to the opposite
side of the river, and employed a part of the men in transporting
our baggage to the opposite shore wile others were directed to collect
the horses; at 10 A.M. we had taken our baggage over and collected
our horses, we then took breakfast, after which we drove our horses
into the river which they swam without accedent and all arrived safe
on the opposite shore.   the river is 150 yds. wide at this place and
extreemly rapid. tho' it may be safely navigated at this season, as
the water covers all the rocks which lie in it's bed to a considerable
debth.   we followed our horses and again collected them, after which
we removed our baggage to a position which we had previously
selected for our permanent camp about half a mile below.[38]   this
was a very eligible spot for defence it had been an ancient habitation
of the indians; was sunk about 4 feet in the ground and raised around
it's outer edge about three ½ feet with a good wall of ea[r]th, the
whole was a circle of about 30 feet in diameter. arround this we
formed our tents of sticks and grass facing outwards and deposited
our baggage within the sunken space under a shelter which we
constructed for the purpose.   our situation was within 40 paces of
the river in an extentsive level bottom thinly timbered with the
longleafed pine.   here we are in the vicinity of the best hunting
grounds from indian information, are convenient to the salmon which

[38] On the east bank of the Clearwater, nearly opposite the town of Kamiah, Idaho.

we expect daily and have an excellent pasture for our horses. the hills to the E and North of us are high broken and but partially timbered; the soil is rich and affords fine grass. in short as we are compelled to reside a while in this neighbourhood I feel perfectly satisfyed with our position.[39]

immediately after we had passed the river Tunnachemootoolt and Hohâstillpilp arrived on the south side with a party of a douzen of their young men; they began to sing in token of friendship as is their custom, and we sent the canoe over for them. they left their horses and came over accompanyed by several of their party we received them at our camp and smoked with them; after some hours Hohâstillpilp with much cerimony presented me with a very eligant grey gelding which he had brought for that purpose. I gave him in return a handkercheif 200 balls and 4 lbs. of powder. with which he appeared perfectly satisfyed.

Collins killed two bear this morning and was sent with two others in quest of the meat; with which they returned in the evening; the mail bear was large and fat the female was of moderate size and reather meagre. we had the fat bear fleaced in order to reserve the oil for the mountains. both these bear were of the speceis common to the upper part of the missouri they may be called white black grizly brown or red bear for they are found of all those colours. perhaps it would not be unappropriate to designate them the variagated bear. we gave the indians who were about 15 in number half the female bear, with the sholder head and neck of the other. this was a great treat to those poor wretches who scarcely taist meat once a month. they immediately prepared a brisk fire of dry wood on which they threw a parsel of smooth stones from the river, when the fire had birnt down and heated the stones they placed them level and laid on a parsel of pine boughs, on these they laid the flesh of the bear in flitches, placing boughs between each course of meat and then covering it thickly with pine boughs; after this they poared on a small quantity of water and covered the who[l]e over

---

[39] The expedition remained in this camp longer than at any other place upon the route, except at Forts Mandan and Clatsop. By analogy it is usually spoken of as Camp Chopunnish, but there is no evidence that the explorers gave it that title (Thwaites).

with earth to the debth of four inches. in this situation they suffered it to remain about 3 hours when they took it out. I taisted of this meat and found it much more tender than that which we had roasted or boiled, but the strong flavor of the pine distroyed it for my pallate.

we have found our stonehorses [stallions] so troublesome that we indeavoured to exchange them with the Chopunnish for mears or gel[d]ings but they will not excha[n]ge altho' we offer 2 for one, we came to a resolution to castrate them and began the operation this evening one of the indians present offered his services on this occasion. he cut them without tying the string of the stone as is usual, and assures us that they will do much better in that way; he takes care to scrape the string very clean and to seperate it from all the adhereing veigns before he cuts it. we shall have an opportunity of judging whether this is a method preferable to that commonly practiced as Drewyer has gelded two in the usual way.

The indians after their feast took a pipe or two with us and retired to rest much pleased with their repast. these bear are tremendious animals to them; they esteem the act of killing a bear equally great with that of an enimy in the field of action. I gave the claws of those which Collins killed to Hohâstillpilp.

[Clark] Wednesday 14th. of May 1806.

after we had crossed the river the Chief called the broken arm or *Tin-nach-e-moo-tolt* another principal Chief *Koh-hâst-'ill-pilp* arived on the opposite side and began to sing. we sent the canoe over and those chiefs, the son of the broken arm and the son of a Great Chief who was killed last year by the Big bellies of Saskasshewin river. those two young men were the two whome gave Capt Lewis and my self each a horse with great serimony in behalf of the nation a fiew days ago, and the latter a most elligant mare & colt the morning after we arived at the village. Hohâstillpilp with much serimoney presented Capt Lewis with an elegant Gray horse which he had brought for that purpose. Capt Lewis gave him in return a Handkerchief two hundred balls and four pounds of powder, with which he appeared perfectly satisfied, and appeared much pleased.

Soon after I had crossed the river and during the time Cap Lewis was on the opposit side John Collins whome we had sent out verry early this morning with Labiech and Shannon on the North Side of the river to hunt, came in and informed me, that he had killed two

Bear at about 5 miles distant on the uplands, one of which was in good order. I imediately de[s]patched Jo. Fields. & P. Wiser with him for the flesh.

we made several attempts to exchange our Stalions for Geldin[g]s or mar[e]s without success   we even offered two for one.   those horses are troublesom and cut each other very much and as we can't exchange them we think it best to *castrate* them and began the opperation this evening   one of the indians present offered his services on this occasion.   he cut them without tying the string of the stone as is usial.   he [s]raped it very clean & seperate it before he cut it.

Collins returned in the evening with the two bears which he had killed in the morning one of them an old hee was in fine order, the other a female with Cubs was meagure. we gave the Indians about us 15 in number two sholders and a ham of the bear to eate which they cooked in the following manner. towit on a brisk fire of dryed wood they threw a parcel of small stones from the river, when the fire had burnt down and heated the stone, they placed them level and laid on a parsel of pine boughs, on those they laid the flesh of the bear in flitches, placeing boughs between each course of meat and then covering it thickly with pine boughs; after this they poared on a small quantity of water, and covered the whole over with earth to the debth of 4 inches.   in this situation they suffered it to remain about 3 hours when they took it out fit for use.

This nation esteem the Killing of one of those tremendeous animals (the Bear) equally great with that of an enemy in the field of action.   we gave the claws of those bear which Collins had killed to Hohâstillpilp.

[Lewis]   Saturday May 17th. 1806.
   it rained moderately the greater part of the day and snowed as usual on the plain. Sergt. Pryor informed me that it was shoe deep this morning when he came down.   it is somewhat astonishing that the grass and a variety of plants which are now from a foot to 18 inches high on these plains sustain no injury from the snow or frost; many of those plants are in blume and appear to be of a tender susceptable texture.   we have been visited by no indians today, an occurrence which has not taken place before since we left the Narrows of the Columbia.   I am pleased at finding the river rise so

rapidly, it now doubt is attributeable to the me[l]ting snows of the mountains; that icy barier which seperates me from my friends and Country, from all which makes life esteemable.—patience, patience

[Clark]   Saturday 17th: May 1806
I frequently consult the nativs on the subject of passing this tremendious barier which now present themselves to our view for [a] great extent.   they all appear to agree as to the time those mountains may be passed which is about the middle of *June*.   At the distance of 18 miles from the river and on the Eastern border of the high Plain the Rocky Mountain commences and presents us with *Winter* here we have Summer, Spring and winter in the short space of twenty or thirty miles.

[Lewis]   Thursday May 22nd. 1806.
Charbono's Child is very ill this evening; he is cuting teeth, and for several days past has had a violent lax, which having suddonly stoped he was attacked with a high fever and his neck and throat are much swolen this evening. we gave him a doze of creem of tartar and flour of sulpher and applyed a poltice of boiled onions to his neck as warm as he could well bear it.

                                                  Friday May 23rd. 1806.
at noon we were visited by 4 indians who informed us they had come from their village on Lewis's river at the distance of two days ride in order to see us and obtain a little eyewater,   Capt. C. washed their eyes and they set out on their return to their village.   our skill as phisicians and the virtue of our medicines have been spread it seems to a great distance.   I sincerely wish it was in our power to give releif to these poor aff[l]icted wretches.
at 1. P.M. Shannon, Colter, Labuish, Cruzatte, Collins, and LaPage returned from hunting without having killed anything except a few pheasants of the dark brown kind, which they brought with them.   These hunters informed us that they had hunted the country deligently betwen the river and Creek for some distance above and below our camp and that there was no game to be found.
all the horses which have been castrated except my poor unfortunate horse appear as if they would do very well.   I am convinced that those cut by the indians will get well much soonest and they

do not swell nor appear to suffer as much as those cut in the common way.

[Clark]   Friday 23rd. May 1806
The child is something better this morning   we apply a fresh poltice of the wild Onion which we repeeted twice in the course of the day.   the swelling does not appear to increas any since yesterday. The 4 Indians who visited us to day informed us that they came from their village on Lewis's river two days ride from this place for the purpose of seeing of us and getting a little eye water   I washed their eyes with some eye water and they all left us at 2 P. M. and returned to the villages on the opposit side of this river.

the hunters informed us that they had hunted with great industry all the country between the river and for some distance above and below without the smallest chance of killing any game.   they inform us that the high lands are very cold with snow which has fallen for every day or night for several [days] past.   our horses which was cut is like to doe well.

[Lewis]   Saturday May 24th. 1806.
The child was very wrestless last night; it's jaw and the back of it's neck are much more swolen than they were yesterday tho' his fever has abated considerably.   we gave it a doze of creem of tartar and applyed a fresh poltice of onions.   we ordered some of the hunters out this morning and directed them to pass Collins's creek if possible and hunt towards the quawmash feilds.   William Bratton still continues very unwell; he eats heartily digests his food well, and has recovered his flesh almost perfectly yet is so weak in the loins that he is scarcely able to walk, nor can he set upwright but with the greatest pain.   we have tried every remidy which our engenuity could devise, or with which our stock of medicines furnished us, without effect.

John Sheilds observed that he had seen men in a similar situation restored by violent sweats.   Bratton requested that he might be sweated in the manner proposed by Sheilds to which we consented. Sheilds sunk a circular hole of 3 feet diamiter and four feet deep in the earth.   he kindled a large fire in the hole and heated well, after which the fire was taken out a seat placed in the center of the hole for the patient with a board at bottom for his feet to rest on; some

hoops of willow poles were bent in an arch crossing each other over
the hole, on these several blankets were thrown forming a secure
and thick orning of about 3 feet high.

the patient being striped naked was seated under this orning in
the hole and the blankets well secured on every side. the patient
was furnished with a vessell of water which he sprinkles on the
bottom and sides of the hole and by that means creates as much
steam or vapor as he could possibly bear, in this situation he was
kept about 20 minutes after which he was taken out and suddonly
plunged in cold water twise and was then immediately returned to
the sweat hole where he was continued three quarters of an hour
longer then taken out covered up in several blankets and suffered
to cool gradually. during the time of his being in the sweat hole,
he drank copious draughts of a strong tea of horse mint. Sheilds
says that he had previously seen the tea of Sinneca snake root used
in stead of the mint which was now employed for the want of the
other which is not to be found in this country. this experiment was
made yesterday; Bratton feels himself much better and is walking
about today and says he is nearly free from pain.

[Clark]   Saturday 24th. May 1806
at 11 A.M. a canoe came down with the Indian man who had
applyed for medical assistance while we lay at the broken arms
village. this man I had given a fiew doses of Flower of Sulphur &
creme of Tarter and derected that he should take the Cold bath
every morning. he conceited himself a little better than he was at
that time. he had lost the use of all his limbs and his fingers are
contracted. We are at a loss to deturmine what to do for this unfortunate man. I gave him a fiew drops of Lodmen and some portable
Supe as medisine.

[Lewis]   Sunday May 25th. 1806.
we caused a sweat to be prepared for the indian Cheif in the same
manner in which Bratton had been sweated, this we attempted but
were unable to succeed, as he was unable to set up or be supported
in the place. we informed the indians that we knew of no releif
for him except sweating him in their sweat houses and giving him
a plenty of the tea of the horse mint which we shewed them. and
that this would probably not succeed as he had been so long in his

present situation. I am confident that this would be an excellent
subject for electricity and much regret that I have it not in my power
to supply it.

Charbono's son is much better today, tho' the swelling on the
side of his neck I beleive will terminate in an ugly imposthume a
little below the ear.   the indians were so anxious that the sick Cheif
should be sweated under our inspection that they requested we
would make a second atte[m]pt today; accordingly the hole was
somewhat enlarged and his father a very good looking old man, went
into the hole with him and sustained him in a proper position during
the operation; we could not make him sweat as copiously as we
wished. after the operation he complained of considerable pain, we
gave him 30 drops of laudanum which soon composed him and he
rested very well.   this is at least a strong mark of parental affection.
they all appear extreemly attentive to this sick man nor do they
appear to relax in their asciduity towards him notwithstand[ing] he
has been sick and helpless upwards of three years.   the Chopunnish
appear to be very attentive and kind to their aged people and treat
their women with more rispect than the nations of the Missouri.

There is a speceis of Burrowing squirel common in these plains
which in their habits somewhat resemble those of the missouri but
are a distinct speceis.[40]   this little animal measures one fo[o]t five
and ½ inches from the nose to the extremity of the tail, of which
the tail occupys 2-¼ inches only; in the girth it is 11 In. the body
is proportionably long, the neck and legs short; the ears are short,
obtusely pointed, and lie close to the head; the aperture of the ear
is larger proportionably than most animals which burrow.   the eyes
are of moderate size, the puple black and iris of a dark sooty brown.
the teeth are like those of the squirel as is it's whole contour.   the
whiskers are full, long and black; it also has some long black hairs
above the eyes.   it has five toes on each foot; the two inner toes of
the fore feet are remarkably short, and have short blont nails.   the
remaining toes on those feet are long, black, slightly curved and
sharply pointed.   the outer and inner toes of the hind feet are not
short yet they are by no means as long as the three toes in the center
of the foot which are remarkably long but the nails are not as long

[40] Columbian ground squirrel (*Citellus columbianus*).

as those of the fore feet tho' of the same form and colour. the hair of the tail tho' thickly inserted on every part rispects the two sides only. this gives it a flat appearance and a long oval form. the tips of the hair which form the outer edges of the tail are white. the base of the hairs are either black or a fox red. the under disk of the tail is an iron grey, the upper a redish brown. the lower part of the jaws, under part of the neck, legs and feet from the body down and belley are of a light brick red. the nose as high as the eyes is of a darker brick red. the upper part of the head neck and body are of a curious brownish grey colour with a cast of the brick red. the longer hair of these parts being of a redish white colour at their extremities, fall togther in such manner as to give it the appearance of being speckled at a little distance. these animals form large ascociations as those of the Missouri, occupying with their burroughs one or sometimes 200 acres of land. the burrows are seperate and are each occupyed perhaps by ten or 12 of those animals. there is a little mound in front of the hole formed of the earth thrown out of the burrow and frequently there are three or four distinct holes forming what I term one burrow with their mouths arround the base of this little mound which seems to be occupied as a watch-tower in common by the inhabitants of those several holes. these mounds are sometimes as much as 2 feet high and 4 feet in diameter, and are irregularly distributed over the tract they occupy at the distance of from ten to thirty or 40 yds. when you approach a burrow the squirrels, one or more, usually set erect on these mounds and make a kind of shrill whistleing nois, something like *tweet, tweet, tweet,* &c. they do not live on grass as those of the missouri but on roots. one which I examined had in his mouth two small bulbs of a speceis of grass, which resemble very much what is sometimes called the grass-nut. the intestins of those little animals are remarkably large for it's size. fur short and very fine. the grass in their villages is not cut down as in those of the plains of the missouri. I preserved the skins of several of these animals with the heads feet and legs entire.

The Black woodpecker[41] which I have frequently mentioned and which is found in most parts of the roky Mountains as well as the

[41] Lewis' woodpecker (*Melanerpes lewis*).

Western and S. W. mountains, I had never an opportunity of examining untill a few days since when we killed and preserved several of them. this bird is about the size of the lark woodpecker or the turtle dove, tho' it's wings are longer than either of those birds. the beak is black, one inch long, reather wide at the base, somewhat curved, and sharply pointed; the chaps are of equal length. around the base of the beak including the eye and a small part of the throat is of a fine crimson red. the neck and as low as the croop in front is of an iron grey. the belly and breast is a curious mixture of white and blood reed which has much the appearance of having been artificially painted or stained of that colour. the red reather predominates. the top of the head back, sides, upper surface of the wings and tail are black, with a g[l]ossey tint of green in a certain exposure to the light. the under side of the wings and tail are of a sooty black. it has ten feathers in the tail, sharply pointed, and those in the centre reather longest, being 2-½ inches in length. the tongue is barbed, pointed, and of an elastic cartelaginous substance. the eye is moderately large, puple black and iris of a dark yellowish brown. this bird in it's actions when flying resembles the small redheaded woodpecke[r] common to the Atlantic states; it's note also somewhat resembles that bird. the pointed tail seems to assist it in seting with more eas or retaining it its resting position against the perpendicular side of a tree. the legs and feet are black and covered with wide imbricated scales. it has four toes on each foot of which two are in rear and two in front; the nails are much curved long and remarkably keen or sharply pointed. it feeds on bugs worms and a variety of insects.

[Clark]   Tuesday 27th. May 1806.

  The Indians were so anxious that the sick Chief (who has lost the use of his limbs) should be sweted under our inspection they requested me to make a 2d. attempt to day; accordingly the hole was enlarged and his father a very good looking old man performed all the drugery &c. we could not make him swet as copously as we wished, being compelled to keep him erect in the hole by means of cords. after the oppiration he complained of considerable pain, I gave him 30 drops of Laudnom which soon composed him and he rested very well. I observe the strongest marks of parental affection. they all appear extreemly attentive to this sick man, nor do they appear to relax in their ascituity towards him notwithstanding he has been sick and helpless for near 5 years. The Chopunnish appeare to be very attentive & kind to their aged people and treat their women with more respect than the nativs on the Missouri.[42]

[Lewis]   Wednesday May 28th. 1806

The sick Cheif was much better this morning he can use his hands and arms and seems much pleased with the prospect of recovering, he says he feels much better than he has for a great number of months. I sincerely wish these sweats may restore him; we have consented that he should still remain with us and repeat these sweats. he set up a great proportion of the day. The Child is also better, he is free of fever, the imposthume is not so large but seems to be advancing to maturity.

since my arrival here I have killed several birds of the *corvus* genus of a kind found only in the rocky mountains and their neighbour-hood.[43] I first met with this bird above the three forks of the Missouri and saw them on the hights of the rocky Mountains but never before had an opportunity of examining them closely. the small *corvus* discribed at Fort Clatsop is a different speceis, tho' untill now I had taken it to be the same, this is much larger and has a loud squawling note something like the mewing of a cat. the beak of this bird is 1-½ inches long, is proportionably large, black and of the form which characterizes this genus. the upper exceeds the under chap a little. the head and neck are also proportionably large. the eye full and reather prominent, the iris dark brown and puple black. it is about the size and somewhat the form of the Jaybird tho reather rounder or more full in the body. the tail is four and a half inches in length, composed of 12 feathers nearly of the same length. the head neck and body of this bird are of a dove colour. the wings are black except the extremities of six large f[e]athers occupying the middle joint of the wing which are white. the under disk of the wing is not of the shining or gr[l]ossy black which marks its upper surface. the two feathers in the center of

---

[42] Although Clark here repeats Lewis's account, he alters pronouns to differentiate his role in the treatment of the chief. Compare the alteration of pronouns in Clark's entries for April 24 and May 14, 1806.

[43] Clark's nutcracker (*Nucifraga columbiana*).

the tail are black as are the two adjacent feathers for half their width the ballance are of a pure white. the feet and legs are black and imbricated with wide scales. the nails are black and remarkably long and sharp, also much curved. it has four toes on each foot of which one is in the rear and three in front. the toes are long particularly that in the rear. This bird feeds on the seed of the pine and also on insects. it resides in the rocky mountains at all seasons of the year, and in many parts is the only bird to be found.

[Clark]   Wednesday May 28th. 1806
    The Sick Chief is much better this morning he can use his hands and arms and seems much pleased with the prospects of recovering, he says he feels much better than he has done for a great number of months.   I sincerly wish that the swetts may restore him.   I have consented to repeet the sweets.

[Lewis]   Thursday May 29th. 1806.
    Bratton is recovering his strength very fast; the Child and the Indian Cheif are also on the recovery. the cheif has much more uce of his hands and arms. he washed his face himself today which he has been unable to do previously for more than twelve months. we would have repeated the sweat today had [it] not been cloudy and frequently rainy,
    a speceis of Lizzard called by the French engages prarie buffaloe are nativ of these plains as well as of those of the Missouri. I have called them the horned Lizzard. they are about the size and a good deel of the figure of the common black lizzard. but their bellies are broader, the tail shorter and their action much slower; they crawl much like the toad. they are of a brown colour with yellowish and yellowish brown spots. it is covered with minute scales intermixed with little horny prosesses like blont prickles on the upper surface of the body. the belly and throat is more like the frog and are of a light yelowish brown colour. arround the edge of the belley is regularly set with little horney projections which give to these edges a serrate figure the eye is small and of a dark colour. above and behind the eyes there are several projections of the bone which being armed at their extremities with a firm black substance has the appearance of horns sprouting out from the head. this part has induced me to distinguish it by the appellation of the *horned Liz-*

zard.[44] I cannot conceive how the engages ever assimilated this animal with the buffaloe for there is not greater analogy than between the horse and the frog. this animal is found in greatest numbers in the sandy open parts of the plains, and appear in great abundance after a shower of rain; they are sometimes found basking in the sunshine but conceal themselves in little holes in the earth much the greater proportion of their time. they are numerous about the falls of the Missouri and in the plains through which we past lately above the Wallahwallahs.

Friday May 30th. 1806

I sent Sergt. Pryor and a party over with the indian canoe in order to raise and secure ours but the debth of the water and the strength of the current baffled every effort. I fear that we have also lost our canoe. all our invalides are on the recovery. we gave the sick Cheif a severe sweat today, shortly after which he could move one of his legs and thyes and work his toes pretty well, the other leg he can move a little; his fingers and arms seem to be almost entirely restored. he seems highly delighted with his recovery. I began to entertain strong hope of his restoration by these sweats.

The reptiles which I have observed in this quarter are the Rattlesnake of the speceis discribed on the Missouri, they are abudant in every part of the country and are the only poisonous snake which we have yet met with since we left St. Louis. the 2 speceis of snakes of an inosent kind already discribed. the common black lizzard, the horned lizzard, a smal green tree-frog, the smal frog which is common to our country which sings in the spring of the year, a large speceis of frog which resorts the water considerably larger than our bull frog, it's shape seems to be a medium between the delicate and lengthy form of our bull frog and that of our land frog or toad as they are sometimes called in the U' States. like the latter their bodies are covered with little pustles or lumps, elivated above the ordinary surface of the body; I never heard them make any sound or noise. the mockerson snake coper head, a number of

---

[44] Short-horned lizard (*Phrynosoma douglassi*) which is "often, although erroneously, called 'horned frog' or 'horned toad.' The name 'prairie buffalo' no doubt arises from its horns, and the way it humps itself when irritated" (Thwaites).

vipers a variety of lizzard, the toad bull frog &c. common to the U'
States are not to be found in this country.

   most of the insects common to the U'States are found here. the
butterflies, common house and blowing flies the horse flies, except
the goald coloured ear fly, tho' in stead of this fly we have a brown
coloured fly about the same size which attaches itself to that part of
the horse and is equally troublesome. the silkworm is also found
here. a great variety of beatles common to the Atlantic states are
found here likewise. except from this order the large cow beatle
and the black beatle usually [c]alled the tumble bug which are not
found here. the hornet, the wasp and yellow wasp or yellow jacket
as they are frequently called are not met with in this quarter. there
is an insect which much resembles the latter only a vast deel larger
which are very numerous particularly in the rocky mountains on the
waters of the Columbia; these build in the ground where they form
a nest like the hornet with an outer covering to the comb in which
they deposit their eggs and raise their young. the sheets of this
comb are attatched to each other as those of the hornets are. their
wings are four of a dark brown colour. the head is black, the body
and abdomen are yellow incircled with transverse rings of black,
they are ferce and sting very severely, we found them troublesome
in frightening our horses as we passed those mountains. the honey
bee is not found here. the bumble bee is.

[Clark]   Friday May 30th. 1806
   I sent Serjt. Pryor and a party over in the Indian canoe in order
to raise and secure ours but the debth of the water and the strength
of the current baffled every effort. I fear that we have also lost our
canoe. all our invalides are on the recovery. we gave the sick Chief
a severe *Swet* to day, shortly after which he could move one of his
legs and thy's and work his toes pritty well, the other leg he can
move a little; his fingers and arms seem to be almost entirely restored. he seems highly delighted with his recovery. I begin to
entertain strong hope of his recovering by these sweats.[45]

   [45] Here Clark copies Lewis's account without distinguishing himself from his co-
commander.

[Lewis] Sunday June 1st. 1806.

This morning Drewyer accompanyed by Hohâstillpilp set out in surch of two tomahawks of ours which we have understood were in the possession of certain indians residing at a distance in the plains on the South side of the Kooskoske; the one is a tomahawk which Capt. C. left at our camp on Musquetoe Creek and the other was stolen from us while we lay at the forks of this and the Chopunnish rivers last fall.

we begin to feel some anxiety with rispect to Sergt. Ordway and party who were sent to Lewis's river for salmon; we have received no inteligence from them since they set out. we desired Drewyer to make some enquiry after the *Twisted hair;* the old man has not been as good as his word with rispect to encamping near us, and we fear we shall be at a loss to procure guides to conduct us by the different routs we wish to pursue from Traveller's rest to the waters of the Missouri.

I met with a singular plant today in blume of which I preserved a specemine; it grows on the steep sides of the fertile hills near this place, the radix is fibrous, not much branched, annual, woody, white and nearly smooth. the stem is simple branching ascending, [2-½ *feet high.*] celindric, villose and of a pale red colour. the branches are but few and those near it's upper extremity. the extremities of the branches are flexable and are bent downward near their extremities with the weight of the flowers. the leaf is sessile, scattered thinly, nearly linear tho' somewhat widest in the middle, two inches in length, absolutely entire, villose, obtusely pointed and of an ordinary green. above each leaf a small short branch protrudes, supporting a tissue of four or five smaller leaves of the same appearance with those discribed. a leaf is placed underneath ea[c]h branch, and each flower. the calyx is a one flowered spathe. the corolla superior consists of four pale perple petals which are tripartite, the central lobe largest and all terminate obtusely; they are inserted with a long and narrow claw on the top of the germ, are long, smooth, & deciduous. there are two distinct sets of stamens, the 1st. or principal consists of four, the filaments of which are capillary, erect, inserted on the top of the germ alternately with the petals, equal, short, membranous; the anthers are also four each being elivated with it's fillament, they are linear and reather flat, erect, sessile, cohering at the base, membranous, longitudinally furrowed, twice as long as the fillament naked, and of a pale perple colour. the second set of stamens are very minute are also four and placed within and opposite to the petals, these are scarcely persceptable while the 1st are large and conspicuous; the filaments are capillary equal, very short, white and smooth. the anthers are four, oblong, beaked, erect, cohering at the base, membranous, shorter than the fillaments, white naked and appear not to form pollen, there is one pistillum; the germ of which is also one, cilindric, villous, inferior, sessile, as long as the 1st. stamens & marked with 8 longitudinal furrows. the single style and stigma form a perfect monapetallous corolla only with this difference, that the style which elivates the stigma or limb is not a tube but solid tho' it's outer appearance is that of the tube of a monopetallous corolla swelling as it ascends and gliding in such manner into the limb that it cannot be said where the style ends, or the stigma begins; jointly they are as long as the corolla, white, the limb is four cleft, sauser shaped, and the margins of the lobes entire and rounded. this has the appearance of a monopetallous flower growing from the center of a four petalled corollar, which is rendered more conspicuous in consequence of the 1st. being white and the latter of a pale perple. I regret very much that the seed of this plant are not yet ripe and it is pro[ba]ble will not be so during my residence in this neighbourhood.[46]

Monday June 2ed. 1806.

McNeal and York were sent on a trading voyage over the river this morning. having exhausted all our merchandize we are obliged to have recourse to every subterfuge in order to prepare in the most ample manner in our power to meet that wretched portion of our journy, the Rocky Mountains, where hungar and cold in their most rigorous forms assail the w[e]aried traveller; not any of us have yet forgotten our suffering in those mountains in September last, and I think it probable we never shall. Our traders Mc.Neal and York were furnished with the buttons which Capt. C. and myself cut off our coats, some eye water and Basilicon which we made for that purpose and some Phials and small tin boxes which I had brought out with Phosphorus. in the evening they returned with about 3

---

[46] Beautiful Clarkia (*Clarkia pulchella*), also called ragged-robin or deerhorn Clarkia.

bushels of roots and some bread having made a successfull voyage, not much less pleasing to us than the return of a good cargo to an East India Merchant. Collins, Sheilds, R & J. Feilds and Shannon set out on a hunting excurtion to the Quawmash grounds on the lower side of Collins's Creek.

our horses many of them have become so wild that we cannot take them without the assistance of the Indians who are extreemly dextrous in throwing a rope and taking them with a noose about the neck; as we frequently want the use of our horses when we cannot get the assistance of the indians to take them, we had a strong pound formed today in order to take them at pleasure.

The men at this season resort their fisheries while the women are employed in collecting roots. both forks of Lewis's river above their junction appear to enter a high Mountainous country. my sick horse being much reduced and apearing to be in such an agoni of pain that there was no hope of his recovery I ordered him shot this evening. the other horses which we casterated are all nearly re-covered, and I have no hesitation in declaring my beleif that the indian method of gelding is preferable to that practiced by ourselves.

Tuesday June 3d. 1806.

Our invalids are all on the recovery; Bratton is much stronger and can walk about with considerable ease. the Indian Cheif appears to be gradually recovering the uce of his limbs, and the child is nearly well; the imposthume on his neck has in a great measure subsided and left a hard lump underneath his left ear; we still con-tinue the application of the onion poltice.

Friday June 6th. 1806

we meet with a beautifull little bird in this neighbourhood about the size and somewhat the shape of the large sparrow.[47] it is reather longer in proportion to it's bulk than the sparrow. it measures 7 inches from the extremity of the beek to that of the tail, the latter occupying 2-½ inches. the beak is reather more than half an inch in length, and is formed much like the virginia nitingale; it is thick and large for a bird of it's size; wide at the base, both chaps convex,

---

[47] Western tanager (*Piranga ludoviciana*).

and pointed, the uper exceeds the under chap a little is somewhat curved and of a brown colour; the lower chap of a greenish yellow. the eye full reather large and of a black colour both puple and iris. the plumage is remarkably delicate; that of the neck and head is of a fine orrange yellow and red, the latter predominates on the top of the head and arround the base of the beak from whence it graduly deminishes & towards the lower part of the neck, the orrange yellow prevails most; the red has the appearance of being laid over a ground of yellow. the breast, the sides, rump and some long feathers which lie between the legs and extend underneath the tail are of a fine orrange yellow. the tail, back and wings are black, e[x]cept a small stripe of yellow on the outer part of the middle joint of the wing, ¼ of an inch wide and an inch in length. the tail is composed of twelve feathers of which those in the center are reather shortest, and the plumage of all the feathers of the tail is longest on that side of the quill next the center of the tail. the legs and feet are black, nails long and sharp; it has four toes on each foot, of which three are forward and one behind; that behind is as long as the two outer of the three toes in front.

Sunday June 8th. 1806
several foot races were run this evening between the indians and our men. the indians are very active; one of them proved as fleet as Drewyer and R. Fields, our swiftest runners. when the racing was over the men divided themselves into two parties and played prison base, by way of exercise which we wish the men to take previously to entering the mountain; in short those who are not hunters have had so little to do that they are geting reather lazy and slouthfull. after dark we had the violin played and danced for the amusement of ourselves and the indians. one of the indians informed us that we could not pass the mountains untill the full of the next moon or about the first of July, that if we attempted it sooner our horses would be at least three days travel without food on the top of the mountain; this information is disagreeable inasmuch as it causes some doubt as to the time at which it will be most proper for us to set out. however as we have no time to loose we will wrisk the chanches and set out as early as the indians generally think it practicable or the middle of this month.

[Clark]   Sunday June 8th. 1806
   one of those Indians informed us that we could not cross the mountains untill the full of the next moon; or about the 1st. of July. if we attempted it Sooner our horses would be three days without eating, on the top of the Mountns.   this information is disagreeable to us, in as much as it admits of some doubt, as to the time most proper for us to Set out.   at all events we Shall Set out at or about the time which the indians Seem to be generally agreed would be the most proper.   about the middle of this month.

[Lewis]   Tuesday June 10th. 1806
   This morning we arrose early and had our horses collected except one of Cruzatt's and one of Whitehouse's, which were not to be found; after a surch of some hours Cruzatt's horse was obtained and the indians promised to find the other and bring it to us at the quawmash flatts where we purpose encamping a few days.   at 11 A. M. we set out with the party each man being well mounted and a light load on a second horse, beside which we have several supenemary horses in case of accedent or the want of provision, we therefore feel ourselves perfectly equiped for the mountains.   we ascended the river hills which are very high and about three miles in extent our course being N. 22°. E. thence N. 15. W. 2m to Collins's creek. thence due North 5 m. to the Eastern border of the quawmash flatts where we encamped near the place we first met with the Chopunnish last fall[48]   the pass of Collins's Creek was deep and extreemly difficult tho' we passed without sustaining further injury than weting some of our roots and bread.   the country through which we passed is extreemly fertile and generally free of stone, is well timbered with several speceis of fir, long leafed pine and larch.
   we had scarcely reached Collins's Creek before we were over taken by a party of Indians who informed us that they were going to the quawmash flatts to hunt; their object I beleive is the expectation of b[e]ing fed by us in which however kind as they have been we must disappoint them at this moment as it is necessary that we should use all frugallaty as well as employ every exertion to provide meat for our journey. they have encamped with us.   we find a great

[48] Weippe Prairie, Idaho.

number of burrowing squirels about our camp of which we killed several; I eat of them and found them quite as tender and well flavored as our grey squirel. saw many sand hill crains and some ducks in the slashey glades about this place.

Thursday June 12th 1806

The Cutnose informed us on the 10th. before we left him that two young men would overtake us with a view to accompany me to the falls of the Missouri.

our camp is agreeably situated in a point of timbered land on the eastern border of an extensive level and beautifull prarie which is intersected by several small branches near the bank of one of which our camp is placed. the quawmash is now in blume and from the colour of its bloom at a short distance it resembles lakes of fine clear water, so complete is this deseption that on first sight I could have swoarn it was water.

Saturday June 14th. 1806.

we had all our articles packed up and made ready for an early departure in the morning. our horses were caught and most of them hubbled and otherwise confined in order that we might not be detained. from hence to traveller's rest we shall make a forsed march; at that place we shal probably remain one or two days to rest ourselves and horses and procure some meat. we have now been detained near five weeks in consequence of the snows; a serious loss of time at this delightfull season for traveling. I am still apprehensive that the snow and the want of food for our horses will prove a serious imbarrassment to us as at least four days journey of our rout in these mountains lies over hights and along a ledge of mountains never intirely destitute of snow. every body seems anxious to be in motion, convinced that we have not now any time to delay if the calculation is to reach the United States this season; this I am detirmined to accomplish if within the compass of human power.

[Clark]   Saturday June 14th. 1806

we expect to set out early, and shall proceed with as much expedition as possible over those snowey tremendious mountains which has detained us near five weeks in this neighbourhood waiting for the Snows to melt sufficient for us to pass over them. and even now I shudder with the expectation with [of] great dificuelties in passing those Mountains, from the debth of snow and the want of grass sufficient to subsist our horses, as about 4 days we Shall be on the top of the Mountain which we have every reason to beleive is covered with snow the greater part of the year.

[Lewis]   Sunday June 15th 1806.

we arrived at Collins's Creek[49] where we found our hunters; the rains have rendered the road very slippery insomuch that it is with much difficulty our horses can get on several of them fell but sustained no injury. after dinner we proceeded up the creek about ½ a mile, passing it three times, thence through a high broken country to an Easterly fork of the same creek about 10-½ miles and incamped near a small prarie in the bottom land. the fallen timber in addition to the slippry roads made our march slow and extreemly laborious on our horses. the country is exceedingly thickly timbered with longleafed pine, some pitch pine, larch, white pine, white cedar or arbor vita of large size, and a variety of firs. the undergrowth principally reedroot[50] from 6 to 10 feet high with all the other speceis enumerated the other day. the soil is good; in some plaices it is of a red cast like our lands in Virginia about the S. W. mountains. Saw the speckled woodpecker, bee martin and log cock or large woodpecker. found the nest of a humming bird, it had just began to lay its eggs.[51] Came *22* Miles today.

[Clark]   Tuesday June 17th. 1806
the road assends the mountain to the hight of the main leading ridges, which divides the waters of the Kooskooske and Chopunnish Riv's.[52] This mountain we ascended about 3 miles when we found ourselves invelloped in snow from 8 to 12 feet deep even on the South Side of the mountain. I was in front and could only prosue the derection of the road by the trees which had been peeled by the nativs for the iner bark of which they scraped and eate, as

---

[49] Lolo Creek, Idaho.
[50] Redstem Ceanothus (*Ceanothus sanguineus*); the genus is generally referred to as buckbrush or chapparal.
[51] Broad-tailed hummingbird (*Selasphorus platycercus*).
[52] North Fork of the Clearwater, and the Lochsa River, in Idaho.

those pealed trees were only to be found scattered promisquisley, I with great difficulty prosued the direction of the road one mile further to the top of the mountain where I found the snow from 12 to 15 feet deep, but fiew trees with the fairest exposure to the Sun; here was Winter with all it's rigors; the air was cold my hands and feet were benumed. we knew that it would require four days to reach the fish weare at the enterance of Colt Creek,[53] provided we were so fortunate as to be enabled to follow the p[r]oper ridge of the mountains to lead us to that place; of this all of our most expert woodsmen and principal guides were extreemly doubtfull; Short of that point we could not hope for any food for our horses not even under wood itself as the whole was covered many feet deep in snow. if we proceeded and Should git bewildered in those Mountains the certainty was that we Should lose all of our horses and consequently our baggage enstrements perhaps our papers and thus eventially resque the loss of our discoveries which we had already made if we should be so fortunate as to escape with life.

the snow bore our horses very well and the traveling was therefore infinately better than the obstruction of rocks and fallen timber which we met with in our passage over last fall when the snow lay on this part of the ridge in detached spop[t]s only. under these circumstances we conceived it madness in this stage of the expedition to proceed without a guide who could certainly conduct us to the fishwears on the Kooskooske, as our horses could not possibly sustain a journey of more than 4 or 5 days without food. we therefore come to the resolution to return with our horses while they were yet strong and in good order, and indeaver to keep them so untill we could precure an indian to conduct us over the Snowey Mountains, and again to proceed as soon as we could precure such a guide, knowing from the appearance of the snows that if we remained untill it had disolved sufficiently for us to follow the road that we should not be enabled to return to the United States within this season.

having come to this resolution, we ordered the party to make a deposit of all the baggage which we had not imediate use for, and also all the roots and bread of Cows which they had except an allowance for a fiew days to enable them to return to some place at

[53] Whitesand Creek.

which we could subsist by hunting untill we precured a guide. we left our instrements, and I even left the most of my papers believing them safer here than to Wrisk them on horse back over the road, rocks and water which we had passed. our baggage being laid on Scaffolds and well covered, we began our retragrade march at 1 P. M. haveing remaind. about three hours on this Snowey mountain. we returned by thc rout we had advanced to hungary Creek, which we assended about 2 miles and encamped. we had here more grass for our horses than the proceeding evening, yet it was but scant. the party were a good deel dejected, tho' not as much so as I had apprehended they would have been. this is the first time since we have been on this tour that we have ever been compelled to retreat or make a retragrade march. it rained on us the most of this evening. on the top of the Mountain the Weather was very fluctiating and uncertain snowed cloudy & fair in a few minets.

[Lewis]   Wednesday June 18th 1806.
We dispatched Drewyer and Shannon to the Chopunnish Indians in the plains beyond the Kooskooske in order to hasten the arrival of the indians who had promised to accompany us or to procure a gu[i]de at all events and rejoin us as soon as possible. we sent by them a rifle which we offered as a reward to any of them who would engage to conduct us to traveller's rest: we also dirrected them if they found difficulty in inducing any of them to accompany us to offer the reward of two other guns to be given them immediately and ten horses at the falls of Missouri.

we had not proceeded far this morning before Potts cut his leg very badly with one of the large knives; he cut one of the large veigns on the inner side of the leg; I found much difficulty in stoping the blood which I could not effect untill I applyed a tight bandage with a little cushon of wood and tow on the veign below the wound. Colter's horse fel with him in passing hungry creek and himself and horse were driven down the creek a considerable distance rolling over each other among the rocks. fortunately [he] escaped without injury or the loss of his gun.

Friday June 20th. 1806.
Labush and Cruzatte returned late in the evening with one deer which the former had killed. we also caught seven salmon trout in

the course of the day. the hunters assured us that their greatest
exertions would not enable them to support us here more than one
or two days longer from the great scarcity of game and the difficult
access of the country, the under brush being very thick and great
quantities of fallen timber. as we shall necessarily be compelled to
remain more than two days for the return of Drewyer and Shannon
we determined to return in the morning as far as the quawmash
flatts[54] and indeavour to lay in another stock of meat for the mountains, our former stock being now nearly exhausted as well as what
we have killed on our return. by returning to the quawmash flats
we shall sooner be informed whether or not we can procure a guide
to conduct us through the mountains; should we fail in procuring
one, we have determined to wrisk a passage on the following plan
immediately, because should we wait much longer or untill the snow
desolves in such manner as to enable us to follow the road we cannot
hope to reach the United States this winter

Monday June 23rd. 1806.

   at 3 P. M. Drewyer Shannon and Whitehouse returned. Drewyer
brought with him three indians who had consented to accompany
us to the falls of the Missouri for the compensation of two guns.
one of those men is the brother of the cutnose and the other two
are the same who presented Capt. Clark and myself each with a
horse on a former occasion at the Lodge of the broken arm. these
are all young men of good character and much respected by their
nation. we directed the horses to be brought near camp this evening
and secured in such manner that they may be readily obtained in
the morning being determined to make an early start if possible.
Colter one of our hunters did not return this evening.

Wednesday June 25th. 1806.

   last evening the indians entertained us with seting the fir trees
on fire. they have a great number of dry lims near their bodies
which when set on fire creates a very suddon and immence blaze
from bottom to top of those tall trees. they are a beatifull object
in this situation at night. this exhibition reminded me of a display

[54] Weippe Prairie.

of fireworks. the natives told us that their object in seting those trees on fire was to bring fair weather for our journey. We collected our horses readily and set out at an early hour this morning. one of our guides complained of being unwell, a symptom which I did not much like as such complaints with an indian is generally the prelude to his abandoning any enterprize with which he is not well pleased.

after dinner we continued our rout to hungary Creek and en-camped about one and a half miles below our encampment of the 16th. inst. the indians continued with us and I beleive are disposed to be faithfull to their engagement. I gave the si[c]k indian a buffaloe robe he having no other covering except his mockersons and a dressed Elkskin without the hair. Drewyer and Sheilds were sent on this morning to hungry Creek in surch of their horses which they fortunately recovered.

Thursday June 26th. 1806.

This morning we collected our horses and set out after an early breakfast or at 6 A. M. we passed by the same rout we had travelled on the 17th. inst. to our deposit on the top of the snowey mountain to the N. E. of hungary Creek. here we necessarily halted about 2 hours to arrange our baggage and prepare our loads. we cooked and made a haisty meal of boiled venison and mush of cows. the snow has subsided near four feet since the 17th. inst. we now measured it accurately and found from a mark which we had made on a tree when we were last here on the 17th. that it was then 10 feet 10 inches which appeared to be about the common debth though it is deeper still in some places. it is now generally about 7 feet.

on our way up this mountain about the border of the snowey region we killed 2 of the small black pheasant and a female of the large dommanicker or speckled pheasant,[55] the former have 16 f[e]athers in their tail and the latter 20 while the common pheasant have only 18. the indians informed us that neither of these speceis drumed; they appear to be very silent birds for I never heared either of them make a noise in any situation.

[55] Franklin's grouse (*Canachites canadensis franklinii*), a subspecies of the spruce grouse.

the indians haistened to be off, and informed us that it was a considerable distance to the place which they wished to reach this evening where there was grass for our horses. accordingly we set out with our guides who lead us over and along the steep sides of tremendious mountains entirely covered with snow except about the roots of the trees where the snow had sometimes melted and exposed a few square feet of the earth.

Friday June 27th. 1806.

the road still continued on the heights of the same dividing ridge on which we had traveled yesterday for nine miles or to our encampment of the (*17th.*) of September last. about one mile short of this encampment on an elivated point we halted by the request of the Indians a few minutes and smoked the pipe. On this eminence the natives have raised a conic mound of stones of 6 or eight feet high and on it's summit erected a pine pole of 15 feet long. from hence they informed us that when passing over with their fami[i]es some of the men were usually sent on foot by the fishery at the entrance of Colt Creek in order to take fish and again me[e]t the main party at the Quawmash glade on the head of the Kooskooske river.

from this place we had an extensive view of these stupendous mountains principally covered with snow like that on which we stood; we were entirely surrounded by those mountains from which to one unacquainted with them it would have seemed impossible ever to have escaped; in short without the assistance of our guides I doubt much whether we who had once passed them could find our way to Travellers rest in their present situation for the marked trees on which we had placed considerable reliance are much fewer and more difficult to find than we had apprehended. these fellows are most admireable pilots; we find the road wherever the snow has disappeared though it be only for a few hundred paces. after smoking the pipe and contemplating this seene sufficient to have damp[ened] the sperits of any except such hardy travellers as we have become we continued our march

[Clark]   Friday June 27th: 1806
our Meat being exhosted we issued a point of *Bears Oil* to a mess which with their boiled roots made an agreeable dish. Jo. Potts leg

which had been much Swelled and inflaimed for several days is
much better this evening and givs him but little pain. we applied
the pounded root & leaves of wild ginger[56] from which he found
great relief. Near our encampment we saw great numbers of the
Yellow lilly with reflected petals in blume; this plant was just as
forward here at this time as it was in the plains on the 10th. of
May. My head has not pained me so much to day as yesterday and
last night.

[Lewis]   Saturday June 28th. 1806.

we continued our rout along the dividing ridge passing one very
deep hollow and at the distance of six miles passed our encampment
of the [15th] of September last, one and a half miles further we
passed the road which leads by the fishery falling in on the wright
immediately on the dividing ridge. about eleven O'clock we arrived
at an untimbered side of a mountain with a Southern aspect just
above the fishery here we found an abundance of grass for our
horses as the Indians had informed us.[57] as our horses were very
hungary and much fatiegued and from information no other place
where we could obtain grass for them within the reach of this evening's travel we determined to remain at this place all night having
come 13 miles only. the water was distant from our encampment
we therefore melted snow and used the water principally. the whole
of the rout of this day was over deep snows.

[Clark]   Saturday June 28th. 1806

we find the travelling on the Snow not worse than without it, as
[the] easy passage it givs us over rocks and fallen timber fully com-
pensates for the inconvenience of sliping, certain it is that we travel
considerably faster on the snow than without it. the snow sinks
from 2 to 3 inches with a horse, is course and firm and seems to be
formed of the larger particles of the Snow; the Surface of the Snow
is reather harder in the morning than after the sun shines on it a
fiew hours, but it is not in that situation so dense as to prevent the
horses from obtaining good foothold.

[56] Long-tailed wild ginger (*Asarum caudatum*).
[57] Mount Marcy, 6875 feet in height (Nicholson).

[Lewis]   Sunday June 29th. 1806.

when we decended from this ridge we bid adieu to the snow.
near the river we f[o]und a deer which the hunters had killed and
left us.   this was a fortunate supply as all our oil was now exhausted
and we were reduced to our roots alone without salt.   the Kooskooske at this place is about 30 yds. wide and runs with great
velocity.   the bed as [of] all the mountain streams is composed of
smooth stones. beyond the river we ascended a very steep acclivity
of a mountain about 2 Miles and arrived at it's summit where we
found the old road which we had pased as we went out, coming in
on our wright.   the road was now much plainer and more beaten,
which we were informed happened from the circumstance of the
Ootslashshoots visiting the fishery frequently from the vally of
Clark's river; tho' there was no appearance of there having been
here this spring.

at noon we arrived at the quawmas flatts[58] on the Creek of the
same name and halted to graize our horses and dine having traveled
12 miles.   we passed our encampment of the (*13th.*) September at
10 ms.   where we halted there is a pretty little plain of about 50
acres plentifully stocked with quawmash and from apperances this
fromes [forms] one of the principal stages or encampments of the
indians who pass the mountains on this road.   we found after we
had halted that one of our pack-horses with his load and one of my
riding horses were left behind.   we dispatched J. Feilds and Colter
in surch of the lost horses.

after dinner we continued our march seven miles further to the
warm springs[59] where we arrived early in the evening and sent out
several hunters, who as well as R. Fields and Drewyer returned
unsuccessful; latc in thc evening Colter and J. Fields joined us with
the lost horses and brought with them a deer which they had killed,
this furnished us with supper.   these warm springs are situated
at the base of a hill of no considerable hight on the N. side and near
the bank of travellers rest creek which at that place is about 10 yards
wide.   these springs issue from the bottoms and through the interstices of a grey freestone rock, the rock rises in iregular mas[s]y

[58] Packer Meadows, Idaho.
[59] Lolo Hot Springs, Montana.

clifts in a circular range arround the springs on their lower side. immediately above the springs on the creek there is a handsome little quamas plain of about 10 acres. the prinsipal spring is about the temperature of the warmest baths used at the hot springs in Virginia. In this bath which had been prepared by the Indians by stoping the run with stone and gravel, I bathed and remained in 19 minutes, it was with dificulty I could remain thus long and it caused a profuse sweat two other bold springs adjacent to this are much warmer, their heat being so great as to make the hand of a person smart extreemly when immerced. I think the temperature of these springs about the same as the hotest of the hot springs in Virginia. both the men and indians amused themselves with the use of a bath this evening. I observed that the indians after remaining in the hot bath as long as they could bear it ran and plunged themselves into the creek the water of which is now as cold as ice can make it; after remaining here a few minutes they returned again to the warm bath, repeating this transision several times but always ending with the warm bath. I killed a small black pheasant near the quamash grounds this evening which is the first I have seen below the snowy region.

[Clark]   Monday June 30th. 1806
we noon'd it at the place we had on the 12 of Septr. last whiles here Shields killed a deer on the N. fork near the road. here a rode leads up the N. fork and passed over to an extensive vally on Clarks river at some distance down that river as our guids inform us. after dinner we resumed our march. soon after setting out Shields killed another deer, and we picked up 3 others which G Drewyer had killed along the road. Deer are very abundant in the neighbourhood of travellers rest of boath Species, also some big horn and Elk. a little before Sunset we arrived at our old encampment on the S. side of the Creek a litle above its enterance into Clarks river. here we Encamped with a view to remain 2 days in order to rest ourselves and horses and make our final arrangements for Seperation. we found no signs of the Oatlashshots haveing been here lately. the Indians express much concern for them and apprehend that the Minnetarries of Fort d[e]Prarie have destroyed them in the course of the last Winter and Spring, and mention the tracts of the bear-footed indians which we saw yesterday as an evidence of their being

much distressed. our horses have stood the journey suprisinly well and only want a fiew days rest to restore them.[60]

[Lewis]　　　　　　　　　　　　　　　Tuesday July 1st. 1806.

This morning early we sent out all our hunters. set Sheilds at work to repair some of our guns which were out of order [*Capt. Clark & myself consurted the following plan viz.*] from this place[61] I determined to go with a small party by the most direct rout to the falls of the Missouri, there to leave Thompson McNeal and goodrich to prepare carriages and geer for the purpose of transporting the canoes and baggage over the portage, and myself and six volunteers to ascend Maria's river with a view to explore the country and ascertain whether any branch of that river lies as far north as Latd. 50. and again return and join the party who are to decend the Missouri, at the entrance of Maria's river. I now called for the volunteers to accompany me on this rout, many turned out, from whom I scelected Drewyer the two Feildes, Werner, Frazier and Sergt. Gass

the other part of the men are to proceed with Capt. Clark to the

[60] In the weather diary for this date, Clark entered the following general description of the route over the mountains:

"Decended the mountain to Travellers rest leaveing these tremendious mountains behind us, in passing of which we have experienced cold and hunger of which I shall ever remember. in passing over this part of the Rocky mountains from Clarks river, to the Quawmash flats from the 14th. to the 19th. of Septr. 1805 we marched through Snow, which fell on us the night of the 14th. and nearly all the day of the 15 in addition to the old [and] rendered the air cool and the way dificuelt. our food was horses of which we eate three. on our return we Set out from the quawmash flats on the 15th. of June and commen[c]ed the assent of the rocky mountains; the air became cool and vegetation backward. on the 16th. we met with banks of Snow and in the hollars and maney of the hill Sides the Snow was from 3 to 4 feet deep, and Scercely any grass Vegetation just commencing where the Snow had melted. on the 17th. at meridian, the Snow became So deep in every derection from 6 to 8 feet deep we could not prosue the road, there being no grass for our horses we were obliged to return to the quawmash flatts to precure meat to live on as well as grass for our horses leaveing our baggage on the Mountains.

"We precured 5 Indians as pilots and on the 24th. of June 1806 we again under took those Snowey region the 26th. we with our baggage arrived at an open place serounded with Snow where there was grass for horses on the 27th. & 28th. also passing over Snow 6 or 8 feet deep all the way, on 29th. passed over but little Snow, but saw great masses of it lying in different directions" (Thwaites).

[61] Traveler's Rest, near Lolo and Missoula, Montana.

head of Jefferson's river where we deposited sundry articles and left our canoes. from hence Sergt. Ordway with a party of 9 men are to decend the river with the canoes; Capt. C. with the remaining ten including Charbono and York will proceed to the Yellowstone river at it's nearest approach to the three forks of the missouri, here he will build a canoe and decend the Yellowstone river with Charbono the indian woman, his servant York and five others to the missouri where should he arrive first he will wait my arrival. Sergt. Pryor with two other men are to proceed with the horses by land to the Mandans and thence to the British posts on the Assinniboin with a letter to Mr. Heney (*Haney*) whom we wish to engage to prevail on the Sioux Ch[i]efs to join us on the Missouri, and accompany them with us to the seat of the general government. these arrangements being made the party were informed of our design and prepared themselves accordingly.

our hunters killed 13 deer in the course of this day of which 7 were fine bucks, deer are large and in fine order. the indians inform us that there are a great number of white buffaloe or mountain sheep of [on] the snowey hights of the mountains West of this river;[62] we had our venison fleeced and exposed in the sun on pole[s] to dry. the dove the black woodpecker, the lark woodpecker, the logcock, the prarie lark, sandhill crain, prarie hen with the short and pointed tail, the robin, a speceis of brown plover, a few curloos, small black birds, ravens hawks and a variety of sparrows as well as the bee martin and the several speceis of Corvus genus are found in this vally. Windsor birst his gun near the muzzle a few days since; this Sheilds cut off and I then exchanged it with the Cheif for the one we had given him for conducting us over the mountains. he was much pleased with the exchange and shot his gun several times; he shoots very well for an inexperienced person.

The little animal found in the plains of the Missouri which I have called the *barking squirrel*[63] weighs from 3 to 3-½ pounds. it's form is that of the squirrel. it's colour is an uniform light brick red grey, the red reather predominating. the under side of the neck and bel[l]y are lighter coloured than the other parts of the body. the legs are

[62] Bitterroot River.
[63] Black-tailed prairie dog (*Cynomys ludovicianus*).

short, and it is wide across the breast and sholders in propotion to it's size, appears strongly formed in that part; the head is also bony muscular and stout, reather more blontly terminated wider and flatter than the common squirrel. the upper lip is split or divided to the nose. the ears are short and lie close to the head, having the appearance of being cut off, in this particular they resemble the guinea pig. the teeth are like those of the squirrel rat &c. they have a false jaw or pocket between the skin and the mustle of the jaw like that of the common ground squ[i]rrel but not so large in proportion to their size. they have large and full whiskers on each side of the nose, a few long hairs of the same kind on each jaw and over the eyes. the eye is small and black. they have five toes on each foot of which the two outer toes on each foot are much sho[r]ter than those in the center particularly the two inner toes of the forefeet, the toes of the fore feet are remarkably long and sharp and seem well adapted to [s]cratching or burrowing those of the hind feet are neither as long or sharp as the former; the nails are black. the hair of this animal is about as long and equally as course as that of the common grey squ[i]rrel of our country, and the hair of the tail is not longer than that of the body except immediately at the extremity where it is somewhat longer and frequently of a dark brown colour. the part of generation in the female is placed on the lower region of the belly between the hinder legs so far forward that she must lie on her back to copolate. the whole length of this animal is one foot five inches from the extremity of the nose to that of the tail of which the tail occupyes 4 inches. it is nearly double the size of the whistleing squirrel of the Columbia. it is much more quick active and fleet than it's form would indicate. these squirrels burrow in the ground in the open plains usually at a considerable distance from the water yet are never seen at any distance from their burrows. six or eight usually reside in one burrow to which there is never more than one entrance. these burrows are of great debth. I once dug and pursued a burrow to the debth of ten feet and did not reach it's greatest debth. they generally associate in large societies placing their burrows near each other and frequently occupy in this manner several hundred acres of land. when at rest above ground their position is generally erect on their hinder feet and rump; thus they will generally set and bark at you as you approach them, their note being much that of the little toy dogs, their yelps are in quick succession and at each they [give] a motion to their tails upwards. they feed on the grass and weeds within the limits of their village which they never appear to exceed on any occasion. as they are usually numerous they keep the grass and weeds within their district very closely graized and as clean as if it had been swept. the earth which they throw out of their burrows is usually formed into a conic mound around the entrance. this little animal is frequently very fat and it's flesh is not unpleasant. as soon as the hard frosts commence it shuts up it's burrow and continues untill spring. it will eat neither grain or meat.

[Clark]   Tuesday July 1st; 1806
                                              on Clarks river

one of the Indians who accompanied us swam Clarks river and examined the country around, on his return he informed us that he had discovered where a Band of the *Tushepaws* had encamped this Spring passed of 64 Lodges, & that they had passed Down Clarks river and that it was probable that they were near the quawmash flatts on a Easterly branch of that river. those guides expressed a desire to return to their nation and not accompany us further, we informed them that if they was deturmined to return we would kill some meat for them, but wished that they would accompy Capt Lewis on the rout to the falls of Missouri only 2 nights and show him the right road to cross the Mountains. this they agreed to do. we gave a medal of the small size to the young man son to the late Great Chief of the Chopunnish Nation who had been remarkably kind to us in every instance, to all the others we tied a bunch of blue ribon about the hair, which pleased them very much. the Indian man who overtook us in the Mountain, presented Capt Lewis with a horse and said that he opened his ears to what we had said, and hoped that Capt Lewis would see the Crovanters [Gros Ventres] of Fort de Prarie and make a good peace that it was their desire to be at peace. shew them the horse as a token of their wishes &c.

[Lewis]   Wednesday July 2ed. 1806.

in the course of the day we had much conversation with the indians by signs, our only mode of communicating our ideas. they informed us that they wished to go in surch of the Ootslashshoots their friends and intended leaving us tomorrow morning, I prevailed on them to go with me as far as the East branch of Clark's River and put me on the road to the Missouri. I gave the Cheif a medal of the small size; he insisted on exchanging names with me according to their custom which was accordingly done and I was called Yo-me-kol-lick which interpreted is *the white bearskin foalded*.

in the evening the indians run their horses, and we had several foot races between the natives and our party with various success. these are a race of hardy strong athletic active men. nothin worthy of notice transpired in the course of the day. Goodrich and Mc.Neal are both very unwell with the pox which they contracted last winter with the Chinnook women this forms my inducement principally for taking them to the falls of the Missouri where during an interval of rest they can use the murcury freely.

I found two speceis of native clover here, the one with a very narrow small leaf and a pale red flower, the other nearly as luxouriant as our red clover with a white flower the leaf and blume of the latter are proportionably large. I found several other uncommon plants specemines of which I preserved.[64]

[Clark]　　　　　　　　　　　　　　　　　Wednesday July 2nd. 1806
Sent out 2 hunters this morning and they killed 2 Deer. the Musquetors has been So troublesom day and night since our arrival in this Vally that we are tormented very much by them and cant' write except under our Bears [i. e., biers].

We gave the second gun to our guides agreeable to our promis, and to each we gave Powder & ball I had the greater part of the meat dried for to subsist my party in the Mountains between the head of Jeffersons & Clarks rivers where I do not expect to find any game to kill. had all of our arms put in the most prime order two of the rifles have unfortunately bursted near the muscle [muzzle], Shields cut them off and they shute tolerable well one which is very short we exchanged with the Indian whoe he had given a longer gun to induce them to pilot us across the Mountains. we caused every man to fill his horn with powder & have a sufficiency of Balls &c.

---

[64] Small-headed clover (*Trifolium microcephalum*) and owls' clover (*Orthocarpus tenuifolius*) (Cutright).

the last day in passing down Travellers rest Creek Capt. Lewis
fell down the side of a Steep Mountain near 40 feet but fortunately
receved no damage. his hors was near falling on him but fortunately
recovered and they both escaped unhurt. I killed a Small grey
squirel and a Common pheasant. Capt. L. showed me a plant in
blume which is sometimes called the ladies slipper or Mockerson
flower.[65] it is in shape and appearance like ours only that the corolla
is white marked with small veigns of pale red longitudinally on the
inner side, and much smaller. The Indians and some of our men
amused themselves in running races on foot as well as with their
horses.

Thursday July 3rd. 1806

We colected our horses and after brackfast I took My leave of
Capt. Lewis and the indians and at 8 A M Set out with [blank space
in MS.][66] Men interpreter Shabono & his wife & child (as an interpreter & interpretes[s] for the Crow Inds. and the latter for the
Shoshoni) with (*50*) horses.

Labeish killed a Deer this evening. We saw great numbers of
deer and 1 bear today. I also observed the burr[ow]ing Squirel of
the Species common about the quawmarsh flatts West of the Rocky
Mountains. Musquetors very troublesom. one man Jo: Potts very
unwell this evening owing to rideing a hard trotting horse; I give
him a pill of Opiom which soon releve[d] him.

Friday July 4th: 1806

This being the day of the decleration of Independence of the
United States and a Day commonly scelebrated by my Country I
had every disposition to selebrate this day and therefore halted early
and partook of a Sumptious Dinner of a fat Saddle of Venison and
Mush of Cows (roots) after Dinner we proceeded on about one
mile to a very large Creek which we assended some distance to find
a foard to cross. in crossing this creek several articles got wet, the
water was so strong, alto' the debth was not much above the horses

---

[65] Mountain lady's slipper (*Cypripedium montanum*).
[66] Clark was accompanied by twenty men, besides the Indian woman and her child (Thwaites).

belly, the water passed over the backs and loads of the horses. those Creeks are emensely rapid

Sunday 6th July 1806

entered an extensive open Leavel plain in which the Indian trail scattered in such a manner that we could not pursue it. the Indian woman wife to Shabono informed me that she had been in this plain frequently and knew it well that the creek which we decended was a branch of Wisdom river[67] and when we assended the higher part of the plain we would discover a gap in the mountains in our direction to the canoes, and when we arived at that gap we would see a high point of a mountain covered with snow in our direction to the canoes.[68] we proceeded on 1 mile and Crossd. a large Creek from the right which heads in a snow Mountain and Fish Creek over which there was a road thro' a gap. we assended a small rise and beheld an open beutifull Leavel Vally or plain of about 20 (*15*) Miles wide and near 60 (*30*) long extending N & S. in every direction around which I could see high points of Mountains covered with snow. I discovered one at a distance very high covered with snow which bore S. 80°. E. The Squar pointed to the gap through which she said we must pass which was *S. 56°: E* she said we would pass the river before we reached the gap.

Tuesday 8th July 1806

after dinner we proceeded on down the forke[69] which is here but small 9 Miles to our encampment of 17 Augt. at which place we Sunk our Canoes & buried some articles, as before mentioned the most of the Party with me being Chewers of Tobacco become so impatient to be chewing it that they scercely gave themselves time to take their saddles off their horses before they were off to the deposit. I found every article safe, except a little damp. I gave to each man who used tobacco about two feet off a part of a role took one third of the ballance myself and put up ⅔ in a box to send down with the most of the articles which had been left at this place, by the canoes to Capt. Lewis.

[67] Big Hole River, east of Gibbon's Pass, Montana.
[68] The cache in Shoshone Cove, south of Dillon, Montana.
[69] At Clark Canyon Reservoir, Montana.

The road which we have traveled from travellers rest Creek to *this place (this place is the head of Jeffer river where we left our canoes)* [is] an excellent road.

Sunday 13th: July 1806

I had all the horses driven across Madicine & gallitines rivers and halted to dine and let the horses feed imediately below the enterance of Gallitine.[70] had all the baggage of the land party taken out of the canoes and after dinner the 6 canoes and the party of 10 men under the direction of Sergt. Ordway set out. previous to their departur[e] I gave instructions how they were to proceed &c. I also wrote to Capt Lewis by Sergt. Ordway. My party now Consists of the following persons Viz: Sergeant N. Pryor, Jo. Shields, G. Shannon William Bratton, Labiech, Windsor, H. Hall, Gibson, Interpreter Shabono his wife & child and my man york; with 49 horses and a colt. the horses feet are very sore and Several of them can scercely proceed on.

The country in the forks between Gallitins & Madisens rivers is a butifull leavel plain covered with low grass. on the lower or N E. Side of Gallitins river the country rises gradually to the foot of a mountain which runs nearly parrelal. I observe Several leading roads which appear to pass a gap of the mountain in a E. N E. direction about 18 or 20 miles distant. The indian woman who has been of great service to me as a pilot through this country recommends a gap in the mountain more south which I shall cross.[71]

[70] At Three Forks, Montana.
[71] Bozeman Pass, Montana.

ELEVEN

Lewis's Shortcut

From Traveler's Rest to the Missouri
July 3–August 12, 1806

[Lewis]   Thursday July 3rd. 1806.

I took leave of my worthy friend and companion Capt. Clark and the party that accompanyed him.   I could not avoid feeling much concern on this occasion although I hoped this seperation was only momentary.   I proceeded down Clark's river[1] seven miles with my party of nine men and five indians.   here the Indians recommended our passing the river which was rapid and 150 yds. wide.   2 miles above this place I passed the entrance of the East branch of Clark's River[2] which discharges itself by two channels; the water of this river is more terbid than the main stream and is from 90 to 120 yds. wide.   as we had no other means of passing the river we busied ourselves collecting dry timber for the purpose of constructing rafts; timber being scarce we found considerable difficulty in procuring as much as made three small rafts.

we arrived at 11 A. M. and had our rafts completed by 3 P. M. when we dined and began to take over our baggage which we effected in the course of 3 hours the rafts being obliged to return several times.   the Indians swam over their horses and drew over

[1] Bitterroot River.
[2] Hellgate River.

their baggage in little basons of deer skins which they constructed in a very few minutes for that purpose. we drove our horses in after them and they followed to the opposite shore. I remained myself with two men who could scarcely swim untill the last; by this time the raft by passing so frequently had fallen a considerable distance down the river to a rapid and difficult part of it crouded with several small Islands and willow bars which were now overflown; with these men I set out on the raft and was soon hurried down with the current a mile and a half before we made shore, on our approach to the shore the raft sunk and I was drawn off the raft by a bush and swam on shore the two men remained on the raft and fortunately effected a landing at some little distance below. I wet the chronometer by this accedent which I had placed in my fob as I conceived for greater security. I now joined the party and we proceeded with the indians about 3 Ms. to a small Creek and encamped at sunset.

I sent out the hunters who soon returned with three very fine deer of which I gave the indians half. These people now informed me that the road which they shewed me at no great distance from our Camp would lead us up the East branch of Clark's river and [to] a river they called Cokahlarishkit or the *river of the road to buffaloe* and thence to medicine river and the falls of the Missouri where we wished to go.

they alledged that as the road was a well beaten track we could not now miss our way and as they were affraid of meeting with their enimies the Minnatares they could not think of continuing with us any longer, that they wished now to proceed down Clark's river in surch of their friends the Shalees. they informed us that not far from the dividing ridge between the waters of this and the Missouri rivers the roads forked they recommended the left hand as the best rout but said they would both lead us to the falls of the Missouri. I directed the hunters to turn out early in the morning and indeavour to kill some more meat for these people whom I was unwilling to leave without giving them a good supply of provision after their having been so obliging as to conduct us through those tremendious mountains. the musquetoes were so excessively troublesome this evening that we were obliged to kindle large fires for our horses these insects torture them in such a manner untill they placed them-

.wood on this river is like that common to the Columbia narrower than that common to the lower part of the Missouri and Mississippi and wider than that on the upper part of the Missouri. the wild rose, service berry, white berryed honeysuckle, seven bark, elder, alder aspin, choke cherry and the broad and narrow leafed willow are natives of this valley. the long leafed pine forms the principal timber of the neighbourhood, and grows as well in the river bottoms as on the hills. the firs and larch are confined to the higher parts of the hills and mountains. the tops of the high moun-tains on either side of this river are covered with snow. the musquetoes have been excessively troub-blesome to us since our arrival at this place.

Thursday July 3rd 1806.

All arrangements being now compleated for carrying into effect the several schemes we had planed for execution on our return, we saddled our horses and set out. I took leave of my worthy friend and companion Capt. Clark and the party that accompanyed him. I could not avoid feeling much concern on this occasion although I hoped this seperation was only momentary. I pro-ceeded down Clarks river seven miles with my party of nine men and five indians. here the Indians recommend-ed our passing the river which was rapid and 150 yds wide. 2 miles above this place I passed the entrance of the East branch of Clark's River which dis-charges itself by two channels; the water of this river is more turbid than the main stream and is from 90 to 120 yds wide. as we had no other means of passing the river we busied ourselves collecting dry timber for the purpose of constructing .... we soon were ....

Manuscript page by Lewis, July 3, 1806.

selves in the smoke of the fires that I realy thought they would become frantic. about an hour after dark the air become so coald that the musquetoes disappeared.

July 7th 1806.

N. 45. E. 2 M. passing the dividing ridge[3] betwen the waters of the Columbia and Missouri rivers at ¼ of a mile. from this gap which is low and an easy ascent on the W. side the fort mountain bears North East, and appears to be distant about 20 Miles. the road for one and ¾ miles decends the hill and continues down a branch.

July 11th 1806.

I sent the hunters down Medicine river[4] to hunt Elk and proceeded with the party across the plain to the white bear Islands which I found to be 8 Ms. distant my course S. 75 E. through a level beautifull and extensive high plain covered with immence hirds of buffaloe. it is now the season at which the buffaloe begin to coppelate and the bulls keep a tremendious roaring we could hear them for many miles and there are such numbers of them that there is one continual roar. our horses had not been acquainted with the buffaloe they appeared much allarmed at their appearance and bellowing. when I arrived in sight of the white-bear Islands[5] the missouri bottoms on both sides of the river were crouded with buffaloe I sincerely beleif that there were not less than 10 thousand buffaloe within a circle of 2 miles arround that place.

I then set all hands to prepare two canoes the one we made after the mandan fassion with a single skin in the form of a bason and the other we constructed of two skins on a plan of our own. we were unable to compleat our canoes this evening. the wind blew very hard. we continued our operations untill dark and then retired to rest. I intend giving my horses a couple of days rest at this place

[3] Lewis crossed the divide by the gap now known as Lewis and Clark's Pass, Montana.

[4] Sun River, Montana.

[5] At Great Falls, Montana.

July 12th. 1806.
the wind abated and we transported our baggage and meat to the opposite shore in our canoes which we found answered even beyond our expectations. we swam our horses over also and encamped at sunset. Musquetoes extreemly troublesome.

14th July
Had the carriage wheels dug up. found them in good order. the iron frame of the boat had not suffered materially. had the meat cut thiner and exposed to dry in the sun. and some roots of cows of which I have yet a small stock pounded into meal for my journey. I find the fat buffaloe meat a great improvement to the mush of these roots. the old cash being too damp to venture to deposit my trunks &c. in I sent them over to the Large island and had them put on a high scaffold among some thick brush and covered with skins. I take this precaution lest some indians may visit the men I leave here before the arrival of the main party and rob them. the hunters killed a couple of wolves, the buffaloe have almost entirely disappeared. saw the bee martin. the wolves are in great numbers howling arround us and loling about in the plains in view at the distance of two or three hundred yards. I counted 27 about the carcase of a buffaloe which lies in the water at the upper point of the large island. these are generally of the large kind. Drewyer did not return this evening.

Tuesday July 15th. 1806.
Dispatched McNeal early this morning to the lower part of portage in order to learn whether the Cash and white perogue remained untouched or in what state they were. the men employed in drying the meat, dressing deerskins and preparing for the reception of the canoes.

Drewyer returned without the horses and reported that after a diligent surch of 2 days he had discovered where the horses had passed Dearborn's river at which place there were 15 lodges that had been abandoned about the time our horses were taken; I have no doubt but they are a party of the Tushapahs who have been on a buffaloe hunt. his horse being much fatiegued with the ride he had given him and finding that the indians had at least 2 days the start of him thought it best to return. his safe return has releived me from great anxiety. I had already settled it in my mind that a white-bear had killed him and should have set out tomorrow in surch of him, and if I could not find him to continue my rout to Maria's river. I knew that if he met with a bear in the plains even he would attack him. and that if any accedent should happen to seperate him from his horse in that situation the chances in favour of his being killed would be as 9 to 10. I felt so perfectly satisfyed that he had returned in safety that I thought but little of the horses although they were seven of the best I had.

a little before dark McNeal returned with his musquet broken off at the breach, and informed me that on his arrival at willow run [*on the portage*] he had approached a white bear within ten feet without discover[ing] him the bear being in the thick brush, the horse took the allarm and turning short threw him immediately under the bear; this animal raised himself on his hinder feet for battle, and gave him time to recover from his fall which he did in an instant and with his clubbed musquet he struck the bear over the head and cut him with the guard of the gun and broke off the breech, the bear stunned with the stroke fell to the ground and began to scratch his head with his feet; this gave McNeal time to climb a willow tree which was near at hand and thus fortunately made his escape. the bear waited at the foot of the tree untill late in the evening before he left him, when McNeal ventured down and caught his horse which had by this time strayed off to the distance of 2 Ms. and returned to camp. these bear are a most tremenduous animal; it seems that the hand of providence has been most wonderfully in our favor with rispect to them, or some of us would long since have fallen a sacrifice to their farosity. there seems to be a sertain fatality attatched to the neighbourhood of these falls, for there is always a chapter of accedents prepared for us during our residence at them.

the musquetoes continue to infest us in such manner that we can scarcely exist; for my own part I am confined by them to my bier at least ¾ths of my time. my dog even howls with the torture he experiences from them, they are almost insupportable, they are so numerous that we frequently get them in our thr[o]ats as we breath.

Thursday July 17th. 1806.
the whole face of the country as far as the eye can reach looks like a well shaved bowling green, in which immence and numerous

herds of buffaloe were seen feeding attended by their scarcely less numerous sheepherds the wolves. we killed a buffaloe cow as we passed throug[h] the plains and took the hump and tonge which furnish ample rations for four men

we arrived at *rose* [*Tansy*]⁶ river where I purposed remaining all night as I could not reach maria's river this evening and unless I did there would be but little probability of our finding any wood and very probably no water either. on our arrival at the river we saw where a wounded and bleading buffaloe had just passed and concluded it was probable that the indians had been runing them and were near at hand. the Minnetares of Fort de prarie and the blackfoot indians rove through this quarter of the country and as they are a viciouis lawless and reather an abandoned set of wretches I wish to avoid an interview with them if possible. I have no doubt but they would steel our horses if they have it in their power and finding us weak should they happen to be numerous wil most probably attempt to rob us of our arms and baggage; at all events I am determined to take every possible precaution to avoid them if possible.

Friday July 18th 1806.
we passed immence herds of buffaloe on our way in short for about 12 miles it appeared as one herd only the whole plains and vally of this creek being covered with them; saw a number of wolves of both speceis, also Antelopes and some horses. after dinner we proceeded about 5 miles across the plain to Maria's river where we arrived at 6 P. M. we killed a couple of buffaloe in the bottom of this river and encamped on it's west side in a grove of cottonwood some miles above the entrance of the creek.

Thursday July 24th 1806.
the air has become extreemly cold which in addition to the wind and rain renders our situation extreemly unpleasant. several wolves⁷ visited our camp today, I fired on and wounded one of them very badly. the small speceis of wolf barks like a dog, they frequently salute us with this note as we pass through the plains.

⁶ The Teton, a tributary of Marias River (Thwaites).
⁷ Coyotes.

Friday July 25th. 1806.

The weather still continues cold cloudy and rainy, the wind also has blown all day with more than usual violence from the N. W. this morning we eat the last of our birds and cows, I therefore directed Drewyer and J. Fields to take a couple of the horses and proceed to the S.E. as far as the main branch of Maria's river which I expected was at no great distance and indeavour to kill some meat; they set out immediately and I remained in camp with R. Fields to avail myself of every opportunity to make my observations should any offer, but it continued to rain and I did not see the sun through the whole course of the day R. Fields and myself killed nine pige[ons] which lit in the trees near our camp on these we dined. late in the evening Drewyer and J. Fields returned the former had killed a fine buck on which we now fared sumptuously. they informed me that it was about 10 miles to the main branch of Maria's River, that the vally formed by the river in that quarter was wide extensive and level with a considerable quantity of timber; here they found some wintering camps of the natives and a great number of others of a more recent date or that had from appearance been evacuated about 6 weeks; we consider ourselves extreemly fortunate in not having met with these people.

I determined that if tomorrow continued cloudy to set out as I now begin to be apprehensive that I shall not reach the United States within this season unless I make every exertion in my power which I shall certainly not omit when once I leave this place which I shall do with much reluctance without having obtained the necessary data to establish it's longitude   as if the fates were against me my chronometer from some unknown cause stoped today, when I set her to going she went as usual.

Saturday July 26th. 1806.

The mor[n]ing was cloudy and continued to rain as usual, tho' the cloud seemed somewhat thiner I therefore posponed seting out untill 9 A. M. in the hope that it would clear off but finding the contrary result I had the horses caught and we set out biding a lasting adieu to this place which I now call camp *disappointment*.[8]

[8] Northeast of Browning, Montana.

the country through which this portion of Maria's river passes to the fork which I ascended appears much more broken than that above and between this and the mountains. I had scarcely ascended the hills before I discovered to my left at the distance of a mile an assembleage of about 30 horses, I halted and used my spye glass by the help of which I discovered several indians on the top of an eminence just above them who appeared to be looking down towards the river I presumed at Drewyer. about half the horses were saddled. this was a very unpleasant sight, however I resolved to make the best of our situation and to approach them in a friendly manner. I directed J. Fields to display the flag which I had brought for that purpose and advanced slowly toward them, about this time they discovered us and appeared to run about in a very confused manner as if much allarmed, their attention had been previously so fixed on Drewyer that they did not discover us untill we had began to advance upon them, some of them deceded the hill on which they were and drove their horses within shot of it's summit and again returned to the hight as if to wate our arrival or to defend themselves. I calculated on their number being nearly or quite equal to that of their horses, that our runing would invite pursuit as it would convince them that we were their enimies and our horses were so indifferent that we could not hope to make our escape by flight; added to this Drewyer was seperated from us and I feared that his not being apprized of the indians in the event of our attempting to escape he would most probably fall a sacrefice.

under these considerations I still advanced towards them; when we had arrived within a quarter of a mile of them, one of them mounted his horse and rode full speed towards us, which when I discovered I halted and alighted from my horse; he came within a hundred paces halted looked at us and turned his horse about and returned as briskly to his party as he had advanced; while he halted near us I held out my hand and becconed to him to approach but he paid no attention to my overtures. on his return to his party they all deceded the hill and mounted their horses and advanced toward us leaving their horses behind them, we also advanced to meet them. I counted eight of them but still supposed that there were others concealed as there were several other horses saddled. I told the two men with me that I apprehended that these were the

Minnetares of Fort de Prarie and from their known character I expected that we were to have some difficulty with them; that if they thought themselves sufficiently strong I was convinced they would attempt to rob us in which case be their numbers what they would I should resist to the last extremity prefering death to that of being deprived of my papers instruments and gun and desired that they would form the same resolution and be allert and on their guard.

when we arrived within a hundred yards of each other the indians except one halted   I directed the two men with me to do the same and advanced singly to meet the indian with whom I shook hands and passed on to those in his rear, as he did also to the two men in my rear; we now all assembled and alighted from our horses; the Indians soon asked to smoke with us, but I told them that the man whom they had seen pass down the river had my pipe and we could not smoke untill he joined us.   I requested as they had seen which way he went that they would one of them go with one of my men in surch of him, this they readily concented to and a young man set out with R. Fields in surch of Drewyer.

I now asked them by sighns if they were the Minnetares of the North which they answered in the affirmative;[9] I asked if there was any cheif among them and they pointed out 3   I did not believe them however I thought it best to please them and gave to one a medal to a second a flag and to the third a handkerchief, with which they appeared well satisfyed.   they appeared much agitated with our first interview from which they had scarcely yet recovered, in fact I beleive they were more allarmed at this accedental interview than we were.   from no more of them appearing I now concluded they were only eight in number and became much better satisfyed with our situation as I was convinced that we could mannage that number should they attempt any hostile measures.   as it was growing late in the evening I proposed that we should remove to the nearest part of the river and encamp together, I told them that I was glad to see them and had a great deel to say to them.

we mounted our horses and rode towards the river which was at but a short distance, on our way we were joined by Drewyer Fields

---

[9] They were Piegan, one of three groups of Algonquian-speaking Blackfeet occupying the Northern Plains.

and the indian. we decended a very steep bluff about 250 feet high to the river where there was a small bottom of nearly ½ a mile in length and about 250 yards wide in the widest part, the river washed the bluffs both above and below us and through it's course in this part is very deep; the bluffs are so steep that there are but few places where they could be ascended, and are broken in several places by deep nitches which extend back from the river several hundred yards, their bluffs being so steep that it is impossible to ascend them; in this bottom there stand t[h]ree solitary trees near one of which the indians formed a large simicircular camp of dressed buffaloe skins and invited us to partake of their shelter which Drewyer and myself accepted and the Fieldses lay near the fire in front of the she[l]ter.[10]

with the assistance of Drewyer I had much conversation with these people in the course of the evening. I learned from them that they were a part of a large band which lay encamped at present near the foot of the rocky mountains on the main branch of Maria's river one ½ days march from our present encampment; that there was a whiteman with their band; that there was another large band of their nation hunting buffaloe near the broken mountains and were on there way to the mouth of Maria's river where they would probably be in the course of a few days. they also informed us that from hence to the establishment where they trade on the Suskasawan river is only 6 days easy march or such as they usually travel with their women and childred[n] which may be estimated at about 150 ms. that from these traders they obtain arm[s] amunition sperituous liquor blankets &c. in exchange for wolves and some beaver skins.

I told these people that I had come a great way from the East up the large river which runs toward the rising sun, that I had been to the great waters where the sun sets and had seen a great many nations all of whom I had invited to come and trade with me on the rivers on this side of the mountains, that I had found most of them at war with their neighbours and had succeeded in restoring peace among them, that I was now on my way home and had left my party at the falls of the missouri with orders to decend that river to the entrance of Maria's river and there wait my arrival and that I had

[10] On Two Medicine River, south of Cut Bank, Montana.

come in surch of them in order to prevail on them to be at peace
with their neighbours particularly those on the West side of the
mountains and to engage them to come and trade with me when
the establishment is made at the entrance of this river to all which
they readily gave their assent and declared it to be their wish to be
at peace with the Tushepahs whom they said had killed a number
of their relations lately and pointed to several of those present who
had cut their hair as an evidence of the truth of what they had
asserted. I found them extreemly fond of smoking and plyed them
with the pipe untill late at night. I told them that if they intended
to do as I wished them they would send some of their young men
to their band with an invitation to their chiefs and warriors to bring
the whiteman with them and come down and council with me at
the entrance of Maria's river and that the ballance of them would
accompany me to that place, where I was anxious now to meet my
men as I had been absent from them some time and knew that they
would be uneasy untill they saw me.   that if they would go with
me I would give them 10 horses and some tobacco.   to this proposition they made no reply

I took the first watch tonight and set up untill half after eleven;
the indians by this time were all asleep, I roused up R. Fields and
laid down myself; I directed Fields to watch the movements of the
indians and if any of them left the camp to awake us all as I apprehended they would attampt to s[t]eal our horses.   this being done
I feel into a profound sleep and did not wake untill the noise of the
men and indians awoke me a little after light in the morning.

July 27th. 1806. Sunday.

This morning at daylight the indians got up and crouded around
the fire, J. Fields who was on post had carelessly laid his gun down
behi[n]d him near where his brother was sleeping, one of the indians
the fellow to whom I had given the medal last evening sliped behind
him and took his gun and that of his brother unperceived by him,
at the same instant two others advanced and seized the guns of
Drewyer and myself, J. Fields seeing this turned about to look for
his gun and saw the fellow just runing off with her and his brother's
he called to his brother who instantly jumped up and pursued the
indian with him whom they overtook at the distance of 50 or 60
paces from the camp s[e]ized their guns and rested them from him

and R. Fields as he seized his gun stabed the indian to the heart with his knife   the fellow ran about 15 steps and fell dead; of this I did not know untill afterwards, having recovered their guns they ran back instantly to the camp;

Drewyer who was awake saw the indian take hold of his gun and instantly jumped up and s[e]ized her and rested her from him but the indian still retained his pouch,   his jumping up and crying damn you let go my gun awakened me   I jumped up and asked what was the matter which I quickly learned when I saw drewyer in a scuffle with the indian for his gun.   I reached to seize my gun but found her gone, I then drew a pistol from my holster and terning myself about saw the indian making off with my gun   I ran at him with my pistol and bid him lay down my gun which he was in the act of doing when the Fieldses returned and drew up their guns to shoot him which I forbid as he did not appear to be about to make any resistance or commit any offensive act, he droped the gun and walked slowly off, I picked her up instantly,   Drewyer having about this time recovered his gun and pouch asked me if he might not kill the fellow which I also forbid as the indian did not appear to wish to kill us,   as soon as they found us all in possession of our arms they ran and indeavored to drive off all the horses   I now hollowed to the men and told them to fire on them if they attempted to drive off our horses, they accordingly pursued the main party who were dr[i]ving the horses up the river and I pursued the man who had taken my gun who with another was driving off a part of the horses which were to the left of the camp.

I pursued them so closely that they could not take twelve of their own horses but continued to drive one of mine with some others; at the distance of three hundred paces they entered one of those steep nitches in the bluff with the horses before them   being nearly out of breath I could pursue no further, I called to them as I had done several times before that I would shoot them if they did not give me my horse and raised my gun, one of them jumped behind a rock and spoke to the other who turned arround and stoped at the distance of 30 steps from me and I shot him through the belly,   he fell to his knees and on his wright elbow from which position he partly raised himself up and fired at me, and turning himself about crawled in behind a rock which was a few feet from him. he overshot me, being bearheaded I felt the wind of his bullet very distinctly. not having my shotpouch I could not reload my peice and as there were two of them behind good shelters from me I did not think it prudent to rush on them with my pistol which had I discharged I had not the means of reloading untill I reached camp; I therefore returned leasurely towards camp

on my way I met with Drewyer who having heared the report of the guns had returned in surch of me and left the Fieldes to pursue the indians, I desired him to haisten to the camp with me and assist in catching as many of the indian horses as were necessary and to call to the Fieldes if he could make them hear to come back that we still had a sufficient number of horses, this he did but they were too far to hear him. we reached the camp and began to catch the horses and saddle them and put on the packs. the reason I had not my pouch with me was that I had not time to return about 50 yards to camp after geting my gun before I was obliged to pursue the indians or suffer them to collect and drive off all the horses. we had caught and saddled the horses and began to arrange the packs when the Fieldses returned with four of our horses; we left one of our horses and took four of the best of those of the indian's; while the men were preparing the horses I put four sheilds and two bows and quivers of arrows which had been left on the fire, with sundry other articles; they left all their baggage at our mercy. they had but 2 guns and one of them they left the others were armed with bows and arrows and eyedaggs. the gun we took with us. I also retook the flagg but left the medal about the neck of the dead man that they might be informed who we were.

we took some of their buffaloe meat and set out ascending the bluffs by the same rout we had decended last evening leaving the ballance of nine of their horses which we did not want. the Fieldses told me that three of the indians whom they pursued swam the river one of them on my horse. and that two others ascended the hill and escaped from them with a part of their horses, two I had pursued into the nitch one lay dead near the camp and the eighth we could not account for but suppose that he ran off early in the contest. having ascended the hill we took our course through a beatifull level plain a little to the S. of East. my design was to hasten to the entrance of Maria's river as quick as possible in the hope of meeting with the canoes and party at that place having no doubt but that they [the Indians] would pursue us with a large party and as there was a band near the broken mountains or probably between them and the mouth of that river we might expect them to receive inteligence from us and arrive at that place nearly as soon as we could, no time was therefore to be lost and we pushed our horses as hard as they would bear.

at 8 miles we passed a large branch 40 yds. wide which I called battle river.   at 3 P. M. we arrived at rose river about 5 miles above where we had passed it as we went out, having traveled by my estimate compared with our former distances and cou[r]ses about 63 ms.   here we halted an hour and a half took some refreshment and suffered our horses to graize; the day proved warm but the late rains had supplyed the little reservors in the plains with water and had put them in fine order for traveling,   our whole rout so far was as level as a bowling green with but little stone and few prickly pears. after dinner we pursued the bottoms of rose river but finding [it] inconvenient to pass the river so often we again ascended the hills on the S. W. side and took the open plains; by dark we had traveled about 17 miles further,   we now halted to rest ourselves and horses about 2 hours, we killed a buffaloe cow and took a small quantity of the meat.

after refreshing ourselves we again set out by moonlight and traveled leasurely, heavy thunderclouds lowered arround us on every quarter but that from which the moon gave us light.   we continued to pass immence herds of buffaloe all night as we had done in the latter part of the day.   we traveled untill 2 OCk in the morning having come by my estimate after dark about 20 ms.   we now turned out our horses and laid ourselves down to rest in the plain very much fatiegued as may be readily conceived.[11] my indian horse carried me very well in short much better than my own would have done and leaves me with but little reason to complain of the robery.

July 28th. 1806.   Monday.

The morning proved fair,   I slept sound but fortunately awoke as day appeared, I awaked the men and directed the horses to be

[11] The bivouac for this night was not far from the site of Fort Benton (Thwaites).

saddled, I was so soar from my ride yesterday that I could scarcely
stand, and the men complained of being in a similar situation however I encouraged them by telling them that our own lives as well
as those of our friends and fellow travellers depended on our exertions at this moment; they were allert soon prepared the horses
and we again resumed our march; the men proposed to pass the
missouri at the grog spring where rose river approaches it so nearly
and pass down on the S. W. side, to this I objected as it would
delay us almost all day to reach the point[12] by this circuetous rout
and would give the enemy time to surprise and cut off the party at
the point if they had arrived there, I told them that we owed much
to the safety of our friends and that we must wrisk our lives on this
occasion, that I should proceed immediately to the point and if the
party had not arrived that I would raft the missouri a small distance
above, hide our baggage and march on foot up the river through the
timber untill I met the canoes or joined them at the falls; I now told
them that it was my determination that if we were attacked in the
plains on our way to the point that the bridles of the horses should
be tied together and we would stand and defend them, or sell our
lives as dear as we could.

we had proceeded about 12 miles on an East course when we
found ourselves near the missouri; we heard a report which we took
to be that of a gun but were not certain; still continuing down the
N. E. bank of the missouri about 8 miles further, being then within
five miles of the grog spring we heared the report of several rifles
very distinctly on the river to our right, we quickly repared to this
joyfull sound and on arriving at the bank of the river had the un-
speakable satisfaction to see our canoes coming down. we hurried
down from the bluff on which we were and joined them striped our
horses and gave them a final discharge imbarking without loss of
time with our baggage. I now learned that they had brought all
things safe having sustaned no loss nor met with any accident of
importance. Wiser had cut his leg badly with a knife and was unable
in consequence to work.

we decended the river opposite to our principal cash which we

[12] At the confluence of the Marias and Missouri rivers, northeast of Fort Benton,
Montana.

proceeded to open after reconnoitering the adjacent country. we found that the cash had caved in and most of the articles burried therin were injured; I sustained the loss of two very large bear skins which I much regret; most of the fur and baggage belonging to the men were injured. the gunpowder corn flour poark and salt had sustained but little injury the parched meal was spoiled or nearly so. having no time to air these things which they much wanted we droped down to the point to take in the several articles which had been buried at that place in several small cashes; these we found in good order, and recovered every article except 3 traps belonging to Drewyer which could not be found. here as good fortune would have it Sergt. Gass and Willard who brought the horses from the falls joined us at 1 P. M. I had ordered them to bring down the horses to this place in order to assist them in collecting meat which I had direceted them to kill and dry here for our voyage, presuming that they would have arrived with the perogue and canoes at this place several days before my return. having now nothing to detain us we passed over immediately to the island in the entrance of Maria's river to launch the red perogue, but found her so much decayed that it was impossible with the means we had to repare her and therefore mearly took the nails and other ironworks about her which might be of service to us and left her.

we now reimbarked on board the white perog[u]e and five small canoes and decended the river about 15 ms. and encamped on the S. W. side near a few cottonwood trees, one of them being of the narrow leafed speceis and was the first of that kind which we had remarked on our passage up the river. we encamped late but having little meat I sent out a couple of hunters who soon returned with a sufficient quantity of the flesh of a fat cow. there are immence quantities of buffaloe and Elk about the junction of the Missouri and Maria's rivers. during the time we halted at the entrance of Maria's river we experienced a very heavy shower of rain and hail attended with violent thunder and lightning.

Tuesday July 29th. 1806.

a violent storm came on from N. W. attended with rain hail Thunder and lightning which continued the greater part of the night. no[t] having the means of making a shelter I lay in the water all night. the rain continued with but little intermission all day.

the currant being strong we proceeded with great rapidity. at 11 A. M. we passed that very interesting part of the Missouri where the natural walls appear, particularly discribed in my outward bound journey. we continued our rout untill late in the evening and encamped on the N. E. side of the river at the same place we had encamped on the 29th. of May 1805. on our way today we killed 9 bighorns of which I preserved the skins and skeletons of 2 females and one male; the flesh of this aninmal is extreemly delicate tender and well flavored; they are now in fine order. their flesh both in colour and flavor much resembles mutton though it is not so strong as our mutton. the eye is large and prominant, the puple of a pale sea green the iris of a light yellowish brown colour. these animals abound in this quarter keeping themselves principally confined to the steep clifts and bluffs of the river. we saw immence hirds of buffaloe in the high plains today on either hand of the river. saw but few Elk. the brown Curloo has left the plains I presume it has raised it's young and retired to some other climate and country. as I have been very particular in my discription of the country as I ascended this river I presume it is unnecesssesary here to add anything further on that subject.

the river is now nearly as high as it has been this season and is so thick with mud and sand that it is with difficulty I can drink it. every little rivulet now discharges a torrant of water bringing down imme[n]ce boddies of mud sand and filth from the plains and broken bluffs.

Saturday August 2ed. 1806.

The morning proved fair and I determined to remain all day and dry the baggage and give the men an opportunity to dry and air their skins and furr. had the powder parched meal and every article which wanted drying exposed to the sun. the day proved warm fair and favourable for our purpose. I permitted the Fieldses to go on a few miles to hunt. by evening we had dryed our baggage and repacked it in readiness to load and set out early in the morning. the river fell 18 inches since yesterday evening. the hunters killed several deer in the course of the day. nothing remarkable took place today. we are all extreemly anxious to reach the entrance of the Yellowstone river where we expect to join Capt. Clark and party.

Thursday August 7th. 1806.

we arrived at the entrance of the Yellowstone river. I landed at
the point and found that Capt. Clark had been encamped at this
place and from appearances had left it about 7 or 8 days. I found a
paper on a pole at the point which mearly contained my name in
the hand wrighting of Capt. C. we also found the remnant of a
note which had been attatched to a peace of Elk'shorns in the camp;
from this fragment I learned that game was scarce at the point and
musquetoes troublesome which were the reasons given for his going
on; I also learnt that he intended halting a few miles below where
he intended waiting my arrival.

I now wrote a note directed to Colter and Collins provided they
were behind, ordering them to come on without loss of time; this
note I wraped in leather and attatched to the same pole which Capt.
C. had planted at the point; this being done I instantly reimbarked
and decended the river in the hope of reaching Capt. C's camp
before night. about 7 miles below the point on the S. W. shore I
saw some meat that had been lately fleased and hung on a pole; I
directed Sergt. Ordway to go on shore [and] examine the place; on
his return he reported that he saw the tracks of two men which
appeared so resent that he beleived they had been there today, the
fire he found at the plce was blaizing and appeared to have been
mended up afresh or within the course of an hour past. he found at
this place a part of a Chinnook hat which my men recognized as
the hat of Gibson; from these circumstances we concluded that Capt.
C's camp could not be distant and pursued our rout untill dark with
the hope of reaching his camp in this however we were disappointed
and night coming on compelled us to encamp

Saturday August 9th. 1806.

The day proved fair and favourable for our purposes. the men
were all engaged dressing skins and making themselves cloathes
except R. & J. Fields whom I sent this morning over the river with
orders to proceed to the entrance of the White earth river in surch
of Capt. C. and to hunt and kill Elk or buffaloe should they find
any convenient to the river. in the evening these men returned
and informed me that they saw no appearance of Capt. Clark or
party. they found no game nor was there a buffaloe to be seen in
the plains as far as the eye could reach. nothing remarkable took

place in the course of the day. Colter and Collins have not yet overtaken us I fear some missfortune has happened them for their previous fidelity and orderly deportment induces me to beleive that they would not thus intentionally delay. the Perogue is not yet sufficiently dry for reparing. we have no pitch and will therefore be compelled to use coal and tallow.

Monday August 11th. 1806.

We set our very early this morning. it being my wish to arrive at the birnt hills by noon in order to take the latitude of that place as it is the most northern point of the Missouri, I enformed the party of my design and requested that they would exert themselves to reach the place in time as it would save us the delay of nearly one day; being as anxious to get forward as I was they plyed their oars faithfully and we proceeded rapidly. I had instructed the small [c]anoes that if they saw any game on the river to halt and kill it and follow on; however we saw but little game untill about 9 A.M. when we came up with a buffaloe swiming the river which I shot and killed; leaving the small canoes to dress it and bring on the meat I proceeded. we had gone but little way before I saw a very large grizzly bear and put too in order to kill it, but it took wind of us and ran off. the small canoes overtook us and informed that the flesh of the buffaloe was unfit for uce and that they had therefore left it.

half after 11 A.M. we saw a large herd of Elk on the N. E. shore and I directed the men in the small canoes to halt and kill some of them and continued on in the perogue to the birnt hills; when I arrived here it was about 20 minutes after noon and of course the observation for the ☉'s meridian Altitude was lost. jus[t] opposite to the birnt hills there happened to be a herd of Elk on a thick willow bar and finding that my observation was lost for the present I determined to land and kill some of them accordingly we put too and I went out with Cruzatte only. we fired on the Elk I killed one and he wounded another, we reloaded our guns and took different routs through the thick willows in pursuit of the Elk; I was in the act of firing on the Elk a second time when a ball struck my left thye about an inch below my hip joint, missing the bone it passed through the left thye and cut the thickness of the bullet across the hinder part of the right thye; the stroke was very severe; I instantly supposed that Cruzatte had shot me in mistake for an Elk as I was dressed in brown leather and he cannot see very well; under this impression I called out to him damn you, you have shot me, and looked towards the place from whence the ball had come, seeing nothing I called Cruzatte several times as loud as I could but received no answer;   I was now preswaded that it was an indian that had shot me as the report of the gun did not appear to be more than 40 paces from me and Cruzatte appeared to be out of hearing of me; in this situation not knowing how many indians there might be concealed in the bushes I thought best to make good my retreat to the perogue, calling out as I ran for the first hundred paces as loud as I could to Cruzatte to retreat that there were indians hoping to allarm him in time to make his escape also; I still retained the charge in my gun which I was about to discharge at the moment the ball struck me.

when I arrived in sight of the perogue I called the men to their arms to which they flew in an instant, I told them that I was wounded but I hoped not mortally, by an indian I beleived and directed them to follow me that I would return & give them battle and releive Cruzatte if possible who I feared had fallen into their hands; the men followed me as they were bid and I returned about a hundred paces when my wounds became so painfull and my thye so stiff that I could scarcely get on; in short I was compelled to halt and ordered the men to proceed and if they found themselves overpowered by numbers to retreat in order keeping up a fire.

I now got back to the perogue as well as I could and prepared my self with a pistol my rifle and air-gun being determined as a retreat was impracticable to sell my life as deerly as possible.   in this state of anxiety and suspense I remained about 20 minutes when the party returned with Cruzatte and reported that there were no indians nor the appearance of any; Cruzatte seemed much allarmed and declared if he had shot me it was not his intention, that he had shot an Elk in the willows after he left or seperated from me.   I asked him whether he did not hear me when I called to him so frequently which he absolutely denied.   I do not beleive that the fellow did it intentionally but after finding that he had shot me was anxious to conceal his knowledge of having done so.   the ball had lodged in my breeches which I knew to be the ball of the short rifles such as that he had, and there being no person out with me but him and no indians that we could discover I have no doubt in my own mind of his having shot me.

with the assistance of Sergt. Gass I took off my cloaths and dressed my wounds myself as well as I could, introducing tents of patent lint into the ball holes, the wounds blead considerably but I was hapy to find that it had touched neither bone nor artery. I sent the men to dress the two Elk which Cruzatte and myself had killed which they did in a few minutes and brought the meat to the river. the small canoes came up shortly after with the flesh of one Elk. my wounds being so situated that I could not without infinite pain make an observation I determined to relinquish it and proceeded on.

we came within eight miles of our encampment of the 15th. of April 1805 and encamped on N. E. side. as it was painfull to me to be removed I slept on board the perogue; the pain I experienced excited a high fever and I had a very uncomfortable night. at 4 P. M. we passed an encampment which had been evacuated this morning by Capt. Clark, here I found a note from Capt. C. informing me that he had left a letter for me at the entrance of the Yelow stone river, but that Sergt. Pryor who had passed that place since he left it had taken the letter; that Sergt. Pryor having been robed of all his horses had decended the Yelowstone river in skin canoes and had overtaken him at this encampment. this I fear puts an end to our prospects of obtaining the Sioux Cheifs to accompany us as we have not now leasure to send and engage Mr. Heney on this service, or at least he would not have time to engage them to go as early as it is absolutely necessary we should decend the river.

Tuesday August 12th. 1806

Being anxious to overtake Capt. Clark who from the appearance of his camps could be at no great distance before me, we set out early and proceeded with all possible expedition at 8 A. M. the bowsman informed me that there was a canoe and a camp he beleived of whitemen on the N. E. shore. I directed the perogue and canoes to come too at this place and found it to be the camp of two hunters from the Illinois by name Joseph Dickson and Forest Hancock.[13] these men informed me that Capt. C. had passed them about noon the day before. they also informed me that they had left the Illinois in the summer [of] 1804 since which time they had been ascended the Missouri, hunting and traping beaver; that they had been robed by the indians and the former wounded last winter by the Tetons of the birnt woods; that they had hitherto been unsuccessfull in their voyage having as yet caught but little beaver, but were still determined to proceed.   I gave them a short discription of the Missouri, a list of distances to the most conspicuous streams and remarkable places on the river above and pointed out to them the places where the beaver most abounded.   I also gave them a file and a couple of pounds of powder with some lead.   these were articles which they assured me they were in great want of.   I remained with these men an hour and a half when I took leave of them and proceeded.

while I halted with these men Colter and Collins who seperated from us on the 3rd i[n]st rejoined us.   they were well no accedent having happened.   they informed me that after proceeding the first day and not overtaking us that they had concluded that we were behind and had delayed several days in waiting for us and had thus been unable to join us untill the present mome[n]t.   my wounds felt very stiff and soar this morning but gave me no considerable pain.   there was much less inflamation than I had reason to apprehend there would be.   I had last evening applyed a poltice of peruvian barks. at 1 P. M. I overtook Capt. Clark and party and had the pleasure of finding them all well.

as wrighting in my present situation is extreemly painfull to me I shall desist untill I recover and leave to my fri[e]nd Capt. C. the continuation of our journal.   however I must notice a singular Cherry which is found on the Missouri in the bottom lands about the beaver bends and some little distance below the white earth river.   this production is not very abundant even in the small tract of country

[13] These men, whom Clark met the previous day, were the first whites, save their own party, which the explorers had seen since the winter at Fort Mandan.   Joseph Dickson was a native of Pennsylvania, who emigrated to St. Clair County, Illinois, in 1802 (Thwaites).

to which it seems to be confined. the stem is compound erect and
subdivided or branching without any regular order it rises to the
hight of eight or ten feet seldom puting up more than one stem
from the same root not growing in cops as the Choke Cherry dose.
the bark is smooth and of a dark brown colour. the leaf is peteolate,
oval accutely pointed at it's apex, from one end a ¼ to 1½ inches
in length and from ½ to ¾ of an inch in width, finely or minutely
serrate, pale green and free from pubessence. the fruit is a globular
berry about the size of a buck-shot of a fine scarlet red; like the
cherries cultivated in the U' States each is supported by a seperate
celindric flexable branch peduncle which issue from the extremities
of the boughs the peduncle of this cherry swells as it approaches
the fruit being largest at the point of insertion. the pulp of this fruit
is of an agreeable ascid flavour and is now ripe. the style and stigma
are permanent. I have never seen it in blume.[14]

---

[14] Pin cherry (*Prunus pennsylvanica*), according to Cutright.

TWELVE

The Homestretch

From the Little Missouri to St. Louis
August 12–September 26, 1806

[Clark]   Thursday 12th. August 1806[1]

Capt Lewis hove in Sight with the party which went by way of the Missouri as well as that which accompanied him from Travellers rest on Clarks river; I was alarmed on the landing of the Canoes to be informed that Capt. Lewis was wounded by an accident. I found him lying in the Perogue, he informed me that his wound was slight and would be well in 20 or 30 days   this information relieved me very much. I examined the wound and found it a very bad flesh wound   the ball had passed through the fleshey part of his left thy below the hip bone and cut the cheek of the right buttock for 3 inches in length and the debth of the ball. Capt. L. informed me the accident happened the day before by one of the men Peter Crusat misstaking him in the thick bushes to be an Elk. Capt Lewis with this Crusat and several other men were out in the bottom Shooting of Elk, and had Scattered in a thick part of the woods in pursute of the Elk. Crusat seeing Capt L. passing through the bushes and taking him to be an Elk from the colour of his cloathes

---

[1] August 12, 1806, was a Tuesday. Clark's datelines remain somewhat askew for the rest of the week. He resumes correct datelines by the following Tuesday, August 19, 1806.

which were of leather and very nearly that of the Elk fired and unfortunately the ball passed through the thy as aforesaid. Capt. Lewis thinking it indians who had Shot him hobbled to the canoes as fast as possible and was followed by Crusat, the Mistake was then discovered. This Crusat is near Sighted and has the use of but one eye, he is an attentive industrious man and one whome we both have placed the greatest confidence in dureing the whole rout.

at 2 P.M. Shannon & Gibson arrived in the Skin canoe with the Skins and the greater part of the flesh of 3 Elk which they had killed a fiew miles above. the two men Dixon & Handcock the two men we had met above came down intending to proceed on down with us to the Mandans. at 3 P M we proceeded on all together haveing left the 2 leather canoes on the bank. a little below the enterance of Shabonos Creek we came too on a large Sand point from the S.E. Side and Encamped. the wind blew very hard from the S W. and Some rain. I washed Capt L. wound which has become Sore and Somewhat painfull to him.

Thursday (*Saturday*) 14th: August 1806
Set out at Sunrise and proceeded on. when we were opposit the Minetares Grand Village we Saw a number of the Nativs viewing of [us] we derected the Blunderbuses fired Several times, Soon after we Came too at a Croud of the nativs on the bank opposit the Village of the Shoe Indians or *Mah-har-has'* at which place I saw the principal Chief of the Little Village of the Menitarre & the principal Chief of the *Mah-har-has*. those people were extreamly pleased to See us. the chief of the little Village of the Menetarras cried Most imoderately, I enquired the cause and was informed it was for the loss of his Son who had been killed latterly by the Blackfoot Indians. after a delay of a fiew minits I proceeded on to the black cats (*Mandan*) Village on the N.E. side of the Missouri where I intended to Encamp but the Sand blew in Such a manner that we deturmined not to continue on that side but return to the side we had left. here we were visited by all the inhabitants of this village who appeared equally as well pleased to see us as those above.

I had soon as I landed despatched Shabono to the Minetarras inviting the Chiefs to visit us, & Drewyer down to the lower Village of the Mandans to ask Mr. Jessomme to come and enterpret for us.

Thursday August 15th. 1806 (*continued*)
Mandans Vilg.

after assembling the Chiefs and Smokeing one pipe, I informed them that I still Spoke the Same words which we had Spoken to them when we first arived in their Country in the fall of 1804. we then envited them to visit their great father the president of the U. States and to hear his own Councils and recieve his Gifts from his own hands as also See the population of a government which can at their pleasure protect and Secure you from all your enimies, and chastize all those who will shut their years to his Councils. we now offer to take you at the expense of our Government and Send you back to your Country again with a considerable present in Merchendize which you will receive of your great Father. I urged the necessity of their going on with us as it would be the means of hastening those Suppl[i]es of Merchindize which would be Sent to their Country and exchanged as before mentioned for a moderate price in Pelteries and furs &c.

the great chief of the Menetaras Spoke, he Said he wished to go down and see his great father very much, but that the Scioux were in the road and would most certainly kill him or any others who should go down they were bad people and would not listen to any thing which was told them. when he Saw us last we told him that we had made peace with all the nations below, Since that time the Seioux had killed 8 of their people and Stole a number of their horses. he Said that he had opened his ears and followed our Councils, he had made peace with the Chyennes and rocky Mountains indians, and repieted the same objecctions as mentioned. that he went to war against none and was willing to recieve all nations as friends. he Said that the Ricaras had Stolen from his people a number of horses at different times and his people had killed 2 Ricaras. if the Sieoux were at peace with them and could be depended on he as also other Chiefs of the villages would be glad to go and See their great father, but as they were all afraid of the Sieoux they should not go down

after smoking a pipe and relateing some passages I recrossed to our Camp. being informed by one of our enterpreters that the 2d. Chief of the Mandans comonly called the little crow intended to accompany us down, I took Charbono and walked to the Village to see this Chief and talk with him on the subject he told me he had deturmined to go down, but wished to have a council first with his people which would be in the after part of the day. I smoked a pipe with the little Crow and returned to the boat.

Colter one of our men expressed a desire to join Some trappers [*the two Illinois Men we met, & who now came down to us*] who offered to become shearers with [him] and furnish traps &c. the offer [was] a very advantagious one, to him, his services could be dispenced with from this down and as we were disposed to be of service to any one of our party who had performed their duty as well as Colter had done, we agreed to allow him the privilage provided no one of the party would ask or expect a Similar permission to which they all agreed that they wished Colter every suckcess and that as we did not wish any of them to Seperate untill we Should arive at St. Louis they would not apply or expect it

The Maharha Chief brought us Some Corn, as did also the Chief of the little village of the Menetarras on mules of which they have Several.

Friday 16th. August 1806

a cool morning. Sent up Sergt. Pryor to the Mandan village for some corn which they offered to give us. he informed that they had more corn collected for us than our Canoes could carry six load of which he brought down. I thanked the Chief for his kindness and informed him that our canoes would not carry any more corn than we had already brought down. at 10 A.M. the Chiefs of the different villages came to see us and smoke a pipe &c. as our swivel could no longer be Serveceable to us as it could not be fireed on board the largest Perogue, we concluded to make a present of it to the Great Chief of the Menitaras (the One Eye) with a view to ingratiate him more Strongly in our favour I had the Swivel Charged and Collected the Chiefs in a circle around it and adressed them with great ceremoney.

The One Eye said his ears would always be open to the word of his great father and Shut against bad council &c. I then [with] a good deel of ceremoney made a preasent of the swivel to the *One Eye* Chief, and told him when he fired this gun to remember the words of his great father which we had given him. this gun had anounced the words of his great father to all the nations which we had seen &c. &c. after the council was over the gun was fired &

delivered, they chief appeared to be much pleased and conveyed it immediately to his village

Saturday 17th. of August 1806

Settled with Touisant Chabono for his services as an enterpreter the price of a horse and Lodge purchased of him for public Service in all amounting to 500$ 33⅓ cents. derected two of the largest of the Canoes be fastened together with poles tied across them So as to make them Study [steady] for the purpose of Conveying the Indians and enterpreter and their families

we were visited by all the principal Chiefs of the Menetarras to take their leave of us at 2 oClock we left our encampment after takeing leave of Colter who also Set out up the river in company with Messrs. Dickson & Handcock. we also took our leave of T. Chabono, his Snake Indian wife and their child [son] who had accompanied us on our rout to the pacific ocean in the capacity of interpreter and interprete[s]s. T. Chabono wished much to accompany us in the said Capacity if we could have provailed [upon] the Menetarre Chiefs to dec[e]nd the river with us to the U. States, but as none of those Chiefs of whoes language he was Conversant would accompany us, his services were no longer of use to the U. States and he was therefore discharged and paid up. we offered to convey him down to the Illinois if he chose to go, he declined proceeding on at present, observing that he had no acquaintance or prospects of makeing a liveing below, and must continue to live in the way that he had done. I offered to take his little son a butifull promising child who is 19 months old to which they both himself & wife wer willing provided the child had been weened. they observed that in one year the boy would be sufficiently old to leave his mother & he would then take him to me if I would be so freindly as to raise the child for him in such a manner as I thought proper, to which I agreed

we droped down to the *Big White Cheifs* Mandan village ½ a mile below on the South Side, all the Indians proceeded on down by land. and I walked to the lodge of the Chief whome I found sorounded by his friends the men were Setting in a circle Smokeing and the womin crying. he Sent his baggage with his wife & son, with the Interpreter Jessomme & his wife and 2 children to the

Canoes provided for them. after Smokeing one pipe, and distributing some powder & lead which we had given him, he informed me that he was ready and we were accompd. to the Canoes by all the village Maney of them Cried out aloud. as I was about to shake with the Grand Cheifs of all the villages there assembled they requested me to Set one minit longer with them which I readily agreed to and directed a pipe to be lit. the Cheifs informed that when we first came to their Country they did not beleive all we Said we then told them. but they were now convinced that every thing we had told them were true, that they should keep in memory every thing which we had said to them, and Strictly attend to our advice, that their young men Should Stay at home and Should no[t] go again to war against any nation, that if any atacted them they should defend themselves, that we might depend on what they said, and requested us to inform their great father. the also requested me to tell the Ricaras to come and see them, not to be afraid that no harm Should be done them, that they were anxious to be in peace with them.

The Seeoux they said they had no dependance in and Should kill them whenever they came into their country to do them harm &c. I told them that we had always told them to defend themselves, but not to strike those nations we had taken by the hand, the Sieoux with whome they were at war we had never seen on our return we Should inform their great father of their conduct towards his faithfull red children and he would take Such Steps as will bring about a lasting peace between them and his faithfull red children. I informed them that we should inform the ricaras what they had requested.

The Grand Chief of the Minetarres said that the Great Cheif who was going down with [us] to see their great father was a[s] well as if he went also, and on his return he would be fully informed of the words of his great father, and requested us to take care of this Gt. Chief. we then saluted them with a gun and set out and proceeded on to *Fort Mandan* where I landed and went to view the old works the houses except one in the rear bastion was burnt by accident, some pickets were standing in front next to the river. we proceeded on to the old Ricara village

Tuesday 19th. of August 1806

Capt. Lewis'es wounds are heeling very fast, I am much in hope
of his being able to walk in 8 or 10 days.

the wind rose and become very strong from the S.E. and a great
appearance of rain. Jessomme the Interpreter let me have a piece
of a lodge and the Squars pitched or Stretched it over Some Sticks,
under this piece of leather I Slept dry, it is the only covering which
I have had Sufficient to keep off the rain Since I left the Columbia.

Wednesday 20th. of August 1806

Saw great number of wolves on the bank some Buffalow & Elk,
tho' not so abundant as near the River Rochejhone.[2] passed the
place where we left the last encampment of Ricaras in the fall 1804
and encamped on a Sandbar from the N.E. Side,   haveing made
81 miles only,   the wind blew hard all day which caused the waves
to rise high and flack over into the Small Canoes in such a manner
as to employ one hand in throwing the water out.   The plains begin
to change their appearance the grass is turning of a yellow colour.
I observe a great alteration in the Current course and appearance of
this pt. of the Missouri.   in places where there was Sand bars in
the fall 1804 at this time the main current passes, and where the
current then passed is now a Sand bar.   Sand bars which were then
naked are now covered with willow several feet high.

Thursday 21te. August 1806

Met three frenchmen Comeing up, they proved to be three men
from the Ricaras two of them Reeved & Greinyea wintered with us
at the mandans in 1804 we Came too, those men informed us that
they were on their way to the Mandans, and intended to go down
to the Illinois this fall.   one of them quit[e] a young lad requested
a passage down to the Illinois,   we concented and he got into a
Canoe to [ply] an Ore.   Those men informd. us that 700 Seeoux
had passed the Ricaras on their way to war with the Mandans &
Menitarras and that their encampment where the Squaws and children wer, was Some place near the Big Bend of this river below.
no ricaras had accompanied them but were all at home,   they also

[2] Yellowstone River.

informed us that no trader had arived at the Ricaras this Season, and that they were informed that the Pania or Ricara Chief who went to the United States last Spring was a year, died on his return at Some place near the Sieoux river &c. those men had nether powder nor lead we gave them a horn of powder and some balls and after a delay of an hour we parted from the 2 men Reevey & Grienway and proceeded on.

Saturday 23rd. August 1806

I observe great quantities of Grapes and choke Cheries, also a speces of currunt which I had never before observed the lea[ve]s is larger than those above, the currt. black and very inferior to either the yellow, red, or perple. at dark we landed on a Small Sand bar under a Bluff on the S W. Side and encamped, this Situation was one which I had Chosen to avoid the Musquetors, they were not very troublesom after we landed. we came only *40* Miles to daye

My Frend Capt. Lewis is recovering fast the hole in his thy where the Ball passed out is closed and appears to be nearly well. the one where the ball entered discharges very well.

Tuesday 26th. of August 1806

as we were now in the country where we were informed the Seioux were assembled we were much on our guard deturmined to put up with no insults from those bands of Seioux, all the arms &c. in perfect order. Capt. L. is Still on the mending hand he walks a little. I have discontinued the tent in the hole where the ball entered, agreeable to his request he tells me that he is fully convinced that the wound is sufficiently heeled for the tents to be discontinued. we made *60* miles to day with the wind ahead greater part of the day.

Friday 29th. August 1806

I with Several of the men went out in pursute of Buffalow. the men killed 2 Bulls near me they were very pore I assended to the high Country and from an eminance I had a view of the plains for a great distance. from this eminance I had a view of a greater number of buffalow than I had ever seen before at one time. I must have seen near 20,000 of those animals feeding on this plain. I have observed that in the country between the nations which are at war with each other the greatest numbers of wild animals are to be found.

Saturday 30th. of August 1806.

Capt. Lewis is mending slowly.   I saw Several men on horseback which with the help of a spie glass I found to be Indians on the high hills to the N. E.   we landed on the S. W. side and I sent out two men to a village of Barking Squirels to kill some of those animals imedeatily after landing about 20 indians was discovered on an eminance a little above us on the opposite Side. One of those men I took to be a french man from his [having] a blanket capo[t]e & a handkerchief around his head.   imediately after 80 or 90 Indian men all armed with fusees & Bows & arrows came out of a wood on the opposite bank about ¼ of a mile below us.   they fired of[f] their guns as a Salute we returned the Salute with 2 rounds.   we were at a loss to deturmin of what nation those indians were.   from their hostile appearance we were apprehensive they were Tetons,   but from the country through which they roved we were willing to believe them either the Yanktons, Pon[c]ars or Mahars either of which nations are well disposed towards the white people.

I deturmined to find out who they were without running any risque of the party and indians,   and therefore took three french men who could Speak the Mahar Pania and some Seeoux and in a Small canoe I went over to a Sand bar which extended Sufficiently near the opposite shore to converse.   imedeately after I set out 3 young men set out from the opposite Side and swam next me on the Sand bar. I derected the men to Speak to them in the Pania and Mahar Languages first neither of which they could understand   I then derected the man who could speak a fiew words of Seioux to inquire what nation or tribe they belong to   they informed me that they were Tetons and their chief was *Tar-tack-kah-sab-bar* or the black buffalow   this chief I knew very well to be the one we had seen with his band at Teton river which band had attempted to detain us in the fall of 1804 as we assended this river and with whome we wer near comeing to blows.   I told those Indians that they had been deef to our councils and ill treated us as we assended this river two years past, that they had abused all the whites who had visited them since.   I believed them to be bad people & should not suffer them to cross to the Side on which the party lay, and directed them to return with their band to their camp, that if any of them come near our camp we Should kill them certainly.

I lef[t] them on the bear [bar] and returned to th[e] party and examined the arms &c those indians seeing some corn in the canoe requested some of it which I refused being deturmined to have nothing to do with these people. Several others swam across one of which understood pania, and as our pania interpreter was a very good one we had it in our power to inform what we wished. I told this man to inform his nation that we had not forgot their treatment to us as we passed up this river &c. that they had treated all the white people who had visited them very badly; robed them of their goods, and had wounded one man whom I had Seen. we viewed them as bad people and no more traders would be Suffered to come to them, and whenever the white people wished to visit the nations above they would come sufficiently Strong to whip any vilenous party who dare to oppose them and words to the same purpote. I also told them that I was informed that a part of all their bands were going to war against the Mandans &c, and that they would be well whiped as the Mandans & Minitarres &[c] had a plenty of Guns Powder and ball, and we had given them a cannon to defend themselves. and derected them to return from the Sand bar and inform their chiefs what we had said to them, and to keep away from the river or we Should kill every one of them &c. &c. those fellows requested to be allowed to come across and make cumerads which we positively refused and I directed them to return imediately which they did and after they had informed the Chiefs &c. as I suppose what we had said to them, they all set out on their return to their camps back of a high hill.

7 of them halted on the top of the hill and blackguarded us, told us to come across and they would kill us all &c of which we took no notice. we all this time were extreamly anxious for the arival of the 2 fields & Shannon whome we had left behind, and were some what consd. as to their Safty. to our great joy those men hove in Sight at 6 P. M. Jo. Fields had killed 3 black tail or mule deer. we then Set out, as I wished to see what those Indians on the hill would act, we steared across near the opposit Shore, this notion put them [in] some agitation as to our intentions, some set out on the direction towards their Camps others walked about on the top

of the hill and one man walked down the hill to meet us and invited us to land to which invitation I paid no kind of attention. this man I knew to be the one who had in the fall 1804 accompanied us 2 days and is said to be the friend to the white people. after we passd him he returned on the top of the hill and gave 3 strokes with the gun he had in his hand. this I am informed is a great oath among the indians. we proceeded on down about 6 miles and encamped on a large Sand bar in the middle of the river   Saw Several indians on the hills at a distance this evening viewing us. our encampment of this evening was a very disagreeable one, bleak exposed to the winds, and the sand wet. I pitched on this Situation to prevent being disturbed by those Scioux in the course of the night as well as to avoid the musquetors.

Monday 1st. of September 1806

Musquitors very troublesom last night, we set out at the usial hour and had not proceeded on far before the fog became so thick that we were oblige[d] to come too and delay half an hour for the fog to pass off which it did in some measure and we again proceded on R. [and] Jo. Fields and Shannon landed on an Island [*Ponceras*][3] to try to kill Some deer which was seen on the beech and the Canoes all passed them

at 9 A. M. we passed the enterance of River *Quiequur* [Qui Court, or Niobrara] which had the Same appearance it had when we passed up water rapid and of a milky white colour   about two miles below the Quicurre,   9 Indians ran down the bank and beckened to us to land, they appeared to be a war party, and I took them to be Tetons and paid no kind of attention to them further than an enquirey to what tribe they belonged,   they did not give me any answer, I presume they did not understand the man who Spoke to them as he Spoke but little of their language.   as one canoe was yet behind we landed in an open commanding Situation out of sight of the indians deturmined to delay untill they came up.

about 15 minits after we had landed Several guns were fired by the indians, which we expected was at the three men behind. I calld out 15 men and ran up with a full deturmination to cover them

[3] At the mouth of Ponca River (Thwaites).

if possible let the number of the indians be what they might. Capt. Lewis hobled up on the bank and formed the remainder of the party in a Situation well calculated to defend themselves and the Canoes &c. when I had proceeded to the point about 250 yards I discovered the Canoe about 1 mile above & the indians where we had left them. I then walked on the Sand beech and the indians came down to meet me I gave them my hand and enquired of them what they were Shooting at, they informed me that they were Shooting off their guns at an old Keg which we had thrown out of one of the Canoes and was floating down. those indians informed me they were Yanktons, one of the men with me knew one of the Indians to be the brother of young Durion's wife.

finding those indians to be Yanktons I invited them down to the boats to Smoke. when we arived at the Canoes they all eagerly Saluted the Mandan Chief, and we all set and smoked Several pipes. I told them that we took them to be a party of Tetons and the fireing I expected was at the three men in the rear Canoe and I had went up with a full intention to kill them all if they had been tetons & fired on the canoe as we first expected, but finding them Yanktons and good men we were glad to see them and take them by the hand as faithfull Children who had opened their ears to our Councils.

at this Island[4] we brought 2 years together or on the 1st. of Sept. 1804 we Encamped at the lower point of this Island. after we all came together we again proceeded on down to a large Sand bar imediately opposit to the place where we met the Yanktons in council at the Calumet Bluffs and which place we left on the 1t. of Sept. 1804. I observed our old flag Staff or pole Standing as we left it.

We came *52* miles to day only with a head wind. the country on either Side are butifull and the plains much richer below the Quequer river than above that river.

Wednesday 3rd September 1806

we Spied two boats & Several men, our party p[l]eyed their ores and we soon landed on the Side of the Boats the men of [these] boats Saluted us with their Small arms I landed & was met by a

[4] The site of Lewis and Clark Lake on the Nebraska–South Dakota border.

Mr. James Airs from Mackanaw by way of Prarie Dechien and St. Louis. this Gentleman is of the house of Dickson & Co. of Prarie de Chian who has a Licence to trade for one year with the Sieoux he has 2 Batteaux loaded with Merchendize for that purpose. This Gentleman receved both Capt. Lewis and my self with every mark of friendship he was himself at the time with a chill of the agu on him which he has had for Several days. our first enquirey was after the President of our country and then our friends and the State of the politicks of our country &c. and the State [of] Indian affairs to all of which enquireys Mr. Aires gave us as Satisfactory information as he had it in his power to have collected in the Illinois which was not a great deel.

this Gentleman informed us of maney changes & misfortunes which had taken place in the Illinois amongst others the loss of Mr. Cady Choteaus house and furniture by fire. for this misfortune of our friend Choteaus I feel my self very much concernd &c. he also informed us that Genl. Wilkinson was the governor of the Louisiana and at St. Louis. 300 of the american Troops had been cantuned on the Missouri a fiew miles above it's mouth, Some disturbance with the Spaniards in the Nackatosh [Natchitoches] Country is the cause of their being called down to that country, the Spaniards had taken one of the U. States frigates in the Mediteranean, Two British Ships of the line had fired on an American Ship in the port of New York, and killed the Capts. brother. 2 Indians had been hung in St. Louis for murder and several others in jale. and that Mr. Burr & Genl. Hambleton fought a Duel, the latter was killed. &c. &c. I am happy to find that my worthy friend Capt. L's is so well as to walk about with ease to himself &c. we made *60* Miles to day

Thursday 4th September 1806.
as we were in want of some tobacco I purposed to Mt. Airs to furnish us with 4 carrots for which we would Pay the amount to any Merchant of St. Louis he very readily agreed to furnish us with tobacco and gave to each man as much as it is necessary for them to use between this and St. Louis, an instance of Generossity for which every man of the party appears to acknowledge.

at 11 A. M. passed the Enterance of the big Sieoux River which is low, and at meridian we came too at Floyds Bluff below the

Enterance of Floyds river and assended the hill, with Capt. Lewis and Several men, found the grave had been opened by the nativs and left half covered. we had this grave completely filled up, and returned to the canoes and proceeded on

at dark the Musquetors became troublesom and continued so all night the party obtained but little Sleep we made *36* miles only to day.

Saturday 6th. September 1806.

at the lower point of Pelecan Island a little above the Petite River de Seeoux we met a tradeing boat of Mr. Og. Choteaux [Auguste Chouteau] of St. Louis bound to the River Jacque to trade with the Yanktons, this boat was in care of a Mr. Henry Delorn, he had exposed all his loading (*to dry*) and sent out five of his hands to hunt they soon arived with an Elk. we purchased a gallon of whiskey of this man (*promised to pay Chateau who would not receive any pay*) and gave to each man of the party a dram which is the first spiritious licquor which had been tasted by any of them since the 4 of July 1805. several of the party exchanged leather for linen Shirts and beaver for corse hats. Those men could inform us nothing more than that all the troops had movd. from the Illinois and that Genl. Wilkinson was prepareing to leave St. Louis. We advised this trader to treat the Tetons with as much contempt as possible and stated to him where he would be benefited by such treatment &c &c.

Sunday 7th September 1806.

we proceeded on with a Stiff Breeze ahead (*note* the *evaperation* on this portion of the Missouri has been noticed as we assended this river, and it now appears to be greater than it was at that time. I am obliged to replenish my ink Stand every day with fresh ink at least 9/10 of which must evaperate.

we came *44* miles to day only.

Monday 8th September 1806

we proceeded on very well all being anxious to get to the River Platt to day they ply'd their orers very well, and we arived at our old encampment at White Catfish Camp 12 miles above the river platt at which place we lay from the 22th to the 26th. of July 1804 here we encamped haveing made *78* Miles to day. The Missouri at this place does not appear to contain more water than it did 1000 Miles above this, the evaperation must be emence; in the last 1000 miles this river receives the water [of] 20 rivers and maney Creeks Several of the Rivers large and the Size of this river or the quantity of water does not appear to increas any.

Tuesday 9th September 1806

passed the enterance of the great river Platt which is at this time low the water nearly clear the current turbelant as usial; below the R. Platt the current of the Missouri becomes evidently more rapid than above and the Snags much more noumerous and bad to pass late in the evening we arived at the Bald pated prarie and encamped imediately opposit our encampment of the 16th. and 17th. of July 1804. haveing made *73* miles only to day. The river bottoms are extencive rich and covered with tall large timber, and the hollows of the reveens may be Said to be covered with timber Such as Oake ash Elm and some walnut & hickory. our party appears extreamly anxious to get on, and every day appears [to] produce new anxieties in them to get to their country and friends. My worthy friend Cap Lewis has entirely recovered   his wounds are heeled up and he can walk and even run nearly as well as ever he could,   the parts are yet tender &c &c. The Musquetors are yet troublesom, tho' not so much so as they were above the River platt. the climate is every day preceptably wormer and air more Sultery than I have experienced for a long time.   the nights are now so worm that I sleep comfortable under a thin blanket, a fiew days past 2 was not more than sufficient.

Friday 12th of September 1806

Met Mr. Mc.Clellin at the St. Michls. Prarie we came too here we found Mr. Jo. Gravelin the Ricaras enterpreter whome we had Sent down with a Ricaras Chief in the Spring of 1805. and old M. Durion the Sieux enterpreter, we examined the instructions of those interpreters and found that Gravelin was ordered to the Ricaras with a Speach from the president of the U. States to that nation and some presents which had been given the Ricara Chief who had visited the U. States and unfortunately died at the City of Washington, he was instructed to teach the Ricaras agriculture & make every enquirey after Capt. Lewis my self and the party. Mr. Durion was enstructed to accompany Gravelin and through his influence pass him with his presents &[c.] by the tetons bands of Sieux, and to provale on Some of the Principal chiefs of those bands not exceeding six to Visit the Seat of the Government next Spring. he was also enstructed to make every enquirey after us. we made Some Small addition to his instructions by extending the number of Chiefs to 10 or 12 or 3 from each band including the Yanktons &c. Mr. Mc.Clellin receved us very politely, and gave us all the news and occurrences which had taken place in the Illinois within his knowledge the evening proveing to be wet and cloudy we concluded to continue all night,

Sunday 14th Septr 1806

at 2 P. M. a little below the lower [end] of the old Kanzas Village we met three large boats bound to the Yanktons and Mahars the property of Mr. Lacroy, Mr. Aiten & Mr. Coutau all from St. Louis, those young men received us with great friendship and pressed on us Some whisky for our men, Bisquet, Pork and Onions, & part of their Stores, we continued near 2 hours with those boats, makeing every enquirey into the state of our friends and country &c. those men were much affraid of meeting with the Kanzas. we Saw 37 Deer on the banks and in the river to day 5 of which we killed those deer were Meager. we proceeded on to an Island near the middle of the river below our encampment of the 1st. of July 1804 and encamped haveing decended only 53 miles to day. our party received a dram and Sung Songs untill 11 oClock at night in the greatest harmoney.

Wednesday 17th September 1806

at 11 A. M. we met a Captain Mc.Clellin late a Capt. of Artily. of the U States Army assending in a large boat. this gentleman an acquaintance of my friend Capt. Lewis was Somewhat astonished to see us return and appeared rejoiced to meet us. we found him a man of information and from whome we received a partial account of the political State of our country, we were makeing enquires and exchangeing answers &c. untill near mid night. this Gentleman informed us that we had been long Since given out [up] by the people of the U S Generaly and almost forgotton, the President of

the U. States had yet hopes of us; we received some civilities of
Capt. Mc.Clellin, he gave us Some Buisquit, Chocolate Sugar &
whiskey, for which our party were in want and for which we made
a return of a barrel of corn & much obliged to him.

Friday 19th of Septr. 1806.

Set out this morning a little after day & proceeded on very well
the men plyd their oares & we decended with great velocity, only
came too once for the purpose of gathering pappows, our anxiety
as also the wish of the party to proceed on as expeditiously as possible
to the Illinois enduce us to continue on without halting to hunt.
we calculate on ariveing at the first Settlements on tomorrow evening
which is 140 miles, and [the] objecet of our party is to divide the
distance into two days, this day to the Osarge River, and tomorrow
to the Charreton a Small french Village. we arived at the Enterance
of Osage River at dark and encamped on the Spot we had encamped
on the 1st. & 2nd. of June 1804 haveing came *72* miles.

a very singular disorder is takeing place amongst our party that of
the Sore eyes. three of the party have their eyes inflamed and
Sweled in Such a manner as to render them extreamly painfull,
particularly when exposed to the light, the eye ball is much inflaimed
and the lid appears burnt with the Sun, the cause of this complaint
of the eye I can't [account] for. from it's sudden appearance I am
willing to believe it may be owing to the reflection of the sun on
the water.

Saturday 20th Septr. 1806

as three of the party was unabled to row from the State of their
eyes we found it necessary to leave one of our crafts and divide the
men into the other Canoes, we left the two Canoes lashed together
which I had made high up the River Rochejhone, those Canoes
we Set a drift and a little after day light we Set out and proceeded
on very well.

the party being extreemly anxious to get down ply their ores very
well, we saw some cows on the bank which was a joyfull Sight to
the party and caused a Shout to be raised for joy at   [blank in MS.]
P M we came in Sight of the little french Village called Charriton[5]

---

[5] La Charette.

the men raised a Shout and Sprung upon their ores and we soon landed opposit to the Village. our party requested to be permited to fire off their Guns which was alowed & they discharged 3 rounds with a harty cheer, which was returned from five tradeing boats which lay opposit the village. we landed and were very politely received by two young Scotch men from Canada one in the employ of Mr. Aird a Mr. [blank space in MS.] and the other Mr. Reed, two other boats the property of Mr. Lacomb & Mr. [blank space in MS.] all of those boats were bound to the Osage and Ottoes. those two young Scotch gentlemen furnished us with Beef flower and some pork for our men, and gave us a very agreeable supper, as it was like to rain we accepted of a bed in one of their tents. we purchased of a citizen two gallons of Whiskey for our party for which we were obliged to give Eight dollars in Cash, an imposition on the part of the citizen. every person, both French and americans seem to express great pleasure at our return, and acknowledged themselves much astonished in seeing us return. they informed us that we were supposed to have been lost long since, and were entirely given out by every person &c.

Sunday 21st Septr. 1806
we arived in Sight of St. Charles, the party rejoiced at the Sight of this hospita[b]l[e] village plyed thear ores with great dexterity and we Soon arived opposit the Town this day being Sunday we observed a number of Gentlemen and ladies walking on the bank, we saluted the Village by three rounds from our blunderbuts and the Small arms of the party, and landed near the lower part of the town. we were met by great numbers of the inhabitants, we found them excessively polite.

Tuesday 23rd of September 1806
Set out decended to the Mississippi and down that river to St. Louis at which place we arived about 12 oClock. we Suffered the party to fire off their pieces as a Salute to the Town. we were met by all the village and received a harty welcom from it's inhabitants &c. here I found my old acquaintance Majr. W. Christy who had settled in this town in a public line as a Tavern Keeper. he furnished us with store rooms for our baggage and we accepted of the invitation of Mr. Peter Choteau and took a room in his house. we payed a

friendly visit to Mr. August Chotau and some of our old friends this
evening.   as the post had departed from St. Louis Capt. Lewis
wrote a note to Mr. Hay in Kahoka [Cahokia] to detain the post at
that place untill 12 tomorrow which was reather later than his usial
time of leaveing it

Wednesday 24th. of September 1806

I sleped but little last night   however we rose early and com-
menc[e]d wrighting our letters   Capt Lewis wrote one to the pres-
idend and I wrote Govr. Harrison & my friends in Kentucky and
Sent of[f] George Drewyer with those letters to Kohoka & delivered
them to Mr. Hays &c.   we dined with Mr. Chotoux to day,   and
after dinner went to a store and purchased some clothes, which we
gave to a Tayler and derected to be made.   Capt. Lewis in opening
his trunk found all his papers wet, and some seeds spoiled.

Thursday 25th of Septr. 1806

had all of our skins &c. suned and stored away in a storeroom of
Mr. Caddy Choteau.   payed some visits of form, to the gentlemen
of St. Louis.   in the evening a dinner & Ball.

Friday 25th [*26*] of Septr. 1806

a fine morning   we commenced wrighting &c.

INDEX

acorns, 300
aged Indians, 89–90
    treatment of, 342–43, 414
Ahwahharways (Wetersoon), 71,
    72, 78, 80, 98, 343
Aird, James, 480, 485
Aiten, Mr., 483
alkali, 102n
Ames, Fisher, xiv
antelope (pronghorn), xviii, 43–
    44, 49–50, 67, 108
  clothing made from, 247, 252
  hunting strategy for, 231–32
ants, 205–6
Arapaho, 69n
arborvita, 281, 282
Arikaras (Ricarees; Rees), 58–64,
    66–70, 73, 76, 81, 97, 98,
    189, 229, 251, 470, 473–75,
    482–83
  aged, 343
  ceremonies with, 62–63
  dress of, 64

lodges of, 63
physical appearance of, 63
Arketarnashar, Arikara Chief, 66–
    70
arrowhead (swamp potato), 313
artichokes, wild, 101, 259n
Assiniboins, 77, 78–79, 86, 91,
    102, 105, 437
  aged, 342–43
  expedition's wariness of, 119,
    122
  scaffolding of dead by, 106
  use of name, 69n
avocets, American, 112n

badgers, 20–21
Baker's (Haley's) Bay, 319n, 320
Barton, Benjamin Smith, xvi
Battle River, 458
beads:
  making of, 92–93
  as ornaments, 253, 300, 366